# Microsoft®

# Office 2000

## Illustrated Introductory, Enhanced Edition

# Microsoft®

# Office 2000

## Illustrated Introductory, Enhanced Edition

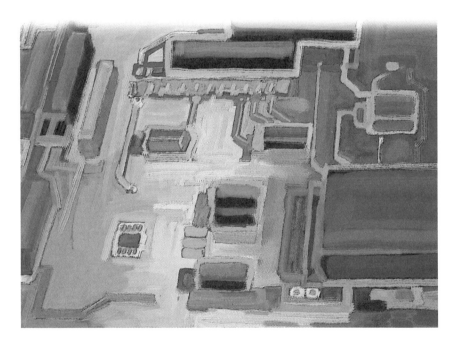

David W. Beskeen ◆ Lisa Friedrichsen
Elizabeth Eisner Reding ◆ Marie L. Swanson

APPROVED COURSEWARE

COURSE
TECHNOLOGY
™
THOMSON LEARNING

Australia • Canada • Mexico • Singapore • Spain • United Kingdom • United States

**COURSE TECHNOLOGY**
™
**THOMSON LEARNING**

# Microsoft® Office 2000 — Illustrated Introductory, Enhanced Edition

David W. Beskeen
Lisa Friedrichsen
Elizabeth Eisner Reding
Marie L. Swanson

**Managing Editor:**
Nicole Jones Pinard

**Product Managers:**
Jennifer A. Duffy, Trisha O'Shea

**Sr. Product Managers:**
Jeanne Herring, Kathryn Schooling

**Associate Product Manager:**
Emeline Elliot

**Editorial Assistant:**
Danielle Roy

**Production Editors:**
Ellina Beletsky, Elena Montillo, Catherine G. DiMassa, Megan Cap-Renzi, Kristen Guevara

**Contributing Authors:** Barbara Clemens, Jessica Evans, Mary Kemper, Nicole J. Pinard

**Developmental Editors:**
Rachel Biheller Bunin, Jennifer A. Duffy, Katherine T. Pinard

**Composition House:**
GEX, Inc.

**QA Manuscript Reviewers:**
Nicole Ashton, John Freitas, Jeff Schwartz, Alex White

**Text Designer:**
Joseph Lee, Black Fish Design

**Cover Designer:**
Doug Goodman, Goodman Designs

# Office 2000 Illustrated Introductory, Enhanced Edition

**What's new to this edition?** In response to our customers needs, we have added coverage of Windows 2000, and a Bonus Exercises unit to this edition. The additional Windows 2000 units provide students with an overview of the operating system. The Bonus Exercises unit offers additional **exercises** for Word, Excel, Access, PowerPoint, Internet Explorer 5, Integration and Publisher. These exercises reinforce the skills learned in the units.

## Office 2000 MOUS Certification Coverage

The Illustrated Series offers a growing number of Microsoft-approved titles, which cover the objectives required to pass the Office 2000 MOUS (Microsoft Office User Specialist) exams. After studying with any of the approved Illustrated titles (see list on inside cover), you will have mastered the Core and Expert skills necessary to pass any Office 2000 MOUS exam. In addition, the **MOUS 2000 Certification Objectives** at the end of the book map to where specific MOUS skills can be found in each lesson and where students can find additional practice.

## What do our Customers Think?

The Illustrated Series responded to Customer Feedback by adding a **Project Files List** at the back of the book for easy reference, changing the **red font** in the steps to green for easier reading, and adding new conceptual lessons to units to give students the extra information they need when learning Office 2000.

# Enhance Any Illustrated Text with these Exciting Products!

Course Technology offers a continuum of solutions to meet your online learning needs. Three Distance Learning solutions enhance your classroom experience: MyCourse.com (hosted by Course Technology), Blackboard, and WebCT.

**MyCourse.com** is an easily customizable online syllabus and course enhancement tool. This tool adds value to your class by offering brand new content designed to reinforce what you are already teaching. MyCourse.com even allows you to add your own content, hyperlinks, and assignments.

**WebCT and Blackboard** are course management tools that deliver online content for eighty-five Course Technology titles. This growing list of titles enables instructors to edit and add to any content made available through WebCT and Blackboard. In addition, you can choose what students access. The site is hosted on your school campus, allowing complete control over the information. WebCT and Blackboard offer their own internal communication system, including internal e-mail, Bulletin Boards, and Chat rooms. For more information please contact your Course Technology sales representative.

**New** to the *Office 2000 Illustrated Introductory, Enhanced* Edition are Office 2000 Projects for Word, Excel, Access and Powerpoint. These capstone Projects are uploaded into Course Technology's Distance Learning Offerings. This content is available through MyCourse, WebCT, and Blackboard. For Additional Office 2000 Projects Course Technology offers Microsoft Office 2000, Illustrated Projects (ISBN 0-7600-6159-9).

## SAM 2000

How well do your students really know Microsoft Office? SAM 2000 is a performance-based testing program that measures students' proficiency in Microsoft Office 2000. You can use SAM 2000 to place students into or out of courses, monitor their performance throughout a course, and help prepare them for the MOUS certification exams.

# Create Your Ideal Course Package with CourseKits™

If one book doesn't offer all the coverage you need, create a course package that does. With Course Technology's CourseKits—our mix-and-match approach to selecting texts—you have the freedom to combine products from more than one series. When you choose any two or more Course Technology products for one course, we'll discount the price and package them together so your students can pick up one convenient bundle at the bookstore.

For more information about any of these offerings or other Course Technology products, contact your sales representative or visit our Web site at:

**www.course.com**

# Preface

**W**elcome to *Office 2000 Illustrated Introductory, Enhanced Edition*. This highly visual book offers users a hands-on introduction to all aspects of Microsoft Office 2000 and also serves as an excellent reference for future use. From individual applications to the improved Web integration features of the software, this book will give your students an excellent overview of the Office 2000 environment. **New** to the *Office 2000 Illustrated Introductory, Enhanced Edition* is coverage of the Windows 2000 operating system as well as an additional Bonus Exercises unit offering exercises developed to reinforce the skills learned within the text.

### ▶ Organization and Coverage

This text is organized into sections that are illustrated by the colored tabs on the sides of the pages. Each section covers basic skills for Microsoft Windows 2000, Microsoft Windows 98, Microsoft Word 2000, Microsoft Excel 2000, Microsoft Access 2000, Microsoft PowerPoint 2000, Microsoft Outlook 2000, Microsoft Internet Explorer 5, Microsoft Publisher 2000, Integrating Office 2000 programs, and Bonus Exercises. In these units students learn how to work with the different applications to create simple documents, spreadsheets, databases, presentations, publications, web pages, and e-mail.

### ▶ About this Approach

What makes the Illustrated approach so effective at teaching software skills? It's quite simple. Each skill is presented on two facing pages, with the step-by-step instructions on the left page, and large screen illustrations on the right. Students can focus on a single skill without having to turn the page. This unique design makes information extremely accessible and easy to absorb, and provides a great reference for after the course is over. This hands-on approach also makes it ideal for both self-paced and instructor-led classes.

Each lesson, or "information display," contains the following elements:

---

Clear step-by-step directions explain how to complete the specific task. What students will type is in green. When students follow the numbered steps, they quickly learn how each procedure is performed and what the results will be.

Each 2-page spread focuses on a single skill.

Concise text introduces the basic principles discussed in the lesson. Procedures are easier to learn when concepts fit into a framework.

---

### Word 2000

# Formatting a Table

You can improve the appearance of a table by adding borders and shading to rows and columns. Changing the alignment of text in a table can also make your tables more attractive and readable. You can format tables automatically with the Table AutoFormat feature, which provides a variety of preset table formats, or you can use the buttons on the Tables and Borders toolbar to apply a variety of formatting effects to your tables, including text alignment, borders, and shading. The Tables and Borders toolbar appears when you click the Tables and Borders button on the Standard toolbar. Table D-1 describes some of the buttons on the Tables and Borders toolbar.  Karen uses the Table AutoFormat command to apply borders, shading, and special formatting to the table, then she changes the alignment of text in the table.

**Steps**

**QuickTip**

You can also click the Table AutoFormat button 📷 on the Tables and Borders toolbar to open the Table AutoFormat dialog box.

1. With the insertion point in the table, click **Table** on the menu bar, then click **Table AutoFormat**
   The Table AutoFormat dialog box opens, as shown in Figure D-9. In this dialog box, you can preview and select different preset table formats.

2. Scroll the list of formats, then click **Grid 8**
   The Preview box shows a sample table formatted with the Grid 8 format option. You can modify the preset formats to highlight important elements in your tables. By default, Word applies special formatting to heading rows and the first column of a table. To emphasize the meeting times in the agenda, you'll apply special formatting to the last column of the table.

3. Make sure the **Heading rows** and **First column check boxes** are selected under Apply special formats to, then click the **Last column check box** to select it
   In the Preview box, the last column of the sample table now appears in bold. AutoFormat automatically adjusts the width of columns in a table to span the width of the page. To retain the column width you set earlier, you'll turn off the AutoFit feature.

4. Clear the **AutoFit** checkbox, then click **OK**
   The table is formatted with the settings you selected.

**Trouble?**

Click the More Buttons button 📷 on the Formatting toolbar to locate buttons that are not visible on your toolbar.

5. Select the **last column**, click the **Align Right button** 📷 on the Formatting toolbar, then deselect the column
   The meeting times are right-aligned. You could also use the alignment buttons on the Tables and Borders toolbar to change the alignment of text in cells. Compare your table to Figure D-10.

6. Type your name at the top of the page, click the **Save button** 📷 on the Standard toolbar, then click the **Print button** 📷 on the Standard toolbar

7. Click **File** on the menu bar, then click **Close**

TABLE D-1: Buttons on the Tables and Borders toolbar

| button | use to | button | use to |
|---|---|---|---|
| Line Style | Determine the line style of borders | Draw Table | Draw a table or cells |
| Line Weight | Determine the thickness of borders | Eraser | Erase or remove a border between cells |
| Border Color | Determine the color of borders | Merge Cells | Combine selected cells into a single cell |
| Outside Borders | Add or remove individual borders | Split Cells | Divide a cell into multiple cells |
| Shading Color | Determine the shade color or pattern of cells | Insert Table | Insert new rows, columns, cells, or a new table |
| Align Top Left | Change the alignment of text in a cell | Distribute Rows Evenly | Make rows the same height |
| Change Text Direction | Change the orientation of text | Distribute Columns Evenly | Make columns the same width |

---

Tips and troubleshooting advice right where you need them—next to the step itself.

Quickly accessible summaries of key terms, toolbar buttons, or keyboard alternatives connected with the lesson material. Students can easily refer to this information when working on their own projects later.

Every lesson features large-size, full-color representations of what the students' screen should look like after completing the numbered steps.

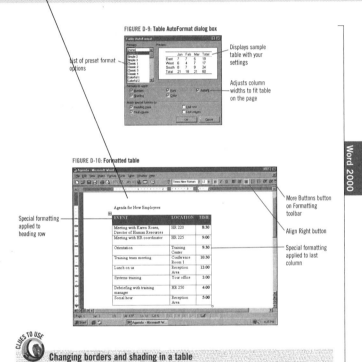

FIGURE D-9: Table AutoFormat dialog box

list of preset format options

Displays sample table with your settings

Adjusts column widths to fit table on the page

FIGURE D-10: Formatted table

Special formatting applied to heading row

More Buttons button on Formatting toolbar

Align Right button

Special formatting applied to last column

Word 2000

### Changing borders and shading in a table

You can add, remove, or alter the borders and shading in a table using the buttons on the Tables and Borders toolbar, shown in Figure D-11, which appears when you click the Tables and Borders button on the Standard toolbar. To change the shading of cells, select the cells you want to format, click the Shading Color list arrow on the Tables and Borders toolbar, then click the shade color and intensity you want to apply to the selected cells. To add or remove borders from a table, select the cells you want to format, then click the Outside Borders list arrow on the Tables and Borders toolbar (or the Formatting toolbar). From the list of border buttons, click the button that corresponds to the border you want to

add or remove. For example, if you want to remove borders from around all the cells in your table, you would select the table, click the Outside Borders list arrow, then click the All Borders button. The border buttons are toggle buttons, which means that you can use them to turn borders on and off. When you remove a border from a table, a gridline appears on the screen. The gridline is a light gray line that represents the edge of the cell, but does not print.

FIGURE D-11: Tables and Borders toolbar

WORKING WITH TABLES  WORD D-9

Clues to Use boxes provide concise information that expands upon one component of the major lesson skill or describes an independent task related to the major lesson skill.

The page numbers are designed like a road map. **Word** indicates the **Word** section, **D** indicates the **4th** unit, and **9** indicate the page within the unit.

# Other Features

The two-page lesson format featured in this book provides the new user with a powerful learning experience. Additionally, this book contains the following features:

### ▶ MOUS Certification Coverage

Each unit opener has a ⌊MOUS⌉ next to it to indicate where Microsoft Office User Specialist (MOUS) skills are covered. In addition, there is a MOUS appendix, which contains a grid for each application that maps to where specific MOUS skills can be found in each lesson and where students can find additional practice. This text, used in conjunction with the Microsoft Office 2000—Illustrated Second Course, 0-7600-6118-1, thoroughly prepares students to learn the skills for PowerPoint 2000, Core and Expert certification, as well as Word 2000, Excel 2000, and Access 2000 Core Certification. The PowerPoint units in this book, in combination with the PowerPoint Instructor's Manual, teach students the skills they need to meet PowerPoint 2000 Core certification.

### ▶ Real-World Case

The case study used throughout the textbook, a fictitious company called MediaLoft, is designed to be "real-world" in nature and introduces the kinds of activities that students will encounter when working with **Microsoft Office**. Students can also enhance their skills by completing the Web Work exercises in each unit by going to the innovative Student Online Companion, available at **www.course.com/illustrated/medialoft**.

### ▶ End-of-Unit Material

Each unit concludes with a Concepts Review that tests students' understanding of what they learned in the unit. The Concepts Review is followed by a Skills Review, which provides students with additional hands-on practice of the skills. The Skills Review is followed by Independent Challenges, which pose case problems for students to solve. At least one Independent Challenge in each unit asks students to use the World Wide Web to solve the problem as indicated by a Web Work icon. The Visual Workshops that follow the Independent Challenges help students develop critical thinking skills. Students are shown completed Web pages or screens and are asked to recreate them from scratch.

# Instructor's Resource Kit

The Instructor's Resource Kit is Course Technology's way of putting the resources and information needed to teach and learn effectively into your hands. With an integrated array of teaching and learning tools that offers you and your students a broad range of technology-based instructional options, we believe this kit represents the highest quality and most cutting edge resources available to instructors today. Many of these resources are available at **www.course.com**. The resources available with this book are:

**MediaLoft Web site** Available at **www.course.com/illustrated/medialoft**, this innovative Student Online Companion enhances and augments the printed page by bringing students onto the Web for a dynamic and continually updated learning experience. The MediaLoft site mirrors the case study used throughout the book, creating a real-world intranet site for this fictitious company, a national chain of bookstore cafés. This Companion is used to complete the Web Work exercise in each unit of this book, and to allow students to become familiar with the business application of an intranet site.

**Instructor's Manual** Available as an electronic file, the Instructor's Manual is quality-assurance tested and includes unit overviews, detailed lecture topics for each unit with teaching tips, an Upgrader's Guide, solutions to all lessons and end-of-unit material, and extra Independent Challenges. The Instructor's Manual is available on the Instructor's Resource Kit CD-ROM, or you can download it from **www.course.com**.

**New** to the *Office 2000 Illustrated Introductory, Enhanced Edition* IM are four capstone Independent Challenges from the Office 2000 Projects text. These capstone projects are available in Word, Excel, Access, and Powerpoint.

**Course Test Manager** Designed by Course Technology, this Windows-based testing software helps instructor's design, administer, and print tests and pre-tests. A full-featured program, Course Test Manager also has an online testing component that allows students to take tests at the computer and have their exams automatically graded.

**Course Faculty Online Companion** You can browse this textbook's password-protected site to obtain the Instructor's Manual, Solution Files, Project Files, and any updates to the text. Contact your Customer Service Representative for the site address and password.

**Project Files** Project Files contain all of the data that students will use to complete the lessons and end-of-unit material. A Readme file includes instructions for using the files. Adopters of this text are granted the right to install the Project Files on any stand-alone computer or network. The Project Files are available on the Instructor's Resource Kit CD-ROM, the Review Pack, and can also be downloaded from **www.course.com**.

**Solution Files** Solution Files contain every file students are asked to create or modify in the lessons and end-of-unit material. A Help file on the Instructor's Resource Kit includes information for using the Solution Files.

**Figure Files** Figure files contain all the figures from the book in bitmap format. Use the figure files to create transparency masters or in a PowerPoint presentation.

**Learning Microsoft Outlook 2000 E-mail** Learning Microsoft Outlook 2000 E-mail is a simulation program designed to imitate the experience of using the mail capabilities of Microsoft Outlook 2000. Using Learning Microsoft Outlook 2000 e-mail, your students will learn to send, receive, forward, and reply to messages, as well as to manage a mailbox. To complete the Microsoft Outlook 2000 unit your students must use a computer that has the Learning Microsoft Outlook 2000 E-mail program installed from either the Review Pack or the Instructor's Resource Kit. Adopters of this text are granted the right to install Learning Microsoft Outlook 2000 E-mail on any standalone computer or network.

**CyberClass** CyberClass is a web-based tool designed for on-campus distance learning. Use it to enhance how you currently run your class, by posting assignments and your course syllabus or holding online office hours. Or, use it for your distance-learning course and offer mini-lectures or conduct online discussion groups; CyberClass can be found at: www.course.com/products/cyberclass/index.html.

# Brief Contents

# Contents

# Contents

## Windows 98

# Office 2000

## Introducing Microsoft Office 2000 Premium

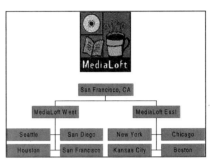

# Internet Explorer 5

## Getting Started with Internet Explorer 5

# Word 2000

## Getting Started with Word 2000

# Contents

## Editing and Proofing Documents — WORD B-1

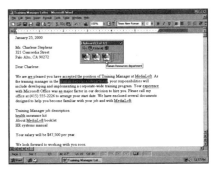

## Formatting a Document — WORD C-1

## Working with Tables           WORD D-1

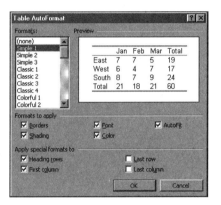

## Excel 2000

## Getting Started with Excel 2000        EXCEL A-1

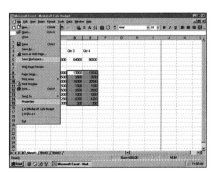

# Contents

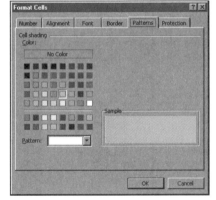

# Working with Charts

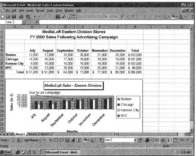

# Integration

# Integrating Word and Excel

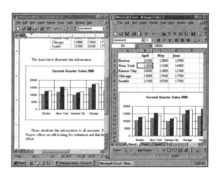

# Access 2000

# Getting Started with Access 2000

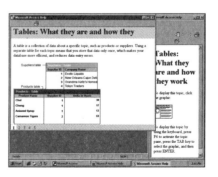

# Contents

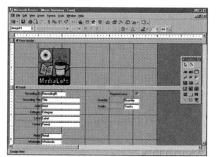

## Integration

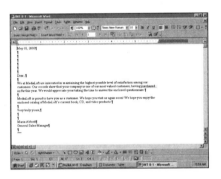

## PowerPoint 2000

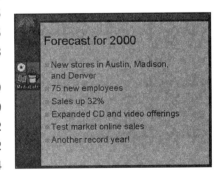

# Contents

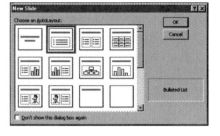

## Enhancing a Presentation

## Integration

## Integrating Word, Excel, Access, and PowerPoint

## Internet Explorer 5

## Creating a Web Publication

# Contents

## Publisher 2000

## Outlook 2000

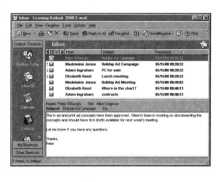

## Bonus Exercises

## Windows 2000 Appendix A

## Windows 98 Appendix A

# Read This Before You Begin

## Project Files

To complete the Lessons and End-of-Unit material in this book, students need to obtain the necessary Project Files. Please refer to the instructions on the inside back cover.

## Installation

Installation offers different options to users through the Setup program, allowing them to choose exactly how to install each feature. Users can complete a typical installation of features onto their hard drive. They now have three additional options:

- Setting a feature to be installed the first time it is used (after a typical install, you are automatically prompted to install a feature on first use unless you specifically choose to install the feature at the time of installation—unless you do a custom or complete installation).

- Installing a feature to run directly from the Office CD or over a network, conserving hard drive space.

- Not installing a feature.

Because of this added flexibility included in the Setup program, some features of Office 2000 covered in the book are not installed as part of the default, typical installation on a standalone computer. These "install on first use" features include the Clip Gallery, templates, and integration functions. They require the user to insert the Office 2000 CD to install the component the first time the feature is used.

To avoid this, make sure that your computer has completed a full installation of Office 2000.

## Toolbars and Menus

Office 2000 features a personalized interface for users. Both the toolbars and menus adapt to your working style. The Standard and Formatting toolbars you see when you start the application for the first time include the most frequently used buttons. Other, less frequently used toolbar buttons are hidden.

To locate a button that is not visible on a toolbar, you need to click the More Buttons button on the right end of either the Standard or Formatting toolbar to see the list of hidden toolbar buttons. When you use buttons from the More Buttons list, the application adds those buttons to the visible toolbar, and moves the buttons you haven't used in a while to the More Buttons list. Similarly, menus adjust to your work habits, so that the commands you use most often automatically appear on shortened menus. Click the double arrow at the bottom of a menu to view additional menu commands.

Personalized toolbars and menus provide a challenge to instructors, as the toolbars and menus will appear differently for each student. To address this challenge, at the beginning of each unit we have instructed students to return their toolbars and menus to the default settings, erasing any personalized settings the application created for a previous user. In addition, each unit begins using the default toolbar and menu settings in screen shots.

We cannot control or predict which buttons will appear on students' toolbars, so we are not able to include instructions to click the More Buttons button in lesson steps. Reminders to use the More Buttons button appear in the margin of lessons, but students learning to use Office 2000 will need to learn how to find buttons that do not appear on their toolbars. Similarly, students will need to learn to use the shortened menus. We have included a Clues to Use explaining personalization features of Office 2000 in the first unit of each application.

## Windows Appendices

Located in the back of the text are appendices for Windows 98 and Windows 2000. These appendices respond to our customers' needs for more detailed information on how to format a disk.

# Getting
## Started with Windows 2000

### Objectives

- ▶ Start Windows and view the Active Desktop
- ▶ Use the mouse
- ▶ Start a program
- ▶ Move and resize windows
- ▶ Use menus, keyboard shortcuts, and toolbars
- ▶ Use dialog boxes
- ▶ Use scroll bars
- ▶ Use Windows Help
- ▶ Close a program and shut down Windows

Microsoft Windows 2000 is an **operating system**, a computer **program**, or set of instructions, that controls how the computer carries out basic tasks such as displaying information on your computer screen and running programs. Windows 2000 helps you save and organize the results of your work as **files**, which are electronic collections of data. Windows 2000 also coordinates the flow of information among the programs, printers, storage devices, and other components of your computer system, as well as among other computers on a network. When you work with Windows 2000, you will notice many **icons**, small pictures intended to be meaningful symbols of the items they represent. You will also notice rectangular-shaped work areas known as **windows**, thus the name of the operating system. These icons, windows, and various other words and symbols create what is referred to as a **graphical user interface** (**GUI**, pronounced "gooey"), through which you interact with the computer. This unit introduces you to basic skills that you can use in all Windows programs.

# Starting Windows and Viewing the Active Desktop

When you turn on your computer, Windows 2000 automatically starts and the Active Desktop appears. The **Active Desktop**, shown in Figure A-1, is where you organize all the information and tools you need to accomplish your computer tasks. You can access, store, share, and explore information seamlessly, whether it resides on your computer, a network, or the **Internet**, a worldwide collection of over 40 million computers linked together to share information. The desktop is called "active" because it offers an interactive link between your computer and the Internet, so that Internet content displayed on your desktop, such as stock prices or weather information, is always up to date. When you start Windows for the first time, the desktop appears with the **default** settings, those preset by the operating system. For example, the default color of the desktop is blue. If any of the default settings have been changed on your computer, your desktop will look different than the one in the figures, but you should be able to locate all the items you need. The bar at the bottom of your screen is called the **taskbar**, which shows what programs are currently running. You use the Start menu, accessed by clicking the **Start button** at the left end of the taskbar, to perform such tasks as starting programs, finding and opening files, and accessing Windows Help. The **Quick Launch toolbar** is next to the Start button; it contains several buttons you can click to start Internet-related programs quickly, and another that you can click to show the desktop when it is not currently visible. Table A-1 identifies the icons and other elements you see on your desktop. If Windows 2000 is not currently running, follow the steps below to start it now.

**Steps**

**Trouble?**

If you don't know your password, see your instructor or technical support person.

**1.** Turn on your computer and monitor

You might see a "Please select the operating system to start" prompt. Don't worry about selecting one of the options; Microsoft Windows 2000 Professional automatically starts after 30 seconds. When Windows starts and the desktop appears, you may see a Log On to Windows dialog box. If so, continue to Step 2. If not, view Figure A-1, then continue on to the next lesson.

**Trouble?**

If the Getting Started with Windows 2000 dialog box opens, move your mouse pointer over the Exit button in the lower-right corner of the dialog box and press the left mouse button once to close the dialog box.

**2.** Enter the correct user name, type your password, then press **[Enter]**

Once the password is accepted, the Windows desktop appears on your screen. See Figure A-1.

## Accessing the Internet from the Active Desktop

Windows 2000 provides a seamless connection between your desktop and the Internet with Internet Explorer. Internet Explorer is an example of a **browser,** a program designed to access the **World Wide Web** (also known as the **WWW,** or simply the **Web**). Internet Explorer is integrated with the Windows 2000 operating system. You can access it by clicking its icon on the desktop or on the Quick Launch toolbar. You can access Web pages, and place Web content such as weather or stock updates on the desktop for instant viewing. This information is updated automatically whenever you connect to the Internet, making your desktop truly active. You can also communicate electronically with other Internet users, using the Windows e-mail and newsreader program, Outlook Express.

FIGURE A-1: Windows Active Desktop

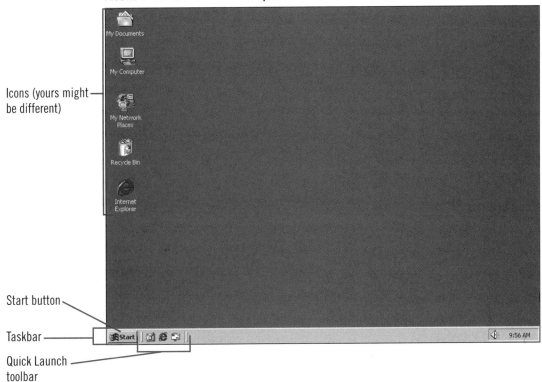

Icons (yours might be different)

Start button

Taskbar

Quick Launch toolbar

TABLE A-1: Elements of the Windows desktop

| desktop element | icon | allows you to |
|---|---|---|
| My Documents folder | | Store programs, documents, graphics, or other files |
| My Computer | | Work with different disk drives and printers on your computer |
| My Network Places | | Open files and folders on other computers and install network printers |
| Recycle Bin | | Delete and restore files |
| Internet Explorer | | Start Internet Explorer to access the Internet |
| Connect to the Internet | | Set up Internet access |
| Start button | Start | Start programs, open documents, search for files, and more |
| Taskbar | | Start programs and switch among open programs |
| Quick Launch toolbar | | Start Internet Explorer, start Outlook Express, and display the desktop |

# Using the Mouse

A **mouse** is a hand-held **input or pointing device** that you use to interact with your computer. Input or pointing devices come in many shapes and sizes; some, like a mouse, are directly attached to your computer with a cable; others function like a TV remote control and allow you to access your computer without being right next to it. Figure A-2 shows examples of common pointing devices. Because the most common pointing device is a mouse, this book uses that term. If you are using a different pointing device, substitute that device whenever you see the term "mouse." When you move the mouse, the **mouse pointer** on the screen moves in the same direction. The **mouse buttons** are used to select icons and commands, which is how you communicate with the computer. Table A-2 shows some common mouse pointer shapes that indicate different activities. Table A-3 lists the five basic mouse actions.  Begin by experimenting with the mouse now.

1. **Locate the mouse pointer on the desktop, then move the mouse across your desk or mousepad**
   Watch how the mouse pointer moves on the desktop in response to your movements; practice moving the mouse pointer in circles, then back and forth in straight lines.

2. **Position the mouse pointer over the My Computer icon**
   Positioning the mouse pointer over an item is called **pointing**.

3. **With the pointer over the My Computer icon, press and release the left mouse button**
   Pressing and releasing the left mouse button is called **clicking** (or single-clicking, to distinguish it from double-clicking, which you'll do in Step 7). When you position the mouse pointer over an icon or any item and click, you select that item. When an item is **selected**, it is **highlighted** (shaded differently from other items), and the next action you take will be performed on that item.

4. **With the My computer icon selected, press and hold down the left mouse button, then move the mouse down and to the right and release the mouse button**
   The icon becomes dimmed and moves with the mouse pointer; this is called **dragging**, which you do to move icons and other Windows elements. When you release the mouse button, the item is positioned at the new location.

5. **Position the mouse pointer over the My Computer icon, then press and release the right mouse button**
   Clicking the right mouse button is known as **right-clicking**. Right-clicking an item on the desktop produces a **pop-up menu**, as shown in Figure A-3. This menu lists the commands most commonly used for the item you have clicked. A **command** is a directive that provides access to a program's features.

6. **Click anywhere outside the menu to close the pop-up menu**

7. **Position the mouse pointer over the My Computer icon, then quickly press and release the left mouse button twice**
   Clicking the mouse button twice quickly is known as **double-clicking**, which, in this case, opens the My Computer window. The **My Computer** window contains additional icons that represent the drives and system components that are installed on your computer.

8. **Click the Close button** ☒ **in the upper-right corner of the My Computer window**

**Trouble?**

If the My Computer window opens during this step, your mouse isn't set with the Windows 2000 default mouse settings. See your instructor or technical support person for assistance. This book assumes your computer is set to all Windows 2000 default settings.

**QuickTip**

When a step tells you to "click," use the left mouse button. If it says "right-click," use the right mouse button.

TABLE A-2: Common mouse pointer shapes

| shape | used to |
|---|---|
| ↖ | Select items, choose commands, start programs, and work in programs |
| I | Position mouse pointer for editing or inserting text; called the insertion point |
| ⧗ | Indicate Windows is busy processing a command |
| ↔ | Change the size of a window; appears when mouse pointer is on the border of a window |
| ⛐ | Select and open Web-based data |

FIGURE A-2: Common pointing devices

Trackball

Trackpoint

Right mouse button

Left mouse button

Intellimouse

Mouse

FIGURE A-3: Displaying a pop-up menu

Selected icon

Pop-up menu

## More about the mouse: Classic style and Internet style

Because Windows 2000 integrates the use of the Internet with its other functions, it allows you to extend the way you click in a Web browser program on the Internet to the way you click in other computer programs. With the default Windows 2000 settings, you click an item to select it and double-click an item to open it. In a Web browser program, however, you point to an item to select it and single-click to open it. Windows 2000 gives you two choices for clicking: with the **Classic style,** you double-click to open items, and with the **Internet style,** you single-click to open items. To switch between styles, double-click the My Computer Icon (or click if you are currently using the Internet style), click Tools on the menu bar, click Folder Options, click the General tab if necessary, click the Single-click to Open an Item option or the Double-click to Open an Item option in the Click items as follows section, and then click OK.

TABLE A-3: Basic mouse techniques

| technique | what to do |
|---|---|
| **Pointing** | Move the mouse to position the mouse pointer over an item on the desktop |
| **Clicking** | Press and release the left mouse button |
| **Double-clicking** | Press and release the left mouse button twice quickly |
| **Dragging** | Point to an item, press and hold the left mouse button, move the mouse to a new location, then release the mouse button |
| **Right-clicking** | Point to an item, then press and release the right mouse button |

**Windows 2000**

# Starting a Program

Clicking the Start button on the taskbar opens the Start menu, which lists submenus for a variety of tasks described in Table A-4. As you become familiar with Windows, you might want to customize the Start menu to include additional items that you use most often. Windows 2000 comes with several built-in programs, called **accessories**. Although not as feature-rich as many programs sold separately, Windows accessories are useful for completing basic tasks. ✎ In this lesson, you start a Windows accessory called **WordPad**, which is a word-processing program you can use to create and edit simple documents.

## Steps

### 1. Click the **Start button** on the taskbar
The Start menu opens.

### 2. Point to **Programs**
The Programs submenu opens, listing the programs and categories for programs installed on your computer. WordPad is in the category called Accessories.

**QuickTip**

Windows 2000 features personalized menus, which list only the commands you've most recently used. Whenever you want to view other commands available on the menu, rest the mouse pointer over the double arrows ⧩ at the bottom of the menu.

### 3. Point to **Accessories**
The Accessories menu, shown in Figure A-4, contains several programs to help you complete common tasks. You want to start WordPad. If you do not see WordPad, rest the mouse pointer over the double arrows at the bottom of Programs submenu and wait. The full menu will open after a few seconds.

### 4. Click **WordPad**
WordPad opens with a blank document window open, as shown in Figure A-5. Don't worry if your window does not fill the screen; you'll learn how to maximize it in the next lesson. Note that a **program button** appears on the taskbar and is highlighted, indicating that WordPad is open.

**TABLE A-4: Start menu categories**

| category | description |
|---|---|
| Windows Update | Connects to a Microsoft Web site and updates your Windows 2000 files as necessary |
| Programs | Displays a menu of programs included on the Start menu |
| Documents | Displays a menu of the most recently opened and recently saved documents |
| Settings | Displays a menu of tools for selecting settings for your system |
| Search | Locates programs, files, folders, people, or computers on your computer network, or finds information and people on the Internet |
| Help | Provides Windows Help information by topic, alphabetical index, or search criteria |
| Run | Opens a program or file based on a location and filename that you type or select |
| Shut Down | Provides options to log off, shut down, or restart the computer |

FIGURE A-4: **Cascading menus**

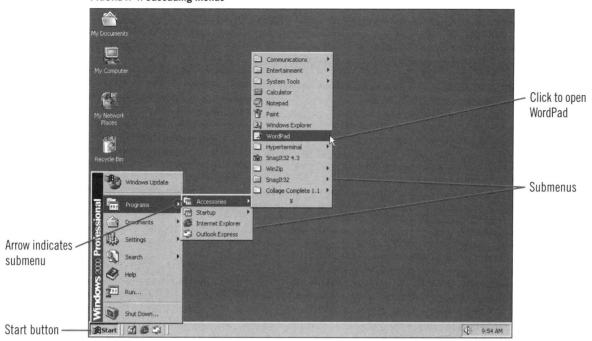

Click to open WordPad

Submenus

Arrow indicates submenu

Start button

FIGURE A-5: **WordPad program window**

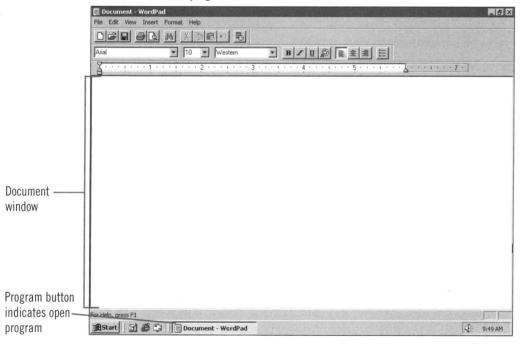

Document window

Program button indicates open program

## The Startup Folder

You can specify one or more programs to open each time you start Windows 2000 by placing shortcuts in the Startup Folder. This might be useful if you know you will be working in the same programs first thing every day. To place a program in the Startup Folder, click the Start button, point to Settings, then click

Taskbar & Start Menu. Click the Advanced tab of the Taskbar and Start Menu Properties dialog box, click Advanced, and then, in the Start Menu folder, locate the shortcut to the program you want to specify, and drag it to the Startup folder.

# Moving and Resizing Windows

One of the powerful features of Windows is the ability to open more than one window or program at once. This means, however, that the desktop can get cluttered with the various programs and files you are using. You can keep your desktop organized by changing the size of a window or moving it. You can do this by clicking the sizing buttons in the upper-right corner of any window and dragging a corner or border of any window that does not completely fill the screen. Practice sizing and moving the WordPad window now.

## Steps

**1.** If the WordPad window does not already fill the screen, click the **Maximize button** in the WordPad window
When a window is **maximized**, it takes up the whole screen.

**2.** Click the **Restore button** in the WordPad window
To **restore** a window is to return it to its previous size, as shown in Figure A-6. The Restore button only appears when a window is maximized.

**3.** Position the pointer on the right edge of the WordPad window until the pointer changes to ↔, then drag the border to the right
The width of the window increases. You can size the height or width of a window by dragging any of the four sides individually.

**QuickTip**

You can resize windows by dragging any corner. You can also drag any border to make the window taller, shorter, wider, or narrower.

**4.** Position the pointer in the lower-right corner of the WordPad window until the pointer changes to ↘, as shown in Figure A-6, then drag down and to the right
The height and width of the window increase proportionally when you drag a corner instead of a side. You can also position a restored window wherever you wish on the desktop by dragging its title bar. The **title bar** is the area along the top of the window that displays the file name and program used to create it.

**5.** Drag the **title bar** on the WordPad window up and to the left, as shown in Figure A-6
The window is repositioned on the desktop. At times, you might wish to close a program window, yet keep the program running and easily accessible. You can accomplish this by minimizing a window.

**QuickTip**

If you have more than one window open and you want to quickly access something on the desktop, you can click the Show Desktop button on the Quick Launch toolbar. All open windows are minimized so the desktop is visible.

**6.** In the WordPad window, click the **Minimize button**
When you **minimize** a window, it shrinks to a program button on the taskbar, as shown in Figure A-7. WordPad is still running, but it is out of your way.

**7.** Click the **WordPad program button** on the taskbar to reopen the window
The WordPad program window reopens.

**8.** Click the **Maximize button** in the upper-right corner of the WordPad window
The window fills the screen.

FIGURE A-6: **Restored program window**

Title bar

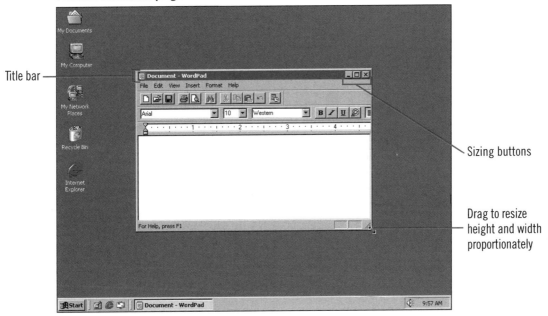

Sizing buttons

Drag to resize height and width proportionately

FIGURE A-7: **Minimized program window**

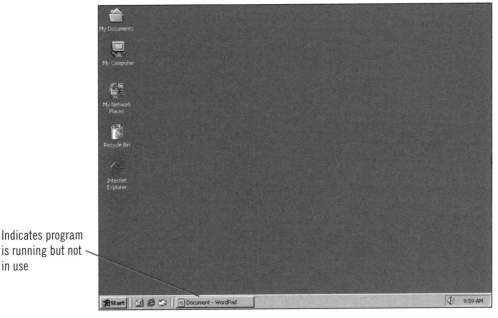

Indicates program is running but not in use

## More about sizing windows

Keep in mind that many programs contain two sets of sizing buttons: one that controls the program window itself and another that controls the window for the file with which you are working. The program sizing buttons are located in the title bar and the file sizing buttons are located below them. See Figure A-8. When you minimize a file window within a program, the file window is reduced to an icon in the lower-left corner of the program window, but the size of the program window remains intact.

FIGURE A-8: **Program and file sizing buttons**

Program window sizing buttons

File window sizing buttons

# Using Menus, Keyboard Shortcuts, and Toolbars

A **menu** is a list of commands that you use to accomplish certain tasks. You've already used the Start menu to start WordPad. Each Windows program also has its own set of menus, which are located on the **menu bar** under the title bar. The menus organize commands into groups of related operations. See Table A-5 for a description of items on a typical menu. **Toolbar buttons** offer another method for executing menu commands; instead of clicking the menu and then the menu command, you simply click the button for the command. A **toolbar** is a set of buttons usually positioned below the menu bar in a Windows program. In Windows 2000, you can customize a toolbar by adding buttons to or removing buttons from toolbars to suit your preferences. You will open the Control Panel, then use a menu and toolbar button to change how the contents of the window appear, and then add and remove a toolbar button.

1. **Click the Start button on the taskbar, point to Settings, then click Control Panel**
   The Control Panel window opens over the WordPad window. The **Control Panel** contains icons for various programs that allow you to specify how your computer looks and performs.

2. **Click View on the menu bar**
   The View menu appears, listing the View commands, as shown in Figure A-9. On a menu, a **check mark** identifies a feature that is currently enabled or "on." To disable or turn "off" the feature, you click the command again to remove the check mark. A **bullet mark** can also indicate that an option is enabled. To disable a bulleted option, you must select another option in its place.

3. **Click Small Icons**
   The icons are now smaller than they were before, taking up less room in the window.

4. **Press [Alt][V] to open the View menu, then press [T] to execute the Toolbars command**
   The View menu appears again, and then the Toolbars submenu appears, with checkmarks next to the commands that are currently selected. You opened these menus using the keyboard. Notice that a letter in each command on the View menu is underlined. These are **keyboard navigation indicators**, indicating that you can press the underlined letter, known as a **keyboard shortcut**, instead of clicking to execute the command.

5. **Press [C] to execute the Customize command**
   The Customize Toolbar dialog box opens. A dialog box is a window in which you make specifications for how you want a task performed; you'll learn more about working in a dialog box shortly. In the Customize Toolbar dialog box, you can add toolbar buttons to the current toolbar, or remove buttons already on the toolbar. The list on the right shows which buttons are currently on the toolbar, and the list on the left shows which buttons are available to add.

6. **Click the Favorites button in the Available toolbar buttons section, then click the Add button**
   As shown in Figure A-10, the Favorites button is added to the Standard toolbar of the Control Panel window.

7. **Click Favorites in the Current toolbar buttons section, click the Remove button, then click Close on the Customize Toolbar dialog box**
   The Favorites button disappears from the Standard toolbar, and the Customize Toolbar dialog box closes.

8. **On the Control Panel toolbar, click the Views button list arrow** ▦▾
   Some toolbar buttons have an arrow, which indicates the button contains several choices. Clicking the button shows the choices.

9. **In the list of View choices, click Details**
   The Details view includes a description of each program in the Control Panel.

Check mark

**FIGURE A-9: Opening a menu**

Menu bar

Commands in View menu

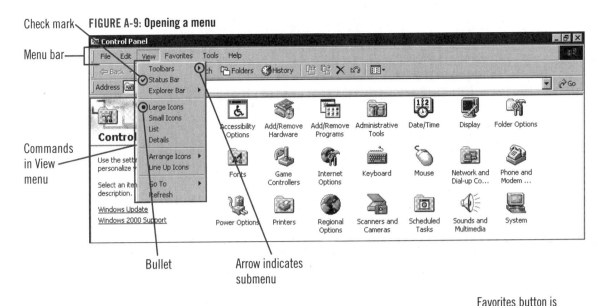

Bullet

Arrow indicates submenu

Favorites button is added to the toolbar

**FIGURE A-10: Customize Toolbar dialog box**

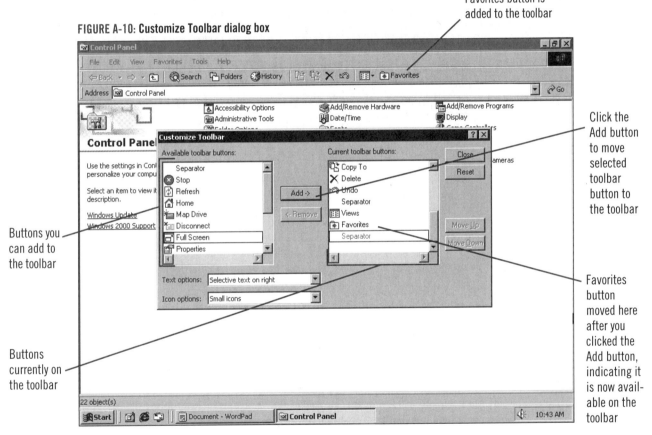

Click the Add button to move selected toolbar button to the toolbar

Buttons you can add to the toolbar

Buttons currently on the toolbar

Favorites button moved here after you clicked the Add button, indicating it is now available on the toolbar

**TABLE A-5: Typical items on a menu**

| item | description | example |
|------|-------------|---------|
| **Dimmed command** | Indicates the menu command is not currently available | Undo    Ctrl+Z |
| **Ellipsis** | Opens a dialog box that allows you to select different or additional options | Save As... |
| **Triangle** | Opens a cascading menu containing an additional list of commands | Zoom    ▶ |
| **Keyboard shortcut** | Executes a command using the keyboard instead of the mouse | Paste    Ctrl+V |
| **Underlined letter** | Indicates the letter to press for the keyboard shortcut | Print Preview |

# Using Dialog Boxes

A **dialog box** is a window that opens when you choose a menu command that is followed by an ellipsis (…), or any command that needs more information before the program can carry out the command you selected. Dialog boxes open in other situations as well, such as when you open a program in the Control Panel. See Figure A-11 and Table A-6 for some of the typical elements of a dialog box. ✎ Practice using a dialog box to control your mouse settings.

1. **In the Control Panel window, double-click the Mouse icon** ✎
   The Mouse Properties dialog box opens, as shown in Figure A-12. **Properties** are characteristics of a specific computer element (in this case, the mouse) that you can customize. The options in this dialog box allow you to control the way the mouse buttons are configured, select the types of pointers that appear, choose the speed of the mouse movement on the screen, and specify what type of mouse you are using. **Tabs** at the top of the dialog box separate these options into related categories.

2. **Click the Motion tab if necessary to make it the front-most tab**
   This tab contains three options for controlling the way your mouse moves. Under Speed, you can set how fast the pointer moves on the screen in relation to how you move the mouse. You drag a **slider** to specify how fast the pointer moves. Under Acceleration, you can click an **option button** to adjust how much your pointer accelerates as you move it faster. When choosing among option buttons, you can select only one at a time. Under Snap to default, there is a **check box**, which is a toggle for turning a feature on or off—in this case, for setting whether or not you want your mouse pointer to move to the default button in dialog boxes.

3. **Under Speed, drag the slider all the way to the left for Slow, then move the mouse pointer across your screen**
   Notice how slowly the mouse pointer moves. After you select the options you want in a dialog box, you need to select a **command button**, which carries out the options you've selected. The two most common command buttons are OK and Cancel. Clicking OK accepts your changes and closes the dialog box; clicking Cancel leaves the original settings intact and closes the dialog box. The third command button in this dialog box is Apply. Clicking the Apply button accepts the changes you've made and keeps the dialog box open so that you can select additional options. Because you might share this computer with others, it's important to return the dialog box options back to the original settings.

4. **Click Cancel**
   The original settings remain intact and the dialog box closes.

FIGURE A-11: Elements of a typical dialog box

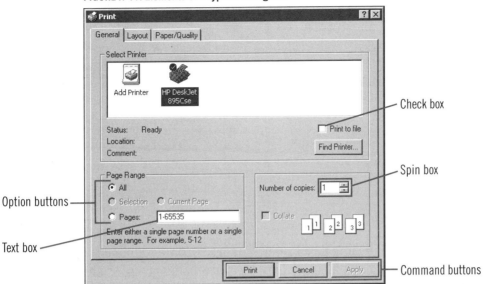

Check box

Spin box

Option buttons

Text box

Command buttons

FIGURE A-12: Mouse Properties dialog box

Tabs

Slider

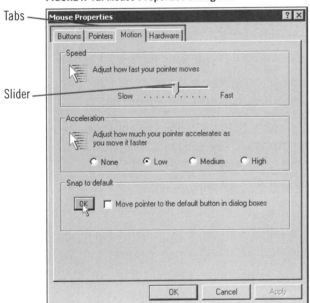

TABLE A-6: Typical items in a dialog box

| item | description | item | description |
|---|---|---|---|
| Check box | A box that turns an option on (when the box is checked) and off (when it is unchecked) | List box | A box containing a list of items; to choose an item, click the list arrow, then click the desired item |
| Text box | A box in which you type text | Spin box | A box with two arrows and a text box; allows you to scroll in numerical increments or type a number |
| Option button | A small circle that you click to select a single dialog box option; you cannot check more than one option button in a list | Slider | A shape that you drag to set the degree to which an option is in effect |
| Command button | A rectangular button in a dialog box with the name of the command on it | Tab | A place in a dialog box where related commands and options are organized |

# Using Scroll Bars

When you cannot see all of the items available in a window, scroll bars appear on the right and/or bottom edges of the window. **Scroll bars** allow you to view the additional contents of the window. There are several ways you can scroll in a window. When you need to scroll only a short distance, you can use the scroll arrows. To scroll the window in larger increments, click in the scroll bar above or below the scroll box. Dragging the scroll box moves you quickly to a new part of the window. See Table A-7 for a summary of the different ways to use scroll bars. ✒️ With the Control Panel window in Details view, you can use the scroll bars to view all of the items in this window.

## Steps

1. In the Control Panel window, drag the **lower-right corner** of the dialog box up toward the upper-left corner until the scroll bars appear, as shown in Figure A-13
   Scroll bars appear only when the window is not large enough to include all the information. After you resize the dialog box, they appear along the bottom and right side of the dialog box. You may have to size your window smaller than the one in the figure for your scroll bars to appear.

2. Click the **down scroll arrow**, as shown in Figure A-13
   Clicking this arrow moves the view down one line.

3. Click the **up scroll arrow** in the vertical scroll bar
   Clicking this arrow moves the view up one line.

4. Click anywhere in the area below the scroll box in the vertical scroll bar
   The view moves down one window's height. Similarly, you can click in the scroll bar above the scroll box to move up one window's height.

5. Drag the **scroll box** all the way down to the bottom of the vertical scrollbar
   The view now includes the items that appear at the very bottom of the window.

6. Drag the **scroll box** all the way up to the top of the vertical scroll bar
   This view shows the items that appear at the top of the window.

7. Click the area to the right of the scroll box in the horizontal scroll bar
   The far right edge of the window comes into view. The horizontal scroll bar works the same as the vertical scroll bar.

8. Click the area to the left of the scroll box in the horizontal scroll bar
   You should return the Control Panel to its original settings.

9. Maximize the Control Panel window, click the **Views button list arrow** 🔲▾ on the Control Panel toolbar, then click **Large Icons**

> **QuickTip**
>
> The size of the scroll box changes to reflect how much information does not fit in the window. A larger scroll box indicates that a relatively small amount of the window's contents is not currently visible; you need to scroll only a short distance to see the remaining items. A smaller scroll box indicates that a relatively large amount of information is currently not visible.

FIGURE A-13: Scroll bars

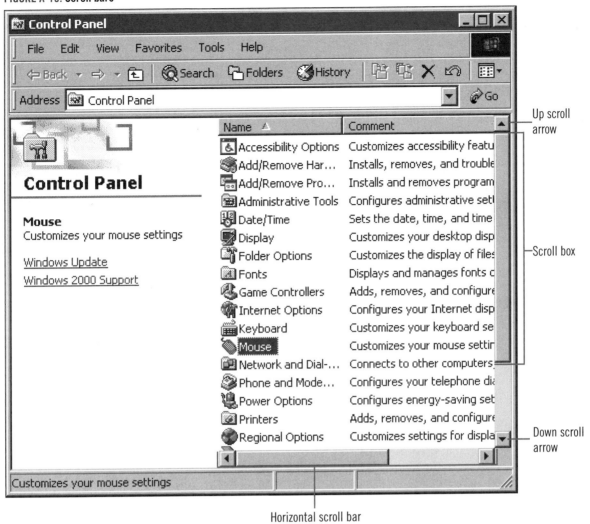

Up scroll arrow

Scroll box

Down scroll arrow

Horizontal scroll bar

TABLE A-7: Using scroll bars in a window

| to | do this |
|---|---|
| Move down one line | Click the down arrow at the bottom of the vertical scroll bar |
| Move up one line | Click the up arrow at the top of the vertical scroll bar |
| Move down one window height | Click in the area below the scroll box in the vertical scroll bar |
| Move up one window height | Click in the area above the scroll box in the vertical scroll bar |
| Move up a large distance in the window | Drag the scroll box up in the vertical scroll bar |
| Move down a large distance in the window | Drag the scroll box down in the vertical scroll bar |
| Move a short distance side-to-side in a window | Click the left or right arrows in the horizontal scroll bar |
| Move to the right one window width | Click in the area to the right of the scroll box in the horizontal scroll bar |
| Move to the left one window width | Click in the area to the left of the scroll box in the horizontal scroll bar |
| Move left or right a large distance in the window | Drag the scroll box in the horizontal scroll bar |

**Windows 2000**

# Using Windows Help

When you have a question about how to do something in Windows 2000, you can usually find the answer with a few clicks of your mouse. **Windows Help** works like a book stored on your computer, with a table of contents and an index to make finding information easier. Help provides guidance on many Windows features, including detailed steps for completing procedures, definitions of terms, lists of related topics, and search capabilities. You can browse or search for information in the Help window, or you can connect to a Microsoft Web site on the Internet for the latest technical support on Windows 2000. You can also access **context-sensitive help**, help specifically related to what you are doing, using a variety of methods such as right-clicking an object or using the question mark button in a dialog box. In this lesson, you get Help on starting a program. You also get information on the taskbar.

**1.** Click the **Start button** on the taskbar, then click **Help**

The Windows Help window opens with the Contents tab in front, as shown in Figure A-14. The Contents tab provides you with a list of Help categories. Each category contains two or more topics that you can see by clicking the book or the category next to it.

**QuickTip**

Click the Glossary category on the Contents tab to access definitions for hundreds of computer terms.

**2.** Click the **Contents tab** if it isn't the front-most tab, click **Working with Programs**, then view the Help categories that are displayed

The Help window contains a selection of topics related to working with programs.

**3.** Click **Start a Program**

Help information for this topic appears in the right pane, as shown in Figure A-15. **Panes** divide a window into two or more sections. At the bottom of the text in the right pane, you can click Related Topics to view a list of topics that may also be of interest to you. Some Help topics also allow you to view additional information about important words; these words are underlined, indicating that you can click them to display a pop-up window with the additional information.

**4.** Click the underlined word **taskbar**, read the definition, then press **[Enter]** or click anywhere outside the pop-up window to close it

**5.** In the left pane, click the **Index tab**

The Index tab provides an alphabetical list of all the available Help topics, like an index at the end of a book. You can type a topic in the text box at the top of the pane. As you type, the list of topics automatically scrolls to try to match the word or phrase you type. You can also scroll down to the topic. In either case, the topic appears in the right pane.

**6.** In the left pane, click the **Search tab**

You can use the Search tab to locate a Help topic using keywords. You enter a word or phrase in the text box and click List Topics; a list of matching topics appears below the text box. To view a topic, double-click it or select the topic, then click Display.

**7.** In the left pane, click the **Favorites tab**

You can add the To Start a Program topic, or any other displayed topic, to the Favorites tab of the Help window by simply clicking the Favorites tab, then clicking the Add button.

**8.** Click the **Web Help button** 🕲 on the toolbar

Information on the Web site for Windows 2000 Help appears in the right pane (a **Web site** is a document or related documents that contain highlighted words, phrases, and graphics that link to other sites on the Internet). To access online support or information, click one of the available options.

**QuickTip**

To get help on a specific Windows program, click Help on the program's menu bar.

**9.** Click the **Close button** ☒ in the upper-right corner of the Windows Help window

The Help window closes.

FIGURE A-14: Windows Help window

Help toolbar

Help tabs

Click to view
alphabetical
list of Help
topics

Click to search
for words and
phrases in
Help topics

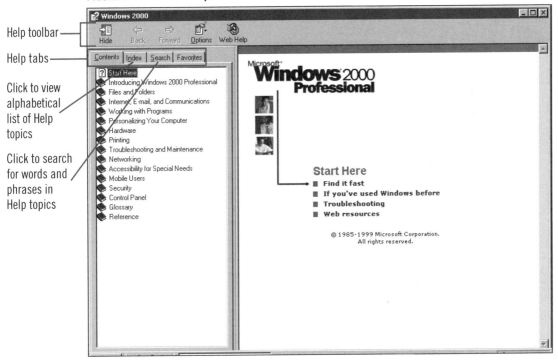

FIGURE A-15: Viewing a Help topic

Help topic

Pointer
changes to
hand pointer
when a topic
is selected

Left pane
contains Help
categories
and topics

Right pane
contains help
on the topic
you select

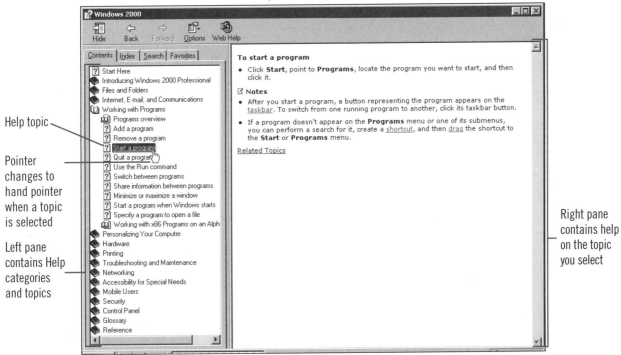

## Context-sensitive help

To receive help in a dialog box, click the Help button in the upper-right corner of the dialog box; the mouse pointer changes to ⤳?. Click the Help pointer on the item for which you need additional information. A pop-up window provides a brief explanation of the selected feature. You can also right-click the button on an item in a dialog box, then click the What's This? button to view the Help explanation.

**Windows 2000**

# Closing a Program and Shutting Down Windows

When you are finished working on your computer, you need to make sure you shut it down properly. This involves several steps: saving and closing all open files, closing all the open programs and windows, shutting down Windows, and finally, turning off the computer. If you turn off the computer while Windows is running, you could lose important data. To **close** programs, you can click the Close button in the window's upper-right corner or click File on the menu bar and choose either Close or Exit. To shut down Windows after all your files and programs are closed, click Shut Down from the Start menu, then select the desired option from the Shut Down dialog box, shown in Figure A-16. See Table A-8 for a description of shut down options. Close all your open files, windows, and programs, then exit Windows.

1. In the Control Panel window, click the **Close button** ☒ in the upper-right corner of the window
   The Control Panel window closes.

2. Click **File** on the WordPad menu bar, then click **Exit**
   If you have made any changes to the open file, you will be prompted to save your changes before the program quits. Some programs also give you the option of choosing the Close command on the File menu in order to close the active file but leave the program open, so you can continue to work in it with a different file. Also, if there is a second set of sizing buttons in the window, the Close button on the menu bar will close the active file only, leaving the program open for continued use.

3. If you see a message asking you to save changes to the document, click **No**
   WordPad closes and you return to the desktop.

**QuickTip**

Complete the remaining steps to shut down Windows and your computer only if you have been told to do so by your instructor or technical support person.

4. Click the **Start Button** on the taskbar, then click **Shut Down**
   The Shut Down Windows dialog box opens, as shown in Figure A-16. In this dialog box, you have the option to log off, shut down the computer, or restart the computer.

5. Click the **What do you want the computer to do? list arrow**

6. If you are working in a lab, click the **list arrow** again and click **Cancel** to leave the computer running; if you are working on your own machine or if your instructor told you to shut down Windows, click **Shut down**, then click **OK**

7. If you see the message "It is now safe to turn off your computer," turn off your computer and monitor
   On some computers, the power shuts off automatically, so you may not see this message.

FIGURE A-16: Shut Down Windows dialog box

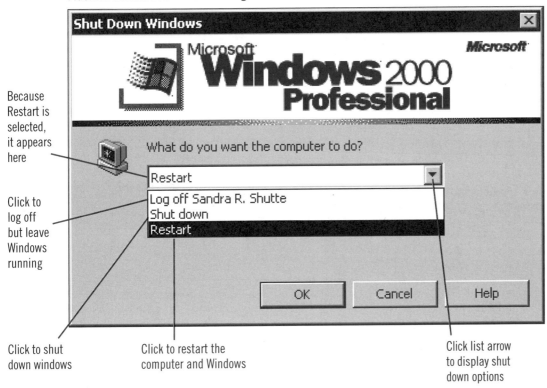

Because Restart is selected, it appears here

Click to log off but leave Windows running

Click to shut down windows

Click to restart the computer and Windows

Click list arrow to display shut down options

## The Log Off command

To change users on the same computer quickly, you can choose the Log Off command from the Shut Down Windows dialog box. When you choose this command, the current user is logged off and Windows 2000 shuts down and automatically restarts, stopping at the point where you need to enter a password. When the new user enters a user name and password, Windows restarts and the desktop appears as usual.

TABLE A-8: Shut down options

| shut down option | function | when to use it |
| --- | --- | --- |
| **Shut down** | Prepares the computer to be turned off | When you are finished working with Windows and you want to shut off your computer |
| **Restart** | Restarts the computer and reloads Windows | When you want to restart the computer and begin working with Windows again (your programs might have frozen or stopped working) |
| **Log off** | Ends your session, then reloads Windows for another user | When you want to end your session but leave the computer running for another user |

# Practice

## ► Concepts Review

Identify each of the items labeled in Figure A-17.

FIGURE A-17

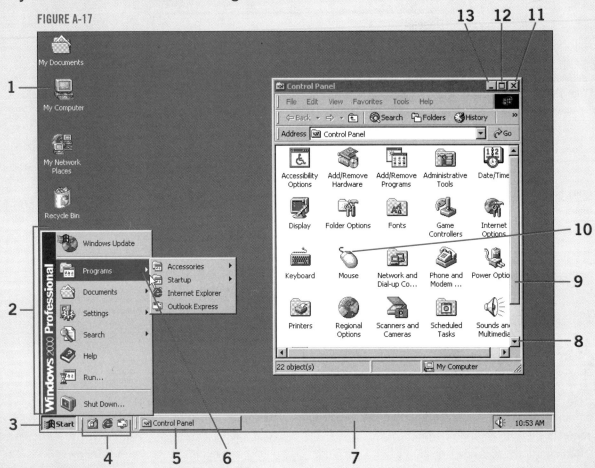

Match each of the statements with the term it describes.

14. Shrinks a window to a button on the taskbar
15. Shows the name of the window or program
16. The taskbar item you first click to start a program
17. Requests more information that you supply before carrying out command
18. Shows the Start button, Quick Launch toolbar, and any currently open programs
19. An input device that lets you point to and make selections
20. Graphic representation of program

a. Taskbar
b. Dialog box
c. Start button
d. Mouse
e. Title bar
f. Minimize button
g. Icon

Select the best answer from the list of choices.

21. The acronym GUI stands for
    a. Grayed user information.
    b. Group user icons.
    c. Graphical user interface.
    d. Group user interconnect.

22. **Which of the following is NOT provided by Windows 2000?**
   a. The ability to organize files
   b. Instructions to coordinate the flow of information among the programs, files, printers, storage devices, and other components of your computer system
   c. Programs that allow you to specify the operation of the mouse
   d. Spell checker for your documents

23. **All of the following are examples of using a mouse, EXCEPT**
   a. clicking the Maximize button.
   b. pressing [Enter].
   c. double-clicking to start a program.
   d. dragging the My Computer icon.

24. **The term for moving an item to a new location on the desktop is**
   a. pointing.　　b. clicking.　　c. dragging.　　d. restoring.

25. **The Maximize button is used to**
   a. return a window to its previous size.
   b. expand a window to fill the computer screen.
   c. scroll slowly through a window.
   d. run programs from the Start menu.

26. **What appears if a window contains more information than can be viewed in the window?**
   a. Program icon　　b. Cascading menu　　c. Scroll bars　　d. Check boxes

27. **A window is active when**
   a. you can only see its program button on the taskbar.
   b. its title bar is dimmed.
   c. it is open and you are currently using it.
   d. it is listed in the Programs submenu.

28. **You can exit Windows by**
   a. double-clicking the Control Panel application.
   b. double-clicking the Program Manager control menu box.
   c. clicking File, then clicking Exit.
   d. selecting the Shut Down command from the Start menu.

## ▶ Skills Review

1. **Start Windows and view the Active Desktop.**
   a. Turn on the computer, if necessary.
   b. After Windows starts, identify as many items on the desktop as you can, without referring to the lesson material.
   c. Compare your results to Figure A-1.

2. **Use the mouse.**
   a. Double-click the Recycle Bin icon.
   b. Drag the Recycle Bin window to the upper-right corner of the desktop.
   c. Right-click the title bar of the Recycle Bin, then click Close.

3. **Start a program.**
   a. Click the Start button on the taskbar, then point to Programs.
   b. Point to Accessories, then click Calculator (rest your pointer on the double arrows to display more menu commands if necessary).
   c. Minimize the Calculator window.

4. **Move and resize windows.**
   a. Drag the Recycle Bin icon to the bottom of the desktop.
   b. Double-click the My Computer icon to open the My Computer window.
   c. Maximize the window, if it is not already maximized.

**d.** Restore the window to its previous size.

**e.** Resize the window until you see the vertical scroll bar.

**f.** Minimize the My Computer window.

**g.** Drag the Recycle Bin back to the top of the desktop.

5. **Use menus, keyboard shortcuts, and toolbars.**

   **a.** Click the Start button on the taskbar, point to Settings, then click Control Panel.

   **b.** Click View on the menu bar, point to Toolbars, then click Standard Buttons to deselect the option and hide the toolbar.

   **c.** Redisplay the toolbar.

   **d.** Press [Alt][V] to display the View menu, then press [L] to view the Control Panel as a list.

   **e.** Note the change, then use keyboard shortcuts to change the view back.

   **f.** Click the Up One Level button to view My Computer.

   **g.** Click the Back button to return to the Control Panel.

   **h.** Click View, click Toolbars, then click Customize.

   **i.** Add a button to the toolbar, remove it, then close the Customize the Toolbar dialog box.

   **j.** Click the Restore button on the Control panel window.

6. **Use dialog boxes.**

   **a.** Double-click the Display icon, then click the Screen Saver tab.

   **b.** Click the Screen Saver list arrow, click any screen saver in the list, then view it in the Preview box above the list.

   **c.** Click the Effects tab.

   **d.** In the Visual effects section, click the Use large icons check box to select it, then click Apply.

   **e.** Note the change in the icons on the desktop and in the Control Panel window.

   **f.** Click the Use large icons check box to deselect it, click the Screen Saver tab, return the screen saver to its original setting, then click Apply.

   **g.** Click the Close button in the Display Properties dialog box, but leave the Control Panel open.

7. **Use scroll bars.**

   **a.** Click View on the Control Panel toolbar, then click Details.

   **b.** Resize the Control Panel window, if necessary, so that both scroll bars are visible.

   **c.** Drag the vertical scroll box down all the way.

   **d.** Click anywhere in the area above the vertical scroll box.

   **e.** Click the down scroll arrow until the scroll box is back at the bottom of the scroll bar.

   **f.** Drag the horizontal scroll box so you can read the descriptions for the icons.

8. **Get Help.**

   **a.** Click the Start button on the taskbar, then click Help.

   **b.** Click the Contents tab, then click Introducing Windows 2000 Professional.

   **c.** Click Tips for New Users, click the Use the Personalized Menus feature, then click Overview of Personalized Menus.

   **d.** Read the topic contents, then click Related Topics.

9. **Close a program and shut down Windows.**

   **a.** Click the Close button to close the Help topic window.

   **b.** Click File on the menu bar, then click Close to close the Control Panel window.

   **c.** Click the Calculator program button on the taskbar to restore the window.

   **d.** Click the Close button in the Calculator window to close the Calculator program.

   **e.** Click the My Computer program button on the taskbar, then click the Close button to close the window.

   **f.** If you are instructed to do so, shut down your computer.

# ▶ Independent Challenges

**1.** Windows 2000 has an extensive help system. In this independent challenge, you will use Help to learn about more Windows 2000 features and explore the help that's available on the Internet.

   **a.** Open Windows Help and locate help topics on adjusting the double-click speed of your mouse and displaying Web content on your desktop.

If you have a printer, print a Help topic for each subject. If you do not have a printer, write a summary of each topic.

   **b.** Follow these steps below to access help on the Internet. If you don't have Internet access, you can't do this step.

      **i.** Click the Web Help button on the toolbar.

      **ii.** Click the link Windows 2000 home page. A browser opens and prompts you to connect to the Internet if you are not already connected.

      **iii.** Write a summary of what you find.

      **iv.** Click the Close button in the title bar of your browser, then disconnect from the Internet and close Windows Help.

**2.** You may need to change the format of the clock and date on your computer. For example, if you work with international clients it might be easier to show the time in military (24-hour) time and the date with the day before the month. You can also change the actual time and date on your computer, to accomodate such things as time zone changes.

   **a.** Open the Control Panel window, then double-click the Regional Options icon.

   **b.** Click the Time tab to change the time to show a 24-hour clock rather than a 12-hour clock.

   **c.** Click the Date tab to change the Short date format to show the date, followed by the month, followed by the year (e.g., 30/3/01).

   **d.** Change the time to one hour later using the Date/Time icon in the Control Panel window.

   **e.** Return the settings to the original time and format, then close all open windows.

**3.** Calculator is a Windows program on the Accessories menu that you can use for calculations you need to perform while using the computer. Follow these guidelines to explore the Calculator and the Help that comes with it:

   **a.** Start the Calculator from the Accessories menu.

   **b.** Click Help on the menu bar, then click Help Topics. The Calculator Help window opens, showing several help topics.

   **c.** View the help topic on how to perform simple calculations, then print it if you have a printer connected.

   **d.** Open the Perform a scientific calculation category, then view the definition of a number system.

   **e.** Determine how many months you have to work to earn an additional week of vacation if you work for a company that provides one additional day of paid vacation for every 560 hours you work. (*Hint:* Divide 560 by the number of hours you work per month.)

   **f.** Close all open windows.

**4.** You can customize many Windows features to suit your needs and preferences. One way you do this is to change the appearance of the taskbar on the desktop. In this challenge, try the guidelines described to explore the different ways you can customize the appearance of the taskbar.

   **a.** Position the pointer over the top border of the taskbar. When the pointer changes shape, drag up an inch.

   **b.** Resize the taskbar back to its original size.

   **c.** Click the Start button on the taskbar, point to Settings, then click Taskbar & Start Menu.

   **d.** In the upper-right corner of the General tab, click the Help button, then click the first check box to view the pop-up window describing it. Repeat this for each check box.

   **e.** Click each check box and observe the effect in the preview area. (*Note:* Do not click OK.)

   **f.** Click Cancel.

## ▶ Visual Workshop

Use the skills you have learned in this unit to customize your desktop so it looks like the one in Figure A-18. Make sure you include the following:

- Calculator program minimized
- Vertical scroll bar in Control Panel window
- Large icons view in Control Panel window
- Rearranged icons on desktop; your icons may be different (*Hint:* If the icons *snap* back to where they were, they are set to be automatically arranged. Right-click a blank area of the desktop, point to Arrange Icons, then click Auto Arrange to deselect this option.)

Use the Print Screen key to make a copy of the screen, then print it from the Paint program. (To print from the Paint program, click the Start button on the taskbar, point to Programs, point to Accessories, then click Paint; in the Paint program window, click Edit on the menu bar, then click Paste; click Yes to fit the image on the bitmap, click the Print button on the toolbar, then click Print in the Print dialog box. See your instructor or technical support person for assistance.)

When you have completed this exercise, be sure to return your settings and desktop back to their original arrangement.

FIGURE A-18

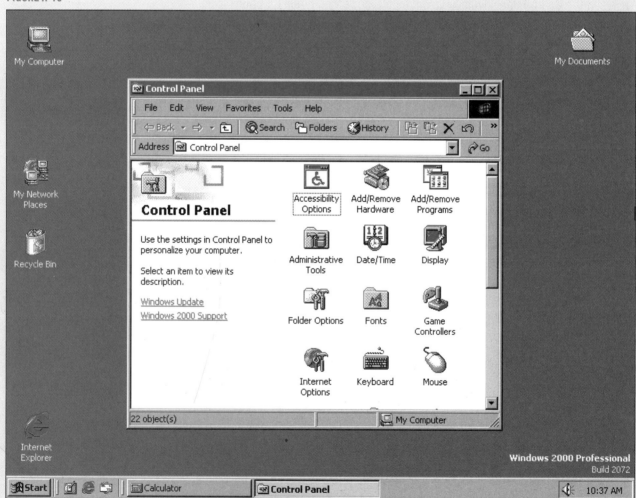

## Windows 2000 — Unit B

# Working
## with Programs, Files, and Folders

### Objectives

- ► Create and save a WordPad document
- ► Open, edit, and save an existing Paint file
- ► Work with multiple programs
- ► Understand file management
- ► View files and create folders with My Computer
- ► Move and copy files with My Computer
- ► Manage files with Windows Explorer
- ► Delete and restore files
- ► Create a shortcut on the desktop

Most of your work on a computer involves using programs to create files. For example, you might use WordPad to create a resumé or Microsoft Excel to create a budget. The resumé and the budget are examples of files, electronic collections of data that you create and save on a disk. In this unit, you learn how to work with files and the programs you use to create them. You create new files, open and edit an existing file, and use the Clipboard to copy and paste data from one file to another. You also explore the file management features of Windows 2000, using My Computer and Windows Explorer. Finally, you learn how to work more efficiently by managing files directly on your desktop.

# Creating and Saving a WordPad Document

As with most programs, when you start WordPad a new, blank **document** (or file) opens. To create a new file, such as a memo, you simply begin typing. Your work is automatically stored in your computer's **random access memory (RAM)** until you turn off your computer, at which point anything stored in the computer's RAM is erased. To store your work permanently, you must save your work as a file on a disk. You can save files either on an internal **hard disk**, which is built into your computer, usually the C: drive, or on a removable 3.5" or 5.25" **floppy disk**, which you insert into a drive on your computer, usually the A: or B: drive. Before you can save a file on a floppy disk, the disk must be formatted. (See the Appendix, "Formatting a Disk," or your instructor or technical support person for more information.) When you name a file, you can use up to 255 characters including spaces and punctuation in the File Name box, using either upper- or lowercase letters. In this lesson, you start WordPad and create a file that contains the text shown in Figure B-1. Then you save the file to Project Disk 1.

## Steps

1. **Click the Start button on the taskbar, point to Programs, point to Accessories, click WordPad, then click the Maximize button if the window does not fill your screen**
   The WordPad program window opens with a new, blank document in the document window. The blinking insertion point I indicates where the text you type will appear.

2. **Type Memo, then press [Enter]**
   Pressing [Enter] inserts a new line and moves the insertion point to the next line.

   **Trouble?**
   If you make a mistake, press [Backspace] to delete the character to the left of the insertion point.

3. **Press [Enter] again, then type the remaining text shown in Figure B-1, pressing [Enter] at the end of each line**
   Now that the text is entered, you can format it. **Formatting** changes the appearance of text to make it more readable or attractive.

   **QuickTip**
   Double-click to select a word or triple-click to select a paragraph.

4. **Click to the left of the word Memo, drag the mouse to the right to highlight the word, then release the mouse button**
   The text is now **selected** and any action you make will be performed on the text.

5. **Click the Center button ▤ on the Formatting toolbar, then click the Bold button on the Formatting toolbar**
   The text is centered and bold.

6. **Click the Font Size list arrow [10 ▼], then click 16 in the list**
   A **font** is a particular shape and size of type. The text is enlarged to 16 point. One **point** is 1/72 of an inch in height. Now that your memo is complete, you are ready to save it to your Project Disk.

7. **Click File on the menu bar, then click Save As**
   The Save As dialog box opens, as shown in Figure B-2. In this dialog box, you specify where you want your file saved and also give your document a name.

   **Trouble?**
   This unit assumes that the Project Disk is in the A: drive. If not, substitute the correct drive any time you are instructed to use the 3½ Floppy (A:) drive. See your instructor or technical support person for help.

8. **Click the Save in list arrow, and then click 3½ Floppy (A:), or whichever drive contains your Project Disk 1**
   The drive containing your Project Disk is now active, meaning that any files currently on the disk appear in the list of folders and files and that the file you save now will be saved on the disk in this drive.

9. **Click the text in the File name text box, type Memo, then click Save**
   Your memo is now saved as a WordPad file with the name "Memo" on your Project Disk. Notice that the WordPad title bar contains the name of the file.

FIGURE B-1: Text to enter in WordPad

Press [Enter] three times to insert blank lines

Bold button          Center button

Document window

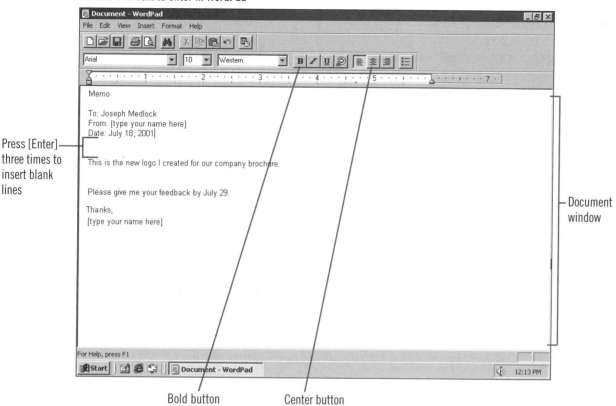

FIGURE B-2: Save As dialog box

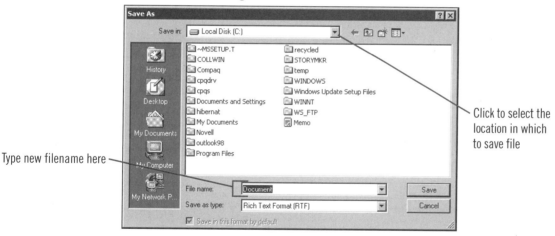

Type new filename here

Click to select the location in which to save file

## Creating a new document

When you want to create a new document in WordPad once the program is already open and another document is active, you can click the New button ☐ on the Standard toolbar. A dialog box opens from which you can choose to create a new Rich Text, Word 6, Text, or Unicode Text document. **Rich Text** documents, the WordPad default document format, can include text formatting and tabs, and be available for use in a variety of other word-processing programs; **Word 6** documents can be opened, edited, and enhanced in Microsoft Word version 6.0 or later without conversion; **Text** documents can be used in numerous other programs because they contain no formatting; and **Unicode Text** documents can contain text from any of the world's writing systems, such as Roman, Greek, and Chinese. You select one of the options by clicking it, and then clicking OK.

# Opening, Editing, and Saving an Existing Paint File

Sometimes you create files from scratch, but often you may want to use a file you or someone else has already created; to do so, you need to **open** the file. Once you open a file, you can **edit** it, or make changes to it, such as adding or deleting text. After editing a file, you can save it with the same filename, which means that you no longer will have the file in its original form, or you can save it with a different filename, so that the original file remains unchanged. ✐ In this lesson, you use **Paint**, a drawing program that comes with Windows 2000, to open a file, edit it by changing a color, then save the file with a new filename to leave the original file unchanged.

1. Click the **Start button** on the taskbar, point to **Programs**, point to **Accessories**, click **Paint**, then click the **Maximize button** if the window doesn't fill the screen
   The Paint program opens with a blank work area. If you wanted to create a file from scratch, you would begin working now.

2. Click **File** on the menu bar, then click **Open**
   The Open dialog box works similarly to the Save As dialog box.

3. Click the **Look in list arrow**, then click 3½ **Floppy (A:)**
   The Paint files on your Project Disk 1 are listed in the Open dialog box, as shown in Figure B-3.

   **QuickTip**
   You can also open a file by double-clicking it in the Open dialog box.

4. Click **Win B-1** in the list of files, and then click **Open**
   The Open dialog box closes and the file named Win B-1 opens. Before you make any changes to a file, you should save it with a new filename, so that the original file is unchanged.

5. Click **File** on the menu bar, then click **Save As**

6. Make sure 3½ **Floppy (A:)** appears in the Save in text box, select the text **Win B-1** in the File name text box if necessary, type **Logo**, then click **Save**
   The Logo file appears in the Paint window, as shown in Figure B-4. Because you saved the file with a new name, you can edit it without changing the original file. You will now use buttons in the **Tool Box**, a toolbar of illustration tools available in Windows Paint, and the **Color Box**, a palette of colors from which you can choose, to modify the graphic.

7. Click the **Fill With Color button** 🪣 in the Tool Box, then click the **Blue color box**, which is the fourth from the right in the first row
   Notice how clicking a button in the Tool Box changes the mouse pointer. Now when you click an area in the image, it will be filled with the color you selected in the Color Box. See Table B-1 for a description of the tools in the Tool Box.

8. Move the pointer into the **white area that represents the sky** until the pointer changes to 🪣, then click
   The sky is now blue.

9. Click **File** on the menu bar, then click **Save**
   The change you made is saved to disk.

FIGURE B-3: **Open dialog box**

List of files ——

Look in list arrow;
click to select the
location of the file

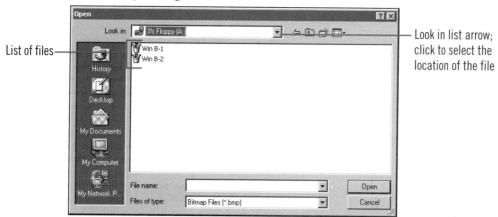

FIGURE B-4: **Paint file saved with new filename**

Name of file
appears in
title bar

Tool Box

Choose this
blue color

Color box ——

Sky area to fill
with color

Fill With Color
button

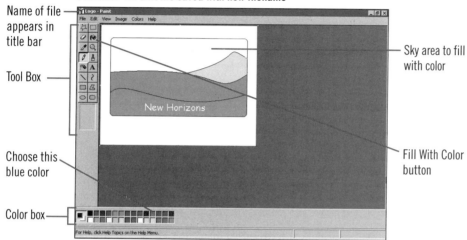

TABLE B-1: **Paint Tool Box buttons**

| tool | description | tool | description |
|------|-------------|------|-------------|
| **Free-Form Select button** | Selects a free-form section of the picture to move, copy, or edit | **Airbrush button** | Produces a circular spray of dots |
| **Select button** | Selects a rectangular section of the picture to move, copy, or edit | **Text button** | Inserts text into the picture |
| **Eraser button** | Erases a portion of the picture using the selected eraser size and foreground color | **Line button** | Draws a straight line with the selected width and foreground color |
| **Fill With Color button** | Fills closed shape or area with the current drawing color | **Curve button** | Draws a wavy line with the selected width and foreground color |
| **Pick Color button** | Picks up a color off the picture to use for drawing | **Rectangle button** | Draws a rectangle with the selected fill style; also used to draw squares by holding down [Shift] while drawing |
| **Magnifier button** | Changes the magnification; lists magnifications under the toolbar | **Polygon button** | Draws polygons from connected straight-line segments |
| **Pencil button** | Draws a free-form line one pixel wide | **Ellipse button** | Draws an ellipse with the selected fill style; also used to draw circles by holding down [Shift] while drawing |
| **Brush button** | Draws using a brush with the selected shape and size | **Rounded Rectangle button** | Draws rectangles with rounded corners using the selected fill style; also used to draw rounded squares by holding down [Shift] while drawing |

# Working with Multiple Programs

A powerful feature of Windows is its capability to run more than one program at a time. For example, you might be working with a document in WordPad and want to search the Internet to find the answer to a question. You can start your browser, a program designed to access information on the Internet, without closing WordPad. When you find the information, you can leave your browser open and switch back to WordPad. Each open program is represented by a program button on the taskbar that you click to switch between programs. You can also copy data from one file to another, (whether the files were created with the same Windows program or not), using the **Clipboard**, a temporary area in your computer's memory, and the Cut, Copy, and Paste commands. See Table B-2 for a description of these commands. ⬤━━ In this lesson, you copy the logo graphic you worked with in the previous lesson into the memo you created in WordPad.

**Trouble?**

If some parts of the image or text are outside the dotted rectangle, click anywhere outside the image, then select the image again, making sure you include everything.

**QuickTip**

To switch between programs using the keyboard, press and hold down [Alt], press [Tab] until the program you want is selected, then release [Alt].

1. Click the **Select button** ⬚ on the Tool Box, and then drag a rectangle around the entire **graphic**

   When you release the mouse button, the dotted rectangle surrounds the selected area, as shown in Figure B-5. Make sure the entire image is inside the rectangle. The next action you take affects the entire selection.

2. Click **Edit** on the menu bar, and then click **Copy**

   The logo is copied to the Clipboard. When you **copy** an object onto the Clipboard, the object remains in its original location and is also available to be pasted into another location.

3. Click the **WordPad program button** on the taskbar

   WordPad becomes the active program.

4. Click in the **first line below the line that ends "for our company brochure."**

   The insertion point indicates where the logo will be pasted.

5. Click the **Paste button** 📋 on the WordPad toolbar

   The contents of the Clipboard, in this case the logo, are pasted into the WordPad file, as shown in Figure B-6.

6. Click the **Save button** 💾 on the toolbar

   The Memo file is saved with the logo inserted.

7. Click the WordPad **Close button**

   Your WordPad document and the WordPad program close. Paint is now the active program.

8. Click the Paint **Close button**; if you are prompted to save changes, click **Yes**

   Your Paint document and the Paint program close. You return to the desktop.

**TABLE B-2: Overview of cutting, copying and pasting**

| Toolbar button | function | keyboard shortcut |
|---|---|---|
| ✂ **Cut** | Removes selected information from a file and places it on the Clipboard | [Ctrl][X] |
| 📋 **Copy** | Places a copy of selected information on the Clipboard, leaving the file intact | [Ctrl][C] |
| 📋 **Paste** | Inserts whatever is currently on the Clipboard into another location within the same file, or in a different file | [Ctrl][V] |

**FIGURE B-5:** Selecting the logo to copy and paste into the Memo file

Select button

Dotted line indicates selected area

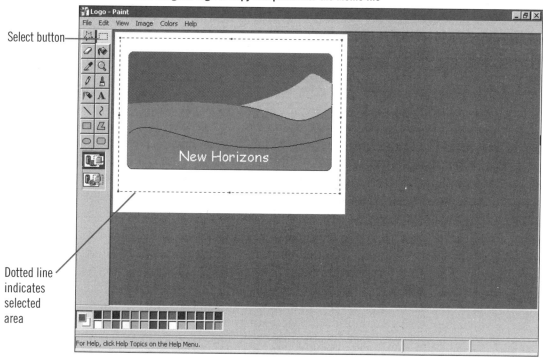

**FIGURE B-6:** Memo with pasted logo

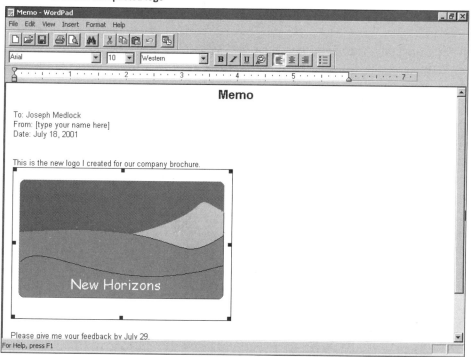

# Understanding File Management

After you have created and saved numerous files using various programs, **file management**, the process of organizing and keeping track of all of your files, can be a challenge. Fortunately, Windows 2000 provides tools to keep everything organized so you can easily locate the files you need, move files to new locations, and delete files you no longer need. There are two main tools for managing your files: My Computer and Windows Explorer. In this lesson, you preview the ways you can use My Computer and Windows Explorer to manage your files.

### Windows 2000 gives you the ability to:

### Create folders in which you can save your files

**Folders** are areas on a floppy disk or hard disk in which you can store files. For example, you might create a folder for your documents and another folder for your graphic files. Folders can also contain additional folders, which creates a more complex structure of folders and files, called a **file hierarchy**. See Figure B-7 for an example of how files can be organized.

**QuickTip**

To browse My Computer using multiple windows, click Tools on the menu bar, and then click Folder Options. In the Folder Options dialog box, click the General tab, and then under Browse Folders, click the Open each folder in its own window option button. Each time you open a new folder, a new window opens, leaving the previous folder's window open so that you can view both at the same time.

### Examine and organize the hierarchy of files and folders

You can use either My Computer or Windows Explorer to see the overall structure of your files and folders. By examining your file hierarchy with these tools, you can better organize the contents of your computer and adjust the hierarchy to meet your needs. Figures B-8 and B-9 illustrate how My Computer and Windows Explorer list folders and files.

### Copy, move, and rename files and folders

If you decide that a file belongs in a different folder, you can move it to another folder. You can also rename a file if you decide a different name is more descriptive. If you want to keep a copy of a file in more than one folder, you can copy it to new folders.

### Delete files and folders you no longer need, as well as restore files you delete accidentally

Deleting files and folders you are sure you don't need frees up disk space and keeps your file hierarchy more organized. The **Recycle Bin**, a space on your computer's hard disk that stores deleted files, allows you to restore files you deleted by accident. To free up disk space, you should occasionally empty the Recycle Bin by deleting the files permanently from your hard drive.

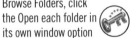

### Locate files quickly with the Windows 2000 Search feature

As you create more files and folders, you may forget where you placed a certain file or you may forget what name you used when you saved a file. With Search, you can locate files by providing only partial names or other factors, such as the file type (for example, a WordPad document or a Paint graphic) or the date the file was created or modified.

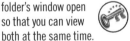

### Use shortcuts

If a file or folder you use often is located several levels down in your file hierarchy (in a folder within a folder, within a folder), it might take you several steps to access it. To save time accessing the files and programs you use frequently, you can create shortcuts to them. A **shortcut** is a link that gives you quick access to a particular file, folder, or program.

FIGURE B-7: Sample file hierarchy

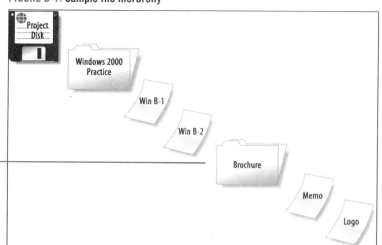

In this hierarchy, Brochure folder is a subfolder of Windows 2000 Practice folder

FIGURE B-8: Brochure folder shown in My Computer

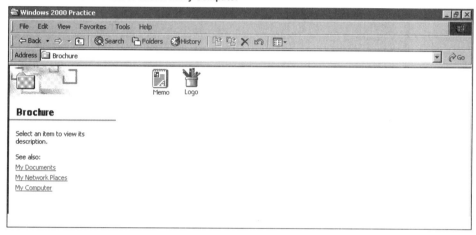

FIGURE B-9: Brochure folder shown in Windows Explorer

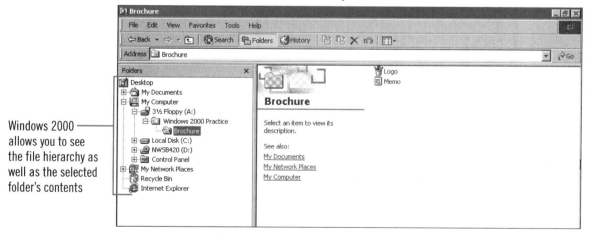

Windows 2000 allows you to see the file hierarchy as well as the selected folder's contents

# Viewing Files and Creating Folders with My Computer

My Computer shows the contents of your computer, including files, folders, programs, disk drives, and printers. You can click the icons representing these various parts of your computer to view their contents or properties. You can manage your files using the My Computer menu bar and toolbar. See Table B-3 for a description of the toolbar buttons. ➤ In this lesson, you begin by using My Computer to move around in your computer's file hierarchy, then you create two new folders on your Project Disk 1 for the files you created.

## Steps

1. Double-click the **My Computer icon** on your desktop, then click the **Maximize button** if the My Computer window does not fill the screen
   My Computer opens and displays the contents of your computer, as shown in Figure B-10. Your window may contain icons for different folders, drives, and printers.

2. Make sure your Project Disk 1 is in the floppy disk drive, then double-click the **3½ Floppy (A:) icon**
   The contents of your Project Disk 1 appear in the window. These are the project files and the files you created using WordPad and Paint. Each file is represented by an icon, which indicates the program that was used to create the file. If Microsoft Word is installed on your computer, the Word icon appears for the WordPad files; if not, the WordPad icon appears.

3. Click the **Address list arrow** on the Address Bar, as shown in Figure B-10, then click **Local Disk (C:)** or the letter for the main hard drive on your computer
   The window changes to show the contents of your hard drive. The **Address Bar** allows you to open and view a drive, folder, or even a Web page. You can also type in the Address Bar to go to a different drive, folder, or Web page. For example, typing "C:\" will display drive C:; typing "E:\Personal Letters" will display the Personal Letters folder on the E: drive, and typing "http://www.microsoft.com" opens Microsoft's Web site if your computer is connected to the Internet.

4. Click the **Back button** on the toolbar
   The Back button displays the previous location, in this case, your Project Disk.

5. Click the **Views button** 🔲 on the toolbar, then click **Details**
   Details view shows not only the files and folders, but also the sizes of the files, the types of files, folders, or drives and the date the files were last modified.

6. Click 🔲, then click **Thumbnails**
   This view offers less information but provides a preview of graphics and a clear view of the contents of the disk.

7. Click **File** on the menu bar, point to **New**, then click **Folder**
   A new folder is created on your Project Disk 1, as shown in Figure B-11. The folder is called "New Folder" by default. It is selected and ready to be renamed. You can also create a new folder by right-clicking in the blank area of the My Computer window, clicking New, then clicking Folder.

8. Type **Windows 2000 Practice**, then press **[Enter]**
   Choosing descriptive names for your folders helps you remember their contents.

9. Double-click the **Windows 2000 Practice folder**, repeat Step 7 to create a new folder in the Windows 2000 Practice folder, type **Brochure** for the folder name, then press **[Enter]**

10. Click the **Up button** 🔲 to return to your Project Disk 1

**FIGURE B-10: My Computer window**

Menu bar

Toolbar

Address bar

Address
list arrow

Your icon
list may
differ

Status bar

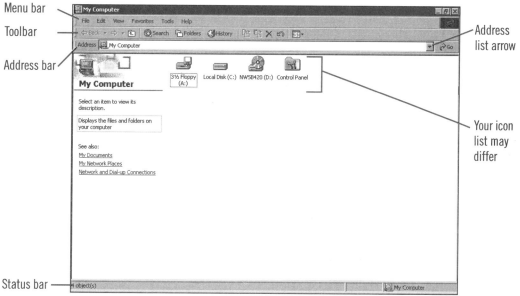

**FIGURE B-11: Creating a new folder**

Back button

Folder is located
on disk in the
A: drive

Type new name here

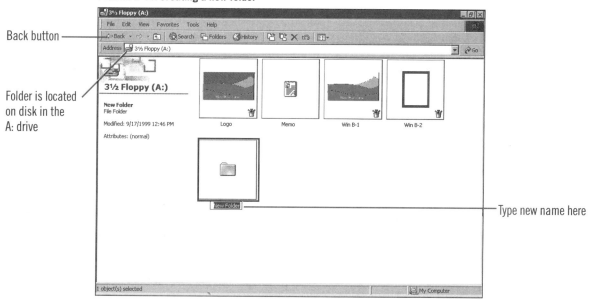

**TABLE B-3: Buttons on the My Computer toolbar**

| button | function |
|---|---|
| | Moves back to the previous location you have already visited |
| | Moves forward to the previous location you have already visited |
| | Moves up one level in the file hierarchy |
| | Opens the Browse For Folder dialog box, to move the selected file to a new location |
| | Opens the Browse For Folder dialog box, to copy the selected file to a new location |
| | Undoes the most recent My Computer operation |
| | Deletes a folder or file permanently |
| | Lists the contents of My Computer using different views |

# Moving and Copying Files with My Computer

You can move a file or folder from one location to another using a variety of methods in My Computer or Windows Explorer. If the file or folder and the location to which you want to move it are both visible on the desktop, you can simply drag the item from one location to the other. You can also use the cut, copy, and paste commands on the Edit menu or the corresponding buttons on the toolbar. Finally you can right-click the file or folder and choose the Send to command to "send" it to another location—most often a floppy disk for **backing up** files. Backup copies are made in case you have computer trouble, which may cause you to lose files. ⬤▬▬ In this lesson, you move your files into the folder you created in the last lesson.

## Steps 1 2 3 4

1. Click **View**, point to **Arrange Icons**, then click **by Name**

   In this view, folders are listed first in alphabetical order, followed by files, also in alphabetical order.

2. Click the **Win B-1 file**, hold down the mouse button and drag the file onto the **Windows 2000 Practice folder**, as shown in Figure B-12, then release the mouse button

   Win B-1 is moved into the Windows 2000 Practice folder.

3. Double-click the **Windows 2000 Practice folder** and confirm that it contains the Win B-1 file as well as the Brochure folder

4. Click the **Up button** 🔲 on the My Computer toolbar, as shown in Figure B-12

   You return to your Project Disk. The Up button shows the next level up in the folder hierarchy.

5. Click the **Logo file**, press and hold down **[Shift]**, then click the **Memo file**

   Both files are selected. Table B-4 describes methods for selecting multiple objects.

6. Click the **Move To button** 🔲 on the 3½ Floppy (A:) toolbar

   The filenames turn gray, and the Browse For Folder dialog box opens, as shown in Figure B-13.

7. Click the **plus sign** ⊞ next to My Computer if you do not see 3½ Floppy (A:) listed, double-click the **3½ Floppy (A:) drive**, double-click the **Windows 2000 Practice folder**, double-click the **Brochure folder**, then click **OK**

   The two files are moved to the Brochure folder. Only the Windows 2000 Practice folder and the Win B-2 file remain.

8. Click the **Close button** in the 3½ Floppy (A:) window

> **QuickTip**
>
> It is easy to confuse the Back button with the Up button. The Back button returns you to the last location you visited, no matter where it is in your folder hierarchy. The Up button displays the next level up in the folder hierarchy, no matter where you last visited.

FIGURE B-12: **Dragging a file from one folder to another**

Up button

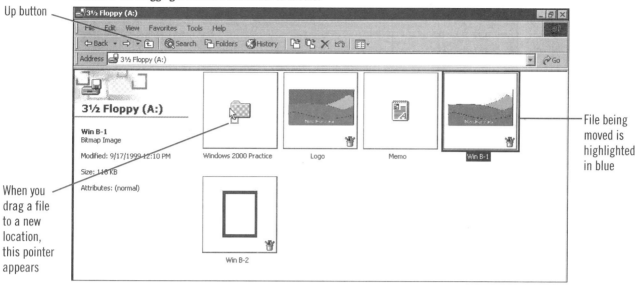

When you drag a file to a new location, this pointer appears

File being moved is highlighted in blue

FIGURE B-13: **Moving files**

Move To button

Copy To button

Click to move files to new location

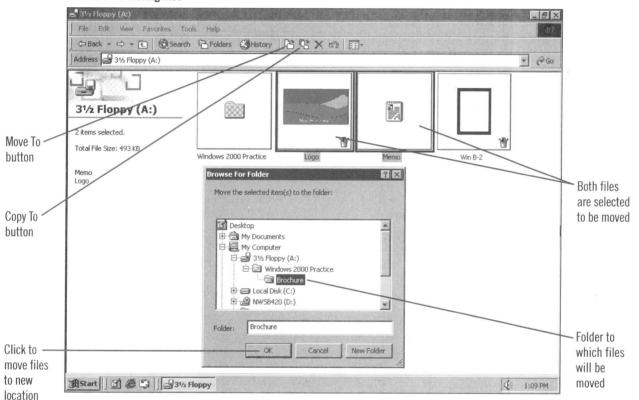

Both files are selected to be moved

Folder to which files will be moved

TABLE B-4: **Techniques for selecting multiple files and folders**

| to select | do this |
| --- | --- |
| **Individual objects not grouped together** | Click the first object you want to select, then press and hold down [Ctrl] as you click each additional object you want to add to the selection |
| **Objects grouped together** | Click the first object you want to select, then press and hold down [Shift] as you click the last object in the list of objects you want to select; all the objects listed between the first and last objects are selected |

**B**
Unit

# Managing Files with Windows Explorer

As with My Computer, you can use Windows Explorer to copy, move, delete, and rename files and folders. However, **Windows Explorer** is more powerful than My Computer: it allows you to see the overall structure of the contents of your computer or network, (the file hierarchy), while you work with individual files and folders within that structure. This means you can work with more than one computer, folder, or file at once. ✐ In this lesson, you copy a folder from your Project Disk 1 onto the hard drive and then rename the folder.

## Steps 1 2 3 4

**Trouble?**

If you do not see the toolbar, click View on the menu bar, point to Toolbars, then click Standard Buttons. If you do not see the Address Bar, click View, point to Toolbars, then click Address Bar.

**1.** Click the **Start button**, point to **Programs**, point to **Accessories**, click **Windows Explorer**, then click the **Maximize button** if the Windows Explorer window doesn't already fill the screen

Windows Explorer opens, as shown in Figure B-14. The window is divided into two areas called **panes**. The left pane, called the **Explorer Bar**, displays the drives and folders on your computer in a hierarchy. The right pane displays the contents of whatever drive or folder is currently selected in the left pane. Each pane has its own set of scroll bars, so that changing what you can see in one pane won't affect what you can see in the other. Like My Computer, Windows Explorer has a menu bar, toolbar, and Address Bar.

**2.** Click **View** on the menu bar, then click **Details** if it is not already selected

Remember that a bullet point next to a command on the menu bar indicates that it's selected.

**Trouble?**

If you cannot see the A: drive, you may have to click the plus sign (+) next to My Computer to view the available drives on your computer.

**3.** In the left pane, scroll to and click **3½ Floppy (A:)**

The contents of your Project Disk 1 appear in the right pane.

**4.** In the left pane, click the **plus sign (+)** next to 3½ Floppy (A:)

You can click the plus sign (+) or minus sign (-) next to any item in the left pane to show or hide the different levels of the file hierarchy, so that you don't always have to look at the entire structure of your computer or network. A plus sign (+) next to a computer, drive, or folder indicates there are additional folders within that object. A minus sign (-) indicates that all the folders of the next level of hierarchy are shown. Clicking the + displays (or "expands") the next level; clicking the - hides (or "collapses") them.

**QuickTip**

When neither a + nor a - appears next to an icon, it means that the item does not have any folders in it, although it may have files, which you can see listed in the right pane by clicking the icon.

**5.** In the left pane, double-click the **Windows 2000 Practice folder**

The contents of the Windows 2000 Practice folder appear in the right pane of Windows Explorer, as shown in Figure B-15. Double-clicking an item in the left pane that has a + next to it displays its contents in the right pane and also expands the next level in the hierarchy in the left pane.

**Trouble?**

If you are working in a lab setting, you may not be able to add items to your hard drive. Skip Steps 6, 7, and 8 if you are unable to complete them.

**6.** In the left pane, drag the **Windows 2000 Practice folder** on top of the **C: drive icon**, then release the mouse button

When you drag files or folders to a different drive, they are copied rather than moved. The Windows 2000 Practice folder and the files in it are copied to the hard disk.

**7.** In the left pane, click the **C: drive icon**

The Windows 2000 Practice folder should now appear in the list of folders in the right pane. You may have to scroll to see it. Now you should rename the folder so you can distinguish the original folder from the copy.

**QuickTip**

You can also rename a selected file by pressing [F2], or using the Rename command on the File menu.

**8.** Right-click the **Windows 2000 Practice folder** in the right pane, click **Rename** in the pop-up menu, type **Practice Copy**, then press **[Enter]**

**WORKING WITH PROGRAMS, FILES, AND FOLDERS**

**FIGURE B-14: Windows Explorer window**

Left pane, also known as Explorer Bar

Your list of folders and files will vary

Contents of the C: drive

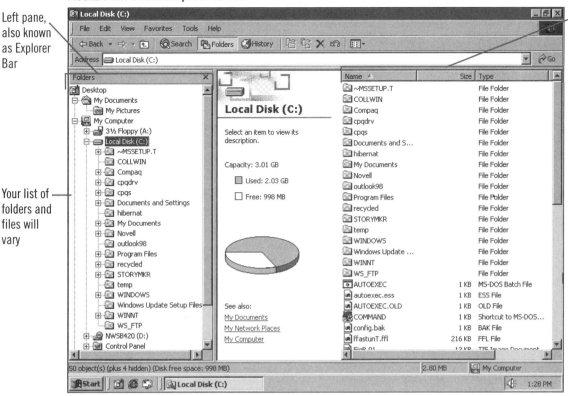

**FIGURE B-15: Contents of Windows 2000 Practice folder**

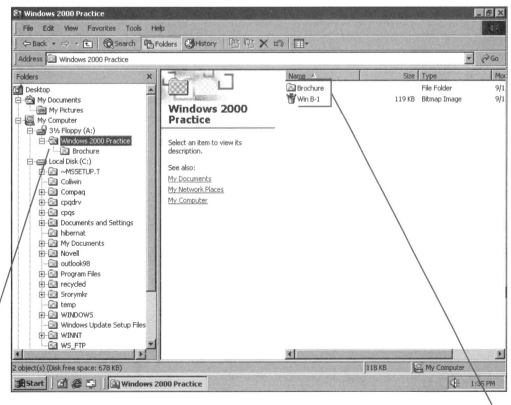

Windows 2000 Practice folder selected in left pane

Contents of Windows 2000 Practice folder appear in right pane

# Deleting and Restoring Files

To save disk space and manage your files more effectively, you should **delete** (or remove) files you no longer need. Because files deleted from your hard drive are stored in the Recycle Bin until you remove them permanently by emptying the Recycle Bin, you can restore any files you might have deleted accidentally. However, if you delete a file from your floppy disk it will not be stored in the Recycle Bin—it will be permanently deleted. See Table B-5 for an overview of deleting and restoring files. There are many ways to delete files and folders from the My Computer and Windows Explorer windows, as well as from the Windows 2000 desktop. In this lesson, you delete a file by dragging it to the Recycle Bin, restore it, and delete a folder by using the Delete command in Windows Explorer.

## Steps

1. Click the **Restore button** on the Windows Explorer title bar
   You should be able to see the Recycle Bin icon on your desktop. If you can't see it, resize or move the Windows Explorer window until it is visible. See Figure B-16.

2. If necessary, scroll until you see the Practice Copy folder in the right pane of Windows Explorer

3. Drag the **Practice Copy folder** from the right pane to the **Recycle Bin** on the desktop, as shown in Figure B-16, then click **Yes** to confirm the deletion if necessary
   The folder no longer appears in Windows Explorer because you have moved it to the Recycle Bin.

4. Double-click the **Recycle Bin icon** on the desktop
   The Recycle Bin window opens, as shown in Figure B-17. Depending on the number of files already deleted on your computer, your window might look different. Use the scroll bar if you can't see the files.

5. Click **Edit** on the Recycle Bin menu bar, then click **Undo Delete**
   The Practice Copy folder is restored and should now appear in the Windows Explorer window. You might need to minimize your Recycle Bin window if it blocks your view of Windows Explorer, and you might need to scroll to the bottom of the right pane to find the restored folder.

6. Click the **Practice Copy folder** in the right pane, click the **Delete button** on the Windows Explorer toolbar (resize the window as necessary to see the button), then click **Yes**
   When you are sure you no longer need files you've moved into the Recycle Bin, you can empty the Recycle Bin. You won't do this now, in case you are working on a computer that you share with other people. But, when you're working on your own machine, simply right-click the Recycle Bin icon, then click Empty Recycle Bin in the pop-up menu.

7. Close the Recycle Bin
   If you minimized the Recycle Bin in Step 4, click its program button to open the Recycle Bin window, and then click the Close button.

FIGURE B-16: Dragging a folder to delete it

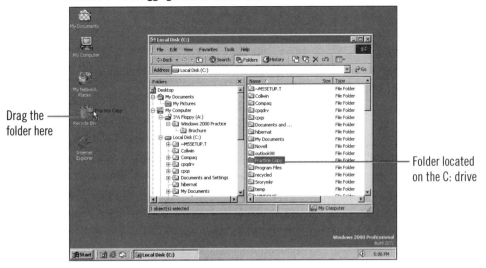

Drag the folder here

Folder located on the C: drive

FIGURE B-17: Recycle Bin window

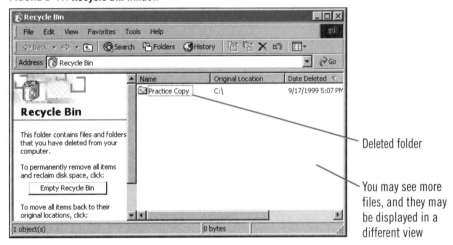

Deleted folder

You may see more files, and they may be displayed in a different view

TABLE B-5: Methods for deleting and restoring files

| ways to delete a file | ways to restore a file from the Recycle Bin |
|---|---|
| Select the file, then click the Delete button on the toolbar | Click the Undo button on the toolbar |
| Select the file, then press [Delete] | Select the file, click File, then click Restore |
| Right-click the file, then click Delete on the pop-up menu | Right-click the file, then click Restore |
| Drag the file to the Recycle Bin | Drag the file from the Recycle Bin to any other location |

## Customizing your Recycle Bin

You can set your Recycle Bin according to how you like to delete and restore files. For example, if you do not want files to go to the Recycle Bin but rather want them to be immediately and permanently deleted, right-click the Recycle Bin, click Properties, then click the Do Not Move Files to the Recycle Bin check box. If you find that the Recycle Bin fills up too fast and you are not ready to delete the files permanently, you can increase the amount of disk space devoted to the Recycle Bin by moving the Maximum Size of Recycle Bin slider to the right. This, of course, reduces the amount of disk space you have available for other things. Also, you can choose not to have the Confirm File Delete dialog box open when you send files to the Recycle Bin. See your instructor or technical support person before changing any of the Recycle Bin settings.

# Creating a Shortcut on the Desktop

When you frequently use a file, folder, or program that is located several levels down in the file hierarchy, you may want to create a shortcut to the object. You can place the shortcut on the desktop or in any other location, such as a folder, that you find convenient. To open the file, folder, or program using the shortcut, double-click the icon. ◄▬▬ In this lesson, you use Windows Explorer to create a shortcut on your desktop to the Memo file.

## Steps 1 2 3 4

**1. In the left pane of the Windows Explorer window, click the Brochure folder**
The contents of the Brochure folder appear in the right pane.

**2. In the right pane, right-click the Memo file**
A pop-up menu appears, as shown in Figure B-18.

**3. Click Create Shortcut in the pop-up menu**
The file named Shortcut to Memo file appears in the right pane. Now you need to move it to the desktop so that it will be accessible whenever you need it.

> **Trouble?**
>
> Make sure to use the right mouse button in Step 4. If you used the left mouse button by accident, right-click the Shortcut to Memo file in the right pane of Windows Explorer, click Delete, and repeat Step 4.

**4. Click the Shortcut to Memo file with the right-mouse button, then drag the shortcut to an empty area of the desktop**
Dragging an icon using the left mouse button copies it. Dragging an icon using the right mouse button gives you the option to copy it, move it, or create a shortcut to it. When you release the mouse button a pop-up menu appears.

**5. Click Move Here in the pop-up menu**
A shortcut to the Memo file now appears on the desktop, as shown in Figure B-19. You might have to move or resize the Windows Explorer window to see it.

**6. Double-click the Shortcut to Memo file icon**
WordPad starts and the Memo file opens (if you have Microsoft Word installed on your computer, it will start and open the file instead). Using a shortcut eliminates the many steps involved in starting a program and locating and opening a file.

**7. Click the Close button in the WordPad or Word title bar**
Now you should delete the shortcut icon in case you are working in a lab and share the computer with others.

> **QuickTip**
>
> Deleting a shortcut deletes only the link; it does not delete the original file or folder to which it points.

**8. On the desktop, click the Shortcut to Memo file, press [Delete], then click Yes to confirm the deletion**
The shortcut is removed from the desktop and is now in the Recycle Bin.

**9. Close all windows, then shut down Windows**

**FIGURE B-18: Creating a shortcut**

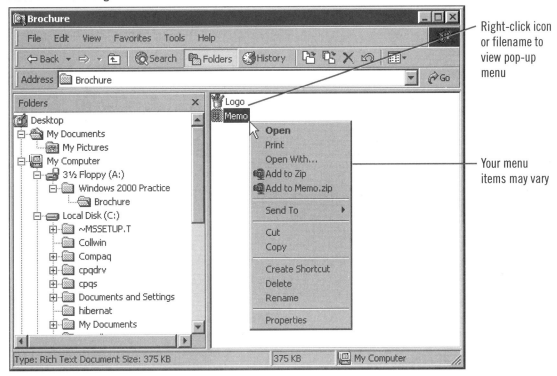

Right-click icon or filename to view pop-up menu

Your menu items may vary

**FIGURE B-19: Shortcut on desktop**

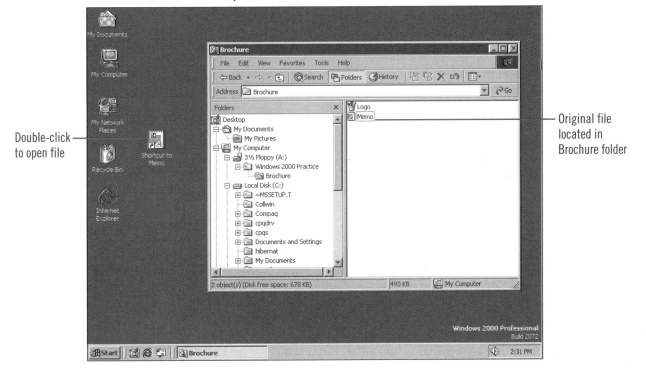

Double-click to open file

Original file located in Brochure folder

### Adding shortcuts to the Start menu

If you do not want your desktop to get cluttered with icons but you would still like easy access to certain files, programs, and folders, you can create a shortcut on the Start menu. Drag the file, program, or folder that you want to add to the Start menu from the Windows Explorer window to the Start button. The file, program, or folder will appear on the first level of the Start menu.

# Practice

## ► Concepts Review

**Label each of the elements of the Windows Explorer window shown in Figure B-20.**

FIGURE B-20

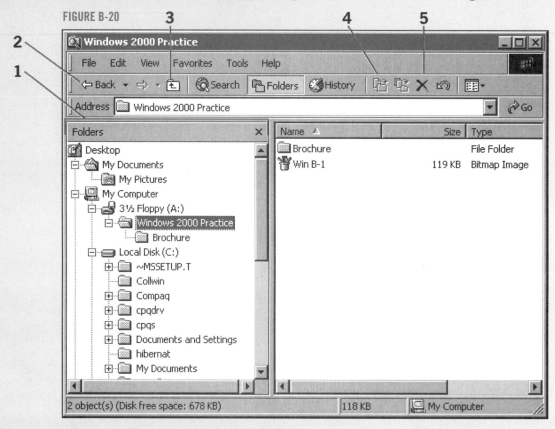

## Match each of the statements with the term it describes.

6. Electronic collections of data

7. Your computer's temporary storage area

8. Temporary location of information you wish to paste into another program

9. Storage areas on your hard drive for files, folders, and programs

10. Structure of files and folders

a. **RAM**
b. **Folders**
c. **Files**
d. **File hierarchy**
e. **Clipboard**

## Select the best answer from the list of choices.

**11. To prepare a floppy disk to save your files, you must first do which of the following?**
  a. Copy work files to the disk
  b. Format the disk
  c. Erase all the files that might be on the disk
  d. Place the files on the Clipboard

**12. You can use My Computer to**
  a. create a drawing of your computer.
  b. view the contents of a folder.
  c. change the appearance of your desktop.
  d. add text to a WordPad file.

**13. Which of the following best describes WordPad?**
  a. A program for organizing files
  b. A program for performing financial analysis
  c. A program for creating basic text documents
  d. A program for creating graphics

14. **Which of the following is NOT a way to move files from one folder to another?**
    a. Open the file and use the Save As command to save the file in a new location
    b. In My Computer or the Windows Explorer, drag the selected file to the new folder
    c. Use the Move To button on the Standard toolbar in the My Computer or the Windows Explorer window
    d. Use the [Ctrl][X] and [Ctrl][V] keyboard shortcuts while in the My Computer or the Windows Explorer window

15. **In which of the following can you view the hierarchy of drives, folders, and files in a split pane window?**
    a. Windows Explorer
    b. Programs
    c. My Computer
    d. WordPad

16. **To restore files that you have sent to the Recycle Bin,**
    a. click File, then click Empty Recycle Bin.
    b. click Edit, then click Undo Delete.
    c. click File, then click Undo.
    d. You cannot retrieve files sent to the Recycle Bin.

17. **To select files that are not grouped together, select the first file, then**
    a. press [Shift] while selecting the second file.
    b. press [Alt] while selecting the second file.
    c. press [Ctrl] while selecting the second file.
    d. click on the second file.

18. **Pressing [Backspace]**
    a. deletes the character to the right of the cursor.
    b. deletes the character to the left of the cursor.
    c. moves the insertion point one character to the right.
    d. deletes all text to the left of the cursor.

19. **The size of a font is measured in**
    a. centimeters.
    b. points.
    c. places.
    d. millimeters.

20. **The Back button on the My Computer toolbar**
    a. starts the last program you used.
    b. displays the next level of the file hierarchy.
    c. backs up the currently selected file.
    d. displays the last location you visited.

# ▶ Skills Review

Use Project Disk 2 to complete the exercises in this section.

1. **Create and save a WordPad file.**
   a. Start Windows, then start WordPad.
   b. Type My Drawing Ability.
   c. Press [Enter] three times.
   d. Save the document as *Drawing Ability* to your Project Disk 2.

2. **Open, edit, and save an existing Paint file.**
   a. Start Paint and open the file Win B-2 on your Project Disk 2.
   b. Inside the picture frame, use the ellipses tool to create a circle filled with purple and then use the rectangle tool to place a square filled with yellow inside the circle.
   c. Save the picture as *First Unique Art* to your Project Disk 2.

3. **Work with multiple programs.**
   a. Select the entire graphic and copy it to the Clipboard, then switch to WordPad.
   b. Place the insertion point in the last blank line, paste the graphic into your document, then deselect the graphic.
   c. Save the changes to your WordPad document.
   d. Switch to Paint.
   e. Using the Fill With Color button, change the color of a filled area of your graphic.
   f. Save the revised graphic with the new name *Second Unique Art* to Project Disk 2.
   g. Select the entire graphic and copy it to the Clipboard.
   h. Switch to WordPad, move the insertion point to the line below the graphic by clicking below the graphic and press [Enter], type This is another version of my graphic. below the first picture, then press [Enter].

   **i.** Paste the second graphic under the text you just typed.

   **j.** Save the changed WordPad document as *Two Drawing Examples* to your Project Disk 2.

   **k.** Exit Paint and WordPad.

**4. View files and create folders with My Computer.**

   **a.** Open My Computer.

   **b.** Double-click the drive that contains your Project Disk 2.

   **c.** Create a new folder on your Project Disk 2 by clicking File, New, then Folder, and name the new folder *Review*.

   **d.** Open the folder to display its contents (it is empty).

   **e.** Use the Address Bar to view your hard drive, usually (C:).

   **f.** Create a folder on the hard drive called *Temporary*, then use the Back button to view the Review folder.

   **g.** Create two new folders in it, one named *Documents* and the other named *Artwork*.

   **h.** Click the Forward button as many times as necessary to move up in the file hierarchy and view the contents of the hard drive.

   **i.** Change the view to Details.

**5. Move and copy files with My Computer.**

   **a.** Use the Address Bar to view your Project Disk 2.

   **b.** Use the [Shift] key to select *First Unique Art* and *Second Unique Art*, then cut and paste them into the Artwork folder.

   **c.** Use the Back button as many times as necessary to view the contents of Project Disk 2.

   **d.** Select the two WordPad files, *Drawing Ability* and *Two Drawing Examples*, then move them into the Review folder.

   **e.** Open the Review folder, select the two WordPad files again, then drag them into the Documents folder.

**6. Manage files with Windows Explorer.**

   **a.** Open Windows Explorer and view the contents of the Artwork folder in the right pane.

   **b.** Select the two Paint files.

   **c.** Drag the two Paint files from the Artwork folder to the Temporary folder on the hard drive to copy them.

   **d.** View the contents of the Documents folder in the right pane.

   **e.** Select the two WordPad files.

   **f.** Repeat Step c to copy the files to the Temporary folder on the hard drive.

   **g.** View the contents of the Temporary folder in the right pane to verify that the four files are there.

**7. Delete and restore files and folders.**

   **a.** Resize the Windows Explorer window so you can see the Recycle Bin icon on the desktop, then scroll in Windows Explorer so you can see the Temporary folder in the left pane.

   **b.** Delete the Temporary folder from the hard drive by dragging it to the Recycle Bin.

   **c.** Click Yes if necessary to confirm the deletion.

   **d.** Open the Recycle Bin, restore the Temporary folder and its files to your hard disk, and then close the Recycle Bin. (*Note:* If your Recycle Bin is empty, your computer is set to automatically delete items in the Recycle Bin.)

   **e.** Delete the Temporary folder again by pressing [Delete]. Click Yes if necessary to confirm the deletion.

**8. Create a shortcut on the desktop.**

   **a.** Use the left pane of Windows Explorer to locate the Windows folder on your hard drive. Select the folder to view its contents in the right pane. (*Note:* If you are in a lab setting, you may not have access to the Windows folder.)

   **b.** In the right pane, scroll through the list of objects until you see a file called Explorer.

   **c.** Drag the Explorer file with the right mouse button to the desktop to create a shortcut.

   **d.** Close Windows Explorer.

   **e.** Double-click the new shortcut to make sure it starts Windows Explorer. Then close Windows Explorer again.

   **f.** Delete the shortcut for Windows Explorer and exit Windows.

# ► Independent Challenges

If you are doing all of the Independent Challenges, you may need to use additional floppy disks. Label the first new disk Project Disk 3, and the next Project Disk 4.

**1.** You have decided to start a bakery business and you want to use Windows 2000 to organize the files for the business.

  **a.** Create two new folders on your Project Disk 3, one named *Advertising* and one named *Customers*.

  **b.** Use WordPad to create a letter inviting new customers to the open house for the new bakery, then save it as *Open House Letter* and place it in the Customers folder.

  **c.** Use WordPad to create a list of five tasks that need to get done before the business opens (such as purchasing equipment, decorating the interior, and ordering supplies), then save it as *Business Plan* to your Project Disk 3, but don't place it in a folder.

  **d.** Use Paint to create a simple logo for the bakery, save it as *Bakery Logo*, and then place it in the Advertising folder.

  **e.** Print the file Bakery Logo, then delete it from your Project Disk 3.

**2.** On your computer's hard drive, create a folder called *IC2*. Follow the guidelines listed here to create the file hierarchy shown in Figure B-21.

  **a.** Start WordPad, create a new file that contains a list. Save the file as *To Do List* to your Project Disk 3 (Project Disk 4 if you are out of space on Project Disk 3).

  **b.** Start My Computer and copy the Open House Letter file on your Project Disk 3 to the IC2 folder. Rename the file *Article*.

  **c.** Copy the Memo file again to the IC2 folder on your hard drive and rename the second copy of the file *Article Two*.

  **d.** Use My Computer to copy any Paint file to the IC2 folder and rename the file *Sample Logo*, then delete the Sample Logo file.

  **e.** Copy the To Do List from your Project Disk 3 to the IC2 folder and rename the file *Important List*.

  **f.** Move the files into the folders shown in Figure B-21.

  **g.** Copy the IC2 folder to your Project Disk 3. Then delete the IC2 folder on your hard drive. Using the Recycle Bin, restore the file called IC2. To remove all your work on the hard drive, delete this folder again.

FIGURE B-21

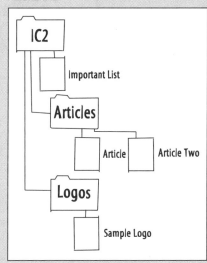

**3.** With Windows 2000, you can access the Web from My Computer and Windows Explorer, allowing you to search for information located not only on your computer or network, but also on any computer on the Internet.

  **a.** Start Windows Explorer, then click in the Address Bar so the current location (probably your hard drive) is selected, type **www.microsoft.com**, then press [Enter].

  **b.** Connect to the Internet if necessary. The Microsoft Web page appears in the right pane of Windows Explorer.

  **c.** Click in the Address Bar, then type **www.course.com**, press [Enter], and then wait a moment while the Course Technology Web page opens.

  **d.** Make sure your Project Disk is in the floppy disk drive, then click 3½ Floppy (A:) in the left pane.

  **e.** Click the Back button list arrow, then click Welcome to Microsoft's Homepage.

  **f.** Capture a picture of your desktop by pressing [Print Screen] located on the upper-right side of your keyboard. (This stores the picture on the Clipboard.) Open the Paint program, paste the contents of the Clipboard into the drawing window, then print it.

  **g.** Close Paint without saving your changes.

  **h.** Close Windows Explorer and disconnect from the Internet.

**4.** Create a shortcut to the drive that contains your Project Disk 3. Then capture a picture of your desktop showing the new shortcut by pressing [Print Screen], located on the upper-right side of your keyboard. The picture is stored temporarily on the Clipboard. Then open the Paint program and paste the contents of the Clipboard into the drawing window. Click No when asked to enlarge the Bitmap. Print the screen, close Paint without saving your changes, then delete the shortcut when you are finished.

# ▶ Visual Workshop

Recreate the screen shown in Figure B-22, which contains the Brochure window in My Computer, two shortcuts on the desktop, and two open files. Press [Print Screen] to make a copy of the screen, (a copy of the screen is placed on the Clipboard), open Paint, click Paste to paste the screen picture into Paint, then print the Paint file.

**FIGURE B-22**

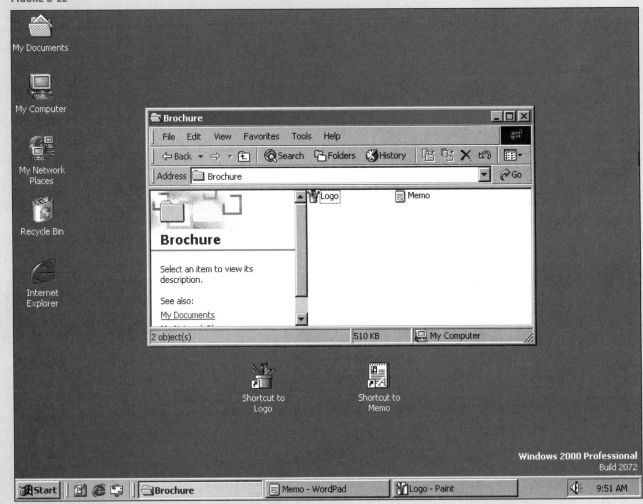

# Getting
## Started with Windows 98

### Objectives

- ► Start Windows and view the Active Desktop
- ► Use the mouse
- ► Start a program
- ► Move and resize windows
- ► Use menus, keyboard shortcuts, and toolbars
- ► Use dialog boxes
- ► Use scroll bars
- ► Get Help
- ► Close a program and shut down Windows

Microsoft Windows 98 is an **operating system**, a computer program that controls how the computer carries out basic tasks such as displaying information on your computer screen and running programs. Windows 98 helps you save and organize the results of your work (such as a resume or a list of addresses) as **files**, which are electronic collections of data. Windows 98 also coordinates the flow of information among the programs, printers, storage devices, and other components of your computer system. When you work with Windows 98, you will notice many **icons**, small pictures intended to be meaningful symbols of the items they represent. You will also notice rectangular-shaped work areas known as **windows**, thus the name of the operating system. This use of icons and windows is called a **graphical user interface** (**GUI**, pronounced "gooey"), which means that you interact with the computer through the use of graphics such as windows, icons, and other meaningful words and symbols. ◀━━ This unit introduces you to basic skills that you can use in all Windows programs.

Windows 98

# Starting Windows and Viewing the Active Desktop

When you turn on your computer, Windows 98 automatically starts and the Active Desktop appears. The **Active Desktop**, shown in Figure A-1, is where you organize all the information and tools you need to accomplish your computer tasks. From the desktop, you can access, store, share, and explore information seamlessly, whether it resides on your computer, a network, or the Internet. The **Internet** is a worldwide collection of over 40 million computers linked together to share information. The desktop is called "active" because, unlike in other versions of Windows, it allows you to access the Internet. When you start Windows for the first time, the desktop appears with the **default** settings, those preset by the operating system. For example, the default color of the desktop is green. If any of the default settings have been changed on your computer, your desktop will look different than in the figures, but you should be able to locate all the items you need. The bar at the bottom of your screen is called the **taskbar**, which shows what programs are currently running. Use the **Start button** at the left end of the taskbar to start programs, find and open files, access Windows Help and so on. The **Quick Launch toolbar** is next to the Start button; it contains buttons you use to quickly start Internet-related programs and show the desktop when it is not currently displayed. The bar on the right side of your screen is called the **Channel Bar**, which contains buttons you use to access the Internet. Table A-1 identifies the icons and other elements you see on your desktop. If Windows 98 is not currently running, follow the steps below to start it now.

1. **Turn on your computer and monitor**
   Windows automatically starts and the desktop appears, as shown in Figure A-1. If you are working on a network at school or at an office, you might see a password dialog box. If so, continue to Step 2. If not, continue to the next lesson.

> **Trouble?**
> If you don't know your password, see your instructor or technical support person.

2. **Type your password, then press [Enter]**
   Once the password is accepted, the Windows desktop appears on your screen.

CLUES TO USE

### Accessing the Internet from the Active Desktop

One of the important differences between Windows 98 and previous versions of Windows is that Windows 98 allows you to access the Internet from the desktop using Internet Explorer, a program that is integrated into the Windows 98 operating system. Internet Explorer is an example of a **browser**, a program designed to access the **World Wide Web** (**WWW, the Web**). One feature of Internet Explorer is that you can use the Favorites command on the Start menu to access places on the Internet that you visit frequently. Also, you can use the Quick Launch toolbar to launch Internet-related programs and the Channel Bar to view Internet channels, which are like those on television but display Internet content. The integration of a browser into the operating system provides a seamless connection between your desktop and the Internet.

**FIGURE A-1:** Windows Active Desktop

Icons (yours might be different)

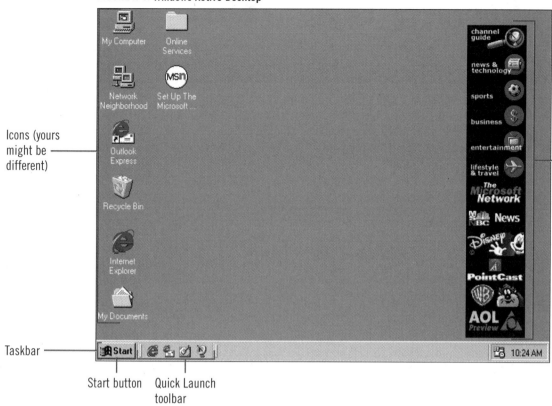

Channel Bar (yours might not be showing)

Taskbar

Start button

Quick Launch toolbar

**TABLE A-1:** Elements of the Windows desktop

| desktop element | allows you to |
| --- | --- |
| **My Computer** | Work with different disk drives and printers on your computer |
| **Network Neighborhood** | Work with different disk drives and printers on a network |
| **Outlook Express** | Start Outlook Express, an electronic mail program |
| **Recycle Bin** | Delete and restore files |
| **Internet Explorer** | Start Internet Explorer, a program you use to access the Internet |
| **My Documents folder** | Store programs, documents, graphics, or other files |
| **Taskbar** | Start programs and switch among open programs |
| **Start button** | Start programs, open documents, find a file, and more |
| **Channel Bar** | Start Internet Explorer and open channels |
| **Quick Launch toolbar** | Start Internet Explorer, start Outlook Express, show the desktop, and view channels |

Windows 98

# Using the Mouse

A **mouse** is a hand-held **input device** that you use to interact with your computer. Input devices come in many shapes and sizes; some, like a mouse, are directly attached to your computer with a cable; others function like a TV remote control and allow you to access your computer without being right next to it. Figure A-2 shows examples of common pointing devices. Because the most common pointing device is a mouse, this book uses that term. If you are using a different pointing device substitute that device whenever you see the term "mouse." When you move the mouse, the **mouse pointer** on the screen moves in the same direction. The **mouse buttons** are used to select icons and commands, which is how you communicate with the computer. Table A-2 shows some common mouse pointer shapes that indicate different activities. Table A-3 lists the five basic mouse actions. Begin by experimenting with the mouse now.

1. **Locate the mouse pointer on the desktop, then move the mouse across your desk or mousepad**
   Watch how the mouse pointer moves on the desktop in response to your movements. Practice moving the mouse pointer in circles, then back and forth in straight lines.

**Trouble?**

If the My Computer window opens, your mouse isn't set with the Windows 98 default mouse settings. See your instructor or technical support person for assistance. This book assumes your computer is set to all Windows 98 default settings

2. **Position the mouse pointer over the My Computer icon**
   Positioning the mouse pointer over an item is called **pointing**.

3. **With the pointer over the My Computer icon, press and release the left mouse button**
   Pressing and releasing the left mouse button is called **clicking** or single-clicking, to distinguish it from double-clicking, which you'll do in Step 7. When you position the mouse pointer over an icon or any item and click, you select that item. When an item is **selected**, it is **highlighted** (shaded differently than other items), and any action you take will be performed on that item.

4. **With the icon selected, press and hold down the left mouse button, then move the mouse down and to the right and release the mouse button**
   The icon becomes dimmed and moves with the mouse pointer; this is called **dragging**, which you use to move icons and other Windows elements. When you release the mouse button, the icon is moved to a new location.

5. **Position the mouse pointer over the My Computer icon, then press and release the right mouse button**
   Clicking the right mouse button is known as **right-clicking**. Right-clicking an item on the desktop displays a **pop-up menu**, as shown in Figure A-3. This menu lists the commands most commonly used for the item you have clicked. A **command** is a directive that provides access to a program's features.

**QuickTip**

When a step tells you to "click," use the left mouse button. If it says "right-click", use the right mouse button.

6. **Click anywhere outside the menu to close the pop-up menu**

7. **Position the mouse pointer over the My Computer icon, then press and release the left mouse button twice quickly**
   Clicking the mouse button twice quickly is known as **double-clicking**, which, in this case, opens the My Computer window. The **My Computer** window contains additional icons that represent the drives and system components that are installed on your computer.

8. **Click the Close button** ✕ **in the upper-right corner of the My Computer window**

TABLE A-2: Common mouse pointer shapes

| shape | used to |
|---|---|
| ▱ | Select items, choose commands, start programs, and work in programs |
| I | Position mouse pointer for editing or inserting text; called the insertion point |
| ⧖ | Indicate Windows is busy processing a command |
| ↔ | Change the size of a window; appears when mouse pointer is on the border of a window |
| 🖑 | Select and open Web-based data |

FIGURE A-2: Common pointing devices

Right mouse button

Left mouse button

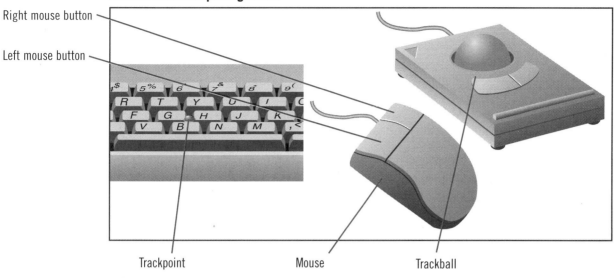

Trackpoint　　　　Mouse　　　　Trackball

FIGURE A-3: Displaying a pop-up menu

Selected icon

Pop-up menu

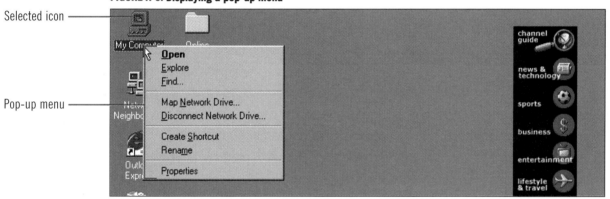

TABLE A-3: Basic mouse techniques

| technique | what to do |
|---|---|
| **Pointing** | Move the mouse to position the mouse pointer over an item on the desktop |
| **Clicking** | Press and release the left mouse button |
| **Double-clicking** | Press and release the left mouse button twice quickly |
| **Dragging** | Point to an item, press and hold the left mouse button, move the mouse to a new location, then release the mouse button |
| **Right-clicking** | Point to an item, then press and release the right mouse button |

## More about the mouse: Classic style and Internet style

Because Windows 98 integrates the use of the Internet with its other functions, it allows you to choose whether you want to extend the way you click on the Internet to the rest of your computer work. With previous versions of the Windows operating system, and with the default Windows 98 settings, you click an item to select it and double-click an item to open it. When you use the Internet, however, you point to an item to select it and single-click to open it. Therefore, Windows 98 gives you two choices for using the mouse buttons: with the **Classic style**, you double-click to open items, and with the **Internet style** or **Web style**, you single-click to open items. To change from one style to another, click the Start button, point to Settings, click Folder Options, then click the Web style, Classic style, or Custom option.

# Starting a Program

To start a program in Windows 98, click the Start button, which lists categories for a variety of tasks described in Table A-4. As you become familiar with Windows, you might want to customize the Start menu to include additional items that you use most often. To start a program from the Start menu, you click the Start menu, point to Programs to open the Programs submenu, then click the program you want to start. Windows 98 comes with several built-in programs, called **accessories**. Although not as feature-rich as many programs sold separately, Windows accessories are useful for completing basic tasks. In this lesson, you start a Windows accessory called **WordPad**, which is a word processing program you can use to create and edit simple documents. Table A-5 describes other popular Windows Accessories.

## Steps

1. **Click the Start button on the taskbar**
   The Start menu opens.

2. **Point to Programs**
   The Programs submenu opens, listing the programs and categories for programs installed on your computer. WordPad is in the category called Accessories.

3. **Point to Accessories**
   The Accessories menu, shown in Figure A-4, contains several programs to help you complete common tasks. You want to start WordPad, which is probably at the bottom of the list.

4. **Click WordPad**
   WordPad opens and a blank document window opens, as shown in Figure A-5. Note that a **program button** appears on the taskbar, indicating that WordPad is open.

**TABLE A-4: Start menu categories**

| category | description |
|---|---|
| Windows Update | Connects to a Microsoft Web site and updates your Windows 98 files as necessary |
| Programs | Opens programs included on the Start menu |
| Favorites | Connects to favorite Web sites or opens folders and documents that you previously selected |
| Documents | Opens the most recently opened and saved documents |
| Settings | Opens tools for selecting settings for your system, including the Control Panel, printers, taskbar and Start menu, folders, icons, and the Active Desktop |
| Find | Locates programs, files, folders, or computers on your computer network, or finds information and people on the Internet |
| Help | Provides Windows Help information by topic, alphabetical index, or search criteria |
| Run | Opens a program or file based on a location and filename that you type or select |
| Log Off | Allows you to log off the system and log on as a different user |
| Shut Down | Provides options to shut down the computer, restart the computer in Windows mode, or restart the computer in MS-DOS mode |

**FIGURE A-4: Cascading menus**

Cascading menus (also called submenus)

Arrow indicates submenu

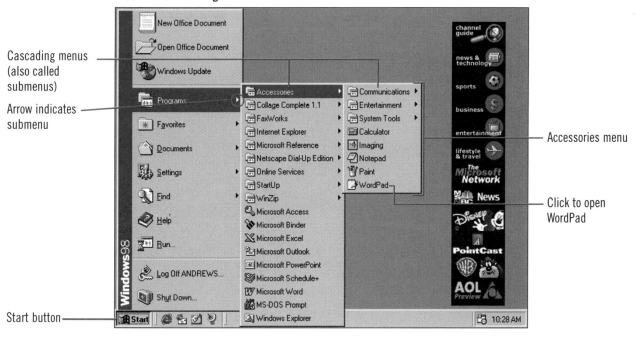

Accessories menu

Click to open WordPad

Start button

**FIGURE A-5: WordPad window**

Blank document window

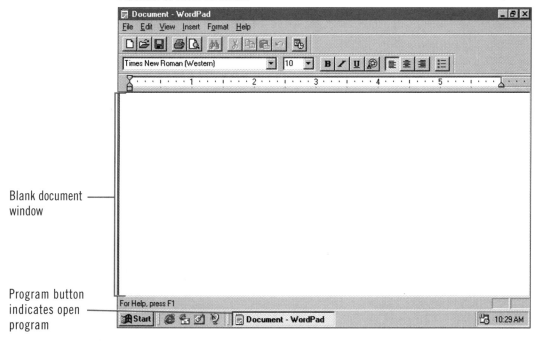

Program button indicates open program

**TABLE A-5: Common Windows Accessories on the Accessories menu**

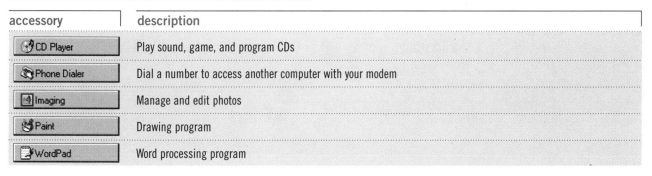

| accessory | description |
|-----------|-------------|
| CD Player | Play sound, game, and program CDs |
| Phone Dialer | Dial a number to access another computer with your modem |
| Imaging | Manage and edit photos |
| Paint | Drawing program |
| WordPad | Word processing program |

# Moving and Resizing Windows

One of the powerful features of Windows is the ability to open more than one window or program at once. This means, however, that the desktop can get cluttered with the various programs and files you are using. One of the ways to keep your desktop organized is by changing the size of a window or moving it. You can do this using the standard borders and sizing buttons that are part of each window. ▰▰▰ Practice sizing and moving the WordPad window now.

## Steps 1 2 3 4

**1.** If the WordPad window does not already fill the screen, click the **Maximize button** 🔲 in the WordPad window.
When a window is **maximized**, it takes up the whole screen.

**2.** Click the **Restore button** 🔲 in the WordPad window
To **restore** a window is to return it to its previous size, as shown in Figure A-6. The Restore button only appears when a window is maximized. In addition to minimizing, maximizing, and restoring windows, you can also change the dimensions of any window.

**3.** Position the pointer on the right edge of the WordPad window until the pointer changes to ↔, then drag the border to the right
The width of the window increases. You can size the height and width of a window by dragging any of the four sides individually. You can also size the height and width of the window simultaneously by dragging the corner of the window.

**4.** Position the pointer in the lower-right corner of the WordPad window until the pointer changes to ↘, as shown in Figure A-6, then drag down and to the right
The height and width of the window increase at the same time. You can also position a restored window wherever you wish on the desktop by dragging its title bar.

**5.** Click the **title bar** on the WordPad window, as shown in Figure A-6, then drag the window up and to the left
The window is repositioned on the desktop. The **title bar** is the area along the top of the window that displays the file name and program used to create it. At times, you might wish to close a program window, yet keep the program running and easily accessible. You can accomplish this by minimizing a window.

**6.** In the WordPad window, click the **Minimize button** ▬
When you **minimize** a window, it shrinks to a program button on the taskbar, as shown in Figure A-7. WordPad is still running, but it is out of your way.

**7.** Click the **WordPad program button** on the taskbar to reopen the window
The WordPad program window reopens.

**8.** Click the **Maximize button** 🔲 in the upper-right corner of the WordPad window
The window fills the screen.

FIGURE A-6: Restored WordPad window

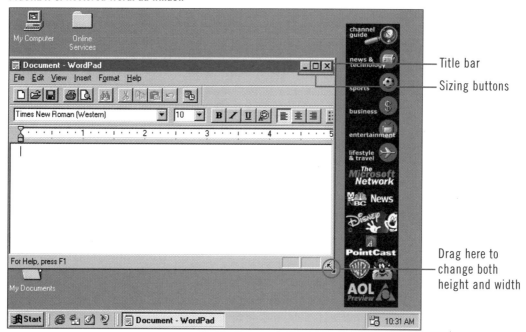

Title bar

Sizing buttons

Drag here to change both height and width

FIGURE A-7: Minimized WordPad window

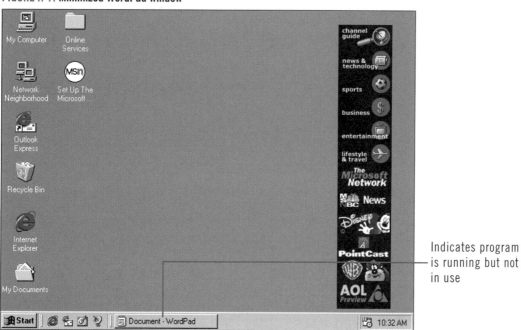

Indicates program is running but not in use

## CLUES TO USE

## More about sizing windows

Many programs contain two sets of sizing buttons: one that controls the program window itself and another that controls the window for the file with which you are working. The program sizing buttons are located in the title bar and the file sizing buttons are located below them. See Figure A-8. When you minimize a file window within a program, the file window is reduced to an icon in the lower-left corner of the program window, but the size of the program window remains intact.

FIGURE A-8: Program and file sizing buttons

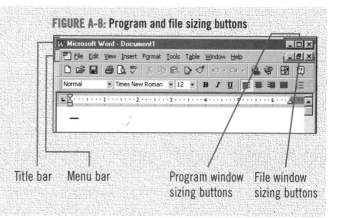

Title bar   Menu bar

Program window sizing buttons

File window sizing buttons

Windows 98

# Using Menus, Keyboard Shortcuts, and Toolbars

A **menu** is a list of commands that you use to accomplish certain tasks. You've already used the Start menu to start WordPad. Each Windows program also has its own set of menus, which are located on the **menu bar** under the title bar. The menus organize commands into groups of related operations. See Table A-6 for examples of what you might see on a typical menu. A **toolbar** is a series of buttons, located under the menu bar, that you click to accomplish certain tasks. Buttons are another method for executing menu commands. ✐ You will open the Control Panel, then use a menu and toolbar button to change how the contents of the window appear.

**QuickTip**

You now have two windows open: WordPad and the Control Panel. The Control Panel is the **active window** (or **active program**) because it is the one with which you are currently working. WordPad is **inactive** because it is open but you are not working with it. Working with more than one window at a time is called **multitasking**.

**1.** Click the **Start button** on the taskbar, point to **Settings**, then click **Control Panel**

The Control Panel window opens over the WordPad window. The **Control Panel** contains icons for various programs that allow you to specify how your computer looks and performs. You use the Control Panel to practice using menus and toolbars.

**2.** Click **View** on the menu bar

The View menu appears, listing the View commands, as shown in Figure A-9. On a menu, a **check mark** identifies a feature that is currently enabled or "on." To disable, or turn "off" the feature, click the command again to remove the check mark. A **bullet mark** can also indicate that an option is enabled. To disable a bulleted option, you must select another option in its place.

**3.** Click **Small Icons**

The icons are now smaller than they were before, taking up less room in the window.

**4.** Press [Alt][V] to open the View menu

The View menu appears again; this time you opened it using the keyboard. Notice that a letter in each command on the View menu is underlined. You can select these commands by pressing the underlined letter. Executing a command using the keyboard is called a **keyboard shortcut**. You might find that you prefer keyboard shortcuts to the mouse if you find it cumbersome to reposition your hands at the keyboard each time you use the mouse.

**5.** Press [T] to select the Toolbars command

The Toolbars submenu appears with check marks next to the commands that are currently selected.

**Trouble?**

If the Text Labels command wasn't selected, clicking the command now will select it, and you will see the labels under the buttons. Click View, click Toolbars, then click Text Labels to deselect it.

**6.** Press [T] to deselect the Text Labels command

The buttons appear without labels below each one; now you can see the entire toolbar.

**7.** On the Control Panel toolbar, position the pointer over the **Views button** 🖾 but do not click yet

When you position the mouse pointer over a button (and other items), a **ScreenTip** appears, showing the name of the item, as shown in Figure A-10. ScreenTips help you learn the names of the various elements in Windows programs.

**8.** Click the **Views button list arrow** 🖾▾

Some toolbar buttons have an arrow, which indicates the button contains several choices. Clicking the arrow shows the choices; clicking the button itself automatically selects the command below the one that was previously selected.

**9.** In the list of View choices, click **Details**

The Details view includes a description of each program in the Control Panel.

FIGURE A-9: Opening a menu

Menu bar

Commands in View menu

Status bar displays description of menu

Arrow indicates submenu

Check mark

Bullet

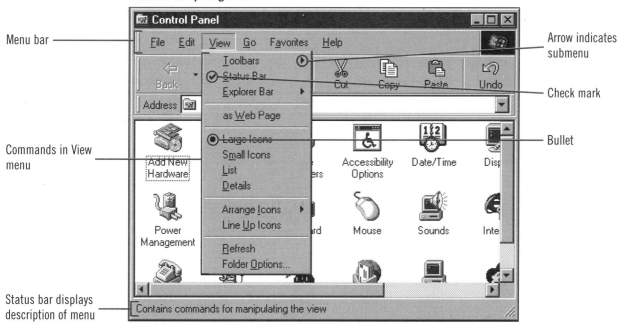

FIGURE A-10: ScreenTip in Control Panel

Toolbar

Position pointer over button to display ScreenTip

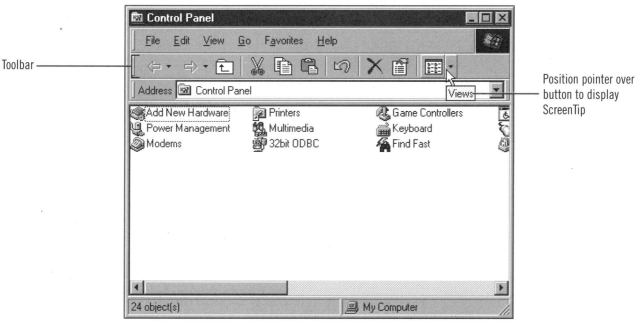

TABLE A-6: Typical items on a menu

| item | description | example |
|------|-------------|---------|
| **Dimmed command** | A menu command that is not currently available | Undo    Ctrl+Z |
| **Ellipsis** | Opens a dialog box that allows you to select different or additional options | Save As... |
| **Triangle** | Opens a cascading menu containing an additional list of commands | Zoom    ▶ |
| **Keyboard shortcut** | A keyboard alternative to using the mouse for executing a command | Paste    Ctrl+V |
| **Underlined letter** | Indicates the letter to press for the keyboard shortcut | Print Preview |

# Using Dialog Boxes

A **dialog box** is a window that opens when you choose a menu command that is followed by an ellipsis (…), or any command that needs more information before the program can carry out the command you selected. Dialog boxes open in other situations as well, such as when you open a program in the Control Panel. See Figure A-11 and Table A-7 for some of the typical elements of a dialog box. ◀▬▬▬ Practice using a dialog box to control your mouse settings.

**Trouble?**

If you can't see the Mouse icon, resize the Control Panel window.

**1.** In the Control Panel window, double-click the **Mouse icon** 🖰

The Mouse Properties dialog box opens, as shown in Figure A-12. **Properties** are characteristic of a specific computer element (in this case, the mouse) that you can customize. The options in this dialog box allow you to control the way the mouse buttons are configured, select the types of pointers that appear, choose the speed of the mouse movement on the screen, and specify what type of mouse you are using. **Tabs** at the top of the dialog box separate these options into related categories.

**2.** Click the **Motion tab** if it is not already the frontmost tab

This tab has two boxes. The first, Pointer speed, has a slider for you to set how fast the pointer moves on the screen in relation to how you move the mouse in your hand. The second, **Pointer trail**, has a check box you can select to add a "trail" or shadow to the pointer on your screen, making it easier to see. The slider in the Pointer trail box lets you determine the degree to which the option is in effect—in this case, the length of the pointer trail.

**3.** In the Pointer trail box, click the **Show pointer trails check box** to select it

**4.** Drag the **slider** below the check box all the way to the right, then move the mouse pointer across your screen

As you move the mouse, notice the pointer trails.

**5.** Click the other tabs in the Mouse Properties dialog box and experiment with the options that are available in each category

After you select the options you want in a dialog box, you need to select a **command button**, which carries out the options you've selected. The two most common command buttons are OK and Cancel. Clicking OK accepts your changes and closes the dialog box; clicking Cancel leaves the original settings intact and closes the dialog box. The third command button in this dialog box is Apply. Clicking the Apply button accepts the changes you've made and keeps the dialog box open so that you can select additional options. Because you might share this computer with others, it's important to return the dialog box options back to the original settings.

**QuickTip**

You can also use the keyboard to carry out commands in a dialog box. Pressing [Enter] is the same as clicking OK; pressing [Esc] is the same as clicking Cancel.

**6.** Click **Cancel** to leave the original settings intact and close the dialog box

FIGURE A-11: **Elements of a typical dialog box**

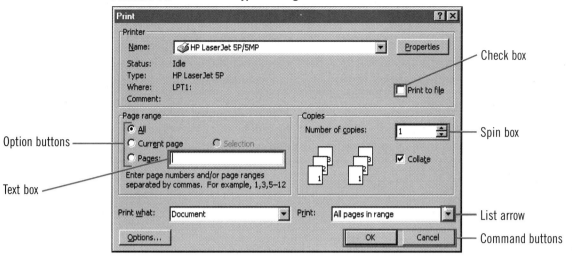

Check box — Option buttons — Text box — Spin box — List arrow — Command buttons

FIGURE A-12: **Mouse Properties dialog box**

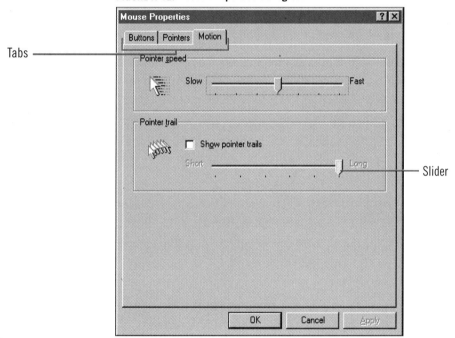

Tabs — Slider

TABLE A-7: **Typical items in a dialog box**

| item | description | item | description |
|---|---|---|---|
| **Check box** | A box that turns an option on (when the box is checked) and off (when it is blank) | **List box** | A box containing a list of items; to choose an item, click the list arrow, then click the desired item |
| **Text box** | A box in which you type text | **Spin box** | A box with two arrows and a text box; allows you to scroll numerical increments or type a number |
| **Option button** | A small circle that selects a single dialog box option; you cannot check more than one option button in a list | **Slider** | A shape that you drag to set the degree to which an option is in effect |
| **Command button** | A rectangular button in a dialog box with the name of the command on it | **Tab** | A place in a dialog box where related commands and options are organized |

# Using Scroll Bars

When you cannot see all of the items available in a window, scroll bars appear on the right and/or bottom edges of the window. **Scroll bars** allow you to display the additional contents of the window. There are several ways you can scroll in a window. When you need to scroll only a short distance, you can use the scroll arrows. To scroll the window in larger increments, click in the scroll bar above or below the scroll box. Dragging the scroll box moves you quickly to a new part of the window. See Table A-8 for a summary of the different ways to use scroll bars. With the Control Panel window in Details view, you can use the scroll bars to view all of the items in this window.

## Steps

**Trouble?**

If you can't see the scroll bars, resize the window until both the horizontal and vertical scroll bars appear. Scroll bars don't appear when the window is large enough to include all the information.

**QuickTip**

The size of the scroll box changes to reflect how many items or the amount of text that does not fit in a window. A larger scroll box indicates that a relatively small amount of the window's contents is not currently visible; you need to scroll only a short distance to see the remaining items. A smaller scroll box indicates that a relatively large amount of information is currently not visible.

1. **In the Control Panel window, click the down scroll arrow, as shown in Figure A-13**
   Clicking this arrow moves the view down one line. Clicking the up arrow moves the view up one line.

2. **Click the up scroll arrow in the vertical scroll bar**
   The screen moves up one line.

3. **Click anywhere in the area below the scroll box in the vertical scroll bar**
   The view moves down one window's height. Similarly, you can click in the scroll bar above the scroll box to move up one window's height.

4. **Drag the scroll box all the way down to the bottom of the vertical scrollbar**
   The view now includes the items that appear at the very bottom of the window. Similarly, you can drag the scroll box to the top of the scroll bar to view the information that appears at the top of the window.

5. **Drag the scroll box all the way up to the top of the vertical scroll bar**
   This view shows the items that appear at the top of the window.

6. **Click the area to the right of the scroll box in the horizontal scroll bar**
   The far right edge of the window comes into view. The horizontal scroll bar works the same as the vertical scroll bar.

7. **Click the area to the left of the scroll box in the horizontal scroll bar**
   You should return the Control Panel to its original settings.

8. **On the Control Panel toolbar, click the Views button list arrow ⊞▾ , click Large Icons, then maximize the Control Panel window**

**FIGURE A-13: Scroll bars in the Control Panel**

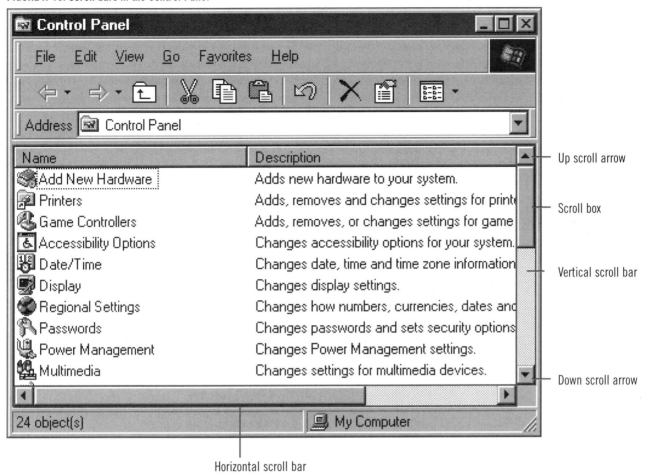

Up scroll arrow

Scroll box

Vertical scroll bar

Down scroll arrow

Horizontal scroll bar

**TABLE A-8: Using scroll bars in a window**

| to | do this |
|---|---|
| **Move down one line** | Click the down arrow at the bottom of the vertical scroll bar |
| **Move up one line** | Click the up arrow at the top of the vertical scroll bar |
| **Move down one window height** | Click in the area below the scroll box in the vertical scroll bar |
| **Move up one window height** | Click in the area above the scroll box in the vertical scroll bar |
| **Move up a large distance in the window** | Drag the scroll box up in the vertical scroll bar |
| **Move down a large distance in the window** | Drag the scroll box down in the vertical scroll bar |
| **Move a short distance side-to-side in a window** | Click the left or right arrows in the horizontal scroll bar |
| **Move to the right one window width** | Click in the area to the right of the scroll box in the horizontal scroll bar |
| **Move to the left one window width** | Click in the area to the left of the scroll box in the horizontal scroll bar |
| **Move left or right a large distance in the window** | Drag the scroll box in the horizontal scroll bar |

Windows 98

# Getting Help

When you have a question about how to do something in Windows 98, you can usually find the answer with a few clicks of your mouse. **Windows Help** works like a book stored on your computer, with a table of contents and an index to make finding information easier. Help provides guidance on many Windows features, including detailed steps for completing a procedure, definitions of terms, lists of related topics, and search capabilities. To open the main Windows 98 Help system, click Help on the Start menu. From here you can browse the Help "book," or you can connect to a Microsoft Web site on the Internet for the latest technical support on Windows 98. To get help on a specific Windows program, click Help on the program's menu bar. You can also access **context-sensitive help**, help specifically related to what you are doing, using a variety of methods such as right-clicking an object or using the question mark button in a dialog box. In this lesson, you get Help on how to start a program. You also get information on the taskbar.

1. **Click the Start button on the taskbar, then click Help**
   The Windows Help dialog box opens with the Contents tab in front, as shown in Figure A-14. The Contents tab provides you with a list of Help categories. Each "book" has several "chapters" that you can see by clicking the book or the name next to the book.

**QuickTip**

When you point to a Help category, the mouse changes to the hand pointer, the Help category is selected, and the text changes to blue and is underlined. This is similar to selecting items on the Internet.

2. **Click the Contents tab if it isn't the frontmost tab, click Exploring Your Computer, then click Work with Programs to view the Help categories**
   The Help window contains a selection of topics related to running programs.

3. **Click Start a Program**
   The Help window appears in the right pane, as shown in Figure A-15. **Panes** divide a window into two or more sections. At the bottom of the right pane, you can click Related Topics to view a list of topics that may also be of interest. Some Help topics also allow you to view additional information about important words; these words are underlined.

4. **Click the underlined word taskbar**
   A pop-up window appears with a definition of the underlined word.

5. **Read the definition, then press [Enter] or click anywhere outside the pop-up window to close it**

6. **In the left pane, click the Index tab**
   The Index tab provides an alphabetical list of all the available Help topics, like an index at the end of a book. You can enter a topic in the text box at the top of the pane. As you type, the list of topics automatically scrolls to try to match the word or phrase you type. You can also scroll down to the topic. In either case, the topic appears in the right pane, as usual.

7. **In the left pane, click the Search tab**
   You can use the Search tab to locate a Help topic using keywords. You enter a word or phrase in the text box and click List Topics; a list of matching topics appears below the text box. To view a topic, double-click it or select the topic, then click Display.

8. **Click the Web Help button [Web Help] on the toolbar**
   Information on the Web page for Windows 98 Help appears in the right pane (a **Web page** is a document that contains highlighted words, phrases, and graphics that link to other pages on the Internet). You could access this Web page by clicking the "Support Online" underlined text.

9. **In the Windows Help window, click the Close button [X] in the upper-right corner of the window**
   Clicking the Close button closes the active window.

**FIGURE A-14: Windows Help dialog box**

Help toolbar

Help tabs

Click to view alphabetical list of Help topics

Click to search for words and phrases used in Help topics

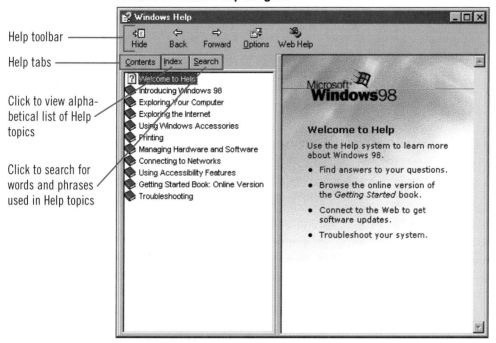

**FIGURE A-15: Viewing Help on starting a program**

Help topic

Hand pointer

Left pane contains Help categories and topics

Right pane contains help on the topic you select

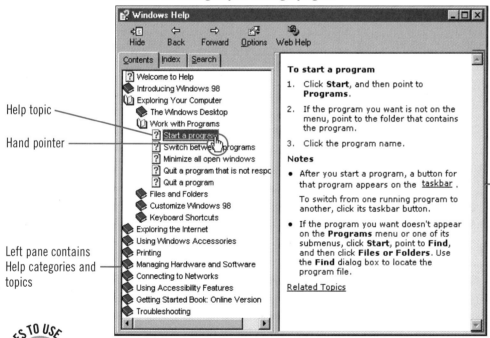

### Context-sensitive help

To receive help in a dialog box, click the Help button ? in the upper-right corner of the dialog box; the mouse pointer changes to ▷?. Click the Help pointer on the item for which you need additional information. A pop-up window provides a brief explanation of the selected feature. You can also click the right mouse button on an item in a dialog box, then click the What's This? button to display the Help explanation. In addition, when you click the right mouse button in a Help topic window, you can choose commands to annotate, copy, and print the contents of the topic window. From the Help pop-up menu, you can also choose to have topic windows always appear on top of the currently active window, so you can see Help topics while you work.

Windows 98

# Closing a Program and Shutting Down Windows

When you are finished working on your computer, you need to make sure you shut it down properly. This involves several steps: saving and closing all open files, closing all the open programs and windows, shutting down Windows, and finally, turning off the computer. If you turn off the computer while Windows is running, you could lose important data. To **close** programs, you can click the Close button in the window's upper-right corner or click File on the menu bar and choose either Close or Exit. To shut down Windows after all your files and programs are closed, click Shut Down from the Start menu, then select the desired option from the Shut Down dialog box, shown in Figure A-16. See Table A-9 for a description of shutdown options. Close all your open files, windows, and programs, then exit Windows.

1. In the Control Panel window, click the **Close button** ☒ in the upper-right corner of the window
   The Control Panel window closes.

2. Click **File** on the WordPad menu bar, then click **Exit**
   If you have made any changes to the open file, you will be prompted to save your changes before the program quits. Some programs also give you the option of choosing the Close command on the File menu in order to close the active file but leave the program open, so you can continue to work in it with a different file. Also, if there is a second set of sizing buttons in the window, the Close button on the menu bar will close the active file only, leaving the program open for continued use.

3. If you see a message asking you to save changes to the document, click **No**
   WordPad closes and you return to the desktop.

**QuickTip**

Complete the remaining steps to shut down Windows and your computer only if you have been told to do so by your instructor or technical support person.

4. Click the **Start button** on the taskbar, then click **Shut Down**
   The Shut Down Windows dialog box opens, as shown in Figure A-16. In this dialog box, you have the option to shut down the computer, restart the computer in Windows mode or restart the computer in MS-DOS mode.

5. Click the **Shut down option button**, if necessary

6. If you are working in a lab, click **Cancel** to leave the computer running and return to the Windows desktop
   If you are working on your own machine or if your instructor told you to shut down Windows, click **OK** to exit Windows.

7. When you see the message **It's now safe to turn off your computer**, turn off your computer and monitor

FIGURE A-16: Shut Down Windows dialog box

Click to shut down Windows

Click to restart computer in Windows mode

Click to restart computer in MS-DOS mode

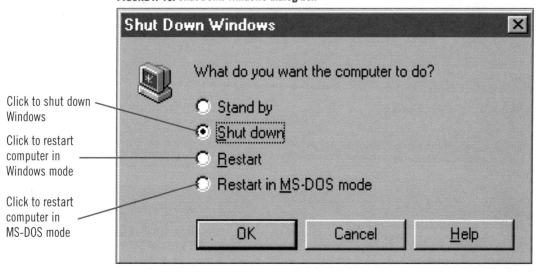

TABLE A-9: Shut down options

| shut down option | function | when to use it |
| --- | --- | --- |
| **Shut down** | Prepares the computer to be turned off | When you are finished working with Windows and you want to shut off your computer |
| **Restart** | Restarts the computer and reloads Windows | When you want to restart the computer and begin working with Windows again (your programs might have frozen or stopped working). |
| **Restart in MS-DOS mode** | Starts the computer in the MS-DOS mode | When you want to run programs under MS-DOS or use DOS commands to work with files |

### The Log Off command

To change users on the same computer quickly, you can choose the Log Off command from the Start menu. This command identifies the name of the current user. When you choose this command, Windows 98 shuts down and automatically restarts, stopping at the point where you need to enter a password. When the new user enters a user name and password, Windows restarts and the desktop appears as usual.

# Practice

## ► Concepts Review

Identify each of the items labeled in Figure A-17.

FIGURE A-17

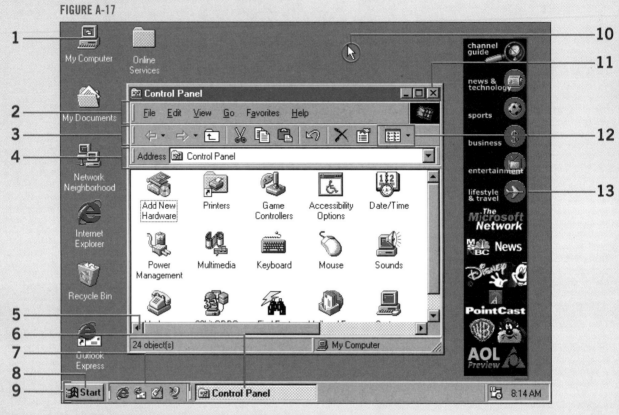

Match each of the statements with the term it describes.

14. Shrinks a window to a button on the taskbar
15. Shows the name of the window or program
16. The item you first click to start a program
17. Requests more information that you supply before carrying out command
18. Shows the Start button, Quick Launch toolbar, and any currently open programs
19. An input device that lets you point to and make selections
20. Graphic representation of program

a. Taskbar
b. Dialog box
c. Start button
d. Mouse
e. Title bar
f. Minimize button
g. Icon

Select the best answer from the list of choices.

21. The acronym GUI means
    a. Grayed user information.
    b. Group user icons.
    c. Graphical user interface.
    d. Group user interconnect.

22. **Which of the following is NOT provided by an operating system?**
    a. Programs for organizing files
    b. Instructions to coordinate the flow of information among the programs, files, printers, storage devices, and other components of your computer system
    c. Programs that allow you to specify the operation of the mouse
    d. Spell checker for your documents

23. **All of the following are examples of using a mouse, EXCEPT**
    a. Clicking the Maximize button.
    b. Pressing [Enter].
    c. Double-clicking to start a program.
    d. Dragging the My Computer icon.

24. **The term for moving an item to a new location on the desktop is**
    a. Pointing.
    b. Clicking.
    c. Dragging.
    d. Restoring.

25. **The Maximize button is used to**
    a. Return a window to its previous size.
    b. Expand a window to fill the computer screen.
    c. Scroll slowly through a window.
    d. Run programs from the Start menu.

26. **What appears if a window contains more information than can be displayed in the window?**
    a. Program icon
    b. Cascading menu
    c. Scroll bars
    d. Check box

27. **A window is active when**
    a. You see its program button on the taskbar.
    b. Its title bar is dimmed.
    c. It is open and you are currently using it.
    d. It is listed in the Programs submenu.

28. **You can exit Windows by**
    a. Double-clicking the Control Panel application.
    b. Double-clicking the Program Manager control menu box.
    c. Clicking File, then clicking Exit.
    d. Selecting the Shut Down command from the Start menu.

# ▶ Skills Review

1. **Start Windows and view the Active Desktop**
   a. Turn on the computer, if necessary.
   b. After Windows starts, identify as many items on the desktop as you can, without referring to the lesson material.
   c. Compare your results to Figure A-1.

2. **Use the mouse**
   a. Double-click the Recycle Bin icon.
   b. Drag the Recycle Bin window to the upper-right corner of the desktop.
   c. Right-click the title bar of the Recycle Bin, then click Close.

3. **Start a program.**
   a. Click the Start button on the taskbar, then point to Programs.
   b. Point to Accessories, then click Calculator.
   c. Minimize the Calculator window.

4. **Practice dragging, maximizing, restoring, sizing, and minimizing windows.**
   a. Drag the Recycle Bin icon to the bottom of the desktop.
   b. Double-click the My Computer icon to open the My Computer window.
   c. Maximize the window, if it is not already maximized.
   d. Restore the window to its previous size.
   e. Resize the window until you see both horizontal and vertical scroll bars.
   f. Resize the window until the horizontal scroll bar no longer appears.

    **g.** Click the Minimize button.

    **h.** Drag the Recycle Bin back to the top of the desktop.

**5. Use menus, keyboard shortcuts, and toolbars**

    **a.** Click the Start button on the taskbar, point to Settings, then click Control Panel.

    **b.** Click View on the menu bar, point to Toolbars, then click Standard Buttons to hide the toolbar.

    **c.** Redisplay the toolbar.

    **d.** Press [Alt][V] to show the View menu, then press [W] to view the Control Panel as a Web page.

    **e.** Note the change, then use the same keyboard shortcuts to change the view back.

    **f.** Click the Up One Level button to view My Computer.

    **g.** Click the Back button to return to the Control Panel.

    **h.** Double-click the Display icon.

**6. Use dialog boxes.**

    **a.** Click the Screen Saver tab.

    **b.** Click the Screen Saver list arrow, select a screen saver, and preview the change but do not click OK.

    **c.** Click the Effects tab.

    **d.** In the Visual effects section, click the Use large icons check box to select it, then click Apply.

    **e.** Note the change in the icons on the desktop and in the Control Panel window.

    **f.** Click the Use large icons check box to deselect it, Click the Screen Saver tab, return the scrren saver to its original setting, then click Apply.

    **g.** Click the Close button in the Display Properties dialog box, but leave the Control Panel open.

**7. Use scroll bars**

    **a.** Click View on the Control Panel toolbar, then click Details.

    **b.** Resize the Control Panel window, if necessary, so that both scroll bars are visible.

    **c.** Drag the vertical scroll box down all the way.

    **d.** Click anywhere in the area above the vertical scroll box.

    **e.** Click the up scroll arrow until the scroll box is back at the top of the scroll bar.

    **f.** Drag the horizontal scroll box so you can read the descriptions for the icons.

**8. Get Help**

    **a.** Click the Start button on the taskbar, then click Help.

    **b.** Click the Contents tab, then click Introducing Windows 98.

    **c.** Click Exploring Your Computer, click Customize Windows 98, then click How the Screen Looks.

    **d.** Click each of the topics and read them in the right pane.

**9. Close a program and shut down Windows.**

    **a.** Click the Close button to close the Help topic window.

    **b.** Click File on the menu bar, then click Close to close the Control Panel window.

    **c.** Click the Calculator program button on the taskbar to restore the window.

    **d.** Click the Close button in the Calculator window to close the Calculator program.

    **e.** Click the My Computer program button on the taskbar, then click the Close button to close the window.

    **f.** If you are instructed to do so, shut down your computer.

# ▶ Independent Challenges

**1.** Windows 98 has an extensive help system. In this independent challenge, you will use Help to learn about more Windows 98 features and explore the help that's available on the Internet.

**a.** Open Windows Help and locate help topics on: adjusting the double-click speed of your mouse; using Print; and, displaying Web content on your desktop.

If you have a printer, print a Help topic for each subject. If you do not have a printer, write a summary of each topic.

**b.** Follow these steps below to access help on the Internet. If you don't have Internet access, you can't do this step.

**i.** Click the Web Help button on the toolbar.

**ii.** Read the introduction, then click the link Support Online. A browser will open and prompt you to connect to the Internet. Once you are connected, a Web site called Support Online will appear.

**iii.** Click the View Popular Topics link. Write a summary of what you find.

**iv.** Click the Close button in the title bar of your browser, then disconnect from the Internet and close Windows Help.

**2.** You may need to change the format of the clock and date on your computer. For example, if you work with international clients it might be easier to show the time in military (24-hour) time and the date with the day before the month. You can also change the actual time and date on your computer, such as when you change time zones.

**a.** Open the Control Panel window, then double-click the Regional Settings icon.

**b.** Click the Time tab to change the time to show a 24-hour clock rather than a 12-hour clock.

**c.** Click the Date tab to change the date to show the day before the month (e.g., 30/3/99).

**d.** Change the time to one hour later using the Date/Time icon in the Control Panel window.

**e.** Return the settings to the original time and format and close all open windows.

**3.** Calculator is a Windows program on the Accessories menu that you can use for calculations you need to perform while using the computer. Follow these guidelines to explore the Calculator and the Help that comes with it:

**a.** Start the Calculator from the Accessories menu.

**b.** Click Help on the menu bar, then click Help topics. The Calculator Help window opens, showing several Help topics.

**c.** View the Help topic on how to perform simple calculations, then print it if you have a printer connected.

**d.** Open the Tips and Tricks category, then view the Help topic on how to find out what a calculator button does.

**e.** View the Help topic (under Tips and Tricks) on how to use keyboard equivalents of calculator buttons, then print the topic if you have a printer connected to your computer.

**f.** Determine how many months you have to work to earn an additional week of vacation if you work for a company that provides one additional day of paid vacation for every 560 hours you work. (*Hint*: First multiply 560 times 5 days, then divide the answer by the number of hours you work in a month.)

**g.** Close all open windows.

**4.** You can customize many Windows features to suit your needs and preferences. One way you do this is to change the appearance of the taskbar on the desktop. In this challenge, try the guidelines described to explore the different ways you can customize the appearance of the taskbar.

**a.** Position the pointer over the top border of the taskbar. When the pointer changes shape, drag up an inch.

**b.** Resize the taskbar back to its original size.

**c.** Click the Start button on the taskbar, then point to Settings, and click Taskbar & Start Menu.

**d.** In the upper-right corner of the Taskbar Properties window, click the Help button, then click each option to view the pop-up window describing the option. You need to click the Help button before clicking each option.

**e.** Click each option and observe the effect in the preview area. (*Note:* Do not click OK.)

**f.** Return the options to their original settings or click Cancel.

# ► Visual Workshop

Use the skills you have learned in this unit to create a desktop that looks like the one in Figure A-18. Make sure you include the following:

- Calculator program minimized
- Scroll bars in Control Panel window
- Details view in Control Panel window
- Rearranged icons on desktop; your icons may be different (*Hint*: If the icons "snap" back to where they were, they are set to be automatically arranged. Right-click a blank area of the desktop, point to Arrange Icons, then click Auto Arrange to deselect it.)
- Channel Bar closed

Use the Print Screen key to make a copy of the screen and then print it from the Paint program (see your instructor or technical support person for assistance.) Be sure to return your settings and desktop back to their original arrangement when you complete this exercise.

FIGURE A-18

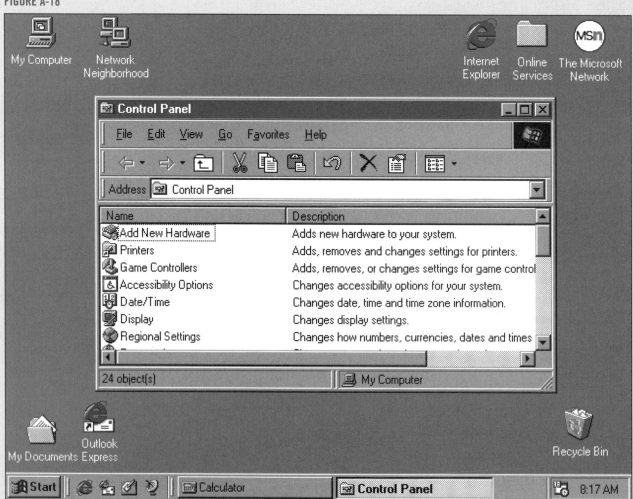

# Working

## with Programs, Files, and Folders

### Objectives

▶ **Create and save a WordPad file**
▶ **Open, edit, and save an existing Paint file**
▶ **Work with multiple programs**
▶ **Understand file management**
▶ **View files and create folders with My Computer**
▶ **Move and copy files using My Computer**
▶ **Manage files with Windows Explorer**
▶ **Delete and restore files**
▶ **Create a shortcut on the desktop**

Most of your work on a computer involves creating files in programs. For example, you might use WordPad to create a resume or Microsoft Excel to create a budget. The resume and the budget are examples of **files**, electronic collections of data that you create and save on a computer. ✎ In this unit, you learn how to work with files and the programs you use to create them. You create new files, open and edit an existing file, and use the Clipboard to copy and paste data from one file to another. You also explore the file management features of Windows 98, using My Computer and Windows Explorer. Finally, you learn how to work more efficiently by managing files directly on your desktop.

**Windows 98**

# Creating and Saving a WordPad File

As with most programs, when you start WordPad a new, blank **document** (or file) opens. To create a new file, such as a memo, you simply begin typing. Your work is automatically stored in your computer's **random access memory (RAM)** until you turn off your computer, at which point the computer's RAM is erased. To store your work permanently, you must save your work as a file on a disk. You can save files either on an internal **hard disk**, which is built into your computer, usually drive C, or on a removable 3.5" or 5.25" **floppy disk**, which you insert into a drive on your computer, usually drive A or B. Before you can save a file on a floppy disk, the disk must be formatted. See the Appendix, "Formatting a Disk," or your instructor or technical support person for more information. When you name a file, you can use up to 255 characters including spaces and punctuation in the File Name box, using either upper or lowercase letters. ➤➤➤ In this unit, you save your files to your Project Disk. If you do not have a Project Disk, see your instructor or technical support person for assistance. First, you start WordPad and create a file that contains the text shown in Figure B-1. Then you save the file to your Project Disk.

1. **Click the Start button on the taskbar, point to Programs, point to Accessories, click WordPad, then click the Maximize button if the window does not fill your screen**
   The WordPad program window opens with a new, blank document. The blinking **insertion point** | indicates where the text you type will appear.

**Trouble?**

If you make a mistake, press [Back Space] to delete the character to the left of the insertion point.

2. **Type Memo, then press [Enter] to move the insertion point to the next line**

3. **Type the remaining text shown in Figure B-1, pressing [Enter] at the end of each line to move to the next line and to insert blank lines**
   Now that the text is entered, you can format it. **Formatting** changes the appearance of text to make it more readable or attractive.

**QuickTip**

Double-click to select a word or triple-click to select a paragraph.

4. **Click in front of the word Memo, then drag the mouse to the right to select the word**
   The text is now **selected** and any action you make will be performed on the text.

5. **Click the Center button ☰ on the Formatting toolbar, then click the Bold button B on the Formatting toolbar**
   The text is centered and bold.

6. **Click the Font Size list arrow ⟨10 ▾⟩, then click 16**
   A **font** is a particular shape and size of type. The text is enlarged to 16 point. One **point** is 1/72 of an inch in height. Now that your memo is complete, you are ready to save it to your Project Disk.

7. **Click File on the menu bar, then click Save As**
   The Save As dialog box opens, as shown in Figure B-2. In this dialog box, you specify where you want your file saved and also give your document a name.

**Trouble?**

This unit assumes that the drive that contains your Project Disk is drive A. If not, substitute the correct drive any time you are instructed to use the 3½ Floppy (A:) drive. See your instructor or technical support person for assistance.

8. **Click the Save in list arrow, then click 3½ Floppy (A:) or whichever drive contains your Project Disk**
   The drive containing your Project Disk is now active, meaning that any files currently on the disk are displayed in the list of folders and files and that the file you save now will be saved on the disk in this drive.

9. **Double-click the text in the File name text box, type Memo, then click Save**
   Your memo is now saved as a WordPad file with the name "Memo" on your Project Disk. Notice that the WordPad title bar contains the name of the file.

FIGURE B-1: Text to enter in WordPad

Bold button

Center button

Press [Enter]
three times
to insert
blank lines

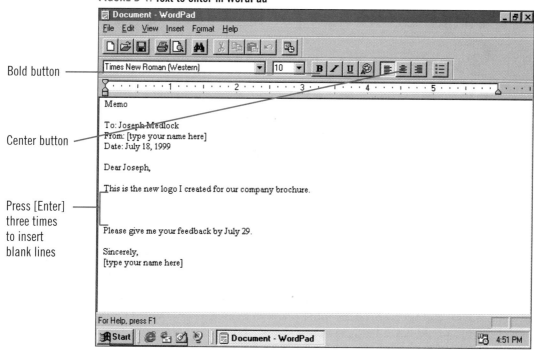

FIGURE B-2: Save As dialog box

Click to select
where to save file

Type new
filename here

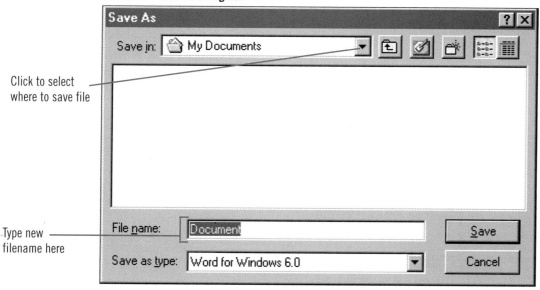

# Opening, Editing, and Saving an Existing Paint File

Sometimes you create files from scratch, but often you may want to reopen a file you or someone else has already created. Once you open a file, you can **edit** it, or make changes to it, such as adding or deleting text. After editing a file, you can save it with the same filename, which means that you no longer will have the file in its original form, or you can save it with a different filename, so that the original file remains unchanged. ✎ In this lesson, you use **Paint**, a drawing program that comes with Windows 98, to open a file, edit it by changing a color, then save the file with a new filename to leave the original file unchanged.

## Steps

**1.** Click the **Start button** on the taskbar, point to **Programs**, point to **Accessories**, click **Paint**, then click the **Maximize button** if the window doesn't fill the screen
The Paint program opens with a blank work area. If you wanted to create a file from scratch, you would begin working now.

**2.** Click **File** on the menu bar, then click **Open**
The Open dialog box works similarly to the Save As dialog box.

**3.** Click the **Look in list arrow**, then click **3½ Floppy (A:)**
The Paint files on your Project Disk are displayed in the Open dialog box, as shown in Figure B-3.

> **QuickTip**
>
> You can also open a file by double-clicking it in the Open dialog box.

**4.** Click **Win B-1** in the list of files, then click **Open**
The Open dialog box closes and the file named Win B-1 opens. Before you make any changes to the file, you decide to save it with a new filename, so that the original file is unchanged.

**5.** Click **File** on the menu bar, then click **Save As**

**6.** Make sure **3½ Floppy (A:)** appears in the Save in text box, select the text **Win B-1** in the File name text box if necessary, type **Logo**, then click **Save**
The Logo file appears in the Paint window, as shown in Figure B-4. Because you saved the file with a new name, you can edit it without changing the original file.

**7.** Click the **Fill With Color button** 🪣 in the Toolbox, click the **Blue color box**, which is the fourth from the right in the first row
Now when you click an area in the image, it will be filled with the color you selected. See Table B-1 for a description of the tools in the Toolbox.

**8.** Move the pointer into the **white area that represents the sky**, the pointer changes to 🪣, then click
The sky is now blue.

**9.** Click **File** on the menu bar, then click **Save**
The change you made is saved.

FIGURE B-3: **Open dialog box**

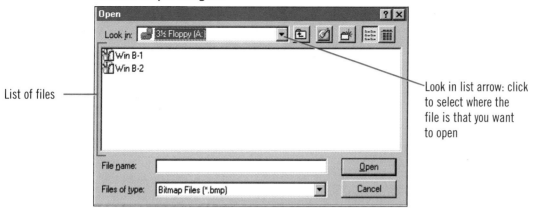

List of files

Look in list arrow: click to select where the file is that you want to open

FIGURE B-4: **Paint file saved with new filename**

Name of file displayed in title bar

Fill With Color button

Choose this blue color

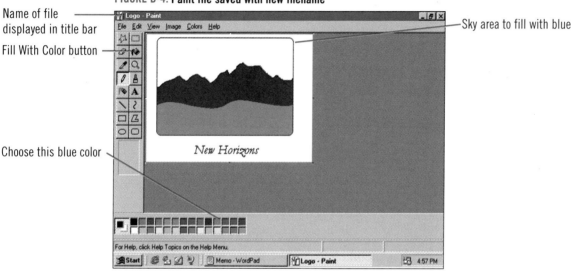

Sky area to fill with blue

TABLE B-1: **Paint Toolbox buttons**

| tool | description | tool | description |
|------|-------------|------|-------------|
| Free-Form Select button | Selects a free-form section of the picture to move, copy, or edit | Airbrush button | Produces a circular spray of dots |
| Select button | Selects a rectangular section of the picture to move, copy, or edit | Text button | Inserts text into the picture |
| Eraser button | Erases a portion of the picture using the selected eraser size and foreground color | Line button | Draws a straight line with the selected width and foreground color |
| Fill With Color button | Fills closed shape or area with the current drawing color | Curve button | Draws a wavy line with the selected width and foreground color |
| Pick Color button | Picks up a color off the picture to use for drawing | Rectangle button | Draws a rectangle with the selected fill style; also used to draw squares by holding down [Shift] while drawing |
| Magnifier button | Changes the magnification; lists magnifications under the toolbar | Polygon button | Draws polygons from connected straight-line segments |
| Pencil button | Draws a free-form line one pixel wide | Ellipse button | Draws an ellipse with the selected fill style; also used to draw circles by holding down [Shift] while drawing |
| Brush button | Draws using a brush with the selected shape and size | Rounded Rectangle button | Draws rectangles with rounded corners using the selected fill style; also used to draw rounded squares by holding down [Shift] while drawing |

# Working with Multiple Programs

A powerful feature of Windows is that you can use more than one program at a time. For example, you might be working with a file in WordPad and want to search the Internet to find the answer to a question. You can start your **browser**, a program designed to access information on the Internet, without closing WordPad. When you find the information, you can leave your browser open and switch back to WordPad. Each program that you have open is represented by a program button on the taskbar that you click to switch between programs. You can also copy data from one file to another, whether the files were created with the same program or not, using the **Clipboard**, a temporary area in your computer's memory, and the Cut, Copy, and Paste commands. See Table B-2 for a description of these commands. ✒══ In this lesson, you copy the logo graphic you worked with in the previous lesson into the memo you created in WordPad.

1. Click the **Select button** ⬚ on the Toolbox, then drag a rectangle around the entire graphic, including the text

   When you release the mouse button, the dotted rectangle indicates the contents of the selection, as shown in Figure B-5. Make sure the entire image and all the text is inside the rectangle. The next action you take affects the entire selection.

2. Click **Edit** on the menu bar, then click **Copy**

   The logo is copied to the Clipboard. When you **copy** an object onto the Clipboard, the object remains in its original location and is also available to be pasted into another location.

3. Click the **WordPad program button** on the taskbar

   WordPad becomes the active program.

4. Click in the **second line** below the line that ends "for our company brochure."

   The insertion point indicates where the logo will be pasted.

5. Click the **Paste button** 📋 on the WordPad toolbar

   The contents of the Clipboard, in this case the logo, are pasted into the WordPad file, as shown in Figure B-6.

6. Click the **Save button** 💾 on the toolbar

   The Memo file is saved with the logo inserted.

7. Click the **Close buttons** in both the WordPad and Paint programs to close all open files and exit both programs

   You return to the desktop.

**TABLE B-2: Overview of cutting, copying, and pasting**

| toolbar button | function | keyboard shortcut |
|---|---|---|
| ✂ Cut | Removes selected information from a file and places it on the Clipboard | [Ctrl][X] |
| 📋 Copy | Places a copy of selected information on the Clipboard, leaving the file intact | [Ctrl][C] |
| 📋 Paste | Inserts whatever is currently on the Clipboard into another location within the same file or in a different file | [Ctrl][V] |

FIGURE B-5: Selecting the logo to copy and paste into the Memo file

Select button

Dotted line indicates selected area

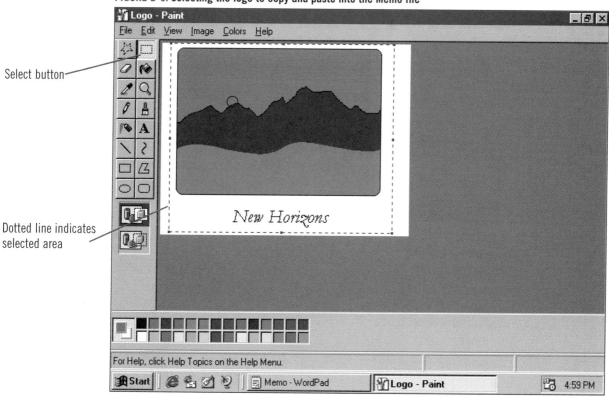

FIGURE B-6: Memo with pasted logo

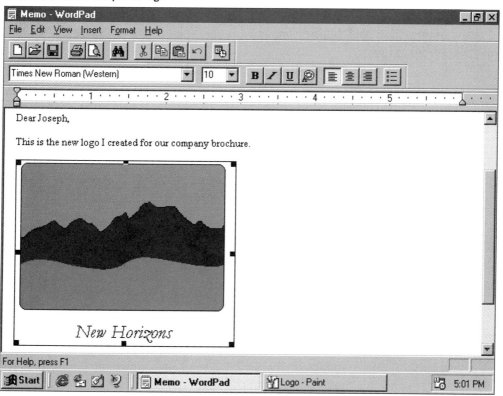

# Understanding File Management

After you have created and saved numerous files using various programs, **file management**, the process of organizing and keeping track of all of your files can be a challenge. Fortunately, Windows 98 provides tools to keep everything organized so you can easily locate the files you need. There are two main tools for managing your files: My Computer and Windows Explorer. In this lesson, you preview the ways you can use My Computer and Windows Explorer to manage your files.

**Details**

### Windows 98 gives you the ability to:

### Create folders in which you can save your files

**Folders** are areas on a floppy disk or hard disk in which you can store files. For example, you might create a folder for your documents and another folder for your graphic files. Folders can also contain additional folders, which creates a more complex structure of folders and files, called a **file hierarchy**. See Figure B-7 for an example of how you could organize the files on your Project Disk.

**QuickTip**

To browse My Computer using multiple windows, click View on the menu bar, then click Folder Options. In the Folder Options dialog box, click the General tab, click Settings, then under Browse folders as follows, click the second option button. Each time you open a new folder, a new window opens, leaving the previous folder's window open so that you can view both at the same time.

### Examine and organize the hierarchy of files and folders

When you want to see the overall structure of your files and folders, you can use either My Computer or Windows Explorer. By examining your file hierarchy with these tools, you can better organize the contents of your computer and adjust the hierarchy to meet your needs. Figures B-8 and B-9 illustrate how My Computer and Windows Explorer display folders and files.

### Copy, move, and rename files and folders

If you decide that a file belongs in a different folder, you can move it to another folder. You can also rename a file if you decide a new name is more descriptive. If you want to keep a copy of a file in more than one folder, you can copy it to new folders.

### Delete files and folders you no longer need, as well as restore files you delete accidentally

Deleting files and folders you are sure you don't need frees up disk space and keeps your file hierarchy more organized. Using the **Recycle Bin**, a space on your computer's hard disk that stores deleted files, you can restore files you deleted by accident. To free up disk space, you should occasionally empty the Recycle Bin by deleting the files permanently from your hard drive.

### Locate files quickly with the Windows 98 Find feature

As you create more files and folders, you may forget where you placed a certain file or you may forget what name you used when you saved a file. With Find, you can locate files by providing only partial names or other factors, such as the file type (for example, a WordPad document, a Paint graphic, or a program) or the date the file was created or modified.

### Preview the contents of a file without opening the file in its program

After locating a particular file, use Quick View to look at the file to verify that it is the one you want. This saves time because you do not need to open the program to open the file; however, if you decide that you want to edit the file, you can open the program right from Quick View. To preview a file, right-click the selected file in My Computer or Windows Explorer, then click Quick View on the pop-up menu. A preview of the file appears in the Quick View window.

**Trouble?**

If the Quick View command does not appear on the pop-up menu, it means that this feature was not installed on your computer. See your instructor or technical support person for assistance.

### Use shortcuts

If a file or folder you use often is located several levels down in your file hierarchy, in a folder within a folder, within a folder, it might take you several steps to access it. To save time accessing the files and programs you use frequently, you can create shortcuts to them. A **shortcut** is a link that gives you quick access to a particular file, folder, or program.

FIGURE B-7: Example of file hierarchy for Project Disk files

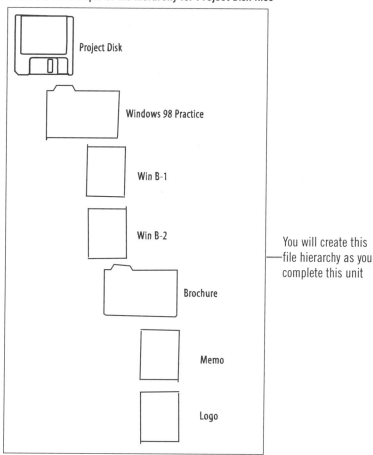

Project Disk

Windows 98 Practice

Win B-1

Win B-2

You will create this file hierarchy as you complete this unit

Brochure

Memo

Logo

FIGURE B-8: Brochure folder shown in My Computer

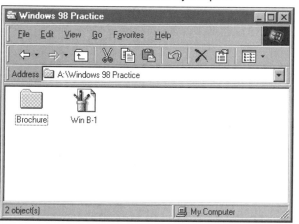

FIGURE B-9: Brochure folder shown in Windows Explorer

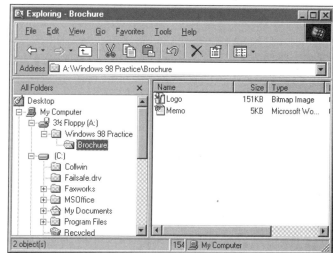

# Viewing Files and Creating Folders with My Computer

My Computer shows the contents of your computer, including files, folders, programs, disk drives, and printers. You can click the icons representing these various parts of your computer to view their contents. You can manage your files using the My Computer menu bar and toolbar. See Table B-3 for a description of the toolbar buttons. ⬤  In this lesson, you begin by using My Computer to move around in your computer's file hierarchy, then you create two new folders on your Project Disk that contain the files you created.

**Steps** 1 2 3 4

**Trouble?**

If you do not see the toolbar, click View on the menu bar, point to Toolbars, then click Standard Buttons. If you do not see the Address Bar, click View, point to Toolbar, then click the Address Bar.

**1.** Double-click the **My Computer icon** on your desktop, then click the **Maximize button** if the My Computer window does not fill the screen
My Computer opens and displays the contents of your computer, as shown in Figure B-10. Your window may contain icons for different folders, drives, printers, and so on.

**2.** Make sure your Project Disk is in the floppy disk drive, then double-click the **3½ Floppy (A:) icon**
The contents of your Project Disk are displayed in the window. These are the project files and the files you created using WordPad and Paint. Each file is represented by an icon, which indicates the program that was used to create the file. If Microsoft Word is installed on your computer, the Word icon appears for the WordPad files; if not, the WordPad icon appears.

**Trouble?**

This book assumes that your hard drive is drive C. If yours differs, substitute the appropriate drive for drive C wherever it is referenced. See your instructor or technical support person for assistance.

**3.** Click the **Address list arrow** on the Address Bar, as shown in Figure B-10, then click **(C:)**, or the letter for the main hard drive on your computer
The window changes to show the contents of your hard drive. The **Address Bar** allows you to open and display a drive, folder, or even a Web page. You can also type in the Address Bar to go to a different drive, folder, or Web page. For example, typing "C:\" will display drive C; typing "E:\Personal Letters" will display the Personal Letters folder on drive E, and typing "http://www.microsoft.com" opens Microsoft's Web site if your computer is connected to the Internet.

**4.** Click the **Back button** on the toolbar
The Back button displays the previous location, in this case, your Project Disk.

**5.** Click the **Views button list arrow** ▦▾ on the toolbar, then click **Details**
Details view shows not only the files and folders, but also the size of the file; the type of file, folder, or drive; and the date the file was last modified.

**6.** Click ▦▾, then click **Large Icons**
This view offers less information but provides a large, clear view of the contents of the disk.

**7.** Click **File** on the menu bar, click **New**, then click **Folder**
A new folder is created on your Project Disk, as shown in Figure B-11. The folder is called "New Folder" by default. It is selected and ready to be renamed. You can also create a new folder by right-clicking in the blank area of the My Computer window, clicking New, then clicking Folder.

**Trouble?**

To rename a folder, click the folder to select it, click the folder name so it is surrounded by a rectangle, type the new folder name, then press [Enter].

**8.** Type **Windows 98 Practice**, then press **[Enter]**
Choosing descriptive names for your folders helps you remember their contents.

**9.** Double-click the **Windows 98 Practice folder**, repeat Step 7 to create a new folder in the Windows 98 Practice folder, type **Brochure** for the folder name, then press **[Enter]**

**10.** Click the **Back button** ⬅ to return to your Project Disk

Menu bar

Toolbar

Address bar

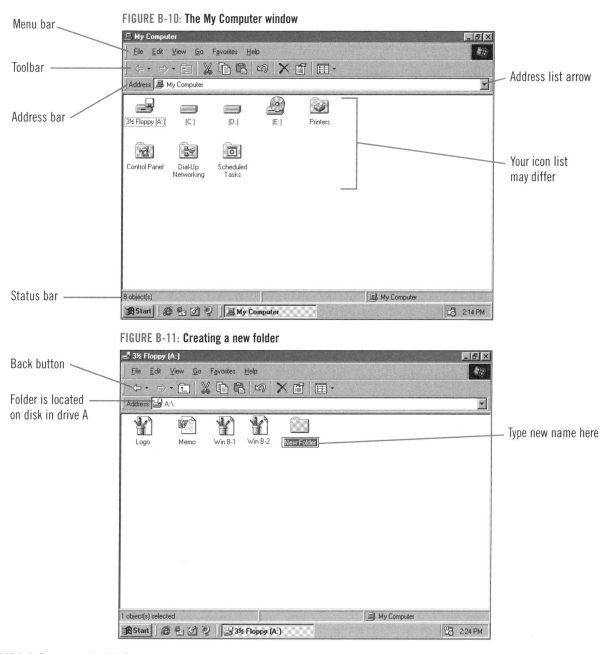

FIGURE B-10: **The My Computer window**

Address list arrow

Your icon list
may differ

Status bar

FIGURE B-11: **Creating a new folder**

Back button

Folder is located
on disk in drive A

Type new name here

TABLE B-3: **Buttons on the My Computer toolbar**

| button | function |
| --- | --- |
| ⇐ | Moves back to the previous location you have already visited |
| ⇒ | Moves forward to the previous location you have already visited |
| 🖿 | Moves up one level in the file hierarchy |
| ✂ | Deletes a folder or file and places it on the clipboard |
| 🗎 | Copies a folder or file |
| 📋 | Pastes a folder or file |
| ↶ | Undoes the most recent My Computer operation |
| ✕ | Deletes a folder or file permanently |
| 🖹 | Shows the properties of a folder or file |
| 🖽 | Lists the contents of My Computer using different views |

# Moving and Copying Files Using My Computer

You can move a file or folder from one location to another using a variety of methods in My Computer or Windows Explorer. If the file or folder and the location to which you want to move it are both visible on the desktop, you can simply drag the item from one location to the other. You can also use the cut, copy and paste commands on the Edit menu or the corresponding buttons on the toolbar. You can also right-click the file or folder and choose the Send to command to "send" it to another location—most often a floppy disk for **backing up** files. Backup copies are made in case you have computer trouble, which may cause you to lose files. In this lesson, you move your files into the folder you created in the last lesson.

### QuickTip

To copy a file so that it appears in two locations, press and hold [Shift] while you drag the file to its new location.

1. Click **View**, click **Arrange Icons**, then click **By Name**
   In this view, folders are listed first in alphabetical order, followed by files, also in alphabetical order.

2. Click the **Win B-1 file**, hold down the mouse button and drag the file onto the **Windows 98 Practice folder**, as shown in Figure B-12, then release the mouse button
   Win B-1 is moved into the Windows 98 Practice folder.

3. Double-click the **Windows 98 Practice folder** and confirm that it contains the Win B-1 file as well as the Brochure folder

### QuickTip

It is easy to confuse the Back button with the Up One Level button. The Back button returns you to the last location you visited, no matter where it is in your folder hierarchy. The Up One Level button displays the next level up in the folder hierarchy, no matter where you last visited.

4. Click the **Up button** 🗀 on the My Computer toolbar, as shown in Figure B–12
   You return to your Project Disk. The Up button displays the next level up in the folder hierarchy.

5. Click the **Logo file**, press and hold [Shift], then click the **Memo file**
   Both files are selected. Table B-4 describes methods for selecting multiple files and folders.

6. Click the **Cut button** ✂ on the 3½ Floppy (A:) toolbar
   The icons for the files are gray, as shown in Figure B-13. This indicates that they've been cut and placed on the Clipboard, to be pasted somewhere else. Instead of dragging items to a new location, you can use the Cut, Copy, and Paste toolbar buttons or the cut, copy, and paste commands on the Edit menu.

7. Click the **Back button** ⇦ to return to the Windows 98 Practice folder, then double-click the **Brochure folder**
   The Brochure folder is currently empty.

8. Click the **Paste button** 📋 on the toolbar
   The two files are pasted into the Brochure folder.

9. Click the **Address list arrow**, then click **3½ Floppy (A:)** and confirm that the Memo and Logo files are no longer listed there and that only the Windows 98 Practice folder and the Win B-2 file remain

10. Click the **Close button** in the 3½ Floppy (A:) window

FIGURE B-12: Dragging a file from one folder to another

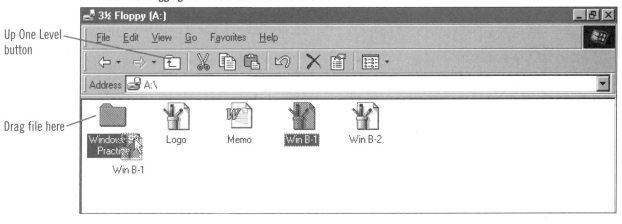

Up One Level
button

Drag file here

FIGURE B-13: Cutting files to move them

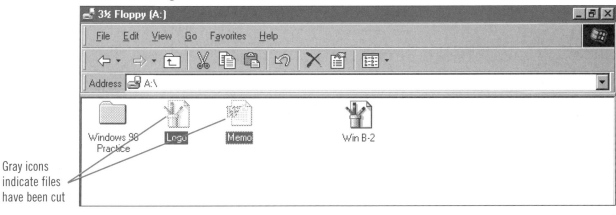

Gray icons
indicate files
have been cut

TABLE B-4: Techniques for selecting multiple files and folders

| to select | use this technique |
| --- | --- |
| **Individual objects not grouped together** | Click the first object you want to select, then press [Ctrl] as you click each additional object you want to add to the selection |
| **Objects grouped together** | Click the first object you want to select, then press [Shift] as you click the last object in the list of objects you want to select; all the objects listed between the first and last objects are selected |

**Windows 98**

# Managing Files with Windows Explorer

As with My Computer, you can use Windows Explorer to copy, move, delete, and rename files and folders. However, Windows Explorer is more powerful than My Computer: it allows you to see the overall structure of the contents of your computer or network, the file hierarchy, while you work with individual files and folders within that structure. This means you can work with more than one computer, folder, or file at once. In this lesson, you copy a folder from your Project Disk onto the hard drive, then rename the folder.

## Steps

**Trouble?**

If you do not see the toolbar, click View on the menu bar, point to Toolbars, then click Standard Buttons. If you do not see the Address Bar, click View, point to Toolbars, then click Address Bar.

1. **Click the Start button, point to Programs, point to Windows Explorer, then click the Maximize button if the Windows Explorer window doesn't already fill the screen**
Windows Explorer opens, as shown in Figure B-14. The window is divided into two sides called **panes**. The left pane, also known as the **Explorer Bar**, displays the drives and folders on your computer in a hierarchy. The right pane displays the contents of whatever drive or folder is currently selected in the left pane. Each pane has its own set of scroll bars, so that changing what you can see in one pane won't affect what you can see in the other. Like My Computer, Windows Explorer has a menu bar, toolbar, and Address Bar.

2. **Click View on the menu bar, then click Details if it is not already selected**

3. **In the left pane, scroll to and click 3½ Floppy (A:)**
The contents of your Project Disk are displayed in the right pane.

**QuickTip**

When neither a + nor a – appears next to an icon, it means that the item does not have any folders in it, although it may have files, which you can display in the right pane by clicking the icon.

4. **In the left pane, click the plus sign (+) next to 3½ Floppy (A:)**
You can use the plus signs (+) and minus signs (-) next to items in the left pane to show or hide the different levels of the file hierarchy, so that you don't always have to look at the entire structure of your computer or network. A plus sign (+) next to a computer, drive, or folder indicates there are additional folders within that object. A minus sign (-) indicates that all the folders of the next level of hierarchy are shown. Clicking the + displays (or "expands") the next level; clicking the – hides (or "collapses") them.

5. **In the left pane, double-click the Windows 98 Practice folder**
The contents of the Windows 98 Practice folder appear in the right pane of Windows Explorer, as shown in Figure B-15. Double-clicking an item in the left pane that has a + next to it displays its contents in the right pane and also expands the next level in the hierarchy in the left pane.

**Trouble?**

If you are working in a lab setting, you may not be able to add items to your hard drive. Skip Steps 6, 7, and 8 if you are unable to complete them.

6. **In the left pane, drag the Windows 98 Practice folder on top of the C: drive icon, then release the mouse button**
The Windows 98 Practice folder and the files in it are copied to the hard disk.

7. **In the left pane, click the C: drive icon**
The Windows 98 Practice folder should now appear in the list of folders in the right pane. Now you should rename the folder so you can distinguish the original folder from the copy.

**QuickTip**

You can also rename a selected file by pressing [F2], or using the Rename command on the File menu.

8. **Right-click the Windows 98 Practice folder in the right pane, click Rename in the pop-up menu, type Practice Copy, then press [Enter]**

**FIGURE B-14:** The Windows Explorer window

Contents of C drive

Left pane, also known as Explorer bar

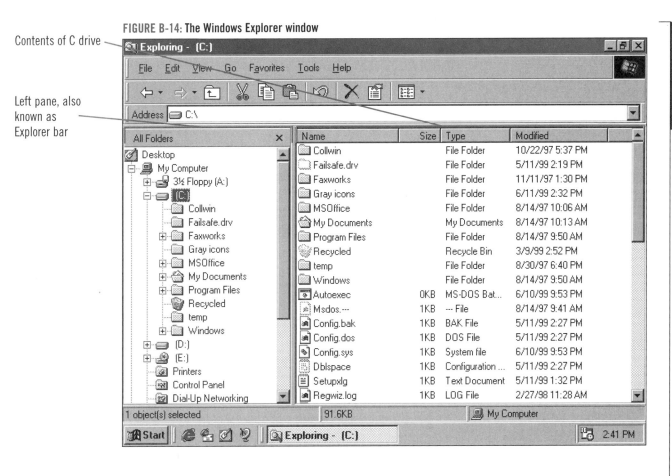

**FIGURE B-15:** Contents of Windows 98 Practice folder

Contents of Windows 98 Practice folder

Windows 98 Practice folder is selected in left pane

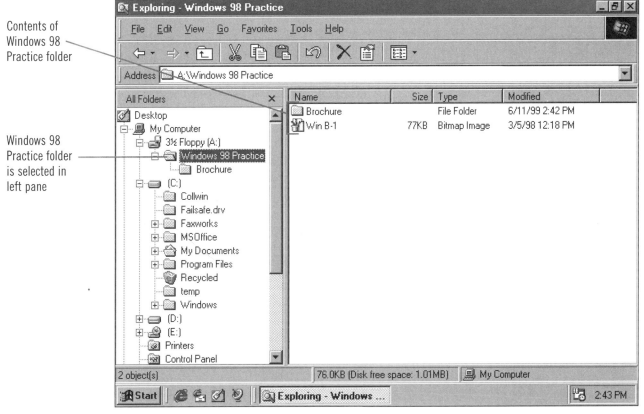

# Deleting and Restoring Files

To save disk space and manage your files more effectively, you should **delete** (or remove) files you no longer need. Because files deleted from your hard drive are stored in the Recycle Bin until you remove them permanently by emptying the Recycle Bin, you can restore any files you might have deleted accidentally. However, if you delete a file from your floppy disk it will not be stored in the Recycle Bin—it will be permanently deleted. See Table B-5 for an overview of deleting and restoring files. ◀────── There are many ways to delete files in Windows 98. In this lesson, you use two different methods for removing files you no longer need. Then, you learn how to restore a deleted file.

1. **Click the Restore button on the Windows Explorer title bar**
   You should be able to see the Recycle Bin icon on your desktop. If you can't see it, resize or move the Windows Explorer window until it is visible. See Figure B-16.

### QuickTip
If you are unable to delete the file, it might be because your Recycle Bin is full, or too small, or the properties have been changed so that files are not stored in the Recycle Bin but are deleted instead. See your instructor or technical support person for assistance.

2. **Drag the Practice Copy folder from the right pane to the Recycle Bin on the desktop, as shown in Figure B-16, then click Yes to confirm the deletion**
   The folder no longer appears in Windows Explorer because you have moved it to the Recycle Bin. Next, you will examine the contents of the Recycle Bin.

3. **Double-click the Recycle Bin icon on the desktop**
   The Recycle Bin window opens, as shown in Figure B-17. Depending on the number of files already deleted on your computer, your window might look different. Use the scroll bar if you can't see the files.

4. **Click Edit on the Recycle Bin menu bar, then click Undo Delete**
   The Practice Copy folder is restored and should now appear in the Windows Explorer window. You might need to minimize your Recycle Bin window if it blocks your view of Windows Explorer, and you might need to scroll the right pane to find the restored folder. Now you should delete the Practice Copy folder from your hard drive.

5. **Click the Practice Copy folder in the right pane, click the Delete button ✕ on the Windows Explorer toolbar, resizing the window as necessary to see the button, then click Yes**
   When you are sure you no longer need files you've moved into the Recycle Bin, you can empty the Recycle Bin. You won't do this now, in case you are working on a computer that you share with other people. But, when you're working on your own machine, simply right-click the Recycle Bin icon, then click Empty Recycle Bin in the pop-up menu.

### Customizing your Recycle Bin

You can set your Recycle Bin according to how you like to delete and restore files. For example, if you do not want files to go to the Recycle Bin but rather want them to be immediately and permanently deleted, right-click the Recycle Bin, click Properties, then click the Do Not Move Files to the Recycle Bin check box. If you find that the Recycle Bin fills up too fast and you are not ready to delete the files permanently, you can increase the amount of disk space devoted to the Recycle Bin by moving the Maximum Size of Recycle Bin slider to the right. This, of course, reduces the amount of disk space you have available for other things. Also, you can choose not to have the Confirm File Delete dialog box open when you send files to the Recycle Bin. See your instructor or technical support person before changing any of the Recycle Bin settings.

FIGURE B-16: Dragging a folder to delete it

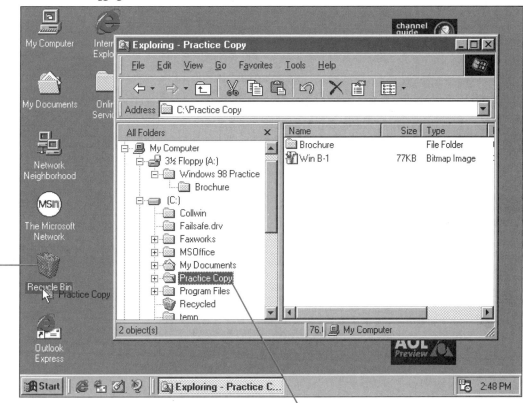

Drag the folder here

Folder located on drive C

FIGURE B-17: The Recycle Bin window

Deleted folder

TABLE B-5: Methods for deleting and restoring files

| ways to delete a file | ways to restore a file from the Recycle Bin |
| --- | --- |
| Select the file, then click the Delete button on the toolbar | Click the Undo button on the toolbar |
| Select the file, then press [Delete] | Select the file, click File, then click Restore |
| Right-click the file, then click Delete on the pop-up menu | Right-click the file, then click Restore |
| Drag the file to the Recycle Bin | Drag the file from the Recycle Bin to any other location |

# Creating a Shortcut on the Desktop

When you use a file, folder, or program frequently, it can be cumbersome to open it if it is located several levels down in the file hierarchy. You can create a shortcut to an object and place the icon for the shortcut on the desktop or any other location you find convenient. To open the file, folder, or program using the shortcut, double-click the icon. A **shortcut** is a link between the original file, folder, or program you want to access and the icon you create. In this lesson, you create a shortcut to the Memo file on your desktop.

## Steps

**1.** In the left pane of the Windows Explorer window, click the **Brochure folder**
The contents of the Brochure folder appear in the right pane.

**2.** In the right pane, right-click the **Memo file**
A pop-up menu appears, as shown in Figure B-18.

**3.** Click **Create Shortcut** in the pop-up menu
The file named Shortcut to Memo file appears in the right pane. Now you need to move it to the desktop so that it will be accessible whenever you need it.

> **QuickTip**
>
> Make sure to use the *right* mouse button in Step 4. If you used the left mouse button by accident, right-click the Shortcut to Memo file in the right pane of Windows Explorer, then click Delete.

**4.** Click the **Shortcut to Memo file** with the right-mouse button, then drag the **shortcut** to an empty area of the desktop
Dragging an icon using the left mouse button copies it. Dragging an icon using the right mouse button gives you the option to copy or move it. When you release the mouse button a pop-up menu appears.

**5.** Click **Move Here** in the pop-up menu
A shortcut to the Memo file now appears on the desktop, as shown in Figure B-19. You might have to move or resize the Windows Explorer window to see it.

**6.** Double-click the **Shortcut to Memo file icon**
WordPad starts and the Memo file opens (if you have Microsoft Word installed on your computer, it will start and open the file instead). Using a shortcut eliminates the many steps involved in starting a program and locating and opening a file.

**7.** Click the **Close button** in the WordPad or Word title bar
Now you should delete the shortcut icon in case you are working in a lab and share the computer with others. Deleting a shortcut does not delete the original file or folder to which it points.

> **QuickTip**
>
> Deleting a shortcut deletes only the link; it does not delete the original file or folder to which it points.

**8.** On the desktop, click the **Shortcut to Memo file** if necessary, press **[Delete]**, then click **Yes** to confirm the deletion
The shortcut is removed from the desktop and is now in the Recycle Bin.

**9.** Close all windows

**FIGURE B-18:** Creating a shortcut

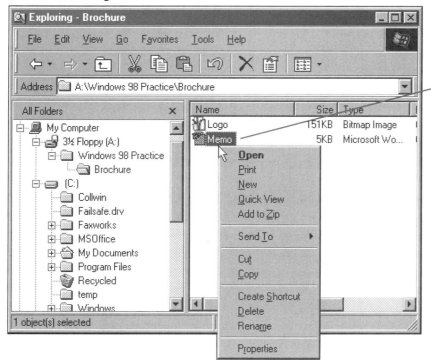

Right-click icon
or filename to
display pop-up
menu. Your
menu items may
differ.

**FIGURE B-19:** Shortcut on desktop

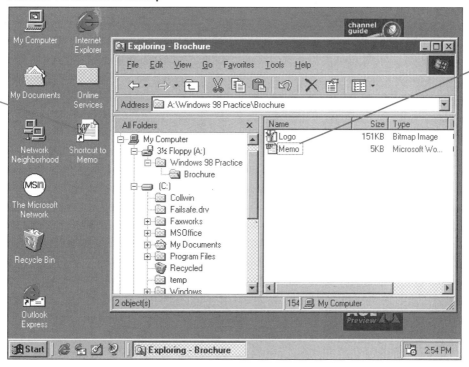

Double-click to
open file

Original file
located in
Brochure folder

### CLUES TO USE

## Adding shortcuts to the Start menu

If you do not want your desktop to get cluttered with
icons but you would still like easy access to certain
files, programs, and folders, you can create a shortcut
on the Start menu. Drag the file, program, or folder

that you want to add to the Start menu from the
Windows Explorer window to the Start button. The
file, program, or folder will appear on the first level of
the Start menu.

# Practice

## ► Concepts Review

Label each of the elements of the Windows Explorer window shown in Figure B-20.

FIGURE B-20

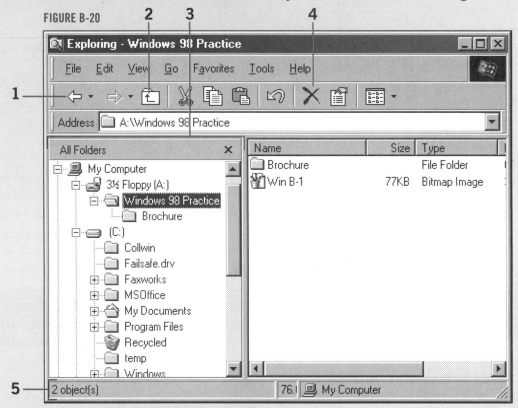

Match each of the statements with the term it describes.

6. Electronic collections of data
7. Your computer's temporary storage area
8. Temporary location of information you wish to paste into another program
9. Storage areas on your hard drive for files, folders, and programs
10. Structure of files and folders

a. RAM
b. Folders
c. Files
d. File hierarchy
e. Clipboard

Select the best answer from the list of choices.

11. To prepare a floppy disk to save your files, you must first do which of the following?
    a. Copy work files to the disk
    b. Format the disk
    c. Erase all the files that might be on the disk
    d. Place the files on the Clipboard

12. You can use My Computer to
    a. Create a drawing of your computer.
    b. View the contents of a folder.
    c. Change the appearance of your desktop.
    d. Add text to a WordPad file.

13. Which of the following best describes WordPad?
    a. A program for organizing files
    b. A program for performing financial analysis
    c. A program for creating basic text documents
    d. A program for creating graphics

**14. Which of the following is NOT a way to move files from one folder to another?**

   **a.** Open the file and use the Save As command to save the file in a new location.

   **b.** In My Computer or the Windows Explorer, drag the selected file to the new folder.

   **c.** Use the Cut and Paste commands on the Edit menu while in the My Computer or the Windows Explorer windows.

   **d.** Use the [Ctrl][X] and [Ctrl][V] keyboard shortcuts while in the My Computer or the Windows Explorer windows.

**15. In which of the following can you view the hierarchy of drives, folders, and files in a split pane window?**

   **a.** Windows Explorer                   **c.** My Computer

   **b.** Programs                         **d.** WordPad

**16. To restore files that you have sent to the Recycle Bin:**

   **a.** Click File, then click Empty Recycle Bin.     **c.** Click File, then click Undo.

   **b.** Click Edit, then click Undo Delete.         **d.** You cannot retrieve files sent to the Recycle Bin.

**17. To copy instead of move a file from one folder to another, drag while pressing**

   **a.** [Shift].                           **c.** [Tab].

   **b.** [Alt].                            **d.** [Ctrl].

**18. To select files that are not grouped together, select the first file, then**

   **a.** Press [Shift] while selecting the second file.    **c.** Press [Ctrl] while selecting the second file.

   **b.** Press [Alt] while selecting the second file.     **d.** Click on the second file.

**19. Pressing [Backspace]**

   **a.** Deletes the character to the right of the cursor.   **c.** Moves the insertion point one character to the right.

   **b.** Deletes the character to the left of the cursor.    **d.** Moves the insertion point one character to the left.

**20. The size of a font is measured in**

   **a.** Centimeters.                      **c.** Places.

   **b.** Points.                          **d.** Millimeters.

**21. The Back button on the My Computer toolbar:**

   **a.** Starts the last program you used.         **c.** Backs up the currently selected file.

   **b.** Displays the next level of the file hierarchy.    **d.** Displays the last location you visited.

# ► Skills Review

If you are doing all of the exercises in this unit, you may run out of space on your Project Disk. Use a blank, formatted disk to complete the exercise if this happens.

**1. Create and save a WordPad file.**

   **a.** Start Windows, then start WordPad.

   **b.** Type a short description of your artistic abilities, pressing [Enter] several times to insert blank lines between the text and the graphic you are about to create.

   **c.** Save the document as "Drawing Ability" to the Windows 98 Practice folder on your Project Disk.

**2. Open and save a Paint file.**

   **a.** Start Paint and open the file Win B-2 from your Project Disk.

   **b.** Inside the picture frame, create your own unique, colorful design using several colors. Use a variety of tools. For example, create a filled circle and then place a filled square inside the circle.

   **c.** Save the picture as "First Unique Art" to the Windows 98 Practice folder on your Project Disk.

**3. Work with multiple programs.**

   **a.** Select the entire graphic and copy it to the Clipboard, then switch to WordPad.

   **b.** Place the insertion point in the last blank line, then paste the graphic into your document.

   **c.** Save the changes to your WordPad document using the same filename.

   **d.** Switch to Paint.

   **e.** Using the Fill With Color button, change the color of a filled area of your graphic.

   **f.** Save the revised graphic with the new name, "Second Unique Art," to the Windows 98 Practice folder.

   **g.** Select the entire graphic and copy it to the Clipboard.

   **h.** Switch to WordPad and type "This is another version of my graphic." below the first picture, then press [Enter]. (*Hint*: To move the insertion point to the line below the graphic, click below the graphic, then press [Enter].)

   **i.** Paste the second graphic under the text you just typed.

   **j.** Save the changed WordPad document as "Two Drawing Examples" to the Windows 98 Practice folder.

   **k.** Close Paint and WordPad.

**4. View files and create folders with My Computer.**

   **a.** Open My Computer, then insert your Project Disk in the appropriate drive if necessary.

   **b.** Double-click the drive that contains your Project Disk.

   **c.** Create a new folder on your Project Disk by clicking File, New, then Folder, and name the new folder "Review."

   **d.** Open the folder to display its contents (it is empty).

   **e.** Use the Address Bar to view your hard drive, usually (C:).

   **f.** Create a folder on the hard drive called "Temporary" then use the Back button to view the Review folder. (*Note:* You may not be able to add items to your hard drive.)

   **g.** Create two new folders in the Review folder. Name one "Documents" and the other "Artwork."

   **h.** Use the Forward button as many times as necessary to view the hard drive.

**5. Move and copy files using My Computer.**

   **a.** Use the Address Bar to view your Project Disk, then open the Windows 98 Practice folder.

   **b.** Select the two Paint files, then cut and paste them into the Artwork folder.

   **c.** Use the Back button as many times as necessary to view the Windows 98 Practice folder.

   **d.** Select the two WordPad files, then move them into the Documents folder.

   **e.** Close My Computer.

**6. View, move and copy files.**

   **a.** Open Windows Explorer and display the contents of the Artwork folder in the right pane.

   **b.** Select the two Paint files.

   **c.** Drag the two Paint files from the Artwork folder to the Temporary folder on the hard drive to copy them.

   **d.** Display the contents of the Documents folder in the right pane.

   **e.** Select the two WordPad files.

   **f.** Repeat Step c to copy the files to the Temporary folder on the hard drive.

   **g.** Display the contents of the Temporary folder in the right pane to verify that the four files are there.

**7. Delete and restore files and folders.**

   **a.** Resize the Windows Explorer window so you can see the Recycle Bin icon on the desktop, then scroll in Windows Explorer so you can see the Temporary folder in the left pane.

   **b.** Delete the Temporary folder from the hard drive by dragging it to the Recycle Bin.

   **c.** Select the Review folder in the left pane, then press [Delete]. Click Yes if necessary to confirm the deletion.

   **d.** Open the Recycle Bin, restore the Review folder and its files to your Project Disk, then close the Recycle Bin. (*Note:* If your Recycle Bin is empty, your computer is set to automatically delete items in the Recycle Bin.)

**8. Create a shortcut on the desktop.**

   **a.** Use the left pane of Windows Explorer to locate the Windows folder on your hard drive. Select the folder to display its contents in the right pane. (*Note:* If you are in a lab setting, you may not have access to the Windows folder.)

   **b.** In the right pane, scroll through the list of objects until you see a file called Explorer.

   **c.** Drag the Explorer file to the desktop to create a shortcut.

   **d.** Close Windows Explorer.

   **e.** Double-click the new shortcut to make sure it starts Windows Explorer. Then close Windows Explorer again.

   **f.** Delete the shortcut for Windows Explorer and exit Windows.

# ▶ Independent Challenges

**If you are doing all of the Independent Challenges, you will need to use a new floppy disk.**

**1.** You have decided to start a bakery business and you want to use Windows 98 to organize the files for the business.
   **a.** Create two new folders on your Project Disk named "Advertising" and "Customers".
   **b.** Use WordPad to create a form letter inviting new customers to the open house for the new bakery, then save it as "Open House Letter" and place it in the Customers folder.
   **c.** Use WordPad to create a list of five tasks that need to get done before the business opens, then save it as "Business Plan" to your Project Disk, but don't place it in a folder.
   **d.** Use Paint to create a simple logo for the bakery, save it as "Bakery Logo", then place it in the Advertising folder.
   **e.** On a piece of paper, draw out the new organization of all the folders and files on your Project Disk, close all open programs, then exit Windows.

**2.** On your computer's hard drive, create a folder called "IC3". Follow the guidelines listed here to create the file hierarchy shown in Figure B-21.
   **a.** Start WordPad, create a new file that contains a list. Save the file as "To Do List" to your Project Disk.
   **b.** Start My Computer and copy the Memo file on your Project Disk to the IC3 folder. Rename the file "Article."
   **c.** Copy the Memo file again to the IC3 folder on your hard drive and rename the second copy of the file "Article Two."
   **d.** Use My Computer to copy any Paint file to the IC3 folder and rename the file "Sample Logo."
   **e.** Copy the To Do List from your Project Disk to the IC3 folder and rename the file "Important List."
   **f.** Move the files into the folders shown in Figure B-21.
   **g.** Copy the IC3 folder to your Project Disk. Then delete the IC3 folder on your hard drive. Using the Recycle Bin, restore the file called IC3. To remove all your work on the hard drive, delete this folder again.

**FIGURE B-21**

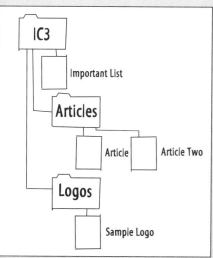

**3.** With Windows 98, you can access the Web from My Computer and Windows Explorer, allowing you to search for information located not only on your computer or network, but also on any computer connected to the Internet.
   **a.** Start Windows Explorer, then click in the Address Bar so the current location (probably your hard drive) is selected, then type "www.microsoft.com"
   **b.** Connect to the Internet if necessary. The Microsoft Web page displays in the right pane of Windows Explorer.
   **c.** Click in the Address Bar, then type "www.course.com", then wait a moment while the Course Technology Web page opens.
   **d.** Make sure your Project Disk is in the floppy disk drive, then click 3½ Floppy (A:) in the left pane.

e. Click the Back button list arrow, then click Welcome to Microsoft Homepage.

f. Capture a picture of your desktop by using [Print Screen]. Save the file as "Microsoft", then print it. See Independent Challenge 4 for instructions.

g. Click the Close button on the Explorer Bar.

h. Close Windows Explorer and disconnect from the Internet.

**4.** Create a shortcut to the drive that contains your Project Disk. Then capture a picture of your desktop showing the new shortcut by pressing [Print Screen], located on the upper-right side of your keyboard. The picture is stored temporarily on the Clipboard. Then open the Paint program and paste the contents of the Clipboard into the drawing window. Click No when asked to enlarge the Bitmap. Save the Paint file as Desktop Picture on your Project Disk and print it. Delete the shortcut when you are finished.

## ▶ Visual Workshop

Recreate the screen shown in Figure B-22, which contains the Brochure window in My Computer, two shortcuts on the desktop, and two files open. Press [Print Screen] to make a copy of the screen, then print it from Paint. See your instructor or technical support person for assistance.

FIGURE B-22

# Introducing

## Microsoft Office 2000 Premium

### Objectives

- ► **Define Office 2000 components**
- ► **Create a document with Word 2000**
- ► **Build a worksheet with Excel 2000**
- ► **Manage data with Access 2000**
- ► **Create a presentation with PowerPoint 2000**
- ► **Browse the World Wide Web with Internet Explorer 5**
- ► **Create a publication with Publisher 2000**
- ► **Manage office tasks with Outlook 2000**

Microsoft Office 2000 is a collection of software programs designed to take advantage of the Windows interface and improve your computer efficiency. When programs are grouped together, as in Office, this grouping is called a suite, and all its components have similar icons, functions, and commands. ◄━━ This unit will introduce you to MediaLoft, a nationwide chain of bookstore cafés that sells books, CDs, and videos in eight locations. By exploring how MediaLoft uses Microsoft Office components, you will learn how each program can be used in a business environment.

# Defining Office 2000 Components

Microsoft Office 2000 contains programs commonly used in businesses. Office is available in several arrangements: Premium, Professional, and Small Business Edition. Office Premium includes Word, Excel, Access, PowerPoint, Outlook, Internet Explorer, Publisher, FrontPage, PhotoDraw, and Office Small Business Tools. Table A-1 displays the icons for each Office program. MediaLoft employees began using Office Premium when the company switched from manual functions to networked personal computers using Windows. All employees use Office to create business documents, communicate, and access the Internet. Figure A-1 shows MediaLoft's organizational chart. Below are some of the ways MediaLoft employees use Office components.

### Create text documents using Word
Word is a **word processing** program used to create documents such as business letters and reports.

### Analyze data using Excel
Excel is a **spreadsheet** program used to analyze data, perform calculations, and create charts. Charts are a visual representation of spreadsheet data.

### Track information using Access
Access is a database management system. A **database** is a collection of related information such as a list of employees, their social security numbers, salaries, and vacation time. A **database management system** organizes databases and allows you to crosscheck information in them.

### Create presentations using PowerPoint
PowerPoint is a **presentation graphics** program used to develop slides or handouts for visual presentations. Figure A-1 was created using PowerPoint.

### Maintain tasks, contacts, schedules, appointments, and e-mail with Outlook
Outlook is an electronic **personal information manager** that you can use to schedule appointments, maintain contacts, and send e-mail and files to people on your network and across the Internet.

### Explore the World Wide Web using Internet Explorer
Internet Explorer is a multimedia **browser** that lets you explore the World Wide Web, allowing you access to a vast array of information resources.

### Create professional publications with Publisher
Publisher is a **desktop publishing** program used to create publications containing text and graphics. Publisher contains predesigned templates that you can use to create newsletters, Web sites, brochures and other publications, or you can create publications from scratch.

### Design Web pages using FrontPage
FrontPage is an **HTML editor** that lets you create attractive web pages. FrontPage makes it simple to create web pages that include graphics and hyperlinks.

### Create graphics with PhotoDraw
PhotoDraw is a graphics program that combines drawing and photo editing tools, enabling you to create professional-looking graphics.

### Share or link text and graphics among programs to increase accuracy
Information from one Office program can be **dynamically linked** to (connected to), or **embedded** in (placed in), another Office program, such as an Excel chart in a PowerPoint slide.

**FIGURE A-1: MediaLoft organizational chart**

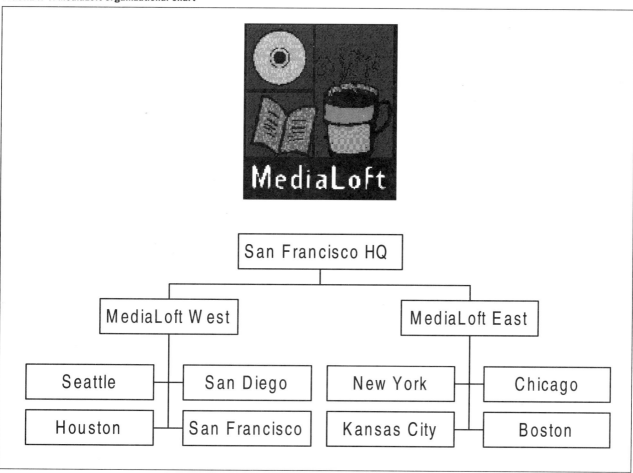

**TABLE A-1: Office program icons**

| icon | program | function |
|------|---------|----------|
| | **Access** | Database program used to create and manage databases |
| | **Excel** | Spreadsheet program used to create spreadsheets |
| | **FrontPage** | HTML editor used to create Web pages |
| | **Internet Explorer** | Browser used to explore the World Wide Web |
| | **Outlook** | Personal information manager used to send e-mail and manage office tasks |
| | **PhotoDraw** | Graphics program used to create graphics |
| | **PowerPoint** | Presentation graphics program used to create presentations |
| | **Publisher** | Desktop publishing program used to create publications |
| | **Word** | Word processing program used to create documents |

# Creating a Document with Word 2000

Word allows you to create, edit and format documents, such as reports, memos, or letters that contain text, tables, and graphics. MediaLoft employees use Word to create documents for the company's Annual Report. The memo requesting information for the report is shown in Figure A-2. The memo contains the kinds of elements that make a document readable and professional-looking.

## Details

**The following are some of the benefits of using Word:**

### Enter text quickly and easily

Word makes it easy to enter text and then edit it later. Rather than having to retype a document, you can rearrange and revise the text.

### Organize information in a table to make it easier to read

Some information is easier to read in tabular form, and it's easy to create and modify a table in Word. Once a table is created, you can edit its contents and modify its appearance using pre-designed formats. You can also sort tabular data without any additional typing: this means you can add entries and then reorganize the data in your table.

### Create error-free copy

You can use Word's spell checker after you finish typing to help you create error-free documents. It compares each word in a document to a built-in dictionary and notifies you if it does not recognize a word. Word's AutoCorrect feature automatically corrects misspelled words as you type them. Word provides several entries for commonly misspelled words, but you can also add your own.

### Combine text and graphics

Using Word, you can combine text and graphics easily. Figure A-2 shows the Word document containing text and graphics as it looks on the screen; Figure A-3 shows the printed memo.

### Add special effects

Word gives you the ability to create columns of text, drop caps (capital letters that take up two or three lines), and WordArt (customized text with a three-dimensional or shadowed appearance), adding a polished quality to your documents.

FIGURE A-2: Memo created in Word

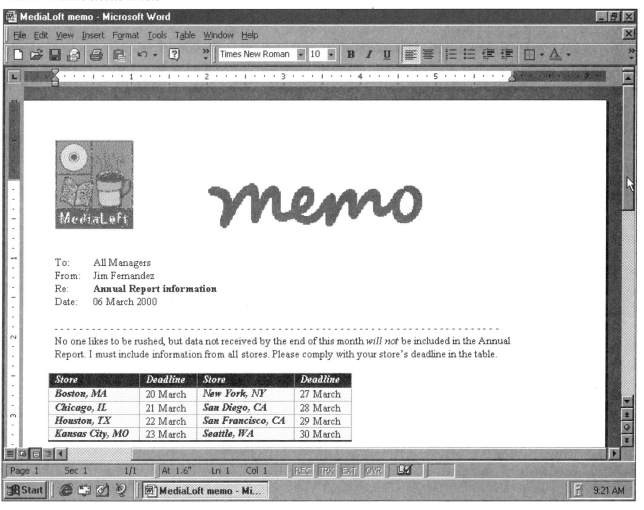

FIGURE A-3: Printout of completed memo

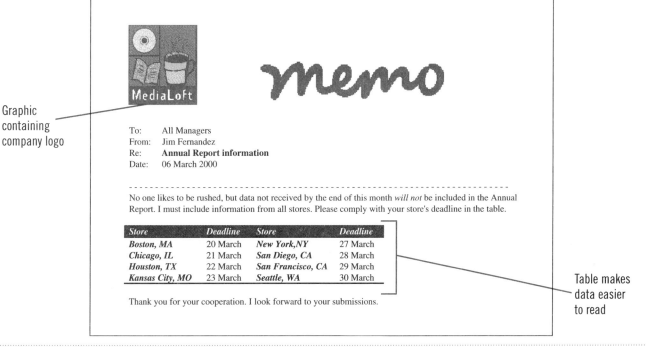

Graphic containing company logo

Table makes data easier to read

# Building a Worksheet with Excel 2000

Excel performs numeric calculations rapidly and accurately. Like traditional paper-based spreadsheets, this electronic spreadsheet contains a **worksheet** area that is divided into columns and rows that form individual **cells**. Cells can contain text, numbers, formulas, or a combination of all three.  MediaLoft's employees use Excel to store and manipulate the sales and other data they have collected. They can then format the data to be inserted into the Annual Report.

## Details

### The following are some of the benefits of using Excel:

 **Calculate results quickly and accurately**

With Excel, you can enter data quickly and accurately using formulas. Excel then calculates the results accordingly.

 **Recalculate easily**

Excel recalculates data easily by updating information automatically when you change or correct an entry.

 **Perform what-if analysis**

Because equations are automatically recalculated, this lets you ask "what-if" and create a variety of business scenarios, such as what if the interest rate on a corporate credit card changes. Anticipating possible outcomes helps you make better business decisions.

 **Complete complex mathematical equations**

Using Excel, you can easily complete complicated math computations using built-in equations. This function tells you what data is needed, and you then fill in the blanks. This saves you valuable time.

 **Create charts**

Excel makes it easy to create charts based on information in a worksheet. With Excel, charts are automatically updated as data changes. The worksheet in Figure A-4 shows a bar chart that illustrates sales revenue for the eight MediaLoft stores.

 **Create attractive output**

You can enhance the overall appearance of the printouts of numeric data using charts, graphics, and text formatting, as shown in Figure A-5.

**FIGURE A-4:** Worksheet created in Excel

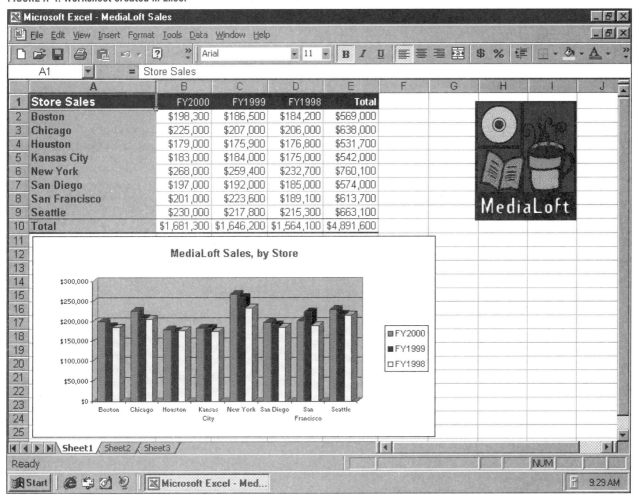

**FIGURE A-5:** Printout of annual revenue data with corresponding chart

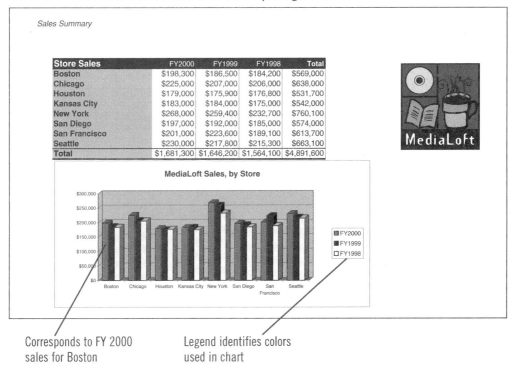

Corresponds to FY 2000
sales for Boston

Legend identifies colors
used in chart

# Managing Data with Access 2000

Access is a database program that you can use to arrange large amounts of data in various groups or databases, such as an inventory of products. The information in the databases can be retrieved in a variety of ways. For example, a database like an inventory list might be arranged alphabetically, by stocking location, or by the number of units on order. A powerful database program, such as Access, lets you look up information quickly, easily, and in a wide variety of ways. ✒️ MediaLoft stores use Access databases to keep track of inventory. Information from these databases is used to generate inventory lists and numbers for the Annual Report.

The following are some of the benefits of using Access:

### Enter data easily

Employees can enter data in an existing table as the database grows or changes. Because Access organizes the data for you, the order in which you enter items is not a concern.

### Retrieve data easily

Access makes it easy for you to specify criteria, or conditions, and then produce a list of all data that conforms to the criteria. You might want to see a list of products by supplier or a list of discontinued products. Figure A-6 shows an inventory table containing music sold at MediaLoft's stores.

### Create professional forms

You can enter data into an on-screen form that you create in Access. Using a form makes entering data more efficient, and you'll be less prone to making errors. Figure A-7 shows a screen form that can be used for data entry.

### Add graphics to printed screen forms and reports

Forms and reports can contain graphic images, text formatting, and special effects, such as WordArt, to make them look more professional. Screen forms can contain graphics. You can preview a screen form before printing it, as shown in Figure A-8, to make sure the form meets your specifications.

FIGURE A-6: Table of inventory items in Access

FIGURE A-7: An on-screen Access data entry form

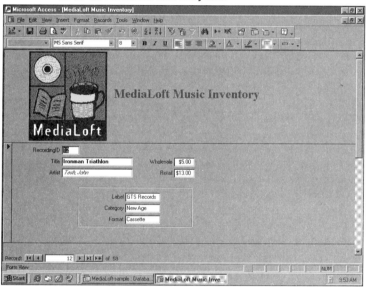

FIGURE A-8: Preview of inventory form created in Access

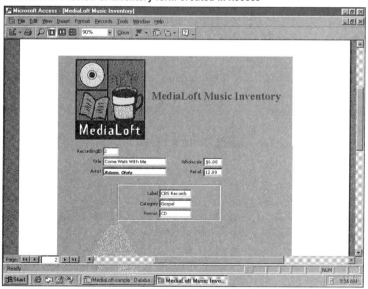

# Creating a Presentation with PowerPoint 2000

In PowerPoint, a **slide** is the work area in which you can create handouts, outlines, speakers' notes and 35mm slides. You can also generate an online slide show in which flowing images appear on a PC monitor. The computer can be hooked up to a projector so a roomful of people can see the demonstration.  Store managers present highlights of the Annual Report to MediaLoft executives using a slide show and notes created in PowerPoint.

## Details

The following are some of the benefits of using PowerPoint:

### Create and edit slides easily
You can enter text directly on a PowerPoint slide, enabling you to see how your slide will look. Editing is accomplished using the same methods as in Word. You can cut, copy, paste, and move slide text simply and easily.

### Combine information from Office programs
You can use data you create in Word, Excel, Access, and other Office programs in your PowerPoint slides. This means that a worksheet you created in Excel, for example, can be inserted on a slide, without your having to retype the information.

### Add graphics
Graphic images, such as clip art, an Excel chart, or a corporate logo, further enhance any presentation. PowerPoint accepts the most commonly available graphic file formats and comes with many clip art images. PowerPoint also allows you to create your own shapes and design your own text. Figure A-9 shows a slide containing a chart created in Excel and a graphic image of a corporate logo.

### Print a variety of presentation materials
In addition to being able to print out a slide, you can also create many other types of printed materials. Notes—containing hints and reminders helpful to whoever delivers the presentation—are invaluable. Figure A-10 shows notes in PowerPoint. You can also print other types of handouts for presentation attendees that contain a reduced image of each slide and a place for handwritten notes.

### Add special effects
You can add special effects, such as transitions from one slide to the next, text and graphics builds within slides, sounds, and videos to make your presentation look professional.

**FIGURE A-9: Slide created in PowerPoint**

Background layout created using PowerPoint template

Logo as a graphic image

Excel chart as a graphic image

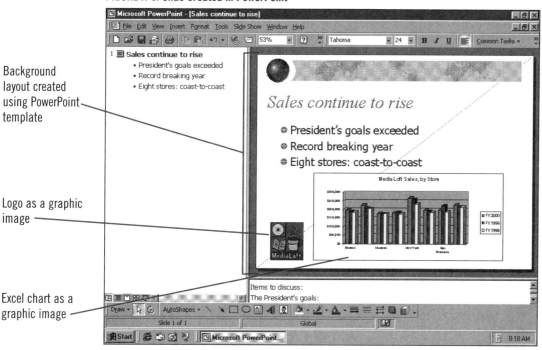

**FIGURE A-10: Notes created in PowerPoint**

A picture of each slide is printed so you know what the audience is seeing

Add your own text to serve as a reminder during a presentation

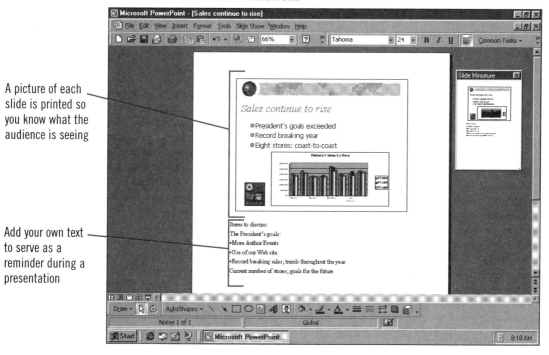

Office 2000

# Browsing the World Wide Web with Internet Explorer 5

The **World Wide Web**—also know as the **Web**—is a subset of the Internet that brings text, graphics, and multimedia information to your desktop. Internet Explorer 5 is a **browser**, a program designed to help you view the graphic images and multimedia data on the Web. Many Web sites let you move to other sites with the click of your mouse using **links**, instructions that take you to different Web site addresses. ◤━━━ MediaLoft employees keep informed on the latest trends and research competitors using Internet Explorer.

The following are some of the benefits of using Internet Explorer:

 **Display Web sites**
Once you're connected to the Internet, you can view interesting and informative Web sites from all around the globe.

 **Move from one Web site to another**
Web page links let you effortlessly move from site to site. You can easily find information related to the topic you're interested in.

 **Save your favorite Web site locations**
Once you've located interesting Web sites, such as the one shown in Figure A-11, you can save their Web site addresses so you can return to them later without performing another search. Internet Explorer makes it easy to compile a list of your favorite locations.

 **Use multimedia**
Video and audio clips are commonly found within Web pages. Internet Explorer allows you to take advantage of these features through its multimedia capabilities.

 **Print Web pages**
As you travel the Web, you may want to print the information you find. You can easily print an active Web page—including its text and graphics.

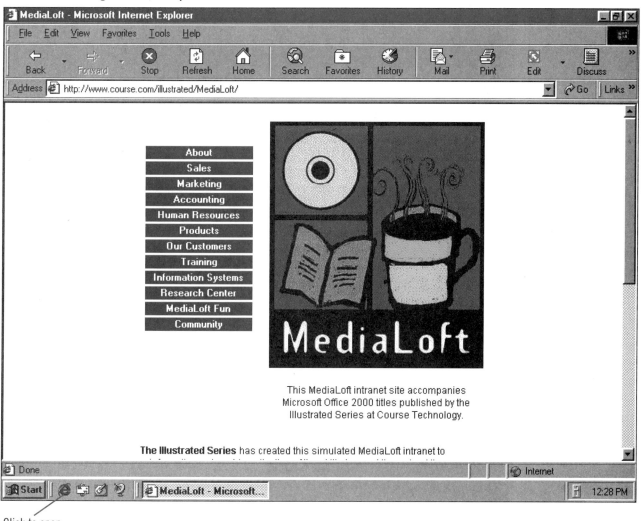

Click to open
Internet Explorer

# Creating a Publication with Publisher 2000

Everyday business documents include letters, spreadsheets, presentations, and databases. Periodically, you may need to create newsletters, brochures, letterhead, and business forms. You can use Publisher to arrange text and images (created in Publisher or in other Office programs) in a **publication**. A publication can contain graphic images and elements created in other programs. ✐ MediaLoft uses Publisher to produce a newsletter that keeps employees informed of news and events within the company, as shown in Figure A-12.

Details

**The following are some of the benefits of using Publisher:**

### Create a wide variety of publications
Publisher's Catalog contains hundreds of predesigned publications that you can easily adapt for your own purposes.

### Add artwork
Artwork adds an important dimension to any publication. You can import images from other programs, create your own artwork using drawing tools available in Publisher, or select from the over 10,000 pieces of clip art that come with Publisher.

### Emphasize text
You can use different fonts and formatting techniques, as well as different font sizes, to add emphasis to your text, as shown in Figure A-13.

### Create logos
Using tools such as WordArt and Publisher's Design Gallery, you can create exciting logos—symbols readily identified with your company or organization.

### Professional tools
Publisher contains a spelling checker that flags errors as you type and helps you check text for accuracy. Snap-to rulers and guides make it simple to align text and images on pages, and "Continued on" and "Continued from" notices help readers follow lengthy stories that don't fit on a single page. Publisher's Design Checker feature lets you check (and correct) your publication for possible design flaws.

### Publish on the Internet
You can easily convert publications into a Web-ready Internet format. For example, you can adapt a brochure for your Web page.

**FIGURE A-12:** Publication created in Publisher

Logo can be added
to publication

Create attractive
tables

Table of contents

Publisher comes
with thousands of
pieces of artwork

Same font,
different sizes

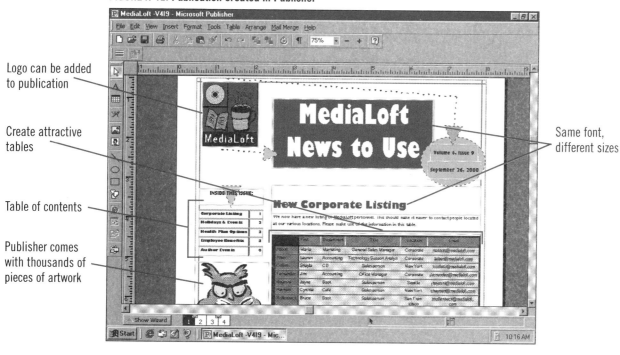

**FIGURE A-13:** Printout of publication

# Managing Office Tasks with Outlook 2000

There's more to office work than creating documents, worksheets, databases, and presentations. Outlook is a personal information manager that helps you manage a typical business day. For example, using the Inbox, you can send electronic mail messages—or **e-mail**—to anyone with an Internet address. Table A-2 describes the other tasks you can perform with Outlook. MediaLoft employees work more efficiently using Outlook to send messages between stores, schedule appointments, and keep track of deadlines.

### The following are some of the benefits of using Outlook:

### Process mail
Use the Inbox to read, forward, reply to, and create e-mail. The Inbox displays unread messages in bold text, so you can tell which messages still need to be read.

### Create an address book
Keep track of e-mail addresses in an address book so that you don't have to type an e-mail address each time you create a new message. You can also create distribution lists so that you can easily send messages to a group of people with whom you communicate frequently, without having to enter each e-mail address over and over.

### Send attachments
In addition to the actual content of a message, you can attach individual files to an e-mail message. This means you can send a colleague a document created in Excel, for example, along with an explanatory message.

**TABLE A-2: Additional Outlook tasks**

| task | description |
| --- | --- |
| **Manage appointments** | Use Calendar to make appointments, plan meetings, and keep track of events |
| **Manage tasks** | Use Tasks to keep track of pending jobs, set priorities, assign due dates, and express completion expectations for tasks |
| **Track contacts** | Use Contacts to record information such as names, addresses, phone numbers, and e-mail addresses for business and personal associates |
| **Maintain a journal of your activities** | Use Journal to track project phases, record activities, and manage your time |
| **Create reminders** | Use Notes—an electronic equivalent to yellow sticky notes—to leave reminders for yourself |

# Getting

# Started with Internet Explorer 5

In this unit, you learn how to use the World Wide Web, examine basic features of Internet Explorer 5, and access Web pages. You need to connect to the Internet to complete this unit. If your computer is not connected to the Internet, check with your instructor or technical support person to get connected, or, if necessary, simply read the lessons without completing the steps to learn about using Internet Explorer. ◀━━ MediaLoft is a chain of café bookstores founded in 1988. MediaLoft stores offer customers the opportunity to purchase books, music, and videotapes while enjoying a variety of exotic coffees, teas, and freshly baked desserts. Alice Wegman is the marketing manager at MediaLoft. Alice needs to determine if MediaLoft should continue its nationwide expansion by opening a store in southern Florida. She decides to use Internet Explorer to find information about other café bookstores in the area.

# Understanding Web Browsers

A **computer network** consists of two or more computers that can share information and resources. An **intranet** is a computer network that connects computers in a local area only, such as computers in a company's office. The **Internet** is a communications system that connects computers and computer networks located around the world. An estimated 40 million computers are currently connected to the Internet through telephone lines, cables, satellites, and other telecommunications media, as shown in Figure A-1. Through the Internet, these computers can share many types of information, including text, graphics, sounds, videos, and computer programs. Anyone who has access to a computer and a connection to the Internet through a computer network or modem can use this rich information source. The **World Wide Web** (the **Web** or **WWW**) is a part of the Internet containing Web pages that are linked together. Web pages contain highlighted words, phrases, or graphics called **hyperlinks**, or simply **links**, that open other Web pages when you click them. Figure A-2 shows a sample Web page. A page's links can also open graphics files or play sound or video files. **Web browsers** are software programs used to access and display Web pages. Web browsers, such as Microsoft Internet Explorer and Netscape Navigator, make navigating the Web easy by providing a graphical, point-and-click environment. This unit features **Internet Explorer 5**, a popular browser from Microsoft that comes with Microsoft Office 2000. Although you only use the Internet Explorer Web browser in this unit, the Internet Explorer 5 suite contains other network communications options that are listed in Table A-1. Alice uses Internet Explorer and the Web to find information about bookstore cafés in southern Florida that might be potential MediaLoft competitors.

### Using Internet Explorer, Alice can:

#### Display Web pages
Alice can access Web pages from all over the world for many business purposes. For example, she can check the pages of competing book retailers to see how they market their products.

#### Use links to move from one Web page to another
Alice can use the hyperlinks on competing book retailers' Web pages to get more specific information about their operations.

#### Play audio and video clips
A Web browser can play audio and video clips if it has been configured to do so and your computer has the appropriate hardware, such as speakers. Alice might find some book retailers' Web sites that include links to short video clips of store interiors or sound clips from audio products that they sell.

#### Search the Web for information
Alice can utilize various search programs in her Web browser to look for more information on bookstore-related topics such as discounts and shipping policies.

#### Save a list of favorite Web pages
Alice can use Internet Explorer to save a list of Web pages that she might need to visit again, such as a page for a competing bookstore. By adding a Web page to her list of favorites, it is easy for her to return to the page later.

#### Print or save the text and graphics on Web pages
If Alice finds information or images that she wants to keep a hard copy of, she can easily print the entire Web page, including any graphics. She can also save the text or graphics on a Web page, or copy this information temporarily to the Clipboard, where it is available for pasting into other Windows programs.

**FIGURE A-1: Internet structure**

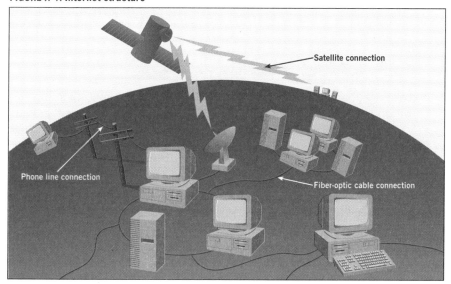

Satellite connection

Phone line connection

Fiber-optic cable connection

**FIGURE A-2: Sample Web page**

Graphic hyperlinks

Text hyperlink

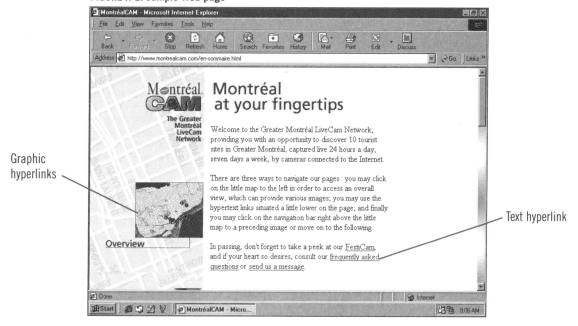

**TABLE A-1: Internet Explorer 5 suite components**

| feature | description |
|---------|-------------|
| FrontPage Express | Provides tools for creating new Web pages and editing existing ones |
| Internet Explorer | Lets you view and print Web pages |
| NetMeeting | Enables you to set up audio and video links to people at different locations for a live discussion |
| Outlook Express | Allows you to read and send e-mail messages as well as read and post messages in newsgroups (discussions organized around specific topics) |
| Personal Web Server | Lets you use your personal computer to host a Web site |
| Web Publishing Wizard | Lets you publish your Web page files, support files, and other Web content files on a Web server |
| Windows Media Player | Lets you listen to and/or view live and prerecorded sounds, images, and videos |

Internet

Internet

# Starting Internet Explorer

Internet Explorer is a Web browser that connects your computer to the Web using an Internet connection. After Internet Explorer 5 is installed, its icon appears on your Windows desktop. You can also start Internet Explorer by clicking the Internet Explorer icon on the Quick Launch toolbar. The exact location of the Internet Explorer icon might vary on different computers. See your instructor or technical support person for assistance if you are unable to locate the Internet Explorer icon or if you do not have an Internet connection. Before Alice can take advantage of the Web's many features to find more information about competing bookstores, she must start Internet Explorer.

## Steps

1. **If you connect to the Internet using a modem and a telephone, follow your normal procedure to establish your connection**

2. **Locate the Internet Explorer icon on your Windows desktop**
   The icon should appear on the left side of your screen, as shown in Figure A-3. If the icon is not on your desktop, click the Start button on the taskbar, point to Programs on the Start menu, and then click Internet Explorer. Skip Step 3.

**Trouble?**

If a Dial-up Connection or an Internet Connection Wizard dialog box opens, you will need to either connect to the Internet or enter your Internet settings to complete the step. See your instructor or technical support person for assistance.

3. **Double-click the Internet Explorer icon on the Windows desktop**
   Internet Explorer opens and displays your home page, which might look different from the one shown in Figure A-4. A **home page** is the first page that opens every time you start Internet Explorer. Your home page might be one for your school, employer, or one that you specify.

4. **If necessary, click the Maximize button on the Internet Explorer title bar to maximize the program window**

### History of the Internet and the World Wide Web

The Internet has its roots in the United States Department of Defense Advanced Research Projects Agency Network (ARPANET), which began in 1969. In 1986, the National Science Foundation formed NSFNET, which replaced ARPANET. NSFNET expanded the foundation of the U.S. portion of the Internet with high-speed, long-distance lines. In 1991, the U.S. Congress further expanded the Internet's capacity and speed and opened it to commercial use.

Over 200 countries now have Internet access.
The World Wide Web was created in Switzerland in 1991 to allow links between documents on the Internet. Software programs designed to access the Web (called Web browsers) use common "point-and-click" interfaces. The first graphical Web browser, Mosaic, was introduced at the University of Illinois in 1993. Microsoft Internet Explorer and Netscape Navigator are two current, popular Web browsers.

FIGURE A-3: Internet Explorer icon on desktop

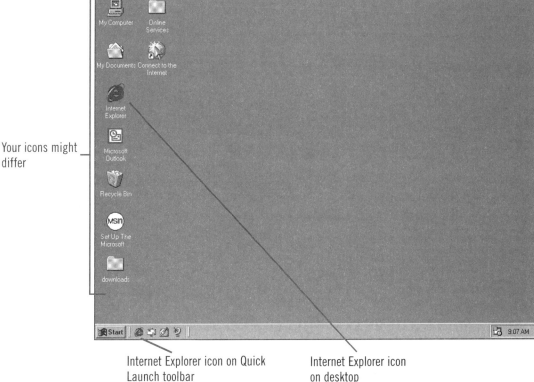

Your icons might
differ

Internet Explorer icon on Quick
Launch toolbar

Internet Explorer icon
on desktop

FIGURE A-4: Sample Web page for Microsoft Corporation

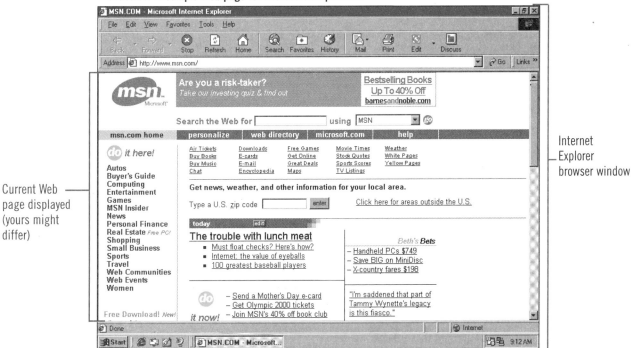

Current Web
page displayed
(yours might
differ)

Internet
Explorer
browser window

Internet

# Exploring the Browser Window

The elements of the Internet Explorer browser window shown in Figure A-5 let you view, print, and search for information on the Web. You can customize the toolbar and Address bar, so your screen might look different than the one shown in Figure A-5. ◢▬▬ Before using, or **surfing**, the Web, Alice needs to become more familiar with the components of the Internet Explorer browser window. Find and compare the elements below, using Figure A-5 as a guide.

## Details

 The **title bar** at the top of the page usually contains the name of the Web page currently displayed in the Web browser window.

 The **menu bar** provides access to most of the browser's features through a variety of commands, similar to other Office programs.

 The **toolbar** provides buttons for many options, such as stopping the transfer of a Web page, moving from one Web page to another, printing Web pages, and searching for information on the Internet. Table A-2 explains these buttons. Many commonly used commands available on menus are more readily accessed using the toolbar buttons.

 The **Address bar** displays the address of the Web page currently opened. The **Uniform Resource Locator** (**URL**), or the Web page's address, appears in the Address bar after you open (or load) the page.

 The **status indicator** (the Internet Explorer logo) animates while a new Web page loads.

 The **Web page area** (or **document window**) is the specific area where the current Web page appears. You might need to scroll down the page to view its entire contents.

 The **vertical scroll bar** allows you to move the current Web page up or down in the browser window. The **scroll box** indicates your relative position within the Web page.

 The **status bar** performs three main functions: 1) displays information about your connection progress whenever you open a new Web page; 2) notifies you when you connect to another Web site; and 3) identifies the percentage of information transferred from the Web server to your browser. The status bar also displays the Web addresses of any links on the Web page when you move your mouse pointer over them.

FIGURE A-5: Elements of the Internet Explorer window

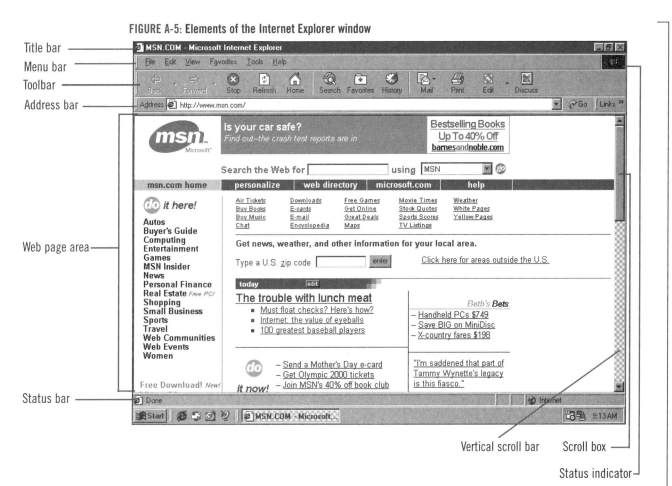

Title bar
Menu bar
Toolbar
Address bar

Web page area

Status bar

Vertical scroll bar    Scroll box

Status indicator

TABLE A-2: Toolbar buttons

| button name | button | description |
| --- | --- | --- |
| Back | ⬅ | Opens the previous page |
| Forward | ➡ | Opens the next page |
| Stop | ⊗ | Stops loading the page |
| Refresh | 🔄 | Refreshes the contents of the current page |
| Home | 🏠 | Opens the home page |
| Search | 🔍 | Opens the Search Assistant in the Explorer Search bar |
| Favorites | ✳ | Opens the Explorer Favorites bar |
| History | 🕘 | Opens the Explorer History bar |
| Mail | 📧 | Displays options for working with mail and news |
| Print | 🖨 | Prints the current Web page |
| Edit | ✎ | Transfers the currently displayed Web page to Microsoft FrontPage for editing |
| Discuss | 🗐 | Lets you add or edit discussion servers and opens the Discussion bar |

Internet

Internet

# Opening and Saving a URL

As you learned in the previous lesson, the address for a Web page is also called a URL. Each Web page has a unique URL beginning with "http" (which stands for Hypertext Transfer Protocol) followed by a colon, two forward slashes, and the Web site's name. After the name of the Web site, another slash and one or more folder names and a filename might appear. For example, in the address http://www.course.com/Illustrated/MediaLoft/community.html, the name of the Web site is *www.course.com*; a folder at that site is *Illustrated*; and within the Illustrated/MediaLoft folder is a file named *community.html*. The Internet Explorer **Favorites list** allows you to create your own list of frequently visited Web pages that you can then access without having to type a URL. After you add a Web page to your Favorites list, you can automatically access that page by clicking the Favorites button on the toolbar and then clicking its name, or by clicking the favorite's name on the Favorites menu. Alice wants to investigate the Web page for a local competitor, Miami Booksellers. Since she will return to this site often as she completes her research, she adds it to her Favorites list.

1. **Click anywhere in the Address bar**
   The current address is highlighted; any text you type replaces it.

2. **Type www.course.com/Illustrated/MediaLoft/MiamiBooksellers/index.html**
   Internet Explorer will automatically add the http:// protocol to the beginning of the address you type after you press [Enter].

3. **Press [Enter]**
   The status bar displays the connection process. After a few seconds, the Web page for Miami Booksellers opens in the Web page area, as shown in Figure A-6.

**QuickTip**

You can change the favorite's default page name by typing a new name in the Name text box.

4. **Click Favorites on the menu bar, click Add to Favorites; if necessary, in the Name text box of the Add Favorite dialog box type Miami Booksellers, then click OK**
   The name and URL for Miami Booksellers are added to your Favorites list.

5. **Click the Back button ⬅ on the toolbar**
   The previous Web page appears in the Web page area.

## Creating and organizing favorites

Once you add a Web page to your Favorites list, returning to that page is much easier. To keep your Favorites list manageable, you only should add pages that you expect to visit again. To add a Web page to your Favorites list, open the Web page in the browser window, click Favorites on the menu bar, click Add to Favorites, then click OK.

If your Favorites list gets too long, you can organize the page names into folders. To add a folder to your Favorites list, click Favorites on the menu bar, click Organize Favorites, and then click the Create Folder button. You can use the buttons or drag and drop to move the favorites into different folders.

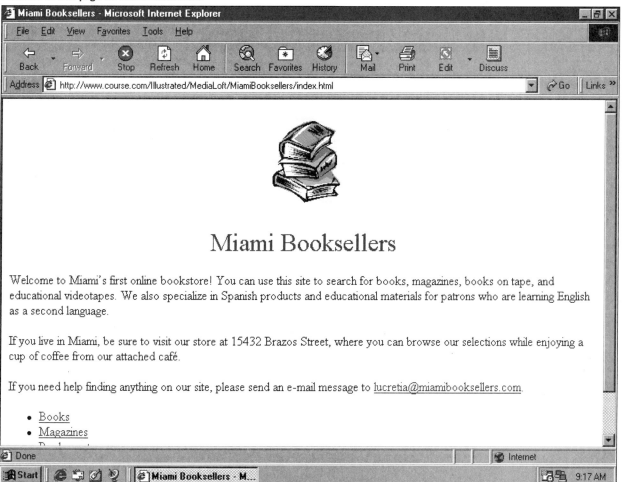

Internet

Internet

# Navigating Web Pages

Hyperlinks enable you to navigate to, or open, another location on the same Web page or jump to an entirely different Web page. You can follow these links to obtain more information about a topic by clicking the highlighted word or phrase. If you change your mind or if a page takes too long to load, you can click the Stop button on the toolbar. While viewing the Web page for Miami Booksellers, Alice decides to investigate the Books link to see what types of books Miami Booksellers features.

## Steps

1. Click **Favorites** on the menu bar

2. Click **Miami Booksellers**
   The Web page for Miami Booksellers that you added to your Favorites list opens in the Web page area.

3. If necessary, click the **vertical scroll bar** to move down the Web page until you see the link **Books**, then place your mouse pointer on the link
   As shown in Figure A-7, the mouse pointer changes to 🖑 when you place it over an active link.

**Trouble?**

If you receive an error message, click a different link on the page. If you want to cancel loading the page, click the Stop button ⊗ on the toolbar.

4. Click **Books**
   The status indicator animates as the new Web page loads. The Books Web page opens in your Web browser window, as shown in Figure A-8.

5. Click the **Home button** 🏠 on the toolbar
   The initial Web page that opens when you start Internet Explorer reappears in your Web browser window.

### Selecting a home page

When you click 🏠, the page that is specified as "home" opens in your Web browser window. When you install Internet Explorer, the default home page is a page at the Microsoft Web site. You can easily select a different home page to open each time you start Internet Explorer or when you click 🏠. Simply open that page in your Web browser window, click Tools on the menu bar, click Internet Options, click the General tab, click Use Current, then click OK to specify the current page as your home page.

**FIGURE A-7: Hyperlinks on Miami Booksellers Web page**

Pointer on hyperlink

Status bar displays URL of hyperlink

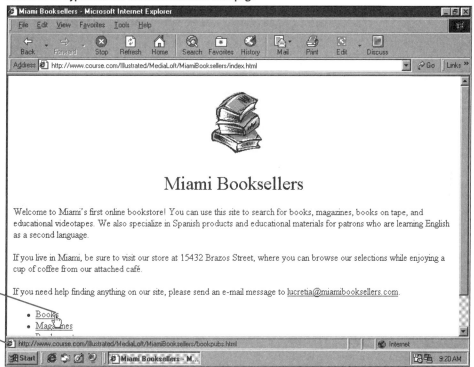

**FIGURE A-8: Books Web page**

Hyperlinks to different book categories

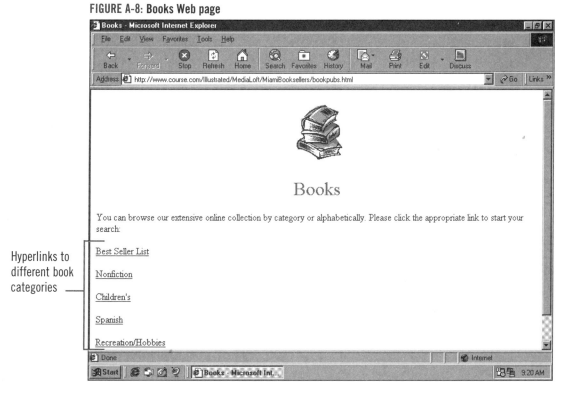

**Internet**

# Getting Help

Internet Explorer provides a Help system with information and instructions on various features and commands. While exploring the Web pages for bookstores, Alice discovers one with very small type. She decides to access the Help system to find instructions for increasing the type's font size.

## Steps

**1.** Click **Help** on the menu bar
The Help menu opens.

**Trouble?**

Don't worry if a different tab is selected. Continue with Step 3.

**2.** Click **Contents and Index**
The Microsoft Internet Explorer Help dialog box opens, as shown in Figure A-9, with the Contents tab selected. Table A-3 explains how each of the three tabs provides a different way to access Help information.

**3.** Click the **Search tab**
The Search tab allows you to search for a specific word or phrase.

**QuickTip**

You can also press [Enter] instead of clicking List Topics to display the relevant topics.

**4.** In the Type in the keyword to find text box, type **font sizes**, then click **List Topics**
As shown in Figure A-10, a list of relevant topics appears in the Select Topic to display list box.

**5.** In the Select Topic to display list box, double-click **Display text larger or smaller**
As shown in Figure A-11, the text in the right pane of the Microsoft Internet Explorer Help window provides information on how to change the font size.

**6.** Click the **Close button** in the upper-right corner of the Microsoft Internet Explorer Help window
The Help window closes.

**TABLE A-3: Help options**

| tab | function |
| --- | --- |
| **Contents** | Lists the categories available in Help |
| **Index** | Lists available Help topics in alphabetical order, and lets you locate specific topics |
| **Search** | Locates the desired Help topic based on the keyword or phrase you enter |

**FIGURE A-9: Microsoft Internet Explorer Help window**

Help tabs —

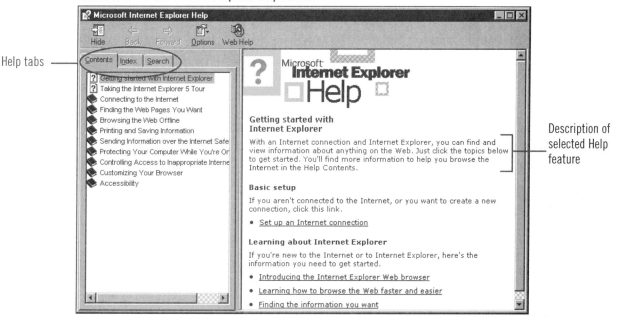

— Description of selected Help feature

**FIGURE A-10: Search tab**

Keywords —

List of topics relevant to keywords —

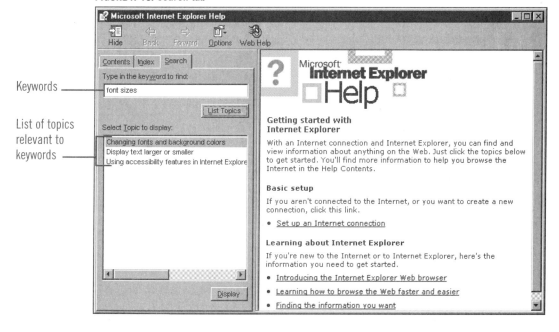

**FIGURE A-11: Help information**

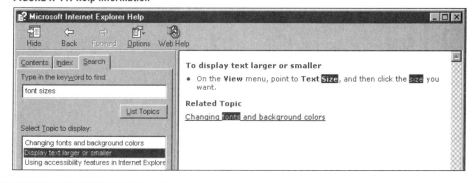

**Internet**

# Printing a Web Page

You can quickly print the Web page that currently appears in the Web page area by clicking the Print button on the toolbar. When you click File on the menu bar, and then click Print, the options in the Print dialog box allow you to specify parameters such as the number of copies and the page ranges you want to print. When you print a Web page, its text and any graphics will appear on your hard copy. Table A-4 explains printing options in more detail. ➤ Alice decides to print two copies of the Miami Booksellers Web page: one for her files and the other to attach to a summary memo that outlines her research results.

## Steps

1. Click the **Back button** on the toolbar to return to the Miami Booksellers home page

**QuickTip**

To print a Web page without changing any settings, click 🖨 on the toolbar.

2. Click **File** on the menu bar, then click **Print**
   The Print dialog box opens, as shown in Figure A-12.

3. In the Copies area, click the **Number of copies up arrow** until the number **2** appears
   The selection of 2 indicates that two copies will be printed.

4. Make sure your computer is connected to a printer that is turned on and contains paper

**Trouble?**

If your computer is not connected to a printer or if an error message appears, see your instructor or technical support person for assistance.

5. Click **OK**
   The Print dialog box closes, and two copies of the current Web page print.

### Copying information from a Web page

As with other Office programs, you can select text or information on a Web page and use the Copy and Paste commands to use the same information in another program, such as Word. You can also save a graphic image from a Web page by right-clicking the image, clicking Save Picture As on the pop-up menu, and then specifying where to save the image. If you just need to copy an image, click the Copy command on the pop-up menu. Using the Copy command saves the text or image to the Clipboard.

Keep in mind that the same laws that protect printed works generally protect information and graphics published on a Web page. Do not use material on a Web page without citing its source and checking the site carefully for any usage restrictions.

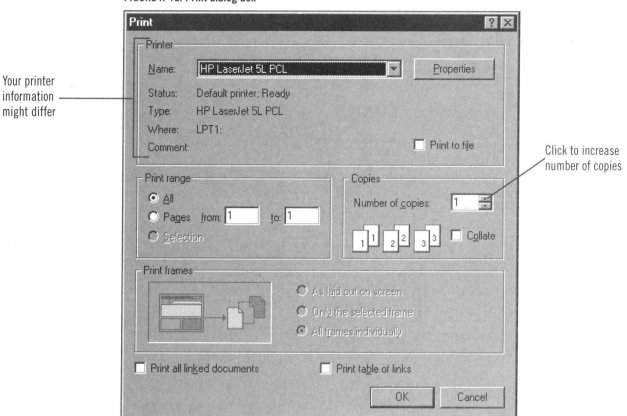

**FIGURE A-12:** Print dialog box

Your printer information might differ

Click to increase number of copies

**TABLE A-4: Printing options**

| option | description |
|---|---|
| **Printer** | Displays information about the name, status, type, and location of the active printer |
| **Properties** | Allows you to specify parameters such as paper size, paper source, and orientation |
| **Print range** | Allows you to choose to print all pages, a range of pages, or a selection on a page |
| **Copies** | Indicates the number of copies of each page to print and their sequence |
| **Print frames** | Allows you to print only the current frame or all frames separately or together |
| **Print all linked documents** | Opens and prints each document referenced by a link on the current page |
| **Print table of links** | Prints links in a table at the end of the document |

Internet

**Internet**

# Searching for Information on the Internet

An estimated 100 to 600 million Web pages and other information sources are available through the Internet. At times, finding the information you want seems like looking for the proverbial needle in the haystack. Luckily, you can use Web **search engines** to help you locate useful information. You simply enter a keyword or phrase describing the information you want to find, and the search engine provides you with a list of related Web sites. Each of these Web sites are listed as hyperlinks so you can quickly and easily continue your search. Alice's final task is to find information about competing bookstores that will help her to recommend a decision about MediaLoft's potential expansion into southern Florida. She decides to use Internet Explorer's built-in shortcuts to conduct her search.

1. Click the **Search button** 🔍 on the toolbar
   As shown in Figure A-13, the Web page area splits into two panes. The **Explorer Search bar** opens in the left pane and contains the **Search Assistant**, which displays a list of search options for finding Web pages, people, businesses, previous searches, or maps. The right pane shows the Web page you were viewing before beginning your search.

2. In the Explorer Search bar, make sure the **Find a Web page option button** is selected, click the **Find a Web page containing text box**, then type **bookstore cafes**
   Now that you've specified your search keywords, you can initiate the search.

3. Click **Search**
   Your search results appear as a list of related Web sites, called **hits**. See Figure A-14. Some search engines list hits by category or topic, whereas others list Web page names. You can click any hyperlink to open the Web page or a list of Web pages for a category.

4. Examine the hit list by scrolling it up or down in the Explorer Search bar, then click a **hyperlink** of your choice
   The related page containing more information about bookstore cafés opens in the right pane. When you finish exploring the hyperlinked site, you can continue or end your search.

5. Click the **Home button** 🏠, then click 🔍
   Your home page appears in the right pane, and then the Explorer Search bar closes.

### Search engines

Many search engines, such as Yahoo, Infoseek, Lycos, WebCrawler, and Excite, can help you locate information on the Internet. These search engines routinely use software programs to methodically catalog, or **crawl**, through the entire Internet and create huge databases with links to Web pages and their URLs. When you enter a keyword or phrase, the search engine examines its database index for relevant information and displays a list of Web sites.

Each search engine differs slightly in the way it formats information, records the number of Internet sites in the database, and how often it updates the database. If you don't find what you need using one search engine, try running the same search using a different search engine or search phrase until you find what you need. Most people develop personal favorites and learn which engine works best in various situations.

**FIGURE A-13: Search Assistant in the Explorer Search bar**

Explorer
Search bar

Enter search
keyword(s) here

Search category
options

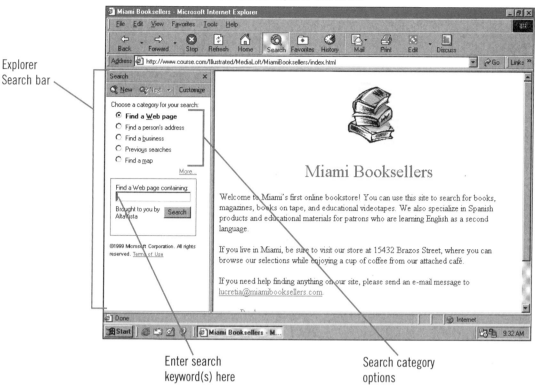

**FIGURE A-14: Bookstore-related Web sites**

Your search engine
might differ

Your results
might differ

Click to open this
category (or Web site)

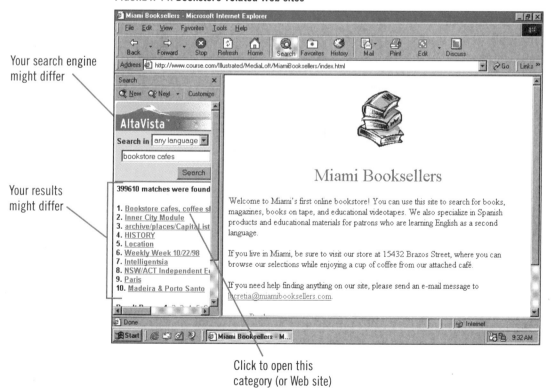

# Exiting Internet Explorer

When you are ready to exit Internet Explorer, you can click the Close button in the upper-right corner of the browser window or select the Close command on the File menu. You do not need to save files before you exit because all files you view with Internet Explorer are already saved on your computer or on another computer connected to the network you are using. ✐ Alice completes her bookstore research on the Web and is ready to exit Internet Explorer.

## Steps

1. **Click File on the menu bar**
   The File menu opens, as shown in Figure A-15.

> **QuickTip**
> You can also exit from Internet Explorer by clicking the Close button in the upper-right corner of the browser window.

2. **Click Close on the File menu**
   The Internet Explorer browser window closes.

3. **If you connected to the Internet by telephone, follow your normal procedure to close your connection**

### Saving or sending a Web page

Before exiting from Internet Explorer, you may want to save a copy of the current page or send someone a copy. By selecting Save As on the File menu, you can choose to save the complete Web page, including any graphics—or just the text from the page—in a file on your computer. If you want to send the complete page to someone, point to Send on the File menu, click Page By E-mail, and then use your e-mail program to address and send the message to the intended recipient.

**FIGURE A-15: Internet Explorer with File menu open**

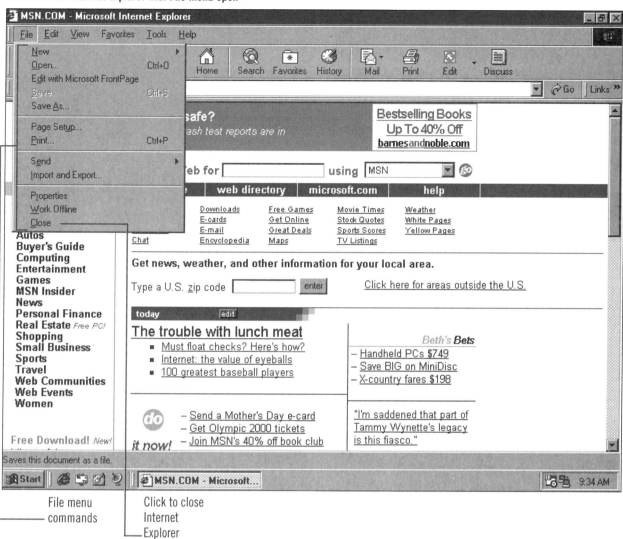

File menu
commands

Click to close
Internet
Explorer

Internet

# Practice

## ► Concepts Review

Label each element of the Internet Explorer browser window shown in Figure A-16.

FIGURE A-16

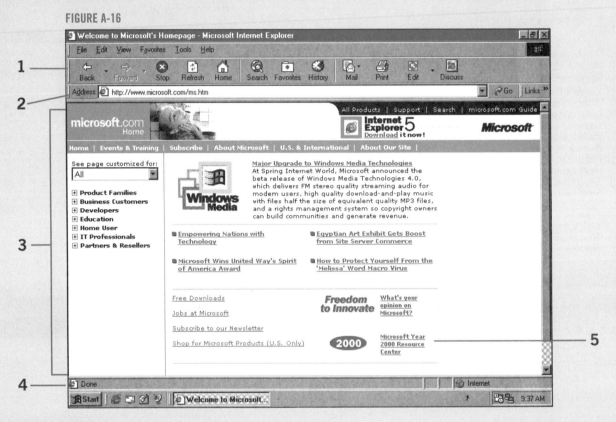

Match each term with the statement that describes it.

6. **Address bar**

7. **Toolbar**

8. **Favorites button**

9. **Status indicator**

10. **Back button**

a. Animates when Internet Explorer loads a page

b. Displays the URL for the currently displayed page

c. Provides shortcuts for options on the menu bar

d. Displays a list of selected Web pages

e. Displays the previously viewed page

## Select the best answer from the list of choices.

11. **Software programs used to access and display Web pages are called**
    - **a.** Web sites.
    - **b.** Web windows.
    - **c.** Web documents.
    - **d.** Web browsers.

12. **If you want to save the name and URL of a file and return to it later, you can add it to a list called**
    - **a.** Favorites.
    - **b.** Bookmarks.
    - **c.** Home pages.
    - **d.** Preferences.

13. **An international telecommunications network that consists of hyperlinked documents is called**
    - **a.** NSFNET.
    - **b.** Netscape Navigator.
    - **c.** Internet Explorer.
    - **d.** the World Wide Web.

14. **Where are the buttons that perform many common functions, such as printing, located in Internet Explorer?**
    - **a.** Address bar
    - **b.** Toolbar
    - **c.** Status bar
    - **d.** Menu bar

15. **Most Web pages are longer than the browser window. Which feature must you use to view the entire page?**
    - **a.** Scroll bar
    - **b.** Status bar
    - **c.** Forward button
    - **d.** Home button

16. **Which of the following URLs is valid?**
    - **a.** http://www.usf.edu
    - **b.** htp://www.usf.edu
    - **c.** http:/www.usf.edu
    - **d.** http//www.usf.edu

17. **Which button should you click if you want to stop a Web page that is currently loading on your computer?**
    - **a.**
    - **b.**
    - **c.**
    - **d.**

18. **Highlighted or underlined words that allow you to navigate to another Web page location are called**
    - **a.** Explorers.
    - **b.** Favorites.
    - **c.** Web browsers.
    - **d.** Hyperlinks.

19. **The URL of the Web page currently displayed in your Web browser window appears in the**
    - **a.** Title bar.
    - **b.** Browser window.
    - **c.** Address bar.
    - **d.** Status bar.

20. **To locate information on a specific topic on the Internet, you can use a**
    - **a.** URL locator.
    - **b.** Web browser.
    - **c.** Favorites list.
    - **d.** Search engine.

## ► Skills Review

1. **Start Internet Explorer.**
   a. Make sure your computer is connected to the Internet.
   b. Start Internet Explorer.

2. **Explore the browser window.**
   a. Identify the toolbar, menu bar, Address bar, status bar, status indicator, URL, browser window, and scroll bars.
   b. Identify the toolbar buttons for printing, searching, viewing favorites, and returning to the home page.
   c. Identify the complete URL of the current Web page.

3. **Open and save a URL.**
   a. Open the Web page www.cnet.com using the Address bar.
   b. Explore the site by using the scroll bars, toolbar, and hyperlinks.
   c. Open the Web page www.loc.gov using the Address bar.
   d. Add the current Web page to your Favorites list.
   e. Click the Home button.
   f. Click the Favorites button.
   g. Click Library of Congress Home Page to return to that page.
   h. Close the Explorer Favorites bar.

4. **Navigate Web pages.**
   a. Open the Web page www.sportsline.com using the Address bar.
   b. Follow the links to investigate the content.
   c. Click the Home button.

5. **Get Help.**
   a. Open Microsoft Internet Explorer Help, then click the Index tab.
   b. Type "search" as your keyword.
   c. Scroll down to the entry "searching the Web" in the index list, then double-click it.
   d. In the Topics Found dialog box, double-click "Finding the information you want."
   e. Read about searching the Web.
   f. Close the Microsoft Internet Explorer Help window.

6. **Print a Web page.**
   a. Open the Web page www.buckinghamgate.com using the Address bar.
   b. Print the first page only.

7. **Search for information on the Internet.**
   a. Open the Search Assistant in the Search Explorer bar.
   b. Type any keyword or phrase for which you would like to find information, then execute the search.
   c. Explore some of the hyperlinks you find and some of the documents that open.
   d. When you finish reviewing the documents you find, close the Search Explorer bar.

8. **Exit Internet Explorer.**
   a. Exit Internet Explorer.

# ► Independent Challenges

**1.** You will soon graduate with a degree in business communications. Before entering the workforce, you want to be sure that you are up to date on recent advances in your field. You decide that checking the Web will provide the most current information. In addition, you can research potential companies for employment opportunities. Use Internet Explorer to open the All Business Network home page at www.all-biz.com. Select a promising site, and then click the Print button to print the page.

**2.** You leave tomorrow for a business trip to Toyko, Japan. You want to be sure that you take the right clothes for the weather and decide that the best place to check weather conditions is the Web. Open two of the following weather sites to determine the weather in Toyko at this time of the year. Use the Print command to print the weather report for Tokyo from two sites.

| | |
|---|---|
| The Weather Channel | www.weather.com |
| CNN Weather | www.cnn.com/WEATHER |
| Yahoo Weather | weather.yahoo.com |

**3.** You work at a newspaper company, and your manager wants to buy a new desktop computer. She assigns you the task of investigating her options. You decide that using the Web is more expedient than traveling to various computer stores. Access the following computer company Web sites, and print a page from the Web site that offers the best deals on prices, service, and shipping options.

| | |
|---|---|
| CompUSA | www.compusa.com |
| Apple | www.apple.com |
| Dell | www.dell.com |

**4.** A recent newspaper article you read listed the URLs of some popular search engines. To compare these search engines, create a chart showing the results of searching for the word "floptical." List each search engine and the number of hits in your chart. Why do you think that each search engine provides different results?

| | |
|---|---|
| Yahoo | www.yahoo.com |
| AltaVista | www.altavista.com |
| Excite | www.excite.com |

Internet

# ▶ Visual Workshop

Use the Search Assistant to find and print the Web page shown in Figure A-17. (*Hint*: Add quotation marks to your search string, for example: "NASA Observatorium Earth Science".)

**FIGURE A-17**

# Getting
## Started with Word 2000

### Objectives

- ► **Define word processing software**
- ► **Start Word 2000**
- ► **View the Word program window**
- ► **Create a document**
- ⌐MOUS⌐ ► **Save a document**
- ⌐MOUS⌐ ► **Preview and print a document**
- ⌐MOUS⌐ ► **Get Help**
- ► **Close a document and exit Word**

Welcome to Microsoft Word 2000. Microsoft Word is a powerful computer program that helps you create documents that communicate your ideas clearly and effectively. It includes sophisticated tools for editing text, creating tables and graphics, formatting pages, and proofing a document, to name just a few of its features. The lessons in this unit introduce you to the basic features of Word and familiarize you with the Word environment as you create a new document. ◄── Karen Rosen is the director of human resources at MediaLoft, a nationwide chain of bookstore cafés selling books, videos, and CDs. Karen's responsibilities include communicating with employees about company policies and benefits. She uses Word to create attractive and professional-looking documents.

**Word 2000**

# Defining Word Processing Software

Microsoft Word is a full-featured word processing program. A **word processing program** is a software program that allows you to create attractive and professional-looking documents quickly and easily. Word processing offers many advantages over typing. The information you type in a word processing document is stored electronically on your computer, so it is easy to revise text and reuse it in other documents. Editing tools allow you to insert and delete text, move information from one part of a document to another, and check spelling and grammar. In addition, you can enhance your documents by changing the appearance of text, adding lines or graphics, and creating tables. Figure A-1 illustrates some of the word processing features you can use to create and enhance your documents using Word.

### Word allows you to:

### Enter and revise text
Using Word's editing tools, you can easily enter and delete text, insert new text in the middle of a sentence, undo a change, and find and replace text throughout a document.

### Copy and move text without retyping
You can copy or move text from one part of a document to another part of the same document, or from one document to a different document.

### Locate and correct spelling mistakes and errors in grammar
Word's proofreading tools identify misspelled words and grammatical errors in your documents. You can correct the mistakes yourself or allow Word to suggest a correction.

### Format text and design pages
By formatting the text and pages in your document to highlight important ideas, you can create documents that convey your message more effectively to your readers. In Word you can change the size and appearance of text, create bulleted or numbered lists, apply formatting styles, and add borders and shading to words and paragraphs. You can also organize text in columns, change margins, line spacing, and paragraph alignment, and adjust tabs and indents

### Align text in rows and columns using tables
You can create tables in Word to present information in an easy-to-read grid of rows and columns. You can format the tables to emphasize important points, and use the information contained in Word tables to create charts and graphs.

### Enhance the appearance of a document using images, lines, and shapes
Word's graphic tools make it easy to illustrate your documents with graphic elements. You can draw lines and shapes, add color, and insert photographs and professionally-designed images into your documents.

### Use Mail Merge to personalize form letters and create mailing labels
Mail merge allows you to customize form letters when you need to send the same letter to many different people. When you perform a mail merge, you merge a standard letter with a separate list of names and addresses. Mail merges are useful for creating labels and for sending frequent correspondence to the same group of people.

**FIGURE A-1: Features of a word processing document**

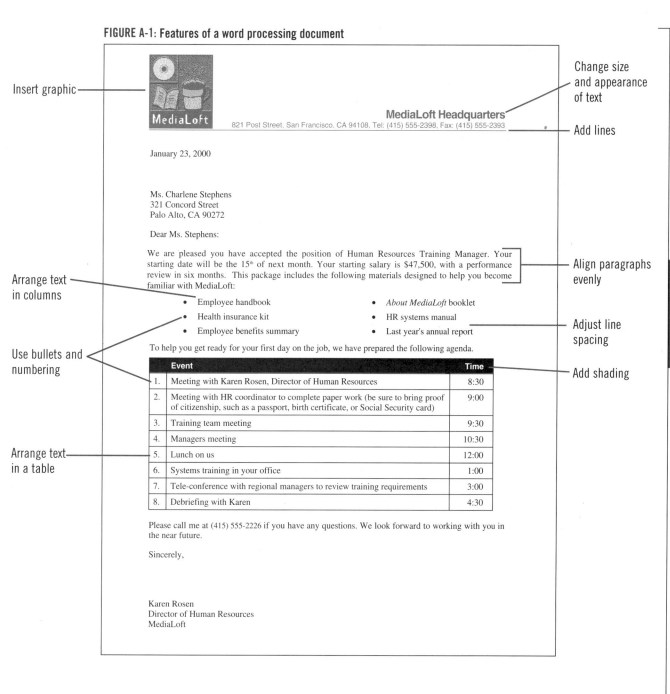

Insert graphic

Change size and appearance of text

Add lines

MediaLoft Headquarters
821 Post Street, San Francisco, CA 94108, Tel: (415) 555-2398, Fax: (415) 555-2393

January 23, 2000

Ms. Charlene Stephens
321 Concord Street
Palo Alto, CA 90272

Dear Ms. Stephens:

We are pleased you have accepted the position of Human Resources Training Manager. Your starting date will be the 15th of next month. Your starting salary is $47,500, with a performance review in six months. This package includes the following materials designed to help you become familiar with MediaLoft:

Align paragraphs evenly

Arrange text in columns

- Employee handbook
- Health insurance kit
- Employee benefits summary

- *About MediaLoft* booklet
- HR systems manual
- Last year's annual report

Adjust line spacing

Use bullets and numbering

To help you get ready for your first day on the job, we have prepared the following agenda.

Add shading

| | Event | Time |
|---|---|---|
| 1. | Meeting with Karen Rosen, Director of Human Resources | 8:30 |
| 2. | Meeting with HR coordinator to complete paper work (be sure to bring proof of citizenship, such as a passport, birth certificate, or Social Security card) | 9:00 |
| 3. | Training team meeting | 9:30 |
| 4. | Managers meeting | 10:30 |
| 5. | Lunch on us | 12:00 |
| 6. | Systems training in your office | 1:00 |
| 7. | Tele-conference with regional managers to review training requirements | 3:00 |
| 8. | Debriefing with Karen | 4:30 |

Arrange text in a table

Please call me at (415) 555-2226 if you have any questions. We look forward to working with you in the near future.

Sincerely,

Karen Rosen
Director of Human Resources
MediaLoft

**Word 2000**

# Starting Word 2000

To start Word, you must first start Windows by turning on your computer. You can start Word on your computer by clicking the Start button on the taskbar, pointing to Programs, and then clicking Microsoft Word on the Programs menu. The Programs menu displays the list of programs installed on your computer, so you can start any program this way. Because computer systems have different setups depending on the hardware and software installed, your procedure for starting Word might be different from the one described below, especially if your computer is part of a network. See your instructor or technical support person if you need assistance. ✎ MediaLoft has just installed Word 2000 on the computers in the Human Resources department. Karen starts Word to familiarize herself with the program.

## Steps

1. **Make sure Windows is open, then click the Start button** 🔲Start **on the taskbar**
   The Start menu appears on the desktop.

2. **Point to Programs on the Start menu**
   The Programs menu opens, as shown in Figure A-2. Your list of programs will depend on the programs installed on your computer.

> **Trouble?**
> If an Office Assistant dialog balloon appears, click Start using Microsoft Word.

3. **Click Microsoft Word on the Programs menu**
   When you start Word, the **Word program window** opens in the most recently used view. **Views** are different ways of displaying a document in Word. Figure A-3 shows the Word program window in Normal view. The lessons in this unit assume you are using Normal view. The Office Assistant may also appear in your program window. The **Office Assistant** is an animated character that appears periodically to provide tips as you work in Word.

> **QuickTip**
> An indented button indicates that a feature is turned on.

4. **Click the Normal View button** 🔲 **in the lower-left corner of the program window if it is not already indented, as shown in Figure A-3**
   The document window changes to Normal view. The blinking vertical line | at the left edge of the document window is called the **insertion point.** It indicates where text will appear when you begin typing. When you start Word, you can enter text and create a new document right away.

5. **Move the mouse pointer around in the Word program window**
   The mouse pointer changes shape depending on where it is in the Word program window. When the mouse pointer is in the document window in Normal view, the pointer changes to an **I-beam** ⌶. Table A-1 describes other Word mouse pointers.

> **Trouble?**
> If the Office Assistant does not appear, continue with Step 8.

6. **If the Office Assistant appears in your program window, move the pointer over the Office Assistant, then click the right mouse button**
   Right-clicking displays a pop-up menu of commands related to the item you click. You can choose to hide the Office Assistant until you want to get help with Word.

7. **Click Hide on the pop-up menu**
   The Office Assistant disappears from the window.

> **Trouble?**
> See your instructor or technical support person for assistance.

8. **Click Tools on the menu bar, click Customize, click the Options tab in the Customize dialog box, click Reset my usage data to restore the default settings, click Yes in the alert box, then click Close**
   You'll learn about restoring default settings for toolbars and menus in the next lesson.

**FIGURE A-2: Starting Word from the desktop**

Displays programs on your computer (your list of programs may be different)

Your taskbar may be different

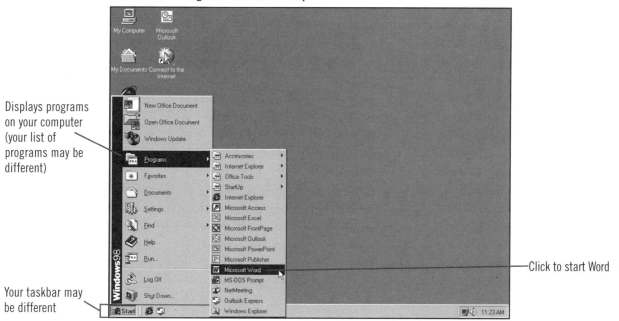

Click to start Word

**FIGURE A-3: Word program window in Normal view**

Insertion point

I-beam pointer

Document window

Normal View button

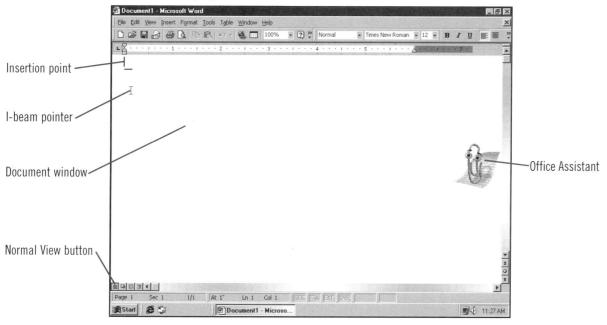

Office Assistant

**ABLE A-1: Pointers in Word**

| pointer | description |
|---|---|
| I | Appears in the document window when working in Normal, Web Layout, and Outline views; use to move the insertion point in the document, or to select text to edit |
| I≡ | Appears in the document window when working in Print Layout view; use to move the insertion point in the document or to select text to edit |
| ⌐ | Appears when you point to a menu, toolbar, ruler, status bar, or other areas that are not part of the document window; use to click a button, menu command, or other element of the Word program window |
| ⌐ | Appears when you point to the left edge of a line of text; use to select a line or lines of text |
| ⌐? | Appears when you click the What's This command on the Help menu; click this pointer over text to view the format settings applied to the text, or click an element of the Word program window or a dialog box to view information about that tool, option, or feature |

# Viewing the Word Program Window

When you start Word, the Word program window opens with a new, blank document in the document window. Refer to your screen and Figure A-4 as you locate the elements of the Word program window described below.

## Details

Trouble?

If your Word program window does not fill your screen, click the Maximize button 🔲 on the title bar.

 The **title bar** displays the name of the document and the name of the program. Until you save the document and give it a name, its temporary name is Document1.

 The **menu bar** lists the names of the menus that contain Word commands. Clicking a menu name displays a list of commands from which you can choose. When you open a menu, you may at first see a short list of commonly used commands. After the menu remains open for a few seconds, additional commands appear on the menu. Menus stay open until you point to another menu, click outside the menu, or press [Esc].

 The **toolbar** contains buttons for the most frequently used commands. Clicking buttons on a toolbar is often faster than using menu commands. By default, there are actually two toolbars in this row. The **Standard toolbar** (on the left) contains buttons for the most commonly used operational commands, such as opening, saving, and printing documents. The **Formatting toolbar** (on the right) contains buttons for the most frequently used formatting commands, such as changing font type and size, applying bold to text, or aligning text. Not all the buttons on the Standard and Formatting toolbars are visible on the screen. To view other buttons, click the **More Buttons button** 🔽 at the right end of each toolbar. Throughout the lessons in this book, you will need to remember to click the More Buttons button if a button you are instructed to click is not visible on your screen. When you use a button from the More Buttons list, Word adds it to your visible toolbar. That's why each user's toolbars look unique. You can return your toolbars to their original state by resetting your usage data. Be sure to read the Clues to Use in this lesson to learn more about working with Word's toolbars. Word also includes toolbars related to other features, such as a toolbar that contains drawing tools.

 The **horizontal ruler** displays tab settings, left and right paragraph indents, and document margins.

 The **document window** is the area where you type text and format and organize the content of your documents. The blinking insertion point is the location where text appears when you type.

 The **vertical and horizontal scroll bars** display the relative position of the text displayed in the document window. You use the scroll bars and **scroll boxes** to view different parts of your document.

 The **view buttons**, which appear in the horizontal scroll bar, allow you to display the document in one of four views: Normal, Web Layout, Print Layout, and Outline. Each view offers features that are useful for working on different types of documents.

 The **status bar** displays the current page number, section number, total number of pages in the document, and the position of the insertion point (in inches, in lines, and in columns, from the upper-left corner of the document).

 **ScreenTips** appear when you place the pointer over a toolbar button or some other element of the Word program window. A ScreenTip is a label that identifies the name of the button or feature.

FIGURE A-4: Elements of the Word program window

Title bar
Menu bar
Standard toolbar (your toolbar buttons may be different)
Horizontal ruler
ScreenTip
More Buttons button on the Standard toolbar
Document window

More Buttons button on the Formatting toolbar
Scroll box
Formatting toolbar (your toolbar buttons may be different)
Divider between Standard and Formatting toolbars

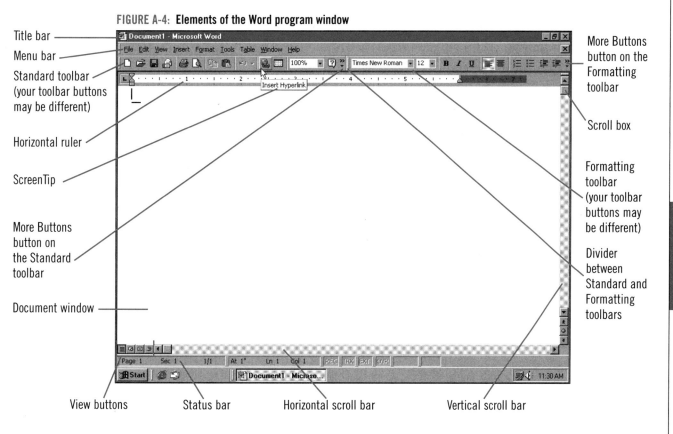

View buttons
Status bar
Horizontal scroll bar
Vertical scroll bar

## Personalized toolbars and menus in Word 2000

Word toolbars and menus modify themselves to your working style. The Standard and Formatting toolbars you see when you first start Word include the most frequently used buttons. To locate a button not visible on a toolbar, click the More Buttons button ⁇ on the Standard or Formatting toolbar to see the list of additional toolbar buttons. As you work, Word adds the buttons you use to the visible toolbars, and moves the buttons you haven't used in a while to the More Buttons list. Similarly, Word menus adjust to your work habits, so that the commands you use most often automatically appear on shortened menus. Click the double arrow at the bottom of a menu to view additional menu commands. You can return toolbars and menus to their default settings by clicking Tools on the menu bar, then clicking Customize. On the

Options tab in the Customize dialog box, click Reset my usage data. An alert box or the Office Assistant appears asking if you are sure you want to do this. Click Yes, then click Close in the Customize dialog box. Resetting your usage data erases changes made automatically to your menus and toolbars. It does not affect the options you set yourself. The lessons in this book assume you are using personalized menus and toolbars, but you can also turn off this feature if you'd like, so that your Standard and Formatting toolbars appear on separate rows, and your menus display the full list of commands. To turn off these features, remove the checks from the Standard and Formatting toolbars share one row and the Menus show recently used commands first checkboxes in the Customize dialog box, then click Close.

**Word 2000**

# Creating a Document

You can begin a new document by simply typing text in the document window. Entering text with a word processor is different from typing with a typewriter. When you reach the end of a line as you type with Word, the insertion point moves to the next line. This feature is called **wordwrap**. You need to press [Enter] only when you want to insert a new line or start a new paragraph. After typing text, you can edit it by inserting new text or by deleting text you want to remove. When you insert or delete text, Word adjusts the spacing of the existing text. Karen uses Word to type a letter offering an internship to Alice Anderson. She begins her letter with the date, then types the inside address, salutation, body, and closing.

## Steps

**Trouble?**

If you type the wrong letter, press [Backspace] to erase the incorrect letter, then type again.

**1.** Type **today's date**, starting with the month (for example, January 21, 2000)

As you type the space after the name of the month, notice that Word's AutoComplete feature displays today's date. You can ignore AutoComplete for now and continue typing the date.

**2.** Press **[Enter]** four times

The first time you press [Enter], the insertion point moves to the start of the next line. Each time you press [Enter] again, you create blank lines.

**3.** Type the following text, pressing **[Enter]** after each line as indicated:

**Ms. Alice Anderson [Enter]**
**456 Goodview Lane [Enter]**
**Palo Alto, CA 90272 [Enter] [Enter]**
**Dear Alice: [Enter] [Enter]**

If you see the Office Assistant, click Cancel in the Office Assistant dialog balloon. If you see a wavy, red line under words it means that these words are not in Word's dictionary and might be misspelled. You can ignore the wavy lines for now. Don't worry if you make typing errors. You can fix them after you finish typing the letter.

**QuickTip**

Word processing programs have made it unnecessary to type two spaces after a period. Typing one space provides enough space after a period to separate sentences because the space is automatically adjusted by the word processing software.

**4.** Type the following, pressing **[Enter]** twice at the end of the paragraph as indicated:

**We are pleased to offer you an internship at MediaLoft. Your experience with Microsoft Office was a major factor in deciding to hire you. Please call my office at (415) 555-2221 to discuss the details. We look forward to working with you this year. [Enter] [Enter]**

**5.** Type **Sincerely**, press **[Enter]** four times, then type your name

Your letter should resemble Figure A-5. Don't be concerned if your text wraps differently than the text shown in the figure. Text wrapping can depend on your monitor or printer. Now that you have finished typing the letter, you can edit it by inserting and deleting text as necessary.

**6.** Position the pointer $\underline{\text{I}}$ after the word **an** (but before the space) in the first sentence then click to place the insertion point

The insertion point is now located between the words "an" and "internship" in the first sentence. Anything you type will be added to the document here.

**Trouble?**

If your typing overwrites existing text, double-click OVR in the status bar to switch back to Insert mode. See your instructor or technical support person for assistance.

**7.** Press **[Backspace]**, press **[Spacebar]**, then type **professional**

Pressing [Backspace] removes the character before the insertion point.

**8.** Place the insertion point between **2** and **1** in the third sentence, press **[Delete]** to remove the character **1**, then type **6**

Pressing [Delete] removes the character after the insertion point. Fix your other typing mistakes using [Backspace] or [Delete], then compare your document to Figure A-6. You'll learn how to save your new document in the next lesson.

FIGURE A-5: Text in a Word document

Blank lines between paragraphs

Red, wavy line indicates an unrecognized word

Text automatically wraps to next line

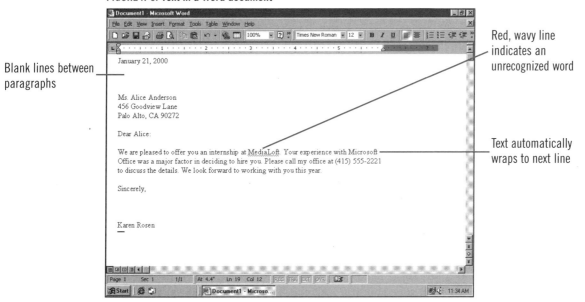

FIGURE A-6: Edited document

New text

Deleted character and inserted text

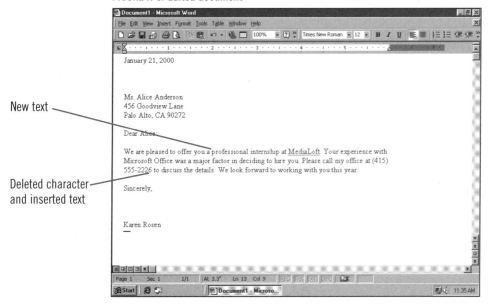

## Working with AutoCorrect

Certain kinds of spelling or typographical errors are automatically corrected as you type. This feature is called **AutoCorrect**. For example, Word corrects some common spelling mistakes (such as typing "adn" instead of "and") as soon as you type the first space or punctuation mark after the word. Similarly, if you type two uppercase letters in a row, the second character is automatically changed to lowercase as you continue typing (except in a state's abbreviation, such as "WA"). If Word makes a correction that you do not want to use, click the Undo button 🔄 on the Standard toolbar. If you type a word that is not in Word's dictionary, the word is underlined with a red, wavy line to indicate it may be misspelled. If you make a possible grammatical error, the error is underlined with a green, wavy line. Right-click red- or green-underlined text to display a pop-up menu of correction options, then click a correction to accept it and remove the underlining.

**Word 2000**

# Saving a Document

When you create a document, the text you enter and the changes you make are only temporarily stored in your computer. To store a document permanently so that you can retrieve and edit it in the future, you must **save** your document to your computer's internal hard disk or to a floppy disk. Documents are saved as **files** on your computer. When you save a document you give it a name, called a **filename**. It's helpful to give your documents brief filenames that describe the contents of the document. It's also a good idea to save your work soon after starting. After saving a document for the first time, save it again every 10 or 15 minutes and always save before printing. When you save after making changes, the document file is updated to reflect your latest revisions. You can save a document using the Save button on the Standard toolbar or the Save command on the File menu. ✏️ Karen saves her letter to Alice Anderson with the filename Intern Offer Letter.

**Steps 1234**

**1.** Insert your Project Disk in the appropriate drive, then click the **Save button** 💾 on the Standard toolbar

The first time you save a document the Save As dialog box opens, as shown in Figure A-7. In this dialog box, you assign a name to the document (replacing the default filename) and indicate the location where you want the file to be stored. The default filename is based on the first few words of the document, in this case today's date.

**2.** Type **Intern Offer Letter** in the File name text box

The name of the current drive or folder appears in the Save in list box. You want to save the file to your Project Disk.

**QuickTip**

This book assumes your Project Disk is in drive A. Substitute the correct drive if this is not the case. See your instructor or technical support person for assistance.

**3.** Click the **Save in list arrow**, then click the drive that contains your Project Disk

Your Save As dialog box should resemble Figure A-8.

**4.** Click **Save**

The document is saved with the name "Intern Offer Letter" on your Project Disk. Notice that the new name of the document appears in the title bar. Depending on your computer's settings in Windows Explorer, the filename in your title bar may include the DOC extension after the period. All Word documents automatically include this extension to help you distinguish Word documents from other files on your disks. Once you save a document as a file, you can continue to work on it in Word, or you can close it. If you continue to work on a file, you should save it again every 10 or 15 minutes and before you close it.

**CLUES TO USE**

### Using the AutoRecover feature

The AutoRecover feature in Word automatically saves your document every few minutes in a temporary file, so that all your work is not lost in case of an interruption to power or some other problem that abruptly stops Word. If Word shuts down unexpectedly, a temporary version of the document you were working on opens automatically the next time you start Word. You can then save the temporary document with a filename and continue to work on it. AutoRecover is not a substitute for using the Save command frequently, so be sure to save a new document right away and to save often. To change how often AutoRecover saves a document, click Tools on the menu bar, click Options, change the number of minutes on the Save tab, then click OK.

FIGURE A-7: Save As dialog box

Save in list box
displays the active
folder or drive

Save in list arrow
changes the active
folder or drive

Default filename

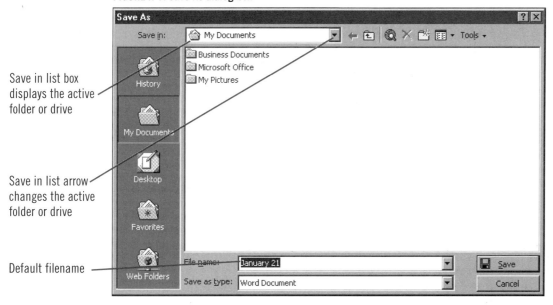

FIGURE A-8: File to be saved to the A drive

Location of Project
Disk (yours may be
different)

Your Project Disk
may contain files
listed here

New filename

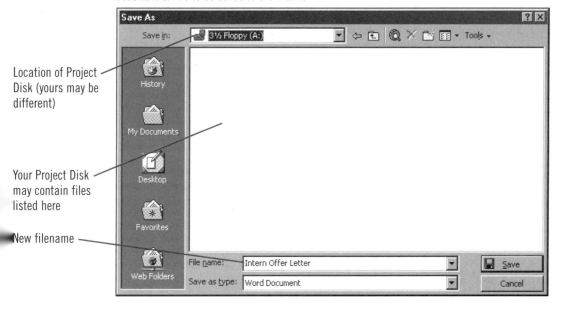

# Previewing and Printing a Document

After saving your document, you can quickly print it by clicking the Print button on the Standard toolbar. When you use the Print button, you print the document using the default print settings. To print a specific page of a document or to choose other printing options, use the Print command on the File menu. Before printing, however, it is good practice to preview the document to see exactly what it will look like when it is printed. When you preview a document you can magnify the page to make it easier to read the text. ▬▬ Karen previews, then prints her letter.

## Steps 1 2 3 4

**Trouble?**

If 🔍 does not appear on your Standard toolbar, click the More Buttons button ≫ to view additional toolbar buttons.

**1. Click the Print Preview button** 🔍 **on the Standard toolbar**

The document appears in the Print Preview window as it will look when it is printed, as shown in Figure A-9.

**2. Move the pointer over the page until it changes to ⊕ , then click the letter**

Clicking with ⊕ magnifies the document in the Print Preview window, allowing you to read the text. When the document is magnified the pointer changes to ⊖ . Clicking with ⊖ reduces the size of the document in the Print Preview window.

**QuickTip**

Click the Print button 🖨 on the Print Preview toolbar to print the document directly from Print Preview.

**3. Examine your letter for mistakes, then click the Close Preview button** Close **on the Print Preview toolbar**

Print Preview closes and the letter appears in the document window. After fixing any mistakes you noticed in Print Preview, you are ready to print your document. You should always save a document right before printing it.

**4. Click File on the menu bar, then click Save**

Any changes you made to the document since the last time you saved it are saved. You can also click the Save button 🖫 on the Standard toolbar or press [Ctrl][S] to save changes.

**Trouble?**

If you are not connected to a printer, ask your instructor or technical support person for assistance.

**5. Click File on the menu bar, then click Print**

The Print dialog box opens, as shown in Figure A-10. The settings in your Print dialog box might be different, depending on your printer. Table A-2 describes some of the options in the Print dialog box.

**6. Click OK**

Clicking OK closes the Print dialog box and prints your document. You can also use the Print button 🖨 on the Standard toolbar to print the document using the default settings.

**TABLE A-2: Options in the Print dialog box**

| print option | use to |
|---|---|
| **Printer Name** | Change the current printer |
| **Properties** | Display the printer's Properties dialog box; use it to change settings for the size or type of paper in your printer, the orientation of the paper, the resolution you want your printer to use, and other printer properties |
| **Page range** | Indicate what pages of a document to print |
| **Copies** | Specify the number of copies to print, and whether or not you want the copies to be collated |
| **Zoom** | Specify the number of pages you want to print on each sheet of paper |
| **Print what** | Select which aspect of a document to print, such as the document itself (the default) or other associated text |
| **Print** | Specify the portion of the document you want to print |

**FIGURE A-9: Print Preview window**

Magnifier button

Zoom list arrow
changes the
size of the doc-
ument in the
window

Close Preview
button

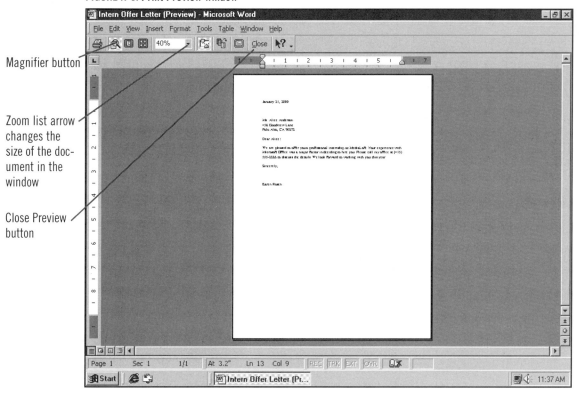

**FIGURE A-10: Print dialog box**

Default printer
(your printer may
be different)

Select the range of
pages to print here

Opens the
Properties dialog
box for the printer

Changes the
number of copies
to print

Prints the
document

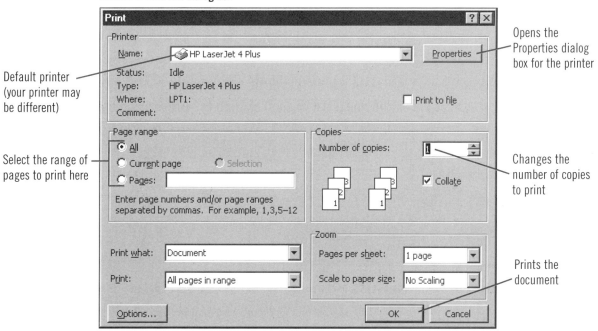

Word 2000

# Getting Help

Word includes an extensive Help system that provides information and instructions about Word features and commands. You can use Help to get as little or as much information as you need, from quick definitions of unfamiliar terms to detailed steps for completing a procedure. The **Office Assistant**, an animated character that provides tips while you are working in Word, is one way to get help. You can also use the Office Assistant to display Help information and discover new features. You can also use the commands on the Help menu, described in Table A-3. Karen uses Help to learn about previewing a document.

1. Click the **Microsoft Word Help button** 🔁 on the Standard toolbar
   The Office Assistant appears, as shown in Figure A-11. Your assistant may look different. In the Office Assistant dialog ballon, you can enter key words or whole questions for which you would like more information.

2. Type **preview documents**, then click **Search**
   The Office Assistant displays topics related to previewing documents.

3. Click **Preview a document before printing**
   The Microsoft Word Help window opens, as shown in Figure A-12. Read the information on previewing a document before you continue. The underlined text in the Help window indicates a link to a related topic.

4. Place the pointer over the underlined topic **edit text in print preview** until the pointer changes to 🖑, then click
   A new Help window opens displaying the steps for editing text in print preview.

5. Click the **Magnifier button** 🔍 in the Help window
   A pop-up description of this button opens. Read the description before you continue.

6. Click the description to close it, then click the **Show button** 📑 on the Help window toolbar
   The Help window expands and displays the Contents, Answer Wizard, and Index tabs. These tabs offer additional methods for searching and accessing Help topics.

7. Click the **Close button** in the Help window to return to Word

8. Click **Help** on the menu bar, then click **Hide the Office Assistant**
   Selecting Hide the Office Assistant hides it temporarily; it will reappear later to give you tips. To turn off the Office Assistant completely, right-click the Assistant, click Options, and deselect the Use the Office Assistant checkbox.

## Using the Contents, Index, and Answer Wizard tabs to get Help

The Contents, Index, and Answer Wizard tabs offer different methods for searching Word's Help system. Use the Contents tab as you would use a table of contents in a book. Scroll through the list of general topics to find the topic that best relates to the topic that interests you, then click the plus sign next to each closed book icon to display a list of subtopics in that topic. Click a subtopic to display information about it in the Help window. The Answer Wizard tab works like the Office Assistant: type a question (or even just the name of the feature you want to learn about), then click Search to display information about your question in the Help window. Use the Index tab to search for topics that relate to a keyword. Type your keyword in the first box, click Search, then double-click the keyword in the second box that best describes your topic. In the third box, click the topic you want to view in the Help window.

FIGURE A-11: Word's Office Assistant

Microsoft Word
Help button

Help topics (your
list of topics may be
different)

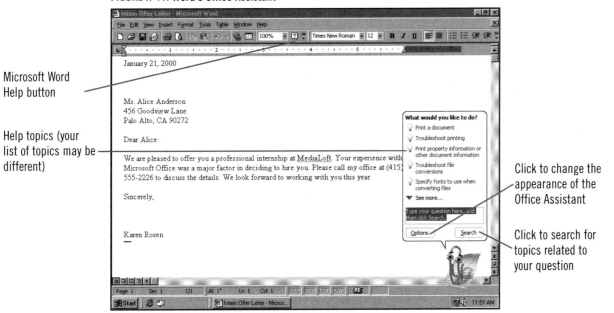

Click to change the
appearance of the
Office Assistant

Click to search for
topics related to
your question

FIGURE A-12: Microsoft Word Help window

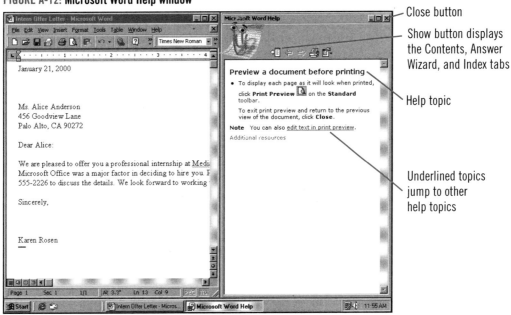

Close button

Show button displays
the Contents, Answer
Wizard, and Index tabs

Help topic

Underlined topics
jump to other
help topics

TABLE A-3: Help menu options

| help menu option | function |
| --- | --- |
| Microsoft Word Help | Opens the Office Assistant if the Office Assistant is turned on; opens the Microsoft Word Help window if the Office Assistant is turned off |
| Show/Hide the Office Assistant | Opens/closes the Office Assistant |
| What's This? | Changes the mouse pointer to ⟨?; click a button or menu option to view a brief explanation |
| Office on the Web | Connects to Microsoft's Web site, where you can find additional information and articles; you must be connected to the Internet to use this option |
| About Microsoft Word | Provides the version and Product ID of Word |

Word 2000

# Closing a Document and Exiting Word

After you save your work on a document, you can close the document. Closing a document removes the document window from the Word program window, but it does not close Word. You should save and close all open documents before exiting Word. Exiting Word closes all open files and the Word program window. You can use the Close and Exit commands on the File menu to close a document and exit Word, or you can use the Close buttons on the menu bar and title bar, as shown in Figure A-13. Table A-4 describes the Close and Exit commands. Karen closes her letter and then exits Word.

**QuickTip**

You can also close a document by clicking the Close Window button on the menu bar.

**1.** Click **File** on the menu bar, then click **Close**

If you saved your document before closing it, the document window closes immediately. If you did not save your changes before closing it, an alert box or the Office Assistant opens, asking if you want to save your changes.

**2.** Click **Yes**, if necessary

The Word program window remains open, as shown in Figure A-14. After you close a document you can use the menus and toolbars to create a new document or to open an existing Word document, or you can exit Word.

**QuickTip**

You can also exit Word by clicking the Close button on the title bar.

**3.** Click **File** on the menu bar, then click **Exit**

The Word program window closes.

TABLE A-4: The Close and Exit commands

| command | function |
| --- | --- |
| **Close** | Closes the current document; leaves Word open so that you can open another document or use Help |
| **Exit** | Closes all open Word files; closes the Word program window and returns you to the Windows desktop |

**FIGURE A-13:** Closing the document and program windows

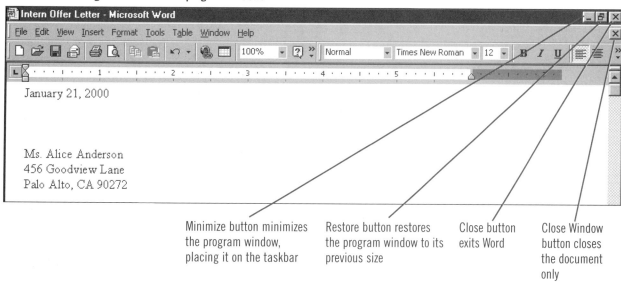

Minimize button minimizes the program window, placing it on the taskbar

Restore button restores the program window to its previous size

Close button exits Word

Close Window button closes the document only

**FIGURE A-14:** Word program window with no documents open

# Practice

## ► Concepts Review

Label each element of the Word program window shown in Figure A-15.

FIGURE A-15

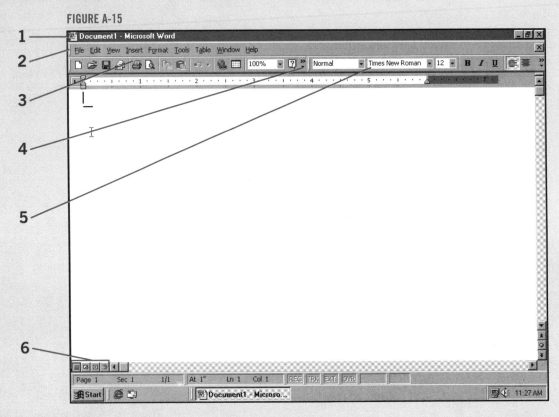

1
2
3
4
5
6

Match each term with the statement that describes it.

7. **Standard toolbar**     a. The part of the Word program window in which you enter text
8. **Formatting toolbar**   b. Identifies the location of the insertion point
9. **Document window**      c. Contains buttons for commands such as Save and Print
10. **Ruler**               d. Changes the spelling of misspelled words as you type
11. **Status bar**          e. Displays tab settings and paragraph and document margins
12. **AutoCorrect**         f. Provides tips and information about using Word
13. **More Buttons button** g. Contains buttons for commands that change the appearance of text
14. **Office Assistant**    h. Displays buttons not currently visible on the toolbar

## Select the best answer from the list of choices.

**15. How is word processing different from typing with a typewriter?**
   **a.** Word processors allow you to enter new text in the middle of a sentence
   **b.** Word processors use word wrap
   **c.** Word processors automatically adjust the spacing between characters
   **d.** All of the above

**16. To view a document as it will look when printed, you**
   **a.** Click File on the menu bar, then click Print.
   **b.** Click the Normal View button on the horizontal scroll bar.
   **c.** Click the Print Preview button on the Standard toolbar.
   **d.** Click View on the menu bar, then click Document Map.

**17. You can get Help in any of the following ways, except**
   **a.** Viewing topics on the Contents tab.
   **b.** Double-clicking anywhere in the document window.
   **c.** Clicking the Microsoft Word Help button on the Standard toolbar.
   **d.** Clicking Help on the menu bar.

**18. The Close command on the File menu**
   **a.** Closes Word without saving any changes.
   **b.** If you have made changes to the document, asks if you want to save them, then closes the document.
   **c.** Closes all open Word documents.
   **d.** Closes the document without saving changes.

**19. To close the Word program window, you must**
   **a.** Click File on the menu bar, then click Close.
   **b.** Click the Exit button on the Standard toolbar.
   **c.** Click File on the menu bar, then click Exit.
   **d.** Click the Close Window button on the menu bar.

**20. The Standard toolbar does not include**
   **a.** The Save button.
   **b.** The More Buttons button.
   **c.** The Bold button.
   **d.** The Print button.

**Skills Review**

1. **Start Word 2000.**
   a. Click the Start button on the Windows taskbar.
   b. Click Microsoft Word on the Programs menu.
   c. Click the Normal View button if necessary.
   d. Hide the Office Assistant if it appears.
   e. Reset your usage data to return your toolbars and menus to the default settings. (*Hint*: Click Tools on the menu bar, click Customize, click the Options tab in the Customize dialog box, click Reset my usage data, click Yes, then click Close.

2. **View the Word program window.**
   a. Identify as many elements of the Word program window as you can.
   b. Click each menu and drag the pointer through all the commands on each menu.
   c. Point to each button on the toolbars and read the ScreenTips.
   d. Click the More Buttons buttons on the Standard and Formatting toolbars and read the ScreenTips for the buttons on the More Buttons lists.

3. **Create a document.**
   a. Begin a short letter to your local newspaper. Type today's date.
   b. In the inside address, type "Editor," the name of the paper, a street address, and the city, state, and zip code. Make up the information if you don't know it.
   c. For a salutation, type "To Whom It May Concern:" (If the Office Assistant appears, click Cancel.)
   d. In the body of the letter, state that you are interested in a career in journalism, and mention that you have strong Word 2000 skills. Request an informational interview with the editors to learn more about working for newpapers.
   e. For a closing, type "Sincerly," press [Enter] four times, then type your name. (Notice that Word corrects your typing for you.)
   f. Insert the sentence "I can be reached at 555-3030." after the last sentence in your letter.
   g. Correct any spelling and grammatical mistakes you made as you typed the letter. (*Hint*: Use the [Backspace] or [Delete] key to correct your typing.)
   h. Using the [Backspace] key, change the inside address to:
   Ms. Alexandra Thomas
   Hamilton Transcript
   35 Conval Street
   Hamilton, NH 02468
   i. Using the [Delete] key, change the salutation to "Dear Ms. Thomas:"

4. **Save a document.**
   a. Click File on the menu bar, then click Save.
   b. Save the document on your Project Disk with the filename "Information Letter."
   c. Change the date on the letter to tomorrow's date.
   d. Save your changes to the letter.

5. **Preview and print a document.**
   a. Click the Print Preview button on the Standard toolbar.
   b. Click to zoom in on the document in Print Preview, then proofread the letter.
   c. Click to zoom out on the document and then close Print Preview.
   d. Print a copy of the letter using the default print settings. (*Hint:* Don't forget to save the document before you print it.)

6. **Get Help.**
   a. Click the Microsoft Word Help button on the Standard toolbar.
   b. Type "Print" in the Office Assistant dialog balloon, then click Search.
   c. Click Print a document, and read about printing more than one copy at a time. (*Hint:* Click "See More" in the dialog balloon if necessary.)
   d. Click the Show button, then type "How do I print a help topic?" on the Answer Wizard tab.
   e. Read about printing a help topic, then close the Help window.
   f. Hide the Office Assistant.

7. **Close a document and exit Word.**
   a. Close the Information Letter document, saving your changes if necessary.
   b. Exit Word.

# ► Independent Challenges

**1.** Your company's employee newsletter includes a technology question-and-answer page. This month you have been asked to write a short article about using Word's toolbars for the page. You consult the Help system to learn more about toolbars before writing your essay.

To complete this independent challenge:

a. Start Word.
b. Use the Office Assistant to search Help for information about using toolbars.
c. Write a brief essay that provides a definition of a toolbar, identifies the two default toolbars, and explains how to display a button that is not visible on a toolbar.
d. Type your name at the top of the document.
e. Proofread your document and correct any errors.
f. Save the document on your Project Disk with the filename "Toolbar Article," then preview and print the document.

**2.** As a co-chair for the Lake City High School class reunion planning committee, you are responsible for recruiting classmates to help with reunion activities. Four reunion subcommittees need volunteers:

- The entertainment committee, which arranges for music, hall rental, and prizes, and organizes different reunion weekend events.
- The hospitality committee, which arranges for lodging discounts and deals with spouses and children of alumni.
- The meals committee, which works with the entertainment committee to coordinate meals at each event.
- The transportation committee, which addresses the logistical issues of transporting alumni to and from airports and to and from reunion events.

Using Word, draft a letter to your fellow alumni asking for volunteers for the four subcommittees.
  To complete this independent challenge:

**a.** Start Word and create a document called "Reunion 2000 Letter" on your Project Disk.
**b.** Type today's date. For the inside address, type any name and address you wish, then add a salutation, such as "Dear Fellow Alum:".
**c.** In the first paragraph, describe the responsibilities of the reunion committee and your need for volunteers.
**d.** In the next paragraph, describe the responsibilities of each of the subcommittees.
**e.** In the final body paragraph, include one more plea to encourage people to sign up, and give instructions for contacting you.
**f.** Include your name and phone number in the closing.
**g.** Correct all spelling and grammatical errors.
**h.** Save your changes, then preview and print the letter.

**3.** Your initiative and enthusiasm for learning to use Word has resulted in you becoming a Word resource for your colleagues. To assist your co-workers in helping themselves (rather than interrupting your own work), you decide to provide them with a summary of Word's built-in Help features.
  To complete this independent challenge:

**a.** Start Word.
**b.** Write a brief essay that describes each of the following help features, including how to access the feature and an example of when you would use it: Microsoft Word Help, Office Assistant, What's This?, and Office on the Web.
**c.** Be sure to create a new paragraph for each topic (separated by a blank line).
**d.** Insert your name at the top of the page, proofread the document, then correct your spelling and grammatical errors.
**e.** Save the document with the filename "Help Overview" on your Project Disk.
**f.** Preview and print a copy of your essay.

**4.** You are an intern in the Human Resources department at MediaLoft. You recently interviewed for a position in the Systems department, and you want to follow up with a thank-you letter to the office manager who interviewed you. You want to make sure you spell his name correctly, so you consult the MediaLoft intranet site. An intranet is a group of connected networks owned by a company or organization that is used for internal purposes. Intranets use Internet software to handle the data communications, such as e-mail and Web pages, within an organization. These pages often provide company-wide information. As with all intranets, the MediaLoft intranet limits access to MediaLoft employees.
  To complete this independent challenge:

**a.** Start Word.

**b.** Connect to the Internet, go to the MediaLoft intranet site at http://www.course.com/illustrated/MediaLoft, then click the link for the About page.

**c.** Write down the address of the San Francisco headquarters.

**d.** Click the link for the Human Resources page, and locate the Personnel database on that page.

**e.** Note the correct spelling of the office manager's name, then disconnect from the Internet.

**f.** Start a thank-you letter to the office manager. Be sure to type today's date, an inside address, and a salutation at the top of the page.

**g.** In the first paragraph, express your thanks for the interview and reiterate how much you learned about the Systems department during your interview.

**h.** In a separate paragraph, mention your experience with Word 2000 and describe a recent project where you used Word.

**i.** Include your name in the closing.

**j.** Proofread your document, correct any mistakes, then save it with the filename "Office Manager Letter" on your Project Disk.

**k.** Preview and print the letter.

# ▶ Visual Workshop

Using the skills you learned in this unit, create the document shown in Figure A-16. Save it on your Project Disk with the filename "Acceptance Letter," then print a copy of the letter.

**FIGURE A-16**

April 2, 2000


Mr. David Matthews
Management Systems Enterprises
Human Resources Department
128 Technology Drive
Needham, MA 02128

Dear Mr. Matthews:

Thank you for offering me the systems coordinator position in your department. I am writing to accept this position under the terms you described in your letter. I am eager to put my Microsoft Office experience to practical use at Management Systems Enterprises.

Again, thank you for your offer. I look forward to working with you and your team.

Sincerely,


Your Name

# Editing
## and Proofing Documents

### Objectives

- ► **Plan a document**
- [MOUS] ► **Open and save a new document**
- [MOUS] ► **Select and replace text**
- [MOUS] ► **Understand the Office Clipboard**
- [MOUS] ► **Move text**
- [MOUS] ► **Copy text**
- [MOUS] ► **Check spelling and grammar**
- [MOUS] ► **Create AutoCorrect entries**
- [MOUS] ► **Find and replace text**

Word's editing and proofing tools make it easy to edit and fine-tune your documents. In this unit, you will learn a variety of techniques for copying and moving text and for replacing specific occurrences of text throughout a document. You will also use Word's proofing tools to find and correct misspelled words and grammatical errors. To begin, you'll create a new document by saving an existing document with a new name, leaving the original unchanged. ✐ Karen Rosen wants to write a letter to the woman she just hired to be the new training manager at MediaLoft, confirming the terms of her employment. She bases this letter on a similar letter she wrote to another recently hired employee.

## Word 2000

# Planning a Document

It is important to plan a document before you create it. Planning a document involves determining the purpose of the document, identifying its audience, developing the content, organizing the content logically, and then deciding the tone the document should take to achieve its purpose. The **tone** of a document is the way it "sounds." It affects how someone feels while reading it. A document's tone should match its audience and purpose. For example, the tone of an invitation to a company picnic is different from the tone of a letter requesting payment for an overdue invoice. Planning a document also involves thinking about its visual appearance. You want the layout and design of a document to complement its purpose, audience, content, organization, and tone. For example, you would never design a business letter to look like a newspaper article. ✒ Karen plans her letter to MediaLoft's new training manager. She jots down her ideas as shown in Figure B-1.

### In planning her letter Karen is careful to:

### Identify the audience and purpose of the document
The audience for this letter is the new training manager. Its purpose is to welcome her to MediaLoft and to confirm the terms of her employment.

### Choose the information and important points to cover in the document
If you later want to add or remove information from a document, you can easily insert and delete text. Karen wants to confirm the new training manager's title, responsibilities, and salary in the letter. She also wants to mention why MediaLoft decided to offer her the position, and to include several enclosures.

### Decide how the information will be organized
If you decide to rearrange the structure of your document later, you can use Word's editing features to move, copy, and cut text. Because the information about the position is most important, Karen decides to present it first, followed by a list of enclosures.

### Choose the tone of the document
You can edit your documents until you achieve exactly the tone you want. The document is being sent to a new employee, so Karen plans to use a businesslike tone that is welcoming and enthusiastic. She wants the new training manager to be excited about her new job and to feel comfortable with her decision to work at MediaLoft.

### Plan the layout and design of the document
Planning the layout of a document involves thinking about its overall appearance: selecting the fonts to use, organizing text under headings, sketching ideas for tables and lists, and planning to include lines and shading to highlight important points and help to organize content, among many other formatting options. If you change your mind about the format of a document, you can make adjustments later. Karen wants to use a simple business letter format for her document.

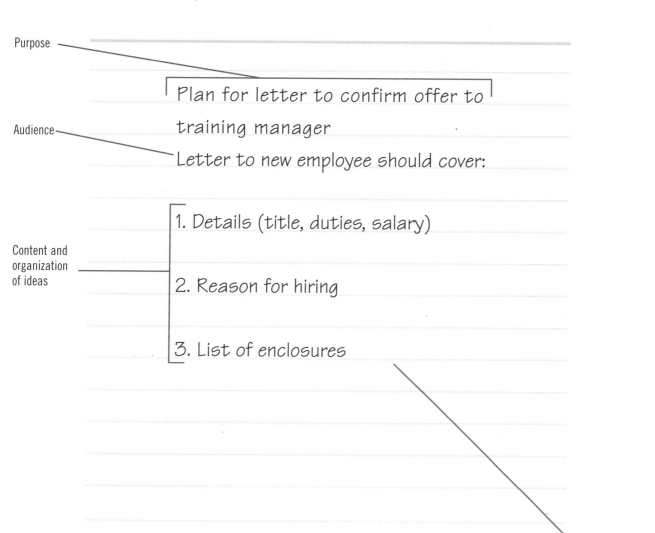

Purpose

Plan for letter to confirm offer to
training manager

Audience

Letter to new employee should cover:

1. Details (title, duties, salary)

Content and
organization
of ideas

2. Reason for hiring

3. List of enclosures

Use a business-
like and positive
tone

ES TO USE

## Creating new documents using wizards and templates

Word includes wizards and templates that help you create a variety of professionally designed documents, including resumes, memos, faxes, letters, and other publications. **Document wizards** are interactive coaches that guide you through the process of creating a document, prompting you to enter information and to choose the design and appearance of a document. **Templates** are pre-formatted documents that contain placeholder text that you replace with your own words. Either method gives you a great head start in developing attractive and effective documents, because wizards and templates offer formatting options that fit many common purposes and tones, such as a professional memo. All you do is provide the text. To create such a document, click File on the menu bar, then click New. In the New dialog box, click the tab containing the type of document you want to create, then double-click the icon for the wizard or template you want to use.

# Opening and Saving a New Document

**Word 2000**

To save time and effort, you can use text from an existing document as the basis for another similar document. When you want to work in an existing document, you must first **open** it, that is, display it in the document window. Using the Save As command, you can save the open document with a different name to create a new document that is a copy. You can then edit the new document without changing the original. Karen wants to use a letter she wrote to a new intern at MediaLoft as the basis for her letter to the new training manager. To preserve the contents of the original document, she creates a new document by saving it with a new name.

**Steps**

1. Start **Word**, click **Tools** on the menu bar, click **Customize**, click the **Options tab** in the Customize dialog box, click **Reset my usage data** to restore the default settings, click **Yes** in the alert box, then click **Close**

**QuickTip**

You can also click File on the menu bar, then click Open, or press [Ctrl][O] to display the Open dialog box.

2. Insert your Project Disk in the appropriate drive, then click the **Open button** 🗁 on the Standard toolbar

   The Open dialog box opens, as shown in Figure B-2. You use this dialog box to navigate the drives and folders on your computer to locate the file you want to open. The Look in list box displays the current drive or folder. You can click the Look in list arrow to display a list of other drives and folders on your computer, or use the buttons in the dialog box to navigate to a different location or to change the way files and folders are displayed in the Open dialog box. Table B-1 describes the function of the buttons in this dialog box.

3. Click the **Up One Level button** 🔼 until you see the drive containing your Project Disk listed in the center of the dialog box

**QuickTip**

A fast way to open a document is to double-click a filename in the Open dialog box.

4. Double-click the drive containing your Project Disk to display its contents

   The files on your Project Disk appear in the Open dialog box, as shown in Figure B-3.

5. Click the filename **WD B-1** in the Open dialog box, then click **Open**

   The file opens in the document window. The filename WD B-1 appears in the title bar.

**QuickTip**

To create a new folder within the current folder, click the Create New Folder button 📁, type a name for the folder, then click OK.

6. Click **File** on the menu bar, then click **Save As**

   The Save As dialog box opens. By saving the file with a new name, you create a new file that is identical to the original file. Changes you make to the new file will not affect the original file.

7. Navigate to the drive or folder where you store your project files (if necessary), type **Training Manager Letter** in the File name text box, then click **Save**

   The original document closes and the Training Manager Letter file is displayed in the document window, ready for you to edit. Note the name of the new document appears in the title bar.

## Save command vs. Save As command

The Save and the Save As commands are different in important ways. Use the Save command the first time you want to name a new document and store it permanently on a disk. When you save a document for the first time, the Save command displays the Save As dialog box, in which you name your document. Using the Save command after naming a file writes your latest changes to the document file on the disk. The Save As command has a different purpose. Use the Save As command to create a new document that is a copy of an existing document. Using Save As allows you to make changes in a copy of a document while leaving the original intact.

FIGURE B-2: Open dialog box

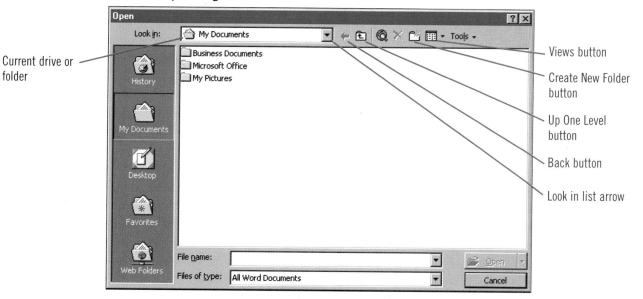

Current drive or folder

Views button

Create New Folder button

Up One Level button

Back button

Look in list arrow

FIGURE B-3: Document file to open

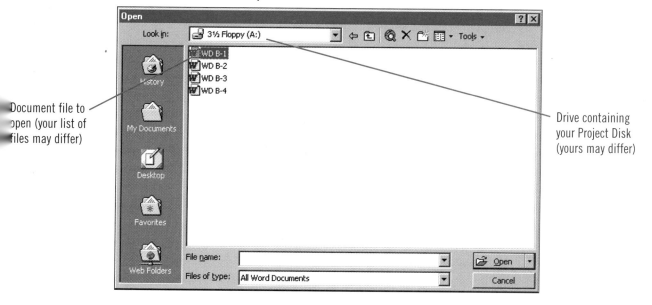

Document file to open (your list of files may differ)

Drive containing your Project Disk (yours may differ)

TABLE B-1: Open dialog box buttons

| button | | function |
| --- | --- | --- |
| ← | Back | Navigates to the previously active folder or drive; the ScreenTip for this button displays the name of the previously active folder or drive |
| ↑ | Up One Level | Navigates to the next highest folder in the folder hierarchy (to the folder or drive that contains the current folder) |
| Q | Search the Web | Connects to the World Wide Web to locate a file |
| × | Delete | Deletes the currently selected file |
| * | Create New Folder | Creates a new folder in the current drive or folder |
| ▦ | Views | Changes the way file information is displayed in the Open dialog box; click to scroll through each view—List, Details, Properties, and Preview—or click the list arrow to choose a view |

# Selecting and Replacing Text

**Word 2000**

Most Word operations require that you **select** text before editing or formatting it. You can select text by clicking before the text you want to select and dragging the mouse pointer across it, or you can use the selection bar to select lines of text. The **selection bar** is the blank area to the left of text. When you click in the selection bar you can select a line, several lines, a paragraph, or the entire document. Table B-2 describes different ways to select text. When you select text and start typing, the text you type replaces the text you selected.  Karen revises her letter by selecting the text she wants to change and replacing it with new text.

You can click anywhere in the document window to deselect text.

1. Click at the start of the text **January 23, 2000** and drag the mouse pointer over the date to select it
The date is selected, as shown in Figure B-4.

2. Type **today's date**
The text you type replaces the selected text.

3. Click before **Alice** in the inside address, drag over **Anderson** to select the entire name, then type **Charlene Stephens**

4. Place the pointer in the **selection bar** to the left of the **second line** in the inside address, when the pointer changes to ⌐ click to select the entire line of text, then type **321 Concordia Street**
Clicking once in the selection bar selects a line of text.

5. Double-click **Alice** in the salutation, then type **Charlene**
Double-clicking a word selects the word.

6. Select **a professional internship** in the first sentence, then type **the position of Human Resources Training Manager**

**Trouble?**
Click the down arrow at the bottom of the vertical scroll bar to display text that is not currently visible in the document window.

7. Select and replace text in the letter using the following table as a guide:

| select: | type: |
|---------|-------|
| an intern | the training manager |
| assisting the training manager and myself on a variety of projects | developing and implementing a corporate-wide training program |
| 9.25 per hour | 47,500 per year |

8. Click the **Save button** 🖫 on the Standard toolbar
The changes you made to the letter are saved. Compare your document with Figure B-5.

## Reversing and repeating changes

Word keeps track of the operations you perform in a document so that you can reverse and repeat any action (with the exception of saving, opening, closing, and printing documents). You can repeat the last action by clicking Edit on the menu bar, and then clicking the Repeat command. The name of the Repeat command changes to reflect your most recent action. You can also press [F4] to repeat the last action. In addition, clicking the Undo button ↶ reverses the most recent change you've made. To reverse a series of changes, click the Undo list arrow ↶ ▾ and scroll through the list of actions to find the last action you want to undo. Click the action and Word reverses all the changes you've made to that point. If you decide to keep a change you just reversed, click the Redo button ↷. To reverse a series of changes, click the Redo list arrow ↷ ▾ and click the last change you want to reverse.

**FIGURE B-4: Selected text**

Selected text ——

Selection bar ——

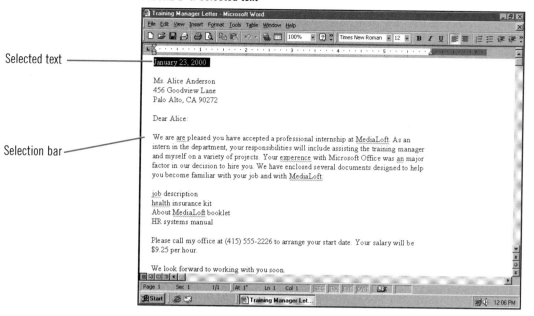

**FIGURE B-5: Edited letter**

——Down Arrow

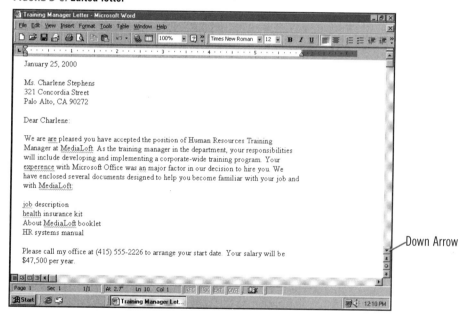

**ABLE B-2: Mouse selection techniques**

| o select | do this |
|---|---|
| word | Double-click the word |
| sentence | Press and hold [Ctrl], then click the sentence |
| paragraph | Triple-click the paragraph, or double-click the selection bar next to the paragraph |
| line of text | Click the selection bar next to the line |
| entire document | Press and hold [Ctrl], then click anywhere in the selection bar, or triple-click the selection bar |
| vertical block of text | Press and hold [Alt], then drag through the text |
| large amount of text | Place the insertion point at the beginning of the text, press and hold [Shift], then click the end of the text |

# Understanding the Office Clipboard

The **Clipboard** is a temporary area in the computer's memory for storing text and graphics that you want to reuse. When you use an Office program such as Word, you use the **Office Clipboard**, which can hold up to 12 items. You can place text or graphics on the Clipboard by selecting the text or graphic and using either the Copy or the Cut command on the Edit menu or the Copy or Cut button on the Standard toolbar. When you **cut** text, you remove it from the document and place it on the Clipboard. When you **copy** text, you place a copy of the text on the Clipboard without removing the original text from the document. After you place an item on the Clipboard it is available for you to **paste**, or insert, into a document using the Paste command. You can paste it into a new location in the same document, or into a different document. Table B-3 describes the commands on the Edit menu that work with the Clipboard. Figure B-6 illustrates how you can use the Office Clipboard to reuse text and graphics from one document in other documents.

### It is important to understand the following about the Office Clipboard:

 Like a physical paper clipboard, the Office Clipboard allows you to place multiple items on it. In Word (and in other Office programs), you can place up to 12 items on the Clipboard.

 Each item you place on the Clipboard can be pasted into a document an unlimited number of times. When you paste an item from the Clipboard, the item remains on the Clipboard until you exceed 12 items and choose to replace it with another item.

 The Clipboard toolbar holds the items copied or cut to the Office Clipboard. You can view the Clipboard toolbar by clicking View on the menu bar, pointing to Toolbars, and then clicking Clipboard. It also appears automatically whenever you cut or copy multiple selections. The Clipboard toolbar is shown in Figure B-7.

 You can review the contents of each item on the Clipboard toolbar by pointing to the item. When you point to an item, a ScreenTip displays its contents.

 To paste an item from the Office Clipboard toolbar, you click the item on the Clipboard to paste it to the location of the insertion point in a document. You can also use the Paste command or the Paste button on the Standard toolbar to paste the most recent item you collected.

 The Office Clipboard is available in all Office applications, so you can use it to paste text and graphics that you have cut or copied from other Office programs into a Word document, and vice versa. For example, you can use the Office Clipboard to insert a spreadsheet or chart created in Excel or a graphic from a PowerPoint presentation into your Word documents.

 Items remain on the Office Clipboard until you close all open Office applications.

**TABLE B-3: The Edit menu Clipboard commands**

| command | description |
| --- | --- |
| Cut | Removes the selected text or graphic from the document and places it on the Clipboard |
| Copy | Copies the selected text or graphic to the Clipboard; the selection remains in the document |
| Paste | Inserts the last item you cut or copied at the insertion point in the document |
| Paste Special | Inserts an item created in another Office program (such as a spreadsheet or a picture) in a document; you can create a link so that changes to the source file are reflected in the document or embed objects so that you can edit the object in its original program |

FIGURE B-6: **Using the Office Clipboard**

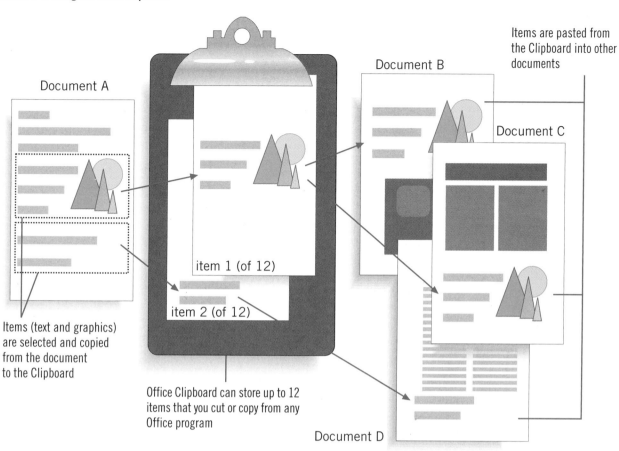

Document A

Document B

Items are pasted from the Clipboard into other documents

Document C

item 1 (of 12)

item 2 (of 12)

Items (text and graphics) are selected and copied from the document to the Clipboard

Office Clipboard can store up to 12 items that you cut or copy from any Office program

Document D

FIGURE B-7: **Clipboard toolbar**

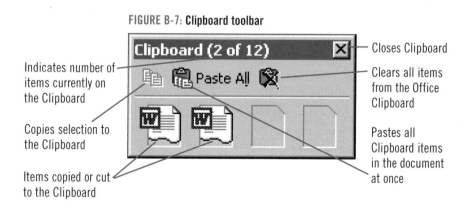

Clipboard (2 of 12)

Paste All

Indicates number of items currently on the Clipboard

Copies selection to the Clipboard

Items copied or cut to the Clipboard

Closes Clipboard

Clears all items from the Office Clipboard

Pastes all Clipboard items in the document at once

**Word 2000**

# Moving Text

You can move text from its current location to a new location in the same document or to a different document. Before you move text, you must select it. To **move** text, use the Cut command or the Cut button to place the text on the Clipboard, then use the Paste command or the Paste button to insert the text from the Clipboard in a new location. You can also move text by selecting it and dragging it to a new location using the mouse. When you drag text, however, it is not placed on the Clipboard. Dragging is a great way to move text when both the text and its new location are visible in the document window at the same time. ✎━━ Karen reorganizes her letter by moving text using both the cut-and-paste and dragging methods. To begin, she displays the Clipboard toolbar.

1. Click **View** on the menu bar, point to **Toolbars**, then click **Clipboard**
   The Clipboard toolbar appears in the document window.

**Trouble?**

If the Clipboard toolbar is in your way, click the toolbar title bar, then drag it to a different location.

2. If the Clipboard toolbar contains items, click the **Clear Clipboard button** 🔳 to empty the Clipboard of previously collected items

3. Select the sentence that begins **Please call...**
   You may need to click the up or down arrows on the vertical scroll bar to display text that is not visible in the document window.

**QuickTip**

Click the More Buttons button ❯ on the Standard toolbar to locate buttons that are not visible on your screen.

4. Click the **Cut button** ✂ on the Standard toolbar
   The sentence is removed from the document and placed on the Clipboard, as shown in Figure B-8. You can also click Edit on the menu bar, then click Cut, or press [Ctrl][X] to cut text.

5. Place the insertion point at the end of the third sentence in the first body paragraph (after the space between **you.** and **We**)

**QuickTip**

You can also click Edit on the menu bar, then click Paste, or press [Ctrl][V] to paste text.

6. Click the **Paste button** 📋 on the Standard toolbar
   The sentence is inserted in the first paragraph.

7. Select **Human Resources** in the first sentence, then press and hold the mouse button over the selected text until the pointer changes to ▯ (do not release the mouse button)

8. Drag the pointer's vertical line in front of the word **department** in the next sentence, as shown in Figure B-9

**Trouble?**

If you make a mistake, click the Undo button ↺ on the Standard toolbar, then repeat Steps 8 and 9.

9. Release the mouse button
   The text is moved from its original location in the first sentence to its new location in the second sentence.

10. Click anywhere in the document window to deselect the text, then click the **Save button** 💾 on the Standard toolbar
    Compare your letter to Figure B-10.

## Working with multiple documents

If you want to copy or cut text from one document and paste it into another, it is easiest to work with both documents open in the program window at the same time. To open multiple documents, you can open one document and then open subsequent documents one by one, or you can open several documents at once by holding [Ctrl] as you click the filename of each document you want to open in the Open dialog box, and then clicking Open. To move between open documents in the document window, click Window on the menu bar, then click the filename of the document you want to display. You can also view multiple documents at once in the program window, by clicking Window on the menu bar, and then clicking Arrange All. All the open documents will appear on the screen, each in its own program window. To activate a document, click its program window. With multiple documents open, you can easily copy and move text between documents by selecting the text you want to copy or move in one document, and then pasting it in another document. To quickly save or close all open documents at the same time, press and hold [Shift] as you click File on the menu bar, then click Save All or Close All.

**FIGURE B-8: Cut item on the Clipboard toolbar**

Item cut from letter

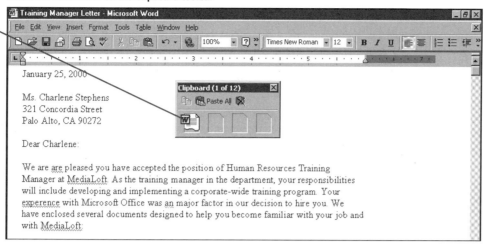

**FIGURE B-9: Dragging to move text**

New location for text

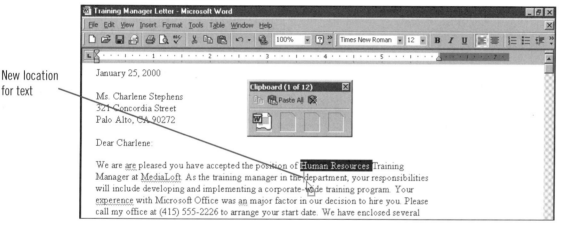

**FIGURE B-10: Moved text in document**

oved text

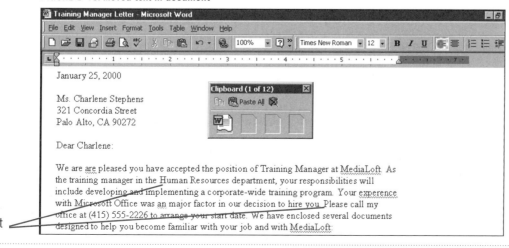

**Word 2000**

# Copying Text

Copying text is similar to moving text, except that when you copy text it remains in its original location. A copy of the text is placed on the Clipboard, available to be pasted in the same document or in another document. Before you copy text you must select it. To copy text to the Clipboard you can use the Copy command on the Edit menu or the Copy button on the Standard toolbar or the Clipboard toolbar. You can also copy text by selecting it and pressing [Ctrl] while you drag it to a new location. When you copy text by dragging it, the selection does not get copied to the Clipboard.  Karen further edits her letter by copying text from one location in the document to another.

## Steps

**QuickTip**

You can also click 📋 on the Clipboard toolbar to copy text to the Clipboard.

1. Select **Training Manager** in the first sentence, then click the **Copy button** 📋 on the Standard toolbar
   The selected text is copied to the Clipboard. You want to place a copy of this text in front of "job description" in the list.

2. Place the insertion point in front of **job description** in the list, then click the **Paste button** 📋 on the Standard toolbar
   "Training Manager" is inserted before "job description." Note that Word automatically inserts a space between "Manager" and "job." "Training Manager" also remains on the Clipboard.

3. Select **Human Resources department** in the second sentence, click **Edit** on the menu bar, then click **Copy**
   The selected text is copied to the Clipboard, as shown in Figure B-11. You want to paste the text "Human Resources department" at the end of the last sentence in the first paragraph.

4. Place the insertion point after **MediaLoft** but before the **colon (:)** in the last sentence of the first paragraph, type **'s**, then press **[Spacebar]**

5. Move the pointer over the items on the Clipboard toolbar until you find **Human Resources department**, then click to paste it at the insertion point
   The text is pasted at the end of the sentence.

6. Select **HR** in the list, then click **Human Resources department** on the Clipboard toolbar
   The pasted text replaces the selected text in the document.

7. Select **MediaLoft** in the first sentence, press and hold **[Ctrl]**, then press and hold the mouse button over the selected text until the pointer changes to 📋

**QuickTip**

Click the Undo button 🔙 on the Standard toolbar if you make a mistake, then try again.

8. Drag the pointer in front of **health insurance kit** in the list to position the pointer's vertical line in front of **health**, release the mouse button, release **[Ctrl]**, then deselect the text
   Pressing [Ctrl] while you drag selected text copies the text to a new location. Compare your document with Figure B-12.

9. Click the **Close button** on the Clipboard toolbar, then click the **Save button** 💾 on the Standard toolbar

**FIGURE B-11: Copying to and from the Clipboard toolbar**

Text copied to the Clipboard

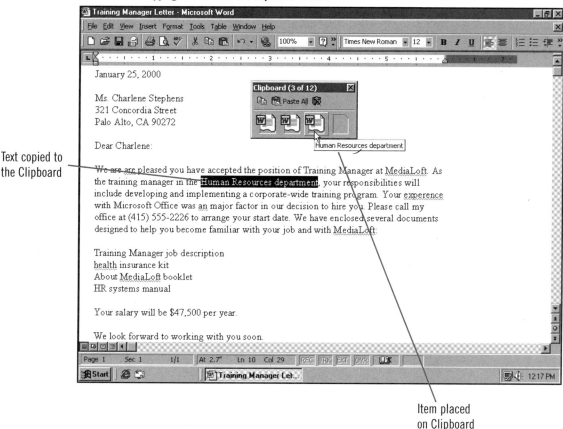

Item placed on Clipboard

**FIGURE B-12: Copied text**

ext copied om here

ext copied here

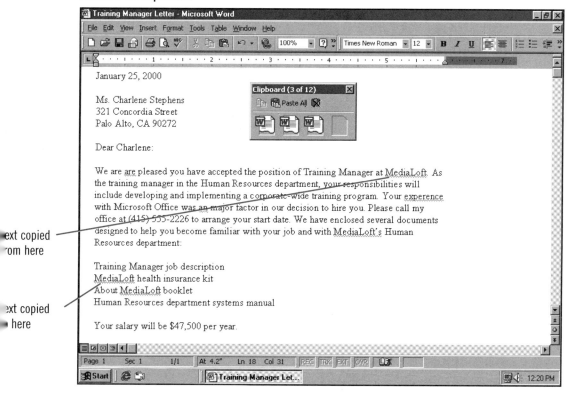

Word 2000

# Checking Spelling and Grammar

**Word 2000**

You can use Word's Spelling, Grammar, and AutoCorrect features to help you identify and correct mistakes in your document. **AutoCorrect** automatically corrects commonly misspelled words as you type. Word also underlines possible spelling and grammatical errors as you type. Words that are not in Word's dictionary are underlined with a red, wavy line. Possible grammatical errors are underlined with a green, wavy line. When you finish creating a document, you can use Word's Spelling and Grammar command to review and correct misspelled words, as well as grammatical errors such as punctuation, sentence fragments, or subject-verb agreement. Although the Spelling and Grammar command catches most errors, there are certain errors it will not find, such as homonyms. For example, if you typed "here" and you meant to use "hear," Word will not identify this as an error. Ultimately, you are still responsible for proofreading your work. Karen uses the Spelling and Grammar command to search her document for errors. Before searching the document, she sets AutoCorrect to ignore the word "MediaLoft," which she knows is not in Word's dictionary because it is underlined in red in her document.

**Trouble?**

If "MediaLoft" is not underlined, click Tools on the menu bar, click Options, click the Spelling & Grammar tab, click Recheck Document, click Yes, click OK, then continue with Step 1.

**1.** Right-click **MediaLoft** in the first sentence to open a pop-up menu

This pop-up menu includes a suggestion for correcting the spelling ("Media Loft") as well as commands for ignoring Word's suggestion and for adding the word to Word's dictionary. Note that Word's suggested correction is wrong in this case.

**2.** Click **Ignore All** on the pop-up menu, right-click **MediaLoft's**, then click **Ignore All**

Clicking Ignore All tells Word to ignore all instances of "MediaLoft" and "MediaLoft's" in the current document, and removes the red, wavy lines under these words.

**Trouble?**

If a word is identified as misspelled, click Ignore to ignore it, or click the correct spelling in the Suggestions list, then click Change.

**3.** Press **[Ctrl][Home]** to move the insertion point to the top of the document, then click the **Spelling and Grammar button** on the Standard toolbar

The Spelling and Grammar dialog box opens. The dialog box indicates that the word "are" is repeated, as shown in Figure B-13. You want to delete the second occurrence of the word.

**4.** Click **Delete**

The second "are" is deleted from the document. Next, "experence" is identified as misspelled. The correct spelling is selected in the Suggestions list.

**Trouble?**

Click the Office Assistant button in the Spelling and Grammar dialog box if the Office Assistant does not open.

**5.** Click **Change**

The correctly spelled word replaces the misspelled word. Next, the Spelling and Grammar dialog box suggests using the word "a" in place of "an." The Office Assistant displays an explanation of the rule that applies to this error, as shown in Figure B-14.

**6.** Read the explanation, then click **Change**

The word "a" is substituted for the incorrect word "an." If you made other errors in your document, you may need to correct them. When Spelling and Grammar check is complete, the dialog box closes.

**7.** When a message box opens saying the Spelling and Grammar check is complete, click **OK** to close it, then proofread the letter for other errors

**8.** Press **[Ctrl][Home]**, then click the **Save button** on the Standard toolbar

**FIGURE B-13:** Spelling and Grammar dialog box

Error in the document

Repeated word

Office Assistant button provides an explanation of grammar errors

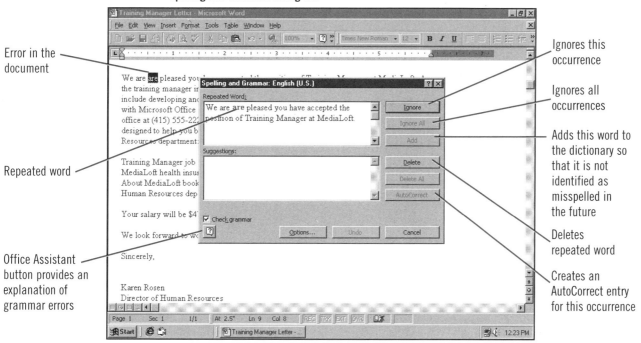

Ignores this occurrence

Ignores all occurrences

Adds this word to the dictionary so that it is not identified as misspelled in the future

Deletes repeated word

Creates an AutoCorrect entry for this occurrence

**FIGURE B-14:** Grammar explanation

Accepts this change

Office Assistant button

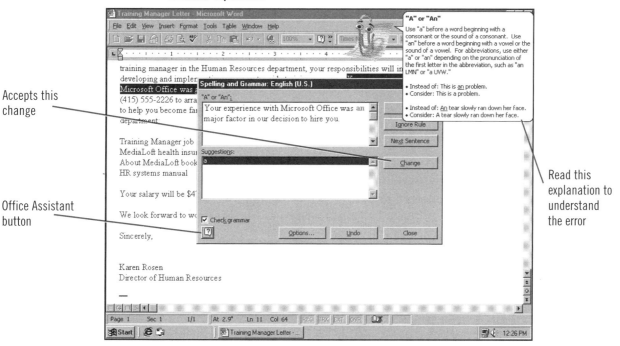

Read this explanation to understand the error

## Using the Thesaurus

You can use Word's Thesaurus to look up synonyms for overused or awkward words in your document. For some words, you can also look up antonyms. To use the Thesaurus, select the word for which you want to find a synonym, click Tools on the menu bar, point to Language, then click Thesaurus. In the Thesaurus dialog box, select the synonym you want to use in your document, then click Replace.

# Creating and Using AutoCorrect Entries

While AutoCorrect automatically corrects hundreds of commonly misspelled words, you can also create your own AutoCorrect entries to help you work more efficiently. You can create entries for text you use frequently, such as your name, title, or the name of your company, or you can create entries for words you often misspell that Word does not correct for you. For example, you could create an AutoCorrect entry for your initials, so that each time you typed your initials Word would automatically insert your name into your document. Karen types "MediaLoft" many times every day. To save time, she creates an AutoCorrect entry that inserts "MediaLoft" whenever she types the abbreviation "ml".

**QuickTip**

To delete an AutoCorrect entry, select it on the AutoCorrect tab, then click Delete.

1. Click **Tools** on the menu bar, then click **AutoCorrect**

   The AutoCorrect dialog box opens, as shown in Figure B-15. The AutoCorrect tab displays the list of existing AutoCorrect entries. Use the tab to enter new text you want to be automatically corrected (such as an abbreviation or a misspelled word) and the text you want to be automatically inserted in its place.

2. Type **ml** in the Replace text box

3. Press **[Tab]** to move the insertion point to the With text box, then type **MediaLoft**

4. Click **Add**, then click **OK**

   Word adds the new AutoCorrect entry to the list of AutoCorrect entries. Every time you type "ml" in a document, Word will replace it with "MediaLoft".

**Trouble?**

If you can't click Add in your AutoCorrect dialog box, someone already created an AutoCorrect entry for "ml". Click Replace, click Yes in the alert box or dialog balloon, then click OK. See your instructor or technical support person for assistance.

5. Press **[Ctrl] [End]** to place the insertion point at the end of the document, then type **ml [Spacebar]**

   "MediaLoft" is inserted after you press [Spacebar], as shown in Figure B-16.

6. Press **[Ctrl] [Home]**, then click the **Save button** 🖫 on the Standard toolbar

### Creating AutoCorrect exceptions

There are some situations when you do not want Word to automatically correct what it assumes to be a mistake. For example, AutoCorrect automatically capitalizes the first character you type after typing a period. However, when you type the abbreviation "Cal." (for California) in the middle of a sentence, you do not want AutoCorrect to capitalize the next character. To avoid this, you can create an AutoCorrect exception. Create an AutoCorrect exception by clicking Tools on the menu bar, clicking AutoCorrect, then clicking Exceptions. In the AutoCorrect Exceptions dialog box, click the tab that includes the type of AutoCorrect exception you want to create: First Letter, INitial CAps, or Other Corrections. Type the text you do not want automatically corrected in the text box on the tab, click Add, then click Close. You can later remove an exception by deleting it from the list of exceptions in the AutoCorrect dialog box.

FIGURE B-15: AutoCorrect dialog box

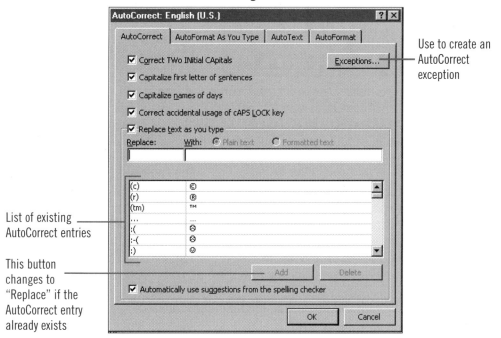

List of existing AutoCorrect entries

This button changes to "Replace" if the AutoCorrect entry already exists

Use to create an AutoCorrect exception

FIGURE B-16: Inserted AutoCorrect entry

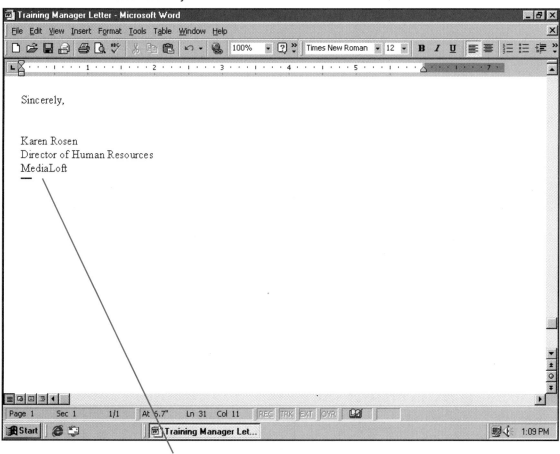

Inserted text

# Finding and Replacing Text

Sometimes you need to replace text throughout a document. In a long document, doing this manually would be time-consuming and prone to error. For example, suppose you just finished writing an announcement of a new beverage for the MediaLoft café, when the marketing department decides that the product name should change from "ChocoShakes" to "CocoShakes". Rather than having to find, select, and replace each instance of "ChocoShakes" in your document, it would be much easier to use the Replace command to search for and replace "ChocoShakes" throughout the document automatically. You have the option to review and replace each occurrence one at a time (so that you can decide in each case whether or not to make the substitution), or you can perform a global replace. A **global replace** changes all occurrences at once. You can also use Word's Find command to locate text in a document. ▶ Karen decides to use the term "position" instead of "job" in her letter. She uses the Replace command to change "job" to "position" throughout the document. When she is finished, she saves, prints, and closes the document.

1. Click **Edit** on the menu bar, click **Replace**, then click **More** in the Find and Replace dialog box if necessary

   The Find and Replace dialog box opens, as shown in Figure B-17. Clicking More in the Find and Replace dialog box reveals additional options for narrowing a search and replace. Table B-4 describes the search options available in the Find and Replace dialog box.

2. Type **job** in the Find what text box

   This text will be replaced.

3. Press **[Tab]** to move the insertion point to the Replace with text box, then type **position**

4. Click **Replace All**

   Clicking Replace All changes all occurrences of "job" to "position" in the document. A message box or balloon reports that two replacements were made.

5. Click **OK** to close the message box or click to close the message balloon, then click **Close**

   The dialog box closes. Compare your document to Figure B-18.

6. Click **Edit** on the menu bar, click **Find**, type **Karen Rosen** in the Find what text box, click **Find Next**, then click **Cancel**

   "Karen Rosen" is selected in the document.

7. Type your name, click the **Save button** 🖫 on the Standard toolbar, then click the **Print button** 🖨 on the Standard toolbar

   A copy of the document prints.

8. Click **File** on the menu bar, click **Close**, click **File** on the menu bar, then click **Exit**

   The documents and Word close.

## Replacing text in Overtype mode

Word's Overtype feature allows you to type over existing text without selecting it first. When you work in Overtype mode, Word replaces the existing text with any new text you type. You can turn on Overtype mode by double-clicking the OVR box on the status bar (it appears in light gray when Overtype is off, and in black when Overtype is on). On some keyboards you can also turn on Overtype by pressing [Insert]. To turn off Overtype mode, double-click the OVR box in the status bar again, or press [Insert].

**FIGURE B-17:** Find and Replace dialog box

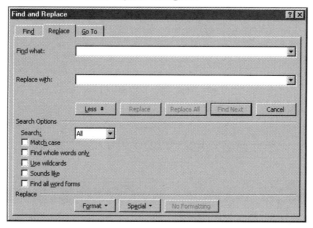

**FIGURE B-18:** Completed document

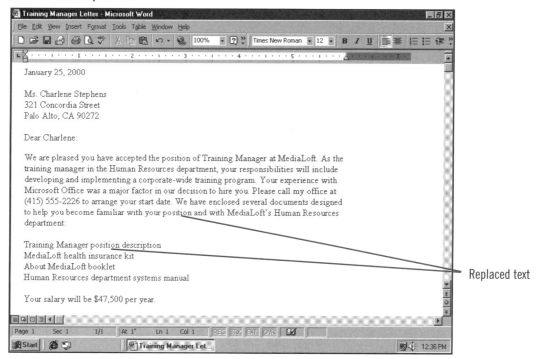

Replaced text

**TABLE B-4:** Search options in the Find and Replace dialog box

| Search option | use to |
|---|---|
| Search | Specify the direction of the search from the current location of the insertion point: Down, Up, or All |
| Match case | Locate only exact matches for the uppercase and lowercase letters entered in the Find what text box; select to find "President" but not "president" |
| Find whole words only | Locate only words that are complete and not part of a larger word; select to locate "Asia" but not "Asian" |
| Use wildcards | Search for a string of characters by using wildcards; select to enter "c*t" to find "cat" and "coat" |
| Sounds like | Locate words that sound like the text in the Find what text box, but have different spellings; select to find "their" and "there" and "they're" |
| Find all word forms | Find and replace all forms of a word; for example, specify "find" in the Find what text box to locate "find," "finds," "found," and "finding" and replace each with the comparable form of the replacement word |

# Practice

## ► Concepts Review

Label each element of the Open dialog box shown in Figure B-19.

FIGURE B-19

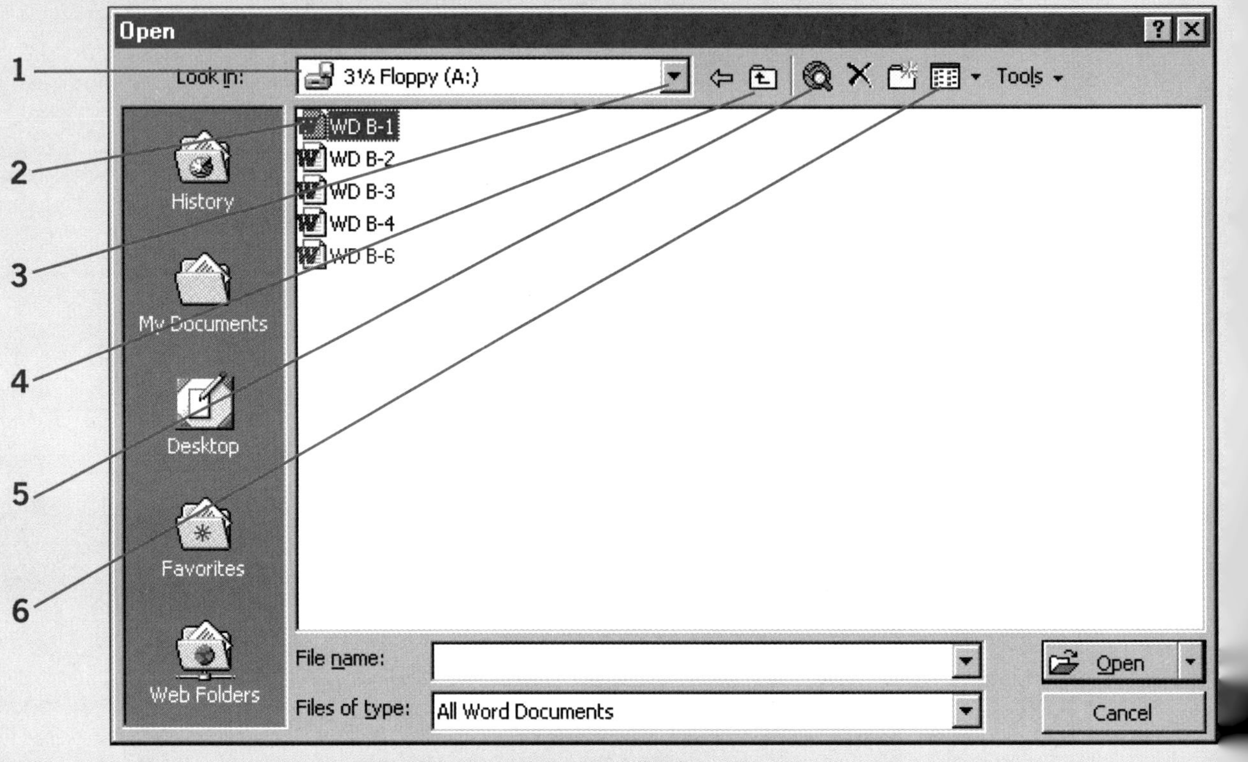

Match each command with the statement that describes it.

7. Copy
8. Paste
9. Spelling and Grammar
10. Thesaurus
11. Cut
12. Replace
13. Save As
14. Paste Special

a. Creates a new document while saving the original document
b. Reviews a document for spelling, punctuation, and usage errors
c. Suggests synonyms and antonyms
d. Removes text from a document and places it on the Clipboard
e. Places text on the Clipboard without removing it from the document
f. Embeds or links an item created in another Office program in a document
g. Locates and replaces occurrences of text in a document
h. Inserts text from the Clipboard in a document

Select the best answer from the list of choices.

15. To place text on the Clipboard, you must first
    a. Click the Copy button.
    b. Click the Cut button.
    c. Click the Paste button.
    d. Select the text.

16. **How many times can you paste an item from the Clipboard into a document?**
    a. Once
    c. 12 times
    b. Twice
    d. An unlimited number of times

17. **Which of the following statements best describes the selection bar?**
    a. The selection bar is the empty area to the left of text in the document window.
    b. To display the selection bar, you must click View on the menu bar, then click Selection Bar.
    c. The selection bar contains up to 12 items that you have copied or pasted to the Clipboard.
    d. The selection bar is the empty area to the right of text in the document window.

18. **Which option is NOT available in the Spelling and Grammar dialog box when a spelling error is identified?**
    a. Add the word to the dictionary
    c. Select a synonym for the word
    b. Add an AutoCorrect entry
    d. Choose a suggested spelling

19. **The Spelling and Grammar feature does not**
    a. Check for words that are repeated.
    c. Automatically correct all misspelled words.
    b. Suggest revisions to make a sentence correct.
    d. Explain grammatical errors.

20. **Which of the following is not true about the AutoCorrect feature?**
    a. AutoCorrect corrects common grammatical errors as you type them.
    b. Words underlined with a wavy line indicate possible spelling or grammatical errors.
    c. You can create AutoCorrect entries.
    d. AutoCorrect corrects commonly misspelled words as you type them.

21. **Using the Find and Replace commands, you can do all of the following *except***
    a. Search for all uses of the passive voice in your document.
    b. Search the document for specified text in a certain direction only.
    c. Substitute all occurrences of a word with another word.
    d. Locate all the different forms of a word in a document.

# ▶ Skills Review

1. **Open and save a new document.**
   a. Start Word.
   b. Open the file WD B-2 from your Project Disk and save it as "Road Map."

2. **Select and replace text.**
   a. Select the date and replace it with today's date.
   b. Select "Wing" in the inside address and replace it with "Carroll."
   c. Select "Wing" in the salutation, then use the Repeat Typing command to replace the name with "Carroll."
   d. Select the street address and replace it with "280 Technology Drive."
   e. Select the line after the street address and delete it.
   f. Undo the deletion, then select "8B" and replace it with "555."

3. **Move text.**
   a. Display the Clipboard toolbar.
   b. Use the cut-and-paste method to move the last two sentences of the first body paragraph to the end of the second body paragraph.
   c. Use the drag method to move the last sentence of the last body paragraph in front of the second sentence in the first body paragraph.

4. **Copy text.**
   a. Copy "Open Roads, Inc." from the first sentence to under "Your Name" in the signature block.
   b. Copy "Open Roads" in the first sentence to in front of "package" in the third sentence.
   c. Close the Clipboard toolbar.

5. **Check spelling and grammar.**
   a. Press [Ctrl][Home], then click the Spelling and Grammar button.
   b. Correct the spelling and grammatical errors in the letter.
   c. Use the Thesaurus to find a substitution for "contact" in the last paragraph, then replace "contact." If the Thesaurus is not installed on your computer, substitute a word of your own.
6. **Create and use AutoCorrect entries.**
   a. Create an AutoCorrect entry for "Account Representative." Use the abbreviation "ar."
   b. Insert a blank line after "Your Name," type "ar," then press [Spacebar].
7. **Find and replace text.**
   a. Press [Ctrl][Home], then use the Replace command to replace all occurrences of "Inc." with "Intl."
   b. Double-click "OVR" in the status bar, place the insertion point in front of "Your Name," then type your name.
   c. Double-click "OVR" in the status bar again to turn Overtype mode off, save your changes, then print the document.
   d. Close the document and exit Word.

# ▶ Independent Challenges

**1.** As the co-chair for the Middleburg reunion planning committee, you are responsible for recruiting classmates to help with reunion activities. One of the other people on your committee drafted a letter to your classmates for you to review and edit. You use the editing and proofing tools in Word to revise the letter.
   To complete this independent challenge:

   a. Start Word, open the file WD B-3 from your Project Disk, and save it as "Reunion Volunteer."
   b. Copy the text "Middleburg" and paste it in front of "memories" in the second body paragraph and in front of "Reunion" in the signature block.
   c. Move the second body paragraph so that it appears immediately before the last body paragraph.
   d. Correct the spelling and grammatical errors in the document.
   e. Replace "Your Name" with your name, save your changes, then print and close the document.

**2.** As an account representative for EasyTemps, a temporary placement service, you often use Word templates to create professional-looking documents. You recently used a template to create a memo to a customer describing your corporate discount program. You use the editing and proofing tools in Word to revise your memo before sending it to the customer.
   To complete this independent challenge:

   a. Start Word, open the file WD B-4 from your Project Disk, and save it as "Discount Proposal."
   b. Copy the company name from the subject line of the memo and paste it in front of "DISCOUNT PROPOSAL" at the top of the document.
   c. Use the Replace command to replace all but the second occurrence of "our" with "EasyTemps."
   d. Move the second-to-last sentence of the memo so that it is the last sentence in the first paragraph.
   e. Use the Thesaurus to look up an alternative word for "sequential," and replace it with a word of your choice.
   f. Correct the spelling and grammatical errors in the document.
   g. Click HERE in the From line, type your name, save your changes, then print and close the document.

**3.** Your boss has recognized you as a Word resource for your colleagues. To help everyone in your department learn to use Word more efficiently, she asks you to create a quick reference list of shortcut keys for the commands you use frequently. The shortcut keys are listed next to the commands on the File and Edit menus.
   To complete this independent challenge:

   a. Start Word and create a new document named "Quick Reference" on your Project Disk.
   b. Open the Edit menu and note the keyboard shortcuts for the Paste, Copy, and Cut commands.
   c. Create an AutoCorrect entry that inserts "[Ctrl]" whenever you type "ct."

**d.** Type a list that includes the name of each command and its keyboard shortcut. Use the new AutoCorrect entry to insert [Ctrl] in your document. (For example, enter "Paste: [Ctrl][V]" for the Paste command.)

**e.** Add keyboard shortcuts for the Undo, Repeat, Find, Replace, New, Open, Save, and Print commands to your list.

**f.** Cut and paste to rearrange your list so the commands appear in alphabetical order.

**g.** Delete the [Ctrl] AutoCorrect entry.

**h.** Type your name at the top of the document, save your changes, then print and close the document.

**4.** You work in the Community Relations Department at MediaLoft. A nonprofit organization called Companies for Kids has approached MediaLoft for information about its corporate sponsorship program. Using the plan shown in Figure B-20, draft a short letter to Companies for Kids, describing MediaLoft's community relations programs.
To complete this independent challenge:

**a.** Start Word, then create a new document using the Letter Wizard. (*Hint:* To start the Letter Wizard, click File on the menu bar, click New, click the Letters & Faxes tab in the New dialog box, click the Letter Wizard, then click OK.)

**b.** Complete the wizard dialog boxes. Use today's date and choose any page design and letter style you wish. Address the letter to Judy Wexler, Director of Companies for Kids, and use any address. Add any other information you want to the letter, making sure to enter your name as the sender. (*Hint:* When you finish entering information in a dialog box, click Next to proceed to the next dialog box.)

**c.** Save the document as "Companies for Kids" on your Project Disk.

**d.** Using Figure B-20 as a guide, type a paragraph in the letter for each topic in the plan. For the second paragraph, collect information from the MediaLoft intranet site.

**e.** Connect to the Internet, go to the MediaLoft intranet site at http://www.course.com/illustrated/MediaLoft, then click the link for the Community page.

**f.** Copy MediaLoft's core assumptions from the Community Relations page on the intranet site to your letter. Disconnect from the Internet when you are done.

**g.** Use editing techniques to rework the text into a readable paragraph. (*Hint:* Delete the bullets.)

**h.** When you finish typing the letter, use the Replace command to locate each occurrence of "valuable" and replace it with "important."

**i.** Correct your spelling and grammatical errors.

**j.** Save your changes, then print and close the document.

**FIGURE B-20**

Plan for letter describing MediaLoft's community

relations policies

Letter to Director of Companies for Kids should cover:

1. Thank you for interest in MediaLoft

2. Describe MediaLoft's core assumptions

3. Suggest a meeting to go over questions/concerns

# ► Visual Workshop

Create the letter shown in Figure B-21, using the Contemporary Letter template. Save it as "Lakeside Letter" on your Project Disk, then print a copy of the letter.

**FIGURE B-21**

128 Lakeview Avenue
Brooklyn Valley, MN 55217

## International Voices

January 26, 2000

Ms. Leslie Ryden
Banquet Caterer
Lakeside Center
North Bay, MN  55509

Dear Ms. Ryden:

I would like to take this opportunity to reaffirm how delighted we are to be conducting International Voices' Vision Conference at the Lakeside Center. We at International Voices believe it is the perfect setting for our conference's objectives.

As you requested, here are my ideas for the informal dinner that will wrap up the day's events. I would be interested in having a low-fat, healthful menu for this meal. Regarding table centerpieces, I liked your idea of arranging international flags drawn by children of International Voices employees.

I hope these general suggestions will be helpful to you as you plan your menu and price proposal. I look forward to confirming our plans by the end of next month.

Sincerely,

Your Name
Conference Coordinator
International Voices

*Children Are The Key To Our Success!*

# Formatting

## a Document

### Objectives

- [MOUS] ▶ **Change fonts and font sizes**
- [MOUS] ▶ **Apply font effects**
- [MOUS] ▶ **Change paragraph alignment**
- [MOUS] ▶ **Indent paragraphs**
- [MOUS] ▶ **Change line spacing**
- [MOUS] ▶ **Change paragraph spacing**
- [MOUS] ▶ **Align text with tabs**
- [MOUS] ▶ **Create bulleted and numbered lists**
- [MOUS] ▶ **Apply borders and shading**

Without some formatting, even a simple document could be almost impossible to read. You can highlight important words or improve the look of a document by changing its typeface or the size of its words. You can organize ideas and add structure to a document by changing the spacing, indentation, and alignment of text in paragraphs. Formatting a document makes it easier to read and easier to understand. ✐ Karen Rosen has drafted a description of the orientation packet for new MediaLoft employees. Before distributing the document to her colleagues, she formats the text and paragraphs to improve the document's organization and to emphasize important topics.

# Changing Fonts and Font Sizes

One of the easiest ways to change the appearance of a document is to change its font. A **font** is a family of characters, which includes letters, numbers, and punctuation, with the same typeface or design. A font can be basic, with clean, simple lines, or more stylized, with a lot of curlicues or a definite "theme." The font you choose affects the tone of your document: stylized fonts can add a note of flamboyance, formality, or sleekness to a document, while a more traditional font can "feel" businesslike or scholarly. You can also change the size of text in your documents by increasing or decreasing the **font size**. Fonts are measured in points (pts). A **point** is ½ of an inch. The bigger the number of points, the larger the size of the font. To quickly change fonts and font size, select the text you want to format, then use the buttons on the Formatting toolbar. ◀ Karen changes the font and font size of the title and headings in her document, so that readers can quickly find the information they need.

**Steps 1 2 3 4**

1. Start **Word**, click **Tools** on the menu bar, click **Customize**, click the **Options tab** in the Customize dialog box, click **Reset my usage data** to restore the default settings, click **Yes** in the alert box, then click **Close**

2. Open the file **WD C-1** from your Project Disk, then save it as **Orientation Packet**
   The document opens in Normal view. The name of the font used in the document appears in the Font list box on the Formatting toolbar, and the font size appears next to it in the Font Size list box. The document is formatted in 12 point Times New Roman.

3. Select the title **New Employee Orientation Packet**, then click the **Font list arrow** on the Formatting toolbar
   The Font list opens with Times New Roman selected, as shown in Figure C-1. The name of each font is formatted in the font so you can see what it looks like. Use the scroll box in the list to view the fonts available on your computer. Fonts you have used recently appear at the top of the list.

4. Click **Arial**
   The font of the selected text changes to Arial. Arial is a font that is commonly used in headings. Titles and headings often appear in a font different from that document's body text.

5. Click the **Font Size list arrow** on the Formatting toolbar, then click **18**
   The size of the title increases to 18 points. The headings should also be formatted in the Arial font.

6. Select the heading **Offer Letter**, click the **Font list arrow**, click **Arial**, click the **Font Size list arrow**, then click **14**
   The heading is formatted in 14 point Arial. Headings in a document are usually larger than body text, but smaller than the title. You'll format each heading in the document in the same way.

7. Click the **down scroll arrow** at the bottom of the vertical scroll bar until the heading **Employee Handbook** appears at the top of your screen
   The Orientation Packet document contains more text than will fit in the document window. **Scrolling** allows you to navigate a document to display the text you want to read or edit in the document window.

8. Select the heading **Employee Handbook**, change the font to **Arial**, change the font size to **14**, then change the font and font size to 14 point Arial (scrolling as needed) for each of the following headings: **Health Insurance Kit**, **Employee Benefits Summary**, and **About MediaLoft © booklet**

9. Deselect the text, then click the **Save button** 🖫 on the Standard toolbar
   Compare your document to Figure C-2.

**FIGURE C-1: Font list**

Formatting toolbar
(yours may differ)

Your font list may
be different

More Buttons button
displays additional
formatting buttons

Font Size list arrow

Font list arrow

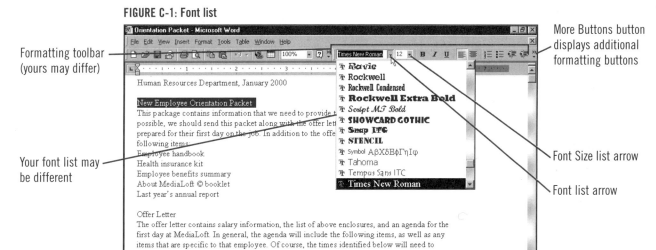

**FIGURE C-2: Formatted document**

Text formatted in
14 point Arial

Click to scroll up
one line

Scroll box

Click to scroll down
one line

Click to scroll up or
down one page

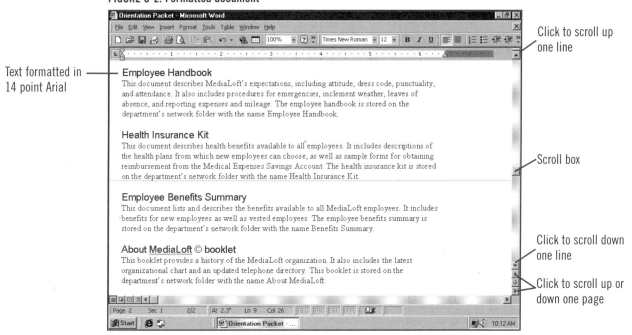

## Scrolling a document

If your document contains more text than will fit in the document window, you need to scroll the document to display the text you want to read or edit. Scrolling changes the position of the document window relative to the document text. You can scroll up or down in a document. Scroll one line at a time by clicking the arrows at the top and bottom of the vertical scroll bar, or scroll one document window at a time by clicking the scroll bar above or below the scroll box. If you want to scroll the document one page at a time, click the up or down double-arrows at the bottom of the scroll bar. You can also drag the scroll box to a new location in the scroll bar to move to a specific page in the document.

**Word 2000**

# Applying Font Effects

You can emphasize words and ideas in a document by changing the font style, such as making text darker (called **bold**) or slanted (called **italics**). Buttons for these and other font effects, including underlining and changing font color, are on the Formatting toolbar. You can also use the Font command on the Format menu to apply additional special effects to text, such as superscripting it (raising text above the line) or adding a shadow. ✎ Karen applies font effects to emphasize important elements in her document, and to italicize the title of the About MediaLoft booklet.

1. Drag the **scroll box** to the top of the vertical scroll bar
   The top of the document appears in the document window.

**QuickTip**

You can also underline text by clicking the Underline button **U** on the Formatting toolbar.

2. Select **New Employee Orientation Packet**, click the **Bold button** **B** on the Formatting toolbar, then deselect the text
   Applying bold to the text makes each character fatter, creating a darker appearance.

3. Select **About MediaLoft** in the list under the first body paragraph, then click the **Italic button** **I** on the Formatting toolbar
   The title of the booklet appears in italics. Next you want to apply the superscript effect to the copyright symbol.

**QuickTip**

Use the Character Spacing tab in the Font dialog box to expand or condense the amount of space between characters, adjust the width or scale of characters, raise or lower characters, and adjust kerning (the spacing between standard character combinations). Formatting character spacing can dramatically affect the appearance of text.

4. Select © (the copyright symbol) after About MediaLoft, click **Format** on the menu bar, then click **Font**
   The Font dialog box opens as shown in Figure C-3. You can use the Font tab to apply many different effects to text, including shadow, superscript, and subscript. You can also change the font, font size, style, and color of text on this tab, and select the style of underline you want to apply to the selected text. Using the Font dialog box, you can apply multiple font effects to text at once. The Preview box on the Font tab displays the combined effects you have chosen for the selected text.

5. Click the **Superscript** check box, click **OK**, then deselect the text
   The copyright symbol is superscripted—formatted in a smaller font size and raised above the line of text.

6. Select **Event & Time** at the top of the list below the second body paragraph, click **Format** on the menu bar, then click **Font**

7. Click **Bold Italic** in the Font style list, click the **Underline style list arrow**, click **Words only**, then click the **Small caps** check box
   The text appears in the Preview box formatted in bold, italic, small caps, with the words (not the spaces between them) underlined. When you change text to small caps, the characters change to uppercase, with the capital letters two points larger than lowercase letters.

8. Click **OK**, deselect the text, then click the **Save button** 🖫 on the Standard toolbar
   Compare your document to Figure C-4.

## Adding color to text

When you want to use color to add visual interest in a document, you can highlight, or apply a transparent layer of color to text, or you can change the color of the text itself. To highlight text, click the Highlight button 🖉 on the Formatting toolbar and then drag the Highlighter pointer over the text you want to highlight. You can change the highlight color by clicking the Highlight list arrow and then clicking a new color. To turn off the Highlighter pointer, simply click the Highlight button again. If you want to change the color of the characters themselves, select the text you want to color, click the Font Color list arrow **A ·** on the Formatting toolbar, and then click a new color.

FIGURE C-3: **Font dialog box**

Change character spacing using this tab

Change font, font style, and font size

Change underline style

Choose from a variety of font effects

Preview of text in the current font, size, and effects

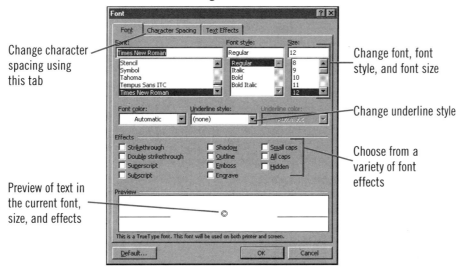

FIGURE C-4: **Completed font formatting**

Text formatted in bold

Text formatted in italics

Superscripted text

Text formatted in small caps, bold, italics, and underlined

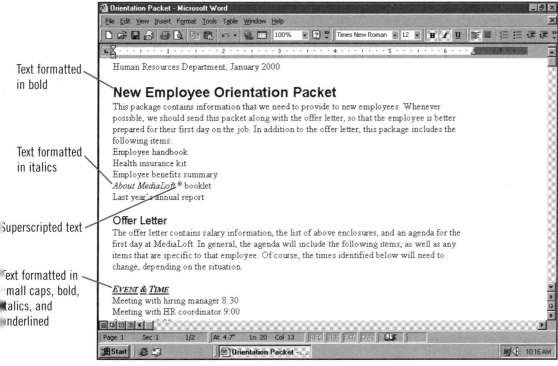

## Serif vs. sans serif fonts

Fonts can be divided into two types: serif and sans serif. A **serif font**, such as Times New Roman, has a small stroke, or a **serif**, at the ends of its characters, as shown in Figure C-5. Serif fonts are typically used in business documents, such as letters and resumes, and as the body text in books and other publications. Fonts without serifs, such as Arial, are known as **sans serif fonts**. Sans serif fonts are often used for headings in a document, or as the main font in other types of publications, such as flyers, brochures, and business cards. In a longer document, serif fonts can be easier to read than sans serif fonts.

FIGURE C-5: **Serif vs. sans serif fonts**

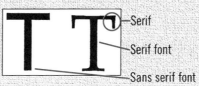

Serif

Serif font

Sans serif font

# Changing Paragraph Alignment

Another way to change the appearance of text in a document is to change the alignment of paragraphs. Paragraphs are aligned relative to the margins in a document. **Margins** are the blank areas between the edge of the text and the edge of the page. By default, text is **left-aligned**, or flush with the left margin. However, you can also **center** a paragraph between margins or **right-align** a paragraph so that its right edge is even with the right margin. You can also **justify** a paragraph so that both the left and right edges are evenly aligned. These paragraph alignment options are available on the Formatting toolbar or with the Paragraph command on the Format menu. When you format a paragraph, Word applies your formatting changes to the paragraph that contains the insertion point. If you wish to format multiple paragraphs, you must first select the paragraphs you want to format. ✎ Karen varies the alignment of paragraphs in her document to make it easier to read.

## Steps

**Trouble?**
Click the More Buttons button on the Formatting toolbar to locate buttons that are not visible on your Formatting toolbar.

1. Select the first line of the document, **Human Resources Department, January 2000**, then click the **Align Right button** 🔳 on the Formatting toolbar
   The text is aligned with the right margin.

2. In the first line, place the insertion point after the comma after **Department**, press **[Backspace]** to remove the comma, then press **[Enter]**
   The new paragraph is also right-aligned, as shown in Figure C-6. When you press [Enter] in the middle of a paragraph, the new paragraph "inherits" the paragraph formatting of the original paragraph.

3. Select **New Employee Orientation Packet**, then click the **Center button** 🔳 on the Formatting toolbar
   The title is centered evenly between the left and right margins. If you change the margins, this text will always remain centered relative to the margins.

4. Scroll down to locate the paragraph that begins **I would like to share …**, place the insertion point in the paragraph, then click the **Justify button** 🔳 on the Formatting toolbar
   Word adjusts the spacing between words of the paragraph so that each line in the paragraph is the same length, and flush with both the left and right margins. Justifying paragraphs eliminates the ragged right edge, and can make your documents look neater.

5. Click the **Save button** 🔳 on the Standard toolbar
   Compare your document to Figure C-7.

### CLUES TO USE

### Using the FormatPainter to copy formatting

You can use Word's FormatPainter to copy text or paragraph formatting to other text that you want to format the same way. This feature is especially useful when you want to copy multiple effects at once. To use the Format Painter, select the text whose formatting you want to copy, then click the FormatPainter button 🖌 on the Standard toolbar. When the pointer changes to 🖌, simply select the text you want to format. The new formatting is automatically applied. If you want to copy the formatting to multiple locations, double-click the FormatPainter button so that the FormatPainter pointer remains active. To turn off the FormatPainter, click the FormatPainter button again.

**FIGURE C-6: Right-aligned text**

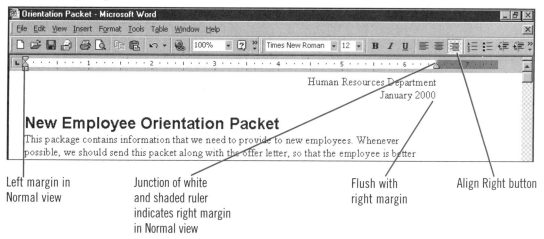

Left margin in
Normal view

Junction of white
and shaded ruler
indicates right margin
in Normal view

Flush with
right margin

Align Right button

Justify button

**FIGURE C-7: Justified text**

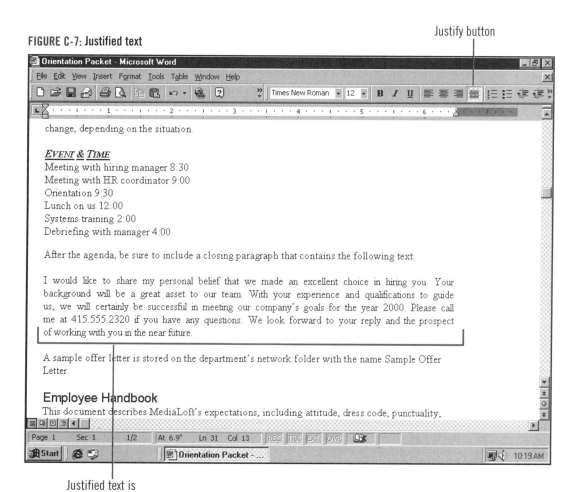

Justified text is
flush with left and
right margins

Word 2000

# Indenting Paragraphs

One way to visually structure a document is to change the indentation of individual paragraphs. When you **indent** text you change the width of the lines in the paragraph. You can modify the indentation from the right or left margins (or both) or you can indent just the first line of a paragraph and leave the remaining lines aligned with the left margin. **Indent markers** on the horizontal ruler show the indent settings for the paragraph that contains the insertion point. You can also drag the indent markers to change a paragraph's indentation. Dragging the Left Indent marker indents an entire paragraph, dragging the First Line Indent marker indents only the first line of the paragraph, and dragging the Right Indent marker indents a paragraph from the right margin. You can also use the Formatting toolbar or the Paragraph command on the Format menu to change a paragraph's indentation. Karen indents several paragraphs to help clarify the structure of her document. She uses the buttons on the Formatting toolbar and the indent markers on the horizontal ruler.

## Steps

**QuickTip**

To indent text with extra precision, click Format on the menu bar, click Paragraph, then enter the amount you want to indent in the Paragraph dialog box.

1. Scroll to the top of the document, select the **five lines** in the list under the first body paragraph (beginning with **Employee handbook**), click the **Increase Indent button** on the Formatting toolbar twice, then deselect the text
Each time you click the Increase Indent button, Word indents the left edge of the text ½ inch from the left margin. Notice that the indent markers on the ruler reflect the indentation, as shown in Figure C-8. (To see the indent markers, place the insertion point in the indented paragraphs.) You can decrease the indentation just as easily.

2. Select the same **five lines**, then click the **Decrease Indent button** on the Formatting toolbar once
The text moves ½ inch to the left. The indent markers on the ruler also move ½ inch to the left. The indent markers indicate how much the selected text is indented. You can also drag the indent markers to change indentation.

**Trouble?**

Be sure to drag the Left Indent marker, not the First Line Indent marker or the Hanging Indent marker. Click the Undo button if you make a mistake, then redo the step.

3. Scroll down to locate the paragraph that begins **I would like to share ...**, place the insertion point in the paragraph, then drag the **Left Indent marker** to the ¾" mark on the horizontal ruler, as shown in Figure C-9
Dragging the Left Indent marker indents all the lines in the paragraph. The left edge of the paragraph is aligned with the ¾" mark on the ruler. You can also use the indent markers to indent text from the right.

4. With the insertion point in the same paragraph drag the **Right Indent marker** to the 5¾" mark on the horizontal ruler
The right edge of the paragraph is indented ¾" from the right margin. You can also indent only the first line of a paragraph by dragging the First Line Indent marker.

5. Scroll to the top of the document, place the insertion point in the first body paragraph that begins **This package contains ...**, then drag the **First Line Indent marker** to the ½" mark on the horizontal ruler, as shown in Figure C-10
Dragging the First Line Indent marker indents only the first line of text in a paragraph.

6. Place the insertion point in the **paragraph** directly below each heading in the document (except "Event & Time"), then drag the **First Line Indent marker** to the ½" mark on the horizontal ruler so that the first line in each paragraph is indented ½"

7. Click the **Save button** on the Standard toolbar

**FIGURE C-8: Indented list**

First Line Indent marker

Hanging Indent marker

Left Indent marker

Indented text

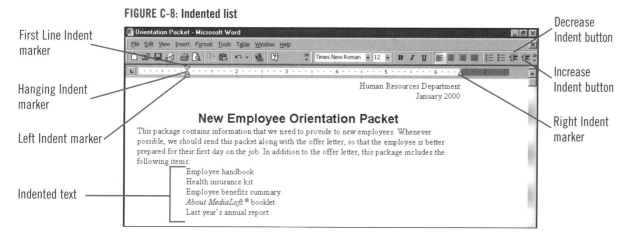

Decrease Indent button

Increase Indent button

Right Indent marker

**FIGURE C-9: Dragging Left Indent marker**

Left Indent marker being dragged to change indent

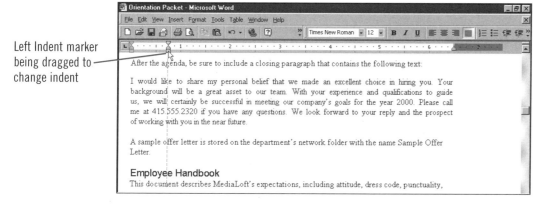

**FIGURE C-10: Dragging First Line Indent marker**

First Line Indent marker being dragged to change indent

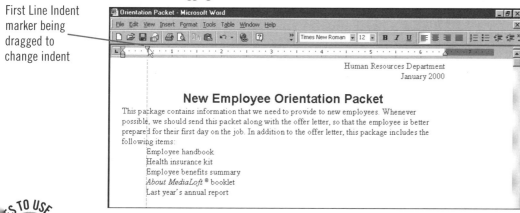

Word 2000

## Using hanging indent paragraph formatting

Sometimes you want a paragraph formatted so that the first line of the paragraph is not indented as much as the text in the remaining lines. This formatting is known as a **hanging indent,** shown in Figure C-11. Notice the arrangement of the indent markers on the horizontal ruler and the indentation of the first and remaining lines of the paragraph. You can create a hanging indent by dragging the Hanging Indent marker on the horizontal ruler or by pressing [Ctrl] [T].

**FIGURE C-11: Hanging indent**

**Bullets** Small symbols in front of items in a list. These symbols may be small circles, squares, check marks, arrows, or other graphics. When you apply bullets (or numbers) to items in a list (called a bulleted list), Word places a tab character after the bullet symbol and formats the paragraph with hanging indent.

# Changing Line Spacing

Another way to make a document easier to read is to increase the amount of spacing between lines. For example, thesis papers or draft versions of documents are often double-spaced to allow space for readers to add written comments. Increase line spacing whenever you want to give a more "open" feel to a document. You use the Paragraph command on the Format menu to change line spacing. Table C-1 describes several keyboard shortcuts for formatting paragraphs. Karen wants to provide space for comments from her colleagues, so she increases the line spacing in the document.

## Steps

1. Scroll to the top of the document, then place the insertion point in the first body paragraph that begins **This package contains ...**

**QuickTip**

You can also display the Paragraph dialog box by right-clicking, then clicking paragraph on the Pop-Up Menu.

2. Click **Format** on the menu bar, then click **Paragraph**
   The Paragraph dialog box opens with the Indents and Spacing tab displayed, as shown in Figure C-12. On this tab you can change the amount of space between lines. You can also change other paragraph format settings, including alignment and indentation.

3. Click the **Line spacing list arrow**, click **1.5 lines**, then click **OK**
   The space between the lines increases to one and a half lines.

4. Scroll down to locate the indented paragraph that begins **I would like to share ...**, then place the insertion point in the paragraph

5. Click **Format** on the menu bar, click **Paragraph**, click the **Line spacing list arrow** click **Double**, then click **OK**
   The space between the lines of the paragraph doubles, as shown in Figure C-13.

6. Click the **Save button** 🖫 on the Standard toolbar

**TABLE C-1: Keyboard shortcuts for aligning text and changing line spacing**

| to | press | to | press |
|----|-------|----|-------|
| Left-align text | [Ctrl] [L] | Format text with 1.5 line spacing | [Ctrl] [5] |
| Center text | [Ctrl] [E] | Single-space text | [Ctrl] [1] |
| Right-align text | [Ctrl] [R] | Double-space text | [Ctrl] [2] |
| Justify text | [Ctrl] [J] | | |

**FIGURE C-12:** Paragraph dialog box

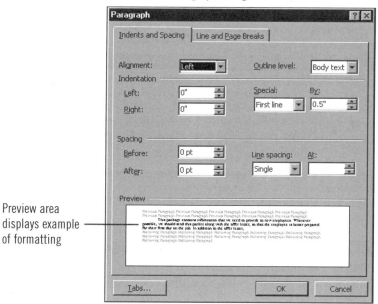

Preview area displays example of formatting

**FIGURE C-13:** New line spacing in a document

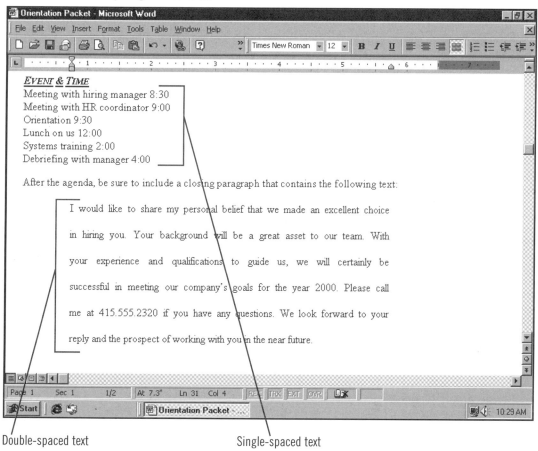

Double-spaced text

Single-spaced text

# Changing Paragraph Spacing

In the same way increasing line spacing can make a document easier to read, adding space between paragraphs can help to visually organize the content of your document. Spacing between lines and paragraphs is measured in points. Because you can set the number of points you want, adjusting paragraph spacing is a much more precise way to format than simply inserting blank lines between paragraphs. Karen increases the paragraph spacing between headings and body text to make the document more readable.

## Steps 1234

1. **Scroll to the top of the document, select New Employee Orientation Packet, click Format on the menu bar, then click Paragraph**

   The Paragraph dialog box opens with the Indents and Spacing tab displayed. You can use this tab to change the amount of space between paragraphs. You want to increase the amount of space after the title.

2. **Click the After up arrow twice, then click OK**

   The space after the paragraph is increased to 12 points. Clicking the Before or After arrows increases or decreases the amount of space above or below a paragraph. Each time you click an up or down arrow, the spacing changes by 6 points. You can also type the specific number of points you want in the Before and After text boxes.

3. **Select the five lines in the list that follows the first body paragraph, click Format on the menu bar, then click Paragraph**

4. **Double-click 0 in the Before text box, type 3, press [Tab] to move the insertion point to the After text box, then type 3**

   Your Paragraph dialog box should resemble Figure C-14.

5. **Click OK, then deselect the text**

   The space before and after each paragraph in the list increases by 3 points, as shown in Figure C-15.

6. **Select the heading Offer Letter, click Format on the menu bar, click Paragraph, click the After up arrow once, then click OK**

   The space between the heading and the paragraph below it increases by 6 points. The other headings should also be formatted with 6 points of space after.

**QuickTip**

You can press [F4] to repeat the last command.

7. **Place the insertion point in each remaining heading in the document (except "Event & Time"), then format each heading with 6 points of space after it**

8. **Click the Save button on the Standard toolbar**

FIGURE C-14: Paragraph spacing in Paragraph dialog box

Spacing Before
up arrow

You can type
specific spacing
settings

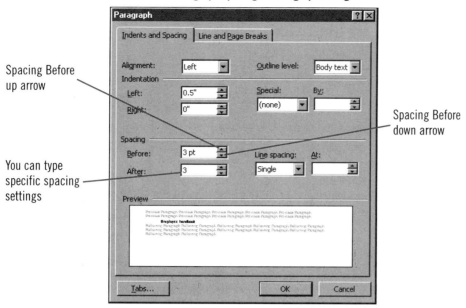

Spacing Before
down arrow

FIGURE C-15: Increased paragraph spacing

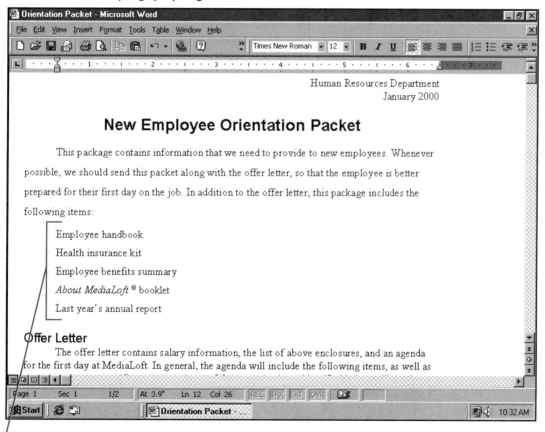

Increased space
before and after
paragraphs

**Word 2000**

# Aligning Text with Tabs

Numerical information (such as tables of financial results) is often easier to read when you align the text with tabs. A **tab** is used to position text at a specific location in the document. You should use tabs rather than the Spacebar to vertically align your text because tabs are more accurate, faster, and easier to change. When you press [Tab] in a document, the insertion point moves to the next tab stop. A **tab stop** is a predefined position in the document to which you can align tabbed text. By default, tab stops are located at every ½" from the left margin, but you can also create and modify tab stops. Table C-2 describes the five types of tabs. Karen uses tabs to align the meeting times listed in the agenda.

## Steps

**QuickTip**

Click the Show/Hide button ¶ on the Standard toolbar to reveal tab symbols (→), paragraph marks (¶), and spaces between characters (•) in your document. Click it again to hide the symbols.

**1.** Scroll to locate the heading **Event & Time**, place the insertion point in front of **Time**, then press **[Tab]**

Pressing [Tab] moves the word "Time" to the next default tab stop at the 1" mark on the horizontal ruler. You can also set your own tab stops.

**2.** At the left end of the horizontal ruler be sure the **Left Tab icon** ⌊ is active, as shown in Figure C-16, then click the **5" mark** on the ruler

If the Left Tab icon is not visible in the tab indicator at the left end of the ruler, click the tab indicator until the Left Tab icon appears. Clicking the ruler moves the tab stop to the 5" mark, and the tabbed text "Time" moves to the new location as shown in Figure C-16. To align the meeting times under this heading, you need to create a tab stop for each line in the agenda. To do this you'll use the Tabs command.

**QuickTip**

You can also adjust the location of a tab stop by dragging the tab marker to a new location on the ruler.

**3.** Select the **six lines** under the heading **Event & Time**, click **Format** on the menu bar, then click **Tabs**

The Tabs dialog box opens. You can use this dialog box to set tab stop position and alignment and to set **tab leaders** (lines or dots that appear in front of the tabbed text). You can also use the Tabs command to clear tabs. You'll set right-aligned tabs with leaders.

**4.** Type **5.3** in the Tab stop position text box, click the **Right option button**, then click the **2.... option button**

Your Tabs dialog box should resemble Figure C-17.

**5.** Click **Set** to create the tab setting, then click **OK**

A new right tab marker appears on the ruler just after the 5¼" mark. You'll insert tabs in front of each of the meeting times.

**6.** Place the insertion point in front of **8:30** in the first line of the agenda, then press **[Tab]**

The time "8:30" is right-aligned with the 5.3" tab stop with a dotted tab leader in front of it.

**QuickTip**

You can remove a tab stop by dragging it off the ruler.

**7.** Place the insertion point in front of each remaining **time** in the agenda, then press **[Tab]**

The times right-align at 5.3".

**8.** Select **&** in the Event & Time heading, then press **[Delete]**

**9.** Click the **Save button** 🖫 on the Standard toolbar

Compare your document to Figure C-18. To see the right-aligned tab marker, place the insertion point in the agenda.

**FIGURE C-16: Setting a tab stop on the ruler**

Left Tab icon in tab indicator

Left-aligned tab marker

Tabbed text

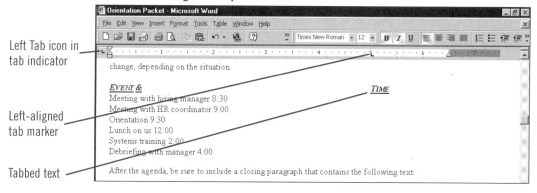

**FIGURE C-17: Tabs dialog box**

**FIGURE C-18: Right-aligned tabs with tab leaders**

Right-aligned tab marker

Right-aligned tabbed text

Tab leader

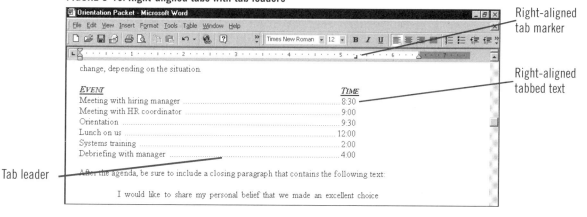

**TABLE C-2: Types of tabs**

| alignment | description | tab indicator |
|---|---|---|
| Left | Text left-aligns at the tab stop and extends to the right | L |
| Center | Text aligns at the middle of the tab stop, extending an equal distance to the left and right | ⊥ |
| Right | Text right-aligns at the tab stop and extends to the left | ⅃ |
| Decimal | Text aligns at the decimal point: text before the decimal point extends to the left, and the text after the decimal point extends to the right (used to align numbers) | ⊥ |
| Bar | Inserts a vertical bar at the tab position | I |

**Word 2000**

# Creating Bulleted and Numbered Lists

In a bulleted list, a **bullet**—a small symbol such as a circle or square—precedes each paragraph in the list. Using the Bullets button on the Formatting toolbar, you can insert a bullet in front of each item in a list. When you want to show items in a sequence, a numbered list best reflects the order or priority of the items. To create a simple numbered list, you can use the Numbering button on the Formatting toolbar. You can also use the Bullets and Numbering command on the Format menu to specify additional bullet and numbering formatting options. Karen draws attention to the lists in her document by formatting them with bullets and numbers.

**Steps**

1. Scroll to the top of the document, select the **five lines** in the list under the first body paragraph, then click the **Bullets button** on the Formatting toolbar
   A bullet appears in front of each item in the list.

**QuickTip**

To access more bullet or number styles, click Customize in the Bullets and Numbering dialog box, then choose from the options in the Customize dialog box.

2. With the list still selected, click **Format** on the menu bar, then click **Bullets and Numbering**
   The Bullets and Numbering dialog box opens with the Bulleted tab displayed, as shown in Figure C-19. In this dialog box, you can choose from seven different bullet styles. Do not be concerned if your bullet styles are different from those shown in the figure. You can customize your styles to use whatever bullet characters you prefer.

3. Click the **check mark box**, then click **OK**
   The bullet character changes to a small check mark.

**QuickTip**

When you add or remove any numbered item, Word renumbers the remaining items in the list.

4. Scroll to the agenda under the "Event Time" heading, select the **six lines** in the agenda, then click the **Numbering button** on the Formatting toolbar
   The agenda becomes a numbered list. You can also change the format of a numbered list in the Bullets and Numbering dialog box.

5. Make sure the six lines of the agenda are selected, then right-click the **agenda**
   A pop-up menu appears.

6. Click **Bullets and Numbering** on the pop-up menu, then click the **Numbered tab** in the dialog box, if it is not already displayed
   The Numbered tab in the Bullets and Numbering dialog box displays additional numbering options.

7. In the first row, click the **uppercase Roman numeral box**, then click **OK**
   The numbers in the list change to Roman numerals.

8. Deselect the text, then click the **Save button** on the Standard toolbar
   Compare your document to Figure C-20.

**CLUES TO USE**

### Creating outline style numbered lists

You can create a simple outline style numbered list by applying an outline numbering scheme from the Outline Numbered tab in the Bullets and Numbering dialog box to a list. To create a new outline, choose a numbering scheme (one that does not include headings), then type your outline, pressing [Enter] after each item in the list. After you have applied an outline numbering scheme to a list, you can increase or decrease the indentation of individual paragraphs to change their level of importance in the outline. For example, to demote an item to a lower level in the outline, click in the paragraph, then click the Increase Indent button on the Formatting toolbar. To promote an item to a higher level, click the Decrease Indent button. You can choose to format outline style numbered lists with a combination of letters and numbers, numbers alone, or bullets, or you can create a custom outline style.

FIGURE C-19: Bullets and Numbering dialog box

Current bullet style ——

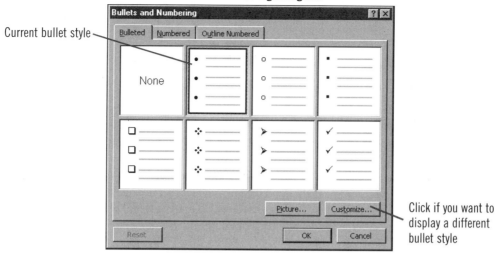

Click if you want to
display a different
bullet style

FIGURE C-20: Bulleted and numbered lists

ulleted
st ——

mbered ——

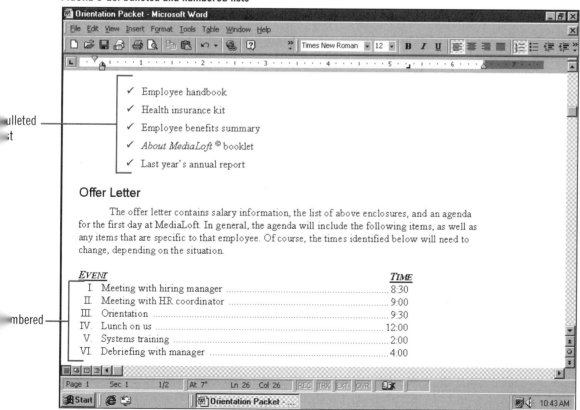

# Applying Borders and Shading

Borders and shading add visual interest to text. **Borders** are lines you can add to the top, bottom, or sides of paragraphs. Preset border settings make it easy to create a box around a paragraph. **Shading** is a transparent color or pattern you apply to a paragraph. With the Tables and Borders toolbar you can apply the borders and shading options you use most often, or you can use the Borders and Shading command on the Format menu to select from additional border and shading options. When you use the Tables and Borders toolbar, Word displays the document in Print Layout view. **Views** are different ways of displaying a document in the document window. Each view provides different features that are especially helpful in different phases of working on a document. Table C-3 describes different views in Word. You can change the document view by clicking the view buttons to the left of the horizontal scroll bar. Karen uses borders to emphasize the headings and adds shading to draw attention to the closing paragraph.

## Steps

### Trouble?

Click the More Buttons button on the Standard toolbar to locate buttons that are not displayed on your Standard toolbar. Click Cancel if the Office Assistant appears.

1. Place the insertion point in the paragraph that begins **I would like to share...**, then click the **Tables and Borders button** on the Standard toolbar
   The Tables and Borders toolbar appears, and the document switches to Print Layout view.

2. Click the **Shading Color list arrow** on the Tables and Borders toolbar, then click the **Gray 20% box**, as shown in Figure C-21
   A transparent gray rectangle covers the paragraph.

3. Scroll to the top of the document, click the **Line Style list arrow** on the Tables and Borders toolbar, then click the **Thick/Thin style** (thick line on top, thin line below) on the Line Style list
   The Thick/Thin line style is now the active line style. It remains in effect for all the borders you create until you change the style again. The pointer also changes to ∅. To apply a border you need to turn off the pointer.

### Trouble?

If a box appears, click the Undo button, click the text, then click again.

4. Click the **Draw Table button** on the Tables and Borders toolbar to turn off the pointer, then select **New Employee Orientation Packet**

5. Click the **Outside Border list arrow** on the Tables and Borders toolbar, then click the **Top Border button**
   A border of a Thick/Thin line appears above the selected text. You'll change to a new line style before adding a border under the selected text.

6. With the text still selected, click the **Line Style list arrow**, click the **Thin/Thick style** (thin line on top, thick line below), then click to turn off the pointer

7. Click the **Top Border list arrow** on the Tables and Borders toolbar, click the **Bottom Border button** on the menu that appears, then deselect the text
   A border appears below the title, as shown in Figure C-22.

8. Click the **Close button** on the Tables and Borders toolbar, place the insertion point in front of **Human Resources Department** at the top of the document, type your name, then press **[Enter]**

9. Click the **Save button** on the Standard toolbar, then click the **Print button** the Standard toolbar

10. Close the document, then exit Word

FIGURE C-21: **Tables and Borders toolbar**

Tables and Borders button

Print Layout View button

Shading Color button

Shading Color list arrow

Click a square to choose a color

Edges of page appear in Print Layout view

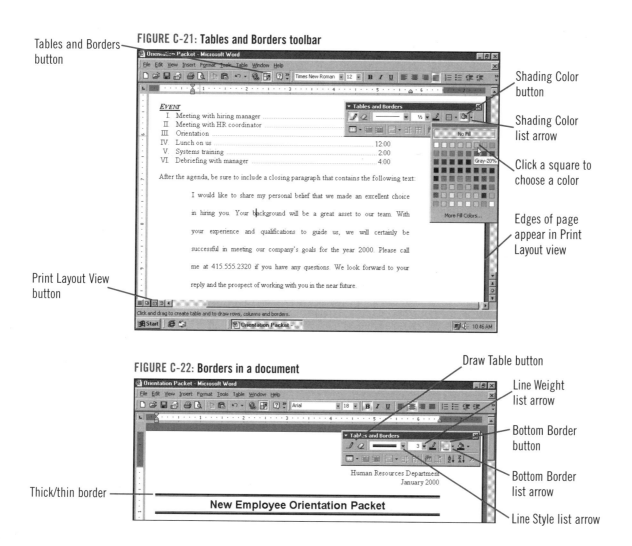

FIGURE C-22: **Borders in a document**

Thick/thin border

Draw Table button

Line Weight list arrow

Bottom Border button

Bottom Border list arrow

Line Style list arrow

Human Resources Department
January 2000

**New Employee Orientation Packet**

TABLE C-3: **Word document views**

| view | displays | use to |
|---|---|---|
| Normal | A simple layout view of the document | Type, edit and format text quickly |
| Print Layout | The document as it will appear when printed on paper, along with the horizontal and vertical rulers | Edit and view the exact placement of text and graphics on the page, adjust margins, and work with columns and tables |
| Outline | Selected levels of headings and body text | View major headings and organize ideas in outline format |
| Web Layout | The document as a Web page | Create a Web page |

ES TO USE

## Adding borders and shading with the Borders and Shading command

The Tables and Borders toolbar includes the most frequently used border and shading options. However, for even more border and shading options use the Borders and Shading command on the Format menu to display the Borders and Shading dialog box. In this dialog box, you can use the Borders tab to select preset box, shadow, and 3-D borders, or design a border of your own using the many line, color, and spacing options available on this tab. Borders can be as simple or as complex as you like. On the Shading tab, you can select a shade pattern, including stripes, checkerboards and grids, and choose the color of the pattern and its background. You can also create a custom shade color and adjust the intensity of the shading you apply to text. Use the Apply to list arrow on both tabs to choose to apply borders or shading to the selected text or to paragraphs.

# Practice

## ► Concepts Review

Label each of the formatting elements shown in Figure C-23.

FIGURE C-23

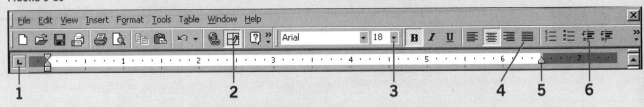

Match each term with the statement that describes it.

| | |
|---|---|
| **7. Font** | **a.** The first line of a paragraph is closer to the left margin than the remaining lines |
| **8. Bold** | **b.** A set of characters of a specific design |
| **9. Hanging indent** | **c.** Both the left and right edges of a paragraph are evenly aligned |
| **10. Tab stop** | **d.** A style that makes text appear darker |
| **11. Justified** | **e.** A set location in the document to which you can align text |

Select the best answer from the list of choices.

12. Which paragraph formatting feature is not available on the Formatting toolbar?
   **a.** Paragraph alignment
   **b.** Line spacing
   **c.** Decrease indentation
   **d.** Borders

13. Which view would you use to best see the margins on a page?
   **a.** Normal
   **b.** Outline
   **c.** Print Layout
   **d.** Web Layout

14. Which of the following statements about tabs is not true?
   **a.** You can use the horizontal ruler to set tab stops.
   **b.** You can use the Tab command on the Format menu to set tab stops.
   **c.** You can use the horizontal ruler to create a tab leader.
   **d.** Tabs are a more accurate way to align text than spaces.

15. Which button on the Tables and Borders toolbar do you click when you want to apply shading to text?
   **a.** Borders
   **b.** Shading
   **c.** Borders and Shading
   **d.** You can not apply shading with a button

**1. Change fonts and font sizes.**

   **a.** Start Word, open the file WD C-2 from your Project Disk, and save it as "Press Release."

   **b.** Format "Press Release" in 26 point Arial Black.

   **c.** Format the second line of text in 20 point Arial.

   **d.** In the second sentence, format "RoadMap" in Arial.

   **e.** Format all occurrences of "Open Roads, Inc." in Arial.

**2. Apply font effects.**

   **a.** Format the heading, "Package Delivery Company …" in bold.

   **b.** In the first body paragraph, format "RoadMap" in bold italics with an underline.

   **c.** Use the Format Painter to apply the same formatting to "RoadMap" in the second body paragraph.

   **d.** Apply superscript formatting to the copyright symbol after the first occurrence of "RoadMap."

   **e.** Format the first occurrence of "Open Roads, Inc." in bold, and apply the All caps effect.

   **f.** Apply the same formatting to all occurrences of "Open Roads, Inc."

**3. Change paragraph alignment.**

   **a.** Center "Press Release" and "Package Delivery Company …".

   **b.** Justify the remaining paragraphs in the document.

   **c.** Type your name and today's date at the bottom of the document, then right-align your name and the date.

**4. Indent paragraphs.**

   **a.** Drag the First Line Indent marker to indent the first line in the first and second body paragraphs ½".

   **b.** Indent the three lines after the first body paragraph one inch.

   **c.** With the insertion point in the last body paragraph, drag the Left Indent marker to the ½" mark on the horizontal ruler.

   **d.** Right-indent the last body paragraph ½" from the right margin.

**5. Change line spacing.**

   **a.** Change the line spacing of the body text (not the headings) to 1.5.

   **b.** Change the line spacing of the last body paragraph to single-spacing.

**6. Change paragraph spacing.**

   **a.** Format "Press Release" with 12 points of space before and 3 points of space after.

   **b.** Format "Package Delivery Company …" with 18 points of space before and 6 points of space after.

   **c.** Format the first body paragraph with 6 points of space after.

**7. Align text with tabs.**

   **a.** Near the bottom, insert a blank line after "Typical shipping prices:".

   **b.** Press [Tab], type "Weight," press [Tab], type "Cost," then press [Enter].

   **c.** Press [Tab], type "Under 1 lb," press [Tab], type "5.25," then press [Enter].

   **d.** Press [Tab], type "1 - 10 lbs," press [Tab], then type "10.75." Do not press [Enter].

   **e.** Select all three lines of the list and place a left-aligned tab stop at the 2" mark.

   **f.** With the same three lines selected, click the tab alignment indicator at the left end of the ruler until you see the decimal tab marker, then place a decimal-aligned tab stop at the 4.5" mark.

   **g.** Press [Enter] at the end of the last item in the list, press [Tab], type "More than 10 lbs," press [Tab], then type "14.50."

   **h.** Remove the decimal tab stop from the first line in the table, then set a new left-aligned tab stop at the 4⅜" mark.

   **i.** Select the next three lines of the table, and format the 4.5" tab stop to have a dotted leader.

   **j.** Underline each word in the first line of the table.

**8. Create bulleted and numbered lists.**

   **a.** Number the three-line list under the first body paragraph.

   **b.** Apply bullets to the list, then change the bullets to another bullet style.

**9. Apply borders and shading.**

   **a.** Apply a thin double line above and below "Press Release."

   **b.** Apply 15% gray shading to the last paragraph.

   **c.** Save your changes to the document, print the document, and exit Word.

# ► Independent Challenges

**1.** As an account representative for Lease For Less, a company that rents office equipment such as fax machines and large copiers, you need to improve the formatting of a customer proposal.

   To complete this independent challenge:

   **a.** Start Word, open the document WD C-3 from your Project Disk, then save it as "Discount Letter."

   **b.** At the top of the document, format the company name in 18 point Arial Black, with the outline effect.

   **c.** Format the company address in 11 point Arial. Right-align the company name and address.

   **d.** Change the font size of the rest of the letter to 12 points.

   **e.** Indent the list of discount rates 1" and format the list as a bulleted list.

   **f.** Justify the body paragraphs in the letter.

   **g.** Type your name in the signature block, and then preview, save, and print the document.

**2.** Your golf league has asked you to design the announcement for the annual tournament. You already entered information about the tournament in a document; now you need to enhance its appearance.

   To complete this independent challenge:

   **a.** Start Word, open the document WD C-4 from your Project Disk, and save it as "Golf Classic."

   **b.** Center the first two lines, change the font to 18 point Arial, bold, italic, and then add 25% gray shading.

   **c.** Indent the first body paragraph one-half inch from the right and left margins.

   **d.** Select the 4 lines under the first body paragraph. Use the Tabs dialog box to format the lines with right tab stops at 1¾" and a left tab stop at 2¼", then press [Tab] before and after "Where", "When", "Who" and "How Much".

   **e.** Center the heading "Schedule." Format this heading in 14 point Arial bold, then add red highlighting.

   **f.** Add numbers to the list of scheduled events.

   **g.** Add a 1½ point border above the line "Send the attached ...", and center the remaining four lines.

   **h.** Double-space the entire document.

   **i.** Replace "Your Name" with your name, preview, save, and print the document.

**3.** As co-chair for your college reunion planning committee, you need to write a memo about upcoming meetings. Yo use Word's Memo Wizard to create the memo. This wizard prompts you to enter information in a series of dialog box and then formats the memo for you. After the memo is created, you adjust the formatting to suit your own preference

   To complete this independent challenge:

   **a.** Start Word and create a new document using the Memo Wizard. (*Hint*: Click File on the menu bar, click New, then double-click Memo wizard on the Memos tab in the New dialog box.)

   **b.** Click Next to begin, click the Professional option button, then click Next to proceed through the wizard.

   **c.** Enter the title "Reunion Memo," the date, your name, and the subject "Meeting dates," clicking Next at the e of each dialog box.

**d.** Enter "Reunion Planning Committee" in the To text box, deselect the CC check box and all other check boxes in the next two dialog boxes, then click Finish.

**e.** Format "Reunion Memo" in 36 point Arial bold, then center the title.

**f.** Type the following memo text:

Thank you for participating in the reunion planning. Here's the schedule for the next three meetings.

| Date | Topic |
|------|-------|
| October 18 | Deciding a theme |
| November 15 | Contacting alums |
| March 20 | Catering options |

**g.** Select the 4 lines of the schedule. Use the Tabs dialog box to set a right tab stop at 3" and a left tab stop at 3½", then use tabs to align the schedule.

**h.** Format the schedule with a double-line 1½ point box around it, 20% gray shading, and 6 points of space below each line, then indent the schedule one inch from both margins.

**i.** Change the font size of the body text to 12 points, then format the schedule headings in 14 point bold.

**j.** Save the memo on your Project Disk as "Reunion Memo," then preview and print the memo.

**4.** As volunteer coordinator at MediaLoft, you are responsible for creating a certificate to award to the volunteer of the month. The name of the winner is posted each month on MediaLoft's intranet site.

To complete this independent challenge:

**a.** Start Word and create a new document called "Volunteer Award" on your Project Disk.

**b.** Connect to the Internet, go to the MediaLoft intranet site at http://www.course.com/illustrated/MediaLoft, click the link for the Community page, then click the link for Volunteer of the Month.

**c.** Copy the name of this month's winner to the Clipboard, then disconnect from the Internet.

**d.** Using Figure C-24 as a guide, enter and format the text on the award certificate. Add the name of the recipient and your name.

**e.** Use Garamond for the font. Format "Volunteer of the Month" in 36 point bold italic and apply the shadow effect. Format "MediaMentors" in 36 point bold and apply the small caps effect. Format all other text in 24 points.

**f.** Center the text and use 1.5 line spacing. Use 12 point spacing before and after "Presented to," "for participating in," "This day," and the date.

**g.** Add a ½ point border under the recipient's name.

**h.** Right-align your name and title, and change the font size to 18 points. Add 60 points of space above your name, then place a ½ point border above your name and indent this line to the 2" mark.

**i.** Add 25% gray shading as shown in the figure.

**j.** Preview, save, and print the certificate.

**FIGURE C-24**

*Volunteer of the Month*

Presented to:

[recipient]

for participating in

**MEDIAMENTORS**

Technology Literacy Program

This day

September 25, 2000

Your Name

Volunteer Coordinator

# ► Visual Workshop

Create the flyer shown in Figure C-25 and save it as "Kids Flyer" on your Project Disk. Use 16 point Garamond for the font and change the font size of the heading to 24 points. Adjust the character spacing of the heading text to expand it and change the scale to 150%. (*Hint*: Use the Character Spacing tab in the Font dialog box.) For the contact information, use a 3 point box border. (*Hint*: Use the Borders and Shading command.) Print a copy of the completed flyer.

FIGURE C-25

## COMPANIES FOR KIDS NEEDS YOUR HELP!

**COMPANIES FOR KIDS** is a non-profit community program that collects toys, clothing, and books for children in local shelters. We depend largely on local businesses to help fund our efforts.

Each weekend **COMPANIES FOR KIDS** sends out corporate teams to collect clothing, books, and toys from the community. Your company may also choose to help our children in any of the following ways:

❖ Provide a monetary donation.

❖ Assemble teams to sort or collect clothing and toys.

❖ Send individuals to spend time with children in local shelters.

We look forward to your company's participation and support in this valuable community program.

**Contact:** Your Name

Fundraising Coordinator

**COMPANIES FOR KIDS**

(415) 555-2020

# Working

## with Tables

| MOUS | ▶ **Create a table**
| MOUS | ▶ **Adjust table rows and columns**
| MOUS | ▶ **Add and delete rows and columns**
| MOUS | ▶ **Format a table**
| MOUS | ▶ **Calculate data in a table**
| MOUS | ▶ **Sort a table**
| MOUS | ▶ **Draw a table**
| MOUS | ▶ **Split and merge cells**

A **table** is text that is arranged in a grid of rows and columns. With Word, you can create a table from scratch or you can convert existing text into a table. Once you have created a table, you can easily modify it, sort and calculate the data in it, and quickly make it attractive using a preset table format. You can also build tables by drawing rows and columns exactly where you want them. Tables are an excellent tool for displaying data that is typically found in lists or columns. ✎ Karen Rosen needs to create an agenda for a new employee, a record of earned vacation days, and a record of employee absences. She decides to format this information in tables to make the documents attractive and easy to use.

# Creating a Table

In a **table**, text is arranged in a grid of rows and columns that is divided by borders. A **column** in a table is text arranged vertically. A **row** is text arranged horizontally. The intersection of a column and a row is called a **cell**. **Borders** surround each cell to help you see the structure of the table. You can create an empty table and then add text to it, or you can convert existing text into a table. When you create a new, blank table, you specify the number of rows and columns you want your table to include. Once the table is created, you can enter information in it. To create a blank table, you can use the Insert Table button on the Standard toolbar, or the Insert Table command on the Table menu. You can later change the structure of the table by adding and deleting rows and columns. ✐ Karen creates a table for tracking employee attendance in a new document. As she works, she adds rows to the table.

## Steps

1. Start **Word**, click **Tools** on the menu bar, click **Customize**, click the **Options tab** in the Customize dialog box, click **Reset my usage data** to restore default settings, click **Yes** in the alert box, then click **Close**

2. Click the **Print Layout View button** on the horizontal scroll bar
   The document displays in Print Layout view and the I-beam pointer changes to $I^{\equiv}$

3. Type **Agenda for New Employees**, then press **[Enter]** twice

**Trouble?**

Click the More Buttons button on the Standard toolbar to locate buttons that are not visible on your toolbar.

4. Click the **Insert Table button** on the Standard toolbar
   A grid opens. You use this grid to indicate the number of rows and columns you want the new table to contain.

5. Click the **second box** in the last row of the grid to select four rows and two columns, as shown in Figure D-1
   A blank table containing four rows and two columns appears in the document.

6. Type **EVENT** in the first cell, then press **[Tab]**
   Pressing [Tab] moves the insertion point to the next cell in the row.

**QuickTip**

Pressing [Shift][Tab] selects the previous cell.

7. Type **TIME**, press **[Tab]**, type **Meeting with Karen Rosen, Director of Human Resources**, press **[Tab]**, type **8:30**, then press **[Tab]**
   Pressing [Tab] at the end of a row moves the insertion point to the next cell in the next row.

8. Type the following text in the table, pressing **[Tab]** to move from cell to cell
   **Meeting with HR coordinator     9:00**
   **Orientation                     9:30**

9. Press **[Tab]**
   Pressing [Tab] with the insertion point in the last cell of a table creates a new blank row at the end of the table, as shown in Figure D-2.

**Trouble?**

If you pressed [Tab] after the last row, click the Undo button on the Standard toolbar to remove the new blank row.

10. Type the following text in the table, pressing **[Tab]** to move from cell to cell, and to add new rows
    **Lunch on us                              12:00**
    **Systems training                          2:00**
    **Tele-conference with regional managers    3:00**
    **Debriefing with training manager          4:00**

11. Click the **Save button** on the Standard toolbar, then save the document with the filename **Agenda** to your Project Disk
    Compare your table to Figure D-3.

**FIGURE D-1: Creating a table**

Your toolbars may differ

Insert Table button

Indicates 4 rows and 2 columns

More Buttons button on Standard toolbar

Drag the lower-right corner of grid to expand number of rows and columns

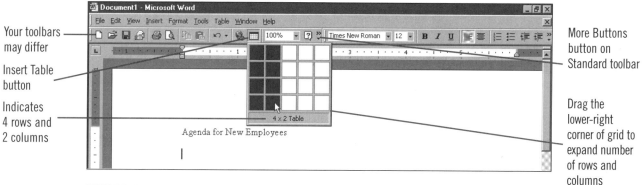

**FIGURE D-2: New row**

Column

Row

New row

Cell

Border

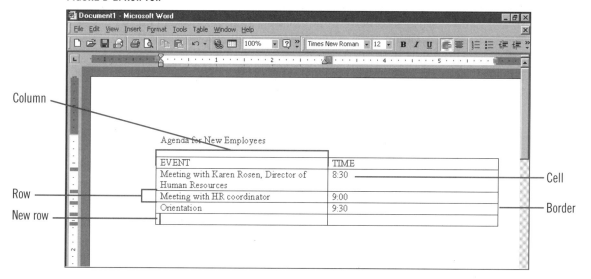

**FIGURE D-3: Text in a table**

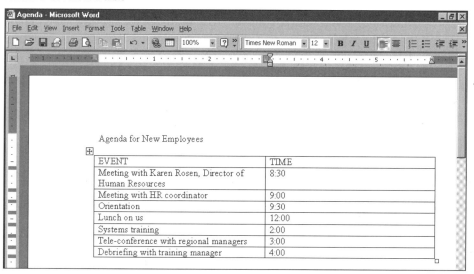

## Converting text to a table

Sometimes it is easier to enter text in your document and convert it into a table than to create a blank table and enter the text in the cells. The text you intend to convert to a table must be formatted with tabs, commas, or paragraph marks so that Word can interpret the formatting and create the table. You can create a table based on existing text by selecting the text and then using the Insert Table button on the Standard toolbar or the Convert Text to Table command on the Table menu. In the Convert Text to Table dialog box, you can specify the number of rows and columns you want in your table, along with other table formatting options.

# Adjusting Table Rows and Columns

Once you create a table, you can easily adjust the size of rows, columns, and individual cells to make your tables easier to read. You can adjust the size of rows and columns by dragging the borders, by using the AutoFit command on the Table menu to resize columns and rows automatically, or by specifying the column width and row height you want using the Table Properties command on the Table menu. ✎ Karen adjusts the height of the rows and the width of the columns in her table.

**Steps**

### Trouble?

If the width of only one cell in the column changes when you adjust the column width, deselect the cell, then click the Undo button 🔄 on the Standard toolbar. If you want to adjust the width of the entire column, make sure no cells are selected.

1. Position the pointer over the **right border of the first column** until the pointer changes to ↔, then drag the border to the 2¼" **mark** on the horizontal ruler

   The first column narrows and the second column widens as shown in Figure D-5. In some cells, the text in the first column wraps onto a second line. Moving the border for the first column resulted in the second column becoming too wide for the text. You can adjust the width of a column to fit the text by double-clicking the column border.

2. Position the pointer over the **right border of the second column** until the pointer changes to ↔, then double-click

   The second column automatically adjusts to fit the text. You can also adjust the table so that all rows are the same height. First you need to select the entire table.

3. Click anywhere in the table, then click the **Table Select icon** ⊞ that appears at the upper-left corner of the table

   The entire table is selected. You can also select a whole table by clicking Table on the menu bar, pointing to Select, and then clicking Table.

4. Click **Table** on the menu bar, point to **AutoFit**, click **Distribute Rows Evenly**, then deselect the table

   All the rows in the table are the same height, as shown in Figure D-6. If you had wanted to make all the columns the same width, you would have clicked Distribute Columns Evenly on the AutoFit menu. You can also use the commands on this menu to adjust the size of columns and rows to fit the text or the document window.

5. Click the **Save button** 💾 on the Standard toolbar

---

### Setting table properties

You can use the Table Properties command to change the structure and format of the tables you create. This command is especially useful when you want to set a specific row height or column width, or when you want to change the alignment of a table on the page. To open the Table Properties dialog box, click Table on the menu bar, then click Table Properties. On the Row, Column, and Cell tabs you can specify an exact height and width for the columns, rows, and cells selected in your table. You can also change the vertical alignment of text in cells on the Cells tab. To change a table's alignment on the page, choose the alignment you want on the Table tab, shown in Figure D-4. You can also specify the width of the table on this tab and set text wrapping options, if any.

**FIGURE D-4: Table Properties dialog box**

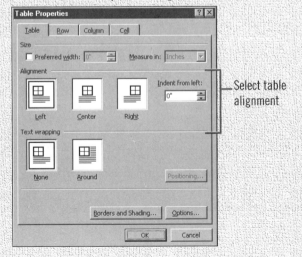

**FIGURE D-5:** Resized columns

Table Select icon

Dragging a column border adjusts the column width

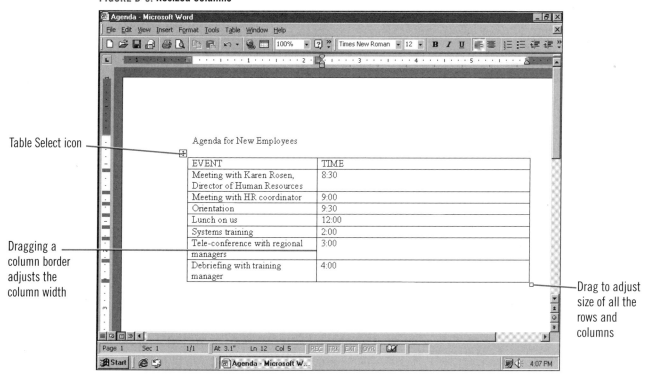

Drag to adjust size of all the rows and columns

**FIGURE D-6:** Resized rows and columns

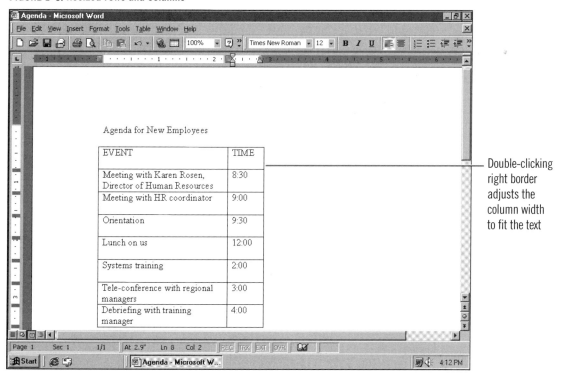

Double-clicking right border adjusts the column width to fit the text

**Word 2000**

# Adding and Deleting Rows and Columns

As you add or remove information in a table, you may need to change the number of rows or columns. You can quickly add or delete rows and columns using the commands on the Table menu or the commands on the pop-up menu for tables. Before you add or delete rows and columns, you must select an existing row or column in the table to indicate where you want to add or remove cells. The easiest way to select a row or column is to use the selection bar. Each row, column, and cell in a table has its own selection bar. Click to the left of a cell or a row to select the whole row, or click above a column to select a whole column. You can also click and drag to select cells, columns, or rows. ▰ Karen adds new rows for new agenda events to the table, and deletes an unnecessary row. She also adds a column to identify the location of each event.

### QuickTip

You can also select a row or column by clicking Table on the menu bar, pointing to Select, and then clicking Row or Column.

1. Click the **selection bar** to the left of the **Lunch on us row** to select it, then click the **Insert Rows button** 🖱 on the Standard toolbar

   A new blank row appears above the row you selected, as shown in Figure D-7. Notice that the Insert Table button changes to the Insert Rows button when a row is selected. If you had selected a column, the button would have changed to the Insert Columns button.

2. In the first cell of the new blank row, type **Training team meeting,** press **[Tab],** then type **10:30**

### QuickTip

To quickly delete a row or column, select it, then press [Shift][Delete] or [Ctrl][X]. You can also click Table on the menu bar, point to Delete, then click Rows or Columns. To remove only the text from a selected row or column, press [Delete].

3. Select the **Tele-conference row,** right-click, then click **Delete Rows** on the pop-up menu

   The selected row is deleted.

4. Place the insertion point in **the last row,** click **Table** on the menu bar, point to **Insert,** click **Rows Below,** type **Social hour,** press **[Tab],** then type **5:00**

5. Select the entire **second column** in the table, then click the **Insert Columns button** ⬆ on the Standard toolbar

   A new blank column appears between the first and second columns. Word places the insertion point in the first cell of the new column when you begin typing.

6. Type **LOCATION**

   The column width adjusts to fit the text.

### QuickTip

To insert a new column at the right end of a table, place the insertion point in the last column, click Table on the menu bar, click Insert, then click Columns to the Right. You can also use the Insert command to insert rows above or below the selected cell.

7. Press **[↓],** then type the following in the remaining cells in the column:
   **HR 220 [↓]**
   **HR 225 [↓]**
   **Training Center [↓]**
   **Conference Room 1 [↓]**
   **Reception Area [↓]**
   **Your office [↓]**
   **HR 250 [↓]**
   **Reception Area**
   Compare your document to Figure D-8.

8. Click the **Save button** 💾 on the Standard toolbar

FIGURE D-7: Inserted row

Insert Rows button

New row

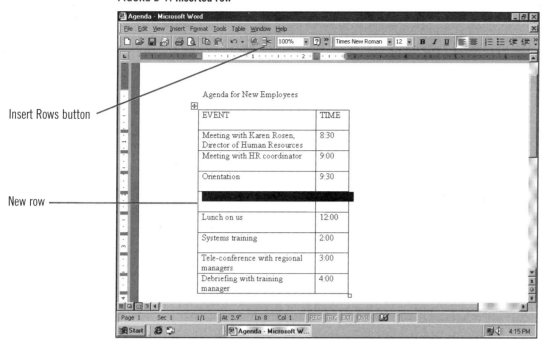

FIGURE D-8: Edited table

nserted column

dded row

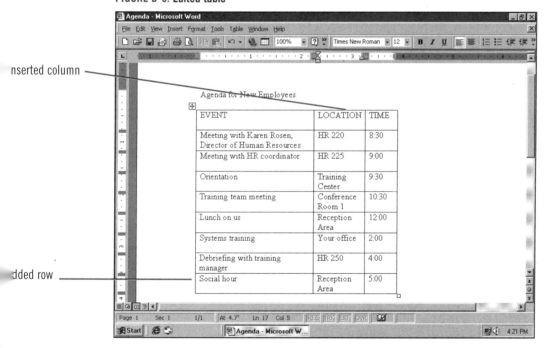

## Copying and moving columns and rows

You can use the same techniques to copy and move columns and rows that you use to copy and move text in a document. Be sure to select the entire row or column you want to copy or move, then click the Cut or Copy buttons to place the selection on the Clipboard. Place the insertion point in the location you want to insert the row or column in the table, then click the Paste button. You can also copy or move rows or columns by clicking and dragging them. Again, select the rows or columns you want to copy or move, click and hold the mouse over the selection until the pointer changes, then drag the selection to the new location in the table and release the mouse button.

**Word 2000**

# Formatting a Table

You can improve the appearance of a table by adding borders and shading to rows and columns. Changing the alignment of text in a table can also make your tables more attractive and readable. You can format tables automatically with the Table AutoFormat feature, which provides a variety of preset table formats, or you can use the buttons on the Tables and Borders toolbar to apply a variety of formatting effects to your tables. Table D-1 describes some of the buttons on the Tables and Borders toolbar. Karen uses the Table AutoFormat command to apply borders, shading, and special formatting to the table, then she changes the alignment of text in the table.

## Steps

**QuickTip**

You can also click the Table AutoFormat button on the Tables and Borders toolbar to open the Table AutoFormat dialog box.

1. **With the insertion point in the table, click Table on the menu bar, then click Table AutoFormat**
   The Table AutoFormat dialog box opens, as shown in Figure D-9.

2. **Scroll the list of formats, then click Grid 8**
   The Preview box shows a sample table formatted with the Grid 8 format option. You can modify the preset formats to highlight important elements in your tables. By default, Word applies special formatting to heading rows and the first column of a table. To emphasize the meeting times in the agenda, you'll apply special formatting to the last column of the table.

3. **Make sure the Heading rows and First column check boxes are selected under Apply special formats to, then click the Last column check box to select it**
   In the Preview box, the last column of the sample table now appears in bold. AutoFormat automatically adjusts the width of columns in a table to span the width of the page. To retain the column width you set earlier, you'll turn off the AutoFit feature.

4. **Clear the AutoFit checkbox, then click OK**
   The table is formatted with the settings you selected.

**Trouble?**

Click the More Buttons button on the Formatting toolbar to locate buttons that are not visible on your toolbar.

5. **Select the last column, click the Align Right button on the Formatting toolbar, then deselect the column**
   The meeting times are right-aligned. You could also use the alignment buttons on the Tables and Borders toolbar to change the alignment of text in cells. Compare your table to Figure D-10.

6. **Type your name at the top of the page, press [Enter], click the Save button on the Standard toolbar, then click the Print button on the Standard toolbar**

7. **Click File on the menu bar, then click Close**

**TABLE D-1: Buttons on the Tables and Borders toolbar**

| button | use to | button | use to |
|--------|--------|--------|--------|
| Line Style | Determine the line style of borders | Draw Table | Draw a table or cells |
| Line Weight | Determine the thickness of borders | Eraser | Erase or remove a border between cells |
| Border Color | Determine the color of borders | Merge Cells | Combine selected cells into a single cell |
| Outside Borders | Add or remove individual borders | Split Cells | Divide a cell into multiple cells |
| Shading Color | Determine the shade color or pattern of cells | Insert Table | Insert new rows, columns, cells, or a new table; determine column width |
| Align Top Left | Change the alignment of text in a cell | Distribute Rows Evenly | Make rows the same height |
| Change Text Direction | Change the orientation of text | Distribute Columns Evenly | Make columns the same width |

FIGURE D-9: Table AutoFormat dialog box

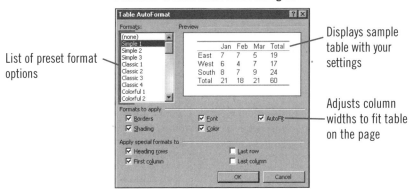

List of preset format options

Displays sample table with your settings

Adjusts column widths to fit table on the page

FIGURE D-10: Formatted table

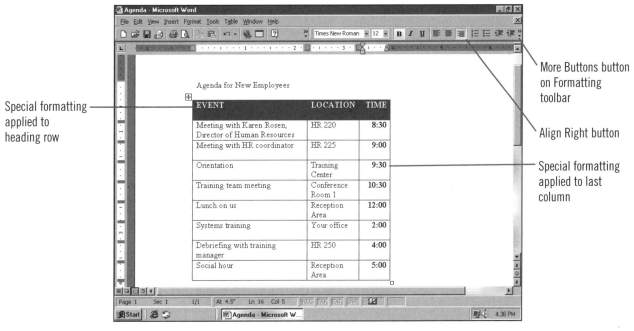

Special formatting applied to heading row

More Buttons button on Formatting toolbar

Align Right button

Special formatting applied to last column

## Changing borders and shading in a table

You can add, remove, or alter the borders and shading in a table using the buttons on the Tables and Borders toolbar, shown in Figure D-11, which appears when you click the Tables and Borders button [icon] on the Standard toolbar. To change the shading of cells, select the cells you want to format, click the Shading Color list arrow [icon] on the Tables and Borders toolbar, then click the shade color and intensity you want to apply to the selected cells. To add or remove borders from a table, select the cells you want to format, then click the Outside Borders list arrow [icon] on the Tables and Borders toolbar (or the Formatting toolbar). From the list of border buttons, click the button that corresponds to the border you want to

add or remove. For example, if you want to remove borders from around all the cells in your table, you would select the table, click the Outside Borders list arrow [icon], then click the All Borders button [icon]. The border buttons are toggle buttons, which means that you can use them to turn borders on and off. When you remove a border from a table, a gridline appears on the screen. The **gridline** is a light gray line that represents the edge of the cell, but does not print.

FIGURE D-11: Tables and Borders toolbar

# Calculating Data in a Table

The Formula command allows you to perform calculations using the numbers in a table. For example, you might want to add the numbers in a row or column to display a total in your table. Word includes built-in formulas that make it easy to quickly perform standard calculations (such as totals or averages). Table D-2 describes several of these formulas. You can also enter your own formulas in a table. To do this, you refer to cells in the table using cell references. A **cell reference** identifies a cell's position in the table. Each cell reference contains a letter (A, B, C....) to identify its column and a number (1, 2, 3....) to identify its row. For example, the cell reference for the first cell in the first row of a table is A1, the second cell in the first row is B1, and so on, as shown in Figure D-12. You can create formulas to multiply, divide, add, and subtract the values of cells. When you change the numbers in a table, you can easily recalculate values associated with those numbers. ➤ Karen has created a table for tracking employee attendance that includes columns for the number of vacation days allowed, taken, and remaining. To calculate each employee's remaining vacation days, she enters a formula in each cell of the Remaining column. She then edits data in the table and updates the associated calculation.

1. Open the file **WD D-1** from your Project Disk, save it with the filename **Department Attendance**, then place the insertion point in the first blank cell in the Remaining column

2. Click **Table** on the menu bar, then click **Formula**

   The Formula dialog box opens, as shown in Figure D-13. Based on the location of the insertion point, Word suggests a formula in the Formula text box—in this case, the built-in SUM formula. Word also suggests which cells to use in the calculation—in this case, the cells to the left of the selected cell. Because you do not want to add the numbers in the Allowed and Taken columns, as Word has suggested, you need to enter a new formula to calculate the remaining vacation days.

3. In the Formula text box, select **=SUM(LEFT)**, then press **[Delete]**

   You must type an equal sign, "=", to indicate that the text that follows it is a formula. You want to enter a formula that subtracts the number of vacation days taken from the number allowed.

4. Type **=D2 – E2**, then click **OK**

   The dialog box closes and 16 appears in the current cell. This is the difference between the value in the fourth column, second row (cell D2) and the fifth column, second row (cell E2).

5. Press **[↓]**, to move the insertion point to **cell F3** (the last cell in the third row), then repeat Steps 2 through 4 using **=D3 – E3** as the formula

   The cells D3 and E3 are the third cells in the fourth and fifth columns. To calculate the other values in the Remaining column, you need to insert a similar formula in each of the empty cells.

6. Press **[↓]**, repeat Steps 2 through 4 using **=D4 – E4** as the formula, then enter the formula for each remaining cell, using **=D5 – E5** and **=D6 – E6** as the formulas

7. Select **7** in cell E6 (the last cell of the fifth column), then type **14**

   If you change a number that is part of a formula, you need to recalculate the formula.

8. Press **[Tab]** to move to the next cell, then press **[F9]**

   Pressing [F9] updates the calculation in the selected cell. "10" now appears in cell E7, as shown in Figure D-14.

9. Deselect the text, then click the **Save button** 🖫 on the Standard toolbar

## QuickTip

Use a plus sign (+) to represent addition; a minus sign (-) for subtraction; an asterisk (*) for multiplication; and a slash (/) for division.

FIGURE D-12: **Cell references in a table**

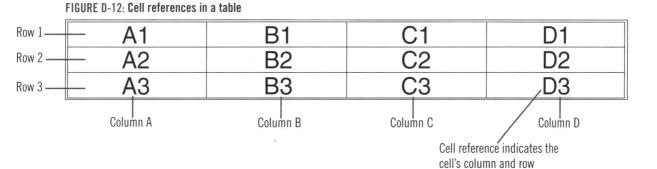

| | | | |
|---|---|---|---|
| Row 1 — | A1 | B1 | C1 | D1 |
| Row 2 — | A2 | B2 | C2 | D2 |
| Row 3 — | A3 | B3 | C3 | D3 |

Column A  Column B  Column C  Column D

Cell reference indicates the
cell's column and row

FIGURE D-13: **Formula dialog box**

Suggested range
of cells

Suggested formula

Displays additional
formulas

**Formula**

Formula:
=SUM(LEFT)

Number format:

Displays number
formatting options

Paste function:  Paste bookmark:

OK  Cancel

FIGURE D-14: **Calculated cells in a table**

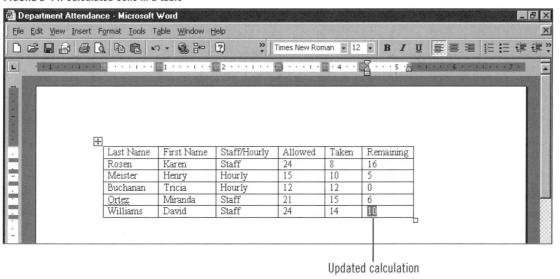

| Last Name | First Name | Staff/Hourly | Allowed | Taken | Remaining |
|---|---|---|---|---|---|
| Rosen | Karen | Staff | 24 | 8 | 16 |
| Meister | Henry | Hourly | 15 | 10 | 5 |
| Buchanan | Tricia | Hourly | 12 | 12 | 0 |
| Ortez | Miranda | Staff | 21 | 15 | 6 |
| Williams | David | Staff | 24 | 14 | 10 |

Updated calculation

TABLE D-2: **Table functions**

| function | description |
|---|---|
| Average | Calculates the sum of specified cells, then divides the sum by the number of cells included in the calculation |
| Count | Displays the number of cells in a specified range of cells |
| Product | Multiplies the values in specified cells |
| Sum | Totals the values of cells above or to the left of the current cell |

# Sorting a Table

Sometimes information in a table is easier to interpret if the rows are **sorted**, that is, arranged in a logical order or sequence. For example, you might sort a department telephone directory by last name, or sort an employee list by date hired. To sort the rows of a table, you must first determine the column (or columns) by which you want to sort. You can sort by a single column or by multiple columns. When you sort by multiple columns, you must select primary, secondary, and sometimes tertiary sort criteria. The primary sort criterion is the first column by which you want to sort. After that, rows are sorted by the additional columns you specify. For example, if you sort an employee list first by a column that contains department names and second by a column that contains employee names, the rows with the same department name would be grouped together, and within those groups employees would be listed alphabetically. For each column, you can sort in ascending or descending order. Sorting in **ascending order** (the default) arranges rows alphabetically (from A to Z) if the sort column contains text, and from smallest to largest if the sort column contains numbers. **Descending order** is the reverse: text is arranged from Z to A and numbers from largest to smallest. Once you group rows by sorting them, you can use the Split Table command on the Table menu to divide a table in two if you wish. Karen sorts the table so that staff and hourly employees are grouped together in the list, and so that employees are listed alphabetically within those groups. She then splits the table to create separate tables for staff and hourly employees.

**1.** Place the insertion point anywhere in the table

You do not need to select the table to sort the entire table, although you do need to select specific rows if you intend to sort only part of a table.

**2.** Click **Table** on the menu bar, then click **Sort**

The Sort dialog box opens, as shown in Figure D-15. In this dialog box, you specify how you want your table sorted. The Sort by drop-down list includes all the columns in the table. You want to sort the table by the information in the Staff/Hourly column, the third column.

**3.** Click the **Sort by list arrow**, then click **Column 3**

You want the staff (which begins with "S") employees to appear before the hourly (which begins with "H") employees in your table, so you must change the sort order to descending, since "S" falls after "H" in the alphabet.

**4.** Click the **Descending option button** in the Sort by section

The rows will be sorted in descending order by the text in the third column. So that the employees are listed alphabetically in each group, you also have to specify the column and sort order of the second sort criterion.

**5.** Click the **Then by list arrow**, then click **Column 1**

Within the Staff and Hourly groups, the rows will be sorted alphabetically by the text in the first column. Your table includes a row of column headings (the first row) that you do not want included in the sort.

**6.** Click the **Header row option button**, click **OK**, then deselect the table

The table is sorted based first on the values in the Staff/Hourly column, and then by the values in the Last Name column, as shown in Figure D-16. The first row of the table (containing the column headings) is not included in the sort. Now that the table is sorted, you can split the table into two separate tables.

**7.** Place the insertion point in the **Tricia Buchanan row**, click **Table** on the menu bar, then click **Split Table**

The table is divided into two tables separated by a blank line, as shown in Figure D-17.

**8.** Click the **Save button** ![] on the Standard toolbar

FIGURE D-15: **Sort dialog box**

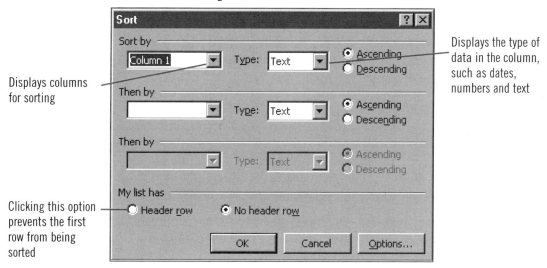

Displays columns for sorting

Displays the type of data in the column, such as dates, numbers and text

Clicking this option prevents the first row from being sorted

FIGURE D-16: **Sorted table**

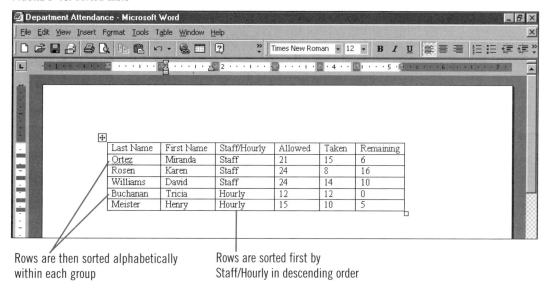

Rows are then sorted alphabetically within each group

Rows are sorted first by Staff/Hourly in descending order

FIGURE D-17: **Split table**

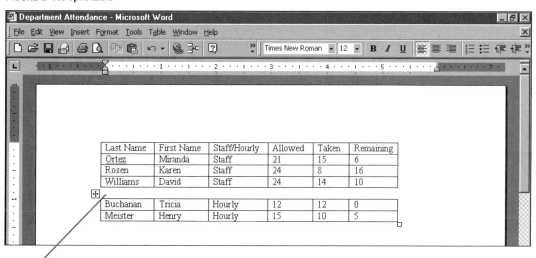

Splitting a table adds a blank line between the two new tables

# Drawing a Table

Sometimes you may not want your table to contain the same number of cells in each row or column. For example, you might need only one cell in the header row or an extra cell in the last column to display an important total. Word's Draw Table feature allows you to customize your tables by drawing cells exactly where you want them. ✎ Karen uses the Draw Table feature to create a table to help her keep track of employees' vacation days and personal days.

## Steps

**QuickTip**

If the Office Assistant opens, click Cancel.

1. **Click the Tables and Borders button 🔲 on the Standard toolbar**
   The Tables and Borders toolbar is displayed, as shown in Figure D-17. Notice that the Draw Table button 🖉 on the Tables and Borders toolbar is indented and the pointer has changed to the Pencil pointer 🖉. You use this pointer to draw a new table.

2. **Click the Down scroll arrow until you see mostly blank space on your screen**
   You'll draw a new table in this blank space in your document.

**Trouble?**

Move the Tables and Borders toolbar by clicking its title bar and dragging it if it blocks the area in which you want to work.

3. **Place the pointer at the left margin near the 2" mark on the vertical ruler, click and drag down and to the right to create a cell about 4" wide and 3" high, then release the mouse button**
   As you drag, dotted lines that represent the cell border appear. Use the vertical and horizontal rulers as guides for determining the size of the cell. The first cell you draw using the Pencil pointer represents the outside border of the table. Next, you'll create smaller cells within the first cell.

**QuickTip**

If you want to remove a line you drew in a table, click the Eraser button 🖉 on the Tables and Borders toolbar, then click and drag along the line you want to erase.

4. **Click the left border of the cell about ½" below the top, drag the pointer straight across to the right border, then release the mouse button**
   You created a row. Next you'll create a column in the table.

5. **Click the new line about 1" from the left border of the table, drag to the bottom border of the table, then release the mouse button**
   Compare your table with Figure D-19.

6. **Keeping the top row intact, draw a line that splits the right column in half**
   The table now has three columns in the second row. The first row is a single column. Next, you'll add more rows to the table.

7. **Draw four lines across the second row to create five new rows, each about ½" high**

8. **Click the Draw Table button 🖉 on the Tables and Borders toolbar to deactivate the Pencil pointer**

9. **Place the insertion point in the first row, type Allowable Absences, press [Tab] twice, type Vacation Days, press [Tab], then type Personal Days**
   Compare the structure of your table to the table shown in Figure D-20. In the next lesson you will use the Tables and Borders toolbar to modify the structure of the table and to format it.

10. **Click the Save button 🔲 on the Standard toolbar**

### Rotating text in a table

When a column heading is much wider than the contents of the other cells in the column, you can improve the appearance of the table by displaying the column heading vertically (rather than horizontally) in a cell. To rotate text in a cell, select the text, then click the Change Text Direction button 🔳 on the Tables and Borders toolbar. Click the button once to rotate the text 90°. Click the button again to change the direction of the vertical text, or to rotate it another 180°. Click the button a third time to return the text to its horizontal position.

FIGURE D-18: **Tables and Borders toolbar**

Draw Table button

Dragging and clicking the Pencil pointer creates lines and cells in a table

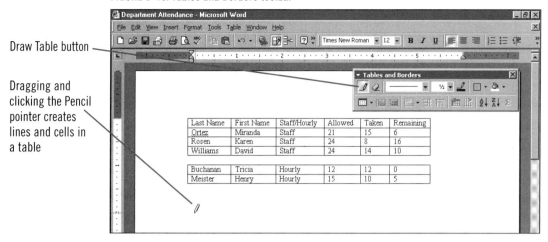

FIGURE D-19: **New column**

Draw a line from here...

...to here

Turns Pencil pointer on and off

Eraser button removes lines/cell boundaries

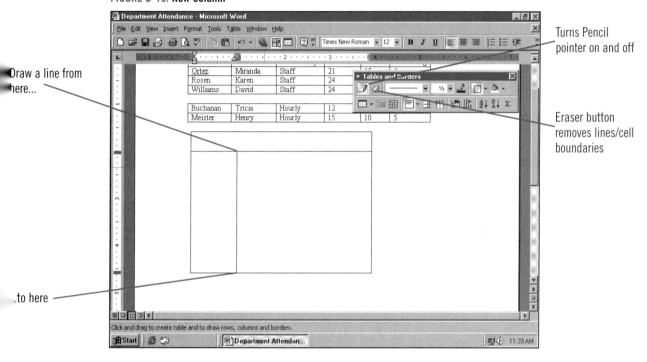

FIGURE D-20: **New rows and columns in a table**

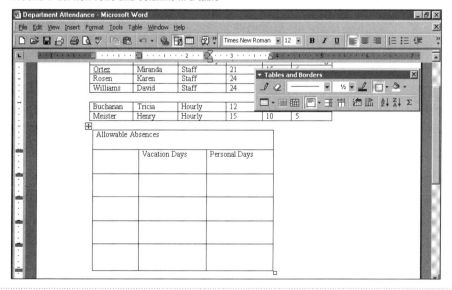

# Splitting and Merging Cells

You can also use the buttons on the Tables and Borders toolbar to modify the structure of a table. In addition to adding or deleting rows and columns, you can change the structure of a table by merging or splitting cells. When you **merge cells**, you combine two or more cells to create one larger cell. When you **split cells** you divide a single cell to create two or more separate cells. To create additional columns in the table, Karen splits existing cells. She also merges two cells to create a single cell. After completing the structure of her table, she adds text, formats the table, and prints her document.

## Steps

1. Select the **8 cells** below the headings in the second and third columns (cells B3 to C6), then click the **Split Cells button** on the Tables and Borders toolbar
   The Split Cells dialog box opens, as shown in Figure D-21. You can split selected cells into rows or columns or both. You'll split the two columns into four columns.

2. Make sure the Number of columns text box displays **4**, click **OK**, then deselect the cells
   The columns are evenly divided into four smaller columns, as shown in Figure D-22.

3. Type **Earned** in cell B3, press **[Tab]**, type **Taken**, press **[Tab]**, type **Earned**, press **[Tab]**, then type **Taken**

4. Click the **Table Select icon** at the upper-left corner of the table to select the table, then click the **Distribute Rows Evenly button** on the Tables and Borders toolbar
   The rows are now all the same height. You can merge cells that you want to combine.

5. Deselect the table, select **cells A2 and A3** (the first two blank cells in the first column) click the **Merge Cells button** on the Tables and Border toolbar, then type **Name**
   The two cells merge to become one cell.

6. Press **[↓]**, type **Miranda Ortez**, press **[↓]**, type **Karen Rosen**, press **[↓]**, then type **David Williams**

7. Select the entire table, click the **Align Top Left list arrow** on the Tables and Borders toolbar, click the **Align Center Left button**, then click in the table
   The text in each cell is left-aligned, but centered vertically.

8. Click the **Table AutoFormat button** on the Tables and Borders toolbar, scroll to the bottom of the Formats list in the Table AutoFormat dialog box, click **Elegant** then click **OK**
   Compare your table to Figure D-23.

9. Close the Tables and Borders toolbar, type your name at the bottom of the document click the **Save button** on the Standard toolbar, then click the **Print button** on the Standard toolbar

10. Click **File** on the menu bar, then click **Exit**

**Trouble?**

If the border between cells B2 and C2 is not aligned with the border between cells C3 and D3, adjust the width of the columns in the second row.

**QuickTip**

You can also click Table on the menu bar, then click Merge Cells to combine cells, or click Split Cells to divide cells.

**FIGURE D-21: Split Cells dialog box**

Split Cells button

Merge Cells button

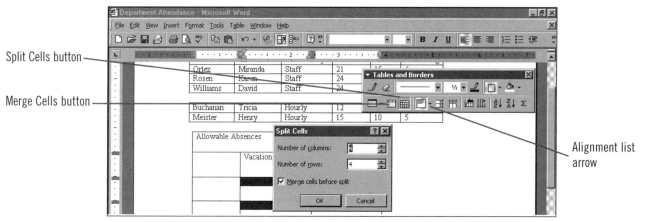

Alignment list arrow

**FIGURE D-22: Split cells in a table**

Table Select icon

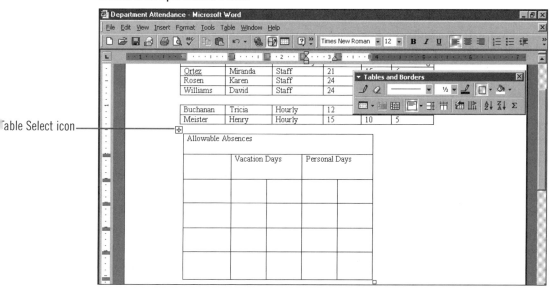

**FIGURE D-23: Completed table**

rged cells

r text may
p differently

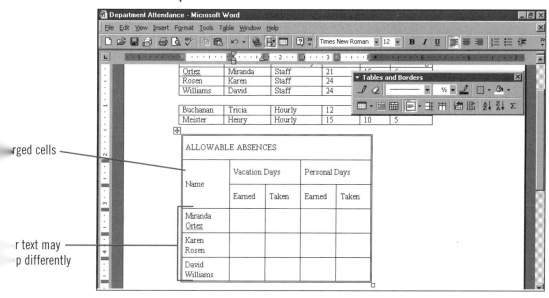

# Practice

## ► Concepts Review

Label each element of the toolbar shown in Figure D-24.

FIGURE D-24

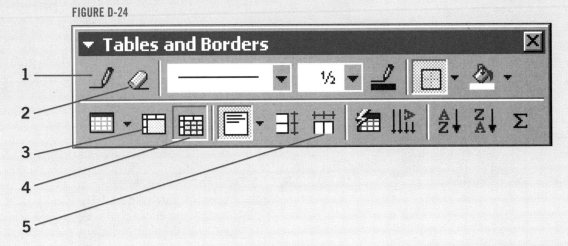

Match each term with the statement that describes it.

6. Gridline
7. Table AutoFormat
8. B3
9. Cell
10. Descending order
11. Ascending order

a. Organizes text from Z to A
b. Adds borders and shading to tables
c. A non-printing cell boundary
d. A cell reference
e. Organizes text from A to Z
f. The intersection of a row and a column

Select the best answer from the list of choices.

12. Which of the following is NOT a way to create a table in Word?
    a. Select tabbed text and click the Insert Table button
    b. Click the Insert Table button and drag to select the number of rows and columns you want
    c. Click the Tables and Borders button, then drag the Pencil pointer
    d. Click Table on the menu bar, then click Table AutoFormat

13. Which statement best describes the commands on the pop-up menu that displays when you right-click a table?
    a. The pop-up menu contains only the commands found on the Table menu
    b. The pop-up menu contains the commands you are likely to use most often when working in a table
    c. The pop-up menu contains Table AutoFormat commands you can use to design a table
    d. The pop-up menu contains the command you use to insert calculations in a table

14. **Which statement best describes how to delete only the text inside a row?**
    a. Select the row, then press [Delete]
    b. With the insertion point in the row, click Table on the menu bar, click Delete Cells, then click Delete Entire Row
    c. Select the row, then click the Cut button
    d. Select the row, then press [Shift][Delete]

15. **To break a table into two separate tables, you**
    a. Insert a new row and erase its borders.
    b. Click the Split Cells button.
    c. Click Table on the menu bar, then click Split Table.
    d. Create a new blank table below the table you want to separate, move the text to the new table, then delete the blank rows from the first table.

16. **To add a new blank row to the bottom of a table, you**
    a. Place the insertion point in the last row, click Table on the menu bar, click Insert, then click Rows Above.
    b. Select the last row, click Table on the menu bar, then click Split Cells.
    c. Place the insertion point in the last cell of the last row, then press [Tab].
    d. Place the insertion point in the last row, then press [Shift] [↓].

17. **Which of the following does NOT adjust the width of a column?**
    a. Double-clicking the right border of a column
    b. Clicking the Right Border button
    c. Dragging a column border
    d. Specifying a column width on the Column tab in the Table Properties dialog box

18. **Which of the following is NOT true of the Table AutoFormat command?**
    a. You can apply special formatting to the last column
    b. You can apply special formatting to the last row
    c. You can see an example of the format in the Table AutoFormat dialog box
    d. You can sort by column or row

19. **Which of the following is a valid cell reference for the first cell in the third column?**
    a. C1                                         c. 1C
    b. A3                                         d. 3A

20. **Which of the following is NOT true about sorting rows in a table?**
    a. The Sort command always sorts all the rows in a table
    b. You can sort a table by more than one column
    c. You can specify not to sort the header row
    d. You can choose the order in which you want rows sorted

# ▶ Skills Review

## 1. Create a table.

**a.** Start Word, type your name at the top of the new document, then press [Enter] twice.

**b.** Use the Insert Table button to create a table that contains 4 rows and 3 columns.

**c.** Enter the following text in the table:

| N | New | Create a new document |
|---|-----|-----------------------|
| O | Open | Open a document |
| D | Delete | Clear selected text |
| S | Save | Save a document |

**d.** Add two new rows to the bottom of the table and enter the following text:

| Y | Repeat | Redo the last action |
|---|--------|----------------------|
| Z | Undo | Undo the last action |

**e.** Save the document as "Quick Table" to your Project Disk.

## 2. Adjust table rows and columns

**a.** Adjust the width of the first two columns to fit the text.

**b.** Drag the right border of the last column to the 2½" inch mark on the horizontal ruler.

**c.** Select the entire table, and distribute the rows evenly.

**d.** Center the table on the page, then save your changes to the table.

## 3. Add and delete rows and columns.

**a.** Add a new row to the bottom of the table.

**b.** Type "P," press [Tab], type "Print," press [Tab], then type "Print the current document."

**c.** Delete the third row of the table.

**d.** Move the last row so that it becomes the fourth row.

**e.** Insert a new column between the first and second columns.

**f.** With the first row selected, insert a new first row at the top of the table.

**g.** In the first cell of the new row, type "CTRL+," press [Tab], type "Menu," press [Tab], type "Command," press [Tab], then type "To do this."

**h.** In the new second column, type "File" in the first four cells in the Menu column.

**i.** Type "Edit" in the remaining cells in the Menu column.

**j.** Save your changes to the table.

## 4. Format a table.

**a.** Display the Tables and Borders toolbar. (*Hint*: Click the Tables and Borders button on the Standard toolbar.)

**b.** Format the table in the Grid 3 preset format.

**c.** Change the shade color of the first row to Lavender. (*Hint*: Use the Shading Color list arrow on the Tables and Borders toolbar.)

**d.** Format the text in the top row in bold.

**e.** Add inside horizontal borders to the table. (*Hint*: Select the table, click the Outside Borders list arrow, then click the Inside Horizontal Border button.)

**f.** Center the text in the first 3 columns of the table.

**g.** Save and print the table, then close the document.

**5. Calculate data in a table.**

   **a.** Open the file WD D-2 from your Project Disk and save it as "Travel Details."

   **b.** Type your name at the top of the document, then press [Enter] twice.

   **c.** In the second cell in the Expense Total column, enter a formula that calculates the sum of the values of the cells to the left. In the Formula dialog box, click the Number format list arrow, then click 0.00.

   **d.** Repeat Step 5c for the remaining cells in the Expense Total column.

   **e.** Replace the Transportation value in the January column with "122.00".

   **f.** Update the transportation calculation in the Expense Total column.

   **g.** Save your changes.

**6. Sort a table.**

   **a.** Sort the table in descending order by the values in the Expense Total column.

   **b.** Sort the table alphabetically by the Expenses column, making sure not to include the heading row in the sort.

   **c.** Apply the Classic 2 preset format, then save your changes.

**7. Draw a table.**

   **a.** Insert several blank lines under the Travel Details table, then use the Pencil pointer to draw a cell 2" high and 3" wide.

   **b.** Draw three lines to create four rows each about ½" high, within the outside border of the new table.

   **c.** Add a vertical line to divide the four rows into two columns.

   **d.** Enter the following text in the table:

   Agenda
   8:30              Opening Ceremonies
   10:00
   12:00             Group Luncheon

   **e.** Save your changes.

**8. Split and merge cells.**

   **a.** Split the empty cell in the third row into two columns, then enter the following in the two new cells: Meeting A for Advisors; Meeting B for Committee Members.

   **b.** Merge the cells in the first row.

   **c.** Adjust the width of the first column so that it is about ½" wide.

   **d.** Adjust the width of the second and third columns in the third row so that they are about the same size.

   **e.** Center the text vertically and horizontally within each cell. (*Hint*: Use the Tables and Borders toolbar to align the text.)

   **f.** Change the direction of the times listed in the first column, so that the text is vertically aligned from bottom to top.

   **g.** Format the table using the Colorful 2 preset format, then center the table on the page.

   **h.** Save, print, close the document, and exit Word.

# Independent Challenges

As the director of marketing for ReadersPlus publishing company, you are responsible for projecting sales for a new book series for beginning readers called "Everyone Reads!" Your manager has asked you to present your sales projections at the upcoming sales meeting. You use Word to prepare a table for your presentation. To complete this independent challenge:

1. Start Word and create a new document called "Projected Sales" on your Project Disk.

2. At the top of the document, type your name and "Projected Sales" (on separate lines), then center these lines.

**c.** Create a table with five rows and five columns.

**d.** Enter the following text:

| Everyone Reads! | West | East | Midwest | South |
|---|---|---|---|---|
| Anthologies Only | 5000 | 7000 | 5800 | 7200 |
| Supplements Only | 2400 | 3500 | 4000 | 1100 |
| Anthologies with Guides | 6800 | 6700 | 9400 | 8200 |
| Complete Package | 6500 | 7500 | 6300 | 7700 |

**e.** Adjust the width of the first column so that the text in each cell fits on one line.

**f.** Add a new row to the bottom of the table, then type "Total" in the first cell.

**g.** Enter a formula in each remaining cell in the last row to calculate the sum of the cells above it.

**h.** Center the entire table horizontally on the page.

**i.** Format the table with the Columns 1 preset format.

**j.** Right-align the numerical values in the table and left-align the first column.

**k.** Center the column headings, make them bold, and change the shading of the first row to light yellow.

**l.** Preview, save, print, then close the document.

**2.** After attending a personal productivity seminar, you decide to become more organized by creating an electronic "To Do" list, a document that you can complete each week. You use Word's Draw Table feature to create the blank "To Do" list.
   To complete this independent challenge:

**a.** Start Word and create a new document called "To Do List" on your Project Disk.

**b.** At the top of the document, type your name and "To Do List" (on separate lines), then center these lines.

**c.** Use the Draw Table button to create a table that contains seven rows and one column (about 5" wide and 5" long). Refer to Figure D-25 as a guide to help you complete the remaining steps.

**d.** Draw a line that divides all but the top row into two columns.

**e.** Make all the rows the same height.

**FIGURE D-25**

**f.** In the top row, type "Things To Do: Week of."

**g.** Starting with the second row in the first column, type the days of the week, starting with "Monday." In the last row, type "Weekend."

**h.** Change the direction of the text in the first column so that it is vertically aligned from bottom to top.

**i.** Make each row 1" high.

**j.** Adjust the width of the first column to fit the text.

**k.** Format the table with the Columns 4 preset format.

**l.** Center the table on the page.

**m.** Center the text in the first column.

**n.** Center the text in the top row both vertically and horizontally, then increase the font size to 20 points. Apply bold formatting to all the text in the table.

**o.** Preview, save, print, then close the document.

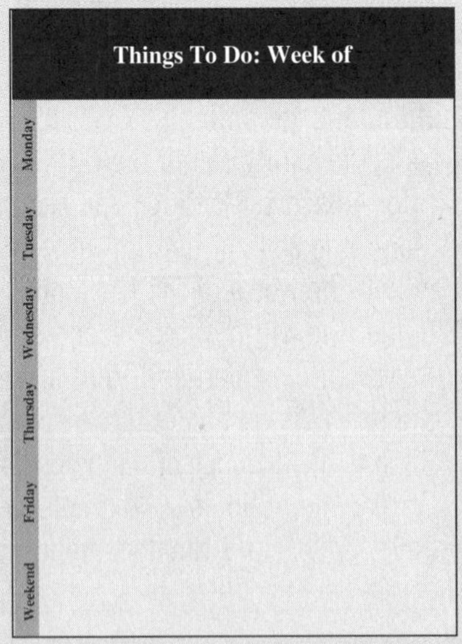

**3.** As a co-chair of the class reunion entertainment committee, you are responsible for keeping track of registration and fees paid for upcoming events. To make it easier to track and update your registration statistics, you create a table showing the distribution of attendees among events, and add formulas to help you calculate registration income.
   To complete this independent challenge:

**a.** Start Word, open the file WD D-3 from your Project Disk, and save it as "Reunion Costs."

**b.** At the top of the document, insert your name and "Reunion Costs" (on separate lines). Add a blank line underneath, then center these lines.

c. Convert the tabbed text to a table.

d. Add a row to the end of the table, and enter "Variety Show" as the event, with 120 attendees at $7 per person.

e. Calculate the total for each row, using a multiplication formula. (*Hint:* For the first row, type "=B2*C2" in the Formula dialog box.)

f. Sort the table rows so that the events are listed in alphabetical order.

g. Add a new row to the bottom of the table and type "Grand Total" in the first cell in this row.

h. Calculate the total of the values in the Total column.

i. Merge the first three cells in the last row.

j. Format the table with the 3D Effects 1 preset format.

k. Format all the rows to be ½" high, and adjust the width of the last column to fit the text.

l. Left, center-align the text in all the cells vertically, and right-align the text in the columns that contain numbers.

m. Preview, save, print, then close the document.

**4.** You are an intern in the Human Resources department at MediaLoft. One of your assignments is to create a memo to all employees that outlines MediaLoft's holidays and events. Rather than type the information, you decide to copy the holidays and events from MediaLoft's intranet site, and then format the table and add more information to it.

To complete this independent challenge:

a. Start Word, click File on the menu bar, click New, then double-click the Elegant Memo template on the Memos tab in the New dialog box.

b. Enter the following in the memo template:
TO: MediaLoft employees
FROM: Your Name
SUBJECT: MediaLoft holidays and events
CC: Karen Rosen

c. Save the document with the filename "MediaLoft Holidays" on your Project Disk.

d. Connect to the Internet, go to the MediaLoft intranet site at http://www.course.com/illustrated/MediaLoft, then click the link for the Human Resources page.

e. Copy the schedule of holidays from the Human Resources page on the intranet site to the body of the memo. Be sure to include the heading "Company Holidays and Events." (Replace the template text in the body of the memo.)

f. Sort the table by type in descending order, and then by date.

g. Split the table to separate holidays and events.

h. Insert a new row at the top of the holidays table and type "MediaLoft Holidays" in the first cell.

i. Insert new row at the top of the event table and type "MediaLoft Events" in the first cell.

j. Copy the second row (column headings) of the holidays table to become the new second row of the events table.

k. Delete the Type column in each table.

l. Add a column to the right end of the events table, type "Location" in the second row, then enter the following in the Location column: "Majestic Towers Hotel," "Civic Center," "Pacific View Park," "Majestic Towers Hotel."

m. Adjust the column widths in each table to fit the text, then merge the cells in the first row of each table.

n. Apply the Classic 2 preset format to each table.

o. Add inside borders to each table.

p. Center the heading for each table, bold the column headings, then center the tables on the page.

q. Preview, save, print, then close the document.

**Visual Workshop**

Create the table shown in Figure D-26 and save it as "Activity Prices" on your Project Disk. Be sure to align the text and the table as shown in the figure. (*Hint*: Make each row 1" high and use the List 7 preset format.)

FIGURE D-26

## Your Name
## Extreme Fitness

| Activity | Price | Sales | Total |
|---|---|---|---|
| Aerobic Classes | $15.00 | 89 | $1335.00 |
| Basketball | $7.00 | 152 | $1064.00 |
| Racquetball | $10.00 | 214 | $2140.00 |
| Swimming | $10.00 | 345 | $3450.00 |
| Total for 2000 | | 800 | $7989.00 |

Unit
A

# Getting
## Started with Excel 2000

### Objectives

► Define spreadsheet software

► Start Excel 2000

► View the Excel window

⌐MOUS⌐ ► Open and save a workbook

⌐MOUS⌐ ► Enter labels and values

⌐MOUS⌐ ► Preview and print a worksheet

⌐MOUS⌐ ► Get Help

► Close a workbook and exit Excel

In this unit, you will learn how to start Microsoft Excel 2000 and use different elements of the Excel window. You will also learn how to open and save existing files, enter data in a worksheet, and use the extensive Help system. Jim Fernandez is the office manager at MediaLoft, a nationwide chain of bookstore cafés selling books, CDs, and videos. MediaLoft cafés also sell coffee and pastries to customers. Jim uses Excel to analyze a worksheet that summarizes budget information for the MediaLoft Café in the New York City store.

# Defining Spreadsheet Software

Microsoft Excel is an electronic spreadsheet program that runs on Windows computers. You use an **electronic spreadsheet** to perform numeric calculations rapidly and accurately. See Table A-1 for common ways spreadsheets are used in business. The electronic spreadsheet that you produce when using Excel is also referred to as a **worksheet**. Excel helps Jim produce professional-looking documents that can be updated automatically so they always have accurate information. Figure A-1 shows a budget worksheet that Jim created using pencil and paper, while Figure A-2 shows the same worksheet Jim created using Excel.

### The advantages of using Excel include:

### Enter data quickly and accurately

With Excel, you can enter information faster and more accurately than when using the pencil-and-paper method. For example, in the MediaLoft NYC Café budget, certain expenses such as rent, cleaning supplies, and products supplied on a yearly plan (coffee, creamers, sweeteners) remain constant for the year. You can copy the expenses that don't change from quarter to quarter, and then use Excel to calculate Total Expenses and Net Income for each quarter by simply supplying the data and formulas.

### Recalculate data easily

Fixing typing errors or updating data using Excel is easy, and the results of a changed entry are recalculated automatically. For example, if you receive updated expense figures for Quarter 4, you simply enter the new numbers and Excel recalculates the worksheet.

### Perform a what-if analysis

One of the most powerful decision-making features of Excel is the ability to change data and then quickly view the recalculated results. Anytime you use a worksheet to answer the question "what if," you are performing a **what-if analysis.** For instance, if the advertising budget for a quarter is increased to $3,600, you can enter the new figure into the worksheet and immediately see the impact on the overall budget.

### Change the appearance of information

Excel provides powerful features for enhancing a spreadsheet so that information is visually appealing and easy to understand. You can use boldface type and shade text headings or numbers to add emphasis to key data in the worksheet.

### Create charts

Excel makes it easy to create charts based on information in a worksheet. With Excel, charts are automatically updated as data changes. The worksheet in Figure A-2 includes a pie chart that graphically shows the distribution of the MediaLoft NYC Café's budget expenses for the year 200

### Share information with other users

Because everyone at MediaLoft is now using Microsoft Office, it's easy to share worksheet data among colleagues. For example, you can complete the MediaLoft budget that your manager started creating in Excel. Simply access the files you need or want to share through the network or from a disk, and then make any changes or additions.

### Create new worksheets from existing ones quickly

It's easy to take an existing Excel worksheet and quickly modify it to create a new one. When you are ready to create next year's budget, you can open the file for this year's budget, save it with a new file name, and use the existing data as a starting point.

**FIGURE A-1**: Traditional paper worksheet

## MediaLoft NYC Café Budget

|  | Qtr1 | Qtr 2 | Qtr 3 | Qtr 4 | Total |
|---|---|---|---|---|---|
| Net Sales | 48,000 | 76,000 | 64,000 | 80,000 | 268,000 |
| Expenses |  |  |  |  |  |
| Salary | 13,000 | 13,000 | 13,000 | 13,000 | 52,000 |
| Rent | 3,500 | 3,500 | 3,500 | 3,500 | 14,000 |
| Advertising | 3,600 | 8,000 | 16,000 | 20,000 | 47,600 |
| Cleaners | 1,500 | 1,500 | 1,500 | 1,500 | 6,000 |
| Pastries | 2,500 | 2,500 | 2,500 | 2,500 | 10,000 |
| Milk/Cream | 1,000 | 1,000 | 1,000 | 1,000 | 4,000 |
| Coffee/Tea | 4,250 | 4,250 | 4,250 | 4,250 | 17,000 |
| Sweeteners | 300 | 300 | 300 | 300 | 1,200 |
| Total Expenses | 29,650 | 34,050 | 42,050 | 46,050 | 151,800 |
|  |  |  |  |  |  |
| Net Income | 18,350 | 41,950 | 21,950 | 33,950 | 116,200 |

**FIGURE A-2**: Excel worksheet

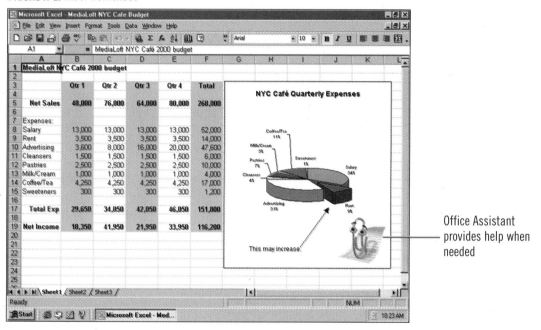

Office Assistant provides help when needed

**LE A-1**: Common business uses for spreadsheets

| eadsheets are used to: | by: |
|---|---|
| intain values | Calculating numbers |
| present values visually | Creating charts based on worksheet figures |
| ate consecutively numbered pages using multiple rkbook sheets | Printing reports containing workbook sheets |
| anize data | Sorting data in ascending or descending order |
| lyze data | Creating data summaries and short-lists using PivotTables or AutoFilters |
| ate what-if data scenarios | Using variable values to investigate and sample different outcomes |

Excel 2000

# Starting Excel 2000

To start any Windows program, you use the Start button on the taskbar. A slightly different procedure might be required for computers on a network and those that use Windows-enhancing utilities. If you need assistance, ask your instructor or technical support person. ✐━━ Jim is ready to begin work on the budget for the MediaLoft Café in New York City. He begins by starting Excel.

**1.** Point to the **Start button** 🅰Start on the taskbar

The Start button is on the left side of the taskbar and is used to start programs on your computer.

**2.** Click 🅰Start

Microsoft Excel is located in the Programs group, which is at the top of the Start menu, as shown in Figure A-3.

**Trouble?**

If you don't see the Microsoft Excel icon, consult your instructor or technical support person.

**3.** Point to **Programs**

All the programs on your computer, including Microsoft Excel, are listed in this area of the Start menu. See Figure A-4. Your program list might look different depending on the programs installed on your computer.

**4.** Click the **Microsoft Excel program icon** on the Programs menu

Excel opens and a blank worksheet appears. In the next lesson, you will familiarize yourself with the elements of the Excel worksheet window.

**FIGURE A-3: Start menu**

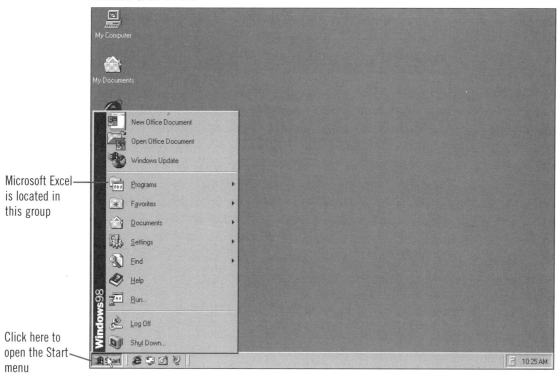

Microsoft Excel
is located in
this group

Click here to
open the Start
menu

**FIGURE A-4: Programs list**

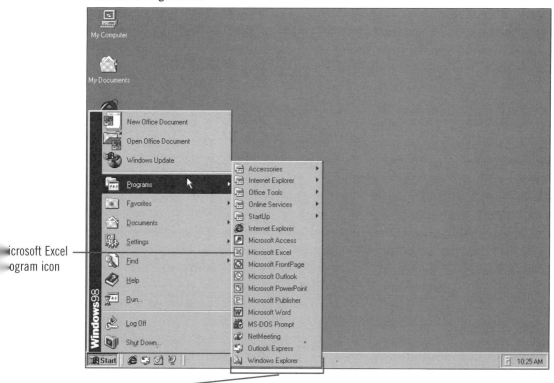

Microsoft Excel
program icon

Your list of programs
might vary

Excel 2000

# Viewing the Excel Window

When you start Excel, the **worksheet window** appears on your screen. The worksheet window includes the tools that enable you to create and work with worksheets.　　　　 Jim needs to familiarize himself with the Excel worksheet window and its elements before he starts working with the budget worksheet. Compare the descriptions below to Figure A-5.

## Details

The **worksheet window** contains a grid of columns and rows. Columns are labeled alphabetically (A, B, C, etc.) and rows are labeled numerically (1, 2, 3, etc.). The worksheet window displays only a tiny fraction of the whole worksheet, which has a total of 256 columns and 65,536 rows. The intersection of a column and a row is a **cell**. Cells can contain text, numbers, formulas, or a combination of all three. Every cell has its own unique location or **cell address**, which is identified by the coordinates of the intersecting column and row. For example, the cell address of the cell in the upper-left corner of a worksheet is A1.

The **cell pointer** is a dark rectangle that highlights or outlines the cell you are working in. This cell is called the **active cell**. In Figure A-5, the cell pointer is located at A1, so A1 is the active cell. To activate a different cell, just click any other cell or press the arrow keys on your keyboard to move the cell pointer elsewhere.

The **title bar** displays the program name (Microsoft Excel) and the filename of the open worksheet (in this case the default filename, Book1). As shown in Figure A-5, the title bar also contains a control menu box, a Close button, and resizing buttons, which are common to all Windows programs.

The **menu bar** contains menus from which you choose Excel commands. As with all Windows programs, you can choose a menu command by clicking it with the mouse or by pressing [Alt] plus the underlined letter in the menu name. When you click a menu, a short list of commonly used commands may appear at first; you can wait or click the double arrows at the bottom of the menu to see expanded menus.

The **name box** displays the active cell address. In Figure A-5, "A1" appears in the name box indicating that A1 is the active cell.

The **formula bar** allows you to enter or edit data in the worksheet.

The **toolbars** contain buttons for frequently used Excel commands. The **Standard toolbar** is located just below the left edge of the menu bar and contains buttons that effect operations within the worksheet. The **Formatting toolbar**—to the right of the Standard toolbar—contains buttons that change the worksheet's appearance. Each button contains a graphic representation of its function. For instance, the face of the Printing button contains a printer. To choose a button, simply click it with the left mouse button. Not all the buttons on the Standard and Formatting toolbar are visible on the screen. To view other toolbar buttons, click the More Buttons button ⃞ at the right end of each toolbar to display a list of additional buttons. Throughout the lessons in this book, you will need to remember to click the More Buttons button if a button you are instructed to click is not visible on your screen. When you use a button from the More Button list, Excel adds it to your visible toolbar. That's why each user's toolbars look unique. Be sure to read the Clues to Use in this lesson to learn more about working with Excel's toolbars.

**Sheet tabs** below the worksheet grid let you keep your work in collections called **workbooks**. Each workbook contains three worksheets by default and can contain a maximum of 255 sheets. **Sheet tabs** can be given meaningful names. **Sheet tab scrolling buttons** help you move from one sheet to another.

The **status bar** is located at the bottom of the Excel window. The left side of the status bar provides a brief description of the active command or task in progress. The right side of the status bar shows the status of important keys such as [Caps Lock] and [Num Lock].

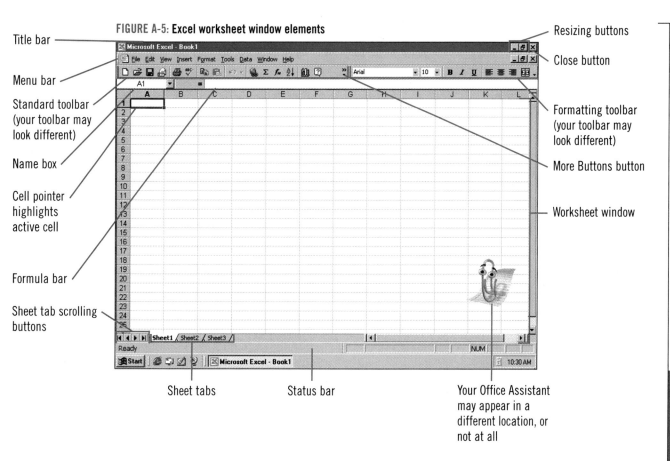

FIGURE A-5: **Excel worksheet window elements**

Title bar

Menu bar

Standard toolbar
(your toolbar may
look different)

Name box

Cell pointer
highlights
active cell

Formula bar

Sheet tab scrolling
buttons

Resizing buttons

Close button

Formatting toolbar
(your toolbar may
look different)

More Buttons button

Worksheet window

Sheet tabs          Status bar          Your Office Assistant
may appear in a
different location, or
not at all

## Personalized toolbars and menus in Excel 2000

Excel toolbars and menus modify themselves to
your working style. The Standard and Formatting
toolbars you see when you first start Excel include
the most frequently used buttons. To locate a button
not visible on a toolbar, click the **More Buttons
button** ⁑ on that toolbar to see the list of additional toolbar buttons. As you work, Excel promotes
the buttons you use to the visible toolbars, and
demotes the buttons you don't use to the More
Buttons list. Similarly, Excel menus adjust to your
work habits, so that the commands you use most
often automatically appear on the shortened menus.
Click the double arrow at the bottom of a menu to
view additional menu commands. You can return
toolbars and menus to their default settings by clicking Reset my usage data on the Options tab of the
Customize dialog box, as shown in Figure A-6.
Resetting your usage data erases changes made automatically to your menus and toolbars. It does not
affect the options you customize.

FIGURE A-6: **Customize dialog box**

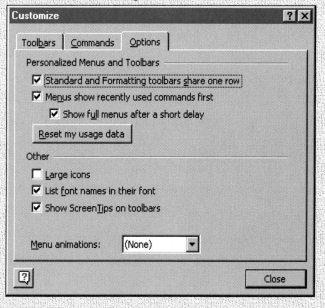

# Opening and Saving a Workbook

Sometimes it's more efficient to create a new worksheet by modifying one that already exists. This saves you from having to retype information that can be reused from previous work. Throughout this book, you will create new worksheets by opening a file from your Project Disk, using the Save As command to create a copy of the file with a new name, and then modifying the new file by following the lesson steps. Use the Save command to store changes made to an existing file. It is a good idea to save your work every 15 minutes or before printing. Saving the files with new names keeps your original Project Disk files intact, in case you have to start the lesson over again or you wish to repeat an exercise. ◄━━━━ Jim wants to complete the New York City MediaLoft Café budget that a member of the accounting staff has been working on. Jim opens the budget workbook and then uses the Save As command to create a copy with a new name.

## Steps 1234

1. Insert your Project Disk in the appropriate disk drive

2. Click the **Open button** 🖼 on the Standard toolbar
   The Open dialog box opens. See Figure A-7.

3. Click the **Look in list arrow,** then click the **drive that contains your Project Disk**
   A list of the files on your Project Disk appears in the Open dialog box.

   > **QuickTip**
   > You could also double-click the filename in the Open dialog box to open the file.

4. Click the file **EX A-1**, then click **Open**
   The file EX A-1 opens.

5. Click **File** on the menu bar, then click **Save As**
   The Save As dialog box opens with the drive containing your Project Disk displayed in the Save in list box. You should save all your files to your Project Disk, unless instructed otherwise.

   > **QuickTip**
   > You can click 💾 or use the shortcut key [Ctrl][S] to save a workbook using the same filename.

6. In the File name text box, select the current file name (if necessary), type **MediaLoft Cafe Budget**, as shown in Figure A-8, then click **Save**
   Both the Save As dialog box and the file EX A-1 close, and a duplicate file named MediaLoft Café Budget opens, as shown in Figure A-9. The Office Assistant may or may not appear on your screen. As you will learn, toolbars and menus change as you work with Excel. It is a good idea to return toolbars and menus to their default settings when you begin these lessons.

7. Click **Tools** on the menu bar, click **Customize,** make sure the Options tab in the Customize dialog box is displayed, click **Reset my usage data** to restore the default settings, click **Yes** in the alert box or dialog balloon, then click **Close**

**FIGURE A-7: Open dialog box**

Click to display a list of available drives and folders

Your folder may differ

Your files and folders display here

The selected filename will appear here

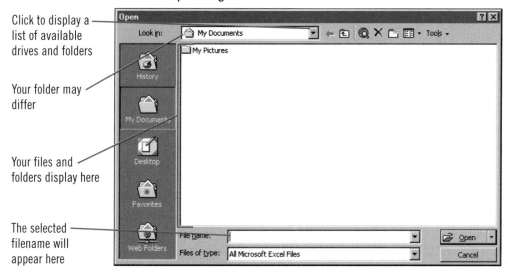

**FIGURE A-8: Save As dialog box**

Current drive or folder (yours may differ)

Your list of files might be different

Type the new filename here

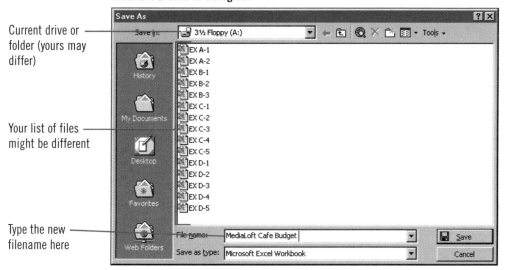

**FIGURE A-9: MediaLoft Cafe Budget workbook**

Because toolbars adapt as you work, your toolbars may not match the figures

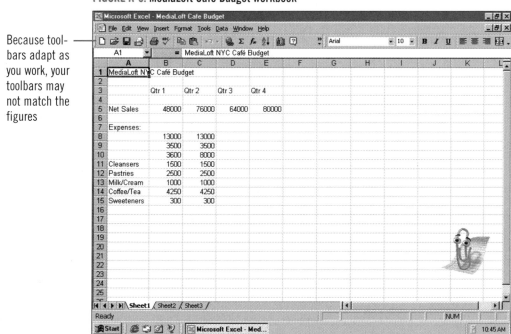

# Entering Labels and Values

Labels are used to identify the data in the rows and columns of a worksheet. They also make your worksheet more readable and understandable. You should try to enter all labels in your worksheet before entering the data. Labels can contain text and numerical information not used in calculations, such as dates, times, or addresses. Labels are left-aligned by default. **Values**, which include numbers, formulas, and functions, are used in calculations. Excel recognizes an entry as a value when it is a number or begins with special symbols: +, -, =, @, #, or $. All values are right-aligned by default. When a cell contains both text and numbers it is not a valid formula; Excel recognizes the entry as a label. Jim needs to enter labels identifying the rest of the expense categories, and the values for Qtr 3 and Qtr 4 into the MediaLoft Café Budget worksheet.

**1.** Click cell **A8** to make it the active cell

Notice that the cell address A8 appears in the name box. As you work, the mouse pointer has a variety of appearances, depending on where it is and what Excel is doing. Table A-2 lists and identifies some mouse pointers. The labels in cells A1:A15 identify the expenses.

**2.** Type **Salary**, as shown in Figure A-10, then click the **Enter button** 🔲 on the formula bar

The label is entered in cell A8 and its contents display in the formula bar. You can also confirm a cell entry by pressing [Enter], pressing [Tab], or by pressing one of the arrow keys on the keyboard. If a label does not fit in a cell, Excel displays the remaining characters in the next cell to the right as long as it is empty. Otherwise, the label is **truncated**, or cut off.

**3.** Click cell **A9**, type **Rent**, press [Enter] to complete the entry and move the cell pointer to cell A10, type **Advertising** in cell A10, then press [Enter]

The remaining expense values have to be added to the worksheet.

**4.** Click cell **D8**, press and hold the left mouse button, drag the ⊹ pointer to cell **E8** then down to cell **E15**, then release the mouse button

Two or more selected cells is called a **range**. The active cell is still cell D8, the cells in the range are shaded in purple. Since entries often cover multiple columns and rows, selecting a range makes working with data entry easier.

**5.** Type **13000**, press [Enter], type **3500** in cell D9, press [Enter], type **16000** in cell D10, press [Enter], type **1500** in cell D11, press [Enter], type **2500** in cell D12, press [Enter], type **1000** in cell D13, press [Enter], type **4250** in cell D14, press [Enter], type **300** in cell D15, then press [Enter]

All the values in the Qtr 3 column have been added. The cell pointer is now in cell E8.

**6.** Using Figure A-11 as a guide, type the remaining values for cells E8 through E15

Before confirming a cell entry you can click the Cancel button on the formula bar or press [Esc] to cancel or delete the entry.

**7.** Type your name in cell **A17**, then click the **Save button** 🔲 on the Standard toolbar

Your name identifies the worksheet as yours when it is printed.

---

## Trouble?

If you notice a mistake in a cell entry after it has been confirmed, double-click the cell, use [Backspace] or [Delete] to make your corrections, then press [Enter]. You can also click Edit on the menu bar, point to Clear, then click Contents to remove a cell's contents.

## QuickTip

To enter a number that will not be used as part of a calculation, such as a telephone number, type an apostrophe (') before the number.

---

**TABLE A-2: Commonly used pointers**

| name | pointer | use to |
|---|---|---|
| **Normal or Cross** | ⊹ | Select a cell or range; indicates Ready mode |
| **I-beam** | I | Edit contents of formula bar |
| **Select** | ⊾ | Select objects and commands |

FIGURE A-10: Worksheet with initial label entered

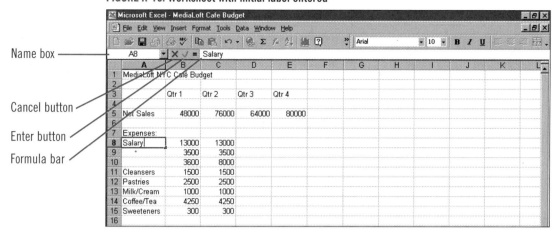

Name box ——
Cancel button ——
Enter button ——
Formula bar ——

FIGURE A-11: Worksheet with new labels and values

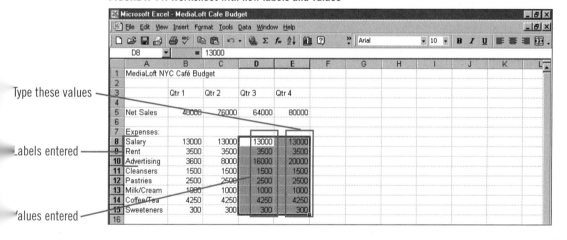

Type these values ——
Labels entered ——
Values entered ——

### Navigating a worksheet

With over a million cells available to you, it is important to know how to move around, or **navigate**, a worksheet. You can use the arrow keys on the keyboard ([↑], [↓], [←], [→]) to move a cell or two at a time, or [Page Up] or [Page Down] to move a screenful at a time. To move a screen to the left press [Alt] [Page Up]; to move a screen to the right press [Alt] [Page Down]. You can also simply use your mouse pointer to click the desired cell. If the desired cell is not visible in the worksheet window, use the scroll bars or the Go To command to move the location into view. To return to the first active cell in a worksheet, click cell A1, or press [Ctrl][Home].

# Previewing and Printing a Worksheet

When a worksheet is completed, you may want to print it to have a paper copy to reference, file, or give to others. You can also print a worksheet that is not complete to review your work when you are not at a computer. Before you print a worksheet, you should save any changes. That way, if anything happens to the file as it is being sent to the printer, you will have your latest work saved to your disk. Then you should preview it to make sure it will fit on a page the way you want. When you preview a worksheet, you see a copy of the worksheet exactly as it will appear on paper. Table A-3 provides additional printing tips. ◀▬▬ Jim is finished entering the labels and values into the MediaLoft Café budget. Since he already saved his changes, he previews and prints a copy of the worksheet to review on the way home.

### 1. Make sure the printer is on and contains paper
If a file is sent to print and the printer is off, an error message appears.

### Trouble?

If 🔍 is not visible on your Standard toolbar, click the More Buttons button ⯈ to view additional toolbar buttons.

### 2. Click the **Print Preview button** 🔍 on the Standard toolbar
A miniature version of the worksheet appears on the screen, as shown in Figure A-13. If there were more than one page, you could click the Next button or the Previous button to move between pages. You can also enlarge the image by clicking the Zoom button.

### 3. Click **Print**
The Print dialog box opens, as shown in Figure A-14. To print, you could also click File on the menu bar, then click Print Preview.

### 4. Make sure that the **Active Sheet(s) option button** is selected and that **1** appears in the Number of copies text box
Adjusting the value in the Number of copies text box enables you to print multiple copies. You could also print the selected range, the values you just entered, by clicking the Selection option button.

### 5. Click **OK**
The Printing dialog box appears briefly while the file is sent to the printer. Note that the dialog box contains a Cancel button. You can use it to cancel the print job provided you can catch it before the file is sent to the printer.

### Using Zoom in Print Preview

When you are in the Print Preview window, you can enlarge the image by clicking the Zoom button. You can also position the mouse pointer over a specific part of the worksheet page, then click it to view that section of the page. Figure A-12 shows a magnified section of a document. While the image is zoomed in, use the scroll bars to view different sections of the page.

**FIGURE A-12: Enlarging the preview using Zoom**

| MediaLoft NYC Café Budget | | | | |
|---|---|---|---|---|
| | Qtr 1 | Qtr 2 | Qtr 3 | Qtr 4 |
| Net Sales | 48000 | 76000 | 64000 | 80000 |
| Expenses: | | | | |
| Salary | 13000 | 13000 | 13000 | 13000 |
| Rent | 3500 | 3500 | 3500 | 3500 |
| Advertising | 3600 | 8000 | 16000 | 20000 |
| Cleansers | 1500 | 1500 | 1500 | 1500 |
| Pastries | 2500 | 2500 | 2500 | 2500 |
| Milk/Cream | 1000 | 1000 | 1000 | 1000 |
| Coffee/Tea | 4250 | 4250 | 4250 | 4250 |
| Sweeteners | 300 | 300 | 300 | 300 |

▶ EXCEL A-12  **GETTING STARTED WITH EXCEL 2000**

FIGURE A-13: **Print Preview screen**

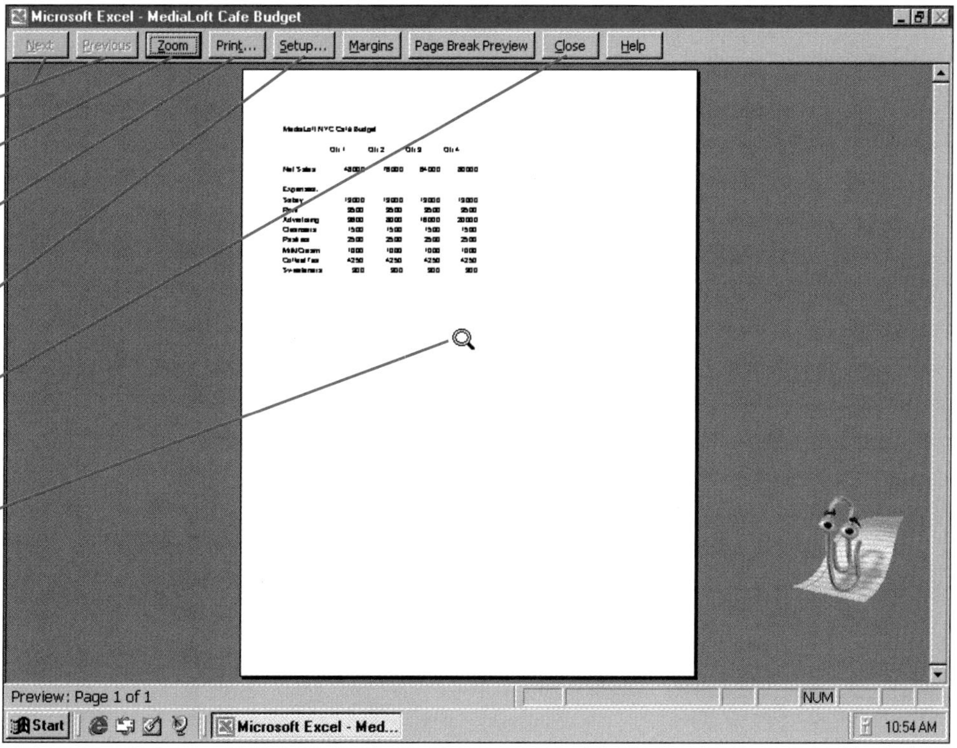

Move to another page

Enlarge the screen image

Print the worksheet

Change print options

Return to worksheet

Mouse pointer enlarges section of sheet when clicked

FIGURE A-14: **Print dialog box**

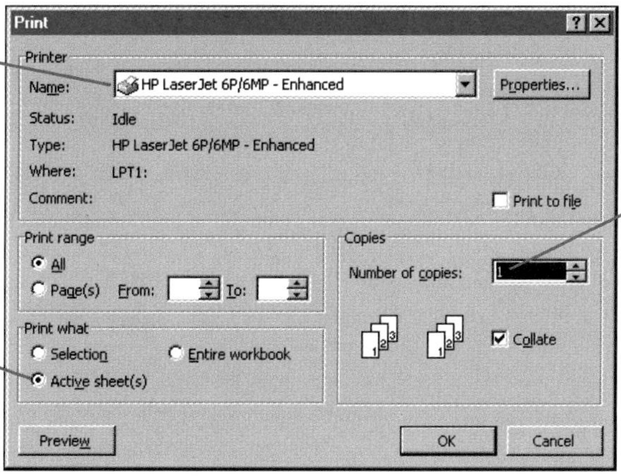

Your printer may differ

Indicates the number of copies to be printed

Prints the current worksheet

TABLE A-3: **Worksheet printing tips**

| before you print | recommendation |
| --- | --- |
| Save your work | Make sure your work is saved to a disk |
| Check the printer | Make sure that the printer is turned on and is online, that it has paper, and that there are no error messages or warning signals |
| Preview the worksheet | Check the formatted image for page breaks, page setup (vertical or horizontal), and overall appearance of the worksheet |
| Check the printer selection | Use the Printer setup command in the Print dialog box to verify that the correct printer is selected |
| Check the Print what options | Verify that you are printing either the active sheet, the entire workbook, or just a selected range |

# Getting Help

Excel features an extensive **Help system** that gives you immediate access to definitions, explanations, and useful tips. The animated Office Assistant provides help in two ways. You can type a keyword to search on, or access a question and answer format to research your help topic. The Office Assistant provides **ScreenTips** (indicated by a light bulb) on the current action you are performing. You can click the light bulb to access further information in the form of a dialog box that you can resize and refer to as you work. In addition, you can press [F1] at any time to get immediate help. ⟍⟋⟍⟋ Jim wants to find out more about ranges so he can work more efficiently with them. He knows he can find more information using the animated Office Assistant.

# Steps

**1.** Click the **Microsoft Excel Help button** 🔲 on the Standard toolbar

An Office Assistant dialog box opens. You can get information by typing a word to search on in the query box, or by typing a question. If the text within the query box is already selected, any typed text will automatically replace what is highlighted. The Office Assistant provides help based on text typed in the query box.

**2.** Type **Define a range**

See Figure A-16.

**3.** Click **Search**

The Office Assistant searches for relevant topics from the help files in Excel and then displays the results.

**4.** Click **See More** if necessary, click **Name cells in a workbook**, then click **Name a cell or a range of cells** in the Microsoft Excel Help window

A Help window containing information about ranges opens. See Figure A-17.

**5.** Read the text, then click the **Close button** on the Help window title bar

The Help window closes and you return to your worksheet.

**6.** Right-click the **Office Assistant**, then click **Hide**

The Office Assistant is no longer visible on the worksheet.

## Changing the Office Assistant

The default Office Assistant character is Clippit, but there are others from which you can choose. To change the appearance of the Office Assistant, right-click the Office Assistant, then click Choose Assistant. Click the Gallery tab, click the Back and Next buttons until you find an Assistant you want to use, then click OK. (You may need to insert your Microsoft Office 2000 CD to perform this task.) Each Office Assistant makes its own unique sounds and can be animated by right-clicking its window and clicking Animate! Figure A-15 shows the Office Assistant dialog box.

**FIGURE A-15: Office Assistant dialog box**

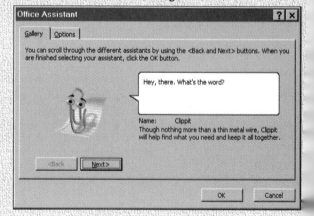

**FIGURE A-16: Office Assistant**

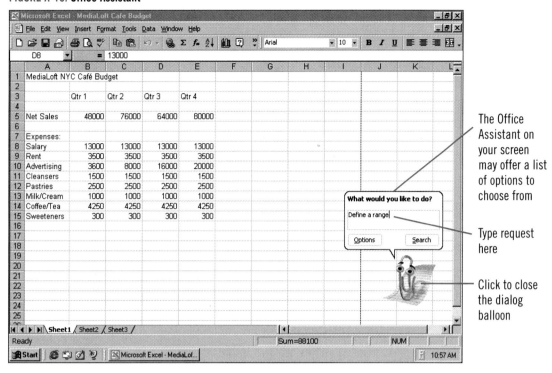

The Office Assistant on your screen may offer a list of options to choose from

Type request here

Click to close the dialog balloon

**FIGURE A-17: Help window**

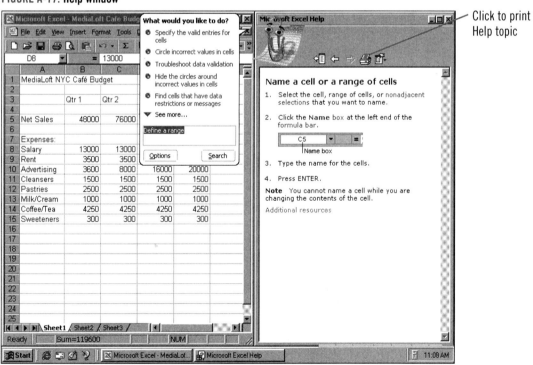

Click to print Help topic

# Closing a Workbook and Exiting Excel

When you have finished working you need to save the file and close it. When you have completed all your work in Excel you need to exit the program. You can exit Excel by clicking Exit on the File menu. Since Jim has completed his work on the MediaLoft Café budget, he is finished using Excel for the day. He closes the workbook and then exits Excel.

**1.** Click **File** on the menu bar

The File menu opens. See Figure A-18.

**2.** Click **Close**

Excel closes the workbook and asks if you want to save your changes; if you have made any changes be sure to save them.

**3.** Click **File** on the menu bar, then click **Exit**

You could also click the program Close button to exit the program. Excel closes and you return to the desktop. Memory is now freed up for other computing tasks.

**FIGURE A-18:** Closing a workbook using the File menu

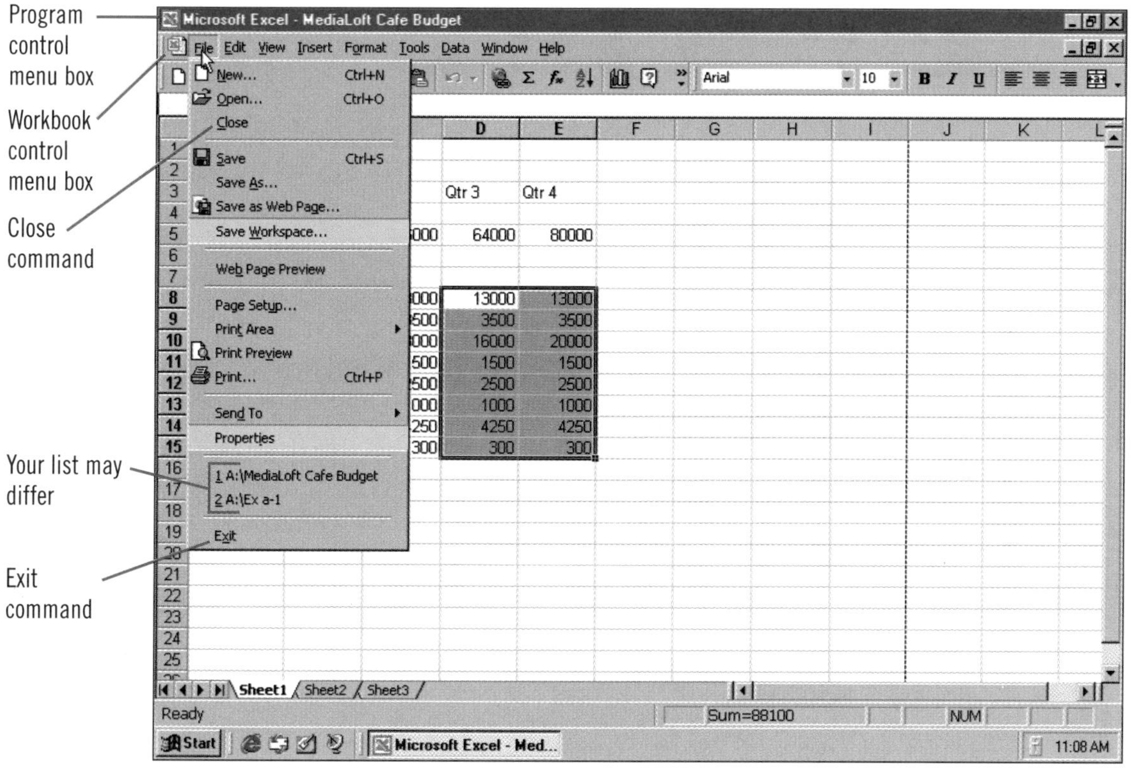

Program control menu box

Workbook control menu box

Close command

Your list may differ

Exit command

| | Microsoft Excel - MediaLoft Cafe Budget |
|---|---|

File  Edit  View  Insert  Format  Tools  Data  Window  Help

| | | | |
|---|---|---|---|
| New... | Ctrl+N | | Σ ƒ* | Arial  ▼ 10 ▼ B I U ≡ ≡ ≡ |
| Open... | Ctrl+O | | |
| Close | | | |
| | | D | E | F | G | H | I | J | K | L |
| Save | Ctrl+S | | |
| Save As... | | Qtr 3 | Qtr 4 |
| Save as Web Page... | | |
| Save Workspace... | | 000 | 64000 | 80000 |
| Web Page Preview | | |
| Page Setup... | | 000 | 13000 | 13000 |
| Print Area | ▶ | 500 | 3500 | 3500 |
| Print Preview | | 000 | 16000 | 20000 |
| Print... | Ctrl+P | 500 | 1500 | 1500 |
| | | 500 | 2500 | 2500 |
| Send To | ▶ | 000 | 1000 | 1000 |
| Properties | | 250 | 4250 | 4250 |
| | | 300 | 300 |
| 1 A:\MediaLoft Cafe Budget | | |
| 2 A:\Ex a-1 | | |
| Exit | | |

Ready                    Sum=88100          NUM

Start   Microsoft Excel - Med...          11:08 AM

# Practice

## ▶ Concepts Review

Label the elements of the Excel worksheet window shown in Figure A-19.

FIGURE A-19

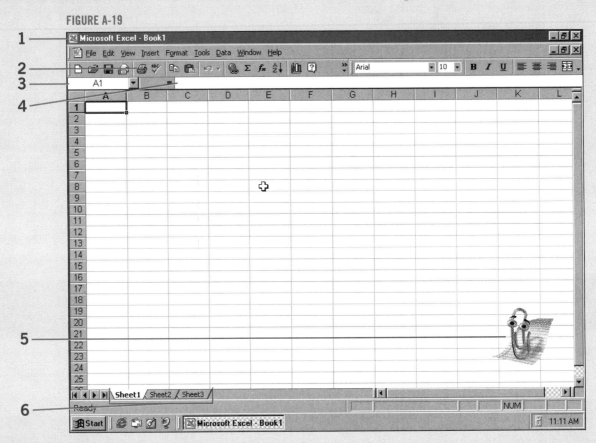

Match each term with the statement that describes it.

7. Cell pointer
8. Button
9. Worksheet window
10. Name box
11. Cell
12. Workbook

a. Area that contains a grid of columns and rows
b. The intersection of a column and row
c. Graphic symbol that depicts a task or function
d. Collection of worksheets
e. Rectangle indicating the active cell
f. Displays the active cell address

## Select the best answer from the list of choices.

13. An electronic spreadsheet can perform all of the following tasks, *except*
    a. Display information visually.
    b. Calculate data accurately.
    c. Plan worksheet objectives.
    d. Recalculate updated information.

14. Each of the following is true about labels, *except*
    a. They are left-aligned by default.
    b. They are not used in calculations.
    c. They are right-aligned by default.
    d. They can include numerical information.

15. Each of the following is true about values, *except*
    a. They can include labels.
    b. They are right-aligned by default.
    c. They are used in calculations.
    d. They can include formulas.

16. What symbol is typed before a number to make the number a label?
    a. "
    b. !
    c. '
    d. ;

17. You can get Excel Help any of the following ways, *except*
    a. Clicking Help on the menu bar.
    b. Pressing [F1].
    c. Clicking .
    d. Minimizing the program window.

8. Each key(s) can be used to confirm cell entries, *except*
    a. [Enter].
    b. [Tab].
    c. [Esc].
    d. [Shift][Enter].

9. Which button is used to preview a worksheet?
    a.
    b.
    c.
    d.

20. **Which feature is used to enlarge a print preview view?**
    a. Magnify
    b. Enlarge
    c. Amplify
    d. Zoom

21. **Each of the following is true about the Office Assistant, *except***
    a. It provides tips based on your work habits.
    b. It provides help using a question and answer format.
    c. You can change the appearance of the Office Assistant.
    d. It can complete certain tasks for you.

# ► Skills Review

1. **Start Excel 2000.**
   a. Point to Programs in the Start menu.
   b. Click the Microsoft Excel program icon.

2. **View the Excel window.**
   a. Identify as many elements in the Excel worksheet window as you can without referring to the unit material.

3. **Open and save a workbook.**
   a. Open the workbook EX A-2 from your Project Disk by clicking the Open button.
   b. Save the workbook as "Totally Together Fashions" by clicking File on the menu bar, then clicking Save As.

4. **Enter labels and values.**
   a. Enter the labels shown in Figure A-20, the Totally Together Fashions worksheet.
   b. Enter values shown in Figure A-20.
   c. Type the label "New Data" in cell A2, then clear the cell contents in A2 using the Edit menu.
   d. Type your name in cell A10.
   e. Save the workbook by clicking the Save button.

FIGURE A-20

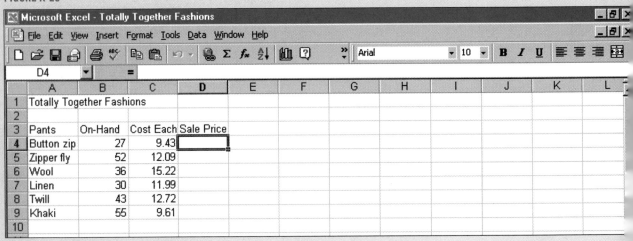

## 5. Preview and print a worksheet.

**a.** Click the Print Preview button.

**b.** Use the Zoom button to see more of your worksheet.

**c.** Print one copy of the worksheet.

## 6. Get Help.

**a.** Click the Office Assistant button if the Assistant is not displayed.

**b.** Ask the Office Assistant for information about changing the Excel Office Assistant.

**c.** Print information offered by the Office Assistant using the Print topic command on the Options menu.

**d.** Close the Help window.

## 7. Close a workbook and exit Excel.

**a.** Click File on the menu bar, then click Close.

**b.** If asked if you want to save the worksheet, click No.

**c.** If necessary, close any other worksheets you might have opened.

**d.** Click File on the menu bar, then click Exit.

# ► Independent Challenges

**1.** The Excel Help feature provides definitions, explanations, procedures, and other helpful information. It also provides examples and demonstrations to show you how Excel features work. Topics include elements such as the active cell, status bar, buttons, and dialog boxes, as well as detailed information about Excel commands and options.

To complete this independent challenge:

**a.** Start Excel and open a new workbook.

**b.** Click the Office Assistant.

**c.** Type a question that will give you information about opening and saving a workbook. (*Hint*: You may have to ask the Office Assistant more than one question.)

**d.** Print the information.

**e.** Return to your workbook when you are finished.

**f.** Exit Excel.

**2.** Spreadsheet software has many uses that can affect the way work is done. Some examples of how Excel can be used are discussed in the beginning of this unit. Use your own personal or business experiences to come up with five examples of how Excel could be used in a business setting.

To complete this independent challenge:

**a.** Start Excel.

**b.** Open a new workbook.

**c.** Think of five business tasks that you could complete more efficiently by using an Excel worksheet.

**d.** Sketch a sample of each worksheet. See Figure A-21, a sample payroll worksheet, as a guide.

**e.** Open a new workbook and save it as "Sample Payroll" on your Project Disk.

**f.** Give your worksheet a title in cell A1, type your name in cell B1.

**g.** Enter the labels shown in Figure A-21.

**h.** Enter sample data for Hours Worked and Hourly Wage in the worksheet.

**i.** Save your work, then preview and print the worksheet.

**j.** Close the worksheet and exit Excel.

FIGURE A-21

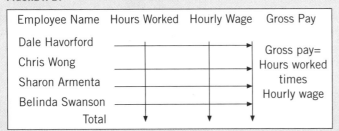

**3.** You are the office manager for Christine's Car Parts, a small auto parts supplier. Although the company is just three years old, it is expanding rapidly, and you are continually looking for ways to make your job easier. Last year you began using Excel to manage and maintain data on inventory and sales, which has greatly helped you to track information accurately and efficiently. The owner of the company has just approved your request to hire an assistant. This person will need to learn how to use Excel. Create a short training document that your new assistant can use as a reference while becoming familiar with Excel.

To complete this independent challenge:

**a.** Draw a sketch of the Excel worksheet window and label the key elements, such as toolbars, title bar, formula bar, scroll bars, etc.

**b.** For each labeled element, write a short description of its use.

**c.** List three ways to get Help in Excel. (*Hint*: Use the Office Assistant to learn all of the ways to get Help in Excel.)

**d.** Create a sketch for three of the following spreadsheet uses: accounts payable schedule, accounts receivable, payroll, list of inventory items, employee benefits data, income statement, cash flow report, or balance sheet. (*Hint*: Make up data for these sketches.)

**e.** Start Excel.

**f.** Create a new workbook and enter the values and labels for a sample spreadsheet. Make sure you have labels in column A. Enter a title for the worksheet and put your name in cell A1.

**g.** Select the range which includes the column labels.

**h.** Use the Print dialog box to print the selected range.

**i.** Preview the entire worksheet.

**j.** Save the workbook as "Christine's Car Parts" on your Project Disk, and then exit Excel.

**4.** To make smart buying decisions, you can use the World Wide Web to gather the most up-to-date information available. MediaLoft employees have access to the Web through the company's intranet. An **intranet** is a group of connected networks owned by a company or organization that is used for internal purposes. Intranets use Internet software to handle the data communications, such as e-mail and Web pages, within an organization. These pages often provide company-wide information. As with all intranets, the MediaLoft intranet limits access to MediaLoft employees.

Imagine that your supervisor at MediaLoft has just given you approval for buying a new computer. Cost is not an issue, and you need to provide a list of hardware and software requirements. You use Excel to create a worksheet using data found on the World Wide Web to support your purchase decision.

To complete this independent challenge:

a. Start Excel, open a new workbook and save it on your Project Disk as "New Computer Data."

b. List the features you want your ideal computer to contain (e.g. CD-ROM drive, etc.).

c. Connect to the Internet, go to the MediaLoft intranet site at http://www.course.com/illustrated/MediaLoft, then click the Research Center link.

d. Use any of the links to computer companies provided at the Research Center to compile your data.

e. Compile data for the components you want. When you find a system that meets your needs, include that in your list. Be sure to identify the system's key features, such as the processor chip, hard drive capacity, RAM, and monitor size. List any extra/upgrade items you want to purchase.

f. When you are finished gathering data, disconnect from the Internet.

g. Make sure all components are listed and totaled. Include any tax and shipping costs the manufacturer charges.

h. Indicate on the worksheet your final purchase decision. Enter your name in one of the cells.

i. Save, preview, and then print your worksheet.

j. Close and exit Excel.

**Excel 2000**

## Visual Workshop

Create a worksheet similar to Figure A-22 using the skills you learned in this unit. Save the workbook as "Carrie's Camera and Darkroom" on your Project Disk. Type your name in cell A11, then preview and print the worksheet.

**FIGURE A-22**

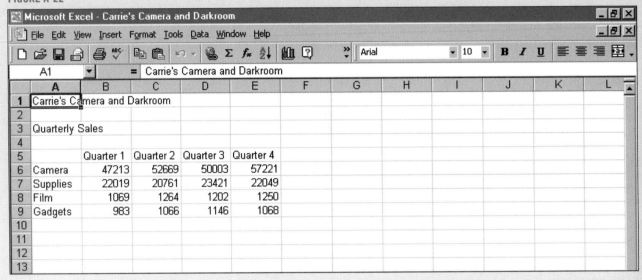

# Building
## and Editing Worksheets

## Objectives

► **Plan and design a worksheet**
[MOUS] ► **Edit cell entries and work with ranges**
[MOUS] ► **Enter formulas**
[MOUS] ► **Introduce Excel functions**
[MOUS] ► **Copy and move cell entries**
[MOUS] ► **Understand relative and absolute cell references**
[MOUS] ► **Copy formulas with relative cell references**
[MOUS] ► **Copy formulas with absolute cell references**
[MOUS] ► **Name and move a sheet**

Using your understanding of the basics of Excel, you can now plan and build your own worksheets. When you build a worksheet, you enter text, values, and formulas into worksheet cells. Once you create a worksheet, you can save it in a workbook file and then print it. Jim Fernandez has received a request from the Marketing department for a forecast of this summer's author events and an estimate of the average number of author appearances. Marketing hopes that the number of appearances will increase 20% over last year's figures. Jim needs to create a worksheet that summarizes appearances for last year and forecasts the summer appearances for this year.

# Planning and Designing a Worksheet

Before you start entering data into a worksheet, you need to know the purpose and approximate layout of the worksheet. You should also familiarize yourself with the mouse pointers you will encounter; refer to Table B-1.  MediaLoft encourages authors to come to stores and sign their books. These author events are great for sales. Jim wants to forecast MediaLoft's 2001 summer author appearances. The goal, already identified by the Marketing department, is to increase the year 2000 signings by 20%. Using the planning guidelines below, work with Jim as he plans this worksheet.

**Details**

### In planning and designing a worksheet it is important to:

### Determine the purpose of the worksheet and give it a meaningful title
Jim needs to forecast summer appearances for 2001. Jim titles the worksheet "Summer 2001 MediaLoft Author Events Forecast."

### Determine your worksheet's desired results, or "output"
Jim needs to begin scheduling author events and will use these forecasts to determine staffing and budget needs if the number of author events increases by 20%. He also wants to calculate the average number of author events since the Marketing department uses this information for corporate promotions.

### Collect all the information, or "input", that will produce the results you want
Jim gathers together the number of author events that occurred at four stores during the 2000 summer season, which runs from June through August.

### Determine the calculations, or formulas, necessary to achieve the desired results
First, Jim needs to total the number of events at each of the selected stores during each month of the summer of 2000. Then he needs to add these totals together to determine the grand total of summer appearances. Because he needs to determine the goal for the 2001 season, the 2000 monthly totals and grand total are multiplied by 1.2 to calculate the projected 20% increase for the 2001 summer season. He'll use the Paste Function to select the Average function, which will determine the average number of appearances for the Marketing department.

### Sketch on paper how you want the worksheet to look; identify where to place the labels and values
Jim decides to put store locations in rows and the months in columns. He enters the data in his sketch and indicates where the monthly totals and the grand total should go. Below the totals he writes out the formula for determining a 20% increase in appearances for 2000. He also includes a label for the location of the average number of events calculations. Jim's sketch of his worksheet is shown in Figure B-1.

### Create the worksheet
Jim enters the labels first to establish the structure of the worksheet. He then enters the values—the data about the events—into his worksheet. Finally, he enters the formulas necessary to calculate totals, averages, and forecasts. These values and formulas will be used to calculate the necessary output. The worksheet Jim creates is shown in Figure B-2.

**FIGURE B-1:** Worksheet sketch showing labels, values, and calculations

## Summer 2001 MediaLoft Author Events Forecast

|          | June       | July       | August       | Total       | Average |
|----------|------------|------------|--------------|-------------|---------|
| Boston   | 15         | 10         | 23           |             |         |
| New York | 14         | 10         | 12           |             |         |
| Seattle  | 12         | 13         | 6            |             |         |
| San Diego| 10         | 24         | 15           |             |         |
| Total    | June Total | July Total | August Total | Grand Total |         |
|          |            |            |              |             |         |
| 20% rise | Total X 1.2|            |              |             |         |

**FIGURE B-2:** Jim's forecasting worksheet

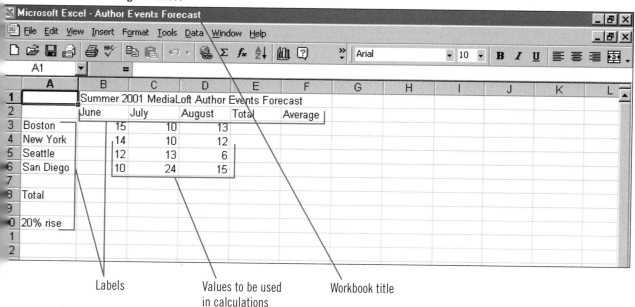

Labels

Values to be used in calculations

Workbook title

**TABLE B-1:** Commonly used pointers

| name | pointer | use to |
|------|---------|--------|
| normal | ✛ | Select a cell or range; indicates Ready mode |
| copy | ↖⁺ | Create a duplicate of the selected cell(s) |
| fill handle | + | Create an alphanumeric series in a range |
| I-beam | I | Edit contents of formula bar |
| move | ↖ | Change the location of the selected cell(s) |

# Editing Cell Entries and Working with Ranges

You can change the contents of any cell at any time. To edit the contents of a cell, you first select the cell you want to edit. Then you have three options: you can click the formula bar, double-click the selected cell, or press [F2]. This puts Excel into Edit mode. To make sure you are in Edit mode, look at the **mode indicator** on the far left side of the status bar. After planning and creating his worksheet, Jim notices that he entered the wrong value for the August Seattle events, and that Houston should be entered instead of San Diego. He fixes the event figures, replaces the San Diego label, and corrects the value for July's Houston events.

**Steps**

1. Start Excel, click **Tools** on the menu bar, click **Customize**, click the **Options tab** in the Customize dialog box, click **Reset my usage data** to restore the default settings, click **Yes**, then click **Close**

2. Open the workbook **EX B-1** from your Project Disk, then save it as **Author Events Forecast**

3. Click cell **D5**
   This cell contains August Seattle events, which you want to change to reflect the correct numbers for the year 2000.

4. Click to **the right of 6** in the formula bar
   Excel goes into Edit mode, and the mode indicator on the status bar displays "Edit." A blinking vertical line called the **insertion point** appears in the formula bar, and if you move the mouse pointer to the formula bar, the pointer changes to $\mathrm{I}$, which is used for editing. See Figure B-3.

5. Press **[Backspace]**, type **11**, then click the **Enter button** on the formula bar
   The value in cell D5 is changed or edited from 6 to 11. Additional modifications can also be made using the [F2] key.

6. Click cell **A6**, then press **[F2]**
   Excel is in Edit mode again, and the insertion point is in the cell.

7. Press **[Backspace]** nine times, type **Houston**, then press **[Enter]**
   The label changes to Houston. If you make a mistake, you can either click the Cancel button on the formula bar *before* accepting the cell entry, or click the Undo button on the Standard toolbar if you notice the mistake *after* you have accepted the cell entry. The Undo button allows you to reverse up to 16 previous actions, one at a time.

**QuickTip**

The Redo command reverses the action of the Undo command. Click the Redo button on the Standard toolbar if you change your mind after an undo.

8. Double-click cell **C6**
   Double-clicking a cell also puts Excel into Edit mode with the insertion point in the cell.

9. Press **[Delete]** twice, then type **14**
   The number of book signings for July in Houston has been corrected. See Figure B-4.

10. Click to confirm the entry, then click the **Save button** on the Standard toolbar

**FIGURE B-3: Worksheet in Edit mode**

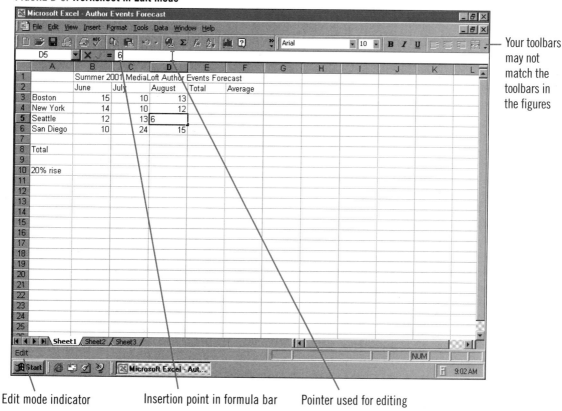

Your toolbars may not match the toolbars in the figures

Edit mode indicator          Insertion point in formula bar          Pointer used for editing

**FIGURE B-4: Edited worksheet**

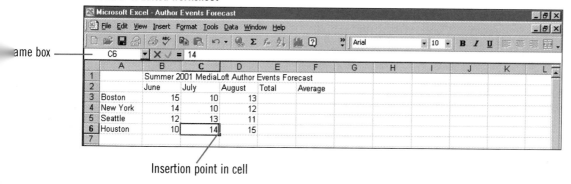

Name box

Insertion point in cell

## Using range names in a workbook

Any group of cells (two or more) is called a range. To select a range, click the first cell and drag to the last cell you want to include in the range. The range address is defined by noting the first and last cells in the range separated by a colon, for example A8:B16. Once you select a range, the easiest way to give it a name is by clicking the name box and typing in a name. Range names—meaningful English names— are usually easier to remember than cell addresses. You can use a range name in a formula (for example, Income-Expenses) or to move around the workbook more quickly. Simply click the name box list arrow, then click the name of the range you want to go to. The cell pointer moves immediately to select that range. To clear the name from a range, click Insert on the menu bar, point to Name, then click Define. Select the range name you want to delete from the Define Name dialog box, click Delete, then click OK.

Excel 2000

# Entering Formulas

You use **formulas** to perform numeric calculations such as adding, multiplying, and averaging. Formulas in an Excel worksheet usually start with the formula prefix—the equal sign (=) and contain cell addresses and range names. Arithmetic formulas use one or more **arithmetic operators** to perform calculations; see Table B-2. Using a cell address or range name in a formula is called **cell referencing**. If you change a value in a cell, any formula containing that cell reference will be automatically recalculated using the new value. In formulas using more than one arithmetic operator, Excel uses the order of precedence rules to determine which operation to perform first. Jim needs to total the values for the monthly author events for June, July, and August, and forecast what the 20% increase in appearances will be. He performs these calculations using formulas.

## Steps

**1. Click cell B8**

This is the cell where you want to enter the calculation that totals the June events.

**2. Type = (the equal sign)**

Placing an equal sign at the beginning of an entry tells Excel that a formula is about to be entered, rather than a label or a value. "Enter" appears on the status bar. The total number of June events is equal to the sum of the values in cells B3, B4, B5, and B6.

**3. Type b3+b4+b5+b6, then click the Enter button ☑ on the formula bar**

Notice that the result of 51 appears in cell B8, and the formula appears in the formula bar. Also, Excel is not case-sensitive: it doesn't matter if you type upper or lower-case characters when you enter cell addresses. See Figure B-5.

**Trouble?**

If the formula instead of the result appears in the cell after you click ☑, make sure you began the formula with = (the equal sign).

**4. Click cell C8, type =c3+c4+c5+c6, press [Tab]; in cell D8, type =d3+d4+d5+d6 then press [Enter]**

The total appearances for July, 47, and for August, 51, appear in cells C8 and D8 respectively.

**5. Click cell B10, type =B8*1.2, then click ☑**

To calculate the 20% increase, you multiply the total by 1.2. The formula in cell B10 multiplies the total events for June, cell B8, by 1.2. The result of 61.2 appears in cell B10 and is the projected value for an increase of 20% over the 51 June events. Now you need to calculate the 20% increase for July and August. You can use the **pointing method**, by which you specify cell references in a formula by selecting the desired cell with your mouse instead of typing its cell reference into the formula. Pointing is a preferred method because it eliminates typing errors.

**6. Click cell C10, type =, then click cell C8**

When you click cell C8, a moving border surrounds the cell. This **moving border**—as well as the mode indicator—indicates the cell that is copied in this operation. Moving border can display around a single cell or a range of cells.

**QuickTip**

Press [Esc] to turn off a moving border.

**7. Type *1.2, then press [Tab]**

The calculated value 56.4 appears in cell C10.

**8. In cell D10, type =, click cell D8, type *1.2, then click ☑**

Compare your results with Figure B-6.

**9. Click the Save button ☐ on the Standard toolbar**

**FIGURE B-5:** Worksheet showing formula and result

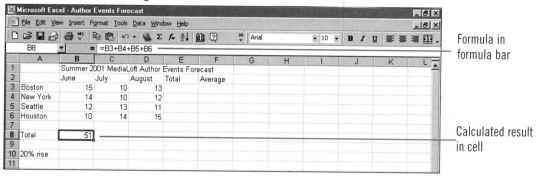

Formula in formula bar

Calculated result in cell

**FIGURE B-6:** Calculated results for 20% increase

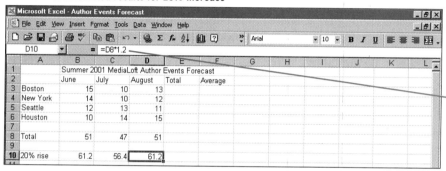

Formula calculates 20% increase over value in cell D8 and displays result in cell D10

**ABLE B-2:** Excel arithmetic operators

| perator | purpose | example |
|---|---|---|
| + | Addition | =A5+A7 |
| - | Subtraction or negation | =A5-10 |
| * | Multiplication | =A5*A7 |
| / | Division | =A5/A7 |
| % | Percent | =35% |
| ^ (caret) | Exponent | =6^2 (same as 6*6) |

ES TO USE

## Order of precedence in Excel formulas

A formula can include several mathematical operations. When you work with formulas that have more than one operator, the order of precedence is very important. If a formula contains two or more operators, such as 4 + .55/4000 * 25, the computer performs the calculations in a particular sequence based on these rules: Operations inside parentheses are calculated before any other operations. Exponents are calculated next, then any multiplication and division—from left to right. Finally, addition and subtraction is calculated from left to right. In the example 4 + .55/4000 * 25, Excel performs the arithmetic operations by first dividing 4000 into .55, then multiplying the result by 25, then adding 4. You can change the order of calculations by using parentheses. For example, in the formula (4+.55)/4000 * 25, Excel would first add 4 and .55, then divide that amount by 4000, then finally multiply by 25.

# Introducing Excel Functions

Functions are predefined worksheet formulas that enable you to do complex calculations easily. Like formulas, functions always begin with the formula prefix = (the equal sign). You can enter functions manually, or you can use the Paste Function to select the function you need from a list. ✏️ Jim uses the SUM function to calculate the grand totals in his worksheet and the AVERAGE function to calculate the average number of author events per store.

**1.** Click cell **E3**

This is the cell where you want to display the total of all author events in Boston for June, July, and August. You use **AutoSum** to create the totals. By default, AutoSum sets up the SUM function to add the values in the cells above the cell pointer. If there are one or fewer values in the cells above the cell pointer, AutoSum adds the values in the cells to the left of the cell pointer—in this case, the values in cells B3, C3, and D3.

> **Trouble?**
>
> If you don't see Σ on your toobar, click the More Buttons button » on the Standard toolbar.

**2.** Click the **AutoSum button** Σ on the Standard toolbar, then click the **Enter button** ☑ on the formula bar

The formula =SUM(B3:D3) appears in the formula bar. The result, 38, appears in cell E3. The information inside the parentheses is the **argument**, or the information to be used in calculating a result of the function. An argument can be a value, a range of cells, text, or another function.

**3.** Click cell **E4**, click Σ , then click ☑

The values for the Boston and New York events are now totaled.

**4.** Click cell **E5**, then click Σ

By default, AutoSum sets up a function to add the two values in the cells above the active cell, as you can see by the formula in the formula bar. You can override the current selection by manually selecting the correct range for this argument.

**5.** Click cell **B5**, drag to cell **D5** to select the range **B5:D5**, then click ☑

As you drag, the argument in the SUM function changes to reflect the selected range, and ScreenTip appears telling you the size of the range by row and column.

**6.** Click cell **E6**, type **=SUM(** , point to cell **B6**, drag to cell **D6**, press **[Enter]**, click ce E8, type **=SUM(** , point to cell **B8**, drag to cell **D8**, press **[Enter]**, click cell **E10**, typ **=SUM(** , point to cell **B10**, drag to cell **D10**, then click ☑ to confirm the entry

See Figure B-7 to verify your results. Now the Paste Function can be used to select the fun tion needed to calculate the average number of author events.

> **Trouble?**
>
> If the Office Assistant opens, click No, don't provide help now.

**7.** Click cell **F3**, then click the **Paste Function button** fx on the Standard toolbar

The Paste Function dialog box opens. See Table B-3 for frequently used functions. The fun tion needed to calculate averages—named AVERAGE—is included in the Most Recen Used function category.

> **QuickTip**
>
> Modify a function's range by clicking the Collapse dialog box button, defining the range with your mouse, then clicking the Expand dialog box button to return to the Paste Function window.

**8.** Click **AVERAGE** in the Function name list box, click **OK**, the AVERAGE dialog b opens; type **B3:D3** in the Number 1 text box, as shown in Figure B-8, then click O

**9.** Click cell **F4**, click fx , verify that **AVERAGE** is selected, click **OK**, type **B4:D4**, cl **OK**, click cell **F5**, click fx , click **AVERAGE**, click **OK**, type **B5:D5**, click OK, click c **F6**, click fx , click **AVERAGE**, click **OK**, type **B6:D6**, then click **OK**

The result in Boston (cell F3) is 12.6667; the result in New York (cell F4) is 12; the resul Seattle (cell F5) is 12; and the result in Houston (cell F6) is 13, giving you the averages all four stores.

**FIGURE B-7:** Worksheet with SUM functions entered

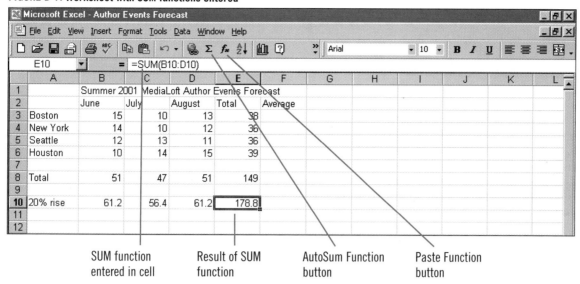

SUM function entered in cell     Result of SUM function     AutoSum Function button     Paste Function button

**FIGURE B-8:** Using the Paste Function to create a formula

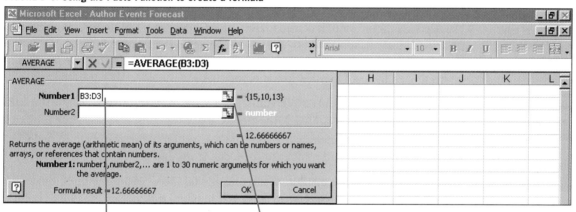

Argument displays here     Click Collapse Dialog Box button to define an argument using your mouse

**TABLE B-3:** Frequently used functions

| function | description |
|---|---|
| SUM(*argument*) | Calculates the sum of the arguments |
| AVERAGE(*argument*) | Calculates the average of the arguments |
| MAX(*argument*) | Displays the largest value among the arguments |
| MIN(*argument*) | Displays the smallest value among the arguments |
| COUNT(*argument*) | Calculates the number of values in the arguments |

### Using the MIN and MAX functions

Other commonly used functions include MIN and MAX. You use the MIN function to calculate the minimum or smallest value in a selected range; the MAX function calculates the maximum or largest value in a selected range. The MAX function is included in the Most Frequently Used function category in the Paste Function dialog box, while the MIN function can be found in the Statistical category. Like AVERAGE, MIN and MAX are preceded by an equal sign and the argument includes a range.

# Copying and Moving Cell Entries

Using the Cut, Copy, and Paste buttons or the Excel drag-and-drop feature, you can copy or move information from one cell or range in your worksheet to another. You can also cut, copy, and paste data from one worksheet to another to make corrections, and add information using the Office Clipboard, which can store up to 12 items. ✎ Jim needs to include the 2001 forecast for spring and fall author events in his Author Events Forecast workbook. He's already entered the spring report in Sheet2 and will finish entering the labels and data for the fall report. Jim copies information from the spring report to the fall report.

**Steps**

1. **Click Sheet 2 of the Author Events Forecast workbook**
   To work more efficiently, existing labels can be copied from one range to another and from one sheet to another. You see that the store names have to be corrected in cells A6:A7.

**QuickTip**

The Cut button 🗶 removes the selected information from the worksheet and places it on the Office Clipboard.

2. **Click Sheet 1, select the range A5:A6, then click the Copy button 📋 on the Standard toolbar**
   The selected range (A5:A6) is copied to the **Office Clipboard**, a temporary storage file that holds the selected information you copy or cut. A moving border surrounds the selected range until you press [Esc] or copy additional information to the Clipboard. To copy the most recent item copied to the Clipboard to a new location, you click a new cell and then use the Paste command.

**Trouble?**

If the Clipboard toolbar does not open, click View on the menu bar, point to toolbars, then click Clipboard.

3. **Click Sheet 2, select the range A6:A7, click the Paste button 📋 on the Standard toolbar, select the range A4:A9, then click 📋**
   The Clipboard toolbar opens when you copy a selection to the already occupied Clipboard. You can use the Clipboard toolbar to copy, cut, store, and paste up to 12 items.

**QuickTip**

To use the pop-up menu, right-click, click Copy, click the target cell, right-click, then click Paste to paste the last item copied to the Clipboard.

4. **Click cell A13, place the pointer on the last 📋 on the Clipboard toolbar, the contents of range A4:A9 display in a ScreenTip, click 📋 to paste the contents in cell A13, then close the Clipboard toolbar**
   The item is copied into the range A13:A18. When pasting an item from the Clipboard into the worksheet, you only need to specify the top left cell of the range where you want the selection to go. The moving border remains active. Now you can use the drag-and-drop technique to copy the Total label, which does not copy the contents to the Clipboard.

5. **Click cell E3, position the pointer on any edge of the cell until the pointer changes to ⬚, then press and hold down [Ctrl]**
   The pointer changes to the copy pointer ⬚⁺. When you copy cells, the original data remains in the original cell. When you move cells, the original data does *not* remain in the original cell.

6. **While still pressing [Ctrl], press and hold the left mouse button, drag the cell contents to cell E12, release the mouse button, then release [Ctrl]**
   As you drag, an outline of the cell moves with the pointer, as shown in Figure B-9, and ScreenTip appears tracking the current position of the item as you move it. When you release the mouse button, the Total label appears in cell E12. You now decide to move the worksheet title over to the left. To use drag and drop to move data to a new cell, do not press [Ctrl].

**Trouble?**

When you drag and drop into occupied cells, Excel asks if you want to replace the existing cells. Click OK to replace the contents with the cell you are moving.

7. **Click cell C1, position the pointer on the edge of the cell until it changes to ⬚, then drag the cell contents to A1**
   Once the labels are copied, you can easily enter the fall events data into the range B13:D1

8. **Using the information shown in Figure B-10, enter the author events data for the fall into the range B13:D16**
   Compare your worksheet to Figure B-10.

FIGURE B-9: Using drag and drop to copy information

Copy button

Paste button

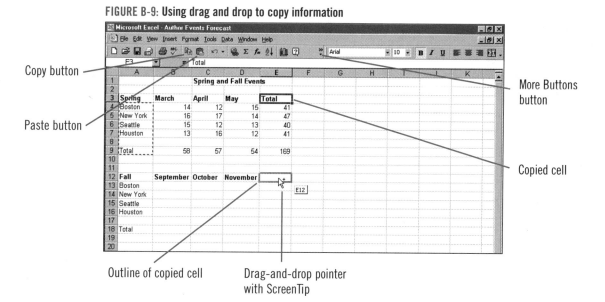

More Buttons
button

Copied cell

Outline of copied cell

Drag-and-drop pointer
with ScreenTip

FIGURE B-10: Worksheet with Fall author event data entered

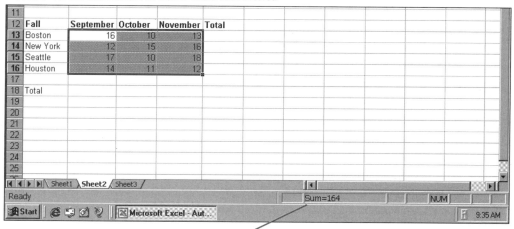

Sum of selected range
displays in status bar

## Using the Office Clipboard

The Office Clipboard lets you copy and paste multiple items such as text, images, tables, or Excel ranges within or between the Microsoft Office applications. The Office Clipboard can hold up to 12 items copied or cut from any Office program. The Clipboard toolbar, shown in Figure B-11, displays the items stored on the Office Clipboard. You choose whether to delete the first item from the Clipboard when you copy the thirteenth item. The collected items remain in the Office Clipboard and are available to you until you close all open Office applications.

FIGURE B-11: The Office Clipboard

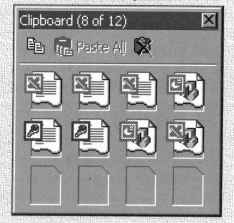

# Understanding Relative and Absolute Cell References

Like a label or value, an existing formula can be copied to a new location. This enables you to work efficiently by copying a working formula to multiple locations. When copied, a cell reference within a formula is automatically copied *relative* to its new location. This is called a **relative reference**. You can, however, choose to copy a cell reference with an absolute reference or a mixed reference. An **absolute reference** always cites a specific cell when the formula is copied. Jim often copies existing worksheet formulas and makes use of many types of cell references.

### Use relative references when cell relationships remain unchanged

When Excel copies a formula, all the cell references change to reflect the new location automatically. Each copied formula is identical to the original, except that the column or row is adjusted for its new location. The outlined cells in Figure B-12 contain formulas that contain relative references. For example, the formula in cell E5 is =SUM(B5:D5). When copied to cell E6, the resulting formula is =SUM(B6:D6). The original formula was copied from row 5 to row 6 within the same column, so the cell referenced in the copied formula increased by one row.

### Use an absolute cell reference when one relationship changes

In most cases, you will use relative cell references—the default. Sometimes, however, this is not what is needed. In some cases, you'll want to reference a specific cell, even when copying a formula. You create absolute references by placing a $ (dollar sign) before both the column letter and row number for a cell's address using the [F4] function key (on the keyboard). Figure B-13 displays the formulas used in Figure B-11. Notice that each formula in range B15:D18 contains both a relative and absolute reference. By using an absolute reference when referring to cell $B$12 in a formula, Excel keeps that cell reference (representing the potential increase) constant when copying that formula.

**FIGURE B-12: Location of relative references**

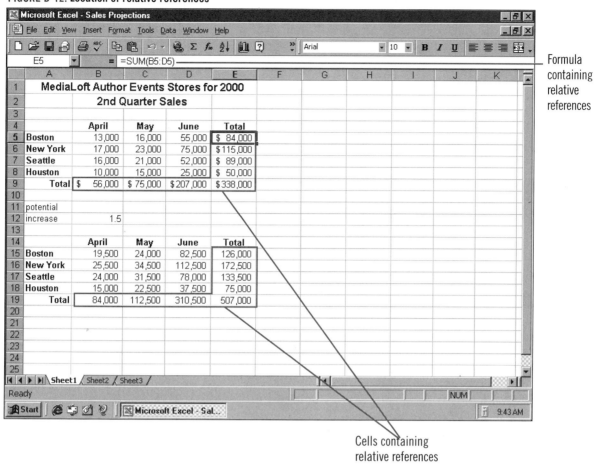

Formula containing relative references

Cells containing relative references

**FIGURE B-13: Absolute and relative reference formulas**

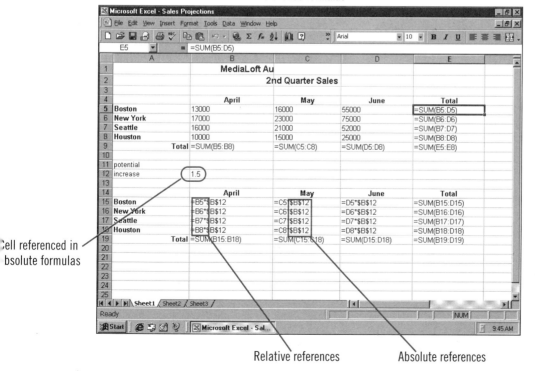

Cell referenced in absolute formulas

Relative references

Absolute references

# Copying Formulas with Relative Cell References

Copying and moving formulas allows you to reuse formulas you've already created. Copying formulas, rather than retyping them, is faster and helps to prevent typing errors. ✎ Jim wants to copy the formulas that total the appearances by region and by month from the spring to the fall. He can use Copy and Paste commands and the Fill Right method to copy this information.

1. **Click cell E4, then click the Copy button** 📋 **on the Standard toolbar**
   The formula for calculating the total number of spring Boston author events is copied to the Clipboard. Notice that the formula =SUM(B4:D4) displays in the formula bar.

2. **Click cell E13, then click the Paste button** 📋 **on the Standard toolbar**
   The formula from cell E4 is copied into cell E13, where the new result of 39 appears. Notice in the formula bar that the cell references have changed, so that the range B13:D13 appears in the formula. This formula contains **relative cell references** which tell Excel to copy the formula to a new cell, but to substitute new cell references so that the relationship of the cells to the formula in its new location remains unchanged. In this case, Excel adjusted the formula so cells D13, C13, and B13—the three cell references immediately to the left of E13—replaced cells D4, C4, and B4, the three cell references to the left of E4.
   Notice that the bottom right corner of the active cell contains a small square, called the **fill handle.** You can use the fill handle to copy labels, formulas, and values. You use the fill handle to copy the formula in cell E13 to cells E14, E15, and E16.

3. **Position the pointer over the fill handle until it changes to ✛, press the left mouse button, then drag the fill handle to select the range E13:E16**
   See Figure B-14.

4. **Release the mouse button**
   Once you release the mouse button, the fill handle copies the formula from the active cell (E13) and pastes it into each cell of the selected range. Again, because the formula uses relative cell references, cells E14 through E16 correctly display the totals for the fall author events.

5. **Click cell B9, click Edit on the menu bar, then click Copy**

6. **Click cell B18, click Edit on the menu bar, then click Paste**
   See Figure B-15. The formula for calculating the September events appears in the formula bar. You can use the Fill Right command to copy the formula from cell B18 to cells C18, D18, and E18.

7. **Select the range B18:E18**

8. **Click Edit on the menu bar, point to Fill, then click Right**
   The rest of the totals are filled in correctly. Compare your worksheet to Figure B-16.

9. **Click the Save button** 💾 **on the Standard toolbar**

**QuickTip**

Click Edit on the menu bar, then click Paste Special to specify components of the copied cell or range prior to pasting. You can selectively copy formulas, values, comments, validation, and formatting attributes, as well as transpose cells or paste the contents as a link.

**QuickTip**

As you drag the fill handle, the contents of the last filled cell appear in the name box.

**Trouble?**

If the Clipboard toolbar opens, click the Close button. If the Office Assistant appears, right-click it, then click Hide.

## CLUES TO USE

### Filling cells with sequential text or values

Often, we fill cells with sequential text: months of the year, days of the week, years, and text plus a number (Quarter 1, Quarter 2, ... ). You can easily fill cells using sequences by dragging the fill handle. As you drag the fill handle, Excel automatically extends the existing sequence. (The contents of the last filled cell appears in the name box.) Use the Fill Series command on the Edit menu to examine all of the available fill series options.

FIGURE B-14: **Selected range using the fill handle**

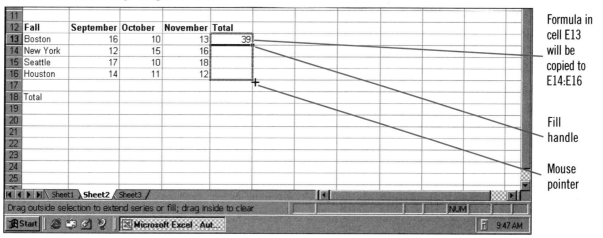

Formula in cell E13 will be copied to E14:E16

Fill handle

Mouse pointer

FIGURE B-15: **Worksheet with copied formula**

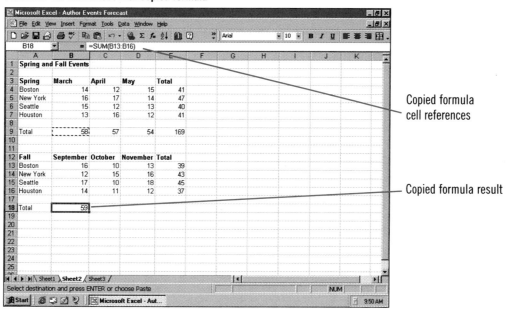

Copied formula cell references

Copied formula result

FIGURE B-16: **Completed worksheet with all formulas copied**

| | A | September | October | November | Total | | | | | | |
|---|---|---|---|---|---|---|---|---|---|---|---|
| 10 | | | | | | | | | | | |
| 11 | | | | | | | | | | | |
| 12 | Fall | September | October | November | Total | | | | | | |
| 13 | Boston | 16 | 10 | 13 | 39 | | | | | | |
| 14 | New York | 12 | 15 | 16 | 43 | | | | | | |
| 15 | Seattle | 17 | 10 | 18 | 45 | | | | | | |
| 16 | Houston | 14 | 11 | 12 | 37 | | | | | | |
| 17 | | | | | | | | | | | |
| 18 | Total | 59 | 46 | 59 | 164 | | | | | | |
| 19 | | | | | | | | | | | |
| 20 | | | | | | | | | | | |
| 21 | | | | | | | | | | | |
| 22 | | | | | | | | | | | |
| 23 | | | | | | | | | | | |
| 24 | | | | | | | | | | | |
| 25 | | | | | | | | | | | |

Sheet1 **Sheet2** Sheet3

Ready                                    Sum=328            NUM

Start    Microsoft Excel - Aut...                          9:49 AM

# Copying Formulas with Absolute Cell References

When copying formulas, you might want a cell reference to always refer to a particular cell address. In such an instance, you would use an **absolute cell reference**. An absolute cell reference always refers to a specific cell address when the formula is copied. You identify an absolute reference by placing a dollar sign ($) before the row letter and column number of the address (for example $A$1). ✎ The staff in the Marketing department hopes the number of author events will increase by 20% over last year's figures. Jim decides to add a column that calculates a possible increase in the number of spring events in 2001. He wants to do a what-if analysis and recalculate the spreadsheet several times, changing the percentage that the number of appearances might increase each time.

1. **Click cell G1, type Change, then press [→]**
   You can store the increase factor that will be used in the what-if analysis in cell H1.

2. **Type 1.1, then press [Enter]**
   The value in cell H1 represents a 10% increase in author events.

3. **Click cell G3, type What if?, then press [Enter]**
   Now you create a formula that references a specific address: cell H1.

4. **In cell G4, type =E4\*H1, then click the Enter button 📝 on the formula bar**
   The result of 45.1 appears in cell G4. This value represents the total spring events for Boston if there is a 10% increase. To determine the value for the remaining stores, you copy the formula in cell G4 to the range G5:G7.

5. **Drag the fill handle to select the range G4:G7**
   The resulting values in the range G5:G7 are all zeros. When you copy the formula it adjusts so the formula in cell G5 is =E5\*H2. Since there is no value in cell H2, the result is 0, an error. You need to use an absolute reference in the formula to keep the formula from adjusting. That way, cell H1 will always be referenced. You can change the relative cell reference to an absolute cell reference using [F4].

6. **Click cell G4, press [F2] to change to Edit mode, then press [F4]**
   When you press [F2], the **range finder** outlines the equation's arguments in blue and green. When you press [F4], dollar signs appear, changing the H1 cell reference to an absolute reference. See Figure B-17.

7. **Click the Enter button 📝 on the formula bar**
   The formula correctly contains an absolute cell reference and the value remains unchanged at 45.1. The fill handle can be used to copy the corrected formula in cell G4 to G5:G7.

8. **Drag the fill handle to select the range G4:G7**
   The correct values for a 10% increase display in cells G4:G7. You complete the what-if analysis by changing the value in cell H1 from 1.1 to 1.25 to indicate a 25% increase in events.

9. **Click cell H1, type 1.25, then click 📝**
   The values in the range G4:G7 change to reflect the 25% increase. Compare your worksheet to Figure B-18. Since events only occur in whole numbers, the numbers' appearance can be changed later.

QuickTip

Before you copy or move a formula, check to see if you need to use an absolute cell reference.

FIGURE B-17: Absolute cell reference in cell G4

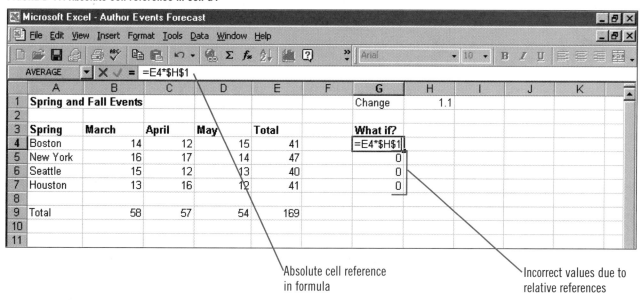

Absolute cell reference
in formula

Incorrect values due to
relative references

FIGURE B-18: Worksheet with what-if value

Absolute cell references
in formulas

## Copying and moving using named ranges

You can give a range of cells an easy-to-remember meaningful name, such as "2001 Sales." If you move the named range, its name moves with it. Like any range, a named range can be referenced absolutely in a formula by using the $ symbol. To copy or move a named range, you can "go to" it quickly by clicking the name box list arrow and selecting its name.

# Naming and Moving a Sheet

Each workbook initially contains three worksheets named Sheet1, Sheet2, and Sheet3. When the workbook is opened, the first worksheet is the active sheet. To move from sheet to sheet, click the desired sheet tab located at the bottom of the worksheet window. Sheet tab scrolling buttons, located to the left of the sheet tabs, allow rapid movement among the sheets. To make it easier to identify the sheets in a workbook, you can rename each sheet and then organize them in a logical way. The name appears on the sheet tab. For instance, sheets within a single workbook could be named for individual salespeople to better track performance goals, and the sheets can be moved so they appear in alphabetical order. ✎ Jim wants to be able to easily identify the actual author events and the forecast sheets. He decides to name two sheets in his workbook, then changes their order.

**Steps** 1 2 3 4

1. **Click the Sheet1 tab**
   Sheet1 becomes active; this is the worksheet that contains the summer information you compiled for the Marketing department. Its tab moves to the front, and the tab for Sheet2 moves to the background.

2. **Click the Sheet2 tab**
   Sheet2, containing the spring and fall data, becomes active. Once you have confirmed which sheet is which, you can rename Sheet1 so it has a name that you can easily remember.

3. **Double-click the Sheet1 tab**
   The Sheet1 text becomes selected with the default sheet name ("Sheet1") selected. You could also click Format in the menu bar, point to Sheet, then click Rename to select the sheet name.

4. **Type Summer, then press [Enter]**
   See Figure B-19. The new name automatically replaces the default name in the tab. Worksheet names can have up to 31 characters, including spaces and punctuation.

**QuickTip**

To delete a worksheet, select the worksheet you want to delete, click Edit on the menu bar, then click Delete sheet. To insert a worksheet, click Insert on the menu bar, then click Worksheet.

5. **Double-click the Sheet2 tab, then rename this sheet Spring-Fall**
   Jim decides to rearrange the order of the sheets, so that Summer comes after Spring-Fall.

6. **Click the Summer sheet tab, then drag it to the right of the Spring-Fall sheet tab**
   As you drag, the pointer changes to 🔖, the sheet relocation pointer. See Figure B-20. The first sheet in the workbook is now the Spring-Fall sheet. When there are multiple sheets in a workbook, the navigation buttons can be used to scroll through the sheet tabs. Click the leftmost navigation button to display the first sheet tab; click the rightmost navigation button to display the last sheet tab. The left and right buttons move one sheet in their respective directions.

7. **Type your name in cell A12, click File on the menu bar, click Print, click the Entire workbook option button, then click the Preview button**
   The Preview screen opens. Each worksheet is displayed on a separate page. You can preview the workbook sheets by clicking the Next and Previous buttons.

8. **Click the Print button on the Preview toolbar**

9. **Save and close the workbook, then exit Excel**

FIGURE B-19: Renamed sheet in workbook

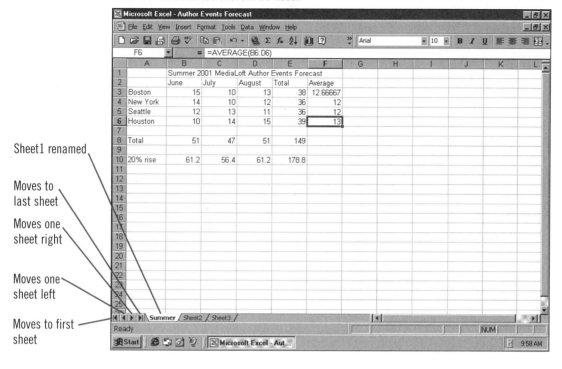

Sheet1 renamed

Moves to
last sheet

Moves one
sheet right

Moves one
sheet left

Moves to first
sheet

FIGURE B-20: Moving Summer after Spring-Fall sheet

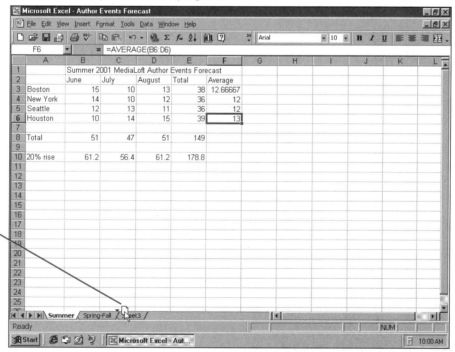

Sheet relocation
pointer

## Moving and copying worksheets

There are times when you may want to move or copy sheets. To move sheets within the current workbook, drag the selected sheet tab along the row of sheet tabs to the new location. To copy, simply press CTRL as you drag the sheet tab and release the mouse button before you release CTRL. Although you have to be careful and carefully check the calculations when doing so, moving and copying worksheets to new workbooks is a relatively simple operation. You must have the workbook that you are copying to, as well as the workbook that you are copying from, open. Select the sheet to copy or move, click File on the menu bar, click Edit, then click Move or Copy sheet. Complete the information in the Move or Copy dialog box. Be sure to click the Create a Copy check box if you are copying rather than moving the worksheet.

# Practice

## ► Concepts Review

Label each element of the Excel worksheet window shown in Figure B-20.

FIGURE B-21

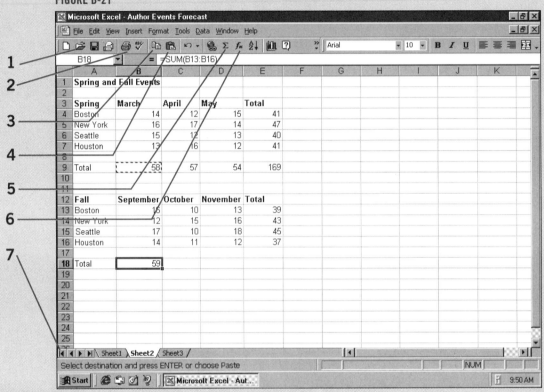

Match the term or button with the statement that describes it.

8. Range
9. Function
10.
11.
12. Formula

a. A predefined formula that provides a shortcut for commonly used calculations
b. A cell entry that performs a calculation in an Excel worksheet
c. A specified group of cells, which can include the entire worksheet
d. Used to copy cells
e. Used to paste cells

Select the best answer from the list of choices.

13. What type of cell reference changes when it is copied?
   a. Absolute
   b. Circular
   c. Looping
   d. Relative

14. What character is used to make a reference absolute?
   a. &
   b. ^
   c. $
   d. @

**15. Which button is used to enter data in a cell?**

  a.       c. 🗎

  b. ✖      d. ✔

# ▶ Skills Review

**1. Edit cell entries and work with ranges.**

  a. Start Excel, open the workbook EX B-2 from your Project Disk and save it as "Office Furnishings."

  b. Change the quantity of Tables to 25.

  c. Change the price of each of the Desks to 250.

  d. Change the quantity of Easels to 17.

  e. Name the range B2:B5 "Quantity" and name the range C2:C5 "Price."

  f. Type your name in cell A20, then save and preview the worksheet.

**2. Enter formulas.**

  a. Click cell B6, then enter the formula B2+B3+B4+B5.

  b. Save your work, then preview the data in the Office Furnishings worksheet.

**3. Introduce Excel functions.**

  a. Type the label "Min Price" in cell A8.

  b. Click cell C8; enter the function MIN(C2:C5).

  c. Type the label "Max Price" in cell A9.

  d. Create a formula in cell C9 that determines the maximum price.

  e. Save your work, then preview the data.

**4. Copy and move cell entries.**

  a. Select the range A1:C6, then copy the range to cell A12.

  b. Use drag and drop to copy the range D1:E1 to cell D12.

  c. Save your work, then preview the worksheet.

**5. Copy formulas with relative cell references.**

  a. Click cell D2, then create a formula that multiplies B2 and C2.

  b. Copy the formula in D2 into cells D3:D5.

  c. Copy the formula in D2 into cells D13:D16.

  d. Save and preview the worksheet.

**6. Copy formulas with absolute cell references.**

  a. Click cell G2 and type the value 1.375.

  b. Click cell E2, then create a formula containing an absolute reference that multiplies D2 and G2.

  c. Use the Office Clipboard to copy the formula in E2 into cells E3:E5.

  d. Use the Office Clipboard to copy the formula in E2 into cells E13:E16.

  e. Change the amount in cell G2 to 2.873.

  f. Save the worksheet.

**7. Name and move a sheet.**

  a. Name the Sheet1 tab "Furniture."

  b. Move the Furniture sheet so it comes after Sheet3.

  c. Name the Sheet2 tab "Supplies."

  d. Move the Supplies sheet after the Furniture sheet.

  e. Save, preview, print and close the workbook, then exit Excel.

# ► Independent Challenges

**1.** You are the box-office manager for Brazil Nuts, a popular jazz band. Your responsibilities include tracking seasonal ticket sales for the band's concerts and anticipating ticket sales for the next season. Brazil Nuts sells four types of tickets: reserved seating, general admission, senior citizen tickets, and student tickets.

The 2000–2001 season includes five scheduled concerts: Spring Hop, Summer Blast, Fall Leaves, Winter Snuggle, and Early Thaw. You will plan and build a worksheet that tracks the sales of each of the four ticket types for all five concerts.

To complete this independent challenge:

a. Think about the results you want to see, the information you need to build into these worksheets, and what types of calculations must be performed.

b. Sketch sample worksheets on a piece of paper to indicate how the information should be laid out. What information should go in the columns? In the rows?

c. Start Excel, open a new workbook and save it as "Brazil Nuts" on your Project Disk.

d. Plan and build a worksheet that tracks the sales of each of the four ticket types for all five concerts. Build the worksheets by entering a title, row labels, column headings, and formulas.

e. Enter your own sales data, but assume the following: the Brazil Nuts sold 1000 tickets during the season; reserved seating was the most popular ticket type for all of the shows except for Winter Snuggle; no concert sold more than 20 student tickets.

f. Calculate the total ticket sales for each concert, the total sales for each of the four ticket types, and the total sales for all tickets. Name the worksheet "Sales Data."

g. Copy the Sales Data worksheet and name the copied worksheet "5% Increase." Modify this worksheet in the workbook so that it reflects a 5% increase in sales of all ticket types.

h. Use named ranges to make the worksheet easier to use. (*Hint*: If your columns are too narrow, position the cell pointer in the column you want to widen. To widen the column, click Format on the menu bar, click Column, click Width, choose a new column width, and then click OK.)

i. Type your name in a worksheet cell.

j. Save your work, preview and print the worksheets, then close the workbook and exit Excel.

**2.** You have been promoted to computer lab manager at Learn-It-All, a local computer training center. It is your responsibility to make sure there are enough computers for students during scheduled classes. Currently, you have five classrooms, four with IBM PCs and one with Macintoshes. Classes are scheduled Monday, Wednesday, and Friday in two-hour increments from 9 a.m. to 5 p.m. (the lab closes at 7 p.m.), and each room can currently accommodate 35 computers.

You plan and build a worksheet that tracks the number of students who can currently use available computers per two-hour class. You create your enrollment data, but assume that current enrollment averages at 80% of each room's daily capacity. Using an additional worksheet, you show the impact of an enrollment increase of 20%.

To complete this independent challenge:

a. Think about how to construct these worksheets to create the desired output.

b. Sketch sample paper worksheets to indicate how the information should be laid out.

c. Start Excel, open a new workbook and save it as "Learn-it-All" on your Project Disk.

d. Build the worksheets by entering a title, row labels, column headings, and formulas. Use named ranges to make the worksheets easier to use, and rename the sheets to identify their contents easily.

e. Use separate sheets for actual enrollment and projected changes.

f. Name each sheet so you know what's on it.

g. Type your name in a worksheet cell.

h. Save your work, preview and print the worksheets, then close the workbook and exit Excel.

**3.** The Beautiful You Salon is a small but growing beauty salon that has hired you to organize its accounting records using Excel. The store hopes to track its supplies using Excel once its accounting records are under control. Before you were hired, one of the bookkeepers entered expenses in a workbook, but the analysis was never completed.

To complete this independent challenge:

**a.** Start Excel, open the workbook EX B-3 and save it as "Beautiful You Finances" on your Project Disk. The worksheet includes labels for functions such as the Average, Maximum, and Minimum amounts of each of the expenses in the worksheet.

**b.** Think about what information would be important for the bookkeeping staff to know.

**c.** Use the existing worksheet to create a list of the types of functions and formulas you will use, and the cells where they will be located. Indicate where you will have named ranges.

**d.** Create your sketch using the existing worksheet as a foundation. Your worksheet should use range names in its formulas and functions.

**e.** Rename Sheet1 "Expenses."

**f.** Type your name in a worksheet cell.

**g.** Save your work, then preview and print the worksheet.

**h.** Close the workbook and exit Excel.

**4.** MediaLoft offers eligible employees a variety of mutual fund options in their 401(k) plan. These mutual funds are posted on MediaLoft's intranet site. As a newly eligible MediaLoft employee, you need to determine which mutual funds you want to invest in.

To complete this independent challenge:

**a.** Start Excel, open a new workbook and save it on your Project Disk as "Mutual Fund Data."

**b.** Connect to the Internet and go to the MediaLoft intranet site at http://www.course.com/illustrated/MediaLoft, click the link for the Human Resources page, then click the Employee Benefits link.

**c.** Copy the available mutual fund data from the intranet site to Sheet1 of your workbook.

**d.** Disconnect from the Internet.

**e.** Name Sheet1 "Current Funds."

**f.** On Sheet2, assume this year's annual contribution to your mutual funds will be $10,000. Name this sheet "Investment."

**g.** Choose no more than 4 of the listed mutual funds for your investment, and decide on a percentage for each fund in your contribution.

**h.** Create formulas that multiply those percentages by the total contribution ($10,000). (*Hint:* Use an absolute reference to determine the dollar amount for each mutual fund.)

**i.** Assume that MediaLoft will match your contribution at a rate of 50¢ to your $1. Create formulas that determine how much your total annual investment will be, including the MediaLoft matching funds.

**j.** Type your name in a worksheet cell.

**k.** Preview, then print the Investment worksheet.

**l.** Save and print your work.

**m.** Exit Excel.

# ► Visual Workshop

Create a worksheet similar to Figure B-22 using the skills you learned in this unit. Save the workbook as "Annual Budget" on your Project Disk. Type your name in cell A13, then preview and print the worksheet. (Your toolbars may look different from those shown in the figure.)

FIGURE B-22

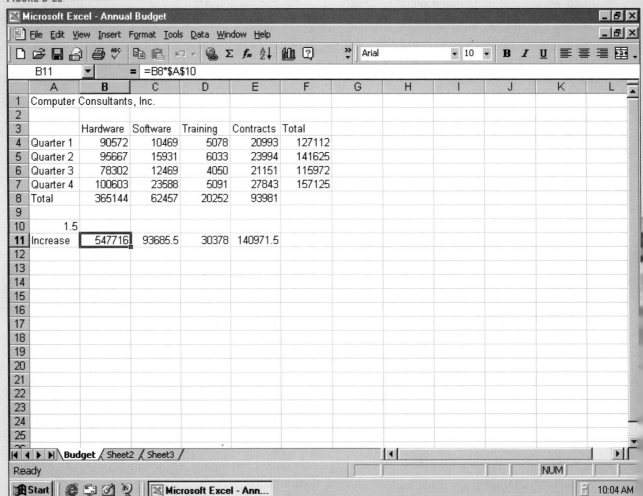

# Formatting
## a Worksheet

### Objectives

- ▶ **Format values**
- ▶ **Use fonts and font sizes**
- ▶ **Change attributes and alignment of labels**
- ▶ **Adjust column widths**
- ▶ **Insert and delete rows and columns**
- ▶ **Apply colors, patterns, and borders**
- ▶ **Use conditional formatting**
- ▶ **Check spelling**

You use Excel's formatting features for a variety of reasons: to make a worksheet more attractive, to make it easier to read, or to emphasize key data. You do this by using colors and different fonts for the cell contents, adjusting column widths, and inserting and deleting columns and rows. The marketing managers at MediaLoft have asked Jim Fernandez to create a workbook that tracks advertising expenses for all MediaLoft stores. Jim has prepared a worksheet for the New York City store containing this information, which can be adapted later for the other stores. Now he uses formatting techniques to make the worksheet easier to read and to call attention to important data.

**Excel 2000**

# Formatting Values

**Formatting** determines how labels and values appear in cells; it does not alter the data in any way. To format a cell, first select it, then apply the formatting. Cells and ranges can be formatted before or after data is entered. If you enter a value in a cell and the cell appears to display the data incorrectly, adjust the cell's format to display the value correctly. The Marketing department has requested that Jim begin by tracking the New York City store's advertising expenses. Jim developed a worksheet that tracks advertising invoices. He entered all the information and now wants to format some of the labels and values. Because some of the changes might also affect column widths, Jim makes all his formatting changes before changing the column widths.

## Steps

1. Start Excel, click **Tools** on the menu bar, click **Customize**, click the **Options tab** in the Customize dialog box, click **Reset my usage data** to restore the default settings, click **Yes**, then click **Close**

2. Open the worksheet **EX C-1** from your Project Disk, then save it as **Ad Expenses**
   The store advertising worksheet appears in Figure C-1. Numeric data can be displayed in a variety of ways, such as having a leading dollar sign. When formatting, you select the range to be formatted up to the last entry in a column or row by selecting the first cell, pressing and holding [Shift], pressing [End], then pressing [→] for the row, or [↓] for the column.

**Trouble?**

Click the More Buttons button to locate buttons that are not visible on your toolbars.

3. Select the range **E4:E32**, then click the **Currency Style button** on the Formatting toolbar
   Excel adds dollar signs and two decimal places to the Cost ea. column data. Excel automatically resizes the column to display all the information supplied by the new formatting. Another option for formatting dollar values is to apply the comma format, which does not include the $ sign.

**QuickTip**

Select any range by clicking the top left cell, pressing and holding [Shift], then clicking the bottom right cell. [Shift] acts as a "connector" for contiguous cells.

4. Select the range **G4:I32**, then click the **Comma Style button** on the Formatting toolbar
   The values in columns G, H, and I display the comma format. You can also format percentages using the Formatting toolbar.

5. Select the range **J4:J32**, click the **Percent Style button** on the Formatting toolbar, then click the **Increase Decimal button** on the Formatting toolbar to show one decimal place
   The % of Total column is now formatted with a percent sign (%) and one decimal place. Dates can be reformatted to display ranges in a variety of ways.

6. Select the range **B4:B31**, click **Format** on the menu bar, then click **Cells**
   The Format Cells dialog box opens with the Number tab in front and the Date format already selected. See Figure C-2. There are many types of date formats from which to choose.

**QuickTip**

The first DD-MM-YY format displays a single-digit date (such as May 1, 2000) as 1-May-00. The second format would display the same date as 01-May-00.

7. Select the (first) format **14-Mar-98** in the Type list box, then click **OK**
   You decide you don't need the year to appear in the Inv Due column.

8. Select the range **C4:C31**, click **Format** on the menu bar, click **Cells**, click **14-Mar** in the Type list box, then click **OK**
   Compare your worksheet to Figure C-3.

9. Save your work

**FIGURE C-1: Advertising expense worksheet**

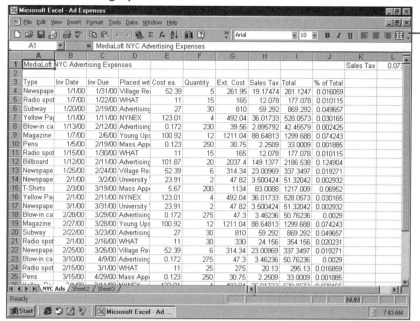

Your toolbars may not match the toolbars in the figures

**FIGURE C-2: Format Cells dialog box**

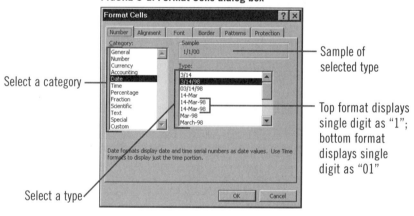

Select a category

Sample of selected type

Top format displays single digit as "1"; bottom format displays single digit as "01"

Select a type

**FIGURE C-3: Worksheet with formatted values**

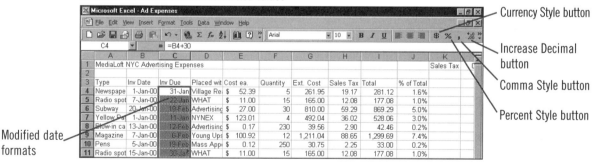

Currency Style button

Increase Decimal button

Comma Style button

Percent Style button

Modified date formats

## Using the Format Painter

A cell's format can be "painted" into other cells using the Format Painter button on the Standard toolbar. This is similar to using drag and drop to copy information, but instead of copying cell contents, you copy only the cell format. Select the cell containing the desired format, then click. The pointer changes to. Use this pointer to select the cell or range you want to contain the painted format.

**Excel 2000**

# Using Fonts and Font Sizes

A **font** is the name given to a collection of characters (letters, numerals, symbols, and punctuation marks) with a specific design. The **font size** is the physical size of the text, measured in units called **points**. The default font in Excel is 10 point Arial. You can change the font, the size, or both of any entry or section in a worksheet by using the Format command on the menu bar or by using the Formatting toolbar. Table C-1 shows several fonts in different sizes. ▬▬▬▬▬ Now that the data is formatted, Jim wants to change the font and size of the labels and the worksheet title so that they are better distinguished from the data.

1. Press **[Ctrl][Home]** to select cell A1

**QuickTip**

You can also open the Format Cells dialog box by right-clicking selected cells, then clicking Format Cells.

2. Click **Format** on the menu bar, click **Cells**, then click the **Font tab** in the Format Cells dialog box
See Figure C-5.

3. Scroll down the **Font list** to see an alphabetical listing of the many fonts available on your computer, click **Times New Roman** in the Font list box, click **24** in the Size list box, then click **OK**
The title font appears in 24 point Times New Roman, and the Formatting toolbar displays the new font and size information. Column headings can be enlarged to make them stand out. You can also change a font and increase the font size using the Formatting toolbar.

4. Select the range **A3:J3**, then click the **Font list arrow** on the Formatting toolbar
Notice that the fonts on this font list actually look like the font they represent.

5. Click **Times New Roman** in the Font list, click the **Font Size list arrow**, then click **14** in the Font Size list
Compare your worksheet to Figure C-6. Notice that some of the column headings are now too wide to display fully in the column. Excel does not automatically adjust column widths to accommodate formatting, you have to adjust column widths manually. You'll learn to do this in a later lesson.

6. Save your work

## Using the Formatting toolbar to change fonts and font sizes

The font and font size of the active cell appear on the Formatting toolbar. Click the Font list arrow, as shown in Figure C-4, to see a list of available fonts. Notice that each font name is displayed in the selected font. If you want to change the font, first select the cell, click the Font list arrow, then click the font you want. You can change the size of selected text in the same way, by clicking the Font Size list arrow to display a list of available point sizes.

**FIGURE C-4: Available fonts on the Formatting toolbar**

Available fonts installed on your computer (yours may differ)

Font list arrow

FIGURE C-5: Font tab in the Format Cells dialog box

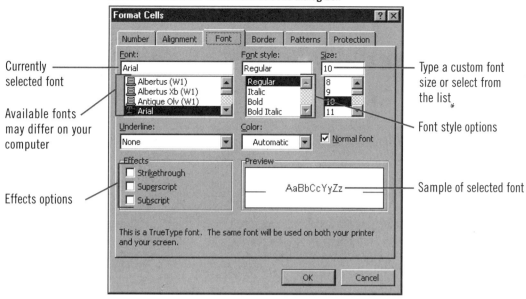

Currently selected font

Available fonts may differ on your computer

Effects options

Type a custom font size or select from the list

Font style options

Sample of selected font

FIGURE C-6: Worksheet with formatted title and labels

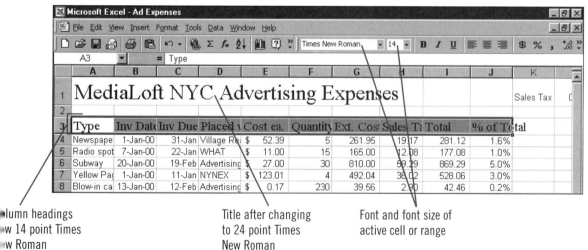

Column headings now 14 point Times New Roman

Title after changing to 24 point Times New Roman

Font and font size of active cell or range

TABLE C-1: Types of fonts

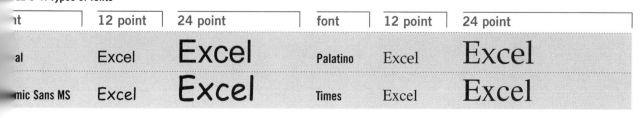

| font | 12 point | 24 point | font | 12 point | 24 point |
|------|----------|----------|------|----------|----------|
| Arial | Excel | Excel | Palatino | Excel | Excel |
| Comic Sans MS | Excel | Excel | Times | Excel | Excel |

# Changing Attributes and Alignment of Labels

**Attributes** are styling features such as bold, italics, and underlining that you can apply to affect the way text and numbers look in a worksheet. You can also change the **alignment** of labels and values in cells to be left, right, or center. Attributes and alignment can be applied from the Formatting toolbar, or from the Alignment tab of the Format Cells dialog box. See Table C-2 for a list and description of the available attribute and alignment buttons. Now that he has applied the appropriate fonts and font sizes to his worksheet labels, Jim wants to further enhance the worksheet's appearance by adding bold and underline formatting and centering some of the labels.

1. Press **[Ctrl][Home]** to move to cell A1, then click the **Bold button** on the Formatting toolbar
   The title Advertising Expenses appears in bold.

2. Select the range **A3:J3**, then click the **Underline button** on the Formatting toolbar
   Excel underlines the text in the column headings in the selected range.

   > **QuickTip**
   > Overuse of any attribute can be distracting and make a workbook less readable. Be consistent, adding emphasis the same way throughout.

3. Click cell **A3**, click the **Italics button** on the Formatting toolbar, then click
   The word "Type" appears in boldface italic type. Notice that the Bold, Italics, and Underline buttons are indented. You can apply one or more attributes to text simultaneously.

4. Click
   Excel removes italics from cell A3 but the bold and underline formatting attributes remain.

   > **QuickTip**
   > Use formatting shortcuts on any selected range: [Ctrl][B] to bold, [Ctrl][I] to italicize, and [Ctrl][U] to underline.

5. Select the range **B3:J3,** then click
   Bold formatting is added to the rest of the labels in the column headings. You want to center the title over the data columns A through J.

6. Select the range **A1:J1**, then click the **Merge and Center button** on the Formatting toolbar
   Merge creates one cell out of the 10 cells across the row, then Center centers the text in that newly created large cell. The title "MediaLoft NYC Advertising Expenses" is centered across ten columns. The alignment within individual cells can be changed using toolbar buttons.

   > **QuickTip**
   > To clear all formatting, click Edit on the menu bar, point to Clear, then click Formats.

7. Select the range **A3:J3**, then click the **Center button** on the Formatting toolbar
   Compare your screen to Figure C-7. Although they may be difficult to read, notice that all the headings are centered within their cells.

8. Save your work

**TABLE C-2: Attribute and Alignment buttons on the Formatting toolbar**

| button | description | button | description |
|---|---|---|---|
| **B** | Bolds text | | Aligns text on the left side of the cell |
| *I* | Italicizes text | | Centers text horizontally within the cell |
| U | Underlines text | | Aligns text on the right side of the cell |
| | Adds lines or borders | | Centers text across columns, and combines two or more selected adjacent cells into one cell |

FIGURE C-7: Worksheet with formatting attributes applied

Title
centered
across
columns

Center
button

Formatting
buttons
indented

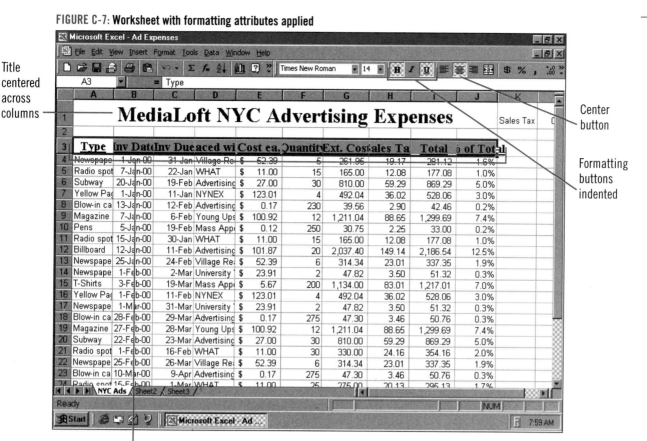

Column headings
centered, bold, and
underlined

## Using AutoFormat

Excel also has 17 predefined worksheet formats to make formatting easier and to give you the option of consistently styling your worksheets. AutoFormats are designed for worksheets with labels in the left column and top rows, and totals in the bottom row or right column. To use AutoFormatting, select the data to be formatted instantly—or place your mouse pointer anywhere within the range to be selected—click Format on the menu bar, click AutoFormat, then select a format from the sample boxes, as shown in Figure C-8.

FIGURE C-8: AutoFormat dialog box

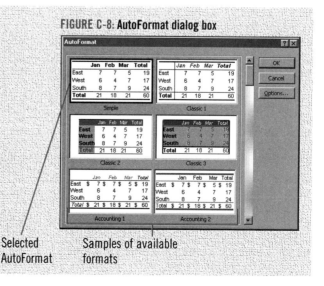

Selected
AutoFormat

Samples of available
formats

Excel 2000

**Excel 2000**

# Adjusting Column Widths

As your worksheet formatting continues, you might need to adjust the width of the columns to make your worksheet more usable. The default column width is 8.43 characters wide, a little less than one inch. With Excel, you can adjust the column width for one or more columns using the mouse or the Column command on the Format menu. Table C-3 describes the commands available on the Format Column menu. You can also adjust the height of rows to accommodate larger font sizes. ✐➤ Jim notices that some of the labels in column A have been truncated and don't fit in the cells. He decides to adjust the widths of the columns so that the labels display fully.

## Steps

1. **Position the pointer on the column line between columns A and B selector buttons**
   The pointer changes to ↔, as shown in Figure C-9. You position the pointer on the right edge of the column that you are adjusting. Then you can drag the column edge, resizing it using the mouse.

2. **Click and drag the ↔ pointer to the right until column A is wide enough to accommodate all of the text entries in column A**
   Yellow Pages is the widest entry. The **AutoFit** feature lets you use the mouse to resize a column so it automatically accommodates the widest entry in a cell.

**QuickTip**

To reset columns to the default width, select the columns, then use the Column Standard Width command on the Format menu. Click OK in the dialog box to accept the default width.

3. **Position the pointer on the column line between columns B and C in the column selector until it changes to ↔, then double-click**
   The width of column B is automatically resized to fit the widest entry, in this case, the column label.

4. **Use AutoFit to resize columns C, D, and J**
   You can also use the Column Width command on the Format menu to adjust several columns to the same width. Columns can be adjusted by selecting any cell in the column.

5. **Select the range F5:I5**

6. **Click Format on the menu bar, point to Column, then click Width**
   The Column Width dialog box appears. Move the dialog box, if necessary, by dragging it by its title bar so you can see the contents of the worksheet. The column width measurement is based on the number of characters in the Normal font (in this case, Arial).

7. **Type 11 in the Column Width text box, then click OK**
   The column widths change to reflect the new settings. See Figure C-10. If "#######" displays after you adjust a column of values, the column is too narrow to display the contents. You need to increase column width until it is wide enough to display the values.

8. **Save your work**

### Specifying row height

The Row Height command on the Format menu allows you to customize row height to improve readability. Row height is calculated in points, units of measure also used for fonts—one inch equals 72 points. The row height must exceed the size of the font you are using. Normally, you don't need to adjust row heights manually. If you format something in a row to be a larger point size, Excel will adjust the row to fit the largest point size in the row. You can also adjust row height by placing the ┼ pointer under the row selector button and dragging to the desired height.

**FIGURE C-9: Preparing to change the column width**

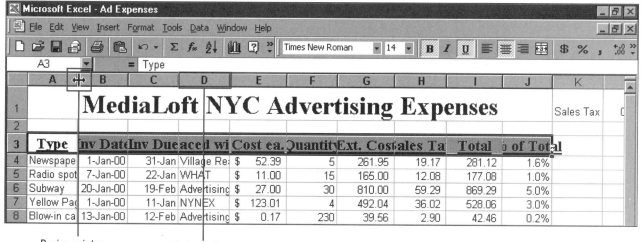

Resize pointer
between columns
A and B

Column D
selector button

**FIGURE C-10: Worksheet with column widths adjusted**

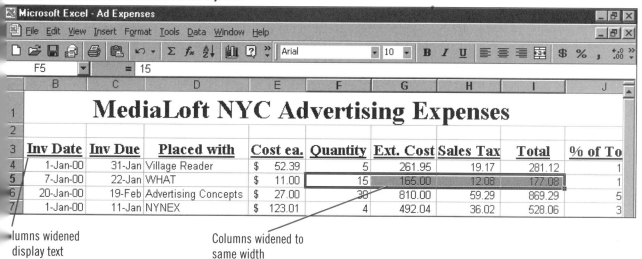

Columns widened
display text

Columns widened to
same width

**TABLE C-3: Format Column commands**

| command | description |
| --- | --- |
| Width | Sets the width to a specific number of characters |
| AutoFit Selection | Fits the widest entry |
| Hide | Hide(s) column(s) |
| Unhide | Unhide(s) column(s) |
| Standard Width | Resets to default widths |

# Inserting and Deleting Rows and Columns

As you modify a worksheet, you might find it necessary to insert or delete rows and columns to keep your worksheet current. For example, you might need to insert rows to accommodate new inventory products or remove a column of yearly totals that are no longer current. ✐——— Jim has already improved the appearance of his worksheet by formatting the labels and values in the worksheet. Now he decides to improve the overall appearance of the worksheet by inserting a row between the last row of data and the totals. Jim has located a row of inaccurate data that should be deleted, as well as a column that is not necessary.

## Steps 1 2 3 4

**1.** Right-click cell **A32**, then click **Insert**

The Insert dialog box opens. See Figure C-11. You can choose to insert a column or a row, or you can shift the data in the cells in the active column right or in the active row down. An additional row between the last row of data and totals will visually separate the totals.

**2.** Click the **Entire Row option button**, then click **OK**

A blank row is inserted between the totals and the Billboard data for March 2000. Excel inserts rows above the cell pointer and inserts columns to the left of the cell pointer. When you insert a new row, the contents of the worksheet shift down from the newly inserted row. Notice that the formula result in cell E33 has not changed. When you insert a new column the contents of the worksheet shift to the right from the point of the new column. To insert a single row, you can also click the row selector immediately below where you want the new row, right-click, and then click Insert. To insert multiple rows, select the same number of rows as you want to insert. A row can easily be selected for deletion using its **row selector button**, the gray box containing the row number to the left of the worksheet.

**3.** Click the **row 27 selector button**

Hats from Mass Appeal Inc. will no longer be part of the advertising campaign. All of row 27 is selected, as shown in Figure C-12.

**4.** Click **Edit** in the menu bar, then click **Delete**

Excel deletes row 27, and all rows below this shift up one row.

**5.** Click the **column J selector button**

The percentage information is calculated elsewhere and is no longer needed in this worksheet.

**6.** Click **Edit** in the menu bar, then click **Delete**

Excel deletes column J. The remaining columns to the right shift left one column. You are satisfied with the appearance of the worksheet and decide to save the changes.

**7.** Save your work

> **QuickTip**
>
> Inserting or deleting rows or columns that are specifically referenced in formulas can cause problems. Be sure to check formulas after inserting or deleting rows or columns.

> **QuickTip**
>
> Use the Edit menu—or right-click the selected row and click Delete—to remove a selected row. Pressing [Delete] removes the contents of a selected row; the row itself remains.

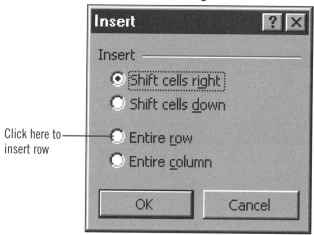

FIGURE C-11: Insert dialog box

Click here to insert row →

FIGURE C-12: Worksheet with row 27 selected

| 24 | Radio spot | 15-Feb-00 | 1-Mar | WHAT | $ | 11.00 | 25 | 275.00 | 20.13 | 295.13 |
| 25 | Pens | 15-Mar-00 | 29-Apr | Mass Appeal, Inc. | $ | 0.12 | 250 | 30.75 | 2.25 | 33.00 |
| 26 | Yellow Pages | 1-Mar-00 | 11-Mar | NYNEX | $ | 123.01 | 4 | 492.04 | 36.02 | 528.06 |
| 27 | Hats | 20-Mar-00 | 4-May | Mass Appeal, Inc. | $ | 7.20 | 250 | 1,800.00 | 131.76 | 1,931.76 |
| 28 | Subway | 20-Mar-00 | 19-Apr | Advertising Concepts | $ | 27.00 | 30 | 810.00 | 59.29 | 869.29 |
| 29 | Newspaper | 1-Apr-00 | 1-May | University Voice | $ | 23.91 | 2 | 47.82 | 3.50 | 51.32 |
| 30 | Subway | 10-Apr-00 | 10-May | Advertising Concepts | $ | 27.00 | 30 | 810.00 | 59.29 | 869.29 |
| 31 | Billboard | 28-Mar-00 | 27-Apr | Advertising Concepts | $ | 101.87 | 20 | 2,037.40 | 149.14 | 2,186.54 |
| 32 | | | | | | | | | | |
| 33 | | | | | $1,169.14 | | 2034 | 16,311.75 | 1,194.02 | 17,505.77 |

|◄ ◄ ► ►|\ NYC Ads / Sheet2 / Sheet3 /

Ready            Sum=77375.83035            NUM

Start    Microsoft Excel - Ad                    8:04 AM

Row 27 selector button

Inserted row

## Using dummy columns and rows

When you add or delete a column or row within a range used in a formula, Excel automatically adjusts the formula to reflect the change. However, when you add a column or row at the end of a range used in a formula, you must modify the formula to reflect the additional column or row. To eliminate having to edit the formula, you can include a dummy column and dummy row which is a blank column or row included at the bottom of—but within—the range you use for that formula, as shown in Figure C-13. Then if you add another column or row to the end of the range, the formula will automatically be modified to include the new data.

FIGURE C-13: Formula with dummy row

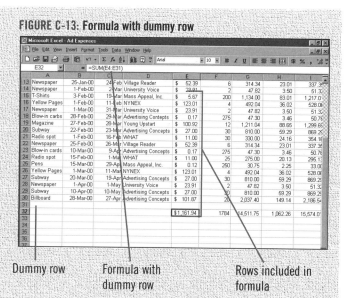

Dummy row          Formula with dummy row          Rows included in formula

# Applying Colors, Patterns, and Borders

You can use colors, patterns, and borders to enhance the overall appearance of a worksheet and to improve its readability. You can add these enhancements using the Patterns tab in the Format Cells dialog box or by using the Borders and Color buttons on the Formatting toolbar. You can apply color or patterns to the background of a cell or range or to cell contents. And, you can apply borders to all the cells in a worksheet or only to selected cells. See Table C-4 for a list of border buttons and their functions. Jim decides to add a pattern, a border, and color to the title of the worksheet. This will give the worksheet a more professional appearance.

## Steps

1. Press **[Ctrl][Home]** to select cell **A1**, then click the **Fill Color list arrow** on the Formatting toolbar
   The color palette appears.

Use color sparingly. Excessive use can divert the reader's attention away from the data in the worksheet.

2. Click **Turquoise** (fourth row, fourth color from the right)
   Cell A1 has a turquoise background, as shown in Figure C-14. Notice that Cell A1 spans columns A-I because of the Merge and Center command used for the title.

3. Click **Format** on the menu bar, then click **Cells**
   The Format Cells dialog box opens.

4. Click the **Patterns tab**, as shown in Figure C-15, if it is not already displayed
   When choosing a background pattern, consider that a high contrast between foreground and background increases the readability of the cell contents.

5. Click the **Pattern list arrow**, click the **Thin Diagonal Crosshatch Pattern** (third row, last pattern on the right), then click **OK**
   A border also enhances a cell's appearance. Unlike underlining, which is a text formatting tool, borders extend the width of the cell.

6. Click the **Borders list arrow** on the Formatting toolbar, then click the **Thick Bottom Border** (second row, second border from the left) on the Borders palette
   It can be difficult to view a border while the cell or range formatted with a border is selected.

7. Click cell **A3**
   The border is a nice enhancement. Font color can distinguish labels in a worksheet.

The default color on the Fill Color and Font Color buttons changes to the last color you selected.

8. Select the range **A3:I3**, click the **Font Color list arrow** on the Formatting tool bar, then click **Blue** (second row from the top, third color from the right) on the palette
   The text changes color, as shown in Figure C-16.

9. Click the **Print Preview button** on the Standard toolbar, preview the first page, click **Next** to preview the second page, click **Close** on the Print Preview toolbar, then save your work

### CLUES TO USE

### Using color to organize a worksheet

You can use color to give a distinctive look to each part of a worksheet. For example, you might want to apply a light blue to all the rows containing one category of data and a light green to all the rows containing another category of data. Be consistent throughout a group of worksheets, and try to avoid colors that are too bright and distracting.

FIGURE C-14: Background color added to cell

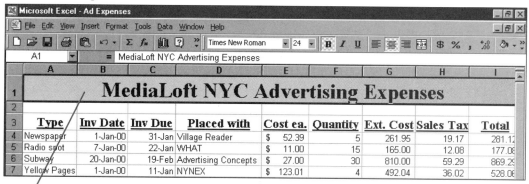

Cell A1 is affected by
fill color

FIGURE C-15: Patterns tab in the Format Cells dialog box

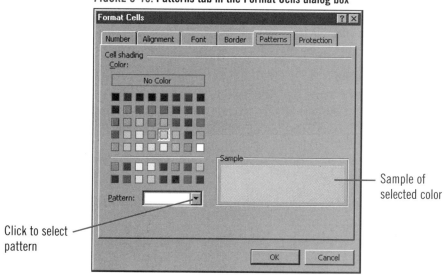

Sample of
selected color

Click to select
pattern

FIGURE C-16: Worksheet with colors, patterns, and border

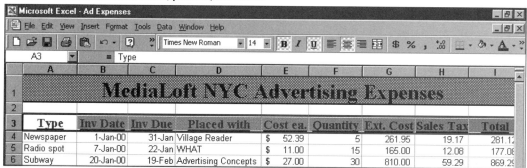

ᴸE C-4: Border buttons

| tton | function | button | function | button | function |
|------|----------|--------|----------|--------|----------|
| | Top Border | | Inside Horizontal Border | | Thick Bottom Border |
| | Bottom Border | | Inside Vertical Border | | Top and Bottom Border |
| | Left Border | | Outside Border | | Top and Double Bottom Border |
| | Right Border | | No Border | | Top and Thick Bottom Border |
| | Inside Border | | Bottom Double Border | | Thick Border |

Excel 2000

# Using Conditional Formatting

Excel 2000

Formatting attributes make worksheets look professional and help distinguish different data. These same attributes can be applied depending on specific outcomes in cells. Automatically applying formatting attributes based on cell values is called **conditional formatting**. If the data meets your criteria, Excel applies the formats you specify. You might, for example, want advertising costs above a certain number to display in red boldface and lower values to display in blue.
Jim wants the worksheet to include conditional formatting so that extended advertising costs greater than $175 display in red boldface. He creates the conditional format in the first cell in the extended cost column.

1. **Click cell G4**
   Use the scroll bars if necessary, to make column G visible.

2. **Click Format on the menu bar, then click Conditional Formatting**
   The Conditional Formatting dialog box opens, as shown in Figure C-17. Depending on the logical operator you've selected (such as "greater than" or "not equal to"), the Conditional Formatting dialog box displays different input fields. You can define up to three different conditions that let you determine outcome parameters, and then assign formatting attributes to each one. The condition is defined first. The default setting for the first condition is "Cell Value Is" "between."

**Trouble?**

If the Office Assistant appears, close it by clicking the No, don't provide help now button.

3. **To change the current condition, click the Operator list arrow, then click greater than or equal to**
   The first condition is that the cell value must be greater than or equal to some value. See Table C-5 for a list of options. You can use a constant, formula, cell reference, or date. Tha value is set in the third box.

4. **Click the Value text box, then type 175**
   Once the value is assigned, the condition's formatting attributes are defined in the Forma Cells dialog box.

5. **Click Format, click the Color list arrow, click Red (third row, first column on the left), clic Bold in the Font style list box, click OK, then click OK to close the Conditional Formattin dialog box**
   The value, 261.95, in cell G4 is formatted in bold red numbers because it is greater than 17 meeting the condition to apply the format. The conditional format, like any other forma ting, can be copied to other cells in a column.

6. **With cell G4 selected, click the Format Painter button 🖌 on the Standard toolba then drag the ➕🖌 Formatting pointer to select the range G5:G30**
   Once the formatting is copied, you reposition the cell pointer to review the results.

7. **Click cell G4**
   Compare your results to Figure C-18. All cells with values greater than or equal to 175 column G are displayed in bold red text.

8. **Press [Ctrl][Home] to move to cell A1**

9. **Save your work**

Click to select
operator

Click to delete
existing condition(s)

Click to add
additional
condition(s)

FIGURE C-17: Conditional Formatting dialog box

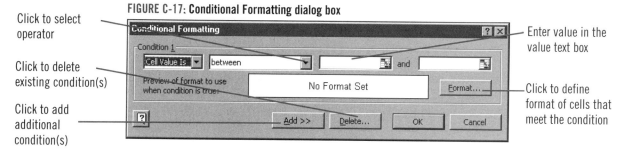

Enter value in the
value text box

Click to define
format of cells that
meet the condition

FIGURE C-18: Worksheet with conditional formatting

Format Painter
button

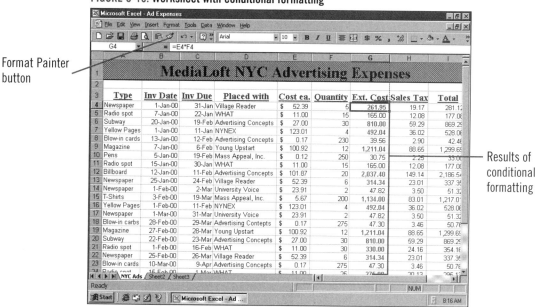

Results of
conditional
formatting

ABLE C-5: Conditional Formatting Options

| option | mathematical equivalent | option | mathematical equivalent |
|---|---|---|---|
| etween | X>Y<Z | Greater than | Z>Y |
| ot between | B≯C≮A | Less than | Y<Z |
| qual to | A=B | Greater than or equal to | A>=B |
| ot equal to | A≠B | Less than or equal to | Z<=Y |

S TO USE

## Deleting conditional formatting

Because it's likely that the conditions you define will change,
any of the conditional formats defined can be deleted. Select the
cell(s) containing conditional formatting, click Format on the
menu bar, click Conditional Formatting, then click the Delete
button. The Delete Conditional Format dialog box opens, as
shown in Figure C-19. Click the checkboxes for any of the
conditions you want to delete, then click OK. The previously
assigned formatting is deleted—leaving the cell's contents intact.

FIGURE C-19: Delete Conditional Format dialog box

**Delete Conditional Format**  ? ☒

Select the condition(s) to delete:

☐ Condition 1

☐ Condition 2

☐ Condition 3

OK        Cancel

**Excel 2000**

# Checking Spelling

You may think your worksheet is complete, but if you haven't checked for spelling errors, you risk undermining the professional value of your work. A single misspelled word can cast doubt on the validity of your numbers. The spell checker in Excel is also shared by Word, PowerPoint, and Access, so any words you've added to the dictionary using those programs are available in Excel. ► Jim has completed the formatting for his worksheet and is ready to check its spelling.

## Steps 1 2 3 4

1. **Click the Spelling button** ⟨ABC⟩ **on the Standard toolbar**
   The Spelling dialog box opens, as shown in Figure C-20, with MediaLoft selected as the first misspelled word in the worksheet. The spell checker starts from the active cell and compares words in the worksheet to those in its dictionary. Any word not found in the dictionary causes the spell checker to stop. At that point, you can decide to Ignore, Change, or Add the word to the active dictionary. For any word, (such as MediaLoft or "Inv", the abbreviation of invoice) you have the option to Ignore or Ignore All cases the spell checker cites as incorrect.

2. **Click Ignore All for MediaLoft**
   The spell checker found the word "cards" misspelled and offers "crabs" as one possible alternative. As words are found, you can choose to ignore them, fix the error, or select from a list of alternatives.

3. **Scroll through the Suggestions list, click cards, then click Change**
   The word "Concepts" is also misspelled and the spell checker suggests the correct spelling.

4. **Click Change**
   When no more incorrect words are found, Excel displays the message box shown i Figure C-21.

5. **Click OK**

6. **Press [Ctrl][Home]**

7. **Type your name in cell A2**

8. **Save your work, then preview and print the worksheet**

9. **Click File on the menu bar, then click Exit to close the workbook and exit Excel**

### Modifying the spell checker

Each of us uses words specific to our profession or task. Because the dictionary supplied with Microsoft Office cannot possibly include all the words that each of us needs, it is possible to add words to the dictionary shared by all the components in the suite. To customize the Microsoft Office dictionary used by th spell checker, click Add when a word that you know t be correct (but was not in the dictionary) is found. From then on, that word will no longer be considere misspelled by the spell checker.

FIGURE C-20: Spelling dialog box

Misspelled word

Type replacement word here or click a suggestion

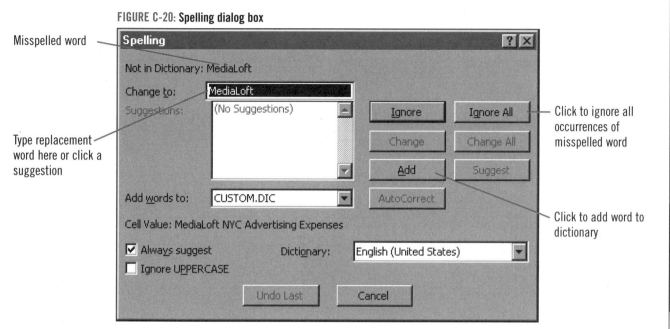

Click to ignore all occurrences of misspelled word

Click to add word to dictionary

FIGURE C-21: Spelling completed alert box

# Practice

## ► Concepts Review

Label each element of the Excel worksheet window shown in Figure C-22.

FIGURE C-22

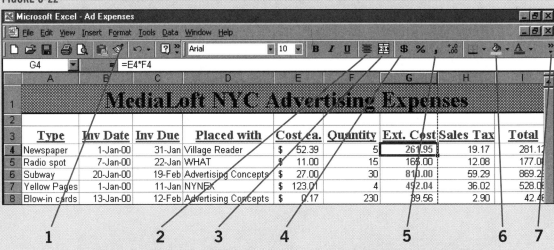

Match command or button with the statement that describes it.

8. Format Cells
9. Edit Delete
10. Format Conditional Formatting
11. 
12. 
13. 

a. Changes appearance of cell depending on result
b. Erases the contents of a cell
c. Checks the spelling in a worksheet
d. Changes the appearance of selected cells
e. Pastes the contents of the Clipboard in the current cell
f. Changes the format to Currency

Select the best answer from the list of choices.

14. Which button increases the number of decimal places in selected cells?
   a. 
   b. 
   c. 
   d. 

15. Each of the following operators can be used in conditional formatting, *except*
   a. Equal to.
   b. Greater than.
   c. Similar to.
   d. Not between.

16. How many conditional formats can be created in any cell?
   a. 1
   b. 2
   c. 3
   d. 4

**17. Which button center-aligns the contents of a single cell?**
   a. [icon]
   c. [icon]
   b. [icon]
   d. [icon]

**18. Which of the following is an example of the comma format?**
   a. $5,555.55
   c. 55.55%
   b. 5555.55
   d. 5,555.55

# ► Skills Review

## 1. Format values.
   a. Start Excel and open a new workbook.
   b. Enter the information from Table C-6 in your worksheet. Begin in cell A1, and do not leave any blank rows or columns.
   c. Add the bold attribute to the equipment descriptions, as well as the Description and Totals labels.
   d. Add the italics attribute to the Price and Sold labels.
   e. Apply the Comma format to the Price and Sold data.
   f. Insert formulas in the Totals column (multiply the price by the number sold).
   g. Apply the Currency format to the Totals data.
   h. Save this workbook as "Sports Equipment" on your Project Disk.

**TABLE C-6**

| Best Sports Supreme, Inc. | | | |
|---|---|---|---|
| Quarterly Sales Sheet | | | |
| Description | Price | Sold | Totals |
| Ski boots | 250 | 1104 | |
| Rollerblades | 175 | 1805 | |
| Baseball bats | 95 | 1098 | |
| Footballs | 35 | 1254 | |

## 2. Use fonts and font sizes.
   a. Select the range of cells containing the column titles.
   b. Change the font of the column titles to Times New Roman.
   c. Increase the font size of the column titles to 14 point.
   d. Resize the columns as necessary.
   e. Select the range of values in the Price column.
   f. Format the range using the Currency Style button.
   g. Resize the columns, if necessary.
   h. Save your changes.

## 3. Change attributes and alignment of labels.
   a. Select the worksheet title Best Sports Supreme, Inc., then click the Bold button to apply boldface to the title.
   b. Use the Merge and Center button to center the title over columns A through D.
   c. Select the label Quarterly Sales Sheet, then click the Underline button to apply underlining to the label.
   d. Select the range of cells containing the column titles, then click the Center button to center the column titles.
   e. Save your changes, then preview and print the workbook.

## 4. Adjust column widths.
   a. Use the AutoFit feature to resize the Price column.
   b. Use the Format menu to resize the Description column to 16 and the Sold column to 9.
   c. Save your changes.

### 5. Insert and delete rows and columns.

a. Insert a new row between rows 4 and 5.

b. Add Best Sports Supreme's newest product—a baseball jersey—in the newly inserted row. Enter "45" for the price and "360" for the number sold.

c. Use the fill handle to copy the formula in cell D4 to cell D5.

d. Add a new column between the Description and Price columns with the title "Location."

e. Delete the "Location" column.

f. Save your changes, then preview the workbook.

### 6. Apply colors, patterns, and borders.

a. Add a border around the value data.

b. Apply a lime background color to the Description column.

c. Apply a green background to the column labels in cells B3:D3.

d. Change the color of the font in the first row of the data to green.

e. Add a pattern fill to the title in Row 1.

f. Type your name in an empty cell, then save your work.

g. Print the worksheet, then close the workbook.

### 7. Use conditional formatting.

a. Open the file EX C-2 from your Project Disk and save it as "Quarterly Report."

b. Create conditional formatting that changes values to blue if they are greater than 2500, and changes them to green if less than 700.

c. Use the Bold button and Center button to format the column headings and row titles.

d. Column A should be wide enough to accommodate the contents of cells A3:A9.

e. AutoFit the remaining columns.

f. Use Merge and Center in Row 1 to center the title over columns A:E.

g. Format the title Reading Room, Inc. using 14 point Times New Roman text. Fill the cell with a color and pattern of your choice.

h. Type your name in an empty cell, then apply a green background and make the text color yellow.

i. Use the Edit menu to clear the cell formats of the cell with your name, then save your changes.

### 8. Check spelling.

a. Check the spelling in the worksheet using the spell checker.

b. Correct any spelling errors.

c. Save your changes, then preview and print the workbook.

d. Save, close the workbook, then exit Excel.

# ▶ Independent Challenges

**1.** Now that the Beautiful You Salon's accounting records are on Excel, they would like you to work on the inventory. Although more items will be added later, enough have been entered in a worksheet for you to begin your modifications.
  To complete this independent challenge:

**a.** Start Excel, open the workbook EX C-3 on your Project Disk, and save it as "BY Inventory."

**b.** Create a formula that calculates the value of the inventory on hand for each item.

**c.** Use an absolute reference to calculate the sale price of each item.

**d.** Use enhancements to make the title, column headings, and row headings more attractive.

**e.** Make sure all columns are wide enough to see the data.

**f.** Add a row under #2 Curlers for "Nail Files," price paid $0.25, sold individually (each), with 59 on hand.

**g.** Before printing, preview the file so you know what the worksheet will look like. Adjust any items as needed, check spelling, and print a copy.

**h.** Use conditional formatting to display which items have 25 or less on hand. Choose colors and formatting.

**i.** Use cell formatting to add borders around the data in the Item column.

**j.** Delete the row with #3 Curlers.

**k.** Type your name in an empty cell, then preview and print the worksheet.

**l.** Save, close the workbook, then exit Excel.

**2.** Continuing your efforts with the Community Action Center, you need to examine the membership in comparison to the community more closely. To make the existing data look more professional and easier to read, you've decided to use attributes and your formatting abilities.
  To complete this independent challenge:

**a.** Start Excel, open the workbook EX C-4 on your Project Disk, and save it as "Community Action."

**b.** Remove any blank columns.

**c.** Format the Annual Revenue column using the Currency format.

**d.** Make all columns wide enough to fit their data.

**e.** Use formatting enhancements, such as fonts, font sizes, and text attributes to make the worksheet more attractive.

**f.** Center-align the contents of cells containing column labels.

**g.** Design conditional formatting so that Number of Employee data greater than 50 employees displays in blue.

**h.** Before printing, preview the file so you know what the worksheet will look like. Adjust any items as needed, check spelling, type your name in an empty cell, save your work, and then print a copy.

**i.** Close the workbook and exit Excel.

**3.** Classic Instruments is a Miami-based company that manufactures high-quality pens and markers. As the finance manager, one of your responsibilities is to analyze the monthly reports from your five district sales offices. Your boss, Joanne Bennington, has just asked you to prepare a quarterly sales report for an upcoming meeting. Since several top executives will be attending this meeting, Joanne reminds you that the report must look professional. In particular, she asks you to emphasize the company's surge in profits during the last month and to highlight the fact that the Northeastern district continues to outpace the other districts.

To complete this independent challenge:

**a.** Plan and build a worksheet that shows the company's sales during the last three months. Make sure you include:

- The number of pens sold (units sold) and the associated revenues (total sales) for each of the five district sales offices. The five Classic Instruments sales districts include: Northeastern, Midwestern, Southeastern, Southern, and Western.
- Calculations that show month-by-month totals and a three-month cumulative total.
- Calculations that show each district's share of sales (percent of units sold).
- Formatting enhancements to emphasize the recent month's sales surge and the Northeastern district's sales leadership.

**b.** Prepare a worksheet plan that states your goal, lists the worksheet data you'll need, and identifies the formulas for the different calculations.

**c.** Sketch a sample worksheet on a piece of paper, indicating how the information should be organized and formatted. How will you calculate the totals? What formulas can you copy to save time and keystrokes? Do any of these formulas need to use an absolute reference? How will you show dollar amounts? What information should be shown in bold? Do you need to use more than one font? More than one point size?

**d.** Start Excel, then build the worksheet with your own sales data. Enter the titles and labels first, then enter the numbers and formulas. Save the workbook as "Classic Instruments" on your Project Disk.

**e.** Make enhancements to the worksheet. Adjust the column widths as necessary. Change the row height of row 1 to 30 points. Format labels and values, and change attributes and alignment.

**f.** Add a column that calculates a 15% increase in sales. Use an absolute cell reference in this calculation.

**g.** Type your name in an empty cell.

**h.** Before printing, preview the file so you know what the worksheet will look like. Adjust any items as needed, check spelling, and then print a copy.

**i.** Save your work before closing the file and exiting Excel.

**4.** As the MediaLoft office manager, you've been asked to assemble data on currently available office suites for use in a business environment. You use the World Wide Web to retrieve information about current software and then post the information on the MediaLoft intranet site. You also create an attractive worksheet for distribution to department managers.
To complete this independent challenge:

a. Start Excel, then open a new workbook and save it as "Software Comparison" on your Project Disk.

b. Connect to the Internet, go to the MediaLoft intranet site at http://www.course.com/illustrated/MediaLoft, then click the link for the Accounting page.

c. Print the Office Suite Analysis, disconnect from the Internet, then enter the data in the Software Comparison workbook.

d. Create a title for the worksheet in cell A1. Use the Merge and Center command to center the title over the worksheet columns.

e. Make sure each column is resized to accommodate its widest contents.

f. Format the labels for each suite manufacturer in bold, 12 point, Times New Roman font.

g. Format the labels for the type of program (for example, spreadsheets) in italics, 12 point, Times New Roman font.

h. Create a background color and a border for the title. Use a pattern to enhance the text.

i. Right-align the label for the suite price.

j. Use conditional formatting so that suites costing more than $375 display in red.

k. Type your name in a visible worksheet cell.

l. Save and print your work, then exit Excel.

# ► Visual Workshop

Create the worksheet shown in Figure C-23, using skills you learned in this unit. Open the file EX C-5 on your Project Disk and save it as "Projected March Advertising Invoices." Create a conditional format in the Cost ea. column so that entries greater than 60 are displayed in red. (*Hint:* The only additional font used in this exercise is Times New Roman. It is 22 points in row 1, and 16 points in row 3.)

FIGURE C-23

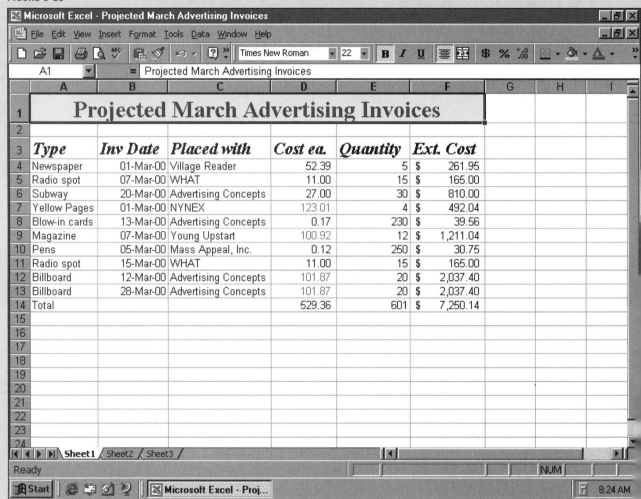

| Type | Inv Date | Placed with | Cost ea. | Quantity | Ext. Cost |
|------|----------|-------------|----------|----------|-----------|
| Newspaper | 01-Mar-00 | Village Reader | 52.39 | 5 | $ 261.95 |
| Radio spot | 07-Mar-00 | WHAT | 11.00 | 15 | $ 165.00 |
| Subway | 20-Mar-00 | Advertising Concepts | 27.00 | 30 | $ 810.00 |
| Yellow Pages | 01-Mar-00 | NYNEX | 123.01 | 4 | $ 492.04 |
| Blow-in cards | 13-Mar-00 | Advertising Concepts | 0.17 | 230 | $ 39.56 |
| Magazine | 07-Mar-00 | Young Upstart | 100.92 | 12 | $ 1,211.04 |
| Pens | 05-Mar-00 | Mass Appeal, Inc. | 0.12 | 250 | $ 30.75 |
| Radio spot | 15-Mar-00 | WHAT | 11.00 | 15 | $ 165.00 |
| Billboard | 12-Mar-00 | Advertising Concepts | 101.87 | 20 | $ 2,037.40 |
| Billboard | 28-Mar-00 | Advertising Concepts | 101.87 | 20 | $ 2,037.40 |
| Total | | | 529.36 | 601 | $ 7,250.14 |

# Working
## with Charts

### Objectives

► **Plan and design a chart**
MOUS ► **Create a chart**
MOUS ► **Move and resize a chart**
MOUS ► **Edit a chart**
MOUS ► **Format a chart**
MOUS ► **Enhance a chart**
MOUS ► **Annotate and draw on a chart**
MOUS ► **Preview and print a chart**

Worksheets provide an effective way to organize information, but they are not always the best format for presenting data to others. Information in a selected range or worksheet can easily be converted to the visual format of a chart. Charts graphically communicate the relationships of data in a worksheet. In this unit, you will learn how to create a chart, how to edit a chart and change the chart type, how to add text annotations and arrows to a chart, and how to preview and print a chart. ◄══ For the annual meeting Jim Fernandez needs to create a chart showing the six-month sales history at MediaLoft for the stores in the eastern division. He wants to illustrate the trend of growth in this division.

# Planning and Designing a Chart

Before creating a chart, you need to plan the information you want your chart to show and how you want it to look. ◆— In early June, the Marketing department launched a regional advertising campaign for the eastern division. The results of the campaign were increased sales during the fall months. Jim wants his chart for the annual meeting to illustrate the growth trend of sales in MediaLoft's eastern division stores and to highlight this dramatic sales increase.

Jim uses the worksheet shown in Figure D-1 and the following guidelines to plan the chart:

### Determine the purpose of the chart, and identify the data relationships you want to communicate visually

You want to create a chart that shows sales throughout MediaLoft's eastern division from July through December. In particular, you want to highlight the increase in sales that occurred as a result of the advertising campaign.

### Determine the results you want to see, and decide which chart type is most appropriate to use

Different charts have different strengths and display data in various ways. How you want your data displayed—and how you want that data interpreted—can help you determine the best chart type to use. Table D-1 describes several different types of charts and when each one is best used. Because you want to compare data (sales in multiple locations) over a time period (the months July through December), you decide to use a column chart.

### Identify the worksheet data you want the chart to illustrate

You are using data from the worksheet titled "MediaLoft Eastern Division Stores" as shown in Figure D-1. This worksheet contains the sales data for the four stores in the eastern division from July through December.

### Sketch the chart, then use your sketch to decide where the chart elements should be placed

You sketch your chart as shown in Figure D-2. You put the months on the horizontal axis (the x-axis) and the monthly sales figures on the vertical axis (the y-axis). The **tick marks** on the y-axis create a scale of measure for each value. Each value in a cell you select for your chart is a **data point**. In any chart, a **data marker** visually represents each data point, which in this case is a column. A collection of related data points is a **data series**. In this chart, there are four data series (Boston, Chicago, Kansas City, and New York), so you include a **legend** to make it easy to identify them.

**FIGURE D-1: Worksheet containing sales data**

```
Microsoft Excel - MediaLoft Sales-Eastern Division                                    _ ☐ X
File  Edit  View  Insert  Format  Tools  Data  Window  Help                            _ ☐ X
```

|   | A | B | C | D | E | F | G | H | I | J | K |
|---|---|---|---|---|---|---|---|---|---|---|---|
| 1 | | MediaLoft Eastern Division Stores | | | | | | | | | |
| 2 | | FY 2000 Sales Following Advertising Campaign | | | | | | | | | |
| 3 | | | | | | | | | | | |
| 4 | | | | | | | | | | | |
| 5 | | July | August | September | October | November | December | Total | | | |
| 6 | Boston | 12,000 | 12,000 | 15,500 | 20,000 | 21,000 | 20,500 | $103,500 | | | |
| 7 | Chicago | 14,500 | 16,000 | 17,500 | 18,000 | 18,500 | 19,000 | $101,000 | | | |
| 8 | Kansas City | 9,500 | 10,000 | 15,000 | 16,000 | 17,000 | 15,500 | $103,500 | | | |
| 9 | New York | 15,000 | 13,000 | 16,500 | 19,000 | 20,000 | 21,000 | $ 83,000 | | | |
| 10 | Total | $ 51,000 | $ 51,000 | $ 64,500 | $ 73,000 | $ 76,500 | $ 76,000 | $391,000 | | | |
| 11 | | | | | | | | | | | |
| 12 | | | | | | | | | | | |

**FIGURE D-2: Sketch of the column chart**

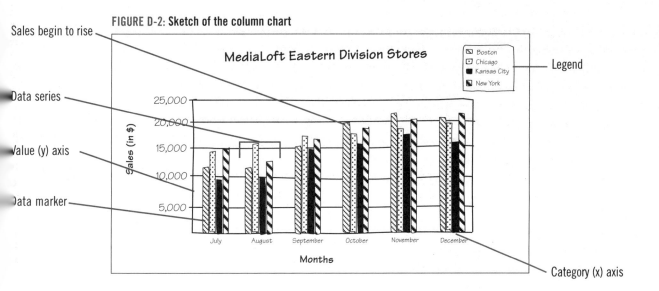

Sales begin to rise

Data series

Value (y) axis

Data marker

Legend

Category (x) axis

**TABLE D-1: Commonly used chart types**

| type | button | description |
|---|---|---|
| area | | Shows how volume changes over time |
| bar | | Compares distinct objects over time using a horizontal format; sometimes referred to as a horizontal bar chart in other spreadsheet programs |
| column | | Compares distinct objects over time using a vertical format; the Excel default; sometimes referred to as a bar chart in other spreadsheet programs |
| line | | Compares trends over even time intervals; similar to an area chart |
| pie | | Compares sizes of pieces as part of a whole; can have slices pulled away from the pie, or "exploded" |
| (scatter) | | Compares trends over uneven time or measurement intervals; used in scientific and engineering disciplines for trend spotting and extrapolation |
| combination | none | Combines a column and line chart to compare data requiring different scales of measure |

# Creating a Chart

To create a chart in Excel, you first select the range containing the data you want to chart. Once you've selected a range, you can use the Excel Chart Wizard to lead you through the process of creating the chart. ◥━━━ Using the worksheet containing the sales data for the eastern division, Jim creates a chart that shows the growth trend that occurred as a result of the advertising campaign.

**Steps** 1234

### Trouble?

Click the More Buttons button ⌄⌄ to locate buttons that are not visible on your toolbars.

**1.** Start Excel, reset your toolbars to their default settings, open the workbook **EX D-1** from your Project Disk, then save it as **MediaLoft Sales-Eastern Division**
You want the chart to include the monthly sales figures for each of the eastern division stores, as well as month and store labels. You don't include the Total columns because the monthly figures make up the totals and these figures would skew the chart.

**2.** Select the range **A5:G9**, then click the **Chart Wizard button** 🛍 on the Standard toolbar
This range includes the cells that will be charted. The Chart Wizard opens. The Chart Wizard - Step 1 of 4 - Chart Type dialog box lets you choose the type of chart you want to create. See Figure D-3. You can see a preview of the chart by clicking and holding the Press and Hold to View Sample button.

**3.** Click **Next** to accept Column, the default chart type
The Chart Wizard - Step 2 of 4 - Chart Source Data dialog box lets you choose the data being charted and whether the series are in rows or columns. You want to chart the effect of sales for each store over the time period. Currently, the rows are accurately selected as the data series, as specified by the Series in option button located under the Data range. Since you selected the data before clicking the Chart Wizard button, Excel converted the range to absolute values and the correct range =Sheet1!$A$5:$G$9 displays in the Data range text box.

**4.** Click **Next**
The Chart Wizard - Step 3 of 4 - Chart Options dialog box shows a sample chart using the data you selected. Notice that the store locations (the rows in the selected range) are plotted according to the months (the columns in the selected range), and that the months were added as labels for each data series. Notice also that there is a legend showing each location and its corresponding color on the chart. Here, you can choose to keep the legend, add a chart title, gridlines, data labels, data table, and add axis titles.

**5.** Click the **Chart title text box**, then type **MediaLoft Sales - Eastern Division**
After a moment, the title appears in the Sample Chart box. See Figure D-4.

**6.** Click **Next**
In the Chart Wizard - Step 4 of 4 - Chart Location dialog box, you determine the placement of the chart in the workbook. You can display a chart as an object on the current sheet, or any other existing sheet, or on a newly created chart sheet. A **chart sheet** in a workbook contains only a chart that is linked to the worksheet data. Displaying the chart as an object in the sheet containing the data will help Jim emphasize his point at the annual meeting.

### Trouble?

If you are using a small monitor, your chart may appear distorted. If so, you'll need to move it to a blank area of the worksheet and then enlarge it before continuing with the lessons in this unit. See your instructor or technical support person for assistance.

**7.** Click **Finish**
The column chart appears and the Chart toolbar opens, either docked, as shown in Figure D-? or floating. Your chart might be in a different location and look slightly different. You will adjust the chart's location and size in the next lesson. The **selection handles**, the small squares at the corners and sides of the chart's border, indicate that the chart is selected. Anytime a chart selected, as it is now, a blue border surrounds the data range, a green border surrounds the r labels, and a purple border surrounds the column labels. If you want to delete a chart, select then press [Delete].

**8.** Save your work

**FIGURE D-3: First Chart Wizard dialog box**

Selected chart

Chart types

Chart sub-types for selected chart

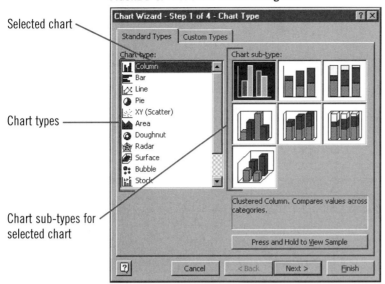

**FIGURE D-4: Third Chart Wizard dialog box**

Type the chart title here

Sample chart

Title added

Legend

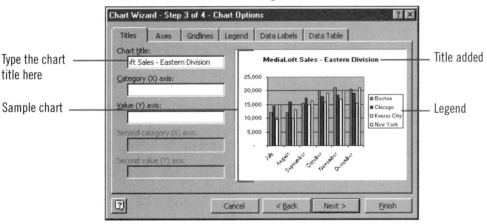

**FIGURE D-5: Worksheet with column chart**

Your toolbars may not match those in the figures

Column labels

Row labels

Data range

Month labels x-axis

Title

Legend

Selection handles

Chart toolbar

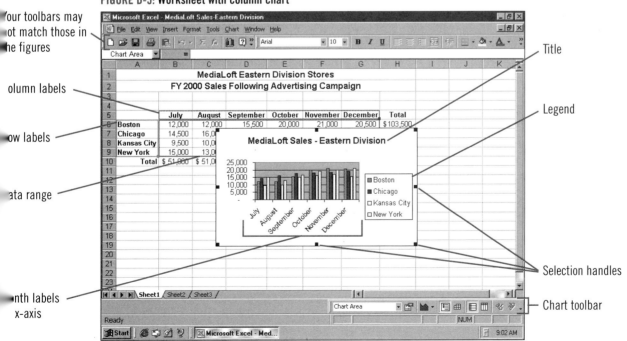

# Moving and Resizing a Chart

Charts are graphics, or drawn **objects**, and are not in a specific cell or range address. You can move a chart anywhere on a worksheet without affecting formulas or data in the worksheet. Resize a chart to improve its appearance by dragging the selection handles. You can even put a chart on another sheet without worrying about cell formulas. Drawn objects such as charts contain other objects that you can move and resize. To move an object, select it, then drag it or cut and copy it to a new location. To resize an object, use the selection handles. When you select a chart object, the name of the selected object appears in the Chart Objects list box on the Chart toolbar, and in the name box. Jim wants to increase the size of the chart and position it below the worksheet data. He also wants to change the position of the legend.

1. **Make sure the chart is still selected, then position the pointer over the chart**
   The pointer shape ⤢ indicates that you can move the chart or use a selection handle to resize it. For a table of commonly used pointers, refer to Table D-2. On occasion, the Chart toolbar obscures your view. You can dock the toolbar to make it easier to see your work.

2. **If the chart toolbar is floating, click the Chart toolbar's title bar, drag it to the right edge of the status bar until it docks, then release the mouse button**
   The toolbar is docked on the bottom of the screen.

3. **Place the ⤢ pointer on the chart, press and hold the left mouse button, using ✛ drag the upper left edge of the chart to the top of row 13 and the left edge of the chart to the left border of column A, then release the mouse button**
   A dotted outline of the chart perimeter appears as the chart is being moved. The chart is in the new location. Resizing a chart doesn't affect the data in the chart, only the way the chart looks on the sheet.

4. **Position the pointer on the right-middle selection handle until it changes to ↔, then drag the right edge of the chart to the right edge of column H**
   The chart is widened. See Figure D-6.

5. **Position the pointer over the top middle selection handle until it changes to ↕, then drag it to the top of row 12**

6. **If the labels for the months do not fully display, position the pointer over the bottom middle selection handle until it changes to ↕, then drag down to display the month**
   You can move the legend to improve the chart's appearance. You want to align the top of the legend with the top of the plot area.

7. **Click the legend to select it, then drag the legend using the ⤢ to the upper-right corner of the chart until it is aligned with the plot area**
   Selection handles appear around the legend when you click it; "Legend" appears in the Chart Objects list box on the Chart toolbar as well as in the name box, and a dotted outline of the legend perimeter appears as you drag. Changing the original Excel data modifies the legend text.

8. **Click cell A9, type NYC, then click** ☑
   See Figure D-7. The legend is repositioned and the legend entry for the New York City store is changed.

9. **Save your work**

**FIGURE D-6:** Worksheet with resized and repositioned chart

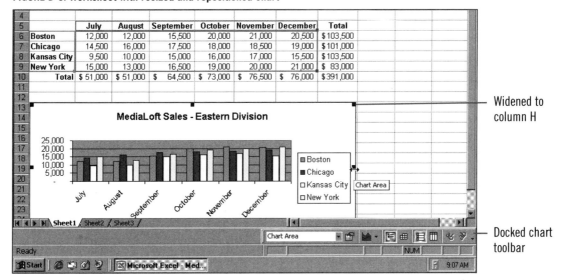

Widened to column H

Docked chart toolbar

**FIGURE D-7:** Worksheet with repositioned legend

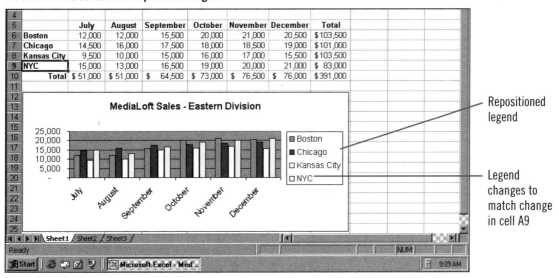

Repositioned legend

Legend changes to match change in cell A9

**TABLE D-2:** Commonly used pointers

| name | pointer | use | name | pointer | use |
|---|---|---|---|---|---|
| Diagonal resizing | ⤢ or ⤡ | Change chart shape from corners | I-beam | I | Edit chart text |
| Draw | + | Create shapes | Move chart | ✛ | Change chart location |
| Horizontal resizing | ↔ | Change chart shape from left to right | Vertical resizing | ↕ | Changes chart shape from top to bottom |

**ES TO USE**

## Identifying chart objects

There are many objects within a chart and Excel makes it easy to identify each of them. Placing your mouse pointer over a chart object causes a ScreenTip for that object to appear, whether the chart is selected or not. If a chart—or any object in it—is selected, the ScreenTips still appear. In addition, the name of the selected chart object appears in the name box and the Chart Object list box on the Chart toolbar.

# Editing a Chart

Once you've created a chart, it's easy to modify it. You can change data values in the worksheet, and the chart will automatically be updated to reflect the new data. You can also easily change chart types using the buttons on the Chart toolbar. Jim looks over his worksheet and realizes he entered the wrong data for the Kansas City store in November and December. After he corrects this data, he wants to see how the same data looks using different chart types.

**Trouble?**

If you cannot see the chart and data together on your monitor, click View on the menu bar, click Zoom, then click 75%.

1. If necessary, scroll the worksheet so that you can see both the chart and row 8, containing the Kansas City sales figures, then place your mouse pointer over the data point to display **Series "Kansas City" Point "December" Value "15,500"**

   As you correct the values, the columns for November and December in the chart automatically change.

2. Click cell **F8**, type **18000** to correct the November sales figure, press [→], type **19500** in cell **G8**, then click ▣

   The Kansas City columns for November and December reflect the increased sales figures. See Figure D-9. The totals are also updated in column H and row 10.

3. Select the chart by clicking anywhere within the chart border, then click the **Chart Type list arrow** ▣▾ on the Chart toolbar

   The chart type buttons appear on the Chart Type palette. Table D-3 describes the chart types available.

4. Click the **Bar Chart button** ▣ on the palette

   The column chart changes to a bar chart. See Figure D-10. You look at the bar chart, take some notes, and then decide to convert it back to a column chart. You now want to see if the large increase in sales would be better presented with a three-dimensional column chart.

**QuickTip**

Experiment with different formats for your charts until you get just the right look.

5. Click the **Chart Type list arrow** ▣▾, then click the **3-D Column Chart button** ▣ on the palette

   A three-dimensional column chart appears. You notice that the three-dimensional column format is more crowded than the two-dimensional format but gives you a sense of volume.

6. Click the **Chart Type list arrow** ▣▾, then click the **Column Chart button** ▣ on the palette

7. Save your work

**CLUES TO USE**

## Rotating a chart

In a three-dimensional chart, columns or bars can sometimes be obscured by other data series within the same chart. You can rotate the chart until a better view is obtained. Double-click the chart, click the tip of one of its axes (select the Corners object), then drag the handles until a more pleasing view of the data series appears. See Figure D-8.

**FIGURE D-8: 3-D chart rotated with improved view of data series**

Click to rotate chart

FIGURE D-9: Worksheet with new data entered for Kansas City

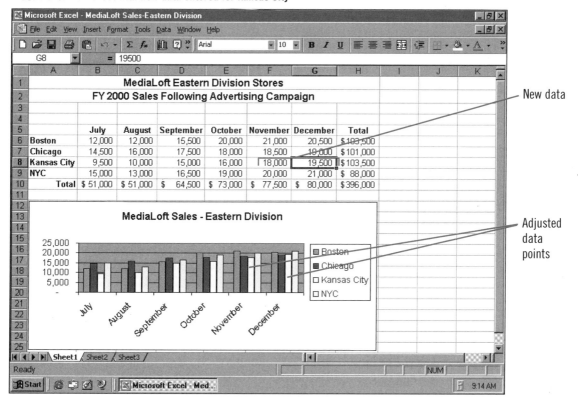

New data

Adjusted
data
points

FIGURE D-10: Bar chart

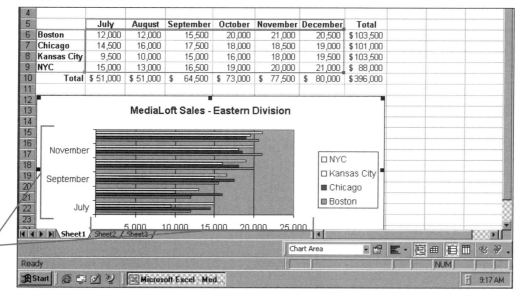

ow and
lumn
ta are
versed

BLE D-3: Commonly used chart type buttons

| ick | to display a | click | to display a | click | to display a | click | to display a |
|---|---|---|---|---|---|---|---|
| | area chart | | pie chart | | 3-D area chart | | 3-D pie chart |
| | bar chart | | (xy) scatter chart | | 3-D bar chart | | 3-D surface chart |
| | column chart | | doughnut chart | | 3-D column chart | | 3-D cylinder chart |
| | line chart | | radar chart | | 3-D line chart | | 3-D cone chart |

Excel 2000

# Formatting a Chart

After you've created a chart using the Chart Wizard, you can easily modify its appearance. Use the Chart toolbar and Chart menu to change the colors of data series and add or eliminate a legend and gridlines. **Gridlines** are the horizontal and vertical lines in the chart that enable the eye to follow the value on an axis. The button that selects the chart type changes to the last chart type selected. The corresponding Chart toolbar buttons are listed in Table D-4. ➤ Jim wants to make some changes in the appearance of his chart. He wants to see if the chart looks better without gridlines, and he wants to change the color of a data series.

## Steps

1. **Make sure the chart is still selected**
   Horizontal gridlines currently appear in the chart.

2. **Click Chart on the menu bar, click Chart Options, click the Gridlines tab in the Chart Options dialog box, then click the Major Gridlines checkbox for the Value (Y) axis to remove the check**
   The gridlines disappear from the sample chart in the dialog box, as shown in Figure D-11. Even though gridlines extend from the tick marks on an axis across the plot area, they are not always necessary to the chart's readability.

   > **QuickTip**
   > Minor gridlines show the values between the tick marks.

3. **Click the Major Gridlines checkbox for the Value (Y) axis, then click the Minor Gridlines checkbox for the Value (Y) axis**
   Both major and minor gridlines appear in the sample.

4. **Click the Minor Gridlines checkbox for the Value (Y) axis, then click OK**
   The minor gridlines disappear, leaving only the major gridlines on the Value axis. You can change the color of the columns to better distinguish the data series.

5. **With the chart selected, double-click any light blue column in the NYC data series**
   Handles appear on all the columns in the NYC data series, and the Format Data Series dialog box opens, as shown in Figure D-12.

   > **QuickTip**
   > Add values, labels, and percentages to your chart using the Data Labels tab in the Chart Options dialog box.

6. **Click the Patterns tab, if necessary, click the fuschia box (in the fourth row, first on the left), then click OK**
   All the columns for the series are fuschia, and the legend changes to match the new color. Compare your finished chart to Figure D-13.

7. **Save your work**

**TABLE D-4: Chart enhancement buttons**

| button | use |
|--------|-----|
| | Displays formatting dialog box for the selected object on the chart |
| | Selects chart type (chart type on button changes to last chart type selected) |
| | Adds/Deletes legend |
| | Creates a data table within the chart |
| | Charts data by row |
| | Charts data by column |
| | Angles selected text downward |
| | Angles selected text upward |

**FIGURE D-11: Chart Options dialog box**

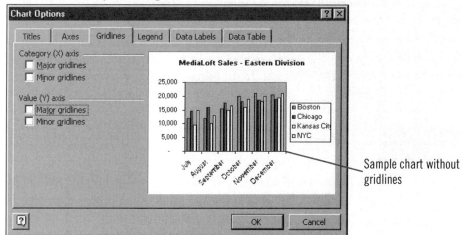

Sample chart without gridlines

**FIGURE D-12: Format Data Series dialog box**

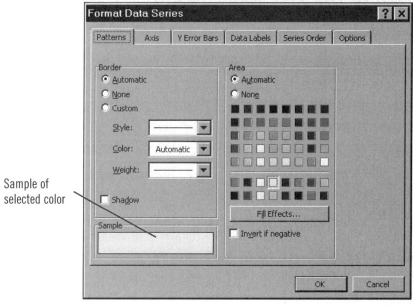

Sample of selected color

**FIGURE D-13: Chart with formatted data series**

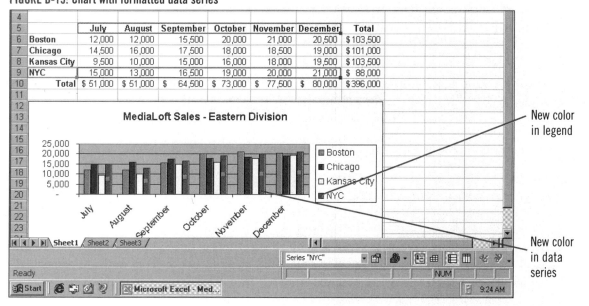

New color in legend

New color in data series

**Excel 2000**

# Enhancing a Chart

There are many ways to enhance a chart to make it easier to read and understand. You can create titles for the x-axis and y-axis, add graphics, or add background color. You can even format the text you use in a chart. Jim wants to improve the appearance of his chart by creating titles for the x-axis and y-axis. He also decides to add a drop shadow to the title.

1. **Make sure the chart is selected, click Chart on the menu bar, click Chart Options, click the Titles tab in the Chart Options dialog box, then type Months in the Category (X) axis text box**
   Descriptive text on the x-axis helps a user understand the chart. The word "Months" appears below the month labels in the sample chart, as shown in Figure D-14.

**QuickTip**

To edit the text, position the pointer over the selected text box until it changes to $I$, click, then edit the text.

2. **Click the Value (Y) axis text box, type Sales (in $), then click OK**
   A selected text box containing "Sales (in $)" appears rotated 90 degrees to the left of the y-axis. Once the Chart Options dialog box is closed, you can move the Value or Category axis titles to new positions by clicking on an edge of the object and dragging it.

3. **Press [Esc] to deselect the Value-axis title**
   Next you decide that a border with a drop shadow will enhance the chart title.

4. **Click the chart title MediaLoft Sales – Eastern Division to select it**
   You can create a drop shadow using the Format button on the Chart toolbar.

**QuickTip**

The Format button ⊞ opens a dialog box with the appropriate formatting options for the selected chart element. The ScreenTip for the button changes depending on the selected object.

5. **Click the Format Chart Title button ⊞ on the Chart toolbar to open the Format Chart Title dialog box, make sure the Patterns tab is selected, then click the Shadow checkbox**
   A border with a drop shadow surrounds the title. You can continue to format the title.

6. **Click the Font tab in the Format Chart Title dialog box, click Times New Roman in the Font list, click Bold Italic in the Font style list, click OK, then press [Esc] to deselect the chart title**
   A border with a drop shadow appears around the chart title, and the chart title text is reformatted.

7. **Click the Category Axis Title, click ⊞, click the Font tab, select Times New Roman in the Font list, then click OK**
   The Category Axis Title appears in the Times New Roman font.

8. **Click the Value Axis Title, click ⊞, click the Font tab, click Times New Roman in the Font list, click OK, then press [Esc] to deselect the title**
   The Value Axis Title appears in the Times New Roman font. Compare your chart to Figure D-1

9. **Save your work**

## Changing text font and alignment in charts

The font and the alignment of axis text can be modified to make it more readable or to better fit within the plot area. With a chart selected, double-click the axis text to be modified. The Format Axis dialog box appears. Click the Font or the Alignment tab, make the desired changes, then click OK.

FIGURE D-14: Sample chart with Category (X) axis text

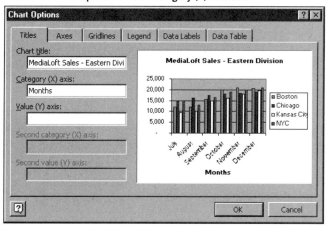

FIGURE D-15: Enhanced chart

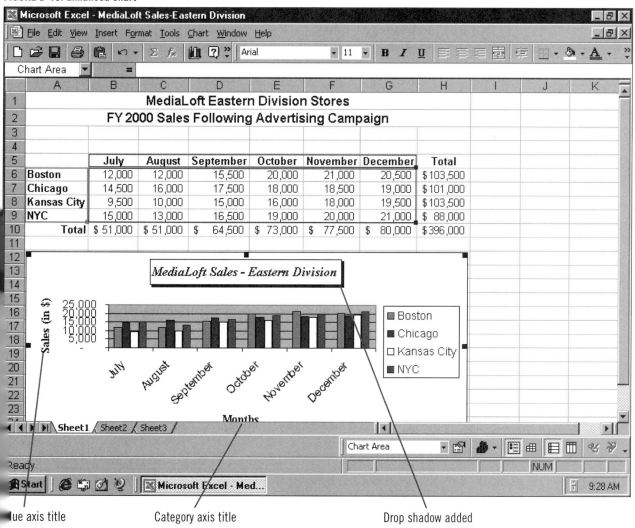

Value axis title          Category axis title          Drop shadow added

# Annotating and Drawing on a Chart

You can add arrows and text annotations to point out critical information in your charts. Text annotations are labels that you add to a chart to further describe the data in it. You can draw lines and arrows that point to the exact locations you want to emphasize. Jim wants to add a text annotation and an arrow to highlight the October sales increase.

## Steps

**1.** Make sure the chart is selected

To call attention to the Boston October sales increase, you can draw an arrow that points to the top of the Boston October data series with the annotation, "Due to ad campaign." With the chart selected, simply typing text in the formula bar creates annotation text.

**2.** Type **Due to ad campaign**, then click the **Enter button**

As you type, the text appears in the formula bar. After you confirm the entry, the text appears in a selected text box within the chart window.

**3.** Point to an edge of the text box so the pointer changes to

> **Trouble?**
>
> If the pointer changes to I or ↔, release the mouse button, click outside the text box area to deselect it, then select the text box and repeat Step 3.

**4.** Drag the text box **above the chart**, as shown in Figure D-16, then release the mouse button

You can add an arrow to point to a specific area or item in a chart using the Drawing toolbar.

**5.** Click the **Drawing button** on the Standard toolbar

The Drawing toolbar appears.

**6.** Click the **Arrow button** on the Drawing toolbar

The pointer changes to + and the status bar displays "Click and drag to insert a AutoShape." When you draw an arrow, the point farthest from where you start will have the arrowhead.

> **QuickTip**
>
> You can insert text and an arrow in the data section of a worksheet by clicking the Text Box button on the Drawing toolbar, drawing a text box, typing the text, and then adding the arrow.

**7.** Position + under the 't' in the word "to" in the text box, press and hold the **left mouse button**, drag the line to the **Boston column in the October sales series**, then release the mouse button

An arrowhead appears, pointing to Boston October sales. The arrowhead is a selected object in the chart and can be resized, formatted, or deleted just like any other object. Compare your finished chart to Figure D-17.

**8.** Click to close the Drawing toolbar

**9.** Save your work

**FIGURE D-16: Repositioning text annotation**

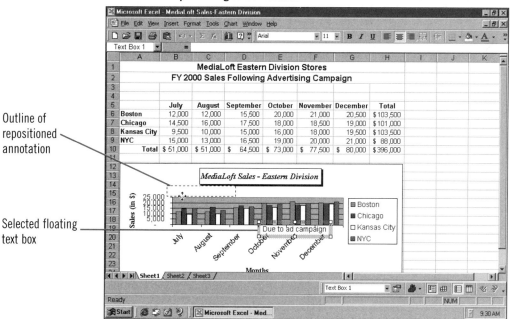

Outline of repositioned annotation

Selected floating text box

**FIGURE D-17: Completed chart with text annotation and arrow**

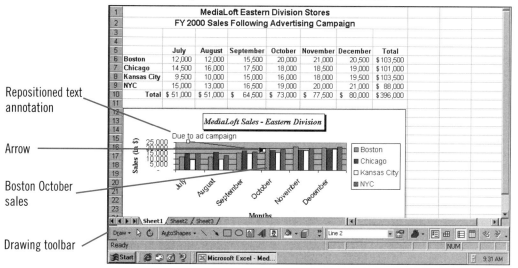

Repositioned text annotation

Arrow

Boston October sales

Drawing toolbar

## Exploding a pie slice

Just as an arrow can call attention to a data series, you can emphasize a pie slice by exploding it, or pulling it away from, the pie chart. Once the pie chart is selected, click the pie to select it, click the desired slice to select only the slice, then drag the slice away from the pie, as shown in Figure D-18. After you change the chart type, you may need to adjust arrows within the chart.

**FIGURE D-18: Exploded pie slice**

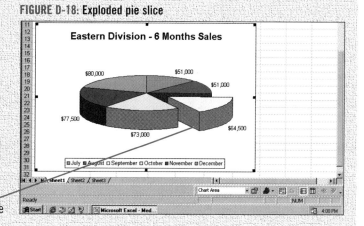

September sales slice pulled from pie

# Previewing and Printing a Chart

After you complete a chart to your satisfaction, you will need to print it. Previewing a chart gives you a chance to see what your chart looks like before you print it. You can print a chart by itself, or as part of the worksheet. ✏️ Jim wants to print the chart for the annual meeting. He will print the worksheet and the chart together, so that the shareholders can see the actual sales numbers for the eastern division stores.

## Steps 1 2 3 4

1. **Press [Esc] twice to deselect the arrow and the chart, click cell A35, type your name, press [Enter], then press [Ctrl][Home]**
   If you wanted to print only the chart without the data, you would leave the chart selected. Including your name on a worksheet insures that you'll be able to identify your work when it is printed.

**Trouble?**

Click Margins on the Print Preview toolbar to display Margin lines in the Print Preview window.

2. **Click the Print Preview button 🔍 on the Standard toolbar**
   The Print Preview window opens. You decide that the chart and data would make better use of the page if they were printed in **landscape** orientation—that is, with the text running the long way on the page. Altering the page setup changes the orientation of the page.

3. **Click Setup on the Print Preview toolbar to open the Page Setup dialog box, then click the Page tab**

4. **Click the Landscape option button in the Orientation section as shown in Figure D-19, then click OK**
   Because each page has a left default margin of 0.75", the chart and data will print too far over to the left of the page. You can change this setting using the Margins tab.

5. **Click Setup, click the Margins tab, click the Center on page Horizontally checkbox, then click OK**
   The data and chart are positioned horizontally on the page. See Figure D-20.

6. **Click Print to display the Print dialog box, then click OK**
   The data and chart print and you are returned to the worksheet. If you want, you can choose to preview (and print) only the chart.

7. **Select the chart, then click the Print Preview button 🔍**
   The chart appears in the Print Preview window. If you wanted to, you could print the chart by clicking the Print button on the Print Preview toolbar.

8. **Click Close on the Print Preview toolbar**

9. **Save your work, then close the workbook and exit Excel**

### Using the Page Setup dialog box for a chart

When a chart is selected, a different Page Setup dialog box opens than when neither the chart nor data is selected. The Center on Page options are not always available. To accurately position a chart on the page, you could click the Margins button on the Print Preview toolbar. Margin lines appear on the screen and show you exactly how the margins display on the page. The exact placement appears in the status bar when you press and hold the mouse button on the margin line. You can drag the lines to the exact setting you want.

FIGURE D-19: **Page tab of the Page Setup dialog box**

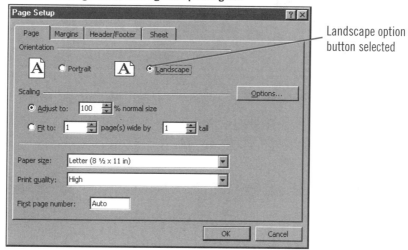

Landscape option button selected

FIGURE D-20: **Chart and data ready to print**

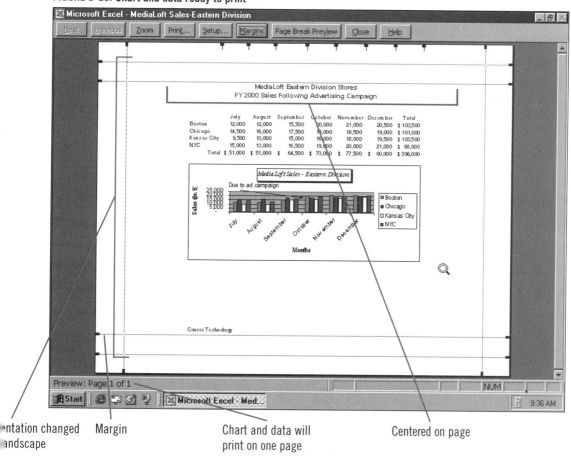

ntation changed    Margin          Chart and data will        Centered on page
andscape                            print on one page

Excel 2000

# Practice

## ► Concepts Review

Label each element of the Excel chart shown in Figure D-21.

FIGURE D-21

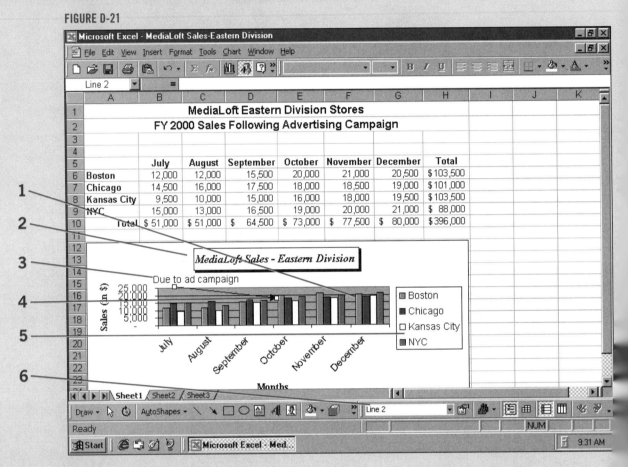

Match each chart type with the statement that describes it.

7. Column
8. Area
9. Pie
10. Combination
11. Line

   **a.** Shows how volume changes over time
   **b.** Compares data as parts of a whole
   **c.** Displays a column and line chart using different scales of measurement
   **d.** Compares trends over even time intervals
   **e.** Compares data over time—the Excel default

**Select the best answer from the list of choices.**

12. The object in a chart that identifies patterns used for each data series is a
    a. Data point.
    b. Plot.
    c. Legend.
    d. Range.

13. What is the term for a row or column on a chart?
    a. Range address
    b. Axis title
    c. Chart orientation
    d. Data series

14. The orientation of a page whose dimensions are 11" by 8½" is
    a. Sideways.
    b. Longways.
    c. Portrait.
    d. Landscape.

15. The Value axis is the
    a. X-axis.
    b. Z-axis.
    c. D-axis.
    d. Y-axis.

16. The Category axis is the
    a. X-axis.
    b. Z-axis.
    c. D-axis.
    d. Y-axis.

17. Which pointer is used to resize a chart object?
    a. I
    b. ↗
    c. ✛
    d. +

**Skills Review**

## 1. Create a chart.

a. Start Excel, open a new workbook, then save it as "Software Usage" to your Project Disk.

b. Enter the information from Table D-5 in your worksheet in range A1:F6. Resize columns and rows.

c. Save your work.

d. Select the range you want to chart.

e. Click the Chart Wizard button.

f. Complete the Chart Wizard dialog boxes and build a column chart on the same sheet as the data, having a different color bar for each department. Title the chart "Software Usage by Department."

g. Save your work.

TABLE D-5

|  | Excel | Word | PowerPoint | Access | Publisher |
|---|---|---|---|---|---|
| Accounting | 22 | 15 | 2 | 2 | 1 |
| Marketing | 13 | 35 | 35 | 5 | 32 |
| Engineering | 23 | 5 | 3 | 1 | 0 |
| Personnel | 10 | 25 | 10 | 2 | 25 |
| Production | 6 | 5 | 22 | 0 | 22 |

## 2. Move and resize a chart.

a. Make sure the chart is still selected.

b. Move the chart beneath the data.

c. Drag the chart's selection handles so it is as wide as the screen.

d. Move the legend below the charted data. (*Hint:* Change the legend's position using the Legend button on the Chart toolbar.)

e. Save your work.

## 3. Edit a chart.

a. Change the value in cell B3 to "6." Notice the change in the chart.

b. Select the chart by clicking it.

c. Click the Chart Type list arrow on the Chart toolbar.

d. Click the 3-D Column Chart button.

e. Rotate the chart to move the data.

f. Change the chart back to a column chart.

g. Save your work.

## 4. Format a chart.

a. Make sure the chart is still selected.

b. Use the Chart Options dialog box to turn off the displayed gridlines.

c. Change the font used in the Category and Value labels to Times New Roman.

d. Turn the major gridlines back on.

e. Change the title's font to Times New Roman.

f. Save your work.

## 5. Enhance a chart.

**a.** Make sure the chart is still selected, click Chart on the menu bar, click Chart Options, then click the Titles tab.

**b.** Click the Category (X) axis text box, then type "Software" in the selected text box below the x-axis.

**c.** Click the Value (Y) axis text box, type "Users" in the selected text box to the left of the y-axis, then click OK.

**d.** Change the legend entry for "Production" to "Art."

**e.** Add a drop shadow to the title.

**f.** Save your work.

## 6. Annotate and draw on a chart.

**a.** Select the chart.

**b.** Create the text annotation "Need More Users."

**c.** Drag the text annotation under the title.

**d.** Click the Arrow button on the Drawing toolbar.

**e.** Click below the text annotation, drag the arrow so it points to the area containing the Access columns, then release the mouse button.

**f.** Save your work.

## 7. Preview and print a chart.

**a.** Deselect the chart and type your name in cell A30.

**b.** Preview the chart and data to see how it will look when printed.

**c.** Change the paper orientation to landscape.

**d.** Center the data and chart horizontally and vertically on the page.

**e.** Click Print in the Print Preview window.

**f.** Select the chart.

**g.** Preview, then print only the chart.

**h.** Save your work, close the workbook, then exit Excel.

# ► Independent Challenges

**1.** You are the operations manager for the Springfield Theater Group. Each year the city of Springfield applies to various state and federal agencies for matching funds. The city's marketing department wants you to create charts for a report that will be used to document the number of productions in previous years. You need to create charts that show the number of previously produced plays.

To complete this independent challenge:

a. Sketch a sample worksheet on a piece of paper describing how you will create the charts. Which type of chart is best suited for the information you need to display? What kind of chart enhancements will be necessary? Will a 3-D effect make your chart easier to understand?

b. Start Excel, open the workbook EX D-2 from your Project Disk, then save it as "Theater Group."

c. Create a column chart for the data.

d. Change at least one of the colors used in a data series.

e. Create at least two additional charts for the same data to show how different chart types display the same data.

f. After creating the charts, make the appropriate enhancements. Include chart titles, legends, and value and category titles.

g. Add data labels.

h. Type your name in a cell in the worksheet.

i. Before printing, preview the file so you know what the charts will look like. Adjust any items as needed.

j. Save your work. Print the worksheet (charts and data).

k. Close the workbook and exit Excel.

**2.** One of your responsibilities at the Beautiful You Salon is to re-create the company's records using Excel. Another i to convince the current staff that Excel can make daily operations easier and more efficient. You've decided to creat charts using the previous year's operating expenses. These charts will be used at the next monthly meeting.

To complete this independent challenge:

a. Decide which data in the worksheet should be charted. Sketch two sample charts. What type of charts are bes suited for the information you need to display? What kind of chart enhancements will be necessary?

b. Start Excel, open the workbook EX D-3 from your Project Disk, and save it as "BY Expense Charts."

c. Create a column chart containing the expense data for all four quarters.

d. Using the same data, create two additional charts using different chart types.

e. Add annotated text and arrows (to the initial chart) highlighting any important data or trends that you can se from the charts.

f. In one chart, change the colors of data series, and in another chart, use black-and-white patterns only.

g. Type your name in a cell in the worksheet.

h. Before printing, preview the file so you know what the charts will look like. Adjust any items as needed.

i. Print the charts. Save your work.

j. Close the workbook and exit Excel.

**3.** The Step Lightly Ad Agency is delighted with the way you've organized their membership roster using Excel. The Board of Directors wants to assess certain advertising expenses and has asked you to prepare charts that can be used in their presentation.

To complete this independent challenge:

**a.** Start Excel, open the workbook EX D-4 from your Project Disk, and save it as "Step Lightly."

**b.** Use the raw data for the sample shown in the range A16:B24 to create charts.

**c.** Decide what types of charts would be best suited for this type of data. Sketch two sample charts. What kind of chart enhancements will be necessary?

**d.** Create at least three different chart types that show the distribution of advertising expenses.

**e.** Add annotated text and arrows highlighting important data, such as the largest expense.

**f.** Change the color of at least one data series.

**g.** Add Category and Value axis titles; add a chart title. Format the titles with a font of your choice. Place a drop shadow around the chart title.

**h.** Type your name in a cell in the worksheet.

**i.** Before printing, preview the file so you know what the charts will look like. Adjust any items as needed. Be sure the chart is placed appropriately on the page.

**j.** Print the charts, save your work, then close the workbook and exit Excel.

**4.** During the second quarter of the year, the New York City MediaLoft store decided to analyze sales by type of book for a three-month period. Sales have been steadily increasing and the manager of the store is planning to renovate the space. Depending on which books sell best for the store location, the manager will reallocate the selling floor space accordingly. To be able to present this information to see which types of books are the best sellers, you will chart the analysis to get a graphical representation of the distributions. You decide to create two types of charts for the same data.

To complete this independent challenge:

**a.** Start Excel, open a new workbook, and save it on your Project Disk as "New York Analysis."

**b.** Connect to the Internet, go to the MediaLoft intranet site at http://www.course.com/illustrated/MediaLoft, then click the link for the Accounting page.

**c.** Copy the New York Analysis data into your worksheet.

**d.** Create a column chart with the data series in rows on the same worksheet as the data. Include a descriptive title and the following text: "Type of Book" in the Category axis, and "Sales" in the Value axis.

**e.** Place the chart on the same sheet as the data.

**f.** Move the chart so that it is below the data and the left side of the chart is in column A.

**g.** Format the legend so that it is placed along the bottom of the chart.

**h.** Change the color of the Science Fiction data series to fuschia.

. Remove the gridlines.

. Using the same data, create a 3-D bar chart (use the Clustered bar with the 3-D visual effect) with the data series in rows on a new sheet.

. Add appropriate title(s) to the worksheet and axes.

. Format the Value axis so the numbers display no decimal places, and a 1000 separator (comma).

. Type your name in a visible cell in the worksheet containing the data.

. Preview the chart and change margins as needed.

. Print the worksheet data and column chart, making setup modifications as necessary.

. Print the 3-D bar chart making any setup modifications as necessary.

. Save the workbook and exit Excel.

# ▶ Visual Workshop

Modify a worksheet using the skills you learned in this unit, using Figure D-22 for reference. Open the file EX D-5 from your Project Disk, and save it as "Quarterly Advertising Budget." Create the chart, then change the data to reflect Figure D-22. Type your name in cell A13, save, preview, and then print your results.

FIGURE D-22

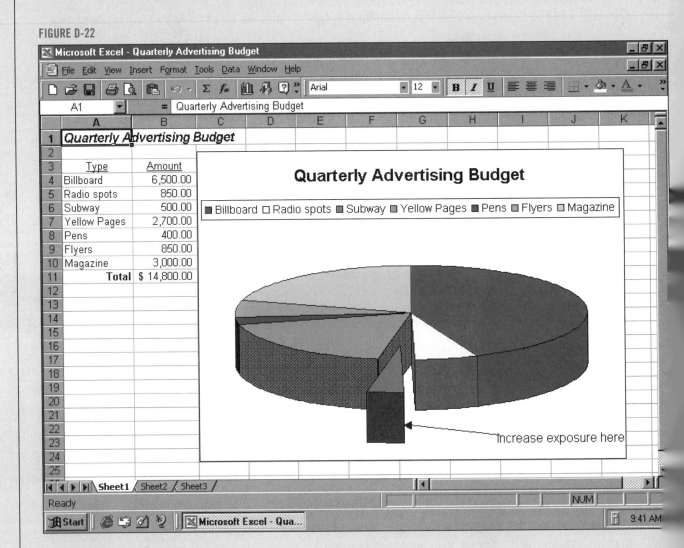

# Integrating
## Word and Excel

Now that you have experienced the power of Word and Excel, it is time to learn how to integrate the programs. When you integrate programs, you combine information from the two programs without retyping anything. Five of the MediaLoft stores noticed that they had an increase in sales soon after they started promoting MediaLoft's participation in a national literacy program. Customers seemed glad to support the stores because they participated in the program. Alice Wegman, the marketing manager for MediaLoft, collected the spring quarter sales data for the five stores so that she could compare the data. She compiled this information in a Word document, and now she wants to add an Excel column chart to her document.

# Opening Multiple Programs

When you are integrating information from one program into another, it is helpful to have both files open at the same time. The Windows environment gives you the ability to have more than one program open at a time. This is sometimes called **multitasking**. ◄━━━ Before integrating the data, Alice starts both Word and Excel. To make integrating the data easier, she aligns each program window side-by-side on the screen.

## Steps 123 4

**1.** Click the **Start button** on the taskbar, point to **Programs**, then click **Microsoft Word** in the Program list

A blank Word document opens and the Word program button appears in the taskbar.

**QuickTip**

It is not necessary to minimize a program window before you start another program.

**2.** Click the **Minimize button** in the program window

The Word program window shrinks into a program button on the taskbar.

**3.** Click the **Start button** on the taskbar, point to **Programs**, then click **Microsoft Excel**

A blank Excel workbook opens, and the Excel program button appears on the taskbar. Notice that the Excel program button appears indented, indicating that it is active.

**4.** Click the **Word program button** on the taskbar

Word maximizes and becomes the active program. Excel is still open, but it is not active, as shown in Figure A-2. Now you'll arrange the program windows so each occupies half the screen.

**5.** Right-click a blank area on the taskbar

The taskbar pop-up menu appears.

**6.** Click **Tile Windows Vertically** on the pop-up menu

The two program windows each occupy half the screen. Compare your screen to Figure A-2. The title bars of both windows are gray, and both program buttons on the taskbar are raised, indicating that neither program window is active.

## Using shortcut keys to switch between open programs

You can switch between open programs by clicking the taskbar buttons or by using the shortcut key combination [Alt][Tab]. Pressing [Alt][Tab] causes the icons and names of open programs (whether or not they are minimized) to appear in the center of the screen, as shown in Figure A-1. To see this on the screen, press and hold [Alt], then press and release [Tab]. If more than one program is open, press and release [Tab] again while still holding down [Alt] to move the selection box to the next icon in the center of the screen. When the program you want to activate is selected, release [Alt].

**FIGURE A-1:** Word program icon in the center of the Excel worksheet

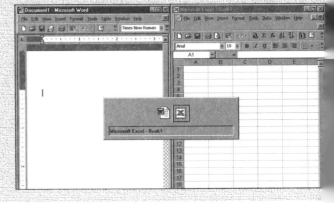

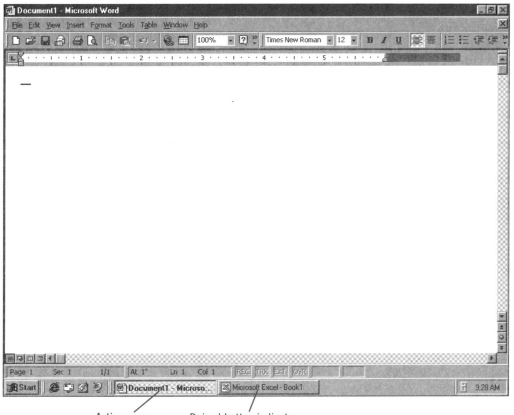

Active program          Raised button indicates
button is indented      program is open but inactive

FIGURE A-3: **Word window and Excel window on screen**

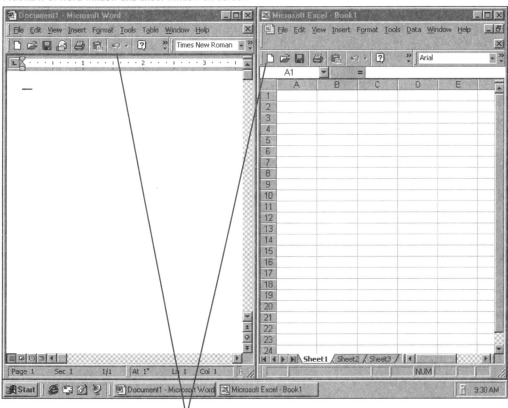

Each program displays its own menu bar
and toolbars (your toolbars may differ)

# Copying Word Data into Excel

Moving or copying information from one program to another is just like moving or copying information within a single program. You can use the Cut, Copy, and Paste commands; buttons on the toolbars; or the drag-and-drop method to move or copy information. The file from which the information is copied is called the **source file**. The file that receives the copied information is called the **target file**. ✎▬▬▬ Alice typed a memo to the five store managers that includes a Word table containing the spring quarter sales data for all five stores. She wants to add an Excel column chart to the memo. Before she can create the column chart in Excel, Alice needs to copy the data from the Word table into an Excel workbook.

**Steps**

1. Click anywhere in the Word program window to make it active

   Just like when two windows are open in the same program, clicking in a window makes that window active.

2. Open the file **INT A-1** from your Project Disk, then save it as **Manager Memo**

   Once the document is open, it can be saved to your Project Disk. Manager Memo appears in the Word program window in Print Layout view.

3. Replace Alice Wegman's name with your name

4. Scroll down until you can see the table and the body of the memo, then click the **right scroll arrow** on the horizontal scroll bar so you can see the entire table, as shown in Figure A-4

   The Word document is the source file, and the Excel workbook is the target file.

5. Position the pointer in the selection bar next to the top row of the table until the pointer changes to ⇗, press and hold the mouse button to select the top row of the table, drag the pointer down until all of the rows are selected, then release the mouse button

6. Press and hold [Ctrl], click in the table so the pointer looks like ▒, drag the pointer to the Excel worksheet, position the outline of the table in the range A1:D6 as shown in Figure A-5, then release the mouse button and [Ctrl]

   The information in the Word table is copied into the Excel worksheet, as shown in Figure A-6. Using drag-and-drop is the easiest way to copy information from a source file to a target file. The data in column A in the worksheet doesn't fit in the column.

7. Position the pointer between column indicators A and B so the pointer looks like ╋ then drag the column indicator to the right until the ScreenTip indicates 10.00

   Column A is resized to fit all the data.

8. Click the **Save button** 🖫 on the Excel Standard toolbar, then save the workbook as **Manager Sales 1** to your Project Disk

   Now that the data is copied into the Excel worksheet, you can easily create the column chart for the memo.

9. Close the **Manager Sales 1** workbook, *but do not exit Excel*

   Do not close the Manager Memo Word file.

## FIGURE A-4: Manager Memo open

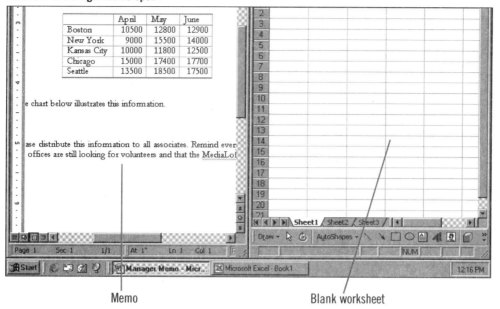

Memo       Blank worksheet

## FIGURE A-5: Word text dragged-and-dropped into an Excel worksheet

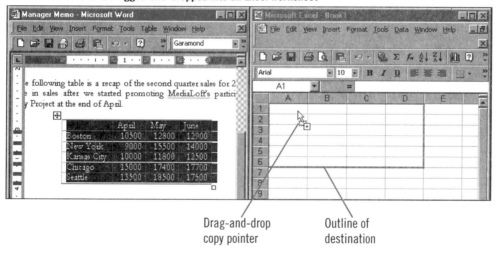

Drag-and-drop      Outline of
copy pointer        destination

## FIGURE A-6: Word table data copied into an Excel worksheet

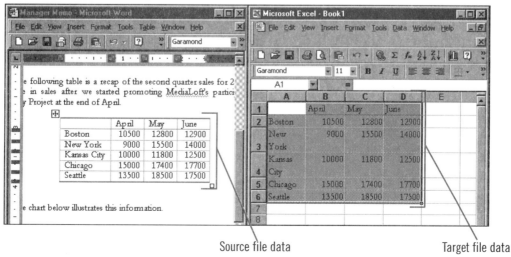

Source file data       Target file data

# Creating a Dynamic Link Between Excel and Word

Sometimes you want the data in two programs to be dynamically linked, not just copied. A **dynamic link**—sometimes called **dynamic data exchange** or **DDE**—means that if the data in the source file is changed, the data in the target file will be automatically updated. Alice created the column chart in Excel using the data that she had copied from the Word file. She decides to link it to the document rather than copy it, so that the Word memo will reflect modifications made in the Excel worksheet.

## Steps 1 2 3 4

1. In the Excel program window, open the file **INT A-2**, then save it as **Manager Sales 2** to your Project Disk

   Manager Sales 2 appears in the Excel worksheet window, as shown in Figure A-7. This file contains the chart created using the data copied from the Word document.

   **QuickTip**

   If the Chart toolbar is in the way, drag it by its title bar to a new location.

2. Position the pointer over a blank area of the **chart** so "Chart Area" appears in the ScreenTip, right-click, then click **Copy** on the pop-up menu

   A moving border appears around the chart and the chart is copied to the Clipboard.

3. Click anywhere in the Word program window to make it active, click the **left scroll arrow** once, then click in the blank paragraph below the sentence that begins "The chart below dramatizes…"

4. Click **Edit** on the Word menu bar, click **Paste Special** to open the Paste Special dialog box, then click the **Paste link option button**

   The As list box in the Paste Special dialog box changes to include the last item copied or cut to the Clipboard.

   **QuickTip**

   Click the scroll buttons to make the chart more visible, if necessary.

5. Make sure **Microsoft Excel Chart Object** is selected in the As list box, then click **O**

   The chart is copied into the Word document, and a dynamic link is created between th Word document and the Excel worksheet. One of the sales figures is incorrect. The Apr sales for New York were actually $12,000.

6. Make the Excel worksheet window active, click cell **B3**, type **12000**, then press **[Enter**

   Watch the chart as the first column in the New York data series increases to reflect the ne data. This change occurs in both the Excel worksheet and in the Word document, as show in Figure A-8. This change did not, however, occur in the table in the Word docume because that table is not linked to the Excel workbook.

7. Click the **Save button** on the Excel Standard toolbar to save the revised wor sheet, then close the workbook and exit Excel

8. Make the Word window active, double-click the cell that indicates the April sales New York, then type **12000**

9. Click the **Maximize button** in the program window, then click on the Wo Standard toolbar

10. Click the **Print Preview button** on the Word Standard toolbar, click the **Print butt** on the Print Preview toolbar, then close the document and exit Word

**FIGURE A-7: Excel worksheet containing chart**

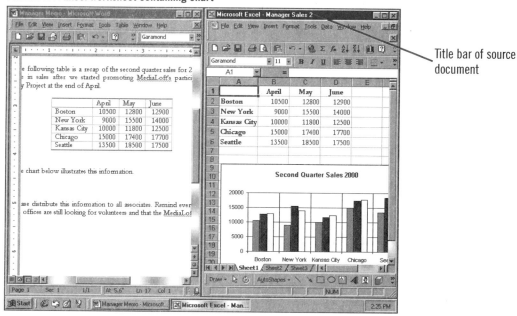

Title bar of source document

**FIGURE A-8: Excel chart linked to Word document**

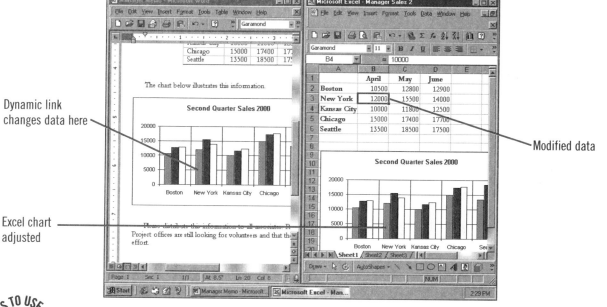

Dynamic link changes data here

Excel chart adjusted

Modified data

## Breaking links

If you are working with a file containing linked data and you decide that you don't want the linked object to change if the source file changes, you can break the link. In other words, you can change the object from a linked object to a pasted object. In the target file, click the object to select it, click Edit on the menu bar, then click Links to open the Links dialog box, shown in Figure A-9. Click the name of the source file, click Break Link, then click OK. The object in the target file is no longer linked to the source file.

**FIGURE A-9: Links dialog box**

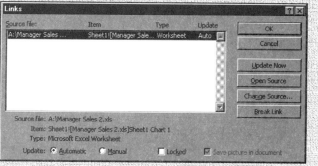

# ▶ Independent Challenges

**1.** The Chamber of Commerce realizes that to improve their advertising coverage, they need to hire an outside consultant. A list of promising consultants is being assembled by other Chamber members. Your job is to create a letter that gives them an overview of the Chamber's advertising efforts.

To complete this independent challenge:

**a.** Open the Excel file INT A-3 from your Project Disk and save it as "Chamber Statistics." Open the Word file INT A-4 from your Project Disk and save it as "Chamber Consultants."

**b.** Examine the chart in the Chamber Statistics workbook. Do you think you can use this chart within a document, or do you need to create other types of charts? What enhancements will need to be added to the charts?

**c.** Examine the Chamber Consultants document and determine what additions you need to make to best inform the prospective consultant.

**d.** Update the date in the Chamber Consultants document to reflect the current date.

**e.** The letter to the board should contain three charts. Create the additional charts you need in Excel. Add any enhancements, such as text annotations and arrows, which you can call attention to in the letter.

**f.** Create the document text to accompany each chart, then paste or link the charts to the document.

**g.** Preview the Chamber Consultants document. When you are satisfied it is complete, add your name to the document, save it, then print a copy.

**h.** Exit Word and Excel.

**2.** Alice Wegman wants to get some demographic data so she can complete her long term marketing plan for MediaLoft's marketing campaigns. The U.S. Census Bureau maintains a variety of current statistics on the World Wide Web. Alice can get population projections by state. She wants to create chart of the projections to use in her marketing plan.

To complete this independent challenge:

**a.** Connect to the Internet, go to the MediaLoft intranet site at http://www.course.com/illustrated/MediaLoft and click the Research Center link. From there, click the link titled US Census Bureau.

**b.** Locate and print Projections of the Total Population of States.

**c.** Open a new Excel workbook and save it to your Project Disk as "Population Projections."

**d.** Enter data for the United States for the years 2005, 2015, and 2025.

**e.** Create at least three charts of this data.

**f.** Open a new Word document and save it to your Project Disk as "Population Analysis."

**g.** Create original text that explains each of the three Excel charts.

**h.** Paste or link each of the charts in the Word document above each one's descriptive text.

**i.** Make sure you include your name in the document, then save and print your work.

**j.** Disconnect from the Internet, then exit Word and Excel.

# Getting
## Started with Access 2000

### Objectives

[MOUS] ► **Define database software**
[MOUS] ► **Learn database terminology**
► **Start Access and open a database**
[MOUS] ► **View the database window**
[MOUS] ► **Navigate records**
[MOUS] ► **Enter records**
[MOUS] ► **Edit records**
[MOUS] ► **Preview and print a datasheet**
[MOUS] ► **Get Help and exit Access**

In this unit, you will learn the purpose, advantages, and terminology of Microsoft Access 2000, a database software. You will also learn how to open a database and how to use the different elements of the Access window. You'll learn how to get help. You'll learn how to navigate through a database, enter and update data, and preview and print data. John Kim is the director of shipping at MediaLoft, a nationwide chain of bookstore cafés that sells books, music, and videos. Recently, MediaLoft switched to Access from an index card system for storing and maintaining customer information. John will use Access to enter and maintain this critical information for MediaLoft.

# Defining Database Software

Microsoft Access 2000 is a database software program that runs on Windows. **Database software** is used to manage data that can be organized into lists of related information, such as customers, products, vendors, employees, projects, or sales. Many small companies record customer, inventory, and sales information in a spreadsheet program such as Microsoft Excel. While this electronic format is more productive than writing information on index cards, Excel still lacks many of the database advantages provided by Access. Refer to Table A-1 for a comparison of the two programs. John reviews the advantages that database software has over a manual index card system.

### Data entry is faster and easier
Before inexpensive microcomputers, small businesses used manual paper systems, such as index cards, to record each customer, sale, and inventory item as illustrated in Figure A-1. Using an electronic database such as Access, you can create on-screen data entry forms, which make managing a database easier, more accurate, and more efficient than using index cards.

### Information retrieval is faster and easier
Retrieving information on an index card system is tedious because the cards have to be physically handled, sorted, and stored. Also, one error in filing can cause serious retrieval problems later. With Access you can quickly search for, display, and print information on customers, sales, or inventory.

### Information can be viewed and sorted in multiple ways
A card system allows you to sort the cards in only one order, unless the cards are duplicated for a second arrangement. Customer and inventory cards were generally sorted alphabetically by name. Sales index cards were usually sorted by date. In this system, complete customer and product information was recorded on each of their individual cards as well as on the corresponding sale cards. This quickly compromises data accuracy. Access allows you to view or sort the information from one or more subjects simultaneously. For example, you might want to know all the customers who purchased a particular product or all the products purchased by particular customer. A change made to the data in one view of Access is automatically updated in every other view or report.

### Information is more secure
Index cards can be torn, misplaced, and stolen. There is no password required to read them, and a disaster, such as a flood or fire, could completely destroy them. You can back up an Access database file on a regular basis and store the file at an offsite location. You can also password protect data so only those users with appropriate security clearances can view or manipulate the data.

### Information can be shared among several users
An index card system is limited to those users who can physically reach it. If one user keeps card for an extended period of time, then others cannot use or update that information. Access databases are inherently multiuser. More than one person can be entering, updating, a using the data at the same time.

### Duplicate data entry is minimized
The index card system requires that the user duplicate the customer and product information each sales card. With Access, you only need to enter each piece of information once. Figure shows a possible structure for an Access database to record sales.

**FIGURE A-1:** Using index cards to organize sales data

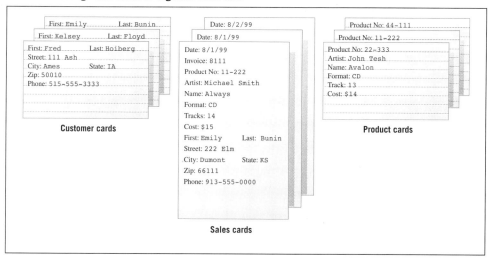

**FIGURE A-2:** Using Access, an electronic relational database, to organize sales data

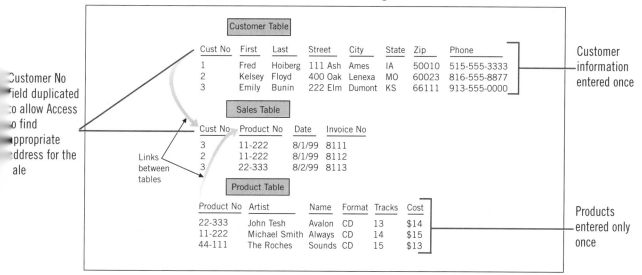

**TABLE A-1:** Comparing Excel to Access

| Feature | Excel | Access |
|---|---|---|
| Layout | Provides a natural tabular layout for easy data entry | Provides a spreadsheet "view" as well as forms which arrange data in a variety of ways |
| Storage | Limited to approximately 65,000 records per sheet | Able to store any number of records up to 2 gigabytes |
| Linked tables | Manages single lists of information | Allows links between lists of information to reduce data entry redundancy |
| Reporting | Limited to a spreadsheet printout | Provides sophisticated reporting features such as multiple headers and footers and calculations on groups of records |
| Security | Very limited | Each user can be given access to only the records and fields they need |
| Multiuser capabilities | Does not allow multiple users to simultaneously enter and update data | Allows multiple users to simultaneously enter and update data |
| Data entry screens | Provides limited data entry screens | Provides the ability to create extensive data entry screens called forms |

# Learning Database Terminology

To become familiar with Access, you need to understand basic database terminology. John reviews the terms and concepts that define a database.

## Details

A **database** is a collection of information associated with a topic (for example, sales of products to customers). The smallest piece of information in a database is called a **field**, or category of information, such as the customer's name, city, state, or phone number. A **key field** is a field that contains unique information for each record. A group of related fields, such as all demographic information for one customer, is called a **record**. In Access, a collection of records for a single subject, such as all of the customer records, is called a **table**, as shown in Figure A-3.

An Access database is a **relational database**, in which more than one table, such as the Customer, Sales, and Product tables, can share information. The term "relational database" comes from the fact that two tables are linked, or related, by a common field.

Tables, therefore, are the most important **object** in an Access database because they contain all of the data within the database. An Access database may also contain six other objects, which serve to enhance the usability and value of the data. The objects in an Access database are tables, queries, forms, reports, pages, macros, and modules, and they are summarized in Table A-2.

Data can be entered and edited in four of the objects: tables, queries, forms, and pages. The relationship between tables, queries, forms, and reports is shown in Figure A-4. Regardless of how the data is entered, it is physically stored in a table object. Data can be printed from a table, query, form, page, or report object. The macro and module objects are used to provide additional database productivity and automation features. All of the objects (except for the page objects, which are used to create Web pages) are stored in one database file.

**TABLE A-2: Access objects and their purpose**

| object | purpose |
| --- | --- |
| Table | Contains all of the raw data within the database in a spreadsheet-like view; tables can be linked with a common field to share information and therefore minimize data redundancy |
| Query | Provides a spreadsheet-like view of the data similar to tables, but a query can be designed to provide the user with a subset of fields or records from one or more tables; queries are created when a user has a "question" about the data in the database |
| Form | Provides an easy-to-use data entry screen, which generally shows only one record at a time |
| Report | Provides a professional printout of data that may contain enhancements such as headers, footers, and calculations on groups of records |
| Page | Creates Web pages from Access objects as well as provides Web page connectivity features to an Access database, also called Data Access Page |
| Macro | Stores a collection of keystrokes or commands, such as printing several reports or displaying a toolbar when a form opens |
| Module | Stores Visual Basic programming code that extends the functions and automated processes of Access |

**FIGURE A-3: Tables contain fields and records**

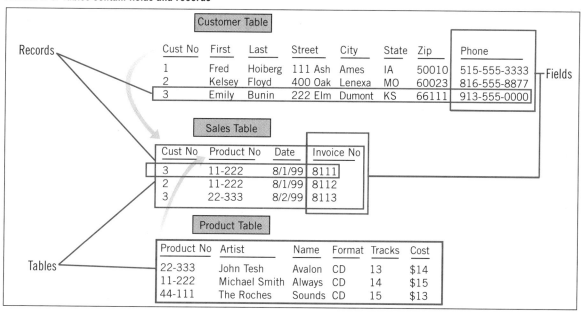

**FIGURE A-4: The relationship between Access objects**

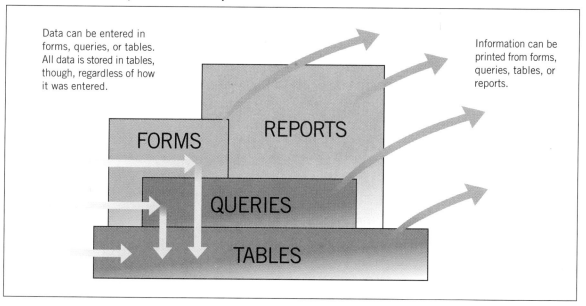

Data can be entered in forms, queries, or tables. All data is stored in tables, though, regardless of how it was entered.

Information can be printed from forms, queries, tables, or reports.

# Starting Access and Opening a Database

You can start Access by clicking the Access icon on the Windows desktop or on the Microsoft Office Shortcut Bar. Since not all computers will provide a shortcut icon on the desktop or display the Office Shortcut Bar, you can always find Access by clicking the Start button on the taskbar, pointing to Programs, and then choosing Access from the Programs menu. You can open a database from within Access or by finding the database file on the desktop, in My Computer, or in Windows Explorer, and then opening it. ▰▰▰▰ John starts Access and opens the MediaLoft-A database.

1. **Click the Start button** 🪟Start **on the taskbar**
   The Start button is in the lower-left corner of the taskbar. You can use the Start menu to start any program on your computer.

> **Trouble?**
>
> If you can't locate Microsoft Access on the Programs menu, point to the Microsoft Office group and look for Access there.

2. **Point to Programs**
   Access is generally located on the Programs menu. All the programs, or applications, stored on your computer can be found here.

3. **Click Microsoft Access**
   Access opens and displays the Access dialog box, from which you can start a new database or open an existing file.

> **QuickTip**
>
> Make a copy of your Project Disk before you use it.

4. **Insert your Project Disk in the appropriate disk drive**
   To complete the units in this book, you need a Project Disk. See your instructor or technical support person for assistance.

5. **Click More Files, then click OK**
   The Open dialog box appears, as shown in Figure A-5. Depending on the databases and folders stored on your computer, your dialog box may look slightly different.

> **Trouble?**
>
> These lessons assume your Project Disk is in drive A. If you are using a different drive, substitute that drive for drive A in the steps.

6. **Click the Look in list arrow, then click 3½ Floppy (A:)**
   A list of the files on your Project Disk appears in the Open dialog box.

7. **Click the MediaLoft-A database file, click Open, then click the Maximize button o** the title bar if the Access window does not fill the screen
   The MediaLoft-A database opens as shown in Figure A-6.

## Personalized toolbars and menus in Office 2000

Office 2000 toolbars and menus modify themselves to your working style. The toolbars you see when you first start a program include the most frequently used buttons. To locate a button not visible on a toolbar, click the More Buttons button at the end of the toolbar to see the list of additional toolbar buttons. As you work, the program adds the buttons you use to the visible toolbars and moves the buttons you haven't used in a while to the More Buttons list. Similarly, menus adjust to your work habits. Short menus appear when you first click a menu command. To view additional menu commands, point to the double-arrow at the bottom of the menu, leave the pointer on the menu name after you've clicked the menu, or double-click the menu name. If you select a command that's not on the short menu, the program automatically adds it to the short menus. You can return personalized toolbars and menus to their original settings by clicking Tools on the menu bar, then clicking Customize. On the Options tab in the Customize dialog box, click Reset my usage data, click Yes to close the alert box, then close the Customize dialog box. Resetting usage data erases changes made automatically to your menus and toolbars. It does not affect the options you customize.

FIGURE A-5: Open dialog box

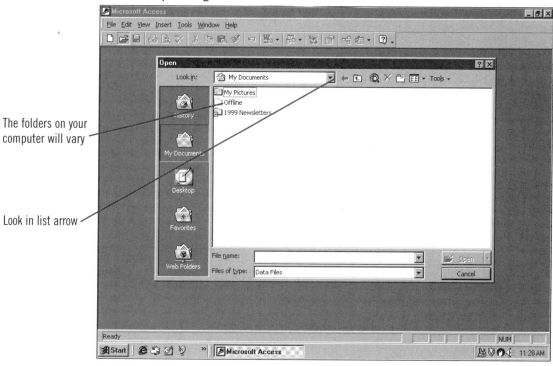

The folders on your computer will vary

Look in list arrow

FIGURE A-6: MediaLoft-A database

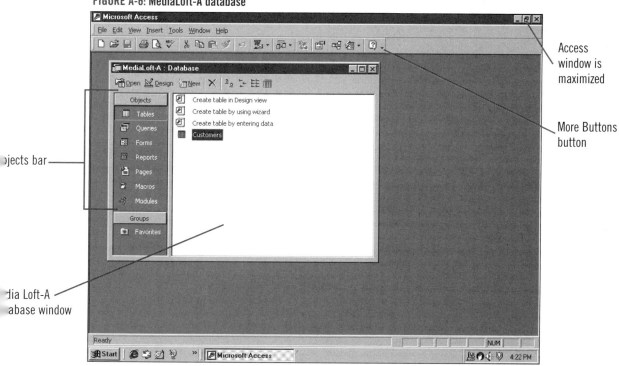

Access window is maximized

More Buttons button

Objects bar

Media Loft-A database window

Access 2000

# Viewing the Database Window

When you start Access and open a database, the **database window** displays common Windows elements such as a title bar, menu bar, and toolbar. Clicking the Objects or Groups buttons on the Objects bar alternatively expands and collapses that section of the database window. If all the objects don't display in the expanded section, click the small arrow at the top or bottom of the section to scroll the list. The **Objects** area displays the seven types of objects that can be accessed by clicking the object type you want. The **Groups** area displays other commonly used files and folders, such as the Favorites folder. ✎ John explores the MediaLoft-A database.

1. **Look at each of the Access window elements shown in Figure A-7**
   The Objects bar on the left side of the database window displays the seven object types. The other elements of the database window are summarized in Table A-3. Because the Tables object is selected, the buttons you need to create a new table or to work with the existing table are displayed in the MediaLoft-A Database window.

2. **Click File on the menu bar**
   The File menu contains commands for opening a new or existing database, saving a database in a variety of formats, and printing. The menu commands vary depending on which window or database object is currently in use.

3. **Point to Edit on the menu bar, point to View, point to Insert, point to Tools, point to Window, point to Help, move the pointer off the menu, then press [Esc] twice**
   All menus close when you press [Esc]. Pressing [Esc] a second time deselects the menu.

4. **Point to the New button ▢ on the Database toolbar**
   Pointing to a toolbar button causes a descriptive **ScreenTip** to automatically appear, providing a short description of the button. The buttons on the toolbars represent the most commonly used Access features. Toolbar buttons change just as menu options change depending on which window and database object are currently in use.

5. **Point to the Open button 🖿 on the Database toolbar, then point to the Save button 🖫 on the Database toolbar**
   Sometimes toolbar buttons or menu options are dimmed which means that they are currently unavailable. For example, the Save button is dimmed because it doesn't make sense to save the MediaLoft-A database right now because you haven't made any changes to it yet.

6. **Click Queries on the Objects bar**
   The query object window provides several ways to create a new query and displays the names of previously created queries, as shown in Figure A-8. There are three previously created query objects displayed within the MediaLoft-A Database window.

7. **Click Forms on the Objects bar, then click Reports on the Objects bar**
   The MediaLoft-A database contains the Customers table, three queries, a customer entry form, and three reports.

## Viewing objects

You can change the way you view the objects in the database window by clicking the last four buttons on the toolbar. You can view the objects as Large Icons 🔳, Small Icons 🔳, in a List 📇 (this is the default view), and with Details 🔳. The Details view shows a longer description of the object, as well as the date the object was last modified and the date it was originally created.

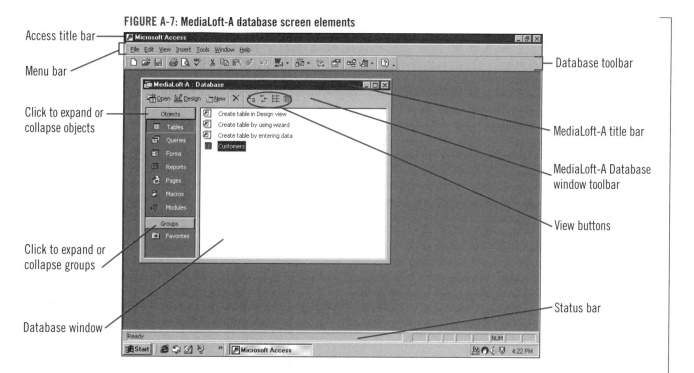

FIGURE A-7: MediaLoft-A database screen elements

Access title bar

Menu bar

Database toolbar

Click to expand or collapse objects

MediaLoft-A title bar

MediaLoft-A Database window toolbar

View buttons

Click to expand or collapse groups

Database window

Status bar

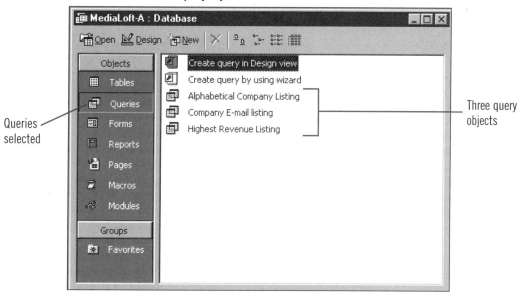

FIGURE A-8: MediaLoft-A query objects

Queries selected

Three query objects

BLE A-3: Elements of the database window

| ement | description |
|---|---|
| atabase toolbar | Contains buttons for commonly performed tasks |
| atabase window | Provides access to the objects within the database |
| enu bar | Contains menus used in Access |
| jects bar | Allows you to view a list of the object type chosen |
| tabase window toolbar | Contains buttons you use to open, modify, create, delete, or view objects |
| tus bar | Displays messages regarding the current database operation |
| e bar | Contains program name (Access) and filename of active database |

# Navigating Records

Your ability to navigate through the fields and records of a database is key to your productivity and success with the database. You navigate through the information in **Navigation mode** in the table's **datasheet**, a spreadsheet-like grid that displays fields as columns and records as rows. John opens the database and reviews the table containing information about MediaLoft's customers.

## Steps

**QuickTip**

You can also double-click an object to open it.

1. **Click Tables on the Objects bar, click Customers, then click the Open button 🖼 on the MediaLoft-A Database window toolbar**
   The datasheet for the Customers table opens, as shown in Figure A-9. The datasheet contains 27 customer records with 13 fields of information for each record. **Field names** are listed at the top of each column. The number of the selected record in the datasheet is displayed in the **Specific Record box** at the bottom of the datasheet window. Depending on the size of your monitor and the resolution of your computer system, you may see a different number of fields. If all of the fields don't display, you can scroll to the right to see the rest.

2. **Press [Tab] to move to Sprint**
   Sprint is the entry in the second field, Company, of the first record.

3. **Press [Enter]**
   The data, Aaron, is selected in the third field, First. Pressing either [Tab] or [Enter] move the focus to the next field. **Focus** refers to which field would be edited if you started typing

4. **Press [ ↓ ]**
   The focus moves to the Kelsey entry in the First field of the second record. The **current record symbol** in the **record selector box** also identifies which record you are navigating. The Next Record and Previous Record **navigation buttons** can also be used to navigate the datasheet.

5. **Press [Ctrl][End]**
   The focus moves to the last field of the last record. You can also use the Last Record navigation button to move to the last record.

6. **Press [Ctrl][Home]**
   The focus moves to the first field of the first record. You can also use the First Record navigation button to move to the first record. A complete listing of navigation keystrokes move the focus between fields and records is shown in Table A-4.

### Changing to Edit mode

If you click a field with the mouse pointer instead of pressing the [Tab] or [Enter] to navigate through the datasheet, you change from Navigation mode to **Edit mode**. In Edit mode, Access assumes that you are trying to edit that particular field, so keystrokes such as [Ctrl][End], [Ctrl][Home], [←], and [→] move the insertion point *within* the field. To return to Navigation mode, press [Tab] or [Enter] which moves the focus to the next field, or press [↑] or [↓] which moves the focus to a different record.

**FIGURE A-9: Customers datasheet**

Current record symbol

Current focus

Records

Record selector box

Specific Record box

Navigation buttons

Field name

| ID | Company | First | Last | Street | City | State | Zip | Phone |
|----|---------|-------|------|--------|------|-------|-----|-------|
| 1 | Sprint | Aaron | Friedrichsen | 111 Ash St. | Kansas City | MO | 66888-1111 | (816) 555-2222 |
| 2 | KGSM | Kelsey | Douglas | 222 Elm St. | Kansas City | MO | 66888-2222 | (816) 555-1111 |
| 3 | JCCC | Douglas | Scott | 333 Oak Dr. | Kansas City | KS | 66777-4444 | (913) 555-8888 |
| 4 | Oliver's | Rachel | Lena | 444 Apple St. | Kansas City | KS | 66777-3333 | (913) 555-7777 |
| 5 | Podiatry Center | Todd | Vandenburg | 555 Birch St. | Lenexa | KS | 66661-0033 | (913) 555-6666 |
| 6 | Mohs Surgery | Glenn | Goldstein | 666 Pine St. | Kansas City | MO | 66886-3333 | (816) 555-3333 |
| 7 | Diabetes Center | Sandie | Anderson | 777 Mulberry Way | Overland Park | KS | 66555-2222 | (913) 555-2222 |
| 8 | Hallmark | Kristen | Reis | 888 Fountain Dr. | Mission Hills | KS | 66222-3333 | (913) 555-1191 |
| 9 | Applebee's | Tom | David | 999 Riverside Dr. | Shawnee | KS | 66111-8888 | (913) 555-5888 |
| 10 | IBM | Daniel | Arno | 123 Wrigley Field | Overland Park | KS | 66333-2222 | (913) 555-3111 |
| 11 | Motorola | Mark | Langguth | 234 Wedd St. | Overland Park | KS | 66333-9988 | (913) 555-1234 |
| 12 | PFS | David | Dahlgren | 987 Front St. | Gladstone | MO | 60011-2222 | (816) 555-9999 |
| 13 | Hills Pets | Jennifer | Bunin | 6788 Poplar St. | Independence | MO | 60222-3333 | (816) 555-6777 |
| 14 | LabOne | Emily | Biheller | 6789 Canyon Pl. | Raytown | MO | 60124-2222 | (816) 555-5555 |
| 15 | Allied Signal | Michael | Davis | 987 Licolnway | Lenexa | KS | 66444-4444 | (913) 555-4444 |
| 16 | Health Midwest | Jane | Eagan | 201 Jackson St. | Overland Park | KS | 66332-9999 | (913) 555-1999 |
| 17 | Cerner | Fritz | Bradley | 887 Winger Rd. | Shawnee | KS | 66111-8887 | (913) 555-1777 |
| 18 | EBC | Carl | Garrett | 444 Metcalf | Overland Park | KS | 66111-7777 | (913) 555-1222 |
| 19 | Royals | Peg | Foxhoven | 554 Stadium Ln. | Raytown | MO | 60124-1111 | (816) 555-4777 |
| 20 | St. Luke's | Amanda | Love | 667 Birdie Ln. | Kansas City | MO | 66888-5555 | (816) 555-3338 |
| 21 | Roche | Brittney | Hill | 887 Foxtrot Ln. | Kansas City | KS | 66777-2222 | (913) 555-4222 |
| 22 | Oak Hill | Callie | Jones | 244 75th St. | Overland Park | MO | 66887-7777 | (913) 555-2211 |

Record: 1 of 27

Total number of records

Fields

Access 2000

**TABLE A-4: Navigation mode keyboard shortcuts**

| Shortcut key | to move to the |
|--------------|----------------|
| [Tab], [Enter] or [→] | Next field of the current record |
| [Shift][Tab] or [←] | Previous field of the current record |
| [Home] | First field of the current record |
| [End] | Last field of the current record |
| [Ctrl][Home] | First field of the first record |
| [Ctrl][End] | Last field of the last record |
| [↑] | Current field of the previous record |
| [↓] | Current field of the next record |
| [Ctrl][↑] | Current field of the first record |
| [Ctrl][↓] | Current field of the last record |
| [ ] | Specific record |

# Entering Records

Adding records to a database is a critical task that is usually performed on a daily basis. You can add a new record by clicking the **New Record button** on the Table Datasheet toolbar or by clicking the New Record navigation button. A new record is always added at the end of the datasheet. You can reorder the records in a datasheet by sorting, which you will learn later. ◢━━ John is ready to add two new records in the Customers table. First he maximizes the datasheet window.

## Steps 1234

1. Click the **Maximize button** on the Customers Table datasheet window title bar
   Maximizing both the Access and datasheet windows displays the most information possible on the screen and allows you to see more fields and records.

2. Click the **New Record button** ▸* on the Table Datasheet toolbar, then press **[Tab]** to move through the ID field and into the Company field
   The ID field is an **AutoNumber** field, which automatically assigns a new number each time you add a record.

3. Type **CIO**, press **[Tab]**, type **Lisa**, press **[Tab]**, type **Lang**, press **[Tab]**, type **420 Locust St.**, press **[Tab]**, type **Lenexa**, press **[Tab]**, type **KS**, press **[Tab]**, type **66111-8899**, press **[Tab]**, type **9135551189**, press **[Tab]**, type **9135551889**, press **[Tab]**, type **9/6/69**, press **[Tab]**, type **lang@cio.com**, press **[Tab]**, type **5433.22**, then press **[Enter]**
   The ID for the record for Lisa Lang is 28. AutoNumber fields should not be used as a counter for how many records you have in a table. Think of the AutoNumber field as an arbitrary but unique number for each record. The value in an AutoNumber field increments by one for each new record and cannot be edited or reused even if the entire record is deleted. The purpose of an AutoNumber field is to uniquely identify each new record. It logs how many records have been added to the datasheet since the creation of the datasheet, and not how many records are currently in the datasheet.

### Trouble?

The ID number for the new records may be different in your database.

4. Enter the new record for Rachel Best shown in the table below

| in field: | type: | in field: | type: |
|---|---|---|---|
| ID | 29 | Zip | 65555-4444 |
| Company | RBB Events | Phone | 913-555-2289 |
| First | Rachel | Fax | 913-555-2889 |
| Last | Best | Birthdate | 8/20/68 |
| Street | 500 Sunset Blvd. | Email | Best@rbb.com |
| City | Manhattan | YTDSales | 5998.33 |
| State | KS | | |

Compare your updated datasheet with Figure A-10.

**FIGURE A-10: Customers table with two new records**

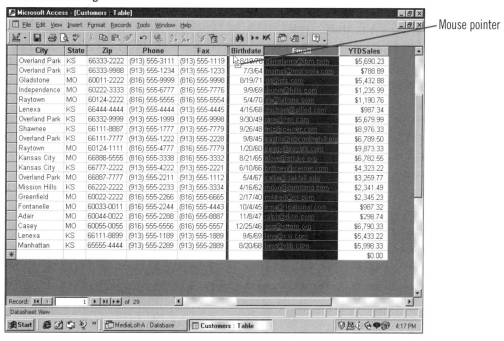

Table Datasheet toolbar

Both windows are maximized

New record button

Two new records

New record button

**FIGURE A-11: Moving a field**

Mouse pointer

## Moving datasheet columns

You can reorganize the fields in a datasheet by dragging the field name left or right. Figure A-11 shows how the mouse pointer changes to ![pointer], as the Email field is moved to the left. The black vertical line represents the new location between the Fax and Birthdate fields. Release the mouse button when you have appropriately positioned the field.

Access 2000

# Editing Records

Updating information in databases is another important daily task required to keep your database current. To change the contents of an existing record, click the field you'd like to change to switch to Edit mode, then type the new information. You can delete any unwanted data by clicking the field and using the [Backspace] and [Delete] keys to delete text to the left and right of the insertion point. Other data entry keystrokes are summarized in Table A-5. John needs to make some corrections to the datasheet of the Customers table. He starts by correcting an error in the Street field of the first record.

## Steps

1. **Press [Ctrl][Home] to move to the first record, click to the right of 111 Ash St. in the Street field, press [Backspace] three times to delete St., then type Dr.**

   When you are editing a record, the **edit record symbol**, which looks like a small pencil, appears in the record selector box to the left of the current record, as shown in Figure A-12.

2. **Click to the right of Hallmark in the Company field in record 8, press [Spacebar], type Cards, then press [↓] to move to the next record**

   You do not need to explicitly save new records or changes to existing records because Access saves the new data as soon as you move to another record or close the data sheet.

3. **Click Shawnee in the City field for record 17, then press [Ctrl][']**

   The entry changes from "Shawnee" to "Overland Park." [Ctrl]['] inserts the data from the same field in the previous record.

4. **Click to the left of EBC in the Company field for record 18, press [Delete] to remove the E, press [Tab] to move to the next field, then type Doug**

   "Doug" replaces the current entry "Carl" in the First field. Notice the edit record symbol in the record selector box to the left of record 18. Since you are still editing this record, you can undo the changes.

5. **Press [Esc]**

   The Doug entry changes back to Carl. Pressing [Esc] once removes the current field's editing changes.

6. **Press [Esc] again**

   Pressing [Esc] a second time removes all changes made to the record you are currently editing. The company entry is restored to EBC. The ability to use the [Esc] key in edit mode to remove data entry changes is dependent on whether or not you are still editing the record (as evidenced by the edit record symbol to the left of the record). Once you move to another record the changes are saved, and you return to Navigation mode. In Navigation mode you can no longer use the [Esc] key to remove editing changes, but you can click the **Undo button** on the Table Database toolbar to undo the last change you made.

7. **Press [↓] to move to Peg in the First field of record 19, type Peggy, then press [↓] to move to record 20**

   Since you are no longer editing record 19, the [Esc] key has no effect on the last change.

**QuickTip**

The ScreenTip for the Undo button displays the action you can undo.

8. **Click the Undo button on the Table Datasheet toolbar**

   You undo the last edit and Peggy is changed back to Peg. Access only allows you to undo your last action. You can also delete a record directly from the datasheet.

9. **Click the Allied Signal ID 15 Record Selector box, click the Delete Record button on the Table Datasheet toolbar, then click Yes to confirm that you want to delete the record**

   You cannot undo a record deletion operation.

Edit record symbol

Insertion point

| ID | Company | First | Last | Street | City | State | Zip | Phone | Fax |
|----|---------|-------|------|--------|------|-------|-----|-------|-----|
| 1 | Sprint | Aaron | Friedrichsen | 111 Ash Dr. | Kansas City | MO | 66888-1111 | (816) 555-2222 | (816) 555-22 |
| 2 | KGSM | Kelsey | Douglas | 222 Elm St. | Kansas City | MO | 66888-2222 | (816) 555-1111 | (816) 555-11 |
| 3 | JCCC | Douglas | Scott | 333 Oak Dr. | Kansas City | KS | 66777-4444 | (913) 555-8888 | (913) 555-8E |
| 4 | Oliver's | Rachel | Lena | 444 Apple St. | Kansas City | KS | 66777-3333 | (913) 555-7777 | (913) 555-77 |
| 5 | Podiatry Center | Todd | Vandenburg | 555 Birch St. | Lenexa | KS | 66661-0033 | (913) 555-6666 | (913) 555-6E |
| 6 | Mohs Surgery | Glenn | Goldstein | 666 Pine St. | Kansas City | MO | 66886-3333 | (816) 555-3333 | (816) 555-22 |
| 7 | Diabetes Center | Sandie | Anderson | 777 Mulberry Way | Overland Park | KS | 66555-2222 | (913) 555-2222 | (913) 555-22 |
| 8 | Hallmark | Kristen | Reis | 888 Fountain Dr. | Mission Hills | KS | 66222-3333 | (913) 555-1191 | (913) 555-11 |
| 9 | Applebee's | Tom | David | 999 Riverside Dr. | Shawnee | KS | 66111-8888 | (913) 555-5888 | (913) 555-8E |
| 10 | IBM | Daniel | Arno | 123 Wrigley Field | Overland Park | KS | 66333-2222 | (913) 555-3111 | (913) 555-11 |
| 11 | Motorola | Mark | Langguth | 234 Wedd St. | Overland Park | KS | 66333-9988 | (913) 555-1234 | (913) 555-12 |
| 12 | PFS | David | Dahlgren | 987 Front St. | Gladstone | MO | 60011-2222 | (816) 555-9999 | (816) 555-99 |
| 13 | Hills Pets | Jennifer | Bunin | 6788 Poplar St. | Independence | MO | 60222-3333 | (816) 555-6777 | (816) 555-77 |
| 14 | LabOne | Emily | Biheller | 6789 Canyon Pl. | Raytown | MO | 60124-2222 | (816) 555-5555 | (816) 555-5E |
| 15 | Allied Signal | Michael | Davis | 987 Licolnway | Lenexa | KS | 66444-4444 | (913) 555-4444 | (913) 555-44 |
| 16 | Health Midwest | Jane | Eagan | 201 Jackson St. | Overland Park | KS | 66332-9999 | (913) 555-1999 | (913) 555-99 |
| 17 | Cerner | Fritz | Bradley | 887 Winger Rd. | Shawnee | KS | 66111-8887 | (913) 555-1777 | (913) 555-77 |
| 18 | EBC | Carl | Garrett | 444 Metcalf | Overland Park | KS | 66111-7777 | (913) 555-1222 | (913) 555-22 |
| 19 | Royals | Peg | Foxhoven | 554 Stadium Ln. | Raytown | MO | 60124-1111 | (816) 555-4777 | (816) 555-77 |
| 20 | St. Luke's | Amanda | Love | 667 Birdie Ln. | Kansas City | MO | 66888-5555 | (816) 555-3338 | (816) 555-33 |
| 21 | Roche | Brittney | Hill | 887 Foxtrot Ln. | Kansas City | KS | 66777-2222 | (913) 555-4222 | (913) 555-22 |
| 22 | Oak Hill | Callie | Jones | 244 75th St. | Overland Park | MO | 66887-7777 | (913) 555-2211 | (913) 555-11 |
| 23 | Farmland | Marjorie | Donald | 556 Cory Ave. | Mission Hills | KS | 66222-2222 | (913) 555-2233 | (913) 555-33 |
| 24 | Cardiac Rehab | Mildred | Wambold | 600 Adair St. | Greenfield | MO | 60022-2222 | (816) 555-2266 | (816) 555-6E |
| 25 | First National | Irma | Mitchell | 800 First St. | Fontanelle | MO | 60033-0011 | (816) 555-2244 | (816) 555-44 |

Record: 1 ▶ ▶| ▶* of 29

Datasheet View

TABLE A-5: Edit mode keyboard shortcuts

| editing keystroke | action |
|-------------------|--------|
| [Backspace] | Deletes one character to the left of the insertion point |
| [Delete] | Deletes one character to the right of the insertion point |
| [F2] | Switches to Edit mode from Navigation mode |
| [Esc] | Undoes the change to the current field |
| [Esc][Esc] | Undoes the change to the current record |
| [F7] | Starts the spell check feature |
| [Ctrl]['] | Inserts the value from the same field in the previous record into the current field |
| [Ctrl][;] | Inserts the current date in a date field |

## Resizing datasheet columns

You can resize the width of the field in a datasheet by dragging the thin black line that separates the field names to the left or right. The mouse pointer changes to ✚ as you resize the field to make it wider or narrower. Release the mouse button when you have resized the field.

# Previewing and Printing a Datasheet

After entering and editing the records in a table, you can print the datasheet to obtain a hard copy of it. Before printing the datasheet, you should preview it to see how it will look when printed. Often you will want to make adjustments to margins and page orientation. ▰▰▰ John is ready to preview and print the datasheet.

**QuickTip**

If you need your name on the printed solution, enter your name as a new record in the datasheet.

1. Click the **Print Preview button** 🔍 on the Table Database toolbar
   The datasheet appears as a miniature page in the Print Preview window, as shown in Figure A-14. The Print Preview toolbar provides options for printing, viewing more than one page, and sending the information to Word or Excel.

2. Click 🔍 on the top of the miniature datasheet
   By magnifying this view of the datasheet, you can see its header, which includes the object name, Customers, in the center of the top of the page and the date on the right.

3. Scroll down to view the bottom of the page
   The footer displays a page number centered on the bottom.

4. Click the **Two Pages button** ▦ on the Print Preview toolbar
   You decide to increase the top margin of the printout.

5. Click **File** on the menu bar, then click **Page Setup**
   The Page Setup dialog box opens, as shown in Figure A-15. This dialog box provides options for changing margins, removing the headings (the header and footer), and changing page orientation from portrait (default) to landscape on the Page tab.

6. Double-click **1"** in the Top text box, type **2**, then click **OK**
   The modified datasheet appears in the window. Satisfied with the layout for the printout, you'll print the datasheet and close the Print Preview window.

7. Click the **Print button** 🖨 on the Print Preview toolbar, then click **Close**
   The datasheet appears on the screen.

## Hiding fields

Sometimes you don't need all the fields of a datasheet on a printout. To temporarily hide a field from viewing and therefore from a resulting datasheet printout, click the field name, click Format on the menu bar, and then click Hide Columns. To redisplay the column, click Format, then Unhide Columns. The Unhide Columns dialog box, shown in Figure A-13, opens. The empty columns check boxes indicate the columns that are hidden. Clicking the check boxes will bring the columns back into view on the datasheet.

**FIGURE A-13:** Unhide Columns dialog box

These fields are currently hidden

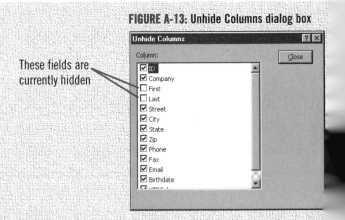

**FIGURE A-14: Datasheet in print preview (portrait orientation)**

Print Preview toolbar

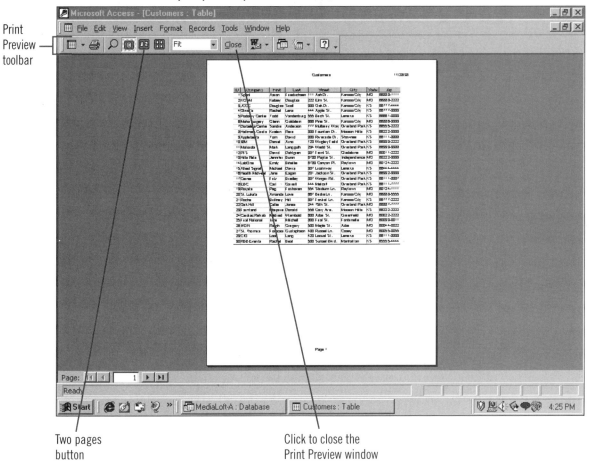

Two pages button

Click to close the Print Preview window

**FIGURE A-15: Page Setup dialog box**

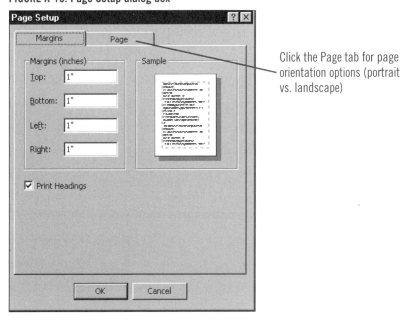

Click the Page tab for page orientation options (portrait vs. landscape)

# Getting Help and Exiting Access

When you have finished working in your database, you need to close the object you were working in, such as a table datasheet, and then close the database. To close a table, click Close on the File menu or click the object's Close button located in the upper-right corner of the menu bar. Once you have closed all open objects, you can exit the program. As with most programs, if you try to exit Access and have not yet saved changes to open objects, Access will prompt you to save your changes. You can use the Help system to learn more about the program and get help. ✎ John has finished working with Access for now, so he closes the Customers table and MediaLoft-A database. Before exiting, he learns more about the Help system, and then exits Access.

1. **Click the Close button for the Customers datasheet**
   The MediaLoft-A database window displays. If you make any structural changes to the datasheet such as moving, resizing, or hiding columns, you will be prompted to save those changes.

2. **Click the Close button for the MediaLoft-A Database, as shown in Figure A-16**
   The MediaLoft-A database is closed, but Access is still running so you could open another database or explore the Help system to learn more about Access at this time.

3. **Click Help on the menu bar, then click Microsoft Access Help**
   The Office Assistant opens and offers to get the help you need. You can further explore some of the concepts you have learned by finding information in the Access Help system. Table A-6 summarizes the options on the Access Help menu, which provides in-depth information on Access features.

4. **Type What is a table, click Search, click Tables: what they are and how they work, then click the graphic as shown in Figure A-17**

5. **Read the information, then click each of the five pages**

6. **Close the Access Help windows**

7. **Click File on the menu bar, then click Exit**
   You have exited Access.

> **Trouble?**
> Do not remove your Project Disk from drive A until you have exited Access.

## CLUES TO USE

### Shutting down your computer

Never shut off a computer before the screen indicates that it is safe to do so. If you shut off a computer during the initial Windows load process (the screen displays the Windows logo and a cloud background at this time) or before the screen indicates that it is safe to do so, you can corrupt your Windows files.

**FIGURE A-16: Closing a database**

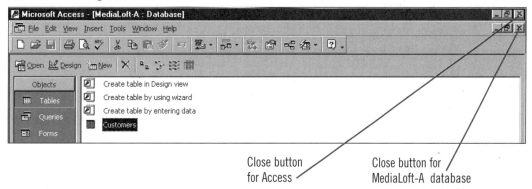

Close button
for Access

Close button for
MediaLoft-A  database

**FIGURE A-17: Access Help window**

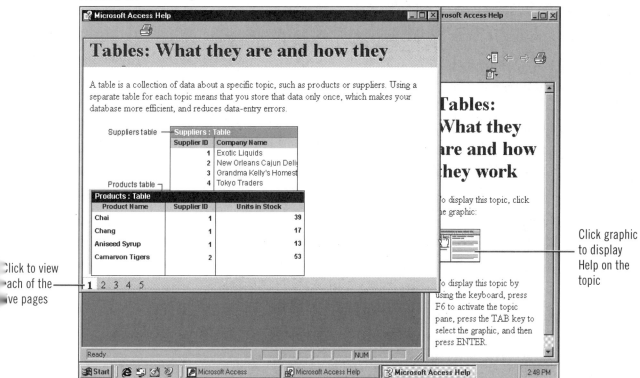

Click to view
each of the
five pages

Click graphic
to display
Help on the
topic

**TABLE A-6: Help menu options**

| menu option | description |
|---|---|
| Microsoft Access Help | Opens the Office Assistant; type a question to open the entire Microsoft Access Help manual in a separate window in which you can search for information by the table of contents, index, or keyword |
| Show the Office Assistant | Presents the Office Assistant, an automated character that provides tips and interactive prompts while you are working |
| Hide the Office Assistant | Temporarily closes the Office Assistant for the working session |
| What's This | Changes the mouse pointer to ⬚?; this special mouse pointer provides a short explanation of the icon or menu option that you click |
| Office on the Web | If you are connected to the Web, provides additional Microsoft information and support articles; this Web-based information is updated daily |
| Detect and Repair | Analyzes a database for possible data corruption and attempts to repair problems |
| About Microsoft Access | Provides the version and product ID of Access |

# Practice

## ► Concepts Review

**Label each element of the Access window shown in Figure A-18.**

FIGURE A-18

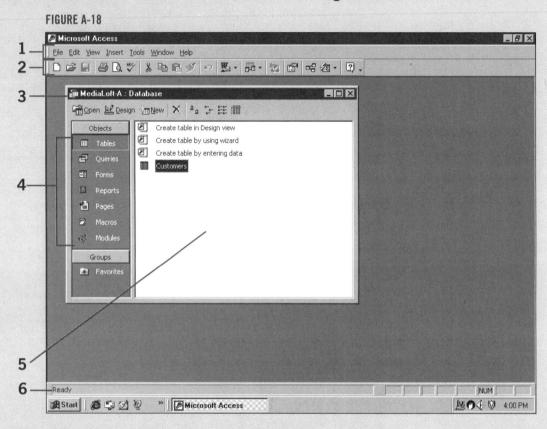

### Match each term with the statement that describes it.

7. Objects
8. Table
9. Record
10. Field
11. Datasheet

a. A group of related fields, such as all the demographic information for one customer
b. A collection of records for a single subject, such as all the customer records
c. A category of information in a table, such as a customer's name, city, or state
d. A spreadsheet-like grid that displays fields as columns and records as rows
e. Seven types of these are contained in an Access database and are used to enter, enhance, and use the data within the database

### Select the best answer from the list of choices.

12. Which of the following is NOT a typical benefit of relational databases?
   a. Easier data entry
   b. Faster information retrieval
   c. Minimized duplicate data entry
   d. Automatic trend analysis

13. Which of the following is NOT an advantage of managing data with a relational database versus a spreadsheet?
   a. Doesn't require preplanning before data is entered
   b. Allows links between lists of information
   c. Provides greater security
   d. Allows multiple users to enter data simultaneously

14. The object that holds all of the data within an Access database
   a. Query
   b. Table
   c. Form
   d. Report

15. The object that provides an easy-to-use data entry screen
   a. Table
   b. Query
   c. Form
   d. Report

16. This displays messages regarding the current database operation
   a. Status bar
   b. Title bar
   c. Database toolbar
   d. Object tabs

# ► Skills Review

1. **Define database software.**
   a. Identify five disadvantages of using a paper system, such as index cards, to organize database information. Write down your answers to this and the following questions using complete sentences.
   b. Identify five advantages of managing database information in Access versus using a spreadsheet product like Excel.

2. **Learn database terminology.**
   a. Explain the relationship between a field, a record, a table, and a database.
   b. Identify the seven objects of an Access database, and explain the main purpose of each.
   c. Which object of an Access database is most important? Why?

3. **Start Access and open a database.**
   a. Click the Start button, point to Programs, then click Microsoft Access.
   b. Insert your Project Disk into the appropriate disk drive, click the Open an existing file option button, click More Files, then click OK.
   c. In the Open dialog box, choose the correct drive, then open the Recycle-A database file.
   d. Identify the following items. (*Hint*: To create a printout of this screen, press [Print Screen] to capture an image of the screen to the Windows clipboard, start any word-processing program, then click the Paste button. Print the document that now contains a picture of this screen, and identify the elements on the printout.)
      - Database toolbar
      - Recycle-A database window
      - Menu bar
      - Object buttons
      - Objects bar
      - Status bar

4. **View the database window.**
   a. Maximize both the Access window and the Recycle-A Database window.
   b. Click each of the objects, then write down the object names of each type that exist in the Recycle-A database.
      - Tables
      - Queries
      - Reports
      - Pages
      - Macros
      - Modules
      - Forms

5. **Navigate records.**
   a. Open the Clubs table.
   b. Press [Tab] or [Enter] to move through the fields of the first record.
   c. Press [Ctrl][End] to move to the last field of the last record.
   d. Press [Ctrl][Home] to move to the first field of the first record.
   e. Click the Last Record navigation button to quickly move to the Oak Hill Patriots record.

### 6. Enter records.

**a.** In the Clubs table, click the New Record button, then add the following records:

| Name | Street | City | State | Zip | Phone | Leader | Club Number |
|------|--------|------|-------|-----|-------|--------|-------------|
| EBC Angels | 10100 Metcalf | Overland Park | KS | 66001 | 555-7711 | Michael Garrett | 8 |
| MOT Friends | 111 Holmes | Kansas City | MO | 65001 | 555-8811 | Aaron Goldstein | 9 |

**b.** Move the Club Number field from the last column of the datasheet to the first column.

### 7. Edit records.

**a.** Change the Name field in the first record from "Jaycees" to "JC Club."

**b.** Change the Name field in the second record from "Boy Scouts #1" to "Oxford Cub Scouts."

**c.** Change the Leader field in the fifth record from "Melanie Perry" to "Melanie Griffiths."

**d.** Enter your name and personal information (make up a club name) as a new record, and enter 99 as the Club Number.

**e.** Delete the record for Club Number 8.

### 8. Preview and print a datasheet.

**a.** Preview the Clubs table datasheet.

**b.** Use the Page Setup option on the File menu to change the page orientation from portrait to landscape.

**c.** Print the Clubs table datasheet.

### 9. Get Help and exit Access.

**a.** Close the Clubs table object, saving the changes.

**b.** Close the Recycle-A database.

**c.** Use Office Assistant to learn more about creating a database.

**d.** Exit Access.

## ▶ Independent Challenges

**1.** Ten examples of databases are given below. For each example, write a brief answer for the following.

**a.** What field names would you expect to find in this database?

**b.** Provide an example of two possible records for each database.

- Telephone directory
- College course offerings
- Restaurant menu
- Cookbook
- Movie listing
- Encyclopedia
- Shopping catalog
- Corporate inventory
- Party guest list
- Members of the House of Representatives

**2.** You are working with several civic groups in your area to coordinate a community-wide cleanup effort. You have start a database called "Recycle-A" that tracks the clubs, their trash deposits, and the trash centers that are participating in this effo To complete this independent challenge:

**a.** Start Access.

**b.** Open the Recycle-A database from your Project Disk, and determine the number of objects of each type that ex in the database:

- Tables
- Queries
- Reports
- Pages
- Macros
- Modules
- Forms

**c.** Open the Deposits table, and answer the following questions:
- How many fields does the table have?
- How many records are there in the table?

**d.** Close the table, then exit Access.

**3.** You are working with several civic groups in your area to coordinate a community-wide cleanup effort. You have started a database called "Recycle-A" that tracks the clubs, their trash deposits, and the trash centers that are participating in this effort.

To complete this independent challenge:

**a.** Start Access and open the Recycle-A database from your Project Disk.

**b.** Add the following records to the Clubs table:

| Club Number | Name | Street | City | State | Zip | Phone | Leader |
| --- | --- | --- | --- | --- | --- | --- | --- |
| 10 | Take Pride | 222 Switzer St. | Olathe | KS | 66001 | 555-2211 | David Reis |
| 11 | Cub Scouts #321 | 333 Ward Pkwy. | Kansas City | MO | 65002 | 555-8811 | Daniel Langguth |

**c.** Edit the following records in the Clubs table. The Street field has changed for Club Number 6 and the Phone and Leader fields have changed for Club Number 7.

| Club Number | Name | Street | City | State | Zip | Phone | Leader |
| --- | --- | --- | --- | --- | --- | --- | --- |
| 6 | Girl Scouts #1 | 55 Oak Terrace | Shawnee | KS | 68777 | 555-4444 | Jonathan Bacon |
| 7 | Oak Hill Patriots | 888 Switzer | Overland Park | KS | 66444 | 555-9988 | Cynthia Ralston |

**d.** If you haven't already, add your name and personal information (make up a club name) and enter 99 as the Club Number. Print the datasheet.

**e.** Close the table, close the database, then exit Access.

**4.** The World Wide Web can be used to collect or research information that is used in corporate databases. MediaLoft often uses their intranet for this purpose. An intranet is a group of connected networks owned by a company or organization that is used for internal purposes. Intranets use internet software to handle the data communications, such as e-mail and Web pages, within an organization. These pages often provide company-wide information. MediaLoft has developed a Web page on the intranet that provides information about their products and customers. Eventually, MediaLoft will tie these Web pages directly to their database so that the information is dynamically tied to their working database. In this exercise, you'll retrieve the new customer information recorded on the intranet Web page, and enter it directly into the MediaLoft-A database.

To complete this independent challenge:

**a.** Connect to the Internet, and use your browser to go to the Medialoft intranet site at
http://www.course.com/illustrated/MediaLoft/

**b.** Click the link for Our Customers.

**c.** Print the page that shows the information for the two new customers.

**d.** Disconnect from the Internet.

**e.** Start Access and open the MediaLoft-A database.

**f.** Open the Customers table.

**g.** Add the new customers to the table. They will become records 30 and 31. Add your name to the table with your personal information as record 32.

**h.** Review your work, print the datasheet, close the MediaLoft A-database, then exit Access.

## ▶ Visual Workshop

Open the Recycle-A database on your Project Disk. Modify the existing Centers table, and enter a new record using your name as the contact and Center Number 99. The Street field for the first record has changed, the Hazardous field for the first two records has changed, and two new records have been added to the datasheet. See Figure A-19. Print the datasheet.

FIGURE A-19

| | Center Number | Name | Street | City | State | Zip | Phone | Contact | Hazard |
|---|---|---|---|---|---|---|---|---|---|
| ⊞ | 1 | Trash 'R Us | 989 Main | Lenexa | KS | 61111 | 555-7777 | Ben Cartwright | ☐ |
| ⊞ | 2 | You Deliver | 12345 College | Overland Park | KS | 63444 | 555-2222 | Jerry Magliano | ☐ |
| ⊞ | 3 | County Landfill | 12444 Pflumm | Lenexa | KS | 64222 | 555-4422 | Jerry Lewis | ☐ |
| ⊞ | 4 | Cans and Stuff | 543 Holmes | Kansas City | MO | 60011 | 555-2347 | Julee Burton | ☑ |
| ⊞ | 5 | We Love Trash | 589 Switzer | Kansas City | KS | 60022 | 555-3456 | Doug Morrison | ☑ |
| * | | | | | | | | | ☐ |

Centers : Table

Record: |◄ ◄ 1 ► ►| ►* of 5

# Using
## Tables and Queries

### Objectives

- MOUS ► **Plan a database**
- MOUS ► **Create a table**
- MOUS ► **Use Table Design view**
- MOUS ► **Format a datasheet**
- MOUS ► **Understand sorting, filtering, and finding**
- MOUS ► **Sort records and find data**
- MOUS ► **Filter records**
- MOUS ► **Create a query**
- MOUS ► **Use Query Design view**

Now that you are familiar with some of the basic Access terminology and features, you are ready to plan and build your own database. Your first task is to create the tables that store the data. Once the tables are created and the data is entered, you can use several techniques for finding specific information in the database, including sorting, filtering, and building queries. ✐ John Kim wants to build and maintain a database containing information about MediaLoft's products. The information in the database will be useful when John provides information for future sales promotions.

# Planning a Database

The first and most important object in a database is the table object because it contains the **raw data**, the individual pieces of information stored in individual fields in the database. When you design a table, you identify the fields of information the table will contain and the type of data to be stored in each field. Some databases contain multiple tables linked together. John plans his database containing information about MediaLoft's products.

### In planning a database it is important to:

### Determine the purpose of the database and give it a meaningful name

The database will store information about MediaLoft's music products. You decide to name the database "MediaLoft," and name the first table "Music Inventory."

### Determine what reports you want the database to produce

You want to be able to print inventory reports that list the products by artist, type of product (CD or cassette), quantity in stock, and price. These pieces of information will become the fields in the Music Inventory table.

### Collect the raw data that will be stored in the database

The raw data for MediaLoft's products might be stored on index cards, in paper reports, and in other electronic formats, such as word-processed documents and spreadsheets. You can use Access to import data from many other electronic sources, which greatly increases your data entry efficiency.

### Sketch the structure of each table, including field names and data types

Using the data you collected, identify the field name and data type for each field in each table as shown in Figure B-1. The **data type** determines what type of information you can enter in a field. For example, a field with a Currency data type does accept text. Properly defining the data type for each field helps you maintain data consistency and accuracy. Table B-1 lists the data types available within Access.

## Choosing between the text and number data type

When assigning data types, you should avoid choosing "number" for a telephone or zip code field. Although these fields generally contain numbers, they should still be text data types. Consider the following: You may want to enter 1-800-BUY-BOOK in a telephone number field. This would not be possible if the field were designated as a number data type. When you sort the fields, you'll want them to sort alphabetically, like text fields. Consider the following zip codes: 60011 and 50011-8888. If the zip code field were designated as a number data type, the zip codes would be interpreted incorrectly as the values 60,011 and 500,118,888; and sort in that order, too.

| Field Name | Data Type |
|---|---|
| RecordingID | AutoNumber |
| RecordingTitle | Text |
| RecordingArtist | Text |
| MusicCategory | Text |
| RecordingLabel | Text |
| Format | Text |
| NumberofTracks | Number |
| PurchasePrice | Currency |
| RetailPrice | Currency |
| Notes | Memo |

TABLE B-1: Data types

| data type | description of data | size |
|---|---|---|
| Text | Text information or combinations of text and numbers, such as a street address, name, or phone number | Up to 255 characters |
| Memo | Lengthy text such as comments or notes | Up to 64,000 characters |
| Number | Numeric information used in calculations, such as quantities | Several sizes available to store numbers with varying degrees of precision |
| Date/Time | Dates and times | Size controlled by Access to accommodate dates and times across thousands of years (for example, 1/1/1850 and 1/1/2150 are valid dates) |
| Currency | Monetary values | Size controlled by Access; accommodates up to 15 digits to the left of the decimal point and 4 digits to the right |
| AutoNumber | Integers assigned by Access to sequentially order each record added to a table | Size controlled by Access |
| Yes/No | Only one of two values stored (Yes/No, On/Off, True/False) | Size controlled by Access |
| OLE Object | Pointers stored that link files created in other programs, such as pictures, sound clips, documents, or spreadsheets | Up to one gigabyte |
| Hyperlink | Web addresses | Size controlled by Access |
| Lookup Wizard | Invokes a wizard that helps link the current table to another table (the final data type of the field is determined by choices made in the wizard; a field created with the lookup data type will display data from another table) | Size controlled through the choices made in the Lookup Wizard |

# Creating a Table

After you plan the structure of the database, your next step is to create the database file itself, which will eventually contain all of the objects such as tables, queries, forms, and reports. When you create a database, first you name it, and then you can build the first table object and enter data. Access offers several methods for creating a table. For example, you can import a table from another data source such as a spreadsheet, or use the Access **Table Wizard**, which provides interactive help to create the field names and data types for each field. John is ready to create the MediaLoft database. He uses the Table Wizard to create the Music Inventory table.

## Steps 1 2 3 4

1. Start Access, click the **Blank Access database option button** in the Microsoft Access dialog box, then click **OK**
   The File New Database dialog box opens.

2. Type **MediaLoft** in the File name text box, insert your Project Disk in the appropriate drive, click the **Save in list arrow**, click the **drive**, then click **Create**
   The MediaLoft database file is created and saved on your Project Disk. The Table Wizard offers an efficient way to plan the fields of a new table.

3. If the Office Assistant appears on your screen, click **Help** on the menu bar, click **Hide the Office Assistant**, then double-click **Create table by using wizard** in the MediaLoft Database window
   The Table Wizard dialog box opens, as shown in Figure B-2. The Table Wizard offers 25 business and 20 personal sample tables from which you can select sample fields. The Recordings sample table, which is in the Personal category of tables, most closely matches the fields you want to include in the Music Inventory table.

4. Click the **Personal option button**, scroll down and click **Recordings** in the Sample Tables list box, then click the **Select All Fields button** >>
   Your Table Wizard dialog box should look like Figure B-3. At this point, you can change the suggested field names to better match your database.

5. Click **RecordingArtistID** in the Fields in my new table list box, click **Rename Field**, type **RecordingArtist** in the Rename field text box, then click **OK**

6. Click **Next**
   The second Table Wizard dialog box allows you to name the table and determine if Access sets the **primary key field**, a field that contains unique information for each record.

7. Type **Music Inventory**, make sure the **Yes, set a primary key for me option button** selected, click **Next**, click the **Modify the table design option button**, then click **Finish**
   The table opens in **Design view**, shown in Figure B-4, which allows you to add, delete, modify the fields in the table. The primary **key field symbol** indicates that the Recording field has been designated as the primary key field.

### Trouble?

If you don't see all the fields in the table, it is because you have different settings on your monitor. Maximize the window to see all the fields, if necessary.

**FIGURE B-2: Table Wizard**

Business and personal categories

Sample fields for the selected table

Select All Fields button

Sample tables

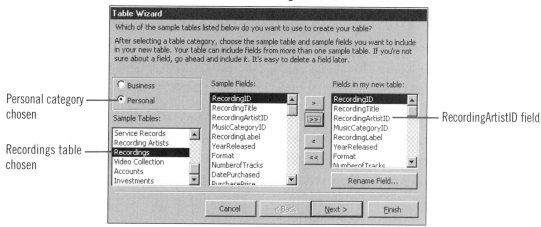

**FIGURE B-3: Table Wizard with Recordings table fields**

Personal category chosen

Recordings table chosen

RecordingArtistID field

**FIGURE B-4: Music Inventory table in Design view**

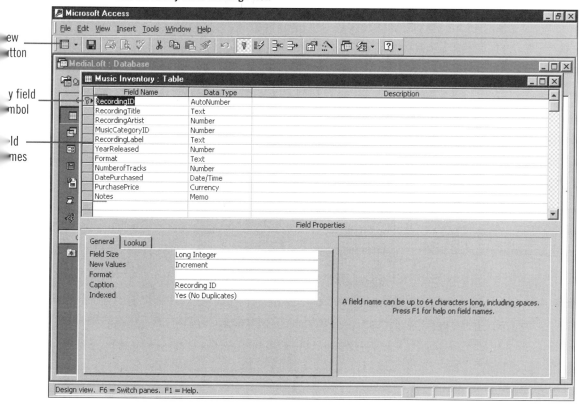

ew
tton

y field
mbol

ld
mes

# Using Table Design View

Each database object has a **Design view** in which you can modify its structure. The Design view of a table allows you to add or delete fields, add **field descriptions**, or change other field properties. **Field properties** are additional characteristics of a field such as its size or default value. Using the Table Wizard, John was able to create a Music Inventory table very quickly. Now in Design view he modifies the fields to meet his needs. MediaLoft doesn't track purchase dates or release dates, but it does need to store retail price information in the database.

**Steps**

1. In the Music Inventory table's Design view, click **DatePurchased** in the Field Name column, click the **Delete Rows button** on the Table Design toolbar, click the **Year Released row selector**, click to delete the field, click the **Notes** field, then click the **Insert Rows button**

   The Year Released and Date Purchased fields are deleted from the table and a new row appears in which you can add the new field name.

2. Type **RetailPrice**, press [Tab], type **C** (for Currency data type), then press [Enter]

   The new field is added to the Music Inventory table, as shown in Figure B-5. The data type of both the RecordingArtist and MusicCategoryID fields should be Text so that descriptive words can be entered in these fields rather than just numbers.

3. Click the **Number** data type in the RecordingArtist field, click the **Data Type list arrow**, click **Text**, click the **Number** data type in the MusicCategoryID field, click the **Data Type list arrow**, then click **Text**

   You must work in the table's Design view to make structural changes to the table.

4. Click to the right of **MusicCategoryID**, press [Backspace] twice, then click the **Save button** on the Table Design toolbar

   A description identifies a field and can list the types of data in that field.

5. Click the **MusicCategory Description cell**, then type **classical, country, folk, gospel, jazz, new age, rap, or rock**

   The **field size property** limits the number of characters allowed for each field.

6. Make sure the **MusicCategory** field is still selected, double-click **50** in the Field Size cell, then type **9**

   The longest entry in the MusicCategory field, "classical," is only nine characters. The finished Music Inventory table Design view should look like Figure B-6.

7. Click the **Datasheet View button** on the Table Design toolbar, click **Yes** to save the table, then type the following record into the new datasheet:

   | in field: | type: | in field: | type: |
   |---|---|---|---|
   | Recording ID | [Tab] | Format | CD |
   | Recording Title | No Words | Number of Tracks | 12 |
   | RecordingArtist | Brickman, Jim | Purchase Price | $10.00 |
   | Music Category ID | New Age | RetailPrice | $13.00 |
   | Recording Label | Windham Hill | Notes | |

   You are finished working with the MediaLoft database for now.

8. Close the Music Inventory table, then close the MediaLoft database

   Data is saved automatically, so you were not prompted to save the record when you closed the datasheet.

FIGURE B-5: Music Inventory table with new RetailPrice field

YearReleased field deleted

DatePurchased field deleted

RetailPrice field added

RetailPrice field is selected

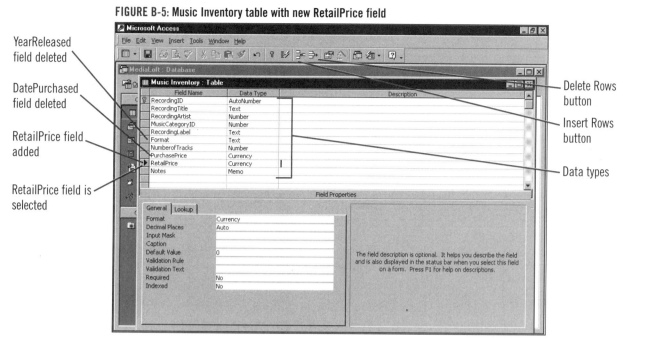

Delete Rows button

Insert Rows button

Data types

FIGURE B-6: Description and field size properties for MusicCategory field

Row selector

MusicCategory field is selected

Field size property changed to 9

Field Properties section

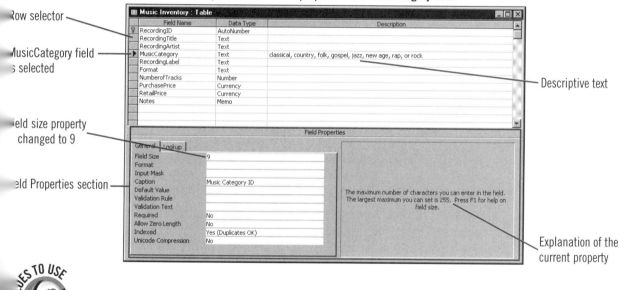

Descriptive text

Explanation of the current property

## Learning about field properties

The properties of a field are the characteristics that define the field. Two properties are required for every field: Field Name and Data Type. Many other properties, such as Field Size, Format (the way the field is displayed on the datasheet), Caption, and Default Value, are defined in the Field Properties section of the table's Design view. As you add more property entries, you are generally restricting the amount or type of data that can be entered in the field, which also increases data entry accuracy. For example, you might change the Field Size property for a State field from the default value of 50 to 2 to eliminate an incorrect entry such as "NYY." The available field properties change depending on the data type of the selected field. For example, there is no Field Size property for a Birth Date field, because Access controls the size of fields with a Date/Time data type. Database designers often insist on field names without spaces because they are easier to reference in other Access objects. The **Caption property**, however, can be used to override the technical field name with an easy-to-read Caption entry when the field name is displayed on datasheets, forms, and reports. When you create a table using the wizard, many fields have Caption properties.

# Formatting a Datasheet

Even though the report object is the primary tool to create professional hard copy output from an Access database, you can print a datasheet too. Although you cannot create fancy headings or insert graphic images on a datasheet, you can change the fonts and colors as well as change the gridlines to dramatically change its appearance. ✎ John has been busy entering MediaLoft's music information in the Music Inventory table (which is stored in the MediaLoft-B database). He has also simplified many of the field names. Now he will print the Music Inventory datasheet using new fonts and colors.

## Steps 1234

1. Click the **Open button** 📂 on the Database toolbar, select the **MediaLoft-B** database from your Project Disk, then click **Open**
   The Music Inventory table has data that was entered by John Kim.

### QuickTip
You can double-click a table object to open it in Datasheet view.

2. Click **Music Inventory** in the Tables Object window, then click the **Open button** 🖼
   Access displays the Music Inventory table, containing 58 records, as shown in Figure B-7. You can change the font and color of the datasheet to enhance its appearance.

3. Click **Format** on the menu bar, click **Font**, click **Comic Sans MS** in the Font list, then click **OK**
   Comic Sans MS is an informal font used for personal correspondence or internal memos. It simulates handwritten text, but is still very readable. You can also change the color and format of the datasheet gridlines.

4. Click **Format** on the menu bar, click **Datasheet**, click the **Gridline Color list arrow** then click **Red**
   The Sample box in the Datasheet Formatting dialog box displays both the vertical and horizontal gridlines as red.

5. Click the **Border list arrow**, click **Vertical Gridline**, click the **Line Styles list arrow**, click **Transparent Border**, as shown in Figure B-8, then click **OK**
   You removed the vertical gridlines separating the fields. You can also change the left and right margins, and change the page orientation from portrait to landscape to fit all the fields across the page.

6. Click **File** on the menu bar, click **Page Setup**, double-click **1"** in the Top text box, type **0.75**, press **[Tab]**, type **0.75** in the Bottom text box, press **[Tab]**, type **0.75** in the Left text box, press **[Tab]**, type **0.75** in the Right text box, click the **Page tab**, click the **Landscape option button**, then click **OK**
   Print Preview displays your formatted datasheet as it will look when printed.

7. Click the **Print Preview button** 🔍 on the Table Datasheet toolbar to preview the finished product, as shown in Figure B-9
   The red gridlines seem a bit too intense for your printout.

8. Click the **Close button** 🔲 on the Print Preview toolbar, click **Format** on the menu bar, click **Datasheet**, click the **Gridline Color list arrow**, click **Silver**, then click **OK**
   Silver is the default gridline color.

Music Inventory : Table

| RecordingID | Title | Artist | Category | Label | Format |
|---|---|---|---|---|---|
| 1 | Gravity | Cook, Jesse | New Age | Columbia | CD |
| 2 | Come Walk With Me | Adams, Oleta | Gospel | CBS Records | CD |
| 3 | Greatest Hits | Winans, BeBe & C | Gospel | Benson | Vinyl |
| 4 | Tribute | Yanni | New Age | MCA | CD |
| 5 | World Café | Tree Frogs | Rap | New Stuff | CD |
| 6 | Relationships | Winans, BeBe & C | Gospel | Capitol | CD |
| 7 | No Words | Brickman, Jim | New Age | Windham Hill | CD |
| 8 | God's Property | Nu Nation | Rap | B-Rite Music | Cassette |
| 9 | Message | 4 Him | Gospel | Benson | CD |
| 10 | Sacred Road | Lantz, David | New Age | Narada | Cassette |
| 11 | Mariah Carey | Carey, Mariah | Rock | Columbia | CD |
| 12 | Ironman Triathlon | Tesh, John | New Age | GTS Records | Cassette |
| 13 | Daydream | Carey, Mariah | Rock | Columbia | CD |
| 14 | Heartsounds | Lantz, David | New Age | Narada | CD |
| 15 | The Roches | Roches, The | Folk | Warner Bros. Reco | Cassette |
| 16 | Can We Go Home Now | Roches, The | Folk | Ryko | CD |
| 17 | Live at the Red Rocks | Tesh, John | New Age | GTS Records | CD |
| 18 | I'll Lead You Home | Smith, Michael | Gospel | Reunion | CD |
| 19 | Winter Song | Tesh, John | New Age | GTS Records | CD |
| 20 | December | Winston, George | New Age | Windham | CD |
| 21 | Time, Love & Tenderness | Bolton, Michael | Rock | Sony Music | CD |
| 22 | Autumn | Winston, George | New Age | Windham | Vinyl |

Record: 1 of 58

FIGURE B-8: Datasheet Formatting dialog box

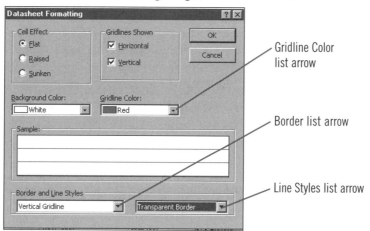

- Gridline Color list arrow
- Border list arrow
- Line Styles list arrow

FIGURE B-9: Previewing the formatted datasheet

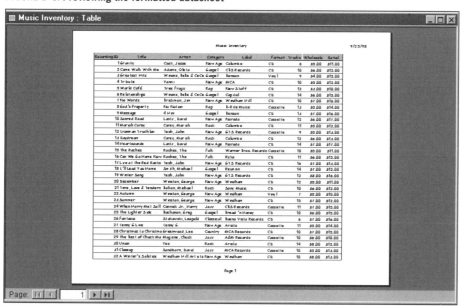

# Understanding Sorting, Filtering, and Finding

The records of a datasheet are automatically sorted according to the data in the primary key field. Often, however, you'll want to view or print records in an entirely different sort order. Or you may want to display a subset of the records, such as those within the same music category or those below a certain retail price. Access makes it easy to sort, find data, and filter a datasheet with buttons on the Table Datasheet toolbar, summarized in Table B-2. John studies the sort, find, and filter features to learn how to find and retrieve information in his database.

 **Sorting** refers to reorganizing the records in either ascending or descending order based on the contents of a field. Text fields sort from A to Z, number fields from the lowest to the highest value, and date/time fields from the oldest date to the date furthest into the future. In Figure B-10 the Music Inventory table has been sorted in ascending order on the Artist field. Notice that numbers sort before letters in an ascending sort order.

 **Filtering** means temporarily isolating a subset of records, as shown in Figure B-11. This is particularly useful because the subset can be formatted and printed just like the entire datasheet. You can produce a listing of all rock music or a listing based on any category, artist, or field in the datasheet. To remove a filter, click the Remove Filter button to view all the records in the datasheet.

 **Finding** refers to locating a specific piece of data, such as "Amy" or "500," within a field or an entire datasheet, similar to finding text in a word-processing document. The Find and Replace dialog box is shown in Figure B-12. The options in this dialog box are summarized below.

- **Find What:** Provides a text box for your search criteria. For example, you might want to find the text "Amy", "Beatles", or "Capitol Records" in the datasheet.

- **Look In:** Determines whether Access looks for the search criteria in the current field (in this case the Artist field) or in all fields.

- **Match:** Determines whether the search criteria must match the whole field's content exactly, any part of the field, or the start of the field.

- **More:** Provides more options to limit your search. For example, it allows you to make your search criteria uppercase- or lowercase-sensitive.

- **Replace tab:** Provides a text box for you to specify "replacement text." In other words, you might want to search for every occurrence of "Compact Disc" and replace it with "CD" by entering "Compact Disc" as your search criteria and "CD" as your replacement text.

**TABLE B-2: Sort, Filter, and Find buttons**

| name | button | purpose |
|---|---|---|
| Sort Ascending | | Sorts records based on the selected field in ascending order (0 to 9, A to Z) |
| Sort Descending | | Sorts records based on the selected field in descending order (Z to A, 9 to 0) |
| Filter By Selection | | Filters records based on selected data and hides records that do not match |
| Filter By Form | | Filters records based on more than one selection criteria by using the Filter By Form window |
| Apply Filter or Remove Filter | | Applies or removes the filter |
| Find | | Searches for a string of characters in the current field or all fields |

FIGURE B-10: Records sorted in ascending order by Artist

Records sorted in
ascending order
by Artist

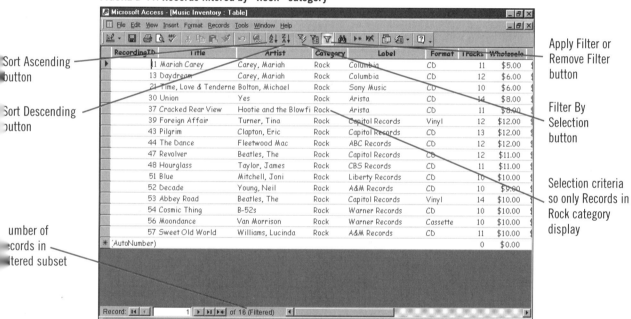

FIGURE B-11: Records filtered by "Rock" category

Sort Ascending
button

Sort Descending
button

umber of
ecords in
ltered subset

Apply Filter or
Remove Filter
button

Filter By
Selection
button

Selection criteria
so only Records in
Rock category
display

FIGURE B-12: Find and Replace dialog box

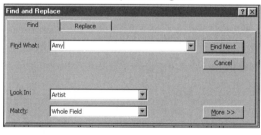

## Using wildcards in Find

Wildcards are symbols you can use as substitutes for characters to find information that matches your find criteria. Access uses these wildcards: the asterisk (*) represents any group of characters, the question mark (?) stands for any single character, and the pound sign (#) stands for a single number digit. For example, to find any word beginning with "S," type "s*" in the Find What text box.

# Sorting Records and Finding Data

Sorting records and quickly finding information in a database are two powerful tools that help you work more efficiently. ⬤ John needs to create several different printouts of the Music Inventory datasheet to satisfy various departments. The Marketing department wants a printout of records sorted by title and artist. The Accounting department wants a printout of records sorted from highest retail price to lowest.

## Steps 1 2 3 4

1. In the Music Inventory datasheet, click **any cell** in the Title field, then click the **Sort Ascending button** ⬆ on the Table Datasheet toolbar
   The records are listed in an A-to-Z sequence based on the data in the Title field, as shown in Figure B-13. Next you'll sort the records according to artist.

2. Click **any cell** in the Artist field, then click ⬆
   The table is sorted alphabetically in ascending order by Artist. You can preview and print a sorted datasheet at any time.

**QuickTip**

Scroll to the right if necessary to see this field.

3. Click **any cell** in the Retail field, then click the **Sort Descending button** ⬇ on the Table Datasheet toolbar
   The records are sorted in descending order on the value in the Retail field. The CD that sells for the highest retail price, "Skyline Firedance," is listed as the first record. To put the records back in their original order, you can click the key field, RecordingID, and click the Sort Ascending button. Access also lets you find all records based on any search word.

4. Click **any cell** in the Title field, then click the **Find button** 🔍 on the Table Datasheet toolbar
   The Find and Replace dialog box opens. You know MediaLoft will want to find the titles that are going to be hot sellers during the Christmas season.

5. Type **Christmas** in the Find What text box, click the **Match list arrow**, then click **Any Part of Field**, as shown in Figure B-14
   Access will find all occurrences of the word "Christmas" in the Title field, whether it is the first, middle, or last part of the title. "Christmas" is the search criteria.

6. Click **Find Next**, then if necessary drag the Find and Replace dialog box up and to the right to better view the datasheet
   If you started the search at the top of the datasheet, "A Family Christmas" is the first title found. You can look for more occurrences of "Christmas."

7. Click **Find Next** to find the next occurrence of the word "Christmas," then click **Find Next** as many times as it takes to move through all the records
   When no more occurrences of the search criteria "Christmas" are found, Access lets you know that no more matching records can be found.

8. Click **OK** when prompted that Access has finished searching the records, then click **Cancel** to close the Find and Replace dialog box

| Music Inventory : Table | | | | | | |
|---|---|---|---|---|---|---|
| RecordingID | Title | Artist | Category | Label | Format | Tracks |
| 55 | A Christmas Album | Grant, Amy | Folk | Reunion Records | CD | 11 |
| 46 | A Family Christmas | Tesh, John | New Age | GTS Records | CD | 14 |
| 32 | A Winter's Solstice | Windham Hill Artists | New Age | Windham | CD | 10 |
| 53 | Abbey Road | Beatles, The | Rock | Capitol Records | Vinyl | 14 |
| 22 | Autumn | Winston, George | New Age | Windham | Vinyl | 7 |
| 51 | Blue | Mitchell, Joni | Rock | Liberty Records | CD | 10 |
| 16 | Can We Go Home Now | Roches, The | Folk | Ryko | CD | 11 |
| 35 | Christmas | Mannheim Steamroller | New Age | Sony Music | CD | 11 |
| 28 | Christmas to Christmas | Greenwood, Lee | Country | MCA Records | CD | 10 |
| 31 | Closeup | Sandborn, David | Jazz | MCA Records | Cassette | 10 |
| 2 | Come Walk With Me | Adams, Oleta | Gospel | CBS Records | CD | 10 |
| 54 | Cosmic Thing | B-52s | Rock | Warner Records | CD | 10 |
| 37 | Cracked Rear View | Hootie and the Blowfi | Rock | Arista | CD | 11 |
| 13 | Daydream | Carey, Mariah | Rock | Columbia | CD | 12 |
| 52 | Decade | Young, Neil | Rock | A&M Records | CD | 10 |
| 20 | December | Winston, George | New Age | Windham | CD | 12 |
| 26 | Fantasia | Stokowski, Leopold | Classical | Buena Vista Records | CD | 6 |
| 40 | Favorite Overtures | Bernstein, Leonard | Classical | CBS Records | Vinyl | 5 |
| 39 | Foreign Affair | Turner, Tina | Rock | Capitol Records | Vinyl | 12 |
| 42 | Garth Brooks Live | Brooks, Garth | Country | Liberty Records | CD | 10 |

Record: 1 of 58

Records are sorted in
ascending order by Title

FIGURE B-14: Specify "Christmas" as the search criteria in the Title field

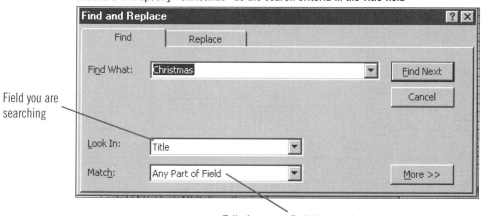

Find and Replace

Find | Replace

Fin_d What: Christmas

Find Next

Cancel

Field you are
searching

Look In: Title

Match: Any Part of Field

More >>

Tells Access to find the search
criteria anywhere in the selected field

## Sorting on more than one field

he telephone book sorts records by last name (**pri-mary sort field**) and when ties occur on the last name (for example, two "Smiths"), it further sorts the records by first name (**secondary sort field**). Access lows you to sort by more than one field using the query object, which you will learn more about later in this unit. Queries allow you to specify more than one sort field in Query Design view, evaluating the sort orders from left to right (the leftmost sort field is the primary sort field).

# Filtering Records

Sorting allows you to reorder all the records of a datasheet. Filtering the datasheet displays only those records that match criteria. **Criteria** are rules or limiting conditions you set. For example, you may want to show only those records where the Category field is equal to "Rap," or where the PurchasePrice field is less than $10. Once you have filtered a datasheet to display a subset of records, you can still sort the records and find data just as if you were working with the entire datasheet. To make sure the Filter By Form grid is clear of any previous entries, you should click the Clear Grid button ⊠. The Accounting department asked John for a printout of cassettes with a retail price of $15 or more. John uses the datasheet's filter buttons to answer this request.

## Steps

1. **In the Music Inventory datasheet, click the RecordingID field, click the Sort Ascending button** 🔼 **on the Table Datasheet toolbar, click any occurrence of Cassette in the Format field, then click the Filter By Selection button** 🏷 **on the Table Datasheet toolbar**
Twelve records are selected, as shown in Figure B-15. Filter By Selection is a fast and easy way to filter the records for an exact match (that is, where Format field value is *equal to* Cassette). To filter for comparative data and to specify more complex criteria (for example where PurchasePrice is *equal to* or *greater than* $15), you must use the Filter By Form feature. See Table B-3 for more information on comparison operators.

> **QuickTip**
>
> If you click the Field List arrow, you can pick an entry from a list of existing entries in that field.

2. **Click the Filter By Form button** 🏷 **on the Table Datasheet toolbar, click the Retail field, then type >=15**
The finished Filter By Form window is shown in Figure B-16. The previous Filter By Selection criteria, "Cassette" in the Format field, is still valid in the grid. Access distinguishes between text and numeric entries by placing quotation marks around text entries. You can widen a column to display the entire criteria. Filter By Form is more powerful than Filter By Selection because it allows you to use comparison operators such as >=. Filter By Form also allows you to enter criteria for more than one field at a time where *both* criteria must be "true" in order for the record to be shown in the resulting datasheet.

3. **Click the Apply Filter button** 🏷 **on the Filter/Sort toolbar, then scroll to the right to display the Retail field**
Only two records are true for both criteria, as shown in Figure B-17. The Record Navigation buttons in the lower-left corner of the datasheet display how many records are in the filtered subset. You can remove the current filter to view all the records in the datasheet at any time by clicking the Remove Filter button.

4. **Click the Remove Filter button** 🏷 **on the Table Datasheet toolbar**
Be sure to remove existing filters before you apply a new filter or you will end up filtering the existing subset of records versus the entire datasheet. Next find all selections produced under the "A&M Records" recording label.

5. **Click any cell in the Label field, click** 🔼**, A&M Records is selected as the Label entry, then click** 🏷
Using both the sort and filter buttons, you quickly found the five records that met the "A&M Records" criteria.

6. **Close the datasheet, then click Yes if prompted to save the changes to the Music Inventory table**
Any filters applied to a datasheet will be removed the next time you open the datasheet, the sort order will be saved.

FIGURE B-15: Music Inventory datasheet filtered for "Cassette" records

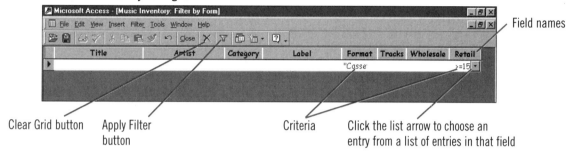

12 records are selected

All records have Cassette in Format field

FIGURE B-16: Filter By Form grid

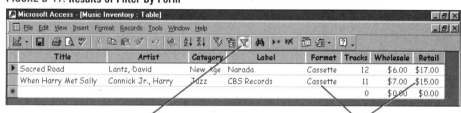

Field names

Clear Grid button

Apply Filter button

Criteria

Click the list arrow to choose an entry from a list of entries in that field

FIGURE B-17: Results of Filter By Form

Filter is applied and the Apply Filter button becomes the Remove Filter button

Both records have Cassette in the Format field and all records have a Retail value >=15

TABLE B-3: Comparison operators

| operator | description | expression | meaning |
|---|---|---|---|
| > | Greater than | >500 | Numbers greater than 500 |
| >= | Greater than or equal to | >=500 | Numbers greater than or equal to 500 |
| < | Less than | <"Bunin" | Names from A through Bunim, but not Bunin |
| <= | Less than or equal to | <="Calloway" | Names from A through, and including, Calloway |
| <> | Not equal to | <>"Cyclone" | Any name except for Cyclone |

TO USE

## Searching for blank fields

Is Null and Is Not Null are two other types of common criteria. Is Null criteria will find all records where no entry has been made in the field. Is Not Null will find all records where there is any entry in the field, even if the entry is 0. Primary key fields cannot have a null entry.

# Creating a Query

A **query** is a database object that creates a datasheet of specified fields and records from one or more tables. It displays the answer to a "question" about the data in your database. You can edit, navigate, sort, find, and filter a query's datasheet just like a table's datasheet. Because a query datasheet is a subset of data, however, it is similar to a filter, but much more powerful. One of the most important differences is that a query is a saved object within the database, which means that it does not need to be recreated each time you want to see that particular subset of data. A **filter** is a temporary view of the data whose criteria is discarded when you remove the filter or close the datasheet. Table B-4 compares the two. ◥▬▬▬▬ John uses a query to correct data in the table and then find all of the music selections in the "country" category.

## Steps 1 2 3 4

**1.** Click **Queries** on the Objects bar, then double-click **Create query by using wizard**
The Simple Query Wizard dialog box opens, allowing you to choose the table or query which contains the fields you want to display in the query. You select the fields in the order you want them to appear on the query datasheet.

**2.** Click **Category** in the Available Fields list, click the **Select Single Field button** `>`, click **Title**, click `>`, click **Artist**, click `>`, click **Tracks**, then click `>`
The Simple Query Wizard dialog box should look like Figure B-18.

**3.** Click **Next**, click **Next** to accept the **Detail option** in the next dialog box, accept the title **Music Inventory Query**, make sure the **Open the query to view information option button** is selected, then click **Finish**
The query's datasheet opens, as shown in Figure B-19, with all 58 records, but with only the four fields that you requested in the query wizard. You can use a query datasheet to edit or add information.

**4.** Double-click **10** in the Tracks cell for record 7, "No Words", then type **11**
This record is now correct in the database.

**5.** Click the **Design View button** 🖉 on the Query Datasheet toolbar
The **Query Design view** opens, showing you a list of fields in the Music Inventory table in the upper portion of the window, and the fields you have requested for the query in the **query design grid** in the lower portion of the window.

**6.** Click the **Criteria cell** for the Category field, then type **country**, as shown in Figure B-2
Query Design view is the view in which you add, delete, or change the order of fields, so the records, or add criteria to limit the number of records shown in the resulting datashe Any change made in Query Design view is saved with the query object.

**7.** Click the **Datasheet View button** 🏢 on the Query Design toolbar
The resulting datasheet has four records that match the criteria "country" in the Catego field. You can save a query with a name that accurately describes the resulting datashe

**8.** Click **File** on the menu bar, click **Save As**, type **Country Music** in the Save Qu 'Music Inventory Query' To text box, click **OK**, then close the query datasheet
Both the Music Inventory Query and Country Music queries are saved in this database objects that you can access in the MediaLoft-B database window.

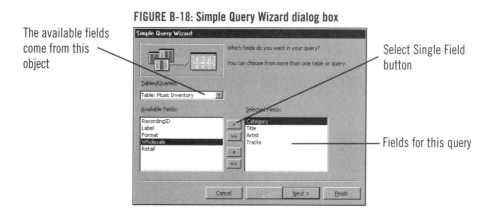

The available fields come from this object

FIGURE B-18: Simple Query Wizard dialog box

Select Single Field button

Fields for this query

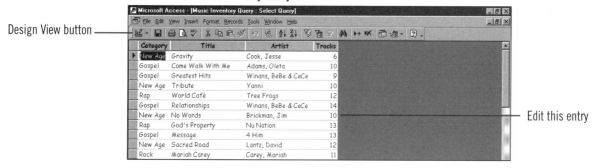

FIGURE B-19: Music Inventory Query datasheet

Design View button

Edit this entry

FIGURE B-20: Query Design view

Datasheet View button

Music Inventory field list

Criteria cell for Category field with country criteria

Query design grid

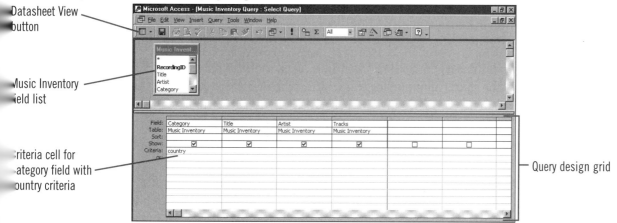

BLE B-4: Queries vs. filters

| aracteristics | filters | queries |
|---|---|---|
| e saved as an object in the database | No | Yes |
| n be used to select a subset of records in a datasheet | Yes | Yes |
| n be used to select a subset of fields in a datasheet | No | Yes |
| resulting datasheet can be used to enter and edit data | Yes | Yes |
| resulting datasheet can be used to sort, filter, and find records | Yes | Yes |
| commonly used as the source of data for a form or report | No | Yes |
| calculate sums, averages, counts, and other types of summary statistics across records | No | Yes |
| be used to create calculated fields | No | Yes |

# Using Query Design View

Every object in the database has a Design view in which you change the structure of the object. You can build a query by using the Query Design view directly or let the Query Wizard help you. In either case, if you want to add criteria to limit the number of records that you view in the datasheet, or if you want to change the fields you are viewing, you must use the query's Design view. ✎▬▬ John wants the Country Music query to also display the Retail field. In addition, he wants to add the folk music records and sort all the records according to the recording artist.

## Steps 1 2 3 4

1. **Click the Country Music query** in the MediaLoft-B Database window, click the **Design button** ☒ in the database window, then click the **Restore button** ⬜ (if the window is maximized)
   Query Design view opens, displaying the current fields and criteria for the Country Music query. To add fields to the query, you can drag the fields from the upper field list and place them in any order in the grid.

> **Trouble?**
> You may have to scroll through the Music Inventory field list to display the Retail field.

2. **Click the Retail field** in the Music Inventory field list, then drag the **Retail field** to the **Tracks Field cell** in the query design grid
   The Query Design view now looks like Figure B-21. The Retail field is added to the query design grid between the Artist and Tracks fields. When you dropped the Retail field into the fourth column position of the query design grid, the Tracks field moved to the right to make room for the new field. You can also change the order of existing fields in the query design grid.

> **QuickTip**
> To remove fields from the query design grid, click the field selector, then press [Delete].

3. In the second column, click **Title**, click the **Title list arrow**, click **Artist**, click **Artist** in the third column, click the **Artist list arrow**, then click **Title**
   You have switched the order of the Title and Artist fields. You can also move fields by dragging them left and right in the query design grid by clicking the field selector, and dragging the field to the new location. The query design grid also displays criteria that limit the number of records in the resulting datasheet.

4. Click the **or: criteria cell** under the "country" criteria of the Category field, then type **folk**
   This additional criteria expression will add the folk selections to the current country selection. You also can enter Or criteria in one cell of the query design grid by entering "country" or "folk" but using two rows of the query design grid inherently joins the criteria in an Or expression.

5. Click the **Sort cell** for the Artist field, click the **Artist Sort list arrow**, then click **Ascending**
   The final Query Design view, as shown in Figure B-22, will find all records that match the Category criteria for "country" or "folk" and sort the records in ascending order by Artist. Notice that text criteria in the query design grid are surrounded by quotation marks (as were filter criteria), but that you did not need to type these characters.

6. Click the **Datasheet view button** ▦ on the Query Design toolbar
   Eight records are displayed in both the country and folk music categories, sorted in ascending order by Artist, as shown in Figure B-23.

7. Click **File** on the menu bar, click **Save As**, type **Country and Folk**, click **OK**, then click the **Print button** 🖨 on the Query Datasheet toolbar

8. Close the query datasheet, close the MediaLoft-B database, then exit Access

**FIGURE B-21: Query Design view with new field, Retail**

Scroll bar for Music Inventory field list

Retail field in Field cell in the fourth column

Field selector

Tracks field moved to the right

Field list arrow

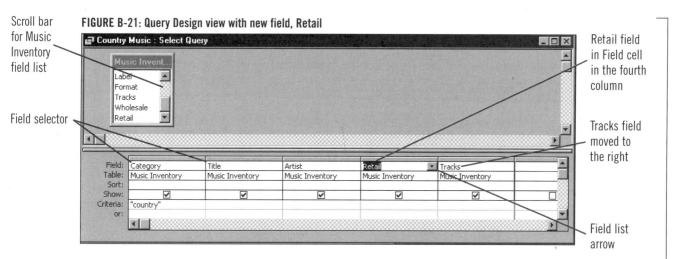

**FIGURE B-22: Adding Or criteria and specifying a sort order**

Field order of Artist and Title fields is changed

Or criteria for the Category field

Sort list arrow

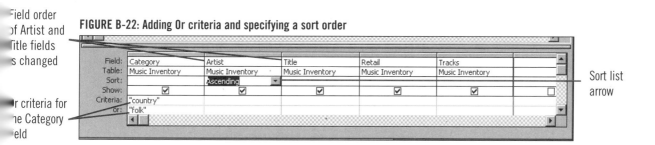

**FIGURE B-23: Final query datasheet**

Only Country or Folk records are displayed

Records are sorted in ascending order by Artist

Eight records are selected

## Understanding And and Or criteria

Criteria placed on different rows of the query design grid are considered Or criteria. In other words, a record may be true for *either* row of criteria in order for it to be displayed on the resulting datasheet. Placing additional criteria in the *same* row, however, is considered the And criteria. For example, if "folk" were in the Category Criteria cell and >10 in the Retail Criteria cell, *both* criteria must be true in order for the record to be displayed in the resulting datasheet.

# Practice

## ► Concepts Review

Label each element of the Select Query window shown in Figure B-24.

FIGURE B-24

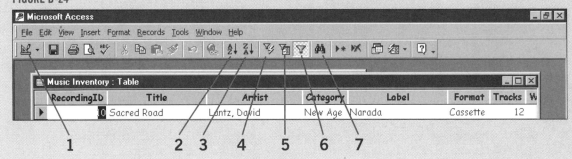

Match each term with the statement that describes it.

8. **Primary key**
9. **Table Wizard**
10. **Filter**
11. **Data type**
12. **Query**

a. Determines what type of data can be stored in each field
b. Provides interactive help to create the field names and data types for each field
c. A database object that creates a datasheet of specified fields and records from one or more tables
d. A field that contains unique information for each record
e. Creates a temporary subset of records

Select the best answer from the list of choices.

13. Which data type would be best for a field that was going to store birth dates?
   a. Text
   b. Number
   c. AutoNumber
   d. Date/Time

14. Which data type would be best for a field that was going to store Web addresses?
   a. Text
   b. Memo
   c. OLE
   d. Hyperlink

15. Which data type would be best for a field that was going to store telephone numbers?
   a. Text
   b. Number
   c. OLE
   d. Hyperlink

16. Each of the following is true about a filter, *except*
   a. It creates a temporary datasheet of records that match criteria.
   b. The resulting datasheet can be sorted.
   c. The resulting datasheet includes all fields in the table.
   d. A filter is automatically saved as an object in the database.

17. Sorting refers to
   a. Reorganizing the records in either ascending or descending order.
   b. Selecting a subset of fields and/or records to view as a datasheet from one or more tables.
   c. Displaying only those records that meet certain criteria.
   d. Using Or and And criteria in the query design grid.

18. Which criteria would be used in a Category field to find all music except that in the rap category?
   **a.** /=/"rap"
   **b.** <>"rap"
   **c.** NULL "rap"
   **d.** IS NULL "rap"

 # Skills Review

### 1. Plan a database.
   **a.** Plan a database that will contain the names and addresses of physicians. You can use the local yellow pages to gather the information.
   **b.** On paper, sketch the Table Design view of a table that will hold this information. Write the field names in one column and the data types for each field in the second column.

### 2. Create a table.
   **a.** Start Access and use the Blank Access database option to create a database. Save the file as "Doctors" on your Project Disk.
   **b.** Use the Table Wizard to create a new table.
   **c.** Make sure the Business option button is selected. In the Sample Tables list, click Contacts.
   **d.** In the Sample Fields list box, choose each of the fields in the following order for your table: ContactID, FirstName, LastName, Address, City, StateOrProvince, PostalCode, Title.
   **e.** Rename the StateOrProvince field as "State."
   **f.** Name the table "Addresses," and allow Access to set the primary key field.
   **g.** Click the Modify the table design option button in the last Table Wizard dialog box, then click Finish.

### 3. Use Table Design view.
   **a.** In the first available blank row, add a new field called "PhoneNumber" with a Text data type.
   **b.** Change the Field Size property of the State field from 20 to 2.
   **c.** Insert a field named "Suite" with a Text data type between the Address and City fields.
   **d.** Add the description "M.D." or "D.O." to the Title field.
   **e.** Save and close the Addresses table, then close the Doctors database, but don't exit Access.

### 4. Format a datasheet.
   **a.** Open the Doctors-B database from your Project Disk. Open the Doctor Addresses table datasheet.
   **b.** Change the font to Arial Narrow, and the font size to 9.
   **c.** Change the gridline color to black, and change the vertical gridline to a transparent border.
   **d.** Change the page orientation to landscape and all of the margins to 0.5". Preview the datasheet (it should fit on one page), then print it.

### 5. Understand sorting, filtering, and finding.
   **a.** On a sheet of paper, identify three ways that you might want to sort an address list, such as the Doctor Addresses datasheet. Be sure to specify both the field you would sort on and the sort order (ascending or descending).
   **b.** On a sheet of paper, identify three ways that you might want to filter an address list, such as the Doctor Addresses datasheet. Be sure to specify both the field you would filter on and the criteria that you would use.

### 6. Sort records and find data.
   **a.** Sort the Doctor Addresses records in ascending order on the Last field, then list the first two doctors on paper.
   **b.** Sort the Doctor Addresses records in descending order on the Zip field, then list the first two doctors on paper.
   **c.** Find the records in which the Title field contains "D.O." How many records did you find?
   **d.** Find the records where the Zip field contains "64012." How many records did you find?

### 7. Filter records.
  **a.** In the Doctor Addresses datasheet, filter the records for all physicians with the Title "D.O."
  **b.** In the Doctor Addresses datasheet, filter the records for all physicians with the title "M.D." in the "64012" zip code, then print the datasheet.

### 8. Create a query.
  **a.** Use the Query Wizard to create a new query based on the Doctor Addresses table with the following fields: First, Last, City, State, Zip.
  **b.** Name the query "Doctors in Missouri," then view the datasheet.
  **c.** In Query Design view, add the criteria "MO" to the State field, then view the datasheet.
  **d.** Change Mark Garver's last name to Garvey.

### 9. Use Query Design view.
  **a.** Modify the Doctors in Missouri query to include only those doctors in Kansas City, Missouri. Be sure that the criteria is in the same row so that both criteria must be true for the record to be displayed.
  **b.** Save the query with the name "Doctors in Kansas City Missouri." Print the query results, then close the query datasheet.
  **c.** Modify the Doctors in Kansas City Missouri query so that the records are sorted in ascending order on the last name, and add "DoctorNumber" as the first field in the datasheet.
  **d.** Print and save the sorted query's datasheet, then close the datasheet.
  **e.** Close the Doctors-B database and exit Access.

## ▶ Independent Challenges

**1.** You want to start a database to track your personal video collection.
To complete this independent challenge:

  **a.** Start Access and create a new database called "Movies" on your Project Disk.
  **b.** Using the Table Wizard, create a table based on the Video Collection sample table in the personal category with the following fields: MovieTitle, YearReleased, Rating, Length, DateAcquired, PurchasePrice.
  **c.** Rename the YearReleased field as "Year" and the PurchasePrice field as "Price."
  **d.** Name the table "Video Collection," and allow Access to set a primary key field.
  **e.** Modify the Video Collection table in Design view with the following changes:
    • Change the Rating field size property to 4.
    • Change the Length field to a Number data type.
    • Change the DateAcquired field name to DatePurchased.
    • Add a field between Rating and Length called "PersonalRating" with a Number data type.
    • In the description of the PersonalRating field, type: My personal rating on a scale from 1 (bad) to 10 (great).
  **f.** Save and close the Video Collection table, and close the Movies database.

**2.** You work for a marketing company that sells medical supplies to doctors' offices.
To complete this independent challenge:

  **a.** Open the Doctors-B database on your Project Disk, then open the Doctors Addresses table datasheet.
  **b.** Filter the records to find all those physicians who live in Grandview, then print the filtered datasheet.
  **c.** Sort the records by last name, change the font size to 12, resize the columns so all the data within each column is visible, change the page orientation to landscape, then print the datasheet.
  **d.** Using the Query Wizard, create a query with the following fields: First, Last, Phone.
  **e.** Name the query "Telephone Query." Sort the records in ascending order by last name, then print the datasheet.

**f.** Add the Title field to the third field position, then delete the First field. Save and close the query.

**g.** Modify the Telephone Query so that the State field is added to the fourth field position. Add criteria so that only those physicians in Missouri are shown on the resulting datasheet.

**h.** Print, save, and close the query. Close the Doctors-B database, then exit Access.

**3.** You want to create a database to keep track of your personal contacts.
To complete this independent challenge:

**a.** Start Access and create a new database called "People" on your Project Disk.

**b.** Using the Table Wizard, create a table based on the Addresses sample table in the Personal category with the following fields: FirstName, LastName, SpouseName, Address, City, StateOrProvince, PostalCode, EmailAddress, HomePhone, Birthdate.

**c.** Name the table Contact Info, allow Access to set the primary key field, and choose the Enter data directly into the table option in the last Table Wizard dialog box.

**d.** Enter at least five records into the table, making sure that two people have the same last name. Use your name for one of the records. You do not have to enter real names and addresses into the other records.

**e.** Press [Tab] to move through the Contact InfoID field.

**f.** Sort the records in ascending order by last name.

**g.** Adjust the column widths, change the datasheet margins, change the paper orientation, and make other adjustments, as necessary, to print the five records on one page.

**h.** Using the Query Wizard, create a query with the following fields from the Contact Info table in this order: LastName, FirstName, Birthdate.

**i.** Name the query Birthday List, and in Query Design view, sort the records in ascending order by LastName and then by FirstName.

**j.** Save the query as Sorted Birthday List, then view the query.

**k.** Change the Birthdate field to 8/20/58 for one of the records in the query datasheet.

**l.** Print the query's datasheet, close the query, then close the People database and exit Access.

**4.** MediaLoft has developed a Web site that provides information about their products and allows viewers to vote for their favorite music collections. In this exercise, you will print the Web page from the MediaLoft intranet site that records the People's choice awards. Then you will enter that information in the database, and create a query that displays only the top records.

**a.** Connect to the Internet, and use your browser to go to the MediaLoft intranet site at http://www.course.com/illustrated/medialoft

**b.** Click the link for Products to go to the Web page summarizing the most popular music selection in several categories as determined by a recent vote of customers.

**c.** Print the People's Choice Web page, then disconnect from the Internet.

**d.** Open the MediaLoft-B database, and then open the Music Inventory table in Design view.

**e.** Add a field called PeoplesChoice at the end of the field list with a Yes/No data type.

**f.** Find the six records listed on the People's Choice Web page (*Hint*: Use the Find and Sort buttons). Then place a checkmark in the PeoplesChoice field in your database for the six records to indicate that they were contest winners.

**g.** Using the Query Wizard, create a query that is based on the Music Inventory table with the following fields: Category, Title, Artist, Retail, PeoplesChoice.

**h.** Show all the Detail records, name the query "Peoples Choice Query," then modify the query so that only those records with "Yes" in the PeoplesChoice field are displayed.

**i.** Save and print the Peoples Choice Query datasheet.

**j.** Close the Peoples Choice Query, close the MediaLoft-B database, then exit Access.

pen the MediaLoft-B database and create a query based on the Music Inventory table that displays the datasheet

# ▶ Visual Workshop

Open the MediaLoft-B database and create a query based on the Music Inventory table that displays the datasheet shown in Figure B-25. Notice that only the Jazz category is displayed and that the records are sorted in a descending order on the Retail field. Save the query as "Jazz Selections" in the MediaLoft-B database.

FIGURE B-25

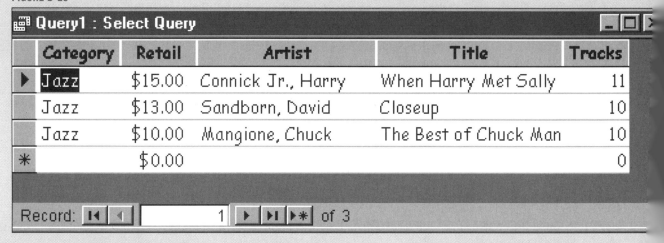

# Using
## Forms

### Objectives

► **Plan a form**
[MOUS] ► **Create a form**
[MOUS] ► **Move and resize controls**
[MOUS] ► **Modify labels**
[MOUS] ► **Modify text boxes**
► **Modify tab order**
[MOUS] ► **Enter and edit records**
[MOUS] ► **Insert an image**

A **form** is an Access database object that allows you to arrange the fields of a record in any layout. Although the datasheet view of a table or query can be used to navigate, edit, and enter new information, all of the fields for one record are sometimes not visible unless you scroll left or right. A form fixes that problem by using the screen to show the fields of only one record at a time. Forms are often the primary object used to enter, edit, and find data. ✎ More people are becoming excited about the MediaLoft music inventory database. They have asked John Kim to create a form to make it easier to access, enter, and update this important inventory data.

# Planning a Form

Properly organized and well-designed forms make a tremendous difference in the productivi[ty] the end user. Since forms are the primary object used to enter and edit data, time spent plann[ing] a form is time well spent. Forms are often built to match a **source document** (for example employment application or a medical history form) to facilitate fast and accurate data entry. N[ow] however, it is becoming more common to type data directly into the database rather than recording it on paper. Form design considerations, such as clearly labeled fields and approp[riate] formatting, are important. Other considerations include how the user tabs from field to f[ield] and what type of **control** is used to display the data. See Table C-1 for more information on f[orm] controls.  John considers the following form design considerations when planning [the] Music Inventory form.

 ### Determine the overall purpose of the form
Have a good understanding of what information you need to gather through the form. T[his] purpose often becomes the form's title such as "Music Inventory Entry Form."

 ### Determine the underlying record source
The **record source** is either a table or query object, and contains the fields and records that [the] form will display.

 ### Gather the source documents used to design your form, or sketch the form by ha[nd] if a paper form does not exist
When sketching the form, be sure to list all the fields and instructions you want the form to dis[play.]

 ### Determine the best type of control to use for each element on the form
Figures C-1 and C-2 show examples of several controls. **Bound controls** display data from [the] underlying record source and are also used to edit and enter new data. **Unbound controls** [do] not change from record to record and exist only to clarify or enhance the appearance of the fo[rm.]

**TABLE C-1: Form Controls**

| name | used to: | bound or unboun[d] |
|---|---|---|
| Label | Provide consistent descriptive text as you navigate from record to record | Unbound |
| Text box | Display, edit, or enter data for each record from an underlying record source | Bound |
| List box | Display a list of possible data entries | Bound |
| Combo box | Display a list of possible data entries for a field, and also provide text box for an entry from the keyboard; a "combination" of the list box and text box controls | Bound |
| Tab control | Create a three-dimensional aspect to a form so that controls can be organized and displayed by clicking the "tabs" | Unbound |
| Check box | Display "yes" or "no" answers for a field; if the box is "checked" it displays "yes" information | Bound |
| Toggle button | Display "yes" or "no" answers for a field; if the button is "pressed," it displays "yes" information | Bound |
| Option button | Display a limited list of possible choices for field | Bound |
| Bound image control | Display OLE data, such as a picture | Bound |
| Unbound image control | Display picture or clip art that doesn't change as you navigate from record to record | Unbound |
| Line and Rectangle controls | Draw lines and rectangles on the form | Unbound |
| Command button | Provide an easy way to initiate a command or run a macro | Unbound |

**FIGURE C-1: Sample Form Controls**

Tab controls

Option group

Labels

List box

Combo box

Text boxes

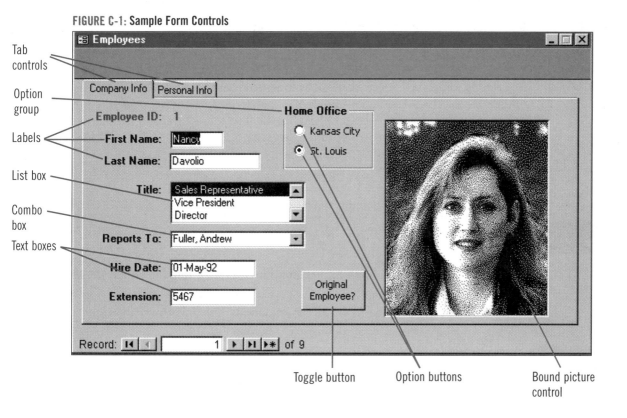

Toggle button    Option buttons    Bound picture control

**FIGURE C-2: Sample Form Controls**

Unbound image

Rectangle

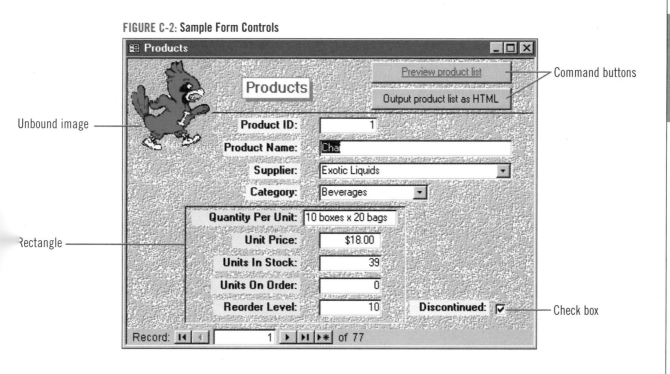

Command buttons

Check box

# Creating a Form

You can create a form from scratch using **Form Design view**, or you can use the **Form Wizard** to create an initial form object that can be modified later if needed. The Form Wizard provides options for selecting fields, an overall layout, a style, and a form title. John created a sketch and made some notes on how he'd like the final Music Inventory form arranged, shown in Figure C-3. He uses the Form Wizard to get started.

1. Start Access, click the **Open an existing file option button**, then open the **MediaLoft-C** database from your Project Disk
   This MediaLoft-C database contains an enhanced Music Inventory table. John added more fields and records.

> **QuickTip**
>
> To hide the Office Assistant, click Help on the menu bar, then click Hide Office Assistant.

2. Click **Forms** on the Objects bar in the MediaLoft-C Database window, then double-click **Create form by using wizard**
   The Music Inventory table includes all of the fields required in the Music Inventory form.

3. Click the **Select All Fields button** >> , click **Next**, click the **Columnar layout option button**, click **Next**, click the **Standard** style, click **Next**, then click **Finish** to accept the name **Music Inventory** for the form
   The Music Inventory form opens in **Form view**, as shown in Figure C-4. Descriptive labels appear in the first column, and text boxes that display data from the underlying records appear in the second column. A check box control displays the yes/no data in the PeoplesChoice field. You can enter, edit, find, sort, and filter records using the form.

> **QuickTip**
>
> Sort, filter, and find buttons work the same way in a form as a datasheet, except that a form generally shows only one record at a time.

4. Click the **Artist text box**, click the **Sort Ascending button** on the Form View toolbar, then click the **Next Record button** to move to the second record
   The "Adams, Oleta" record is second when the records are sorted in ascending order by recording artist.

5. Click the **Last Record button** on the Music Inventory form
   Neil Young's "Decade" is the last record when the records are sorted in ascending order.

6. Click the **Close button** on the Music Inventory form title bar to close the form
   The new Music Inventory form object appears in the Forms section of the MediaLoft-C Database window.

**CLUES TO USE**

## Using AutoForm

You can quickly create a form by clicking a table or query object in the database window, and then clicking the New Object:AutoForm button on the Database toolbar. AutoForm offers no prompts or dialog boxes; it instantly creates a form that displays all the fields in the previously chosen table or query using the same options as those you chose the last time you used the Form Wizard.

**FIGURE C-3:** Sketch of Music Inventory form

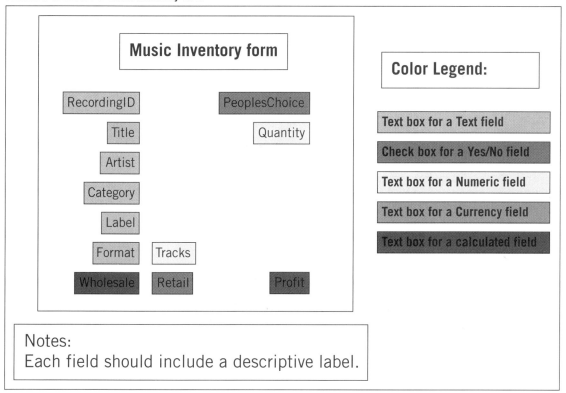

**FIGURE C-4:** Music Inventory form

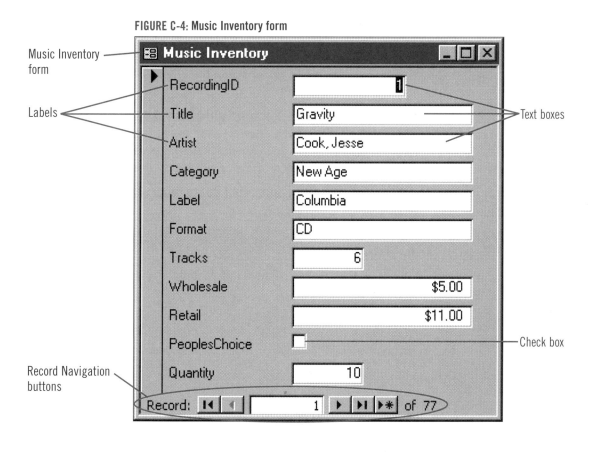

Access 2000

# Moving and Resizing Controls

After you create a form, you can modify the size, location, and appearance of existing controls in Form Design view. Form Design view also allows you to add or delete controls. John moves and resizes the controls on the form to better match his original design.

**Steps**

> **Trouble?**
> Be sure you open the Design view of the Music Inventory form and not the Music Inventory table.

1. Click the **Music Inventory form**, click the **Design button** in the MediaLoft-C Database window, then click the **Maximize button** to maximize the Design view of the Music Inventory form

   The Design view of the Music Inventory form opens. The **Toolbox toolbar** contains buttons that allow you to add controls to the form. The **field list** contains the fields in the underlying object. You can toggle both of these screen elements on and off as needed. Widening the form gives you more room to reposition the controls.

2. Click the **Toolbox button** on the Form Design toolbar to toggle it off (if necessary), click the **Field List button** to toggle it off (if necessary), place the pointer on the right edge of the form, then when the pointer changes to +, drag the right edge to the **6"** mark on the horizontal ruler

   The form is expanded so that it is 6" wide, as shown in Figure C-5. Before moving, resizing, deleting, or changing a control in any way, you must select it.

3. Click the **PeoplesChoice check box**

   Squares, called **sizing handles**, appear in the corners and on the edges of the selected control. When you work with controls, the mouse pointer shape is very important. Pointer shapes are summarized in Table C-2.

> **Trouble?**
> If you make a mistake, immediately click the Undo button and try again.

4. Place the pointer on the **selected control**, when the pointer changes to ✋, drag the control so that the left edge of the label is at the **4"** mark on the horizontal ruler and the bottom edge is aligned with the **RecordingID text box**

   The text boxes appear as white rectangles in this form. When you move a bound control, such as a text box or check box, the accompanying unbound label control to its left moves with it. The field name for the selected control appears in the Object list box.

> **QuickTip**
> You can move controls one pixel at a time by pressing [Ctrl] and an arrow key. You can resize controls one pixel at a time by pressing [Shift] and an arrow key.

5. Select and move the **Quantity** and **Tracks text boxes** using the ✋ pointer to match their final locations as shown in Figure C-6

   Resizing controls also improves the design of the form.

6. Click the **Retail text box**, then use the ↔ pointer to drag the middle-right edge sizing handle left to the **2"** mark, click the **Wholesale text box**, then drag the middle-right edge sizing handle left to the **2"** mark

   Moving and resizing controls requires great concentration and mouse control. Don't worry if your screen doesn't *precisely* match the next figure, but *do* make sure that you understand how to use the move and resize mouse pointers used in Form Design view. Precision and accuracy are naturally developed with practice, but even experienced form designers regularly rely on the Undo button.

7. Click the **Form View button** on the Form Design toolbar, click the **Artist text box**, click the **Sort Descending button**, then click the **Sort Ascending button** on the Form View toolbar

   Your screen should look like Figure C-7.

FIGURE C-5: Design view of the Music Inventory form

Form View button

Horizontal ruler

Field List button

Labels

Vertical ruler

Text boxes

Toolbox button

6" mark

Right edge of form

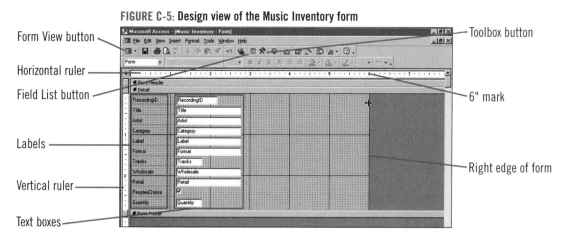

FIGURE C-6: Controls have been moved

Object list box

Text boxes have
been moved

PeoplesChoice label
and check box have
been moved

"Move" mouse
symbol

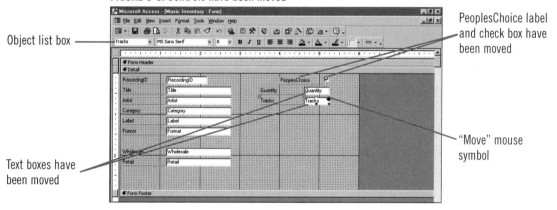

FIGURE C-7: Reorganized Music Inventory form

Check box

Text boxes

Labels

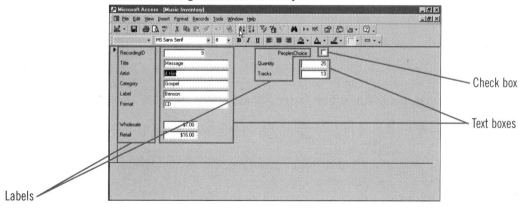

**ᴮLE C-2: Form Design view mouse pointer shapes**

| ᴬᵖe | when does this shape appear? | action |
|---|---|---|
| ⟩ | When you point to any nonselected control on the form; it is the default mouse pointer | Single-clicking with this mouse pointer *selects* a control |
| ·ᵎ· | When you point to the edge of a selected control (but not when you are pointing to a sizing handle) | Dragging this mouse pointer moves all selected controls |
| ◆ | When you point to the larger sizing handle in the upper-left corner of a selected control | Dragging this mouse pointer *moves only the single control* where pointer is currently positioned, not other controls that may also be selected |
| → ↕ ↖ ↗ | When you point to any sizing handle (except the larger one in the upper-left corner) | Dragging this mouse pointer *resizes* the control |

# Modifying Labels

When you create a form with the Form Wizard, it places a label to the left of each text box with the field's name. Often, you'll want to modify those labels to be more descriptive or user friendly. You can modify a label control by directly editing it in Form Design view, or you can make the change in the label's property sheet. The **property sheet** is a comprehensive listing of all **properties** (characteristics) that have been specified for that control. John modifies the Music Inventory form's labels to be more descriptive.

## Steps

**Trouble?**

If you double-click a label, you will open its property sheet. Close the property sheet by clicking its Close button, then single-click the label again.

**1.** Click the **Design View button** on the Form View toolbar, click the **RecordingID label** to select it, click between the **g** and **I** in the RecordingID label, then press **[Spacebar]** to insert a space

Directly editing labels in Form Design view is tricky because you must select the label and then precisely click where you want to edit it. You can also open the label's property sheet and modify the Caption property to change the displayed text.

**2.** Click the **Title label**, click the **Properties button** on the Form Design toolbar, then click the **Format tab**, as shown in Figure C-8

The Caption property controls the text displayed by the label control, and the property can be found on either the Format or the All tabs. The All tab is an exhaustive list of all the properties for a control.

**Trouble?**

Be sure to modify the Title label control and not the Title text box control. Text box controls must reference the *exact* field name in order to display the data within that field.

**3.** Click to the left of **Title** in the Caption property text box, type **Recording**, press **[Spacebar]**, then click to toggle the property sheet off

Don't be overwhelmed by the number of properties available for each control on the form. Over time, you may want to learn about most of these properties, but in the beginning, you'll be able to make the vast majority of the property changes through menu and toolbar options rather than by accessing the property sheet itself. Labels can be aligned so that they are closer to their respective text boxes.

**4.** Click the **Recording ID label**, then click the **Align Right button** on the Formatting (Form/Report) toolbar

The Recording ID label is now much closer to its associated text box. See Table C-3 for a list of techniques to quickly select several controls so that you can apply alignment and formatting changes to many controls simultaneously.

**5.** Click the **0.5"** mark on the horizontal ruler to select the first column of controls, as shown in Figure C-9, then click

All the labels in the first column are right-aligned and next to their text boxes.

**6.** Click the **Save button** on the Form Design toolbar, then click the **Form View button** on the Form Design toolbar

The Music Inventory form is saved, and you can see that the labels are close to the data in the first column.

FIGURE C-8: Looking at a label's property sheet

Recording ID label has been changed

Title label is chosen

Caption property

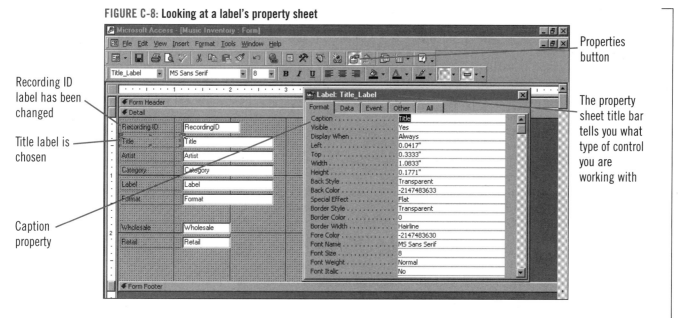

Properties button

The property sheet title bar tells you what type of control you are working with

FIGURE C-9: Selecting several labels at the same time

Clicking the 0.5" mark on the ruler

All labels in the first column are selected

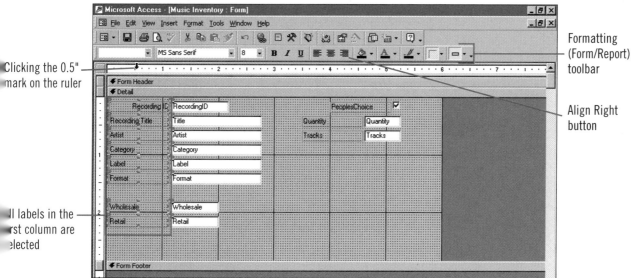

Formatting (Form/Report) toolbar

Align Right button

TABLE C-3: Selecting more than one control

| technique | description |
|-----------|-------------|
| click, [Shift]+click | Click a control, then press and hold [Shift] while clicking other controls; each one will be selected |
| drag a selection box | If you drag a selection box (an imaginary box you create by dragging the pointer in Form Design view), every control that is in or touched by the edges of the box will be selected |
| click in the ruler | If you click in either the horizontal or vertical ruler you will select all controls that intersect the selection line (an imaginary line you create by clicking the ruler) |
| drag in the ruler | If you drag through either the horizontal or vertical ruler you will select all controls that intersect the selection line as it is dragged through the ruler |

# Modifying Text Boxes

Text boxes are generally used to display data from underlying fields and are therefore *bound* to that field. You can also use a text box as a **calculated control** which is not directly bound to a field but rather uses information from a field to calculate an answer. ✎ John wants the Music Inventory form to calculate the profit for each record. He uses a text box calculated control to find the difference between the Retail and Wholesale fields.

## Steps 1 2 3 4

**Trouble?**

The Toolbox toolbar may be floating or docked on the edge of your screen. Drag the title bar of a floating toolbar or the top edge of a docked toolbar to move it to a convenient location.

1. Click the **Design View button** 🖾 on the Form View toolbar, click the **Toolbox button** 🛠 on the Form View toolbar, click the **Text Box button** [abl] on the Toolbox toolbar, the pointer changes to ⁺[abl], click just below the Retail text box on the form, then if necessary move the new text box and label control to align with the controls above it
Your screen should look like Figure C-10. Adding a new text box *automatically* added a new label with the default caption "Text22:". You can access the text box's property sheet to bind it to an underlying field or expression, or you can create the calculated expression directly in the text box.

**Trouble?**

The number in the caption "Text22" varies depending on how many controls you add to the form.

2. Click **Unbound** in the new text box, type **=[Retail]-[Wholesale]**, then press **[Enter]**
When referencing field names within an expression, you *must* use square brackets and type the field name exactly as it appears in the Table Design view. You do not need to worry about uppercase and lowercase letters. The label for any expression should be descriptive.

3. Click the **Text22: label** to select it, click the **Text22: label** again to edit it, double-click **Text22**, type **Profit** as the new caption, then press **[Enter]**
The calculated text box control and associated label are modified.

**Trouble?**

If your calculated control did not work, return to Design view, click the calculated control, press [Delete], then repeat steps 1 through 4.

4. Click the **Form View button** 🖽 to view your changes, click the **Ascending Sort button** 🛂 on the Form View toolbar
Your screen should look like Figure C-11. The first record is $5 wholesale and sells for $11.00 retail so the profit is calculated as $6. You can use Form Design view to make a few more changes to clarify the form.

5. Click 🖾, click the **Calculated text box**, then click the **Properties button** 🖃 on the Form Design toolbar
By default, the values in text boxes that contain numeric and currency fields are right-aligned. Text boxes that contain fields with other data types or those that start as unbound controls are left-aligned. Monetary values should be right-aligned and display with a dollar sign and cents.

**Trouble?**

Properties are not listed in alphabetical order so you may have to scroll up or down the property sheet to find the Format and Text Align properties.

6. Click the **Format tab** in the Text Box property sheet, click the **Format property text box**, click the **Format property list arrow**, scroll and click **Currency**, click the **Text Align property text box**, scroll and click the **Text Align property list arrow**, then click **Right**

7. Click the **Properties button** 🖃, switch the position of the **Retail and Wholesale text boxes**, move and align the **Profit label**, resize the **calculated text box** (as shown Figure C-12), then click the **Form View button** 🖽
The calculated profit value should display as $6.00 and be right-aligned within the text box.

**FIGURE C-10:** Adding a calculated text box

Toolbox button

Toolbox toolbar

Click to add a text box control

New label

New text box

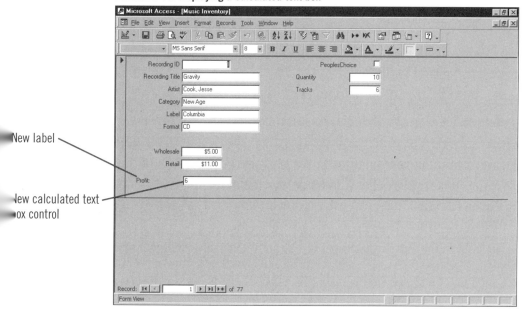

**FIGURE C-11:** Displaying a calculated text box

New label

New calculated text box control

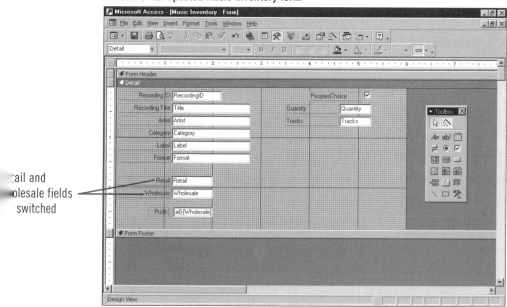

**FIGURE C-12:** Updated Music Inventory form

tail and wholesale fields switched

# Modifying Tab Order

Once all of the controls have been added, moved, and resized on the form, you'll want to check and probably modify the tab order. The **tab order** is the order in which the **focus** (the active control) moves as you press [Tab] in Form view. Since the form is the primary object by which users will view, edit, and enter data, careful attention to tab order is essential to maintain their productivity and satisfaction with the database. John checks the tab order of the Music Inventory form, then changes the tab order as necessary in Form Design view.

## Steps

1. Press **[Tab]** 11 times watching the focus move through the bound controls of the form
   Currently, focus moves back and forth between the left and right columns of controls. For efficient data entry, you want the focus to move down through the first column of text boxes before moving to the second column.

2. Click the **Design View button** 🖋 on the Form View toolbar, click **View** on the menu bar, then click **Tab Order**
   The Tab Order dialog box opens in which you can drag fields up or down to change their tab sequence. The Tab Order dialog box allows you to change the tab order of controls in three sections: Form Header, Detail, and Form Footer. Right now, all of the controls are positioned in the form's Detail section. See Table C-4 for more information on form sections.

3. Click the **Retail row selector** in the Custom Order list, drag it up to position it just below Format, click the **Wholesale row selector**, drag it under Retail, click the **Tracks row selector**, then drag it under Quantity as shown in Figure C-13
   With the change made, test the new tab order.

4. Click **OK** in the Tab Order dialog box, then click the **Form View button** 🖼 on the Form Design toolbar
   Although nothing visibly changes on the form, the tab order is different.

5. Press **[Enter]** 10 times to move through the fields of the form with the new tab order
   You should now be moving through all of the text boxes of the first column, with the exception of the calculated field, before you move to the second column.

6. Click the **Save button** 💾 on the Form View toolbar

**FIGURE C-13:** Tab Order dialog box

Tab Order dialog box with Detail section chosen

Form Header section

Detail section

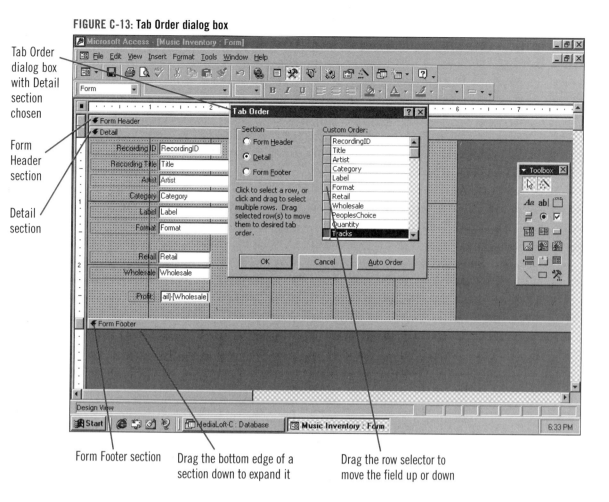

Form Footer section

Drag the bottom edge of a section down to expand it

Drag the row selector to move the field up or down

**LE C-4: Form sections**

| tion | description |
|------|-------------|
| m Header | Controls placed in the Form Header print only once at the top of the printout; by default, this section is not "opened" in Form Design view, but can be expanded by dragging its bottom edge in Form Design view. |
| ail | Controls placed in the Detail section print once for every record in the underlying table or query object; all controls created by the Form Wizard are placed in this section |
| n Footer | Controls placed in the Form Footer print only once at the end of the printout; by default, this section is not "opened" in Form Design view, but it can be expanded by dragging its bottom edge down in Form Design view |

# Entering and Editing Records

The most important reasons for using a form are to find, enter, or edit records to the underlying object. You can also print a form, but you must be careful because printing a form often produces a very long printout because of the vertical orientation of the fields. John uses the Music Inventory form to add a new record to the underlying Music Inventory table. Then he prints the form with the data for only the new record.

## Steps 1234

**QuickTip**

A New Record button is also on the Navigation buttons.

**1.** Click the **New Record button** ▸∗ on the Form View toolbar

A new, blank record is displayed. The text "(AutoNumber)" appears in the Recording ID field, which will automatically increment when you begin to enter data. The Specific Record box indicates the current record number.

**QuickTip**

To enter a check in a check box press [Spacebar].

**2.** Click the **Recording Title text box**, type **The Dance**, then enter the rest of the information shown in Figure C-14

Notice that the Profit text box shows the calculated result of $4.00. The new record is stored as record 78 in the Music Inventory table.

**Trouble?**

Don't click the Print button on the Form View toolbar because *all* of the records in the underlying object will print.

**3.** Click **File** on the menu bar, click **Print** to open the Print dialog box, click the **Selected Record(s) option button** in the Print Range section, then click **OK**

Forms are also often used to edit existing records in the database.

**4.** Click the **Recording Title text box**, click the **Find button** 🔍 on the Form View toolbar to open the Find and Replace dialog box, type **Mermaid Avenue** in the Find What text box, then click **Find Next**

Record 77 appears behind the Find and Replace dialog box, as shown in Figure C-15.

**5.** Click **Cancel** in the Find and Replace dialog box, press [Tab] five times to go to the Retail field, type **20**, then press [Tab]

Editing either the Wholesale or Retail fields automatically updates the calculated Profit field. Forms are also a great way to filter the records to a specific subset.

**6.** Click **Pop** in the Category text box, then click the **Filter By Selection button** 🎛 the Form View toolbar

Twelve records were found that matched the "Pop" criteria. Previewing the records helps determine how many pages the printout would be.

**7.** Click the **Print Preview button** 🔍 on the Form View toolbar

Since about three records print on a page, your printout would be four pages long.

**8.** Click the **Close button** on the Print Preview toolbar, then click the **Remove Filter button** 🔽 on the Form View toolbar so that all 78 records in the Music Inventory table are available

FIGURE C-14: Entering a new record into a form

Edit record symbol ————

New Record button

Calculated text box automatically displays the answer

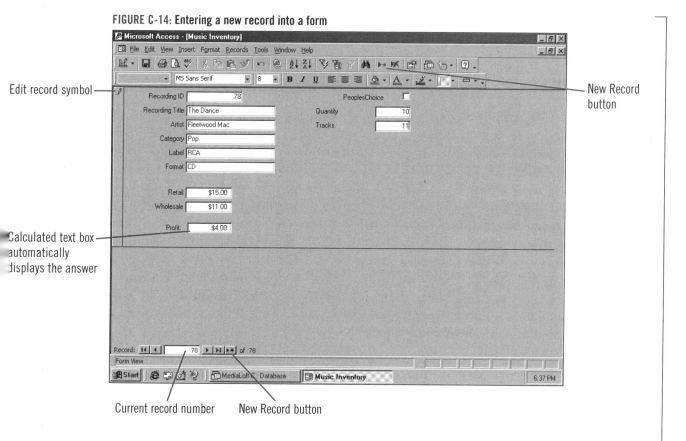

Current record number    New Record button

FIGURE C-15: Finding "Mermaid Avenue" using a form

rmaid Avenue nd in Title field

Find button

rd 77 —

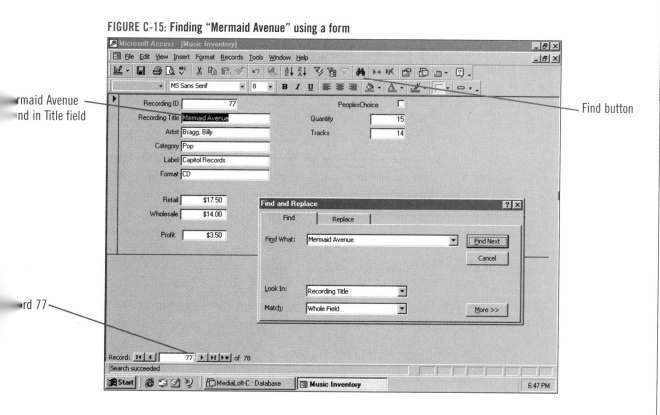

# Inserting an Image

Graphic images, such as pictures, a logo, or clip art, can add style and professionalism to a form. If you add a graphic image as an unbound image to the Form Header, the image will appear at the top of the form in Form view and once at the top of the printout when printing records through a form. ◢◣ John adds the MediaLoft logo and a descriptive title to the Form Header section.

## Steps 1 2 3 4

1. Click the **Design View button** 🔲 on the Form View toolbar, place the pointer on the bottom edge of the Form Header, the pointer changes to ✚, then drag the bottom of the Form Header section to the **1"** mark on the vertical ruler
   The Form Header section is open.

2. Click the **Image button** 🔲 on the Toolbox toolbar, the pointer changes to ⁺🖾, then click in the **Form Header section** at the **1"** mark on the horizontal ruler
   The Insert Picture dialog box opens. The MediaLoft image file you want to insert in the Form Header is on the Project Disk.

3. Click the **Look in list arrow**, click the drive containing your Project Disk, click **smallmedia**, then click **OK**
   The MediaLoft logo appears in the Form Header, surrounded by handles, as shown in Figure C-16. Form header titles add a finishing touch to a form.

### QuickTip
If you need your name on the printed solution, enter your name as a label below the MediaLoft Music label.

4. Click the **Label button** 🅰 on the Toolbox toolbar, the pointer changes to ⁺A, click to the right of the **MediaLoft logo** in the Form Header section, type **MediaLoft Music** then press **[Enter]**
   Labels can be formatted to enhance the appearance on the form.

5. Click the **Font Size list arrow**, click **24**, point to the **upper-right resizing handle** then drag the ⬈ pointer so that the label **MediaLoft Music** is completely displayed
   If you double-click a label's sizing handle, the label will automatically adjust to display the entire caption.

6. Click the **Form View button** 🔲 on the Form Design toolbar
   You can go directly to a specific record by typing the record number in the specific record box.

7. Click in the **specific record box** on the Record Navigation buttons, type **11**, then press **[Enter]**
   Compare your form with Figure C-17.

8. Click **File** on the menu bar, click **Print**, click the **Selected Record(s) option button** then click **OK**

9. Click the **Close button** on the Music Inventory form, then click **Yes** to save changes if necessary

10. Close the MediaLoft-C database, then exit Access

FIGURE C-16: Adding an image to the Form Header section

1" mark on the ruler

MediaLoft logo

Label button

Image button

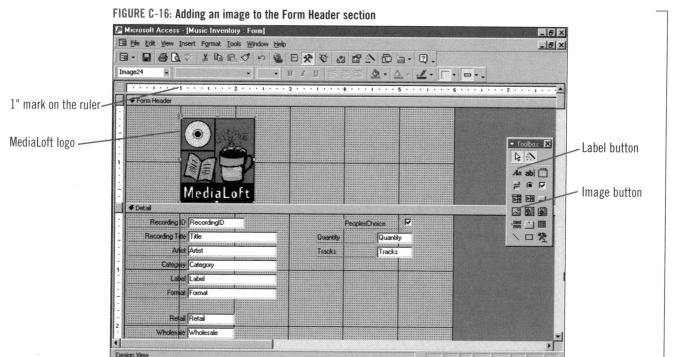

FIGURE C-17: The final Music Inventory form

MediaLoft logo

ew label serves as
rm title

Form Header
section

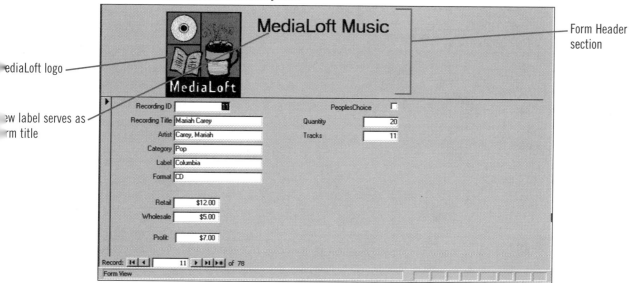

Access 2000

TO USE

## Creating a hyperlink from an image

nce an image is added to a form, you can convert it
a hyperlink by using its property sheet to modify
e control's **Hyperlink Address** property in Form
esign view. Depending on what you enter for the
yperlink Address property, clicking the hyperlinked
age in Form view opens another file, Access object,

Web address, or e-mail address. For example,
C:\Colleges\JCCCDescriptions.doc is the Hyperlink
Address property entry to link a Word document at
the specified drive and folder location;
http://www.jccc.net creates a link between the image
and the specified Web address.

# Practice

## ▶ Concepts Review

Label each element of the Form Design window shown in Figure C-18.

FIGURE C-18

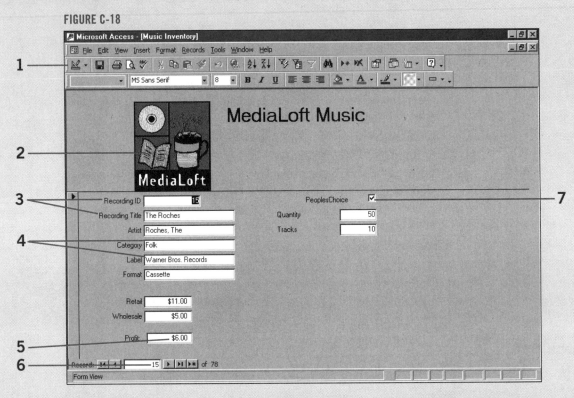

Match each term with the statement that describes it.

8. Sizing handles
9. Detail section
10. Bound control
11. Tab order
12. Form
13. Calculated control

a. An Access database object that allows you to arrange the fields of a record any layout; you use it to enter, edit, and delete records

b. Displays data from a field in the underlying record source

c. Black squares that appear in the corners and edges of the selected control

d. The way in which the focus moves from one bound control to the next

e. Uses a text box and an expression to display an answer

f. Controls placed here print once for every record in the underlying table or query object

Select the best answer from the list of choices.

14. **Every element on a form is called a**
    a. Property.
    b. Control.
    c. Piece.
    d. Handle.

15. **The pointer used to resize a control is**
    a. ✛
    b. ↔
    c. ✋
    d. 👆

16. **The most common bound control is the**
    a. Label.
    b. Text box.
    c. Combo box.
    d. Check box.

17. **The most common unbound control is the**
    a. Label.
    b. Text box.
    c. Combo box.
    d. Image.

18. **The _____ view is used to modify form controls.**
    a. Form
    b. Datasheet
    c. Print Preview
    d. Design

## ▶ Skills Review

### 1. Plan a form.

**a.** Plan a form to use for the data entry of business contacts by looking at several business cards.

**b.** Write down the organization of the fields on the form. Determine what type of control you will use for each bound field.

**c.** Identify the labels you would like to display on the form.

### 2. Create a form.

**a.** Start Access and open the Membership-C database from your Project Disk.

**b.** Click the Forms button in the Membership-C Database window, then double-click the Create form by using wizard option.

**c.** Base the form on the Contacts table, and include all of the fields.

**d.** Use a Columnar layout, a Standard style, and title the form "Contact Entry Form."

**e.** Display the form with data.

### 3. Move and resize controls.

**a.** Open and maximize the Design View window for the Contact Entry Form.

**b.** Widen the form so that the right edge is at the 6" mark on the horizontal ruler.

**c.** Move the LNAME text box and corresponding label to the right of the FNAME text box.

**d.** Move the DUESOWED and DUESPAID text boxes and corresponding labels to the right of the address controls.

**e.** Resize the PHONE and ZIP text boxes to be the same size as the CITY text box.

**f.** Move the PHONE text box and corresponding label between the FNAME and COMPANY controls.

### 4. Modify labels.

**a.** Right align all of the labels.

**b.** Modify the FNAME label to FIRST NAME, the LNAME label to LAST NAME, the DUESOWED label to DUES OWED, and the DUESPAID label to DUES PAID.

### 5. Modify text boxes.

**a.** Add a new text box below the DUESPAID text box.

**b.** Type the expression =[DUESOWED]-[DUESPAID] in the new unbound text box. (*Hint*: Remember that you must use the *exact field names* in a calculated expression.)

**c.** In the property sheet for the new calculated control, change the Format property to Currency.

**d.** Right align the new calculated text boxes.

**e.** Change the calculated text box label from Text20: to BALANCE.

**f.** Move and resize the new calculated control and label so that it is aligned beneath the DUESOWED and DUES PAID controls.

### 6. Modify tab order.

**a.** Change the Tab order so that pressing [Tab] moves the focus through the text boxes in the following order: FNAME, LNAME, PHONE, COMPANY, STREET, CITY, STATE, ZIP, DUESOWED, DUESPAID, BALANCE text box

## 7. Enter and edit records.

**a.** Use the Contact Entry Form to enter the following new records:

|  | FIRST NAME | LAST NAME | PHONE | COMPANY | STREET |
|---|---|---|---|---|---|
| Record 1 | Jane | Eagan | 555-1166 | Cummins Construction | 1515 Maple St. |
| Record 2 | Mark | Daniels | 555-2277 | Motorola | 1010 Green St. |

|  | CITY | STATE | ZIP | DUES OWED | DUES PAID |
|---|---|---|---|---|---|
| 1 con't. | Fontanelle | KS | 50033- | $50.00 | $25.00 |
| 2 con't. | Bridgewater | KS | 50022- | $50.00 | $50.00 |

**b.** Print the Mark Daniels record.

**c.** Find the Lois Goode record, enter IBM in the Company text box, then print that record.

**d.** Filter for all records with a Zip entry of 64145. How many records did you find?

**e.** Sort the filtered 64145 zip code records in ascending order by Last Name, then print the first one.

## 8. Insert an image.

**a.** In Form Design view, expand the Form Header section to the 1" mark on the vertical ruler.

**b.** Use the Image control to insert the handin1.bmp file found on your Project Disk in the Form Header.

**c.** Centered and below the graphic file, add the label MEMBERSHIP INFORMATION in a 24-point font. Be sure to resize the label so that all of the text is visible.

**d.** Add your name as a label in the Form Header section.

**e.** View the form using the Form view.

**f.** Print the selected record.

**g.** Close the form, close the database, then exit Access.

# Independent Challenges

1. As the office manager of a cardiology clinic, you need to create a new patient data entry form. To complete this independent challenge:

**a.** Open the Clinic-C database from your Project Disk.

**b.** Using the Form Wizard, create a form that includes all the fields in the Demographics table, using the Columnar layout and Standard style. Title the form "Patient Entry Form."

**c.** In Form Design view, widen the form to the 6" mark, then move the DOB, Gender, Ins Code, and Entry Date controls to a second column to the right of the existing column. DOB should be next to Last Name.

**d.** Switch the positions of the State and Zip controls.

**e.** Modify the Medical Record Number label to MR Number, the Address 1 label to Address, the DOB label to Birthday, and the Ins Code label to Insurance.

**f.** Change the tab order so State is above Zip.

**g.** Use the newly created form to add a record using your own personal information. Enter 2000 for the MR Number, BCBS for the Insurance, and 2/1/00 for the Entry Date.

**h.** Print the form with the new record you just added about yourself.

**i.** Close the Patient Entry Form, close the Clinic-C database, then exit Access.

**2.** As office manager of a cardiology clinic you want to build a form that quickly calculates a height to weight ratio value based on information in the Outcomes Data table.

To complete this independent challenge:

**a.** Open the Clinic-C database from your Project Disk.

**b.** Using the Form Wizard, create a form based on the Outcomes Data table with only the following fields: MR#, Height, and Weight.

**c.** Use the Columnar layout and Standard style, and name the form "Height to Weight Ratio Form."

**d.** In Design view, widen the form to the 4" mark on the horizontal ruler, then add a text box to the right half of the form.

**e.** Close the Field list if necessary.

**f.** Enter the expression =[Height]/[Weight] in the unbound text box.

**g.** Modify the calculated expression's label from Text6: (the number may vary) to Ratio.

**h.** Resize the Ratio label so that it is closer to the calculated expression control, then right-align the Ratio label.

**i.** Change the format property of the calculated control to Fixed.

**j.** Open the form header and enter your name as a label.

**k.** View the form.

**l.** Print the form for the record for MR# 006494.

**m.** Sort the records in descending order by Height, then print the record with the tallest height entry.

**n.** Close the Height to Weight Ratio Form, close the Clinic-C database, then exit Access.

**3.** As office manager of a cardiology clinic you want to build a form to enter new insurance information.

To complete this independent challenge:

**a.** Open the Clinic-C database from your Project Disk.

**b.** Using the Form Wizard, create a form based on the Insurance Company Information table, and include all of the fields.

**c.** Use the Columnar layout, Standard style, and accept the default title for the form "Insurance Company Information."

**d.** Change the label Insurance Company Name to just "Insurance Company."

**e.** Resize the State text box so that it is the same size as the City text box.

**f.** Expand the Form Header section, and add the graphic image Medical.bmp found on your Project Disk to the left side of the Form Header section.

**g.** Add a label "Insurance Entry Form" and another for your name to the right of the medical clip art in the Form Header section.

**h.** Increase the size of the Insurance Entry Form label to 18 points. Resize the label to display the entire caption.

**i.** Switch to Form view, then find and print the Cigna record.

**j.** Filter for all records with a State entry of KS. Print those records.

**k.** Close the Insurance Company Information Form, close the Clinic-C database, then exit Access.

**4.** As a new employee in the Market Research department for MediaLoft, you use the World Wide Web to find information on competitors' Web sites, specifically as it relates to Web-based forms.

To complete this independent challenge:

**a.** Connect to the Internet, use your browser to go to the MediaLoft intranet site at http://www.course.com/illustrated/ MediaLoft, then click the link for the Research Center.

**b.** Click the link for www.amazon.com, and explore its Web site until you find a Web-based form that requests information about you as a customer or an order that you'd like to place. Print that online form.

**c.** Use the MediaLoft Research Center to find the home pages of at least three other Internet-based book and/or music stores.

**d.** Find and print one Web-based data entry form from each of the three sites that you found. (*Note*: You may have to pretend that you are actually making an online purchase in order to view and print these forms, so be sure to cancel the transaction if you do not intend to purchase any products. Never enter credit card or payment information if you are not serious about finalizing the sale.)

**e.** Disconnect from the Internet.

**f.** Draw a sketch to design a form that MediaLoft can use to take orders online. You can use the Music Inventory table in the MediaLoft database as your guide for product information.

**g.** List all the fields, the data types, and any labels and images for your order form.

## ▶ Visual Workshop

Using the Clinic-C database, create the form based on the Demographics table, as shown in Figure C-19. Notice that the label "Patient Form" is 24 points and has been placed in the Form Header section. The clip art, medstaff.bmp, can be found on the Project Disk. The image has been placed on the right side of the Detail section, and many controls had to be resized in order for it to fit. Also notice that the labels are right-aligned. You also need to correct the gender entry for this record.

FIGURE C-19

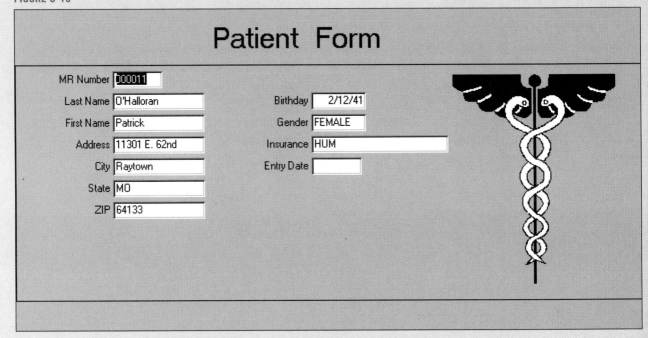

# Using

## Reports

### Objectives

MOUS ► **Plan a report**

MOUS ► **Create a report**

MOUS ► **Group records**

MOUS ► **Change the sort order**

MOUS ► **Modify an expression**

MOUS ► **Align controls**

MOUS ► **Format controls**

► **Create mailing labels**

A **report** is an Access object used to create printouts. You cannot enter or edit data through a report. Although data displayed in a report can be viewed on the screen, it is usually sent to a printer. Access reports can be based on the fields and records of either a table or a query object, can include extensive formatting embellishments such as clip art and lines, and can include professional headers and footers. Reports can also include meaningful calculations such as subtotals on groups of records. ✐ John Kim wants to produce reports that he can distribute to MediaLoft employees who do not yet have access to the MediaLoft database.

Access 2000

# Planning a Report

Without clear communication, the accuracy and integrity of information being discussed can be questioned, misinterpreted, or obscured. Hard copy reports are often the primary tool used to communicate database information at meetings, with outsiders, and with top executives. Although the **Report Wizard** can help you create an initial report object that you can later modify, the time spent planning your report not only increases your productivity but also ensures that the overall report meets its intended objectives. John has been asked to provide several reports on a regular basis to the MediaLoft executives. He plans his first report that summarizes inventory quantities within each music category.

## Steps

John uses the following guidelines to plan his report:

### Identify a meaningful title for the report

The title should clearly identify the purpose of the report and be meaningful to those who will be reading the report. The title is created with a label control placed in the **Report Header** section. **Sections** are the parts of the report that determine where a control will display on the report. See Table D-1 for more information on report sections. Just like forms, every element on a report is a control.

### Determine the information (the fields and records) that the report will show

You can base a report on a table, but usually you create a query to gather the specific fields from the one or more tables upon which to base the report. Of course, using a query also allows you to set criteria to limit the number of records displayed by the report.

### Determine how the fields should be laid out on the report

Most reports display fields in a horizontal layout across the page, but you can arrange them in any way you want. Just as in forms, bound text box controls are used on a report to display the data stored in the underlying records. These text boxes are generally placed in the report **Detail** section

### Determine how the records should be sorted and/or grouped within the report

In an Access report, the term **grouping** refers to sorting records *plus* providing a section before the group of records called the **Group Header** section and a section after the group of record called the **Group Footer** section. These sections include additional controls that often contain calculated expressions such as a subtotal for a group of records. The ability to group records is extremely powerful and only available through the report object.

### Identify any other descriptive information that should be placed at the end of the report or at the top or bottom of each page

You will use the **Report Footer**, **Page Header**, and **Page Footer** sections for these descriptive controls. John has sketched his first report in Figure D-1.

**FIGURE D-1: Sketch of the Quantities Report**

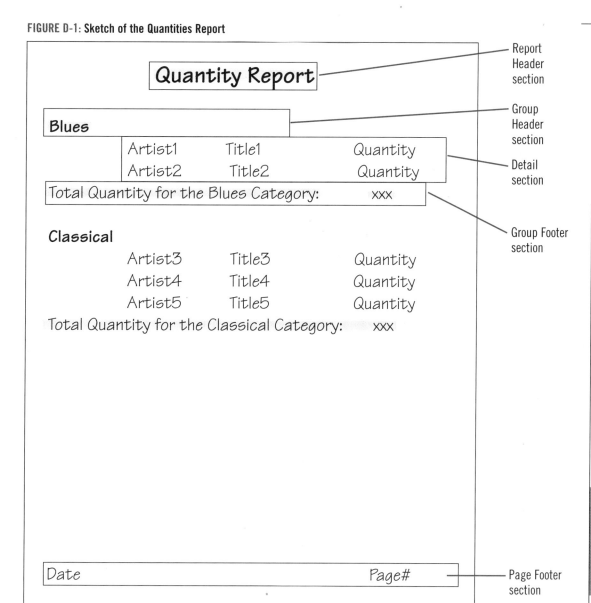

Report Header section

Group Header section

Detail section

Group Footer section

Quantity Report

Blues

| Artist1 | Title1 | Quantity |
| Artist2 | Title2 | Quantity |

Total Quantity for the Blues Category: xxx

Classical

| Artist3 | Title3 | Quantity |
| Artist4 | Title4 | Quantity |
| Artist5 | Title5 | Quantity |

Total Quantity for the Classical Category: xxx

Date                                    Page#

Page Footer section

**Access 2000**

**TABLE D-1: Report sections**

| section | where does this section print? | which controls are most commonly placed there? |
|---|---|---|
| Report Header | At the top of the first page of the report | Label controls containing the report title; can also include clip art, a logo image, or a line separating the title from the rest of the report |
| Page Header | At the top of every page (but below the report header on page one) | Descriptive label controls often acting as column headings for text box controls in the Detail section |
| Group Header | Before every group of records | Text box control for the field by which the records are grouped |
| Detail | Once for every record | Text box controls for the rest of the fields |
| Group Footer | After every group of records | Text box controls containing calculated expressions, such as subtotals or counts, for the records in that group |
| Page Footer | At the bottom of every page | Text box controls containing page number or date expression |
| Report Footer | At the end of the entire report | Text box controls containing expressions such as grand totals or counts that calculate an answer for all of the records in the report |

# Creating a Report

You can create reports in Access in **Report Design view**, or you can use the **Report Wizard** to help you get started. The Report Wizard asks questions that guide you through the initial development of the report, similar to the Form Wizard. In addition to questions about which object the report is based, which fields you want to view in the report, and the style and layout of the report, the Report Wizard also asks how you want report records to be grouped and sorted. John uses the Report Wizard to create the Quantities Report he planned on paper.

1. Start Access, click the **Open an existing file option button**, then open the **MediaLoft-D** database from your Project Disk
   This database contains an enhanced Music Inventory table and several queries from which you will base your reports.

2. Click **Reports** on the Objects bar in the MediaLoft-D Database window, then double-click **Create report by using wizard**
   The Report Wizard dialog box opens. You'll use the Selection Quantities query for this report. Another way to quickly create a report is by selecting a table or query, clicking the New Object list arrow on the Database toolbar and then selecting AutoReport. AutoReport, however, does not give you a chance to review the options provided by the Report Wizard.

3. Click the **Tables/Queries list arrow**, click **Query: Selection Quantities**, click **Category** in the Available Fields list, click the **Select Single Field button** `>`, click **Title**, click `>`, click **Artist**, click `>`, click **Quantity**, then click `>`
   The first dialog box of the Report Wizard should look like Figure D-2. The Report Wizard also asks grouping and sorting questions that determine the order and amount of detail provided on the report.

**Trouble?**

You can always click Back to review previous dialog boxes within a wizard.

4. Click **Next**, click **Next** to move past the grouping levels question, click the **first sort order list arrow** in the sort order dialog box, then click **Category**
   At this point you have not specified any grouping fields, but specified that you want the fields sorted by Category. You can use the Report Wizard to specify up to four sort fields in either an ascending or descending sort order for each field.

5. Click **Next**, click **Next** to accept the **Tabular** layout and **Portrait** orientation, click **Corporate** for the style, click **Next**, type **Quantities Report** for the report title, verify that the **Preview the report option button** is selected, then click **Finish**
   The Quantities Report opens in Print Preview, as shown in Figure D-3. It is very similar to the sketch created earlier. Notice that the records are sorted by the Category field.

## Why reports should be based on queries

Although you can use the first dialog box of the Report Wizard to select fields from different tables without first creating a query to collect those fields into one object, it is not recommended. If you later decide that you want to add more fields to the report or limit the number of records in the table, you will find it very easy to add fields or criteria to an underlying query object to meet these new needs. To accomplish this same task without using an intermediary query object requires that you change the properties of the report itself, which most users find more difficult.

**FIGURE D-2: First Report Wizard dialog box**

Base the report on the Selection Quantities query

Select Single Field button

Fields selected for the report

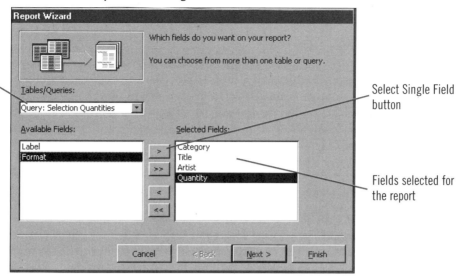

Report Header

Page Header

**FIGURE D-3: Quantities Report in Print Preview**

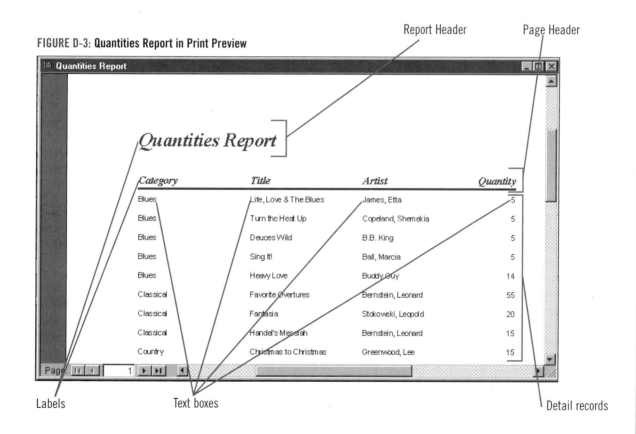

Labels

Text boxes

Detail records

# Grouping Records

Grouping refers to sorting records on a report *plus* providing an area above and below the group of records in which additional controls can be placed. These two sections of the report are called the Group Header and Group Footer. You can create groups on a report through the Report Wizard, or you can change an existing report's grouping and sorting fields in Report Design view. Just as with forms, you make all structural changes to a report in the object's Design view. John wants to group the Quantities Report by Category instead of simply sorting it by Category. In addition, he wants to add controls to the Group Header and Group Footer to clarify and summarize information within the report.

### Trouble?

If a property has a predetermined set of options, a list arrow will display when you click that property's text box in the property sheet.

1. Click the **Design View button** 🔳 on the Print Preview toolbar to switch to Report Design view, as shown in Figure D-4

   Report Design view shows you the sections of the report as well as the controls within each section. Labels and text boxes are formatted similarly in Report Design view. You can click a control and then click the Properties button to view the title bar of the property sheet to determine the nature of a control. Report Design view is where you change grouping and sort fields.

2. Click the **Sorting and Grouping button** 📇 on the Report Design toolbar, click the **Group Header text box**, click the **Group Header list arrow**, click **Yes**, click the **Group Footer text box**, click the **Group Footer list arrow**, then click **Yes**

   Specifying "Yes" for the Group Header and Group Footer properties opens those sections of the report in Report Design view.

3. Click 📇 to close the dialog box, click the **Category text box** in the Detail section, then drag the **textbox** with the ✋ pointer directly up into the Category Header section

   By placing the Category text box in the Category Header, it will print once for each new group rather than once for each record. You can add calculated subtotal controls for each category of records by placing a text box in the Category Footer section.

### QuickTip

The Field list, Toolbox toolbar, and property sheet may or may not be visible, but you can turn them on and off by clicking their respective toggle buttons. You can move them by dragging their title bars.

4. If the Toolbox toolbar is not visible, click the **Toolbox button** 🛠 on the Report Design toolbar, click the **Text Box button** 📦 on the Toolbox toolbar, then click in the **Category Footer section** directly below the Quantity text box

   Your screen should look like Figure D-5. You can use the label and text box controls in the Category Footer section to describe and subtotal the Quantity field respectively.

5. Click the **Text13: label** in the Category Footer section to select it, double-click **Text13**, type **Subtotal**, then press **[Enter]**

### Trouble?

If you double-click the edge of a control, you open the control's property sheet.

6. Click the **unbound text box control** in the Category Footer section to select it, click the **unbound text box control** again to edit it, then type **=sum([Quantity])**

   The expression that calculates the sum of the Quantity field is now in the unbound text box control. Calculated expressions start with an equal sign. When entering an expression, the field name must be referenced exactly and surrounded by square brackets.

7. Click the **Print Preview button** 🔍 on the Report Design toolbar, then scroll through the report as necessary

   The new report that groups and summarizes records by Category appears, as shown Figure D-6. Since the Category text box was moved to the Category Header section, it prints only once per group of records. Each group of records is trailed by a Group Footer that includes the Subtotal label as well as a calculated field that subtotals the Quantity field.

8. Click **Close** on the Print Preview toolbar, click the **Save button** 💾, then click the **Quantities Report Close button** to close the report

   The Quantities Report is now an object in the MediaLoft-D Database window.

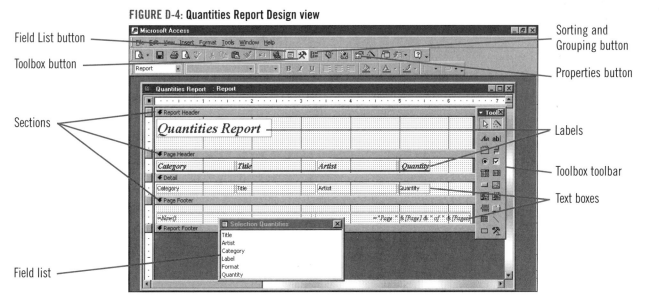

FIGURE D-4: Quantities Report Design view

Field List button

Toolbox button

Sections

Field list

Sorting and Grouping button

Properties button

Labels

Toolbox toolbar

Text boxes

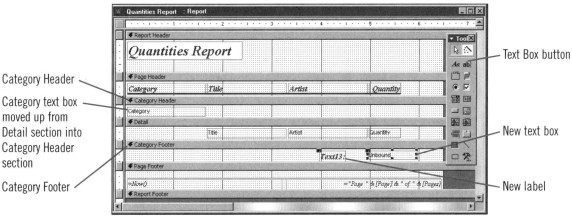

FIGURE D-5: Adding controls to the group footer section

Category Header

Category text box moved up from Detail section into Category Header section

Category Footer

Text Box button

New text box

New label

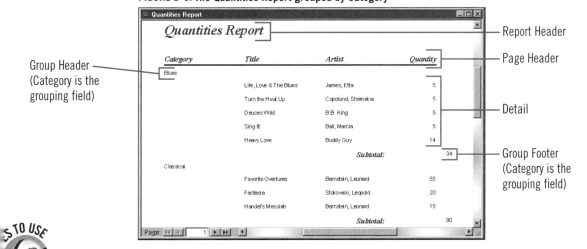

FIGURE D-6: The Quantities Report grouped by Category

Group Header (Category is the grouping field)

Report Header

Page Header

Detail

Group Footer (Category is the grouping field)

STO USE

## Adding a field to a report

Clicking the Field List button 🔲 on the Report Design toolbar toggles the field list of the underlying table or query object. To add a field from this list to the report, simply drag it from the Field list to the appropriate position on the report. This action creates both a label control that displays the field name and a text box control that displays the value of the field from the underlying records.

# Changing the Sort Order

Grouping records is really just sorting them with the additional ability to create a Group Header or Group Footer section on the report. The grouping field acts as a primary sort field. You can define further sort fields too. When you further sort records within a group, you order the Detail records according to a particular field. The Report Wizard prompts you for group and sort information at the time you create the report, but you can also group and sort an existing report by using the Sorting and Grouping dialog box in Report Design view. ✍ John wants to modify the Quantities Report so that the Detail records are sorted by the Artist field within the Category group.

**Steps** 1234

1. Click the **Quantities Report** in the MediaLoft-D Database window, then click the **Design button** 📐
   The Quantities Report opens in Report Design view.

2. Click the **Sorting and Grouping button** 📇 on the Report Design toolbar, click the **second row Field/Expression text box**, click the **Field/Expression list arrow**, then click **Artist**
   The Sorting and Grouping dialog box looks like Figure D-7. There is no Sorting and Grouping indicator in the Artist row selector. Both the Group Header and Group Footer Group properties are "No" which indicates that the Artist field is providing a sort order only.

3. Click 📇 to toggle the Sorting and Grouping dialog box off, then click the **Print Preview button** 🔍 on the Report Design toolbar
   Part of the report is shown in Print Preview, as shown in Figure D-8. You can use the buttons on the Print Preview toolbar to view more of the report.

4. Click the **One Page button** 🔲 on the Print Preview toolbar to view one miniature page, click the **Two Pages button** 🔳 to view two miniature pages, click the **Multiple Pages button** 🔠, then drag to **1x4 Pages** in the grid as shown in Figure D-9
   The Print Preview window displays the four pages of the report in miniature. Regardless of the zoom magnification of the pages, however, you can click the **Zoom pointer** 🔍 to quickly toggle between two zoom magnifications.

5. Point to the **last subtotal** on the last page of the report with the 🔍 pointer, click to read the number **92**, then click again to return the report to its former four-page magnification level

6. Click the **Close** button on the Print Preview toolbar, then click the **Save button** 💾 on the Report Design toolbar

FIGURE D-7: Specifying a sort order

Sorting and
Grouping indicator

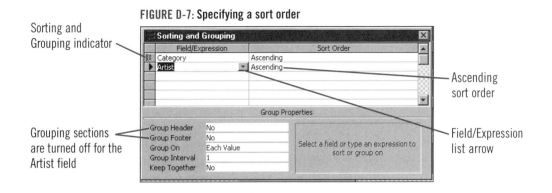

Ascending
sort order

Grouping sections
are turned off for the
Artist field

Field/Expression
list arrow

FIGURE D-8: The Quantities Report sorted by Artist

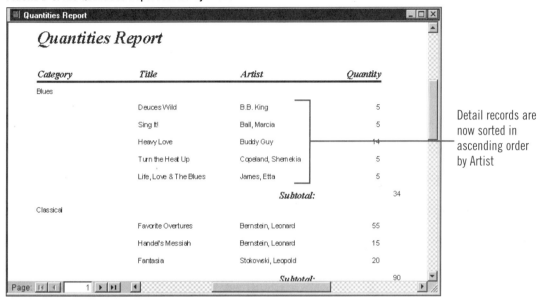

Detail records are
now sorted in
ascending order
by Artist

FIGURE D-9: Print Preview

One Page
button

Two Pages
button

Multiple
Pages button

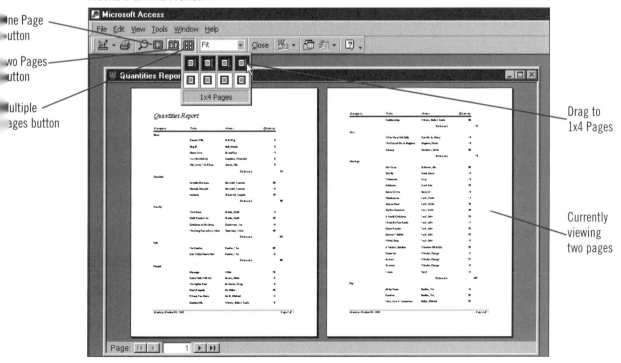

Drag to
1x4 Pages

Currently
viewing
two pages

Access 2000

# Modifying an Expression

An **expression** is a combination of fields, operators (such as +, -, / and *) and functions that result in a single value. A **function** is a built-in formula provided by Access that helps you quickly create a calculated expression. See Table D-2 for examples of common expressions that use Access functions. Notice that every calculated expression starts with an equal sign, and when it uses a function, the arguments for the function are placed in parentheses. **Arguments** are the pieces of information that the function needs to create the final answer. Calculated expressions are entered in text box controls. John adds a calculated expression to the Quantities Report that uses the Count function to count the number of records within each music category.

## Steps

1. Make sure the Quantities Report is in Report Design view, click the **=Sum([Quantity])** **text box** in the Category Footer section, click the **Copy button** on the Report Design toolbar, click in a **blank area** in the left part of the Category Footer section, then click the **Paste button** on the Report Design toolbar

    The text box and accompanying label are copied and pasted, as shown in Figure D-10. Modifying a copy of the existing calculated expression control helps reduce errors and saves on keystrokes.

2. Click the copied **Subtotal label** in the Category Footer section to select it, double-click **Subtotal** to select the text, type **Count**, then press **[Enter]**

    The label is only descriptive text. The text box is the control that actually calculates the count.

3. Click the copy of the **=Sum([Quantity])** **text box** to select it, double-click **Sum** to select it, type **count**, then press **[Enter]**

    The expression now counts the number of records in each group.

4. Click the **Print Preview button** on the Report Design toolbar to view the updated report, click the **One Page button** on the Print Preview toolbar, then scroll and zoom as shown in Figure D-11

### Using the Office Clipboard

The Office Clipboard works together with the Windows Clipboard to let you copy and paste multiple items within or between the Office applications. The Office Clipboard can hold up to 12 items copied or cut from any Office program. The Clipboard toolbar displays the items stored on the Office Clipboard. The collected items remain on the Clipboard and are available to you until you close all open Office applications.

**FIGURE D-10:** Copying and pasting a calculated control

Copy button

Paste button

New label control

New text box control

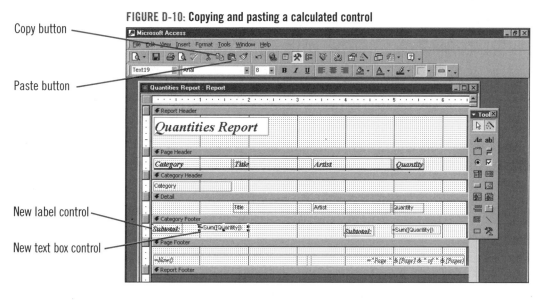

**FIGURE D-11:** Previewing the Count calculated control

New label control

New text box control

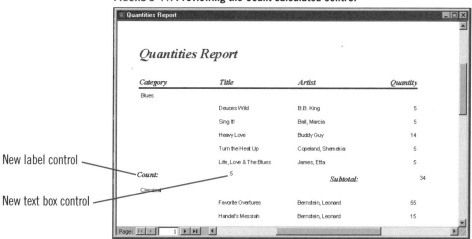

**TABLE D-2:** Common Access expressions

| category | sample expression | description |
|---|---|---|
| Arithmetic | =[Price]*1.05 | Multiplies the Price field by 1.05 (adds 5% to the Price field) |
| Arithmetic | =[Subtotal]+[Shipping] | Adds the value of the Subtotal field to the value of the Shipping field |
| Page Number | =[Page] | Displays the current page number, such as 5, 6, or 10 |
| Page Number | ="Page "&[Page] | Displays the word "Page," a space, and the current page number, such as Page 5, Page 6, or Page 10 |
| Text | =[FirstName]&" "&[LastName] | Displays the value of the FirstName and LastName fields in one control separated by a space |
| Text | =Left([ProductNumber],2) | Uses the **Left** function to display the first two characters in the ProductNumber field |
| Aggregate | =Avg([Freight]) | Uses the **Avg** function to display an average of the values in the Freight field |
| Aggregate | =Count([FirstName]) | Uses the **Count** function to display the number of records that contain an entry in the FirstName field |
| Aggregate | =Sum([Tracks]) | Uses the **Sum** function to display the total value from the Tracks field |
| Date | =Date() | Uses the **Date** function to display the current date in the form of mm-dd-yy, such as 10-23-00 or 11-14-01 |

# Aligning Controls

Once the information that you want to present has been added to the appropriate section of a report, you may also want to rearrange the data on the report. By aligning controls in columns and rows, you can present your information so it is easier to understand. There are several **alignment** commands that are important to understand. You can left-, right-, or center-align a control *within its own border*, or you can align the edges of controls *with respect to one another.* John aligns several controls on the Quantities Report to improve the readability and professionalism of the report. His first task is to right-align all of the controls in the Category Footer.

## Steps 1 2 3 4

1. **Click the Design View button 🔲 on the Print Preview toolbar, then click in the vertical ruler to the left of the Count label in the Category Footer section**
   All four controls in the Category Footer section are selected. Text boxes that display numeric fields are right-aligned by default; the labels and text boxes you added in the Category Footer section that display calculated expressions are left-aligned by default. You can use the same techniques for selecting controls in Report Design view as you did in Form Design view.

2. **Click the Align Right button 🔳 on the Formatting (Form/Report) toolbar**
   Your screen should look like Figure D-12. Now the information displayed by the control is right-aligned within the control.

3. **With the four controls still selected, click Format on the menu bar, point to Align, then click Bottom**
   The bottom edges of the four controls are now aligned with respect to one another. The Align command on the Format menu refers to aligning controls with respect to one another. The Alignment buttons on the Formatting toolbar refer to aligning controls within their own borders. You can also align the right or left edges of controls in different sections.

4. **Click the Quantity label in the Page Header section, press and hold [Shift], click the Quantity text box in the Detail section, click the =Sum([Quantity]) text box in the Category Footer section, release [Shift], click Format on the menu bar, point to Align, then click Right**
   The right edges of the Quantity label, Quantity text box, and Quantity calculated control are aligned. With the edges at the same position and the information right-aligned within the controls, the controls form a perfect column on the final report. You can extend the line in the Page Header section to better define the sections on the page.

5. **Click the blue line in the Page Header section, press and hold [Shift], point to the right sizing handle, when the pointer changes to ↖, drag the handle to the 6" mark, then release [Shift]**
   By pressing [Shift] when you draw or resize a line, the line remains perfectly horizontal as you drag it left or right.

   > **Trouble?**
   > Don't drag beyond the 6" mark or the printout will be wider than one sheet of paper.

6. **Click the Print Preview button 🔍 on the Report Design toolbar, then scroll and zoom**
   Your screen should look like Figure D-13.

**FIGURE D-12:** Working with the alignment buttons

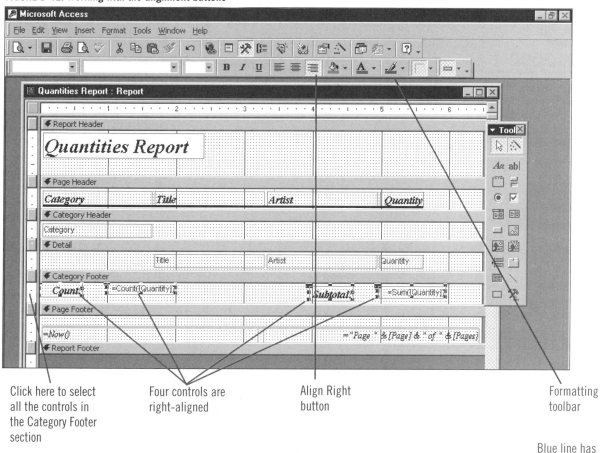

Click here to select
all the controls in
the Category Footer
section

Four controls are
right-aligned

Align Right
button

Formatting
toolbar

Blue line has
been widened

**FIGURE D-13:** Controls are aligned

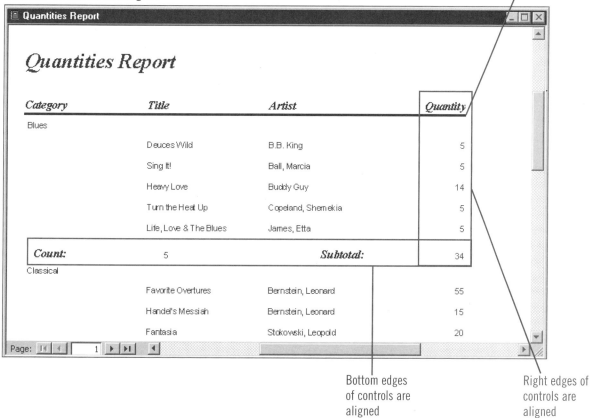

Bottom edges
of controls are
aligned

Right edges of
controls are
aligned

# Formatting Controls

**Formatting** refers to enhancing the appearance of the information. Table D-3 lists several of the most popular formatting commands which can be used with either forms or reports. Although the Report Wizard provides many formatting embellishments on a report, you often want to improve upon the report's appearance to fit your particular needs. ◢▬▬ John doesn't feel that the music category information is prominent on the report, so he wants to format that control to change its appearance.

## Steps

**QuickTip**

If you need your name on the printed solution, add a label to the Report Header that displays your name.

**1.** Click the **Design View button** 📐 on the Print Preview toolbar, click the **Toolbox button** 🛠 to toggle it off, then click the **Category text box** in the Category Header section
Before you can format any control, it must be selected.

**2.** Click the **Font size list arrow** on the Formatting (Form/Report) toolbar, click **11**, then click the **Bold button** **B**
Increasing the font size and applying bold are common ways to make information more visible on a report. You can also change the colors of the control.

**Trouble?**

If the default color on the Font/Fore Color button is red, click the button.

**3.** With the Category text box still selected, click the **Font/Fore Color** list arrow **A·**, then click the **Red box** (third row, first column on the left), as shown in Figure D-14.
Many buttons on the Formatting (Form/Report) toolbar include a list arrow that you can click to reveal a list of choices. When you click the color list arrow, a palette of available colors is displayed. You can change the background color of the Category text box using the palette.

**4.** With the Category text box still selected, click the **Fill/Back Color list arrow** 🎨·, then click the **light gray box** (fourth row, first column on the right)
When you print colors on a black and white printer, they become various shades of gray. So, unless you always print to a color printer, be careful about relying too heavily on color for matting, especially background shades that often become solid black boxes when printed on a black and white printer or fax machine. Fortunately, Access allows you to undo your last command if you don't like the change you've made. You must pay close attention, however, because you can only undo your very last command.

**5.** With the Category text box still selected, click the **Undo button** ↩ on the Report Design toolbar to remove the background color, click the **Line/Border Color list arrow** 🖌·, then click the **blue box** (second row, third column from right)

**6.** Click the **Print Preview button** 🔍 on the Report Design toolbar
The screen should look like Figure D-15.

**7.** Click **File** on the menu bar, click **Print**, type **1** in the From text box, type **1** in the text box, click **OK**, then click **Close** on the Print Preview toolbar
The first page of the report is printed.

**8.** Click the **Save button** 💾, then close the Quantities Report

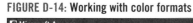

FIGURE D-14: Working with color formats

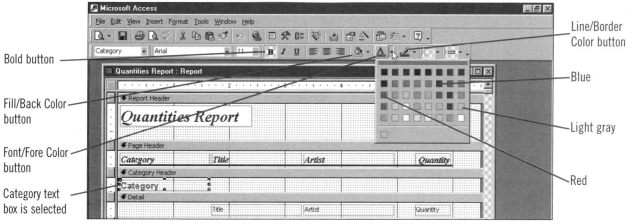

- Bold button
- Fill/Back Color button
- Font/Fore Color button
- Category text box is selected
- Line/Border Color button
- Blue
- Light gray
- Red

FIGURE D-15: Formatted Quantities Report

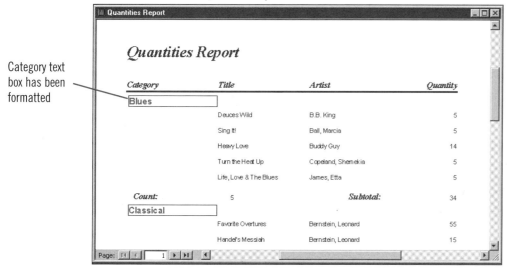

- Category text box has been formatted

Access 2000

**BLE D-3: Popular formatting commands**

| utton | button name | description |
|---|---|---|
| B | **Bold** | Toggles bold on or off for the selected control(s) |
| I | **Italic** | Toggles italics, on or off for the selected control(s) |
| U | **Underline** | Toggles underline on or off for the selected control(s) |
| | **Align Left** | Left-aligns the selected control(s) within its own border |
| | **Center** | Center-aligns the selected control(s) within its own border |
| | **Align Right** | Right-aligns the selected control(s) within its own border |
| | **Fill/Back Color** | Changes the background color of the selected control(s) |
| | **Font/Fore Color** | Changes the text color of the selected control(s) |
| | **Line/Border Color** | Changes the border color of the selected control(s) |
| | **Line/Border Width** | Changes the style of the border of the selected control(s) |
| | **Special Effect** | Changes the special visual effect of the selected control(s) |

# Creating Mailing Labels

Mailing Labels are used for many business purposes such as identifying paper folders and providing addresses for mass mailings. Once you enter raw data into your Access database, you can easily create mailing labels from this data using the **Label Wizard**. John has been asked to create labels for the display cases in the MediaLoft stores with the Artist and Title fields only. The labels are to be printed in alphabetical order by Artist and then by Title. John uses the Label Wizard to get started.

## Steps

**Trouble?**

If you don't see Avery, click English units of measure, click the Filter by manufacturer list arrow, then click Avery.

1. Click **Reports** on the Objects bar in the MediaLoft-D Database window, click the **New button**, click **Label Wizard** in the New Report dialog box, click the **Choose the table or query where the object's data comes from list arrow**, click **Music Inventory**, then click **OK**

   The Label Wizard dialog box opens requesting that you specify information about the characteristics of the label, as shown in Figure D-16. Avery 5160 labels are one of the most popular sizes. Avery 5160 label sheets have three columns and ten rows of labels for a total of 30 label per page.

2. Click **5160**, then click **Next**

   The next wizard dialog box allows you to change the font, font size, and other text attributes. Larger fonts will be easier to read and will fit on this label since there are only two fields of information.

**Trouble?**

If your system doesn't have the Comic Sans MS font, choose another font appropriate for music labels.

3. Click the **Font size list arrow**, click **11**, click the **Font name list arrow**, scroll and click **Comic Sans MS** (a sample appears in the Sample box), then click **Next**

   The next wizard dialog box, which shows you the prototype label, allows you choose which fields you want to include in each label as well as their placement. Any spaces or punctuation that you want on the label must be entered from the keyboard. Also, if you want to put a field on a new line, you must press [Enter] to move to a new row of the prototype label.

**QuickTip**

You can double-click the field name in the Available Fields list to move it to the Prototype label list.

4. Click **Artist**, click the **Select Single Field button**, press [Enter], click **Title**, then click

   Your screen should look like Figure D-17.

5. Click **Next**

   The next wizard dialog box asks about sorting.

6. Double-click **Artist** for your primary sort field, double-click **Title** for your secondary sort field, then click **Next**

   You should give your labels a descriptive name.

7. Type **Artist-Title Labels** to name the report, click **Finish**, then click the **Zoom pointer** to see a full page of labels

   The labels should look like Figure D-18.

8. Click **Close** on the Print Preview toolbar to see the Artist-Title Labels report in Design view, click the **Save button**, then click the **Print button**

9. Click **File** on the menu bar, then click **Exit** to exit Access

**FIGURE D-16:** Label Wizard

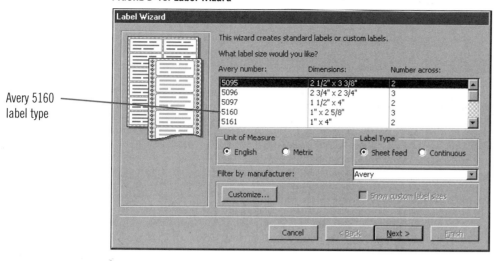

Avery 5160 label type

**FIGURE D-17:** The prototype label

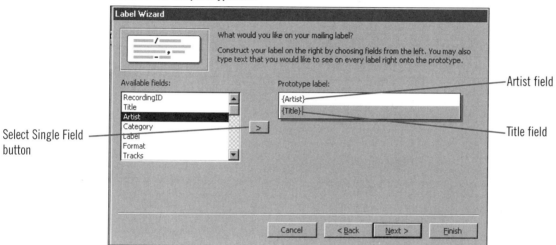

Artist field

Title field

Select Single Field button

**FIGURE D-18:** The Artist-Title Labels report

Labels are 3 columns by 10 rows on each page

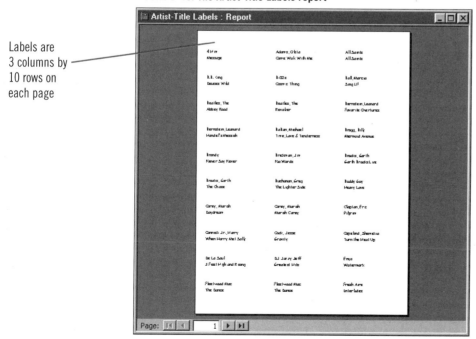

# Practice

## ► Concepts Review

Label each element of the Report Design window shown in Figure D-19.

FIGURE D-19

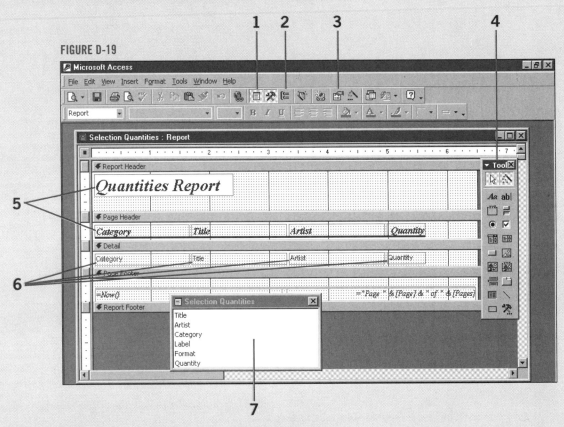

## Match each term with the statement that describes it.

| | |
|---|---|
| 8. Function | a. Part of the report that determines where a control will display on the report |
| 9. Section | b. Sorting records *plus* providing a section before and after the group of records |
| 10. Detail section | c. An Access object used to create paper printouts |
| 11. Report | d. Enhancing the appearance of the information |
| 12. Formatting | e. A built-in formula provided by Access that helps you quickly create a calculated expressi |
| 13. Grouping | f. Prints once for every record |

Select the best answer from the list of choices.

14. Press and hold which key to select more than one control in Report Design view?
    a. [Ctrl]
    b. [Alt]
    c. [Shift]
    d. [Tab]

15. Which type of control is most likely found in the Detail section?
    a. Label
    b. Text box
    c. Combo box
    d. List box

16. Which type of control is most likely found in the Page Header section?
    a. Label
    b. Combo box
    c. Command button
    d. Bound image

7. A calculated expression is most often found in which report section?
    a. Report Header
    b. Detail
    c. Formulas
    d. Group Footer

3. Which of the following would be the appropriate expression to count the number of records using the FirstName field?
    a. =Count(FirstName)
    b. =Count[FirstName)
    c. =Count{FirstName}
    d. =Count([FirstName])

. To align the edges of several controls with respect to one another, you use the alignment commands on the
    a. Formatting toolbar.
    b. Standard toolbar.
    c. Print Preview toolbar.
    d. Format menu.

# ▶ Skills Review

## 1. Plan a report.

a. Pretend that you are looking for a job. Plan a report to use for tracking job opportunities. To gather the raw data for your report, find a newspaper with job listings in your area of interest.

b. Identify the Report Header, Group Header, and Detail sections of the report by using sample data based on the following information:

- The title of the report should be "Job Opportunity Report."
- The records should be grouped by job title. For example, if you are interested in working with computers, job titles might be "Computer Operator" or "Computer Analyst." Include at least two job title groupings in your sample report.
- The Detail section should include information on the company, contact, and telephone number for each job opportunity.

## 2. Create a report.

a. Start Access and open the Club-D database on your Project Disk.

b. Use the Report Wizard to create a report based on the Contacts table.

c. Include the following fields for the report:
   STATUS, FNAME, LNAME, DUESOWED, DUESPAID

d. Do not add any grouping or sorting fields.

e. Use the Tabular layout and Portrait orientation.

f. Use a bold style and title the report "Contact Status Report."

g. Preview the first page of the new report.

## 3. Group records.

a. In Report Design view, open the Sorting and Grouping dialog box, and group the report by the STATUS field in ascending order. Open both the Group Header and Group Footer sections, then close the dialog box.

b. Move the STATUS text box in the Detail section up to the left edge of the STATUS Header section.

c. Preview the first page of the new report.

## 4. Change the sort order.

a. In Report Design view, open the Sorting and Grouping dialog box, then add LNAME as a sort field in ascending order immediately below the STATUS field.

b. Preview the first page of the new report.

## 5. Modify an expression.

a. In Report Design view, add a text box control in the STATUS Footer section directly below the DUESOWED text box in the Detail section.

b. Delete the accompanying label to the left of the unbound text box.

c. Add a text box control in the STATUS Footer section directly below the DUESPAID text box in the Detail section.

d. Delete the accompanying label to the left of the unbound text box by clicking the label, then pressing [Delete].

e. Add an unbound label to the report header, and type your name as the label.

f. Modify the text boxes so that they subtotal the DUESOWED and DUESPAID fields respectively. The calculated expressions will be =Sum([DUESOWED]) and =Sum([DUESPAID]).

g. Preview both pages of the report, then print both pages of the report.

### 6. Align controls.

**a.** In Report Design view, right-align the new calculated controls in the STATUS Footer section.

**b.** Select the DUESOWED text box in the Detail section, and the =Sum([DUESOWED]) calculated expression in the STATUS Footer, then right-align the controls with respect to one another.

**c.** Select the DUESPAID text box in the Detail section, and the =Sum([DUESPAID]) calculated expression in the STATUS Footer, then right-align the controls with respect to one another.

### 7. Format controls.

**a.** Select the two calculated controls in the STATUS Footer, click the Properties button, then change the Format property on the Format tab to Currency. Close the property sheet.

**b.** Select the STATUS text box in the STATUS Header section, change the font size to 12 points, bold and italicize the control, then change the background color to bright yellow.

**c.** Preview the report, check the new totals, save the report, print it, then close the report.

### 8. Create mailing labels.

**a.** Use the Label Wizard and the Contacts table to create mailing labels using Avery 5160 labels.

**b.** The text should be formatted as Arial, 10 points, Light font weight, black, with no italic or underline attributes.

**c.** The prototype label should be organized as follows:
FNAME LNAME
COMPANY
STREET
CITY, STATE ZIP

**d.** Sort the labels by the ZIP field.

**e.** Name the report "Mailing Labels."

**f.** Print the first page of the labels, save the report, then close it.

**g.** Exit Access.

# ▶ Independent Challenges

**1.** You have been hired to create several reports for a physical therapy clinic.
To complete this independent challenge:

a. Start Access and open the Therapy-D database from your Project Disk.
b. Using the Report Wizard, create a report using all of the fields from the Location Financial Query.
c. View your data by Survey, group by Street, sort in ascending order by PatientLast, and sum both the AmountSent and AmountRecorded fields.
d. Use the Stepped layout, Portrait orientation, and Soft Gray style.
e. Name the report "Location Financial Report."
f. Modify the AmountSent and AmountRecorded labels in the Page Header section to "Sent" and "Recorded" respectively.
g. Change the font/fore color of the labels in the Page Header section to bright blue.
h. Widen the Street text box label in the Street Header section to twice its current size, and change the border color to bright blue.
i. Save and print the report.
j. Exit Access.

**2.** You have been hired to create several reports for a physical therapy clinic.
To complete this independent challenge:

a. Start Access and open the Therapy-D database from your Project Disk.
b. Using the Report Wizard, create a report using all of the fields from the Therapist Satisfaction Query except for the Initials and First fields.
c. View the data by Survey. Do not add any grouping levels and do not add any sorting levels.
d. Use the Tabular layout, Portrait orientation, and Casual style.
e. Title the report "Therapist Satisfaction Report," then print the report.
f. In Report Design view, group the report by Last, and open both the Group Header and Group Footer sections.
g. Further sort the records by PatientLast.
h. Move the Last text box from the Detail section up into the Last Header section.
i. Remove bold from all of the labels in the Page Header section.
j. Add text boxes in the Last Footer section directly below the Courtesy and Knowledge text boxes in the Detail section. Enter the calculated controls =Avg([Courtesy]) and =Avg([Knowledge]) respectively. Delete their accompanying labels, and resize the new calculated controls so that they are a little narrower than the Courtesy and Knowledge text boxes in the Detail section.
k. Open the property sheet for the two new calculated controls, and change the Format property on the Format t to "Fixed."
l. Right-align the two new calculated controls within their own borders. Also, align the right edge of the =Avg([Courtesy]) control with respect to the Courtesy text box in the Detail section. Right-align the edges of the =Avg([Knowledge]) and Knowledge text boxes with respect to each other.
m. Align the top edges of the new calculated controls.
n. Drag the right edge of the report to the left so the report is 6½" wide (if necessary).
o. Save, preview, and print the report.
p. Exit Access.

**3.** Use the knowledge and skills that you have acquired about Access to create an attractive report that includes information about colleges and universities that offer programs in computer science. Create a database containing this information, and then design a report that displays the data. Gather information from libraries, friends, and the Web to enter into the database.

To complete this independent challenge:

**a.** Start Access and create a new database called "Colleges" on your Project Disk. Include any fields you feel are important, but make sure you include the institution's name, state, and whether it is a 4- or 2-year school.

**b.** Find information on schools that offer programs in computer science. If you are using the Web, use any available search engines.

**c.** Compile a list of at least 15 institutions, and enter the 15 records into a table named "Computer Science Schools."

**d.** Create a report that includes all the fields in the table Computer Science Schools, and group by the field that contains the information on whether it is a 4- or 2-year school.

**e.** Sort the records in ascending order by the state, then by the institution's name.

**f.** Use an appropriate style and title for your report. Insert your initials at the end of the report title so you can identify it.

**g.** Save, preview, and print the report.

**h.** Exit Access.

**4.** As an assistant in the marketing department at MediaLoft, you are often asked to create mailing labels for the MediaLoft store locations. You have decided to create a small database that stores information about the stores so that you can quickly create the labels using the Label Wizard.

To complete this independent challenge:

**a.** Start Access and create a new database on your Project Disk called "MediaLoft Locations."

**b.** Connect to the Internet, use your browser to go to the MediaLoft intranet site at http://www.course.com/illustrated/MediaLoft, then click the About link for the page with the MediaLoft store locations.

**c.** Print the Web page that displays the store locations.

**d.** Disconnect from the Internet, and switch to the Access window.

**e.** Create a table called "Stores" with the following fields (each field's data type should be Text): StoreName, Street, City, State, Zip, Phone

**f.** Using the Stores datasheet, type each store location into the database. Pay close attention to capitalization and spelling.

**g.** Using the Label Wizard, create mailing labels with the store address information on Avery 5160 labels.

**h.** Format the label with any decorative font, a 12-point font size, and bright red text.

**.** Use the following label prototype:
StoreName
Street
City, State Zip
Name the label report "Store Address Labels," and print the report.

**.** Save and close the report, then exit Access.

# ▶ Visual Workshop

Use the Club-D database on your Project Disk to create the report based on the CONTACTS table shown in Figure D-20. The Report Wizard and the Corporate style were used to create this report. Note that the records are grouped by the CITY field and sorted within each group by the LNAME field. A calculated control that counts the number of records is displayed in the Group Footer.

**FIGURE D-20**

## *Membership by City*

| CITY | LNAME | FNAME | PHONE |
|------|-------|-------|-------|
| *Bridgewater* | | | |
| | Daniels | Mark | 555-2277 |
| Count:  1 | | | |
| *Fontanelle* | | | |
| | Eagan | Jane | 555-1166 |
| Count:  1 | | | |
| *Industrial Airport* | | | |
| | Braven | Mary | 555-7002 |
| Count:  1 | | | |
| *Kansas City* | | | |
| | Alman | Jill | 555-6931 |
| | Bouchart | Bob | 555-3081 |
| | Collins | Christine | 555-3602 |
| | Diverman | Barbara | 555-0401 |
| | Duman | Mary Jane | 555-8844 |
| | Eahlie | Andrea | 555-0401 |
| | Eckert | Jay | 555-7414 |
| | Hammer | Mike | 555-0365 |
| | Hubert | Holly | 555-6004 |
| | Mackintosh | Helen | 555-9414 |
| | Mayberry | Mitch | 555-0401 |
| | Olson | Marcie | 555-1388 |
| | Parton | Jeanette | 555-8773 |
| | Walker | Shirley | 555-0403 |
| Count:  14 | | | |

# Integrating
## Word, Excel, and Access

### Objectives

► **Merge data between Access and Word**
► **Use Mail Merge to create a form letter**
► **Export an Access table to Excel**

You have learned how to use Word, Excel, and Access individually to accomplish specific tasks more efficiently. Now you learn how to integrate files created with these programs so that you can use the best features of each one. In preparation for the upcoming annual report, Maria Abbott, the general sales manager for MediaLoft, wants to establish a profile of MediaLoft's corporate customers that she can incorporate into the report. To do this, she mails a survey to these customers. She also wants to export the Access database of corporate customer names and addresses into an Excel worksheet so that she can create an Excel chart showing corporate sales by state.

# Merging Data Between Access and Word

Companies often keep a database of customer names and addresses, which they use to send form letters to their customers. With Microsoft Office, you can combine, or **merge**, data from an existing Access table with a Word document to automatically create personalized form letters. Maria wants to survey MediaLoft's corporate customers. She wrote a form letter using Word. She wants to merge her form letter with the customer names and addresses that already exist in an Access table.

**QuickTip**

If you plan to do the steps in this unit again, be sure to make and use a copy of the Word file INT B-1 and the Access file MediaLoft-IB.

1. **Start Access, open the file MediaLoft-IB from your Project Disk, click Tables on the Objects bar if necessary, click Customers, then click Open**
   The database window for the file MediaLoft-IB opens. The Customers table is the **data source** for the mail merge.

2. **Click Tools on the menu bar, point to Office Links, then click Merge It with MS Word**
   The Microsoft Word Mail Merge Wizard dialog box opens, as shown in Figure B-1. The Mail Merge Wizard links your data to a Microsoft Word document. The customer survey form letter already exists as a Word document, so the default option, Link your data to an existing Microsoft Word document, is correct.

3. **Click OK**
   The Select Microsoft Word Document dialog box opens.

4. **Select the file INT B-1 from your Project Disk, then click Open**
   Word opens and the document INT B-1 appears in the document window. The Mail Merge toolbar appears below the Standard and Formatting toolbars. Table B-1 describes the buttons on the Mail Merge toolbar. The document you just opened is the **main document** for the mail merge.

**Trouble?**

If the Access window appears on top, click the Word program button on the taskbar.

5. **If the Word program window does not fill the screen, click the Word program window Maximize button**
   Compare your screen to Figure B-2.

6. **Replace Maria Abbott's name with your name**

7. **Click File on the Word menu bar, click Save As, then save the document as Survey Form Letter to your Project Disk**

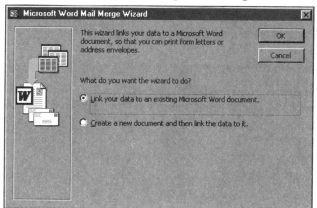

Your toolbars
may differ

FIGURE B-2: **Main document**

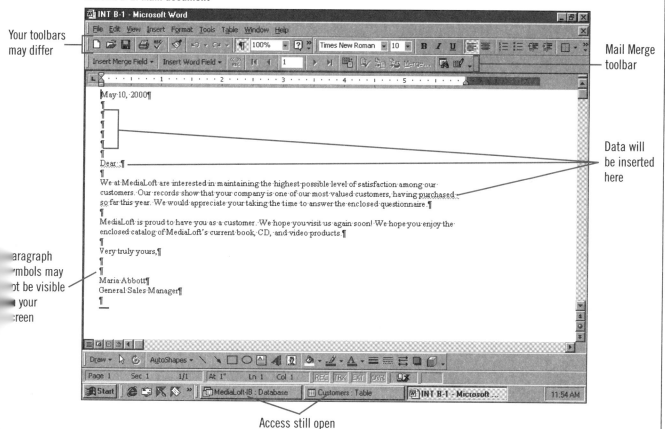

Mail Merge
toolbar

Data will
be inserted
here

aragraph
mbols may
t be visible
your
creen

Access still open

**BLE B-1: Mail Merge buttons**

| me | button | name | button |
|---|---|---|---|
| »| View Merged Data | | Check for Errors |
| ◄ | First Record | | Merge to New Document |
| | Previous Record | | Merge to Printer |
| | Go to Record | Merge... | Start Mail Merge |
| | Next Record | | Find Record |
| | Last Record | | Edit Data Source |
| | Mail Merge Helper | | |

Integration 2000

# Using Mail Merge to Create a Form Letter

Once you have opened and linked the form letter and the Access table, you are ready to insert **merge fields**, placeholders for the merged data, into the letter. When you perform the mail merge, Access looks for the merge fields in the main document and replaces them with the appropriate fields from the data source. After opening the data source and selecting the main document, Maria needs to insert merge fields into the main document.

## Steps

**Trouble?**

If you can't see the paragraph symbols, click the Show/Hide ¶ button ¶ on the Standard toolbar. You may need to click the More Buttons button on the Standard toolbar to locate ¶.

1. **In the Word document, position the pointer in the second empty paragraph below the date, then click the Insert Merge Field menu button on the Mail Merge toolbar**
   A list of fields in the Access database appears, as shown in Figure B-3. The first merge field you need to insert is the First field in the inside address, representing each customer's first name.

2. **Click First**
   The First field is inserted between angled brackets in the form letter.

3. **Press [Spacebar], click the Insert Merge Field menu button on the Mail Merge toolbar, click Last, then press [↓]**

4. **Continue inserting the merge fields and typing the text shown in Figure B-4, being sure to include the fields in the salutation and in the body of the letter, then save the document**
   Make sure you insert a comma and a space after the City merge field and a space after the State merge field.

5. **Click the View Merged Data button on the Mail Merge toolbar**
   Before you merge the data, it's a good idea to check that the merged data appears correctly in the main document. The data from the first record (Aaron Friedrichsen at Sprint) appears in the main document, as shown in Figure B-5. There are several ways to merge the main document with the data source. If you want to merge the main document with records that meet certain criteria, click the Start Mail Merge button on the Mail Merge toolbar, then set query options. If you want to merge the files directly to the printer, click the Merge to Printer button on the Mail Merge toolbar. It's a good idea to merge the documents into one new document so that you can examine the final product and make any necessary corrections before you print.

6. **Click the Merge to New Document button on the Mail Merge toolbar**
   Form Letters1 appears in the title bar as the title of the Word document. You should see the first form letter with Aaron Friedrichsen's data on your screen.

7. **Click on the Standard toolbar, then save the document as Survey Letters to your Project Disk**

8. **Click File on the menu bar, click Print, click the Current page option button to print only the first form letter, then click OK**
   The first form letter prints.

9. **Click File on the menu bar, click Exit, then click No to save changes to Survey Form Letter**
   Word closes and returns you to Access.

FIGURE B-3: **List of fields in Access database**

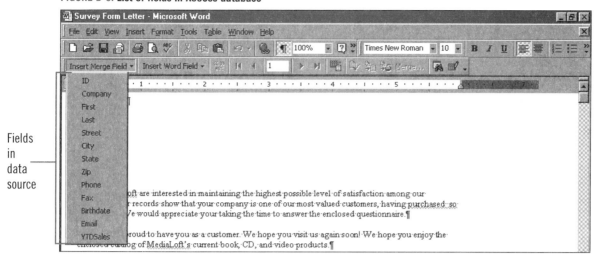

Fields
in
data
source

FIGURE B-4: **Main document with merge fields inserted**

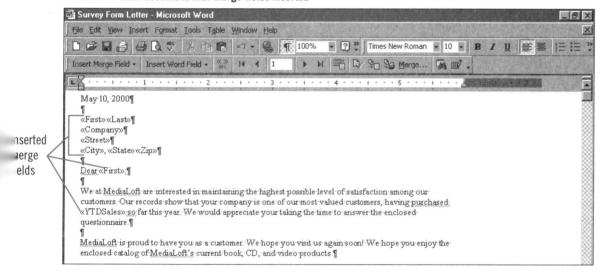

Inserted
merge
fields

FIGURE B-5: **Main document with merged data**

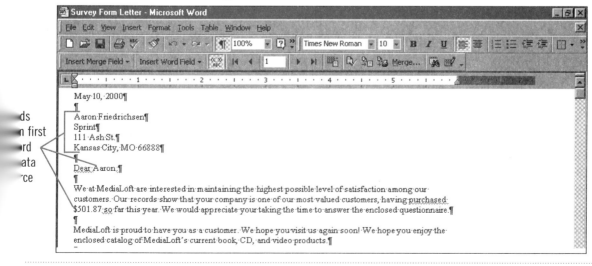

ds
in first
rd
ata
ce

# Exporting an Access Table to Excel

You can export data in an Access table to Excel and several other applications. When you export a table, a copy of the data is created in a format acceptable to the other application, and the original data remains intact. Maria wants to export the Customers table in the MediaLoft-IB database into Excel so that she can analyze the data. Later, she will create a chart that shows the distribution of MediaLoft's corporate customer sales.

## Steps 1234

1. Make sure the Customers table is active

2. Click **Tools** on the menu bar, point to **Office Links**, then click **Analyze It with MS Excel**
   The exported data appears in an Excel workbook named Customers that contains only one worksheet, also named Customers. When you import data into Excel, only one worksheet is supplied, although you can add more.

3. If necessary, click the Excel program window **Maximize button**
   Maria will not need the Phone, Fax, Birthdate, or Email columns.

4. Select the **I through L column selector buttons**, click **Edit** on the menu bar, click **Delete**, then press **[Home]** to return to cell A1
   All the remaining columns are now visible on the screen.

5. Click **Data** on the menu bar, then click **Sort**
   The Sort dialog box opens, as shown in Figure B-6. Notice that the Header row option button at the bottom of the dialog box is selected. This means that the first row in the worksheet will not be sorted.

6. Click the **list arrow** in the **Sort by** section, scroll down and click **State**, click the list arrow in the first **Then by** section, scroll down and click **YTD Sales**, then click **OK**
   The data is now sorted by state, and within each state, by year-to-date sales. Compare your screen to Figure B-7.

### QuickTip
The Excel file created is automatically saved in the same folder as the Access file.

7. Click the **Save button** on the Standard toolbar
   A message might appear telling you that the workbook was created in a previous version Excel.

8. Click **Yes** to update it, if necessary

9. Click **File** on the menu bar, click **Page Setup**, click the **Page tab**, click the **Landscape option button**, click **Print**, then click **OK**

10. Click , click **File** on the menu bar, click **Exit** to exit Excel, in the Access program window, click **File** on the menu bar, then click **Exit** to exit Access

CLUES TO USE

### Exporting an Access table to Word

You can export an Access table to Microsoft Word by using the Publish It with MS Word feature. To export a table, open the Access database with the table you want to export, click the table, click Tools on the menu bar, point to Office Links, then click Publish It with MS Word. An Access wizard automatically opens Word, exports the table data, creates a new table with the database information, and saves the Word file with the same name as the Access table.

FIGURE B-6: Sort dialog box

Sort on State first —————

Sort on YTDSales second —————

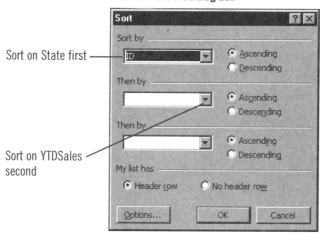

Sorted on YTDSales second

Sorted on state first

FIGURE B-7: Excel worksheet with sorted data

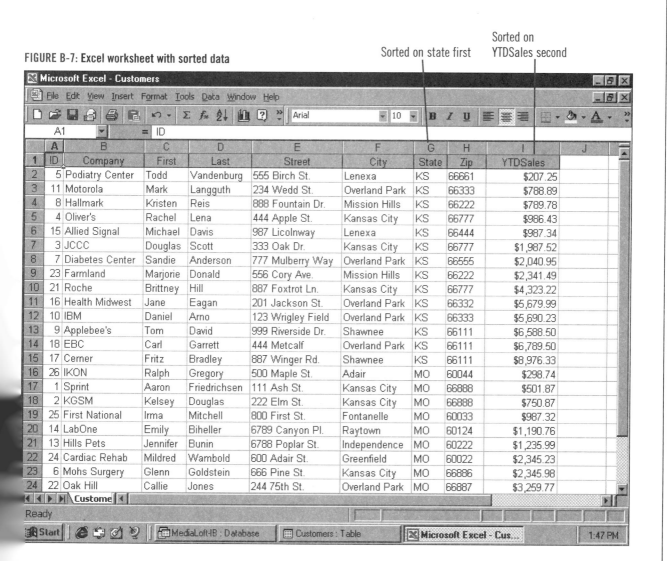

# ▶ Independent Challenges

**1.** As the administrator for Monroe High School, you want to keep track of student records and generate reports for the principal and school district. You need to create a database containing information about the current students enrolled in the high school. Once the database table is complete, export the table information to Excel and Word to create reports.

To complete this independent challenge:

**a.** Decide what fields should be included in the database. Include fields for student's first name, last name, address, phone number, gender (male or female), birth date, grade level, and cumulative grade point average (GPA).

**b.** Save the new database file as "Student Records," then create the student table called "Student Info."

**c.** Create a form to facilitate the entry of your student records, then print one record to show a sample of the form.

**d.** Add 20 records to your table, then sort the students by last name and then by first name.

**e.** Export the Student Info table to an Excel worksheet, then resize the columns to fit the table.

**f.** Scroll down to row 23 and enter your name in cell 23.

**g.** Print out your results, then save the changes to your worksheet. (Note that the Excel file is automatically saved as Student Info to your Project Disk.)

**h.** Use the Publish It With MS Word command to export the Student Info table to a Word table, resize columns to fit the table, sort the table by grade level and then by last name, then format the table to make the document more attractive.

**i.** Press [Ctrl] [Home], type your name, then press [Enter].

**j.** Save the changes to your Student Info document, then print it.

 **2.** MediaLoft sponsors the Pleasantown Players, a regional theater group that is supported by ticket revenues and private donations. As an employee of the MediaLoft Human Resources department, you have been asked to help the theater group by writing a fund raising letter and merging it with a database of selected MediaLoft corporate customers. To maximize your results, you decide to send out the initial mailing to those customers who have spent more than $2,000 at MediaLoft so far this year. To complete the task, you need to modify the current Customers table and create a query to find the appropriate customers. Once the database query is complete, you create a form letter, which you merge with the data stored in the query.

To complete this independent challenge:

**a.** In the MediaLoft-IB database on your Project Disk, create a query to find corporate customers who have spent more than $2,000 at MediaLoft so far this year. You are going to merge this query with a form letter, so make sure you include all the fields you will merge into the letter in the query.

**b.** Create a main document (form letter) in Word using all the fields you feel are necessary. In the letter, you want to tell customers how important it is to support local, nonprofessional theater. For the letter content, tell the customers about the Pleasantown Players, using information you learn from MediaLoft's intranet site: Connect to the Internet, go to www.course.com/illustrated/MediaLoft, click the Community link, click the Corporate Sponsorships link, then click the Pleasantown Players link. Use any of the information you find at this Web site to add informative, persuasive facts to your funding request.

**c.** Type your name in the signature block in the letter.

**d.** Save the main document as "Funding Letter" to your Project Disk.

**e.** Merge the document Funding Letter and the query you created into a new document named "Pleasantown Letters."

**f.** Print the current page of the Pleasantown Letters file.

# Getting
## Started with PowerPoint 2000

### Objectives

- ▶ **Define presentation software**
- ▶ **Start PowerPoint 2000**
- MOUS ▶ **Use the AutoContent Wizard**
- MOUS ▶ **View the PowerPoint window**
- ▶ **View a presentation**
- MOUS ▶ **Save a presentation**
- MOUS ▶ **Get Help**
- MOUS ▶ **Print and close the file, and exit PowerPoint**

Microsoft PowerPoint 2000 is a presentation program that transforms your ideas into professional, compelling presentations. With PowerPoint, you can create slides to use as an electronic slide show, as 35-mm slides, and as transparency masters to display on an overhead projector. Maria Abbott is the general sales manager at MediaLoft, a nationwide chain of bookstore cafés that sells books, CDs, and videos at eight locations. Maria needs to familiarize herself with the basics of PowerPoint and learn how to use PowerPoint to create professional presentations.

# Defining Presentation Software

**Presentation software** is a computer program you use to organize and present information. Whether you are giving a sales pitch or explaining your company's goals and accomplishments, presentation software can help make your presentation effective and professional. You can use PowerPoint to create 35-mm slides, overheads, speaker's notes, audience handouts, outline pages, or on-screen presentations. Table A-1 explains the items you can create using PowerPoint. Maria wants to create a presentation to review sales techniques at a monthly meeting of store managers. She is not familiar with PowerPoint, so she gets right to work exploring its capabilities. Figure A-1 shows an overhead she created using a word processor for a recent presentation. Figure A-2 shows how the same overhead might look in PowerPoint.

## Maria can easily complete the following tasks using PowerPoint:

### Create slides to display information

With PowerPoint, you can present information on full-color slides with interesting backgrounds, layouts, and clip art. Full-color slides have a more powerful impact than traditional black-and-white overheads.

### Enter and edit data easily

Using PowerPoint, you can enter and edit data quickly and efficiently. When you need to change a part of your presentation, you can use the advanced word-processing and outlining capabilities of PowerPoint to edit your content rather than re-create your slides.

### Change the appearance of information

By exploring the capabilities of PowerPoint, you will discover how easy it is to change the appearance of your presentation. PowerPoint has many features that can transform the way text, graphics, and slides look.

### Organize and arrange information

Once you start using PowerPoint, you won't have to spend a lot of time making sure your information is correct and in the right order. With PowerPoint, you can quickly and easily rearrange and modify any piece of information in your presentation.

### Incorporate information from other sources

Often, when you create presentations, you use information from other sources. With PowerPoint, you can import information from spreadsheet, database, and word-processing files prepared in programs such as Microsoft Excel, Microsoft Access, Microsoft Word, and Corel WordPerfect, as well as graphics from a variety of sources.

### Show a presentation on any computer running Windows 98 or Windows 95

PowerPoint has a powerful feature called the PowerPoint Viewer that you can use to show your presentation on computers running Windows 98 or Windows 95 that do not have PowerPoint installed. The PowerPoint Viewer displays a presentation as an on-screen slide show.

Forecast for 2000

- New stores in Austin, Madison,
  and Denver
- 75 new employees
- Sales up 32%
- Expanded CD and video offerings
- Test market online sales
- Another record year!

FIGURE A-2: PowerPoint overhead

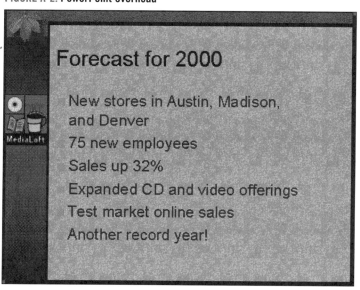

TABLE A-1: Items you can create using PowerPoint

| Item | use |
| --- | --- |
| on-screen presentations | Run a slide show directly from your computer |
| Web presentations | Broadcast a presentation on the Web or on an intranet that others can view, complete with video and audio |
| online meetings | View or work on a presentation with your colleagues in real time |
| 35-mm slides | Use a film-processing bureau to convert PowerPoint slides to 35-mm slides |
| black-and-white overheads | Print PowerPoint slides directly to transparencies on your black-and-white printer |
| color overheads | Print PowerPoint slides directly to transparencies on your color printer |
| speaker notes | Print notes that help you remember points about each slide when you speak to a group |
| audience handouts | Print handouts with two, three, or six slides on a page |
| outline pages | Print the outline of your presentation to show the main points |

PowerPoint 2000

# Starting PowerPoint 2000

To start PowerPoint, you must first start Windows, and then click the Start button on the taskbar and point to the Programs folder, which usually contains the PowerPoint program icon. If the PowerPoint icon is not in the Programs folder, it might be in a different location on your computer. If you are using a computer on a network, you might need to use a different starting procedure. Maria starts PowerPoint to familiarize herself with the program.

## Steps

1. **Make sure your computer is on and the Windows desktop is visible**
   If any program windows are open, close or minimize them.

2. **Click the Start button on the taskbar, then point to Programs**
   The Programs menu opens, showing a list of icons and names for all your programs, as shown in Figure A-3. Your screen might look different, depending on which programs are installed on your computer.

**Trouble?**
If you have trouble finding Microsoft PowerPoint on the Programs menu, check with your instructor or technical support person.

3. **Click Microsoft PowerPoint on the Programs menu**
   PowerPoint starts, and the PowerPoint startup dialog box opens, as shown in Figure A-4. This allows you to choose how you want to create your presentation or to open an existing presentation.

4. **If a dialog balloon connected to the Office Assistant appears, click OK to close it**

### Creating a PowerPoint shortcut icon on the desktop

You can make it easier to start PowerPoint by placing a shortcut on the desktop. To create the shortcut, click the Start button, then point to Programs. On the Programs menu, point to Microsoft PowerPoint, then right-click Microsoft PowerPoint. In the pop-up menu that appears, click Create Shortcut. Windows places a shortcut icon named PowerPoint (2) on the Programs menu. Drag this icon to your desktop where it will look like 🖻. In the future, you can start PowerPoint by simply double-clicking this icon, instead of using the Start menu. You can edit or change the name of the shortcut by right-clicking the shortcut icon, clicking Rename on the pop-up menu, and then editing as you would any item name in Windows.

**FIGURE A-3: Programs menu**

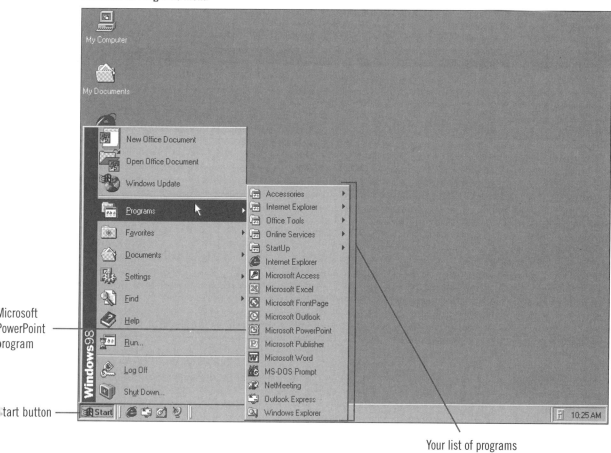

Microsoft
PowerPoint
program

Start button

Your list of programs
will be different

**FIGURE A-4: PowerPoint startup dialog box**

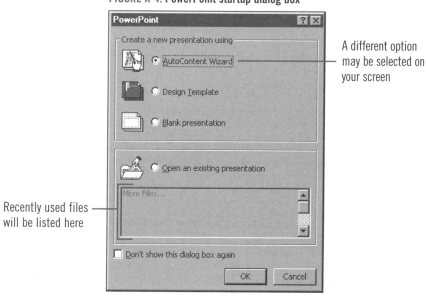

A different option
may be selected on
your screen

Recently used files
will be listed here

PowerPoint 2000

# Using the AutoContent Wizard

When PowerPoint first starts, the startup dialog box opens. The startup dialog box gives you four options for starting your presentation. See Table A-2 for an explanation of all the options in the PowerPoint startup dialog box. The first option, the AutoContent Wizard, is the quickest way to create a presentation. A **wizard** is a series of steps that guides you through a task (in this case, creating a presentation). Using the AutoContent Wizard, you choose a presentation type from the wizard's list of sample presentations. Then you indicate what type of output you want. Next, you type the information for the title slide and the footer. The AutoContent Wizard then creates a presentation with sample text you can use as a guide to help formulate the major points of your presentation.　Maria decides to start her presentation by opening the AutoContent Wizard.

## Steps

1. **In the startup dialog box, click the AutoContent Wizard option button to select it, then click OK**
   The AutoContent Wizard dialog box opens, as shown in Figure A-5. The left section outlines the contents of the AutoContent Wizard and places a green box next to the current screen name. The text on the right side explains the purpose of the wizard.

> **Trouble?**
> If the Office Assistant is in your way, drag it out of the way.

2. **Click Next**
   The Presentation type screen appears. This screen contains category buttons and types of presentations. Each presentation type contains suggested text for a particular use. By default, the presentation types in the General category are listed.

3. **Click the category Sales/Marketing, click Selling a Product or Service in the list on the right, then click Next**
   The Presentation style screen appears, asking you to choose an output type.

4. **If necessary, click the On-screen presentation option button to select it, then click Next**
   The Presentation options screen requests information that will appear on the title slide of the presentation and in the footer at the bottom of each slide.

5. **Click in the Presentation title text box, then type Selling MediaLoft Products**

> **QuickTip**
> To start the AutoContent Wizard when PowerPoint is already running, click File on the menu bar, click New, click the General tab, then double-click the AutoContent Wizard icon.

6. **Press [Tab], then type your name in the Footer text box**

7. **Make sure the Date last updated and Slide number check boxes are selected**

8. **Click Next, then click Finish**
   The AutoContent Wizard opens the presentation based on the Selling a Product or Service presentation type you chose. Sample text for each slide is listed on the left, and the title slide appears on the right side of the screen. Compare your screen to Figure A-6.

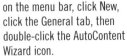

### About Wizards and the PowerPoint installation

As you use PowerPoint, you may find that not all AutoContent Wizards are available to you. The wizards available depend on your PowerPoint installation. A basic installation gives you a minimal set of wizards, templates, and other features. Some may be installed so that the program requests the CD "on first use" the first time you request that feature. If you find that a feature you want is not installed, insert the Office CD as directed. If you are working on a networked computer in a lab, see your technical support person for assistance.

**FIGURE A-5: AutoContent Wizard opening screen**

Current screen name

Click to move to
next screen

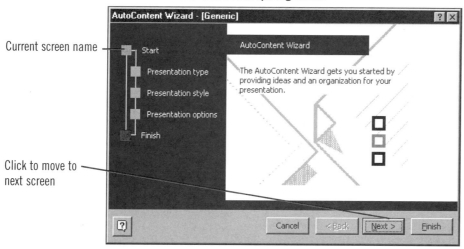

**FIGURE A-6: Presentation created with the AutoContent Wizard**

Presentation
title

Registered
user's name

Office
Assistant
may not
appear on
your screen

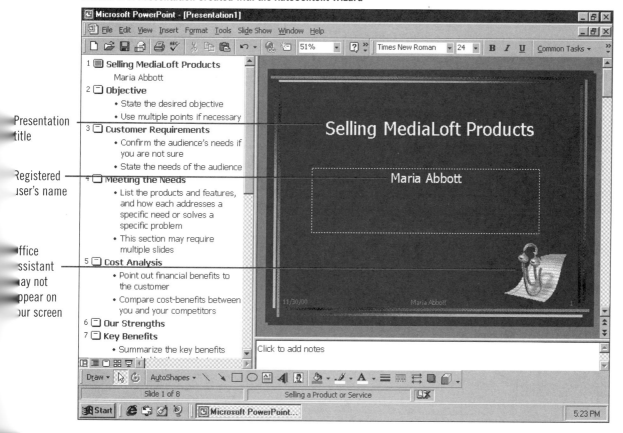

**TABLE A-2: PowerPoint startup dialog box options**

| option | description |
|---|---|
| AutoContent Wizard | Helps you determine the content and organization of your presentation by creating a title slide and an outline using ready-made text for the category you choose |
| Design Template | Opens the New Presentation dialog box, containing PowerPoint design templates; you can click a template to see a preview of it |
| Blank presentation | Opens the New Slide dialog box, allowing you to choose a predesigned slide layout for the first slide, then opens a presentation with no predefined content or design |
| Open an existing presentation | Opens the Open dialog box, allowing you to open a previously created presentation; you can preview a selected presentation before opening it |

# Viewing the PowerPoint Window

After you make your selection in the PowerPoint startup dialog box, the Presentation window opens within the PowerPoint window, and the presentation you just created or opened appears. PowerPoint has different **views** that allow you to see your presentation in different forms. By default, the PowerPoint window opens in **Normal view**, which is divided into three **panes** or sections: the Outline pane, the Notes pane, and the Slide pane. Each pane is described below. You move around in each pane by using its scroll bars. Maria examines the elements of the PowerPoint window. Find and compare the elements described below, using Figure A-7 as a guide.

## Details

 The **title bar** contains the program name, the title of the presentation, a program Control Menu button, resizing buttons, and the program Close button.

 The **menu bar** contains the names of the menus you use to choose PowerPoint commands, as well as the resizing and Close buttons for the maximized presentation window. When you click a menu name, a list of commands from which you can choose opens.

 The **toolbar** contains buttons for commonly used commands. There are actually two toolbars in this row: **Standard**, which contains buttons for the most frequently used commands, such as copying and pasting; and **Formatting**, which contains buttons for the most frequently used formatting commands, such as changing font type and size, as well as the Common Tasks drop-down menu. The **Common Tasks menu** contains three tasks typically performed in PowerPoint: New Slide, Slide Layout, and Assign Design Template. The Common Tasks menu button may be the only button visible on the Formatting toolbar. By default, the two toolbars appear on one row on your screen when PowerPoint first opens. The contents of the toolbars change depending on which options you have recently selected, but you can reset the toolbars back to their default options if you wish. Be sure to read the Clues to Use in this lesson to learn more about working with PowerPoint's toolbars.

 The **Presentation window** contains the Outline, Slide, and Notes panes. It is the "canvas" where you type text, organize your content, work with lines and shapes, and view your presentation.

 The **Outline pane** displays your presentation text in the form of an outline, without graphics. In this pane, it is easy to move text on or among slides by dragging to reorder the information.

 The **Slide pane** contains the current slide in your presentation, including all text and graphics. You can use this pane's vertical scroll bar to view other slides in the presentation.

 The **Notes pane** lets you type in speaker notes for any slide. Speaker notes are for your reference when you make a presentation, such as reminders of other points you want to make during the presentation. They are not visible to the audience when you make a slide presentation. You can print a copy of your presentation with your notes showing under each slide and refer to this copy as you speak.

 The **Office Assistant** is an animated character that provides help. The character on your screen might be different. You can hide the Office Assistant, but it will reappear if you use the Help system. If another user turned off the Office Assistant, it may not appear on your screen. When the Office Assistant has a style tip, a light bulb appears in the presentation window.

 The **Drawing toolbar**, located below the Presentation window, contains buttons and menus that let you create lines, shapes, and special effects.

 The **view buttons**, at the bottom of the Outline pane, allow you to quickly switch between PowerPoint views.

 The **status bar**, located at the bottom of the PowerPoint window, shows messages about what you are doing and seeing in PowerPoint, including which slide you are viewing.

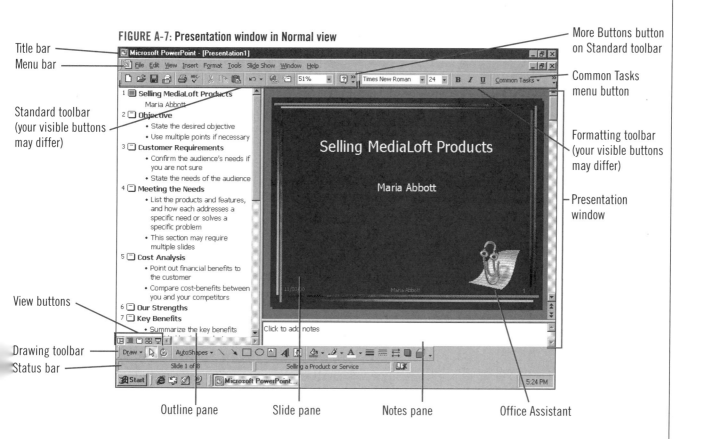

FIGURE A-7: Presentation window in Normal view

Title bar

Menu bar

Standard toolbar (your visible buttons may differ)

View buttons

Drawing toolbar

Status bar

More Buttons button on Standard toolbar

Common Tasks menu button

Formatting toolbar (your visible buttons may differ)

Presentation window

Outline pane          Slide pane          Notes pane          Office Assistant

## Personalized toolbars and menus in PowerPoint 2000

PowerPoint toolbars and menus modify themselves to your working style. The Standard and Formatting toolbars you see when you first start PowerPoint include the most frequently used buttons. To locate a button not visible on a toolbar, click the **More Buttons button** ⚋ at the right end of each toolbar to see the list of additional toolbar buttons. (Because the Standard and Formatting toolbars are on the same line, there are two More Buttons buttons in the row below the menu bar, one for the Standard toolbar and one for the Formatting toolbar.) Throughout the lessons in this book, you will need to remember to click the More Buttons button if a button you are instructed to click is not visible on your screen. As you work, PowerPoint adds the buttons you use to the visible toolbars, and moves the buttons you haven't used in a while to the More Buttons list. Similarly,

PowerPoint menus adjust to your work habits. Short menus appear when you first click a menu command. To view additional menu commands, point to the double-arrow at the bottom of the menu, leave the pointer on the menu name after you've clicked the menu, or double-click the menu name. You can return toolbars and menus to their default settings. Click Tools on the menu bar, click Customize, then click the Options tab in the Customize dialog box. On the Options tab, click Reset my usage data. An alert box or the Office Assistant appears asking if you are sure you want to do this. Click Yes to close the alert box or the dialog balloon, then click Close in the Customize dialog box. Resetting your usage data erases changes made automatically to your menus and toolbars. It does not affect the options you customize.

# Viewing a Presentation

This lesson introduces you to the six PowerPoint views: Normal view, Slide view, Outline view, Slide Sorter view, Notes Page view, and Slide Show view. Each PowerPoint view shows your presentation in a different way and allows you to manipulate your presentation differently. To move easily among the PowerPoint views, use the view buttons located to the left of the horizontal scroll bar, as shown in Figure A-8. Table A-3 provides a brief description of the PowerPoint view buttons and views. ◀━━━ Maria examines each PowerPoint view, starting with Normal view.

## Steps

1. **In the Outline pane, click the small slide icon ▭ next to slide 3 to view the Customer Requirements slide in the Slide pane**
   Notice that in Normal view you can easily view the Outline, Slide, and Notes panes.

2. **Click the Previous Slide button ▲ at the bottom of the vertical scroll bar twice so that slide 1 (the title slide) appears**
   The scroll box in the vertical scroll bar moves back up the scroll bar. The gray slide icon in the Outline pane indicates which slide is displayed in the Slide pane. Both the status bar and the Outline pane indicate the number of the slide you are viewing. As you scroll through the presentation, notice the sample text on each slide created by the AutoContent Wizard.

3. **Click the Outline View button ▤ to the left of the horizontal scroll bar**
   PowerPoint switches to Outline view, which is simply the Outline pane enlarged. See Figure A-8 The Slide pane contains a miniature view of the selected slide.

4. **Click the Slide View button ▣**
   The Slide pane enlarges, the Notes pane disappears, and the Outline pane is reduced to a lis of slide numbers and icons that you can click to view other slides. Compare your screen t Figure A-9.

**QuickTip**

Double-click any slide in Slide Sorter view to return to that slide in the previous view.

5. **Click the Slide Sorter View button ▦**
   A miniature image of each slide in the presentation appears in this view. You can examin the flow of your slides and easily move them to change their order.

6. **Click the Slide Show button ▱**
   The first slide fills the entire screen. In this view, you can practice running through yo slides as they would appear in an electronic slide show.

7. **Click the left mouse button, press [Enter], or press [Spacebar] to advance throu the slides one at a time until you see a black slide, then click once more to return Slide Sorter view**
   After you view the last slide in Slide Show view, a black slide indicating that the slide sh is finished appears. When you click the black slide (or press [Spacebar] or [Enter]), y automatically return to Slide Sorter view, the view you were in before you ran the slide sho

**QuickTip**

To switch to Notes Page view, you must choose Notes Page from the View menu. To switch to Slide and Outline views, you must use the view buttons.

8. **Click View on the menu bar, then click Notes Page**
   Notes Page view appears, showing a reduced image of the title slide above a large box. Y can enter text in this box and then print the notes page for your own use to help you reme ber important points about your presentation.

**FIGURE A-8: Outline View**

Slide icon

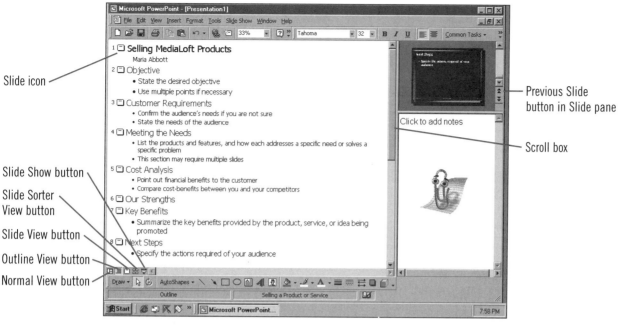

Previous Slide button in Slide pane

Scroll box

Slide Show button
Slide Sorter View button
Slide View button
Outline View button
Normal View button

**FIGURE A-9: Slide view**

Click Slide icon to view other slides

Slide pane is larger

Previous Slide button

**LE A-3: View buttons**

| tton | button name | description |
|------|-------------|-------------|
| | **Normal View** | Displays the Outline, Slide, and Notes panes at the same time; use this view to work on your presentation's content, layout, and notes concurrently |
| | **Outline View** | Widens the outline pane to view the title and main topics in the form of an outline; use this view to enter and edit the text of your presentation |
| | **Slide View** | Widens the slide pane so it occupies most of the presentation window; displays one slide at a time; use this view to modify slide content and enhance a slide's appearance |
| | **Slide Sorter View** | Displays a miniature picture of all slides in the order in which they appear in your presentation; use this view to rearrange and add special effects to your slides |
| | **Slide Show** | Displays your presentation as an electronic slide show |

**PowerPoint 2000**

# Saving a Presentation

To store your presentation permanently, you must save it as a file on a disk. As a general rule, you should save your work about every 10 or 15 minutes and before printing. You use the Save As command on the File menu to save your presentation for the first time or to save an existing presentation under a different name. Use the Save command to save your changes to a file without changing its name. In this lesson, you save your presentation to your Project Disk. ◄═══ Maria saves her presentation as "Sales Presentation."

## Steps

**1.** Click **File** on the menu bar, then click **Save As**

The Save As dialog box opens. See Figure A-10.

**2.** Make sure your Project Disk is in the appropriate drive, click the **Save in list arrow**, then click the **drive** that contains your Project Disk

A default filename placeholder, which PowerPoint takes from the presentation title you entered, appears in the File name text box. If your disk contains any PowerPoint files, their filenames appear in the white area in the center of the dialog box.

**Trouble?**

Don't worry if you see the extension .ppt after the filename in the title bar or in the list of filenames, even though you didn't type it. Windows can be set up to show or not show the file extensions.

**3.** In the **File name text box**, drag to select the default presentation name if necessary type **Sales Presentation**, then click **Save**

Windows 98 allows you to have filenames up to 255 characters long and permits you to use lower- or uppercase letters, symbols, numbers, and spaces. The Save As dialog box closes and the new filename appears in the title bar at the top of the Presentation window. You decide you want to save the presentation in Outline view instead of in Notes Page view.

**4.** Click the **Outline View button** 🔲

The presentation view changes from Notes Page view to Outline view.

**QuickTip**

To save a file quickly, you can press the shortcut key combination [Ctrl][S].

**5.** Click the **Save button** 💾 on the Standard toolbar

The Save command saves any changes you made to the file to the same location you specified when you used the Save As command. Save your file frequently while working with it to protect the presentation.

### Saving fonts with your presentation

When you create a presentation, it uses the fonts that are installed on your computer. If you need to open the presentation on another computer, the fonts might look different if that computer has a different set of fonts. To preserve the look of your presentation on any computer, you can save, or **embed**, the fonts in your presentation. Click File on the menu bar, then click Save As. The Save As dialog box opens. Click Tools, then click Embed TrueType fonts from the drop-down list. Finally, click Save. Now the presentation will look the same on any computer that opens it. This option, however, significantly increases the size of your presentation on disk, so only use this option when necessary. You can freely embed any TrueType font that comes with Windows. You can embed other TrueType fonts only if they have no license restrictions.

Current
drive
(yours may
differ)

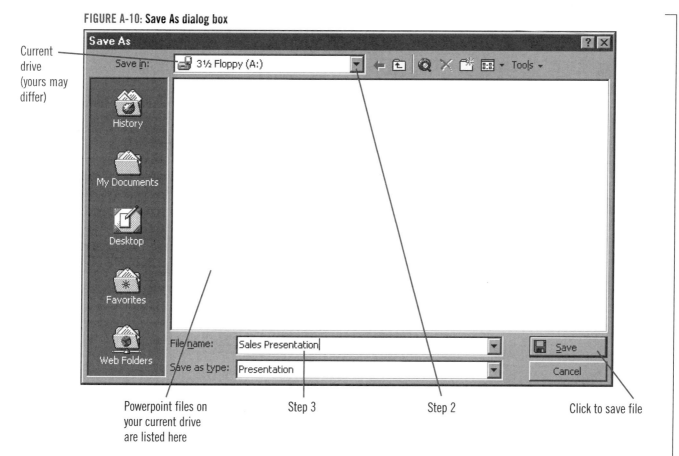

Powerpoint files on
your current drive
are listed here

Step 3

Step 2

Click to save file

PowerPoint 2000

# PowerPoint 2000

# Getting Help

PowerPoint has an extensive Help system that gives you immediate access to definitions, reference information, and feature explanations. Help information appears in a separate window that you can move and resize. ✐ Maria likes the way the AutoContent Wizard helped her create a presentation quickly, and she decides to find out more about it.

## Steps

### Trouble?

If the Microsoft PowerPoint Help dialog box opens instead of the Office Assistant, someone turned the Office Assistant off. Click the Close button in the Help window, click Help on the menu bar, click Show the Office Assistant, then repeat step 1. If there is no space in the dialog balloon to type the question, click OK, then repeat Step 1.

### QuickTip

To quickly open the Office Assistant dialog balloon, click the animated character, click the Microsoft PowerPoint Help button [?] on the Standard toolbar, or press [F1].

### QuickTip

To turn off the Office Assistant completely, right-click the Assistant, click Options, deselect the Use the Office Assistant checkbox, then click OK.

**1.** Click **Help** on the menu bar, then click **Microsoft PowerPoint Help**
If the Office Assistant wasn't already open, it opens. A balloon-shaped dialog box opens near the Office Assistant. The dialog balloon may contain a tip related to the current slide. The question "What would you like to do?" appears at the top of the dialog balloon. It also contains topics related to what is currently on-screen and the last few commands you executed. Below this list is a space for you to type your question. Finally, at the bottom of the dialog balloon are two buttons. Clicking the Options button opens a dialog box that allows you to change Office Assistant options. Clicking the Search button searches PowerPoint Help topics for topics related to the question you type.

**2.** Type **AutoContent Wizard**, then click **Search**
The dialog balloon closes and reopens with five topics related to the AutoContent Wizard listed under "What would you like to do?" See Figure A-11. If you click the See more option, two more topics appear. The mouse pointer changes to 🖑 when it is positioned over the topics.

**3.** Click **Create a new presentation**
The Microsoft PowerPoint Help window opens, containing information about creating a new presentation. See Figure A-12. Read the information in the window.

**4.** Click **Create a presentation based on suggested content and design** in the Microsoft PowerPoint Help window
You may need to scroll down to see this. Another Help window opens listing the steps to follow for using the AutoContent Wizard. Read through the steps.

**5.** Click the **Show button** 🖽 at the top of the window
The Help window expands to include three tabs: Contents, Answer Wizard, and Index. The Contents tab contains Help topics organized in outline form. To open a Help window about a topic, double-click it. On the Answer Wizard tab, you can search for a key word in all the Help topics. The Index tab contains an alphabetical list of Help topics. Type the word you want help on in text box 1, and the list in box 2 scrolls to that word. Click Search to view related subjects in text box 3, then click the topic you want to read about.

**6.** Click the **Close button** on the Microsoft PowerPoint Help Window to close it
The Help Topics dialog box closes, and you return to your presentation. The rest of the figures in this text will not show the Office Assistant.

**7.** Click **Help** on the menu bar, then click **Hide the Office Assistant**
If you have hidden the Office Assistant several times, it may open a dialog balloon asking if you want to turn it off permanently.

**8.** If a dialog balloon opens asking if you want to turn off the Office Assistant permanently, click the option you prefer in the Office Assistant dialog balloon, then click O
Selecting Hide the Office Assistant only hides it temporarily; it will reappear later to give you tip

**FIGURE A-11: Office Assistant dialog balloon**

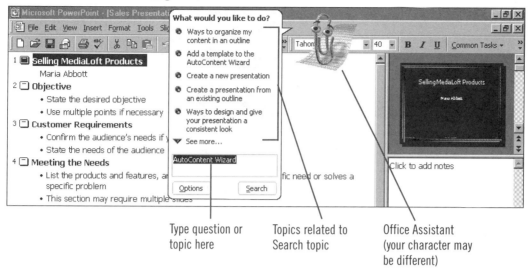

Type question or topic here

Topics related to Search topic

Office Assistant (your character may be different)

**FIGURE A-12: Help window**

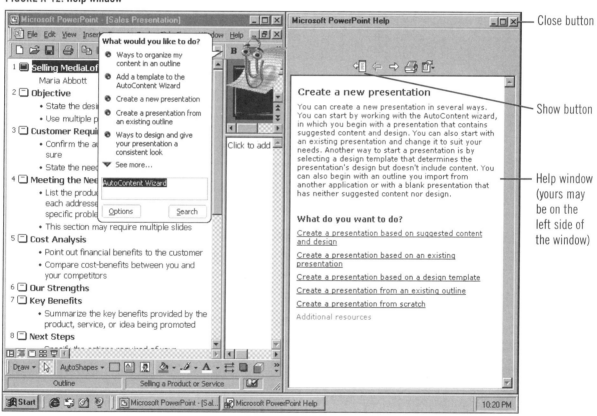

Close button

Show button

Help window (yours may be on the left side of the window)

## What do I do if I see a lightbulb on a slide?

If you have the Office Assistant on, you may see a yellow lightbulb in your presentation window. The lightbulb is part of the PowerPoint Help system and it can mean several things. First, the Office Assistant might have a suggestion for appropriate clip art for that slide. Second, the Office Assistant might have a helpful tip based on the task you are performing. This is known as a context-sensitive tip. Third, the Office Assistant might have detected a style, such as a word in the slide title that should be capitalized, which is inconsistent with preset style guidelines. When you see a lightbulb, you can click it, read the dialog balloon, then click the option you prefer, or you can ignore it. If the Office Assistant is hidden or turned off, the lightbulbs do not appear.

# Printing and Closing the File, and Exiting PowerPoint

You print your presentation when you have completed it or when you want to review your work. Reviewing hard copies of your presentation at different stages of production gives you an overall perspective of its content and look. When you are finished working on your presentation, close the file containing your presentation and exit PowerPoint. Maria needs to go to a meeting, so after saving her presentation, she prints the slides and notes pages of the presentation so she can review them later; then she closes the file and exits PowerPoint.

**1.** Click **File** on the menu bar, then click **Print**

The Print dialog box opens, similar to Figure A-13. In this dialog box, you can specify which slide format you want to print (slides, audience handouts, notes pages, etc.) as well as the number of pages to print and other print options. The default option, Slides, and the Grayscale check box are already selected in the Print what area at the bottom of the dialog box.

**QuickTip**

If the Office Assistant appears offering you help with printing, click No in the dialog balloon.

**2.** In the Print range section in the middle of the dialog box, click the **Slides option button** to select it, type **3** to print only the third slide, then click **OK**

The third slide prints. Because the Grayscale check box is selected by default, the black background does not print. If you have a black-and-white printer, the slide prints in shades of gray. To save paper, it's often a good idea to print in handout format, which lets you print up to nine slides per page.

**3.** Click **File** on the menu bar, then click **Print**

The Print dialog box opens again.

**QuickTip**

The options you choose in the Print dialog box remain there until you close the presentation. To quickly print the presentation with the current Print options, click the Print button 🖨 on the Standard toolbar.

**4.** Click the **All option button** in the Print range section, click the **Print what list arrow**, click **Handouts**, click the **Slides per page list arrow** in the Handouts section, then click **6**

The PowerPoint black-and-white option can help you save toner.

**5.** Click the **Pure black and white check box** to select it, then click **OK**

The presentation prints as audience handouts on two pages. If you have a black-and-white printer, the presentation prints without any gray tones.

**6.** Click **File** on the menu bar, then click **Print**

The Print dialog box opens again.

**QuickTip**

To print slides in a size appropriate for overhead transparencies, click File, click Page Setup, and click the Slides sized for list arrow. Select Overhead. Then print or copy your slides onto transparency film.

**7.** Click the **Print what list arrow**, click **Outline View**, then click **OK**

The presentation outline prints. Notice that you can print any view from the Print dialog box, regardless of the current view.

**8.** Click **File** on the menu bar, then click **Close**

If you have made changes to your presentation, a Microsoft PowerPoint alert box opens asking you if you want to save changes you have made to the Sales Presentation file, as shown in Figure A-14.

**9.** If necessary, click **Yes** to close the alert box

**10.** Click **File** on the menu bar, then click **Exit**

The Presentation window and the PowerPoint program close, and you return to the Windows desktop.

FIGURE A-13: Print dialog box

Your printer name
may be different

Step 2

Step 5

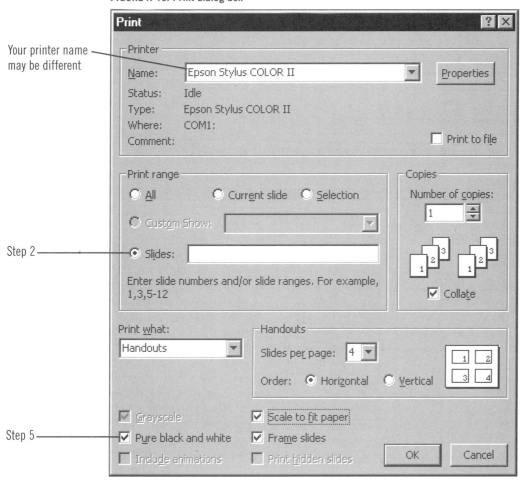

FIGURE A-14: Save changes alert box

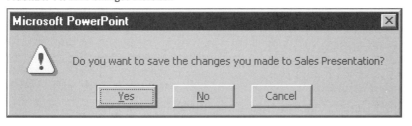

ES TO USE

## Viewing your presentation in gray scale or black and white

Viewing your presentation in pure black and white or in grayscale (using shades of gray) is very useful when you will be printing a presentation on a black-and-white printer and you want to make sure your text will be readable. To see how your color presentation looks in grayscale when you are in any view (except Slide Show View), click the Grayscale Preview button ▣ on the Standard toolbar. To see how your slide looks in pure black and white, hold down [Shift] and press ▣, which is now called the Pure Black and White button. If you don't like the way an object looks in black and white or grayscale view, you can change its shading. Right-click a slide object, point to Black and White, and choose from the options on the pop-up menu.

# Practice

## ► Concepts Review

**Label the elements of the PowerPoint window shown in Figure A-15.**

FIGURE A-15

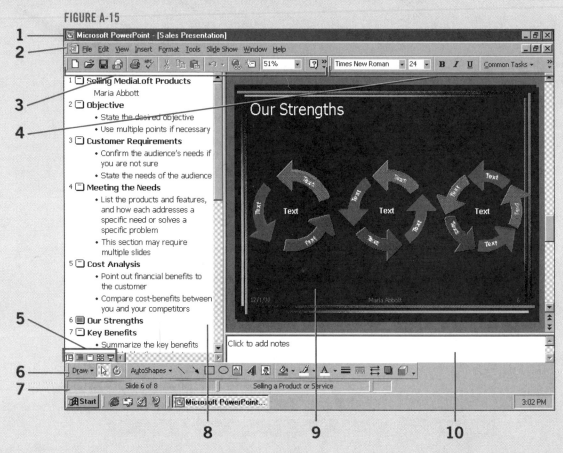

**Match each term with the statement that describes it.**

11. AutoContent Wizard
12. Presentation window
13. Slide Sorter view
14. Normal view
15. Outline pane

a. The area where you work on your presentation
b. Shows slide numbers and small slide icons
c. Series of dialog boxes that guides you through creating a presentatio
   and produces a presentation with suggestions for content
d. Displays the Outline, Slide, and Notes panes
e. Shows all your slides in the same window

## Select the best answer from the list of choices.

**16. PowerPoint can help you create all of the following, *except***
- **a.** 35-mm slides.
- **b.** A movie.
- **c.** An on-screen presentation.
- **d.** Outline pages.

**17. The buttons you use to switch between the PowerPoint views are called**
- **a.** PowerPoint buttons.
- **b.** View buttons.
- **c.** Screen buttons.
- **d.** Toolbar buttons.

**‘8. All of the following are PowerPoint views, *except***
- **a.** Slide view.
- **b.** Notes Page view.
- **c.** Outline view.
- **d.** Current Page view.

**‘9. The animated character that appears on the screen when you click the Microsoft PowerPoint Help button is the**
- **a.** Office Helper.
- **b.** Office Assistant.
- **c.** Assistant Paper Clip.
- **d.** PowerPoint Assistant.

**◢. The view that allows you to view your electronic slide show with each slide filling the entire screen is called**
- **a.** Electronic view.
- **b.** Slide Sorter view.
- **c.** Presentation view.
- **d.** Slide Show view.

**Which wizard helps you create and outline your presentation?**
- **a.** Pick a Look Wizard
- **b.** Presentation Wizard
- **c.** AutoContent Wizard
- **d.** OrgContent Wizard

**How do you switch to Notes Page view?**
- **a.** Click the Notes Page View button to the left of the horizontal scroll bar
- **b.** Click View on the menu bar, then click Notes Page
- **c.** Press [Shift] and click in the Notes pane
- **d.** All of the above

**23. How do you save changes to your presentation after you have saved it for the first time?**

   **a.** Click Save As on the File menu, select a filename from the list, then assign it a new name

   **b.** Click the Save button on the Standard toolbar

   **c.** Click Save As on the File menu, then click Save

   **d.** Click Save As on the File menu, specify a new location and filename, then click Save

#  Skills Review

**1. Start PowerPoint and use the AutoContent Wizard.**

   **a.** Start the PowerPoint program, selecting the AutoContent Wizard option.

   **b.** In the AutoContent Wizard, select a presentation category and type. (*Hint:* If you see a message saying you need to install the feature, insert your Office 2000 CD in the appropriate drive and click OK. See your technical support person for assistance.)

   **c.** Select the output options of your choice.

   **d.** Enter appropriate information for the opening slide, enter your name as the footer text, and complete the wizard to show the first slide of the presentation.

**2. View the PowerPoint window.**

   **a.** Identify as many elements of the PowerPoint window as you can without referring to the unit material.

   **b.** For any elements you cannot identify, refer to the unit.

**3. View a presentation.**

   **a.** View each slide in the presentation to become familiar with its content.

   **b.** When you are finished, return to slide 1.

   **c.** Change to Outline view and review the presentation contents.

   **d.** Change to Notes Page view and see if the notes pages in the presentation contain text, then return to slide 1

   **e.** Examine the presentation contents in Slide Sorter view.

   **f.** View all the slides of the presentation in Slide Show view, and end the slide show to return to Slide Sorter vie

**4. Save a presentation.**

   **a.** Change to the view in which you would like to save your presentation.

   **b.** Open the Save As dialog box.

   **c.** Make sure your Project Disk is in the correct drive.

   **d.** Save your presentation as "Practice."

   **e.** Embed the fonts in your presentation.

   **f.** Save your changes to the file.

   **g.** Go to a different view than the one you saved your presentation in.

   **h.** Save the changed presentation.

## 5. Get Help.

**a.** If the Office Assistant is open, click it. If it is not on your screen, open it.

**b.** In the text box, type "Tell me about Help" and click Search.

**c.** Select the topic, "Display tips and messages through the Office Assistant."

**d.** Click the Show button to open the Help window containing the Contents, Answer Wizard, and Index tabs.

**e.** On the Contents tab, double-click any book icon to view the Help subjects (identified by page icons), then click the page icons to review the Help information. Explore a number of topics that interest you.

**f.** When you have finished exploring the Contents tab, switch to the Index tab.

**g.** In the Type keywords text box, type a word you want help with.

**h.** Click a word in the list in box 2 if it did not jump to the correct word, then click Search.

**i.** Click a topic in the list in box 3 and read about it.

**j.** Explore a number of topics that interest you.

**k.** When you have finished exploring the Index tab, close the Help window and hide the Office Assistant.

## 6. Print and close the file, and exit PowerPoint.

**a.** Print slides 2 and 3 as slides in grayscale. (*Hint:* In the Slides text box, type 2-3.)

**b.** Print all the slides as handouts, 6 slides per page, in pure black and white.

**c.** Print all the slides in Outline view.

**d.** Resize the slides for overhead transparencies then print slides 1 and 2 in grayscale.

**e.** Close the file, saving your changes.

**f.** Exit PowerPoint.

# ► Independent Challenges

**1.** You have just gotten a job as a marketing assistant at Events, Inc., a catering firm specializing in clambakes and barbecues for large company events. John Hudspeth, the marketing manager, has some familiarity with PowerPoint. He has printed his presentation on a black-and-white printer, but he cannot see all of his text, and he wants to know how to solve this problem.

To complete this independent challenge:

**a.** If PowerPoint is not already running, start it. When the startup dialog box opens, click Cancel. If PowerPoint is already running, go to step b.

**b.** Use PowerPoint Help to find the answer to John's question.

**c.** Write down which Help feature you used (Office Assistant, Index, etc.) and the steps you followed.

**d.** Print the Help window that shows the information you found. (*Hint:* Click the Print button at the top of the Help window.)

**e.** Exit PowerPoint.

**2.** You are in charge of marketing for ArtWorks, Inc, a medium-size start-up company that produces all types of art for corporations to enhance their work environment. The company has a regional sales area that includes three neighboring northeastern states. The president of ArtWorks has asked you to plan and create the outline of the PowerPoint presentation he will use to convey his marketing plan to the sales department.

To complete this independent challenge:

**a.** If necessary, start PowerPoint and choose the AutoContent Wizard option button. (*Hint:* If PowerPoint is already running, click File, click New, click the General tab, and double-click AutoContent Wizard.)

**b.** Choose the Sales/Marketing category, then choose Marketing Plan from the list.

**c.** Assign the presentation an appropriate title, and include your name as the footer text.

**d.** Scroll through the outline the AutoContent Wizard produces. Does it contain the type of information you thought it would?

**e.** Plan and take notes on how you would change and add to the sample text created by the wizard. What information do you need to promote ArtWorks to companies?

**f.** Switch views. Run through the slide show at least once.

**g.** Save your presentation to your Project Disk with the name "ArtWorks."

**h.** Print your presentation as Handouts (6 slides per page).

**i.** Close and exit PowerPoint.

**3.** You have recently been promoted to sales manager at Buconjic Industries. Part of your job is to train sales representatives to go to potential customers and give presentations describing your company's products. Your boss wants you to find an appropriate PowerPoint presentation template that you can use for your next training presentation to recommend strategies to the sales representatives for closing sales. She wants a printout so she can evaluate it.

To complete this independent challenge:

**a.** If necessary, start PowerPoint and choose the AutoContent Wizard option. (*Hint:* If PowerPoint is already running, click File on the menu bar, click New, click the General tab, and double-click the AutoContent Wizard.)

**b.** Examine the available AutoContent Wizards and select one that you could adapt for your presentation. (*Hint:* If you see a message saying you need to install additional templates, insert your Office 2000 CD in the appropriate drive and click OK. If you are working in a networked computer lab, see your technical support person for assistance.)

**c.** Enter an appropriate slide title and your name as the footer text.

**d.** Print the presentation as an outline, then print the first slide in pure black and white.

**e.** Write a brief memo to your boss describing which wizard you think will be most helpful, referring to specific slides in the outline to support your recommendations.

**f.** Save the presentation as "Sales Training" and exit PowerPoint.

**4.** MediaLoft offers several health care plans to its employees. One of them is AllCare, a health maintenance organization in Memphis, Tennessee. AllCare is offering a new health plan that they would like to present to MediaLoft employees. The director of human resources, Karen Rosen, has heard that you can use PowerPoint 2000 to place presentations on the Internet as Web pages. Because MediaLoft employees are at different locations around the country, Karen is considering putting a PowerPoint presentation on the MediaLoft intranet site to inform employees about the new plan. An intranet is a group of connected networks owned by a company or organization that is used for internal purposes. Intranets use Internet software to handle the data communications, such as e-mail and web pages, within an organization. These pages often provide company-wide information. As with all intranets, the MediaLoft intranet limits access to MediaLoft employees. However, Karen is not sure how this PowerPoint feature works and she would like you to learn about it and give her a brief overview of the subject at the next departmental meeting.

You decide to learn the basics from the PowerPoint Help system, then explore the MediaLoft intranet site yourself to get a better feel for the subject. Then you will be better able to discuss the topic at the meeting.

To complete this independent challenge:

**a.** If necessary, start PowerPoint and use the Office Assistant Search feature. Type the words "Opening a presentation on the Internet" in the Office Assistant dialog box.

**b.** When the Assistant displays a list of topics, select the topic, "Open a file on a Web server by using PowerPoint." Read the information in the Help window.

**c.** Connect to the Internet, go to the MediaLoft intranet site at http://www.course.com/illustrated/MediaLoft.

**d.** Click each link on the MediaLoft page to become more familiar with the company.

**e.** Click the Human Resources link, where you will find a presentation about MediaLoft's current health plans. This presentation has been saved in HTML format so that it is a Web page you can view with your browser. Click the MediaLoft Health Plan Options link to start the presentation, then click at the bottom of each slide to move through the presentation. Click the Back button in your browser window to return to the Human Resources page.

**f.** Disconnect from the Internet, and write a brief memo to Karen explaining how placing presentations on the intranet site will help her communicate the AllCare plan to MediaLoft employees. Attach any Web page print-outs that support your recommendations. Include any other options you may have learned about.

**g.** Exit PowerPoint.

# ▶ Visual Workshop

Create the presentation shown in Figure A-16 using the Business Plan AutoContent Wizard in the Corporate category. Save the presentation as "Web Plan" on your Project Disk. Print the slides as handouts, six slides per page, in black and white.

**FIGURE A-16**

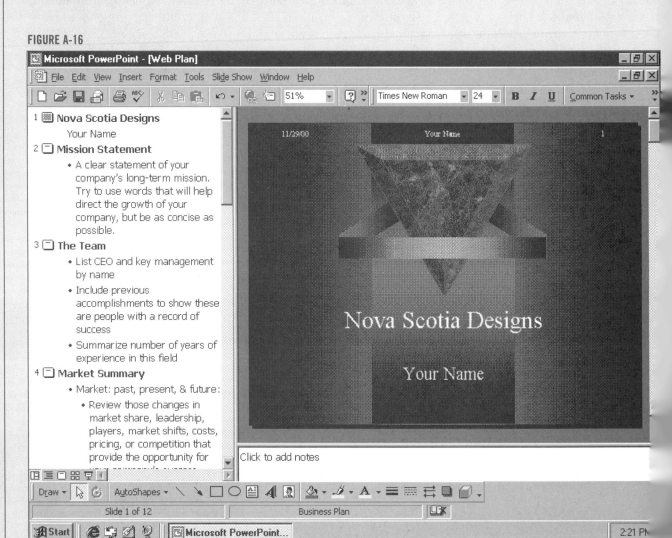

# PowerPoint 2000

Unit
B

# Creating
## a Presentation

### Objectives

- ► **Plan an effective presentation**
- MOUS ► **Choose a look for a presentation**
- MOUS ► **Enter slide text**
- MOUS ► **Create a new slide**
- MOUS ► **Work in Outline view**
- MOUS ► **Enter notes**
- MOUS ► **Check spelling in the presentation**
- MOUS ► **Evaluate a presentation**

Now that you are familiar with PowerPoint basics, you are ready to plan and create your own presentation. To do this, you enter and edit text and choose a slide design. PowerPoint helps you accomplish these tasks with the AutoContent Wizard and with a collection of professionally prepared slide designs, called **design templates**, which can enhance the look of your presentation. In this unit, you create a presentation using a design template. ◄━━ Maria Abbott needs to prepare a presentation on MediaLoft's sales for the upcoming annual meeting for store managers. She begins by planning her presentation.

# Planning an Effective Presentation

Before you create a presentation using PowerPoint, you need to plan and outline the message you want to communicate and consider how you want the presentation to look. When preparing the outline, you need to consider where you are giving the presentation and who your audience will be. It is also important to know what resources you might need, such as a computer or projection equipment. ▰▰▰ Using Figure B-1 and the planning guidelines below, follow Maria as she outlines the presentation message.

## Details

In planning a presentation it is important to:

 **Determine the purpose of the presentation, the location, and the audience**
Maria needs to present the highlights of MediaLoft's 1999 sales at the yearly company meeting for store managers in a large room at a business center.

 **Determine the type of output—black-and-white or color overhead transparencies, on-screen slide show, or 35-mm slides—that best conveys your message, given time constraints and computer hardware availability**
Because Maria is speaking in a large room and has access to a computer and projection equipment, an on-screen slide show is the best choice.

 **Determine a look for your presentation that will help communicate your message**
You can choose one of the professionally designed templates that come with PowerPoint, modify one of these templates, or create one of your own. Maria wants to establish an upbeat, friendly relationship with the store managers, so she will choose an artistic template.

 **Determine the message you want to communicate, then give the presentation meaningful title and outline your message**
Maria wants to highlight the previous year's accomplishments. See Figure B-1.

 **Determine what additional materials will be useful in the presentation**
You need to prepare not only the slides themselves but supplementary materials, including speaker notes and handouts for the audience. Speaker notes will allow Maria to stay on track and deliver a concise message.

1. Media Loft
   - -1999 Sales Report to Managers
   - -Maria Abbott
   - -General Sales Manager
   - -January 26, 2000
2. 1999: A Banner Year
   - -Overall sales set new record
   - -3 new locations
   - -Book sales post biggest increase
   - -CDs and videos close behind
   - -Café sales steady
3. 1999 Sales by Division
   - -Overall product sales up 22%
   - -MediaLoft East sales up 25%
   - -MediaLoft West sales up 21%
4. The Star: MediaLoft East
   - -Book sales up 29%
   - -CD sales up 25%
   - -Video sales up 20%

**PowerPoint 2000**

# Choosing a Look for a Presentation

To help you design your presentation, PowerPoint provides 44 design templates so you don't have to spend time creating the right presentation look. A **design template** has borders, colors, text attributes, and other elements arranged in a specific format that you can apply to all the slides in your presentation. You can use a design template as is, or you can modify any element to suit your needs. Unless you know something about graphic design, it is often easier and faster to use or modify one of the templates supplied with PowerPoint. No matter how you create your presentation, you can save it as a template for future use. ◢◤ Maria doesn't have a lot of time but wants to create a good-looking presentation, so she uses an existing PowerPoint template.

**QuickTip**

If PowerPoint is already running, click File on the menu bar, then click New.

1. Start PowerPoint, click the **Design Template option button** in the PowerPoint startup dialog box, then click **OK**

   The New Presentation dialog box opens, containing three tabs. See Table B-1 for an overview of the tabs.

2. Click the **Design Templates tab**

   This lists the 44 PowerPoint design templates.

3. Click the **right scroll arrow** if necessary, then click the **Sumi Painting icon** once

   A miniature version of the selected template appears in the Preview box on the right side of the dialog box, as shown in Figure B-2.

4. Click **OK**

   The New Slide dialog box opens, showing 24 AutoLayouts. An **AutoLayout** is a slide containing placeholders for text and graphics. The first AutoLayout is selected, and its name, Title Slide, appears on the right side of the dialog box. Because the first slide of the presentation is the title slide, this layout is appropriate.

5. Click **OK**

   A blank title slide, containing placeholders for title and subtitle text, appears in the Slide pane. The background of the slide and the graphics are part of the Sumi Painting design template you chose. Notice that the name of the template is in the status bar. Notice also that there is a slide icon for slide 1 in the Outline pane.

6. Click **Window** on the menu bar, then click **Arrange All**

   This step adjusts your presentation window so it matches the figures in this book. Compare your screen to Figure B-3.

7. Click **Tools** on the menu bar, click **Customize**, click the **Options tab** in the Customize dialog box, click **Reset my usage data** to restore your toolbars to the default settings, click **Yes**, then click **Close**

8. Click the **Save button** 🖫 on the Standard toolbar, then save your presentation **1999 Sales Report** to your Project Disk

**TABLE B-1: New Presentation dialog box tabs**

| tab | contains | use |
|---|---|---|
| **General** | A blank presentation and the AutoContent Wizard | To create a presentation from scratch, or to use one of 24 preformatted presentations with suggested content |
| **Design Templates** | 44 design templates with backgrounds and text formats | To create a presentation with a predesigned template that contains text and graphic designs that coordinate well with each other |
| **Presentations** | 24 design templates that contain suggested content for specific uses | To create a presentation based on suggested content |

FIGURE B-2: Design Templates tab in the New Presentation dialog box

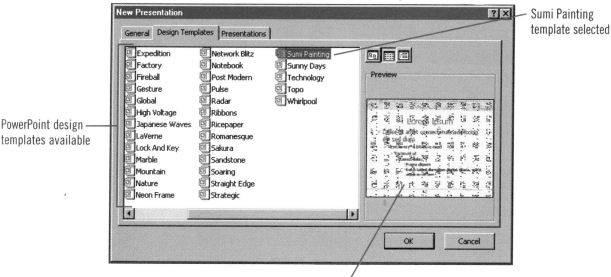

Sumi Painting template selected

PowerPoint design templates available

Miniature version of selected template

FIGURE B-3: Title slide with template design

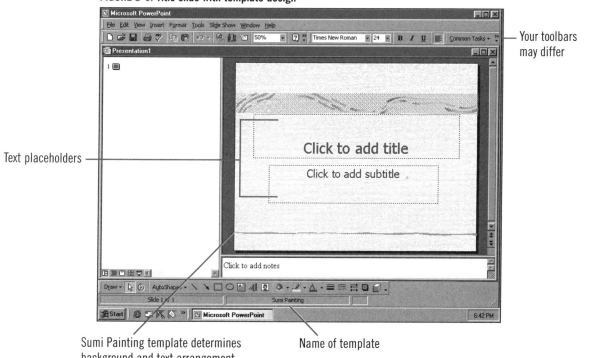

Your toolbars may differ

Text placeholders

Sumi Painting template determines background and text arrangement

Name of template

TO USE

## Applying a design template to an existing presentation

ou can apply a design template to a presentation at
y time. Open the presentation to which you want to
ply the template. Click the Common Tasks menu
tton on the Formatting toolbar, then click Apply
sign Template on the drop-down menu. You can
select Apply Design Template on the Format
nu. The Apply Design Template dialog box opens
h the Presentations Designs folder open. This list

of templates is similar to the list that appears on the
Design Templates tab in the New Presentation dialog
box. Select the template you want to apply. A preview
appears in the preview box on the right. Then click
Apply. The Apply Design Template dialog box closes
and the slide text and background now reflect the
template you chose.

# Entering Slide Text

Now that you have applied a template to your new presentation, you are ready to enter text into the title slide. The title slide has two **text placeholders**, boxes with dashed line borders where you enter text. The first text placeholder on the title slide is the **title placeholder** labeled "Click to add title." The second text placeholder on the title slide is the **main text placeholder** labeled "Click to add subtitle." To enter text in a placeholder, simply click the placeholder and then type your text. After you enter text in a placeholder, the placeholder becomes a text object. An **object** is any item on a slide that can be manipulated. Objects are the building blocks that make up a presentation slide. ✎ Maria begins working on her presentation by entering the title of the presentation in the title placeholder.

## Steps 123 4

1. **Move the pointer over the title placeholder labeled "Click to add title" in the Slide pane**
   The pointer changes to $I$ when you move the pointer over the placeholder. In PowerPoint, the pointer often changes shape, depending on the task you are trying to accomplish. Table B- describes the functions of the most common PowerPoint mouse pointer shapes.

2. **Click the title placeholder**
   The **insertion point**, a blinking vertical line, indicates where your text will appear in the title placeholder. A **selection box**, the slanted line border, appears around the title placeholder indicating that it is selected and ready to accept text. See Figure B-4.

### Trouble?

If you press a wrong key, press [Backspace] to erase the character, then continue to type.

3. **Type MediaLoft**
   In the Slide pane, PowerPoint center-aligns the title text within the title placeholder, which is now a text object. Notice that the text appeared in the Ouline pane as you typed.

4. **Click the main text placeholder in the Slide pane**
   A wavy, red line may appear under the word "MediaLoft" in the title object indicating that the automatic spellchecking feature in PowerPoint is active. Don't worry if it doesn't appear on your screen.

5. **Type 1999 Sales Report to Managers, then press [Enter]**
   In the Outline pane, this text appears indented under the slide title.

6. **Type Maria Abbott, press [Enter], type General Sales Manager, press [Enter], then type January 26, 2000**
   Compare your title slide to Figure B-5.

7. **Click outside the main text object in a blank area of the slide**
   Clicking a blank area of the slide deselects all selected objects on the slide.

8. **Click the Save button 🖫 on the Standard toolbar to save your changes**

FIGURE B-4: Selected title placeholder

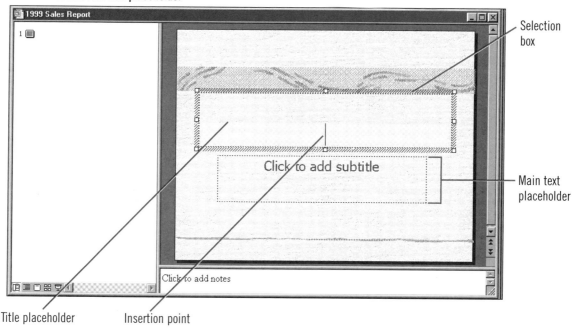

FIGURE B-5: Title slide with text

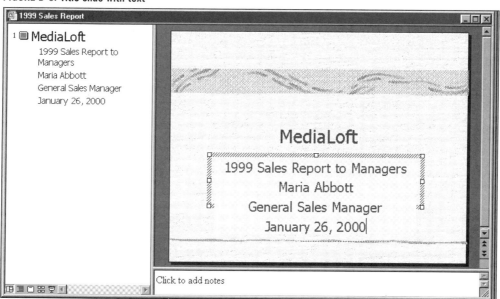

E B-2: PowerPoint mouse pointer shapes

| pe | description |
| --- | --- |
| | Appears when you select the Selection tool; use this pointer to select one or more PowerPoint objects |
| | Appears when you move the pointer over a text object; use this pointer, called the I-beam, to place the insertion point where you want to begin typing or selecting text |
| | Appears when you move the pointer over a bullet, slide icon, or object; use this pointer to select title or paragraph text |
| | Appears when you select a drawing tool; use this pointer, called the cross-hair cursor, to draw shapes |

**PowerPoint 2000**

# Creating a New Slide

To help you create a new slide easily, PowerPoint offers 24 predesigned AutoLayouts, which include a variety of placeholder arrangements for objects including titles, main text, clip art, graphs, charts, and media clips. You have already used the title slide AutoLayout. Table B-3 describes the different placeholders you'll find in the AutoLayouts. ➤ To continue developing the presentation, Maria needs to create a slide that states the main theme of her presentation.

## Steps

**Trouble?**

If you don't see the New Slide button on your toolbar, click the More Buttons button on the Standard toolbar.

**QuickTip**

To delete a slide, select it in the Outline pane, display it in the Slide pane or select it in Slide Sorter view, click Edit on the menu bar, and then click Delete Slide.

1. **Click the New Slide button on the Standard toolbar**
   The New Slide dialog box opens, showing the different AutoLayouts. (Click the down scroll arrow to view more.) This is the same dialog box from which you chose the title slide layout. The title for the selected AutoLayout appears in a Preview box to the right of the layouts, as shown in Figure B-6. You can choose a layout by clicking it. The Bulleted List AutoLayout is already selected.

2. **Click OK**
   A new slide appears after the current slide in your presentation. In the Slide pane, it contains a title placeholder and a main text placeholder for the bulleted list. Notice that the status bar indicates Slide 2 of 2. A new slide icon for slide 2 appears in the Outline pane.

3. **Click next to the slide icon for slide 2 in the Outline pane, then type 1999: Banner Year**
   As you type, the text appears in the Slide pane also.

4. **Click the main text placeholder in the Slide pane**
   You can type text in either pane. The insertion point appears next to a bullet in the main text placeholder.

5. **Type Overall sales set new record, then press [Enter]**
   A new bullet automatically appears when you press [Enter].

6. **Press [Tab]**
   The new first-level bullet indents and becomes a second-level bullet.

7. **Type 3 new locations, then press [Enter]**
   This bullet should actually be a first-level bullet.

8. **Click to the left of the 3 that you just typed, then press [Shift][Tab]**
   The item changes back to a first-level bullet.

9. **Click after the word locations, press [Enter], then enter the next three bulleted items as shown in Figure B-7**

10. **Click the Save button on the Standard toolbar**
    Your changes are saved to your Project Disk.

**FIGURE B-6:** New Slide dialog box

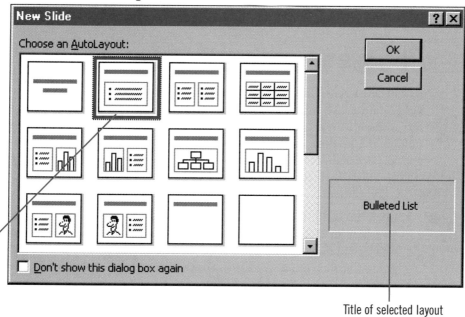

Default AutoLayout

Title of selected layout

**FIGURE B-7:** New slide with bulleted list

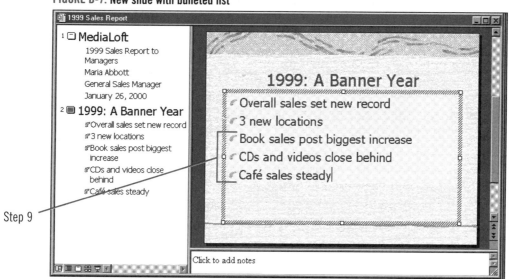

Step 9

**LE B-3: AutoLayout placeholder types**

| ceholder | symbol | description |
|---|---|---|
| lleted List | | Inserts a short list of related points |
| Art | | Inserts a picture from the Clip Gallery |
| rt | | Inserts a chart created with Microsoft Graph |
| anization Chart | | Inserts an organizational chart |
| e | | Inserts a table |
| a Clip | | Inserts a music, sound, or video clip |
| ct | | Inserts an external object such as WordArt, an equation, a spreadsheet, or a picture |

# Working in Outline View

As you have learned, you can enter your presentation text in the Slide or Outline pane in Normal view. You can also enter text in Slide or Outline view. If you want to focus on the presentation text without worrying about how it looks, Outline view can be a good choice. As in a regular outline, the headings, or **titles**, appear first; then under them, the subpoints, or **main text**, appear. The main text appears as one or more lines of bulleted text indented under a title. Maria switches to Outline view to enter text for two more slides.

## Steps

1. **Click the Outline View button** 📖 **to the left of the horizontal scroll bar**
   Switching to Outline view enlarges the Outline pane; the Slide and Notes panes become smaller and move to the right side of the screen. The blinking insertion point is in the title of slide 2 (the slide you just created). The Outlining toolbar appears on the left side of the screen.

2. **Click anywhere in the last text bullet, press [Shift], then click the New Slide button** 🗐 **on the Standard toolbar**
   Pressing [Shift] while clicking 🗐 inserts a new slide with the same AutoLayout as the current slide. A slide icon 🔲 appears next to the slide number when you add a new slide to the outline. See Figure B-8. Text you enter next to a slide icon becomes the title for that slide. The Outlining toolbar is helpful when working in Outline view.

3. **Right-click any toolbar, then click Outlining**
   Table B-4 describes the buttons available on the Outlining toolbar. Because the third slide is a bulleted list like the second slide, you can insert a new slide with the same layout as Slide 2.

4. **Type 1999 Sales by Division, press [Enter], then click the Demote button** 📤 **on the Outlining toolbar**
   A new slide was inserted when you pressed [Enter], but because you want to enter the main text for the slide you just created, you indented this line to make it part of slide 3. You can also press [Tab] to indent text one level.

5. **Type Overall product sales up 22%, then press [Enter]; type MediaLoft East sales up 25%, then press [Enter]; type MediaLoft West sales up 21%, then press [Enter]**

6. **Press [Shift][Tab]**
   The bullet changes to a new slide icon.

7. **Type The Star: MediaLoft East, press [Ctrl][Enter], type Book sales up 29%, press [Enter], type CD sales up 25%, press [Enter], then type Video sales up 20%**
   Pressing [Ctrl][Enter] while the cursor is in title text creates a bullet. Pressing [Ctrl][Enter] while the cursor is in the main text creates a new slide with the same layout as the previous slide. Two of the bulleted points you just typed for slide 4 are out of order.

8. **Position the pointer to the left of the last bullet in slide 4, then click**
   The pointer changes from ⌶ to ✛. PowerPoint selects the entire line of text.

9. **Click the Move Up button** 🔼 **on the Outlining toolbar**
   The third bullet point moves up one line and trades places with the second bullet point shown in Figure B-9.

10. **Right-click any toolbar, click Outlining to close the Outlining toolbar, click Normal View button** 🖼, **click the Previous Slide button** 🔼 **below the vertical scroll bar in the Slide pane three times to view each slide, then save your work**
    When you are finished viewing all the slides, Slide 1 of 4 should appear in the status bar.

FIGURE B-8: Outline view

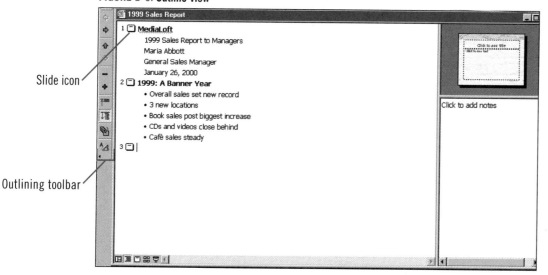

Slide icon

Outlining toolbar

FIGURE B-9: Bulleted item moved up in Outline view

Demote button

Move Up button

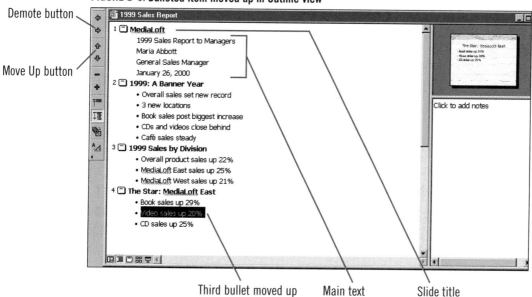

Third bullet moved up       Main text       Slide title

TABLE B-4: Outlining toolbar commands

| button | button name | description |
|---|---|---|
| | Promote | Indents selected text one tab to the left |
| | Demote | Indents selected text one tab to the right |
| | Move Up | Moves the selection above the previous line |
| | Move Down | Moves the selection below the next line |
| | Collapse | Shows only the titles of the selected slide |
| | Expand | Shows all levels of the selected slide |
| | Collapse All | Shows only the titles of all slides |
| | Expand All | Shows all levels of all slides |
| | Summary Slide | Creates a new bulleted slide containing only the titles of selected slides; good for creating an agenda slide |
| | Show Formatting | Shows or hides all character formatting |

# Entering Notes

So you don't have to rely on your memory when you give your presentation in front of a group, you can create notes that accompany your slides. You can enter notes in either the Notes pane or in Notes Page view. The notes you enter do not appear on the slides themselves; they are private notes. You can print these pages and refer to them during your presentation. If you want to provide pages on which your audience can take notes, print the notes pages, but leave the text placeholder blank. You can also insert graphics on the notes pages if you use Notes Page view. To make sure she doesn't forget how she will present the slide information, Maria enters notes to her slides.

## Steps 123 4

1. **Click in the Notes pane**
   The placeholder text in the Notes pane disappears and the blinking insertion point appears, as shown in Figure B-10.

**Trouble?**

If you don't see a red, wavy line under the words "MediaLoft" and "Welcom," don't worry. Someone else may have turned this feature off on your machine.

2. **Type Welcom to MediaLoft's Year 2000 company meeting.**
   Make sure you typed "Welcome" without the "e" as shown. The red, wavy line under the words "MediaLoft" and "Welcom" means that these words are not in the Microsoft Office dictionary.

3. **Click the Next Slide button ⬆, click in the Notes pane, then type I'm happy to share with you a brief overview of the success MediaLoft has achieved in the last year.**
   As you type, text automatically wraps to the next line.

4. **Click ⬆ to go to the third slide, click the Notes pane, then type Due to our recor year in 1998, MediaLoft's 1999 goals were very aggressive. Our overall produc sales were up an amazing 22%, with the eastern division edging out the wester division. Of course, they did get 2 of the 3 new stores, so they had an advantag there.**

**Trouble?**

If you don't see Notes Page on the View menu, point to the double arrow at the bottom of the menu. If you don't see the Zoom list arrow, click the More Buttons button 🔅 on the Standard toolbar.

5. **Click View on the menu bar, click Notes Page, click the Zoom list arrow on th Standard toolbar, then click 100%**
   Because the note on slide 3 is so long, it is easier to read in Notes Page view. See Figure B-1

6. **Click ⬆, click in the notes placeholder, then type As you can see, the book sal for MediaLoft East were remarkable. We had been concerned about the growth online booksellers, but there appears to be no substitute for actually holding book and sipping a cup of cappuccino.**

7. **Press [Enter], then type Thank you all for your hard work and support, and I lo forward to working with you all in the new millennium!**

**QuickTip**

You can also increase the size of the Notes pane in Normal view by dragging the separator line between the Notes pane and the Slide pane.

8. **Click the Normal View button 🔲, then drag the scroll box in the Slide pane verti scroll bar all the way to the top to return to slide 1**

FIGURE B-10: **Insertion point in the Notes pane**

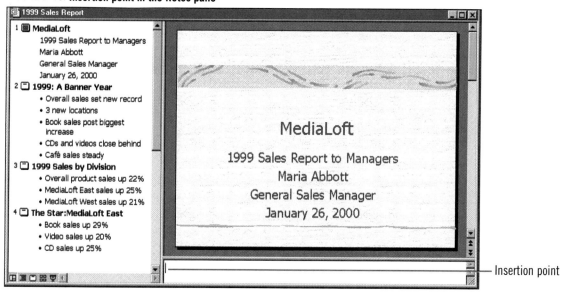
Insertion point

FIGURE B-11: **Slide 3 in Notes Page view**

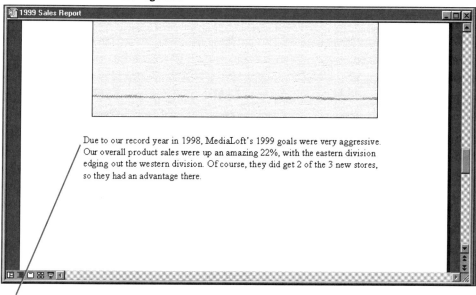
Speaker notes

## Adding slide footers and headers

To customize your slides, notes pages, or handouts with information, such as your company or product name, the slide number, or the date, you can add headers and footers. To add a header or footer, click View on the menu bar, then click Header and Footer. Each checked element in the Header and Footer dialog box is included as part of the header or footer. Each check box corresponds to a different footer area. The date and time appear in the left footer area. The slide number appears in the right footer area, and any footer text you add appears in the middle. Click the check boxes and watch to see in which of the three footer areas the footer element appears. On the Slide tab, you can add only footers. To have the footer appear on only the current slide, click Apply; to have footers appear on all the slides, click Apply to All. On the Notes and Handouts tab, you can choose to add headers and footers, so they appear on all the pages.

# Checking Spelling in the Presentation

As your work nears completion, you need to review and proofread your presentation thoroughly for errors. You can use the spellchecking feature in PowerPoint to check for and correct spelling errors. The spellchecking feature compares the spelling of all the words in your presentation against the words contained in its electronic dictionary. You still must proofread your presentation for punctuation, grammar, and word-usage errors, however. The spellchecker recognizes only misspelled words, not misused words. For example, the spellchecker would not identify "The Test" as an error even if you had intended to type "The Best." ✒️ Maria has finished adding and changing text in the presentation, so she checks her work.

**Steps** 1 2 3 4

**QuickTip**

If your spellchecker doesn't find the word "MediaLoft," then a previous user may have accidentally added it to the custom dictionary. Skip steps 1 and 2 and continue with the lesson.

**1.** Click the **Spelling button** 🔤 on the Standard toolbar

PowerPoint begins to check the spelling in your entire presentation. When PowerPoint finds a misspelled word or a word it doesn't recognize, the Spelling dialog box opens, as shown in Figure B-12. For an explanation of the commands available in the Spelling dialog box, see Table B-5. In this case, PowerPoint does not recognize "MediaLoft" on slide 1. It suggests that you replace it with two separate words "Media" and "Loft," which it does recognize. You want the word to remain as you typed it.

**2.** Click **Ignore all**

Clicking Ignore All tells the spellchecker to ignore all instances of this word in this presentation. The next word the spellchecker identifies as an error is the word "Welcom" on the notes for slide 1. In the Suggestions list box, the spellchecker suggests "Welcome."

**3.** Click **Welcome** in the Suggestions list box, then click **Change**

If PowerPoint finds any other words it does not recognize, either change them or ignore them. When the spellchecker finishes checking your presentation, the Spelling dialog box closes, and a PowerPoint alert box opens with a message saying the spelling check is complete.

**QuickTip**

The spellchecker does not check the text in pictures or embedded objects. You'll need to spell check text in imported objects, such as charts or Word documents, using their original application.

**4.** Click **OK**

The alert box closes.

**5.** Click **View** on the menu bar, then click **Header and Footer**

Before you print your final presentation, placing your name in the footer helps you identify your printout if you are sharing a printer.

**6.** On the Slide tab, make sure the **Footer check box** is selected, click in the **Footer text box**, then type your name

**7.** Click the **Notes and Handouts tab**, type your name in the Footer text box, then click **Apply to All**

Now your name will print on slides, notes pages, and handouts.

**8.** Click **File** on the menu bar, then click **Print**

**9.** Click the **Print what list arrow**, click **Notes Pages**, click the **Pure black and white check box** to select it, click the **Frame Slides check box** to select it, then click OK

The notes pages print with a frame around each page.

**10.** Save your presentation, then return to **slide 1** in Normal view

FIGURE B-12: Spelling dialog box

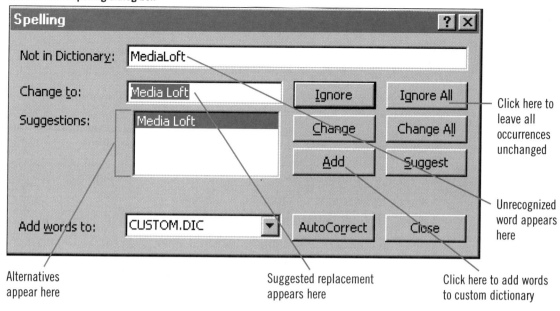

| Spelling | ? X |
|----------|-----|

Not in Dictionary: MediaLoft

Change to: Media Loft        [Ignore]   [Ignore All] ── Click here to leave all occurrences unchanged

Suggestions: Media Loft       [Change]   [Change All]

                              [Add]      [Suggest] ── Unrecognized word appears here

Add words to: CUSTOM.DIC ▼   [AutoCorrect]  [Close]

Alternatives appear here          Suggested replacement appears here          Click here to add words to custom dictionary

TABLE B-5: Spelling dialog box commands

| command | description |
|---------|-------------|
| Ignore/Ignore all | Continues spellchecking, without making any changes to the identified word (or all occurrences of the identified word) |
| Change/Change All | Changes the identified word (or all its occurrences) to the suggested word |
| Add | Adds the identified word to your custom dictionary; spellchecker will not flag it again |
| Suggest | Suggests an alternative spelling for the identified word |
| AutoCorrect | Adds suggested word as an AutoCorrect entry for the highlighted word |
| Add words to | Lets you choose a custom dictionary where you store words you often use but that are not part of the PowerPoint dictionary |

TO USE

## Checking spelling as you type

PowerPoint checks your spelling as you type. If you type a word that is not in the electronic dictionary, a wavy, red line appears under it. To correct the error, right-click the misspelled word. A pop-up menu appears with one or more suggestions. You can select a suggestion, add the word you typed to your custom dictionary, or ignore it. To turn off automatic

spellchecking, click Tools on the menu bar, then click Options to open the Options dialog box. Click the Spelling and Style tab, and in the Spelling section click the Check spelling as you type check box to deselect it. To temporarily hide the wavy, red lines, select the Hide spelling errors in this document check box.

# Evaluating a Presentation

As you create a presentation, keep in mind that good design involves preparation. An effective presentation is both focused and visually appealing. A planned presentation is easy for the speaker to present and easy for the audience to comprehend. The visual elements (colors, graphics, and text) can strongly influence audience attention and interest and can determine the success of your presentation. Maria evaluates her presentation's effectiveness. Her final presentation is shown in Slide Sorter view in Figure B-13. For contrast, Figure B-14 shows a poorly designed slide.

1. Click the **Slide Show button** 🖳, then press **[Enter]** to move through the slide show

2. When you are finished viewing the slide show, click the **Slide Sorter View button** 🔳
   Maria decides that slide 4 should come before slide 3.

3. Drag **slide 4** to the left until you see a thin black line between slides 2 and 3, then release the mouse button
   The thin, black line indicates the slide's position.

4. When you are finished evaluating your presentation according to the following guidelines, exit PowerPoint, saving changes when prompted

## Details

**In evaluating a presentation it is important to:**

### Keep your message focused
Don't put everything you are going to say on your presentation slides. Keep the audience anticipating further explanations to the key points shown on your slides. For example, Maria's presentation focuses the audience's attention on last year's sales numbers and sales by division because she included only the sales percentage increases and the breakdown of the sales by division. She supplemented the slides with notes that explain the reasons for the increases.

### Keep the design simple, easy to read, and appropriate for the content
Use appropriate fonts, font sizes, and background colors. A design template makes the presentation consistent. If you design your own layout, do not add so many elements that the slides look cluttered. Use the same design elements consistently throughout the presentation; otherwise your audience will get confused. The design template Maria used for the sales presentation is simple; the horizontal bar on each slide gives the presentation an interesting, somewhat artistic look appropriate for a friendly presentation to company employees.

### Choose attractive colors that make the slide easy to read
Use contrasting colors for slide background and text, so that the slides are easy to read. If you are giving your presentation on a computer, you can use almost any combination of colors.

### Keep your text concise
Limit each slide to six words per line and six lines per slide. Use lists and symbols to help prioritize your points visually. Your presentation text provides only the highlights; use notes give more detailed information.

### Choose fonts and styles that are easy to read and emphasize important text
As a general rule, use no more than two fonts in a presentation and vary font size. Use bold italic selectively. Do not use text smaller than 18 points. In the design template Maria used titles are 44-point Tahoma and the main text is 32-point Tahoma.

### Use visuals to help communicate the message of your presentation
Commonly used visuals include clip art, photographs, charts, worksheets, tables, and more. Whenever possible, replace text with a visual, but be careful not to overcrowd your slides.

**FIGURE B-13:** The final presentation

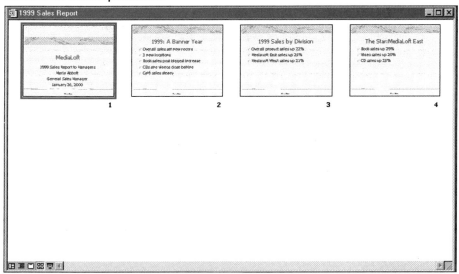

**FIGURE B-14:** A poorly designed slide in Slide view

Text too small

Graphic obscures text and does not relate to slide message

Too many fonts

Not enough contrast

Too many words

Lines add clutter

Too many colors

## Using design templates

You are not limited to the templates in PowerPoint; you can either modify a PowerPoint template or create your own presentation template. For example, you might want to use your company's color as a slide background or incorporate your company's logo on every slide. If you modify an existing template, you can keep, change, or delete any color, graphic, or font. To create a new template, click File on the menu bar, then click New. On the General tab, double-click Blank Presentation, then select the Blank AutoLayout. Add the design elements you want, then use the Save As command on the File menu to name and save your customized design. Click the Save as type list arrow, and choose Design template,

then name your template. PowerPoint will automatically add a .pot file extension to the filename. You can then use your customized template as a basis for future presentations. To apply a template from another presentation, open the presentation you want to change, then choose Apply Design Template from the Format menu. In the Apply Design Template dialog box, choose Presentations and Shows in the Files of type list box. Then navigate to and double-click the presentation whose design you want to apply. That presentation's template will be applied to your current presentation.

# Practice

## ► Concepts Review

**Label each element of the PowerPoint window shown in Figure B-15.**

FIGURE B-15

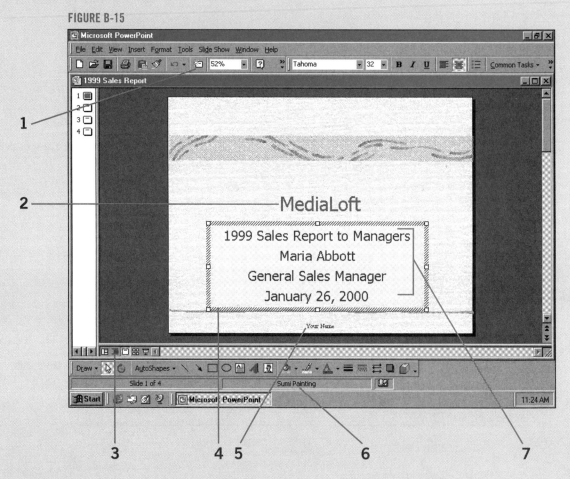

**Match each term with the statement that describes it.**

8. **Selection box**
9. **Insertion point**
10. **Slide icon**
11. **Design template**

a. A specific design, format, and color scheme that is applied to all the slides in a presentation

b. A blinking vertical line that indicates where your text will appear in a text object

c. A box of slanted lines containing prompt text in which you can enter text

d. In Outline view, the symbol that represents a slide

**Select the best answer from the list of choices.**

12. The ⊥ pointer shape appears for which one of the following tasks?
   a. Entering text
   b Switching views
   c. Choosing a new layout
   d. Inserting a new slide

**13. To move a slide up to a new position in Outline view**
- **a.** Click ➡
- **b.** Click ⬆
- **c.** Press [Tab]
- **d.** Click ✚

**14. When the spellchecker identifies a word as misspelled, which of the following is not a choice?**
- **a.** To ignore this occurrence of the error
- **b.** To change the misspelled word to the correct spelling
- **c.** To have the spellchecker automatically correct all the errors it finds
- **d.** To ignore all occurrences of the error in the presentation

**15. When you evaluate your presentation, you should make sure it follows which of the following criteria?**
- **a.** The slides should include every piece of information to be presented so the audience can read it.
- **b.** The slides should use as many colors as possible to hold the audience's attention.
- **c.** Lots of different typefaces will make the slides more interesting.
- **d.** The message should be clearly outlined without a lot of extra words.

**16. According to the unit, which of the following is *not* a guideline for planning a presentation?**
- **a.** Determine the purpose of the presentation
- **b.** Determine what you want to produce when the presentation is finished
- **c.** Determine which type of output you will need to best convey your message
- **d.** Determine who else can give the final presentation

**17. Which of the following statements is *not* true?**
- **a.** You can customize any PowerPoint template.
- **b.** The spellchecker will identify "there" as misspelled if the correct word for the context is "their."
- **c.** Speaker notes do not appear during the slide show.
- **d.** PowerPoint has many colorful templates from which to choose.

**8. Which of the following is *not* a method for changing text levels in the Outline pane or Outline view?**
- **a.** ⬆
- **b.** ➖
- **c.** ⬅
- **d.** Drag selected text

## ► Skills Review

**1. Choose a look for a presentation.**
- **a.** Start PowerPoint if necessary and open a new presentation by clicking the Design Template option button or by clicking New on the File menu.
- **b.** Display the Design Templates tab.
- **c.** Review the PowerPoint design templates and examine the preview of each one when the template is available.
- **d.** When you have finished reviewing the templates, open a new presentation using the Mountain template. (*Hint:* If you see a message saying you need to install additional templates, insert the Office 2000 CD in the appropriate drive and click OK. See your technical support person for assistance.)
- **e.** In the New Slide dialog box, select the Title Slide AutoLayout.
- **f.** Save the presentation as "Weekly Goals" to your Project Disk.
- **g.** Go to Slide view and apply the Bold Stripes template from the Design Templates folder.

**PowerPoint 2000**

**h.** Apply the template from the 1999 Sales Report presentation you created in the unit, and print slides 1 and 2 as Handouts in Grayscale, 6 slides per page.

**i.** Save the presentation.

## 2. Enter slide text.

**a.** In the Slide pane in Normal view or in Slide view, enter the text "Product Marketing" in the title placeholder.

**b.** In the main text placeholder, enter "Les Bolinger."

**c.** On the next line of the placeholder, enter "Manager."

**d.** On the next line of the placeholder, enter "Aug. 2, 2000."

**e.** Display and examine the different pointer shapes in PowerPoint. Refer back to Table B-2 to help you display the pointer shapes.

**f.** Deselect the text objects.

## 3. Create new slides.

**a.** Open the New Slide dialog box, and click each of the AutoLayouts. Identify each AutoLayout by its name in the Preview box.

**b.** Select the Bulleted List AutoLayout.

**c.** Type "Weekly Meeting for Marketing Groups" in the title placeholder.

**d.** Create a new bulleted list slide.

**e.** Enter the text from Table B-5 into the new slide.

TABLE B-5

| | |
|---|---|
| (Slide title) | Goals for the Week |
| (Main text object, first indent level) | Les |
| (Main text object, second indent level) | Interview for new marketing rep |
| | Discuss new procedures with Pacific Rim marketing reps |
| | Prepare for weekly division meeting next Mon. |

## 4. Work in Outline view.

**a.** Switch to Outline view

**b.** Create a new bulleted list slide after the last one.

**c.** Enter the text from Table B-6 into the new slide.

**d.** Create a new bulleted list slide after the last one.

**e.** Enter the text from Table B-7 into the new slide.

**f.** Move slide 5 up to the slide 4 position.

TABLE B-6

| | |
|---|---|
| (Slide title) | Goals for the Week |
| (Main text object, first indent level) | John |
| (Main text object, second indent level) | Revise product marketing report |
| | Set up plan for the annual sales meeting |
| | Thurs.—fly to Phoenix for sales meeting planning session |

## 5. Enter notes.

**a.** Go to slide 3 and place the insertion point in the Notes pane.

**b.** Enter the following notes:
I am interviewing new candidates for the product marketing position.
The following week, each of you will interview the candidates who meet initial qualifications.
I need all reports for the weekly meeting by Fri.
Reminder of the company profit sharing party next Fri. Work half day.
Open agenda for new division items.

**c.** View slide 5.

**d.** Enter the following notes:
I need the marketing report by Wed.
John: Come by my office later this afternoon to review the sales meeting plan.
Open agenda for new division items.

TABLE B-7

| | |
|---|---|
| (Slide title) | Goals for the Week |
| (Main text object, first indent level) | April |
| (Main text object, second indent level) | Complete division advertising plan for next year |
| | Establish preliminary advertising budget for division VP |
| | Investigate new advertising agencies for company |

   **e.** View slide 4.

   **f.** Enter the following speaker's notes:

      I need to review the advertising company list by Fri.

      April: See me about weekly division report after this meeting.

      Status on the advertising budget and next year's advertising plan.

      Open agenda for new division items.

   **g.** Switch to Slide view.

**6. Check spelling in the presentation.**

   **a.** Perform a spelling check on the document and change any misspelled words. Ignore any words that are correctly spelled but that the spellchecker doesn't recognize.

   **b.** Add your name to the footer on all sides and on all notes and handouts.

   **c.** Add "Product Marketing Presentation" to the left side of the header for Notes and Handouts.

   **d.** Save the presentation.

**7. Evaluate your presentation.**

   **a.** View slide 1 in Slide Show view, then move through the slide show.

   **b.** Go to Slide Sorter view, then delete slide 2.

   **c.** Drag slide 4 so that it comes before slide 3.

   **d.** Evaluate the presentation using the points described in the lesson as criteria.

   **e.** Print the Notes pages in Pure black and white, with a frame around the page.

   **f.** Customize the template text by adding the date and time to the left side of the slide footer, then save your new design as a template called Weekly Goals Template.

   **g.** Print the Notes pages in Grayscale with a frame around the page.

# ► Independent Challenges

**1.** You have been asked to give a one-day course at a local adult education center. The course is called "Personal Computing for the Slightly Anxious Beginner" and is intended for adults who have never used a computer. One of your responsibilities is to create presentation slides that outline the course materials.

   Plan and create presentation slides that outline the course material for the students. Create slides for the course introduction, course description, course text, grading policies, and a detailed syllabus. For each slide, include speaker notes to help you stay on track during the presentation.

   Create your own course material, but assume the following: the school has a computer lab with IBM-compatible computers and Microsoft Windows software; each student has a computer; the prospective students are intimidated by computers but want to learn; and the course is on a Saturday from 9 to 5, with a one-hour lunch break.

   To complete this independent challenge:

  **a.** Think about the results you want to see, the information you need, and the type of message you want to communicate.

  **b.** Write an outline of your presentation. What content should go on the slides? On the notes pages?

  **c.** Start PowerPoint and create the presentation by choosing a design template and entering the title slide text.

  **d.** Create the required slides as well as an ending slide that summarizes your presentation.

  **e.** Add speaker notes to the slides.

  **f.** Check the spelling in the presentation.

  **g.** Save the presentation as "Class 1" to your Project Disk.

  **h.** View the slide show, then view the slides in Slide Sorter view. Evaluate your presentation, delete any unnecessary slides, and adjust it as necessary so that it is focused, clear, concise, and readable.

  **i.** Add your name as a footer, then print the slides and notes pages.

**2.** You are the training director for Events, Inc, a company that coordinates special events, including corporate functions, weddings, and private parties. Events, Inc regularly trains groups of temporary employees that they can call on as coordinators, kitchen and wait staff, and coat checkers for specific events. The company trains 10 to 15 new workers a month for the peak season between May and September. One of your responsibilities is to orient new temporary employees at the next training session.

Plan and create presentation slides that outline your employee orientation. Create slides for the introduction, agenda, company history, dress requirements, principles for interacting successfully with guests, and safety requirements. For each slide, include speaker notes that you can use during the presentation.

Create your own presentation and company material, but assume the following: the new employee training class lasts four hours, and your orientation lasts 15 minutes; the training director's presentation lasts 15 minutes; and the dress code requires uniforms, supplied by Events, Inc (white for daytime events, black and white for evening events).

To complete this independent challenge:

a. Think about the results you want to see, the information you need, and the type of message you want to communicate for this presentation.

b. Write a presentation outline. What content should go on the slides? On the notes pages?

c. Start PowerPoint and create the presentation by choosing a design template, and entering the title slide text.

d. Create an ending slide that summarizes your presentation.

e. Add speaker notes to the slides.

f. Check the spelling in the presentation.

g. Save the presentation as "Training Class" to your Project Disk.

h. View the slide show, then view the slides in Slide Sorter view. Evaluate your presentation, delete any unnecessary slides, and make any changes necessary so that the final version is focused, clear, concise, and readable. Adjust any items as needed.

i. Add your name as a footer, then print the slides and notes pages.

**3.** You are an independent distributor of natural foods in Tucson, Arizona. Your business, Harvest Natural Foods, has grown progressively since its inception eight years ago, but sales and profits have plateaued over the last nine months. In an effort to stimulate growth, you decide to acquire two major natural food dealers, which would allow Harvest Natural Foods to expand its territory into surrounding states. Use PowerPoint to develop a presentation that you can use to gain a financial backer for the acquisition.

To complete this independent challenge:

a. Start PowerPoint and open a new presentation. Choose the Nature design template. Add "Growth Plan" as the main title on the title slide, and "Harvest Natural Foods" as the subtitle.

b. Save the presentation as "Harvest Proposal" to your Project Disk.

c. Add five more slides with the following titles: slide 2–Background; slide 3–Current Situation; slide 4–Acquisition Goals; slide 5–Our Management Team; slide 6–Funding Required.

d. Enter text into the text placeholders of the slides. Use both Slide and Outline views to enter text.

e. Create a new slide at the end of the presentation. Enter concluding text on the slide, summarizing the main points of the presentation.

f. Add speaker notes that you can use during the presentation.

g. Check the spelling in the presentation.

h. View the presentation as a slide show. Evaluate and save your presentation.

i. Add your name as a footer in the notes and handouts, print the slides as handouts, six per page, and then print the presentation outline.

**WEB WORK**

**4.** The Literacy Project is a nationwide nonprofit organization that provides free reading and English-language tutoring for adults. Traditionally, the state government has provided most of the funding for the project. However, due to recent state budget cuts, it has become necessary to solicit private corporations and private trusts for grants. MediaLoft has a corporate sponsorship program that works with the Literacy Project. MediaLoft donates books and supplies, encourages interaction between their employees and the program, and helps them raise funds. Karen Rosen, MediaLoft's director of human resources, has appointed you to develop a PowerPoint presentation that the Literacy Project can take to local businesses and trust fund boards to build support. MediaLoft will then loan the Project a portable computer and monitor whenever they need to present the presentation.

The presentation is intended to be a "first contact" with businesses, that will lay the groundwork for a fund-raising proposal at a later date. Therefore, the presentation should educate the corporate audience about the subject of literacy and the need for the Literacy Project, rather than solicit funds directly.

To complete this independent challenge:

a. Connect to the Internet, go to the MediaLoft intranet site at http://www.course.com/illustrated/MediaLoft and click the Community link. Scroll down to and click the Literacy Project link, and read the information it contains.

b. Start PowerPoint, open a new presentation, and apply an appropriate design template, keeping in mind your business audience. Add "Literacy Project" as the main title on the title slide, and add "Improving Tomorrow's Workforce While Building Your Community" as the subtitle.

c. Create a presentation of at least five slides that will educate the corporate audience and convince them of a need for the Literacy Project. Use both Slide and Outline panes or views to enter text.

d. Create a new slide at the end of the presentation. Enter concluding text on the slide, summarizing your main points.

e. Apply a different design template to the presentation. If you don't care for the results, reapply the original design template.

f. Add speaker notes to the slides.

g. Spellcheck the presentation.

h. Save the presentation as "Literacy Presentation" to your Project Disk. Disconnect from the Internet when you are done.

i. View the presentation as a slide show and evaluate your presentation. Delete any unnecessary slides. Save any changes you make.

j. Add you name as a footer, then print the slides as handouts, six per page, and print the outline.

# ► Visual Workshop

Create the marketing presentation shown in Figures B-16 and B-17. Save the presentation as "Sales Project" to your Project Disk. Review your slides in Slide Show view, add your name as a footer, then print the first slide of your presentation in Slide view and print the outline.

FIGURE B-16

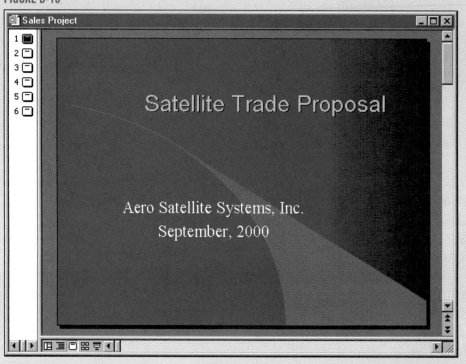

FIGURE B-17

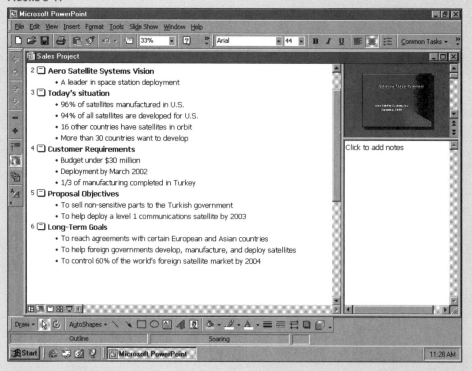

# Modifying
## a Presentation

### Objectives

- ▶ Open an existing presentation
- ▶ Draw and modify an object
- ▶ Edit drawing objects
- ▶ Understand aligning, grouping, and stacking objects
- ▶ Align and group objects
- ▶ Add and arrange text
- ▶ Format text
- ▶ Customize the color scheme and background
- ▶ Correct text automatically

After you create the basic outline of your presentation and enter text, you need to add visuals to your slides to communicate your message in the most effective way possible. In this unit, you open an existing presentation; draw and modify objects; add, arrange, and format text; change a presentation color scheme; and automatically correct text. After Maria Abbott reviews her presentation, she continues to work on the Sales Report presentation. Maria uses the PowerPoint drawing and text-editing features to bring the presentation closer to a finished look.

PowerPoint 2000

# Opening an Existing Presentation

Sometimes the easiest way to create a new presentation is by changing an existing one. Revising a presentation saves you from typing duplicate information. You simply open the file you want to change, then use the Save As command to save a copy of the file with a new name. Whenever you open an existing presentation in this book, you will save a copy of it with a new name to your Project Disk—this keeps the original file intact. Saving a copy does not affect the original file. ✐ Maria wants to add visuals to her presentation, so she opens the presentation she has been working on.

1. Start PowerPoint and insert your Project Disk into the appropriate disk drive

**QuickTip**

If PowerPoint is already running, click the Open button 🗁 on the Standard toolbar.

2. Click the **Open an existing presentation option button** in the PowerPoint startup dialog box, click **More Files** in the scrollable window, then click **OK**
   The Open dialog box opens. See Figure C-1.

3. Click the **Look in list arrow**, then locate the drive that contains your Project Disk

4. Click the drive that contains your Project Disk
   A list of the files on your Project Disk appears in the Open dialog box.

**Trouble?**

If the Open dialog box on your screen does not show a preview box, click the Views list arrow 🔡 in the toolbar at the top of the dialog box, then select Preview.

5. Click **PPT C-1**
   The first slide of the selected presentation appears in the preview box on the right side of the dialog box.

6. Click **Open**
   The file named PPT C-1 opens in Slide view.

7. Click **File** on the menu bar, then click **Save As**
   The Save As dialog box opens. See Figure C-2. The Save As dialog box works just like the Open dialog box.

**QuickTip**

When you save copies of files, you may want to use a naming system to help you stay organized and differentiate different versions of a document. Many people use the name of the original file followed by consecutive numbers (1, 2, 3 . . . ) or letters (a, b, c . . . ) to designate revisions of the same document or presentation.

8. Make sure the Save in list box shows the drive containing your Project Disk and that the current filename in the File name text box is selected, then type **1999 Sale Report 1**
   Compare your screen to the Save As dialog box in Figure C-2.

9. Click **Save** to close the Save As dialog box and save the file
   PowerPoint creates a copy of PPT C-1 with the name 1999 Sales Report 1 on your Project Disk and closes PPT C-1.

10. Click **Window** on the menu bar, then click **Arrange All**
    Your screen now matches those shown in this book. If you have another PowerPoint presentation open and it appears next to this presentation, close it, then repeat step 10.

FIGURE C-1: **Open dialog box**

Step 3 —

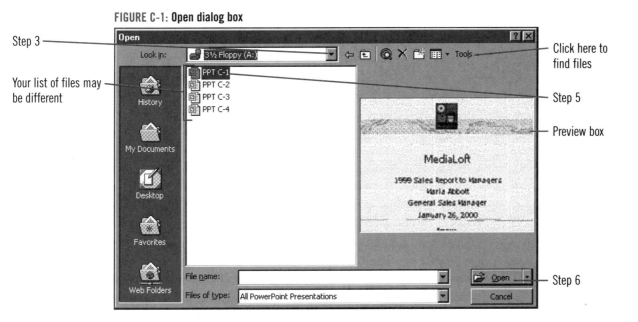

Your list of files may be different —

Click here to find files —

Step 5 —

Preview box —

Step 6 —

FIGURE C-2: **Save As dialog box**

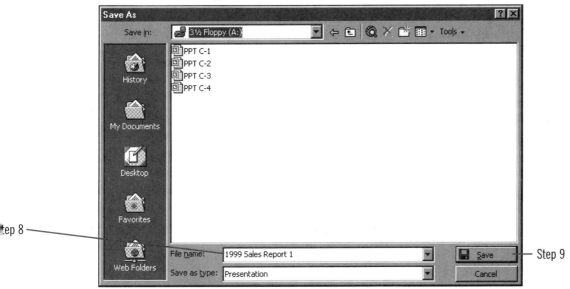

tep 8 —

Step 9 —

## Searching for a file by properties

If you can't find a file, you can search for it using the PowerPoint Find dialog box, which you open from the Tools menu in the Open dialog box. (See Figure C-1.) To search for a file, open the Open dialog box, click the Tools menu button on the toolbar at the top of the dialog box, then click Find on the drop-down list. The Find dialog box opens. You can specify criteria PowerPoint should use to search by clicking the list arrows in the Property, Condition, and Value boxes at the bottom of the dialog box. A property is any aspect of a presentation, such as its filename, title, contents, size, or format. For example, you can specify that you want to find a presentation whose filename (property) includes (condition) the words "sales presentation" (value). Once you've specified criteria, click Add to List. To specify where PowerPoint should search for the file, click the Look in list arrow and select the drive or folder you want to search. To include subfolders in the search, click the Search subfolders check box to select it. Click Find Now to start the search. PowerPoint closes the Find dialog box and lists the folders and files that meet your criteria in the Look in list box in the Open dialog box.

# Drawing and Modifying an Object

The drawing capabilities of PowerPoint allow you to draw and modify lines, shapes, and pictures to enhance your presentation. Lines and shapes that you create with the PowerPoint drawing tools are objects that you can modify and move at any time. These drawn objects have graphic attributes that you can change, such as fill color, line color, line style, shadow, and 3-D effects. To add drawing objects to your slides, use the buttons on the Drawing toolbar at the bottom of the screen above the status bar. Maria decides to draw an object on slide 4 of her sales report presentation to add impact to her message.

## Steps

1. Click **Tools** on the menu bar, click **Customize**, click the **Options tab** in the Customize dialog box, click **Reset my usage data** to restore the default settings, click **Yes** in the alert box or dialog balloon that opens, then click **Close**
This restores the default settings to your toolbars.

2. In the Outline pane, click the **slide icon** ⊟ for slide 4
The 1999 Sales by Division slide appears.

3. Press and hold **[Shift]**, then click the **main text object**
A dotted selection box with small boxes called **sizing handles** appears around the text object. If you click a text object without pressing [Shift], a selection box composed of slanted lines appears indicating the object is active, but not selected. When an entire object is selected, you can change its size, shape, or attributes.

**Trouble?**

If you are not satisfied with the size of the text object, resize it again.

4. Position the pointer over the right, middle sizing handle, then drag the sizing handle to the left until the text object is about half its original size
When you position the pointer over a sizing handle, it changes to ↔. It points in different directions depending on which sizing handle it is positioned over. When you drag a text object's sizing handle, the pointer changes to ┼, and a dotted outline representing the size of the text object appears. See Figure C-3.

**QuickTip**

Position the pointer on top of a button to see its name.

5. Click the **AutoShapes menu button** on the Drawing toolbar, point to **Stars and Banners**, then click the **Up Ribbon button** 🎀 (third row, first item)
After you select a shape from the AutoShapes menu and move the pointer over the slide, the pointer changes to ┼.

**QuickTip**

To create a circle or square, click the Oval or Rectangle button on the Drawing toolbar, then press [Shift] while dragging the pointer.

6. Position ┼ in the blank area of the slide to the right of the text object, press **[Shift]**, drag down and to the right to create a ribbon object, as shown in Figure C-4, then release the mouse button and release **[Shift]**
When you release the mouse button, a ribbon object appears on the slide, filled with the default color and outlined with the default line style, as shown in Figure C-4. Pressing [Shift] while you create the object keeps the object's proportions as you change its size.

7. If your ribbon object is not approximately the same size as the one shown in Figure C-4, press **[Shift]** and drag one of the sizing handles to resize the object

8. Click the **Line Color list arrow** 🖍▾ on the Drawing toolbar, then click the **light purple square** (the third square from the right, called Follow Accent Scheme Color)
PowerPoint applies the purple color to the selected object's outline.

9. Click the **Fill Color list arrow** 🪣▾ on the Drawing toolbar, then click the **dark purple square** (the fourth square from the left, called Follow Title Text Scheme Color)
PowerPoint fills the ribbon with the dark purple color.

FIGURE C-3: Resizing a text object

Step 2 ————

Dotted outline ————

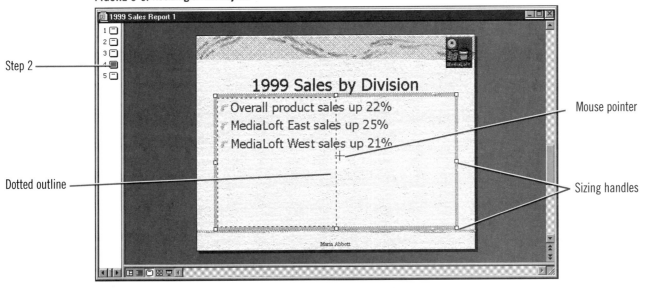

Mouse pointer

Sizing handles

FIGURE C-4: Slide showing ribbon object

## Using the Drawing toolbar

The Drawing toolbar contains many useful buttons for drawing and modifying objects on PowerPoint slides (See Figure C-5). You use the buttons on the left, including the Draw menu button, to manipulate objects. When you click the Draw menu button, a menu of commands useful for manipulating objects opens. The buttons in the middle section are used to create objects on your slides. You use the buttons in the far right section to modify objects once they have been created. To find out about a particular button, point to it to see its name in a ScreenTip, or click Help on the menu bar, click What's This, then click the button to see a brief description.

FIGURE C-5: The Drawing toolbar

# Editing Drawing Objects

Often, a drawn object does not match the slide or presentation "look" you are trying to achieve. PowerPoint allows you to manipulate the size and shape of objects on your slide. You can alter the appearance of any object by changing its shape, as you did when you resized the text object in the previous lesson, or by adjusting the object's dimensions. You also can cut, copy, and paste objects and add text to most PowerPoint shapes. ✏️ Maria changes the shape of the ribbon object, then makes two copies of it to help emphasize each point on the slide.

## Steps

1. **Click the ribbon object to select it, if necessary**
   In addition to sizing handles, small yellow diamonds called **adjustment handles** appear. You change these handles to change the appearance of an object, usually its most prominent feature, like the size of an arrow head, or the proportion of a ribbon's center to its "tails."

2. **Drag the bottom, right sizing handle to the right about 1"**

3. **Position the pointer over the middle of the selected ribbon object so that it changes to ⬥, then drag the ribbon so that the top of the ribbon aligns with the top of the first bullet**
   A dotted outline appears as you move the ribbon object to help you position it. Compare your screen to Figure C-6 and make any necessary adjustments.

4. **Position ⬥ over the ribbon object, then press and hold [Ctrl]**
   The pointer changes to ⬥, indicating that PowerPoint will make a copy of the ribbon object when you drag the mouse.

5. **While holding down [Ctrl], drag the ribbon object down the slide until dotted lines indicate that the copy aligns with the second bullet, then release the mouse button**
   An exact copy of the first ribbon object appears. See Figure C-7.

6. **Position the pointer over the second ribbon object, press and hold [Ctrl], then drag a copy of the ribbon object down the slide until it aligns with the third bullet**
   Compare your screen to Figure C-7.

7. **Click the top ribbon object, then type 22%**
   The text appears in the center of the object. The text is now part of the object, so if you move the object, the text will move with it.

8. **Click the middle ribbon object, type 25%, then click the bottom ribbon object and type 21%**
   The graphics you have added reinforce the slide text. The ribbon shape suggests achievement, and the numbers, which are the focus of this slide, are prominent. The dark text hard to read on the dark background.

9. **Press and hold [Shift], click the other two ribbon objects, click the Font Color arrow 🔽 on the Drawing toolbar, then click the white square**
   Make sure the bottom ribbon object is still selected when you select the other two object. The text changes to white.

10. **Click a blank area of the slide to deselect the objects, then save your presentation**

FIGURE C-6: Slide showing resized ribbon object

Adjustment handles

Step 2

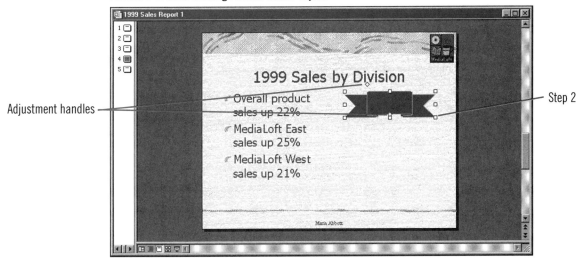

FIGURE C-7: Slide showing duplicated ribbon object

Step 5

Step 6

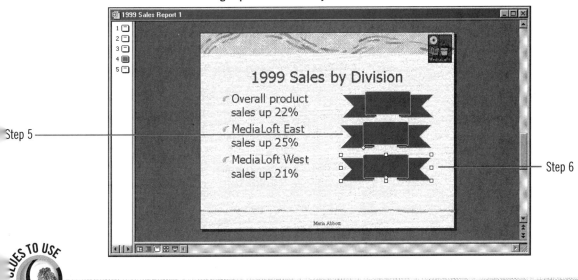

## Using the Office Clipboard

In this lesson, you copied objects using the Ctrl-Drag technique. You can also copy objects using the Office Clipboard, which lets you copy and paste multiple items. You can store up to 12 text or graphic items on the Office Clipboard. See Figure C-8. When you copy a second item within any Office program, the program automatically places the second item on the Office Clipboard. If you put 12 items on the Office Clipboard and then copy a thirteenth item, the program asks you if you want to remove the first item. You can check the contents of a particular item on the Office Clipboard by holding the pointer over it to display a ScreenTip. You can then paste one or more of the items from the Office Clipboard to a slide in your PowerPoint presentation. Just click the item you want to paste on the Clipboard toolbar and PowerPoint inserts it in the presentation. To paste all the items on the Clipboard, click Paste All on the Clipboard toolbar. The items you collect on the Office Clipboard remain there until you quit all Office programs. To clear the Office Clipboard, click Clear Clipboard on the Clipboard toolbar. You can copy and paste items among any of the Office programs.

FIGURE C-8: Clipboard toolbar

# Understanding Aligning, Grouping, and Stacking Objects

As you work in PowerPoint, you often work with multiple objects on the same slide. These may be text objects or graphics objects, such as clip art, drawings, photos, tables, or charts. When you have more than one object on a slide, you want to make sure they look organized and neat and that they help communicate your message effectively. You can accomplish this by aligning, grouping, and stacking the objects using the commands on the Draw menu on the Drawing toolbar.

### Aligning objects

When you **align** objects, you place their edges (or their centers) on the same plane. For example, you might align squares vertically so that their left edges are in a straight vertical line. Or you might align a series of circles horizontally so that their centers are in a straight horizontal line. You align objects in PowerPoint by first selecting the objects you want to align. Next, click the Draw menu button on the Drawing toolbar, point to Align or Distribute, then select one of the three horizontal alignment commands (Align Left, Align Center, or Align Right), or one of the three vertical alignment commands (Align Top, Align Middle, or Align Bottom). Aligning saves you time, because you don't have to drag each object individually. The PowerPoint Align commands make your slides look neater and more professional because they can do a better job than most people can do by manually dragging objects with the mouse and aligning them "by eye." See Figure C-9.

### Grouping objects

When you **group** objects, you combine two or more objects into one object. For example, instead of having to move four squares, you could group them and then only have to move one object that contains the four squares. It's often helpful to group objects that you have aligned so that when you move the group, the alignment among the objects remains the same. To group objects on a PowerPoint slide, you first select the objects, click the Draw menu button on the Drawing toolbar, and then click Group. You can easily ungroup objects by clicking a grouped object and then selecting the Ungroup command on the Draw menu. See Figure C-10.

### Stacking objects

When you **stack** objects, you determine their order in a stack—that is, which ones are in the front and which are in back. You can easily move objects on top of each other to create effects. For example, you'll often want to place a word on top of a circle or square, or place graphics on top of other graphics. To control the stacking order of objects on a PowerPoint slide, you select the object whose order you want to adjust, click the Draw menu button on the Drawing toolbar, point to Order, and then click one of the four Order commands: Bring to Front, Send to Back, Bring Forward, or Send Backward. See Figure C-11.

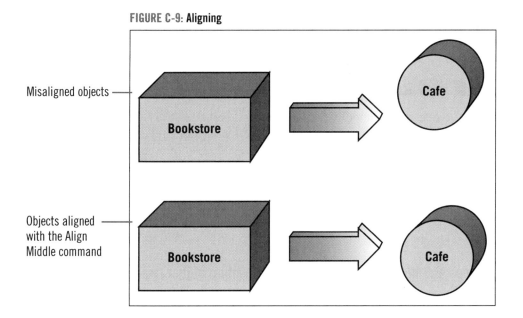

FIGURE C-9: Aligning

Misaligned objects

Objects aligned with the Align Middle command

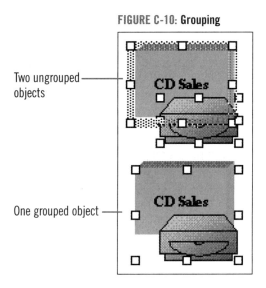

FIGURE C-10: Grouping

Two ungrouped objects

One grouped object

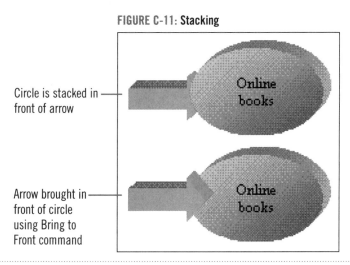

FIGURE C-11: Stacking

Circle is stacked in front of arrow

Arrow brought in front of circle using Bring to Front command

PowerPoint 2000

# Aligning and Grouping Objects

After you create objects, modify their appearance, edit their size and shape, and position them on the slide, you can align and group them. The Align command aligns objects relative to each other by snapping the selected objects to an invisible grid of evenly spaced vertical and horizontal lines. The Group command groups objects into one object to make editing and moving them much easier. Maria aligns, groups, and positions the ribbon objects. Then she copies the grouped ribbon object and pastes it on the next slide.

## Steps

1. Press and hold **[Shift]**, then click **each ribbon object** to select all three objects

2. Click the **Draw menu button** on the Drawing toolbar, then point to **Align or Distribute**
   A menu of alignment and distribution options appears. The top three options align objects horizontally; the next three options align objects vertically.

3. Click **Align Center**
   The ribbon objects align on their centers, as shown in Figure C-12.

4. Click the **Draw menu button**, then click **Group**
   The ribbon objects group to form one object without losing their individual attributes. Notice the sizing handles now appear around the outer edge of the grouped object, not around each individual object.

5. Right-click a blank area of the slide, then click **Guides** on the pop-up menu
   The PowerPoint guides appear as gray dotted lines on the slide. (The dotted lines might be very faint on your screen.) The guides intersect at the center of the slide. They will help you position the ribbon object on the slide.

6. Position ⌖ over the **vertical guide** in a blank area of the slide, press and hold the mouse button until the pointer changes to a guide measurement box, then drag the guide to the right until the guide measurement box reads approximately **1.75**

7. Press **[Shift]**, drag the grouped ribbon object over the vertical guide until the center sizing handles are approximately centered over the vertical guide
   Pressing [Shift] while you drag an object constrains its movement to vertical or horizontal.

**Trouble?**

Click the More Buttons button [?] to locate buttons that are not visible on a toolbar.

8. Right-click the ribbon object, click **Copy** on the pop-up menu, click the **Next Slide button** [▼], then click the **Paste button** [📋] on the Standard toolbar
   Slide 5 appears and the grouped ribbon object from slide 4 is pasted onto slide 5. Notice that the position of the pasted ribbon object on slide 5 is the same as it was on slide 4.

9. Triple-click the **top ribbon object**, type **29%**, triple-click the **middle ribbon object**, type **20%**, triple-click the **bottom ribbon object**, type **25%**, then click in a blank area of the slide
   You do not have to ungroup the objects in order to change the text on them.

10. Click **View** on the menu bar, then click **Guides** to hide the guides
    Compare your screen to Figure C-13.

FIGURE C-12: Aligned ribbon objects

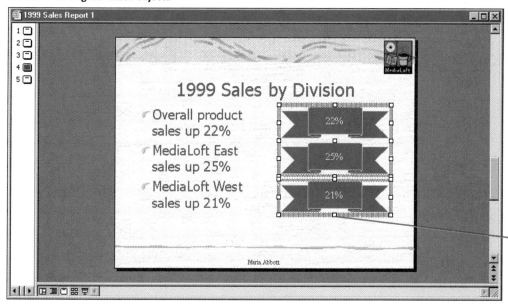

Objects aligned horizontally on their centers

FIGURE C-13: Slide 5 showing pasted ribbon objects

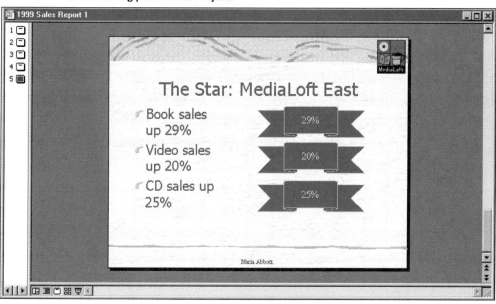

## More ways to change objects

You can change the appearance of an object by rotating or flipping it, or by making it three-dimensional. To rotate or flip an object, select it, click the Draw menu button on the Drawing toolbar, point to Rotate or Flip, then click one of the available menu commands, as shown in Figure C-14. Clicking a Flip command creates a mirror image. Clicking a Rotate command turns an object 90°. To make an object three-dimensional, select it, click the 3-D button, and click one of the options shown on the 3-D menu in Figure C-15. To add a shadow to an object, click the Shadow button on the Drawing toolbar, then click one of the buttons on the pop-up menu.

FIGURE C-14: Rotate or Flip submenu    FIGURE C-15: 3-D menu

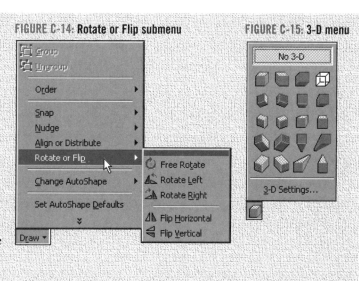

# Adding and Arranging Text

Using the advanced text editing capabilities of PowerPoint, you can easily add, insert, or rearrange text. On a PowerPoint slide, you can enter text in prearranged text placeholders. If these text placeholders don't provide the flexibility you need, you can use the Text Box button on the Drawing toolbar to create your own text objects. With the Text Box button, you can create two types of text objects: a text label, used for a small phrase inside a box where text doesn't automatically wrap to the next line, and a word-processing box, used for a sentence or paragraph where the text wraps inside the boundaries of a box. Maria already added a slide to contain a quote from a recent review. Now, she uses the Text Box button to create a word-processing box on slide 3 in which to enter the quote.

## Steps

1. Click the **slide icon** 🗀 for slide 3 in the Outline pane

2. Click the **Text Box button** 🖾 on the Drawing toolbar

3. Position the pointer about ½" from the left side of the slide and about even with the top of the picture already on the slide, then drag a word-processing box toward the picture so that your screen looks like Figure C-16
   After you click 🖾, the pointer changes to ↓. When you begin dragging, an outline of the box appears, indicating how wide a text object you are drawing. After you release the mouse button, an insertion point appears inside the text object, ready to accept text.

4. Type **Modeled on the café bookstore, MediaLoft takes the concept to new heights!**, press **[Enter]**, then type **Business Day, August 1999**
   Notice that the word-processing box increases in size as your text wraps inside the object. There is a mistake in the quote. It should read "bookstore café" not "café bookstore."

5. Double-click Ⅰ on the word **bookstore** to select it
   When you select a word, the pointer changes from Ⅰ to ⏳.

6. Position the pointer on top of the selected word and press and hold the mouse button
   The pointer changes to ⏳. A dotted insertion line indicates where PowerPoint will place the word when you release the mouse button.

7. Drag the word **bookstore** to the left of the word **café** in the quote, then release the mouse button

8. If necessary, drag the text box to reposition it so that it looks similar to Figure C-

9. Click a blank area of the slide outside the text object, then save your changes
   The text object is deselected. Your screen should look similar to Figure C-17.

### QuickTip
Notice that after you type the word café and press [Spacebar], the PowerPoint AutoCorrect feature automatically inserts an accent over the e in café.

### QuickTip
You also can use the Cut and Paste buttons on the Standard toolbar and the Cut and Paste commands on the Edit menu to move a word.

### QuickTip
To create a text label in which text doesn't wrap, click 🖾, position ↓ where you want to place the text, then click once and enter the text.

## Inserting slides from other presentations

To copy slides, open both presentations in Slide Sorter view, select the desired slides, then paste them into the current presentation. To insert slides, click Insert on the menu bar, then click Slides from Files. Click the Browse button in the Slide Finder dialog box, then locate the presentation from which you want to copy slides. In the Select slides section, select the slide(s) you want to insert, click Insert, then click Close. The new slides automatically take on the design of the current presentation.

FIGURE C-16: Slide showing word-processing box ready to accept text

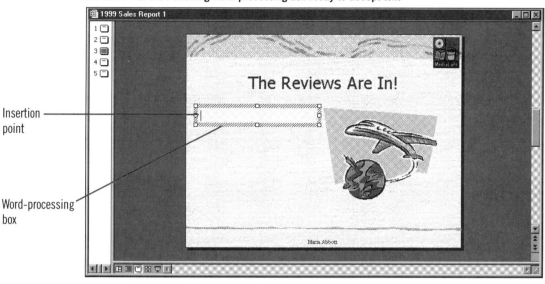

Insertion point

Word-processing box

FIGURE C-17: Slide after adding text to the word-processing box

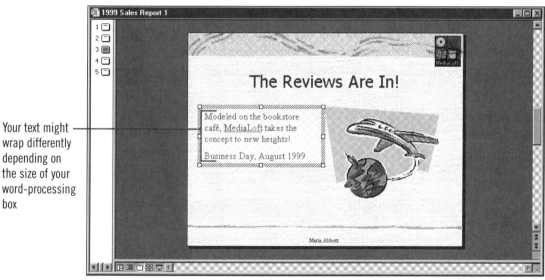

Your text might wrap differently depending on the size of your word-processing box

S TO USE

## Importing text from Microsoft Word

You may want to create a presentation on a subject you wrote about earlier using Microsoft Word 2000. You can easily save time creating a presentation by importing the Word outline. You can import an outline to create a new presentation, or you can import an outline into an existing presentation. To create a new presentation from a Word outline, click the Open button 📄 on the Standard toolbar. Then in the Files of type list box, click All outlines, and double-click the name of the file you want to import. (You may receive a message asking you to insert the Office CD so the program can install

a converter.) To insert an outline into an existing presentation, click the slide after which you want to insert the new information in the Outline pane or Outline view. Click Insert on the menu bar, then click Slides from Outline. Make sure the Files of type text box displays All Files, click the name of the file you want to import, then click Insert. When you import a Word outline, PowerPoint automatically creates slides containing the items from your outline, using the Outline level 1 heads as slide titles, and the lower level items as body text on the slides.

# Formatting Text

Once you have entered and arranged the text in your presentation, you can change and modify the way the text looks to emphasize your message. Important text needs to be highlighted in some way to distinguish it from other text or objects on the slide. Less important information needs to be deemphasized. For example, if you have two text objects on the same slide, you could draw attention to one text object by changing its color or size. To change the way text looks, you need to select it, and then choose a Formatting command. ◢◢◣◣ Maria uses some of the commands on the Formatting and Drawing toolbars to change the way the review quote looks.

## Steps

**1.** On slide 3, press **[Shift]**, then click the **text box**

If a text box is already active because you have been entering text in it, you can select the entire text box by clicking on its edge with ⬚⬚. The entire text box is selected. Any changes you make will affect all the text in the selected text box. Changing the text's size and appearance will help emphasize it.

**Trouble?**

Click the More Buttons button ⬚ to locate buttons that are not visible on your toolbar.

**2.** Click the **Increase Font Size button** 🅰 on the Formatting toolbar twice

Note that after you click 🅰 once, it moves to the Formatting toolbar. The text increases in size to 32 points.

**3.** Click the **Italic button** 🔲 on the Formatting toolbar

The text changes from normal to italic text. The Italic button, like the Bold button, is a toggle button, which you click to turn the attribute on or off.

**4.** Click the **Font Color list arrow** 🔲 on the Drawing toolbar

The Font Color menu appears, showing the eight colors used in the current presentation and More Font Colors, which lets you choose additional colors.

**5.** Click **More Font Colors**, then in the Colors dialog box, click the **Standard tab**

**6.** In the color hexagon, click the **blue color cell** in the third row from the top, fourth from right, then click **OK**

The Current color and the New color appear in the box in the lower-right corner of the dialog box. The text in the word-processing box changes to the blue color.

**7.** Click the **Font list arrow** on the Formatting toolbar

A list of available fonts opens, as shown in Figure C-18. A double line at the top of the font list may separate the fonts most recently used from the complete list of available fonts.

**8.** Click the scroll arrows if necessary, then click **Arial**

The Arial font replaces the original font in the text object.

**QuickTip**

To automatically wrap text in an AutoShape, drag a text box in the desired width, type your text, then group the two objects.

**9.** Drag the pointer over the text **Business Day, August 1999**, click the **Font Size arrow** on the Formatting toolbar, click **18,** then click the **Align right button** 🔲 the Formatting toolbar

The pointer changes to ⌶ when you drag it over text. The source text is now smaller and right-aligned. Only the selected text is affected by the formatting command, not the entire text object.

**10.** Drag the text box to center it vertically, click a blank area of the slide outside text object to deselect it, then click the **Save button** 🔲 on the Standard toolbar

Compare your screen to Figure C-19.

FIGURE C-18: Font list open

Your list of fonts might be different

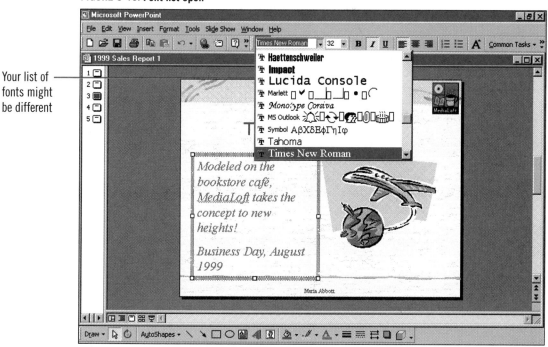

FIGURE C-19: Slide showing formatted text box

Arial, 32-point italic type

Arial, 18-point, right-aligned italic type

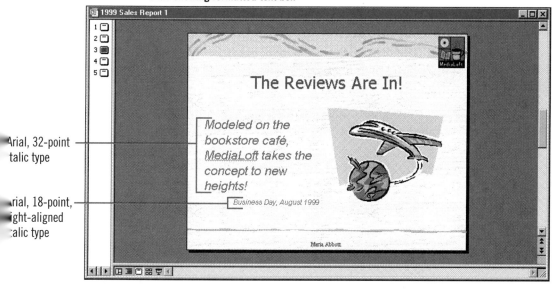

TO USE

## Replacing Text and Attributes

As you review your presentation, you may decide to replace certain words or fonts throughout the entire presentation. You can automatically modify words, sentences, fonts, text case, and periods. To replace specific words or sentences, use the Replace command on the Edit menu. To change a font, use the Replace Fonts command on the Format menu. To automatically add or remove periods from title or body text and to automatically change the case of title or body text, click Options on the Tools menu, click the Spelling and Style tab, then click Style Options to open the Style Options dialog box. Click the Case and End Punctuation tab. The options on the Visual Clarity tab in the Style Options dialog box control the legibility of bulleted text items on the slides.

PowerPoint 2000

# Customizing the Color Scheme and Background

Every PowerPoint presentation has a set of eight coordinated colors, called a **color scheme**, that determines the main colors for the slide elements in your presentation: slide background, text and lines, title text, shadows, fills, and accents. See Table C-1 for a description of the slide color scheme elements. The **background** is the area behind the text and graphics. Every design template has a default color scheme that you can use, or you can create your own. You can also change the background color and appearance independent of changing the color scheme. ▰▰▰▰ Maria decides she doesn't like the color scheme or the white background, so she decides to change it.

## Steps

1. Click **Format** on the menu bar, then click **Slide Color Scheme**

   The Color Scheme dialog box opens with the Standard tab active. See Figure C-20. The number of preset color schemes available depends on the elements in the current presentation. The current color scheme is selected with a black border.

**QuickTip**

To apply a new color scheme to only selected slides, switch to Slide Sorter view, select the slides you want to change, then click Apply instead of Apply to All in the dialog box.

2. Click the second color scheme in the top row, then click **Apply to All**

   The dialog box closes, and the new color scheme is applied to all the slides in the presentation. In this case, the new color scheme changes the color of the slide graphics, but the text and background remain the same.

3. Click **Format** on the menu bar, then click **Background**

   The Background dialog box opens.

4. In the Background fill section, click the **list arrow** below the preview of the slide click **Fill Effects**, then click the **Gradient tab**, as shown in Figure C-21

5. In the Colors section, click the **Two colors option button**, click the **Color 2 list arrow**, click **More Colors** on the drop-down menu, click the **Standard tab**, click the **orange color cell** in the fifth row from the bottom, the sixth color from the right, then click **OK**

**QuickTip**

Note that if you click the Preset option button, you can choose from a variety of predesigned backgrounds. To add a textured background to a slide, click the Texture tab, select any texture, read its name below the texture icons, click OK, then click Apply or Apply to All.

   The horizontal shading style is selected, as is the first of the four variants, showing that the background is shaded from color 1 (white) on the top to color 2 (orange) on the bottom.

6. In the Shading Styles section, click the **Diagonal up option button**, click the **upper-left variant**, click **OK**, then click **Apply to All**

   The background is now shaded from white (upper-left) to orange (lower-right). The ribbons on slides 4 and 5 would look better in plum.

7. Click the **slide icon** ▭ for slide 4, click **Format** on the menu bar, click **Slide Color Scheme**, then click the **Custom tab**

   The eight colors for the selected color scheme appear.

8. In the Scheme colors section, click the **Accent and hyperlink color box**, then click **Change Color**

   The Accent and Hyperlink Color dialog box opens.

9. Click the **Standard tab**, click the **plum color cell** in the fifth row from the bottom, the far right, as shown in Figure C-22

   The Current color and the New color appear in the box in the lower-right of the dialog

10. Click **OK**, click **Add As Standard Scheme**, then click **Apply to All**

    PowerPoint updates the color scheme on all your slides, and the ribbons change to plum. The next time you open the Color Scheme dialog box in this presentation, your new scheme will appear, along with the existing schemes.

FIGURE C-20: **Color Scheme dialog box**

Current color
scheme has
black border

Choose this
color scheme

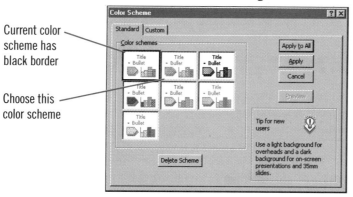

FIGURE C-21: **Gradient tab of Fill Effects dialog box**

Step 5

Shading styles
section

Shading variants
of selected
shading style

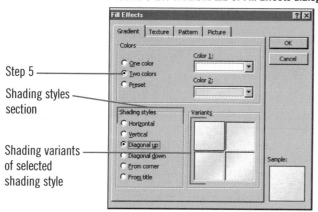

FIGURE C-22: **Standard tab in the Accent and Hyperlink Color dialog box**

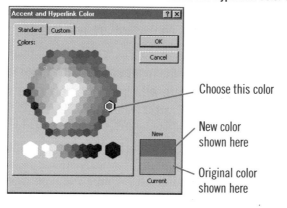

Choose this color

New color
shown here

Original color
shown here

‹LE C-1: **Color scheme elements**

| ‹eme element | description |
|---|---|
| ‹kground color | Color of the slide's canvas, or background |
| ‹t and lines color | Used for text and drawn lines; contrasts with the background color |
| ‹dows color | Color of the shadow of the text or other object; generally a darker shade of the background color |
| ‹e text color | Used for slide title; like the text and line colors, contrasts with the background color |
| ‹ color | Contrasts with both the background and the text and line colors |
| ‹nt color | Colors used for other objects on slides, such as bullets |
| ‹nt and hyperlink colors | Colors used for accent objects and for hyperlinks you insert |
| ‹nt and followed hyperlink color | Color used for accent objects and for hyperlinks after they have been clicked |

# Correcting Text Automatically

As you enter text into your presentation, the AutoCorrect feature in PowerPoint automatically replaces misspelled words and corrects some capitalization mistakes, whether on slides or in speaker notes, without bringing up a dialog box or a menu. For example, if you type "THursday" instead of "Thursday," PowerPoint corrects it as soon as you type it. If there is a word you often type incorrectly, for example, if you type "tehm" instead of "them," you can create an AutoCorrect entry that corrects that misspelled word whenever you type it in a presentation. After reviewing the presentation, Maria uses the AutoCorrect feature as she adds one more slide, thanking the employees for their support.

1. Click the **slide icon** ▭ for slide 5 in the Outline pane, hold down **[Shift]**, then click the **New Slide button** 🖼 on the Standard toolbar
   A new slide 6 with the bulleted list AutoLayout appears.

2. Click **Tools** on the menu bar, then click **AutoCorrect**
   The AutoCorrect dialog box opens, as shown in Figure C-23. The top part of the dialog box contains check boxes that have PowerPoint automatically change two capital letters at the beginning of a word to a single capital letter, capitalize the first letter of a sentence and the names of days, and correct capitalization errors caused by accidental use of the Caps Lock key. The fifth check box, Replace text as you type, tells PowerPoint to change any of the mistyped words listed on the left in the scroll box in the lower part of the dialog box with the correct word listed on the right. The scroll box contains customized entries. For example, if you type (c), PowerPoint will automatically change it to ©, the copyright symbol. See Table C-2 for a summary of AutoCorrect options.

3. Click any check boxes that are not selected

4. In the Replace text as you type section, click the **down scroll arrow** to view all the current text replacement entries, noticing that there is already an entry to automatically replace cafe with café, then click **OK**
   To test the AutoCorrect feature, you decide to enter incorrect text on the sixth slide. As you type text in the following step, watch what happens to that word when you press [Spacebar].

5. Click the **title placeholder**, then type **THank You**
   As soon as you pressed [Spacebar] after typing the word "THank," PowerPoint automatically corrected it to read "Thank." You'll make another intentional error in the next step.

6. Click the **main text placeholder**, type **Sales reps adn managers**, then press **[Enter]**
   As soon as you pressed [Spacebar] after typing the word "adn," PowerPoint automatically corrected it to read "and."

7. Type **CDVision(tm) advisors**, then click outside the main text object
   As soon as you typed the closing parenthesis, PowerPoint automatically changed the (tm) to the trademark symbol ™.

8. Click the **Slide Sorter View button** 🔡, then compare your screen to Figure C-24

9. Click **View** on the menu bar, click **Header and Footer**, click the **Notes and Handouts tab**, click in the **Footer text box**, type your name, then click **Apply to All**
   Now your name appears in the slide footer when you print the presentation, making it easier to find your printout if you are sharing the printer.

10. Save your presentation, print the slides as handouts, six slides to a page, then PowerPoint

FIGURE C-23: AutoCorrect dialog box

Automatic correction options

Type your own custom AutoCorrect entries here

Default AutoCorrect entries

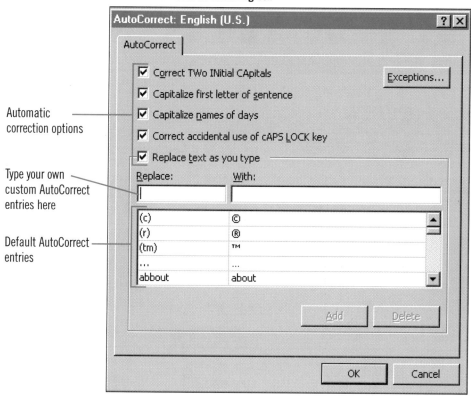

FIGURE C-24: The final presentation

w slide with
rected text

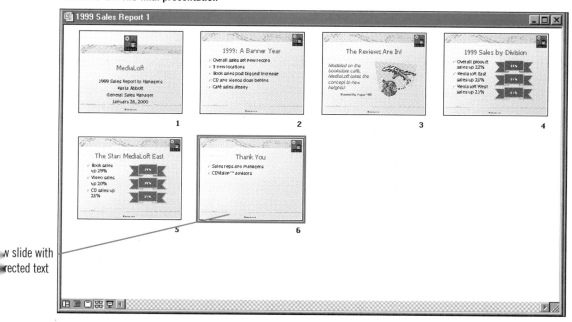

**LE C-2: AutoCorrect options**

| ion | action |
|---|---|
| n off AutoCorrect | Click to remove all the check marks in the AutoCorrect dialog box |
| t an AutoCorrect entry | Select the entry in the list, click in the With text box, correct the entry, and click Replace |
| te an AutoCorrect entry | Highlight the entry in the scroll box and click Delete |
| ame an AutoCorrect entry | Select the entry in the list, click in the Replace text box, click Delete, type a new name in the Replace box, and click Add |

# Practice

## ► Concepts Review

Label the elements of the PowerPoint window shown in Figure C-25.

FIGURE C-25

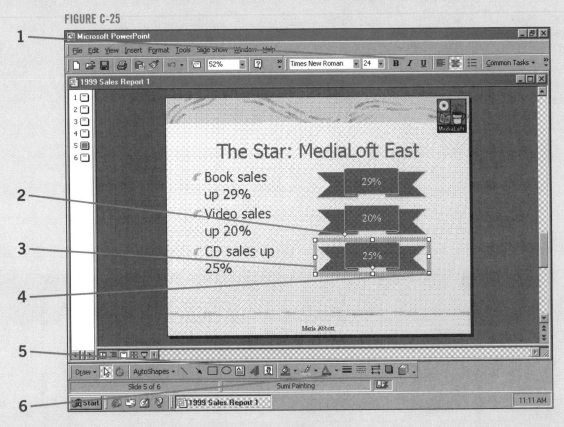

Match each term or button with the statement that describes it.

7. Word-processing box
8. Text label
9. [image]
10. [image]
11. Sizing handles

a. Button that changes the text color
b. Creates a text object on a slide
c. Small boxes that surround an object when it is selected
d. A text object that does not word wrap
e. A text object made by dragging to create a box after clicking the Text Box button

Select the best answer from the list of choices.

12. How do you change the size of a PowerPoint object?
  a. Drag a sizing handle
  b. Click the Resize button
  c. Drag the adjustment handle
  d. You can't change the size of a PowerPoint object
13. What would you use to position objects at a specific place on a slide?
  a. PowerPoint placeholders
  b. PowerPoint guides and rulers
  c. PowerPoint grid lines
  d. PowerPoint anchor lines

# ► Skills Review

**Open an existing presentation.**

**a.** Open the file PPT C-2 from your Project Disk.

**b.** Save it as "Cafe Report."

**Draw and modify an object.**

**a.** On slide 3, add the AutoShape Lightning Bolt from the Basic Shapes category on the AutoShapes menu. Make it as large as possible from the upper-left corner of the slide. It should partially cover the text.

**b.** On the Line Color pop-up menu, click No Line.

**c.** Change the fill color to the dark pink color named Follow Accent and Hyperlink Scheme Color.

**d.** Click the Shadow button on the Drawing toolbar, then click the Shadow Style 2 button.

**e.** Use the appropriate Flip command from the Draw menu on the Drawing toolbar to change the direction of the bolt so it points from the upper-right to the lower-left.

**f.** Send the object to the back, then deselect the object and save the document.

**Edit drawing objects.**

**a.** On slide 6, resize the arrow object so it is about ½" shorter.

**b.** Make two copies of the arrow and arrange them to the right of the first one so that they are pointing in succession to the purple box.

**c.** Insert the text "Products" on the left arrow object, "Satisfaction" on the middle arrow, and on the right arrow, insert "Growth." Enlarge the arrows so that all the text fits and then reposition them as necessary.

**Align and group objects.**

**a.** On slide 6, place a text box on the cube, enter "Success" in it, center the text box on the cube, then group the text box and the cube.

**b.** Select the four graphics on slide 6 and align their middles.

**c.** Change the objects' text font to Arial italic. Enlarge the cube as necessary so the word "Success" fits in it.

**d.** Select only the three arrow objects, click the Draw menu button on the Drawing toolbar, then point to Align or Distribute, and click Distribute Horizontally.

**e.** Group the three arrow objects and the cube.

**f.** Display the guides, then move the vertical guide left to about 4.17, and the horizontal guide down to about 2.50.

**g.** Align the grouped object so its bottom-left resize handle snaps to where the guides intersect. If your object does not snap to the guides, click the Draw menu button, point to Snap, and make sure the To Grid command on the Snap menu is selected (it should look indented).

**h.** Right-click in an empty area of the slide, then hide the guides.

**Add and arrange text.**

**a.** Add a fourth item to slide 2 that reads "Next steps."

**b.** Near the bottom of the slide, below the graphic, create a word-processing box about 3" wide, and in it enter the text "A relaxing café is a reading haven."

**c.** Drag the word "relaxing" in front of the word "reading."

**d.** Open the presentation PPT C-3 in Slide Sorter view and copy slide 3 ("The Reviews Are In!") to the Clipboard, then close the PPT C-3 presentation. In the Cafe Report presentation, switch to Slide Sorter view, then paste the copied slide after slide 5.

**e.** Use the Slides from Files command on the Insert menu to insert slide 2 ("1999: A Banner Year") from the PPT C-3 presentation after slide 6 ("The Reviews Are In!") in the Cafe Report presentation.

**f.** Switch to Outline view, import the Word file PPT C-4 to the end of the presentation. Check each slide's formatting. (*Hint:* If the program tells you that you need to install this feature, insert your Office 2000 CD and click OK.).

### 6. Format text.

**a.** Go to slide 2 in Slide view and select the entire word-processing box so that formatting commands will ap to all the text in the box.

**b.** Change the font color to the purple color in the current color scheme, then increase its size once.

**c.** Select the entire main text object.

**d.** Click the Bullets button on the Formatting toolbar to add bullets to the list.

**e.** Go to slide 8, drag to select all the text on the cube, then change the text color to light blue.

**f.** Go to slide 2, select the entire main text object, then click the Center alignment button.

**g.** Use the Replace command on the Edit menu to replace all occurrences of "sellers" with "performers." Ma sure you capitalize the second occurrence.

**h.** On slide 2, replace the font of the main text object and the word-processing box with Arial.

**i.** Use the Replace Fonts command on the Format menu to change all instances of the Times New Roman fo in the presentation to Arial.

**j.** Go to slide 1 and change the title text font to Arial Black, 48 points.

**k.** Deselect the text object, then save your changes.

### 7. Customize the color scheme and background.

**a.** Open the Color Scheme dialog box.

**b.** Click the upper-left color scheme then apply it to all the slides.

**c.** Open the Background dialog box, then the Fill Effects dialog box.

**d.** On the Gradient tab, select a two-color gradient, picking the light brown that represents Follow Accent an Followed Hyperlink Scheme color as the first color, and the off-white that represents the Follow Backgroun Scheme color as the second color. Select the Diagonal up option and the first variant. Apply this backgrou to all slides.

**e.** Open the Color Scheme dialog box.

**f.** On the Custom tab, change the color of the Title text on all slides to a brighter shade of purple.

**g.** Add the new scheme as a Standard Scheme, and check that it is available on the Standard tab.

**h.** Add the Canvas texture to the background of slide 1.

### 8. Correct text automatically.

**a.** Go to slide 5 and turn on Caps Lock.

**b.** After the third bullet, add a fourth bullet that reads "Herbal teas." Notice how PowerPoint reverses the ca talization as soon as you press [Spacebar].

**c.** For the next bullet, enter the text "Give additional suggestions by thursday." and press [Spacebar]. Notice that PowerPoint automatically capitalizes the word "Thursday" for you.

**d.** Check the spelling in the presentation and make any necessary changes.

**e.** Go to slide 1, view the final slide show, and evaluate your presentation.

**f.** Add your name to the footer of all notes and handouts.

**g.** Save your changes, print the slides as handouts, six slides per page, and then close the presentation an exit PowerPoint.

## ► Independent Challenges

**1.** In this unit, you learned that when you work with multiple objects on a PowerPoint slide, there are three to arrange them so your information appears neat and well organized. Write a one-page summary explaining ho perform each of these tasks in PowerPoint:

**a.** Lining up objects so that their tops, bottoms, sides or middles are in a straight line.

**b.** Combining multiple objects into one object, and why you would want to do this.

**c.** Adjusting objects so that one is in front of or in back of another.

**2.** You work for Chicago Language Systems (CLS), a major producer of language teaching CD-ROMs with accompanying instructional books. Twice a year, the company holds title meetings to determine the new title list for the following production term and to decide which current CD titles need to be revised. As the director of acquisitions, you chair the September Title Meeting and present the basic material for discussion.

To complete this independent challenge:

**a.** Open the file PPT C-5 on your Project Disk and save it as "Title Meeting 9-26-00".

**b.** Add an appropriate design template to the presentation.

**c.** Insert the Word Outline PPT C-6 from your Project Disk after slide 6. Examine each of the three new slides and apply Italic formatting to all product and Book titles.

**d.** Format the text so that the most important information is the most prominent.

**e.** Add appropriate shapes that amplify the most important parts of the slide content. Format the objects using color and shading. Use the Align, Group, and stacking commands to organize your shapes.

**f.** Evaluate the color scheme and the background colors. Make any changes you feel will enhance the presentation.

**g.** Spell check, view the final slide show, and evaluate your presentation. Make any necessary changes.

**h.** Add your name as footer text on the handouts, save the presentation and print the slides as handouts.

**3.** The Software Learning Company is dedicated to the design and development of instructional software that helps college students learn software applications. You need to design five new logos for the company that incorporate the new company slogan: "Software is a snap!" The marketing group will decide which of the five designs looks best. Create your own presentation slides, but assume that the company colors are blue and green.

To complete this independent challenge:

**a.** Sketch your logos and slogan designs on a piece of paper. What text and graphics do you need for the slides?

**b.** Create a new blank presentation, and save it as "Software Learning" to your Project Disk.

**c.** Create five different company logos, each one on a separate slide. Use the shapes on the AutoShapes menu, and enter the company slogan, using the Text tool. (*Hint*: Use the Title only AutoLayout.) The logo and the marketing slogan should match each other in tone, size, and color; and the logo objects should be grouped together to make it easier for other employees to copy and paste. Use shadings and shadows appropriately.

**d.** Add a background color if it is appropriate for your logo design.

**e.** Spell check, view the final slide show, and evaluate your presentation. Make any necessary changes.

**f.** Add your name as footer text, save the presentation, and print the slides and notes pages (if any).

**4.** MediaLoft management is planning to offer 401(k) retirement plans to its employees. The Human Resources Department has asked you to construct a presentation containing general information about 401(k) plans for all MediaLoft employees.

To complete this independent challenge:

**a.** Connect to the Internet, use your browser to go to http://www.course.com/illustrated/medialoft, and click the Human Resources link. Click the Employee Benefits: 401(k) Plans link, and read the information listed there.

**b.** Use the information you learn from the MediaLoft site to construct a presentation about 401(k) plans that MediaLoft's employees will find useful and interesting. On the title slide, title the presentation "401(k) Plans: What Employees Need to Know". The presentation should contain at least five slides, including the title slide. It should explain what 401(k) plans are, why someone should have one, and what their advantages are. Disconnect from the Internet when you are done.

**c.** Save the presentation as "401(k) Plans" to your Project Disk.

**d.** Apply a template to the presentation, customize the slide background, create a new color scheme, and save the color scheme as a standard scheme.

**e.** Use text formatting as necessary to make text visible and help emphasize important points. At least one slide should contain two or more drawing objects with text in them. Customize their size and color.

**f.** Add your name as a footer to the slides and handouts, spell check the presentation, view the final presentation, save the final version, then print the slides and handouts.

# ► Visual Workshop

Create a one-slide presentation that looks like the one shown in Figures C-26. Use a text box for each bullet. Add your name as a footer on the slide. Group the objects in each logo. Save the presentation as "Bowman Logos" to your Project Disk, then print the slide in Slide view. (*Hint:* The top design uses the 3-D menu.) If you don't have the exact fonts, use something similar.

FIGURE C-26

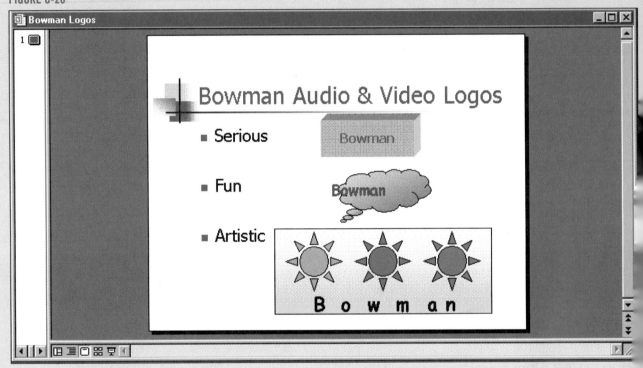

**Unit D**

# Enhancing
## a Presentation

### Objectives

- [MOUS] ► **Insert clip art**
- [MOUS] ► **Insert, crop, and scale a picture**
- [MOUS] ► **Embed a chart**
- [MOUS] ► **Enter and edit data in the datasheet**
- [MOUS] ► **Format a chart**
- [MOUS] ► **Use slide show commands**
- [MOUS] ► **Create tables in PowerPoint**
- [MOUS] ► **Set slide show timings and transitions**
- [MOUS] ► **Set slide animation effects**

After completing the content of your presentation, you can supplement your slide text with clip art or graphics, charts, and other visuals that help communicate your content and keep your slide show visually interesting. In this unit, you learn how to insert three of the most common visual enhancements: a clip art image, a picture, and a chart. These objects are created in other programs. After you add the visuals, you rehearse the slide show and add special effects. ►►►► Maria Abbot has changed her presentation based on feedback from her colleagues. Now she wants to revise the sales presentation to make it easier to understand and more interesting to watch.

# Inserting Clip Art

PowerPoint has more than 1000 professionally designed images, called **clip art**, that you can place in your presentation. Using clip art is the easiest and fastest way to enhance your presentations. In Microsoft Office, clip art is stored in a file index system called a **gallery** that sorts the clip art into categories. You can open the Clip Gallery in one of three ways: double-click a clip art placeholder from an AutoLayout; use the Insert Clip Art button 🖼 on the Drawing toolbar; or choose Picture, then Clip Art on the Insert menu. As with drawing objects, you can modify clip art images by changing their shape, size, fill, or shading. Clip art is the most widely used method of enhancing presentations, and it is available from many sources outside the Clip Gallery, including the World Wide Web (WWW) and collections on CD-ROMs. ✍ Maria wants to add a picture from the Clip Gallery to one of the slides and then adjust its size and placement.

## Steps 1 2 3 4

1. Start PowerPoint, open the presentation **PPT D-1** from your Project Disk, save it as **1999 Sales Presentation 2**, click **Window** on the menu bar, click **Arrange All**, then click the **slide icon** 🖵 for slide 2 in the outline pane
   The 1999: A Banner Year slide appears.

2. Click **Tools** on the menu bar, click **Customize**, click the **Options tab** in the Customize dialog box, click **Reset my usage data** to restore the default settings, click **Yes** in the alert box or dialog balloon, then click **Close**

**Trouble?**

Click the More Buttons button 🔽 to locate buttons that are not visible on your toolbar.

3. Click the **Common Tasks menu button** on the Formatting toolbar, then click **Slide Layout**
   The Slide Layout dialog box opens with the Bulleted List AutoLayout selected.

4. Click the **Text & Clip Art AutoLayout** (third row, first column), then click **Apply**
   PowerPoint applies the Text and Clip Art AutoLayout to the slide, which makes the existing text object narrower, automatically reduces its font size from 32 points to 28 points, and inserts a clip art placeholder, where you will place the clip art object.

**QuickTip**

If you open the Clip Gallery via the icon in the Drawing toolbar or the Picture command on the Insert menu, you will see three tabs: Pictures, Sounds, and Motion Clips.

5. Double-click the **clip art placeholder**
   The Microsoft Clip Gallery dialog box opens with the Pictures tab visible, similar to Figure D-1.

6. Scroll down to and click the **Flags category**
   If the Flags category doesn't appear, select a different category.

7. Position the mouse pointer over the **Mountains graphic** whose ScreenTip says "mountains", click the **graphic**, then on the pop-up menu, click the **Insert Clip icon** 🖾 (the top icon)
   The picture of the mountain with a flag on it appears on the right side of the slide. In addition the Picture toolbar might open automatically. If you don't have the Mountains picture in your Clip Gallery, select a similar picture. If you use the Insert Clip Art button 🖼 on the Drawing toolbar or the Picture command on the Insert menu to insert a clip art image, the Clip Gallery stays open, which is useful in situations where you want to insert more than one picture at a time.

8. Place the pointer over the lower-right sizing handle and drag the handle up and to the left about ½"

**QuickTip**

You can also use the keyboard arrow keys to reposition any selected object by small increments.

9. With the clip art object still selected, hold down **[Shift]**, click the **bulleted list**, click the **Draw menu button** on the Drawing toolbar, point to **Align or Distribute**, click **Align Middle**, then click in a blank area to deselect the objects
   The text object and the clip art object align vertically. Compare your screen to Figure D-2 and make any necessary corrections.

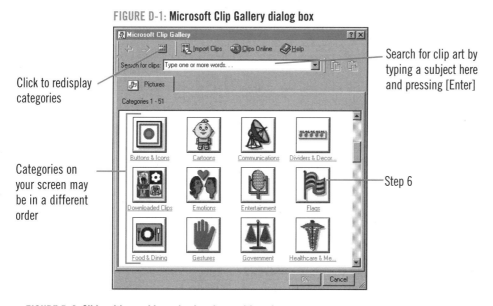

FIGURE D-1: Microsoft Clip Gallery dialog box

Click to redisplay categories

Search for clip art by typing a subject here and pressing [Enter]

Categories on your screen may be in a different order

Step 6

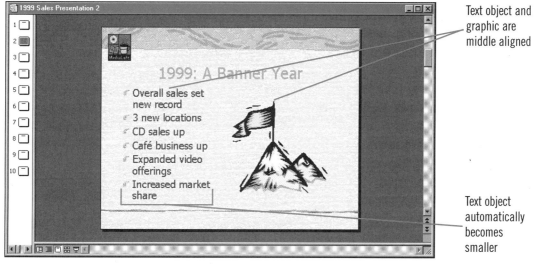

FIGURE D-2: Slide with graphic resized and repositioned

Text object and graphic are middle aligned

Text object automatically becomes smaller

## Find more clips online

you can't find the clips you need in the Clip allery, you can easily use clips from the Clip allery Live Web site. To get clips from the icrosoft Clip Gallery Live Web site, click Clips nline in the Insert ClipArt dialog box, then click K. This will launch your Web browser and auto- atically connect you to the site. Read carefully d accept the License Agreement, which specifies w you are permitted to use clips from this site. e Clip Gallery Live window opens. You can pre- ew and download (import) clips from four tabs: ip Art, Pictures (photographs), Sounds, and otion (animated graphics). You can search the e by keyword or browse by category. Each clip u download is automatically inserted into the ip Gallery. Figure D-3 shows some of the clip t in the Transportation category.

FIGURE D-3: Microsoft Clip Gallery Live Web site

# Inserting, Cropping, and Scaling a Picture

A picture in PowerPoint is a scanned photograph, a piece of line art, clip art, or other artwork that is created in another program and inserted into a PowerPoint presentation. You can insert 20 types of pictures using the Insert Picture command. As with other PowerPoint objects, you can move or crop an inserted picture. Cropping a picture means to hide a portion of the picture if you don't want to include all of the original. Although you can easily change a picture's size by dragging a corner resize handle, you can also scale it to change its size by a specific percentage. ▰▰▰ Maria inserts a picture that has previously been saved to a file, crops and scales it, and then adjusts its background.

## Steps

**QuickTip**

If you want to go to a particular slide but aren't sure what the number is, drag the vertical scroll box in the Slide pane to see both the slide number and the slide title.

1. Go to **slide 6**, titled "Reasons for Our Growth," click the **Common Tasks menu button** on the Formatting toolbar, click **Slide Layout**, click the **Text & Object AutoLayout** (fourth row, first column), then click **Apply**

2. Double-click the **object placeholder**
   The Insert Object dialog box opens.

3. Click the **Create from file option button** to select it
   The dialog box changes to include a text box that will contain the filename of the object you will insert.

4. Click **Browse**, click the **Look in list arrow**, click the drive containing your Project Disk click **PPT D-2** in the Look in list, click **OK**, then click **OK** in the Insert Object dialog box
   The picture appears on the slide, and the Picture toolbar automatically opens. See Figure D-4 The slide would have more impact without the sun image.

**Trouble?**

If the Picture toolbar does not appear, right-click the picture, then click Show Picture Toolbar on the pop-up menu.

5. Click the **Crop button** ⊞ on the Picture toolbar, then place the cursor over the top middle sizing handle of the tree picture
   The pointer changes to ⊹.

6. Drag the top edge downward until the dotted line indicating the top edge of the picture is below the sun image, as shown in Figure D-5
   As you drag with the cropping tool, the pointer changes to ⌐. But now the picture need to be larger to fill the space.

7. Click a blank area of the slide to deselect the cropping tool and leave the picture selected

**QuickTip**

You can change the colors of a bitmapped graphic by double-clicking it, which will open Microsoft Paint. Use the Fill Color tool in Paint to recolor portions of the graphic.

8. Click the **Format Picture button** 🖼 on the Picture toolbar, click the **Size tab**, und Scale, make sure the **Lock aspect ratio check box** is selected, click and hold t **Height up arrow** until the Height and Width percentages reach **275%**, then click
   When you are scaling a picture and Lock aspect ratio is checked, the ratio of height to wid remains the same. Although you cannot change the colors in this bitmapped (.bmp) obj in PowerPoint, you can change its background.

9. With the image still selected, click the **Set Transparent Color button** 🖼 on the Pict toolbar, then click the **white background** in the image with the pointer 🖊
   The white background is no longer visible, and the tree contrasts well with the backgrou

10. Drag the graphic to center it in the blank space, deselect it, then save your chan
    See Figure D-6.

**FIGURE D-4:** Inserted picture object and Picture toolbar

Picture toolbar may appear in a different position on your screen

Inserted picture object

Crop button

Set Transparent Color button

**FIGURE D-5:** Using the cropping pointer to crop out the sun image

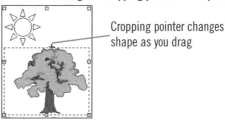

Cropping pointer changes shape as you drag

**FIGURE D-6:** Completed slide with the cropped and resized graphic

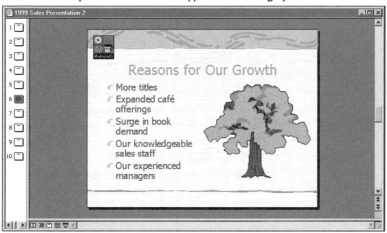

## Graphics in PowerPoint

You can insert pictures with a variety of graphics file formats, or file types, in PowerPoint. Most of the clip art that comes with PowerPoint is in **Windows metafile** format and has a **.wmf** file extension. A graphic in .wmf format can be ungrouped into its separate PowerPoint objects and then edited with PowerPoint drawing tools. You can recolor a .wmf graphic by selecting it and clicking the Recolor picture icon on the Picture toolbar, which lets you replace each color in the graphic with another color. You can also recolor any portion of an ungrouped .wmf graphic by selecting it and using the Fill Color drawing tool. If you ungroup a .wmf graphic and find that it has too

many parts, you can regroup them using the Group command on the Draw menu. The clip art you inserted in the last lesson is in .wmf format, and the tree picture you inserted in this lesson is in .bmp format.

You can also save PowerPoint slides as graphics and then use them in other presentations, in graphics programs, and on Web pages. Display the slide you want to save, then click Save As from the File menu. In the Save As dialog box, click the Save as type list arrow, and scroll to the desired graphics format. Name the file, click OK, then click the desired option when the alert box appears asking if you want to save all the slides or only the current slide.

**PowerPoint 2000**

# Embedding a Chart

Often, the best way to communicate information is with a visual aid such as a chart. PowerPoint comes with a program called **Microsoft Graph** (often called **Graph**) that you use to create graph charts for your slides. A **graph object** is made up of two components: a **datasheet**, containing the numbers you want to chart, and a **chart**, which is the graphical representation of the datasheet. Table D-1 lists the Graph chart types. When you insert a Graph object into PowerPoint, you are actually embedding it. **Embedding** an object means that the object copy becomes part of the PowerPoint file, but you can double-click on the embedded object to display the tools of the program in which the object was created. You can use these tools to modify the object. If you modify the embedded object, the original object file does not change. ✍ Maria wants to embed a Graph object in the slide containing the 1999 revenue by quarter.

## Steps 1 2 3 4

**1.** Go to **slide 5**, titled "1999 Revenue by Quarter," click the **Common Tasks menu button** on the Formatting toolbar, then click **Slide Layout**
The Slide Layout dialog box opens with the Title only Layout selected.

**2.** Click the **Chart AutoLayout** (second row, far right), then click **Apply**
The Chart AutoLayout, which contains a chart placeholder, appears on the slide.

**3.** Double-click the **chart placeholder**
Microsoft Graph opens and embeds a default datasheet and chart into the slide, as shown in Figure D-7. The Graph datasheet consists of rows and columns. The intersection of a row and a column is called a **cell**. Cells are referred to by their row and column location; for example, the cell at the intersection of column A and row 1 is called cell A1. Cells along the left column and top row of the datasheet typically contain **data labels** that identify the data in a column or row; for example, "East" and "1st Qtr" are data labels. Cells below and to the right of the data labels contain the data values that are represented in the Graph chart. Each column and row of data in the datasheet is called a **data series**. Each data series has corresponding **data series markers** in the chart, which are graphical representations such as bars, columns, or pie wedges. The PowerPoint Standard and Formatting toolbars have been replaced with the Microsoft Graph Standard and Formatting toolbars, and the menu bar has changed to include Microsoft Graph commands.

**4.** Move the pointer over the datasheet
The pointer changes to ✛. Cell A1 is the **active cell**, which means that it is selected. The active cell has a heavy black border around it.

**5.** Click cell **B3**, which currently has the value 46.9 in it
Cell B3 is now the active cell.

**6.** Click a blank area of the Presentation window to exit Graph and deselect the chart object
Compare your slide to Figure D-8.

FIGURE D-7: **Datasheet and chart in the PowerPoint window**

Graph menu bar

Graph Formatting
toolbar

Data labels

Chart

Active cell

Datasheet containing
default data

Data marker
corresponds to
data series

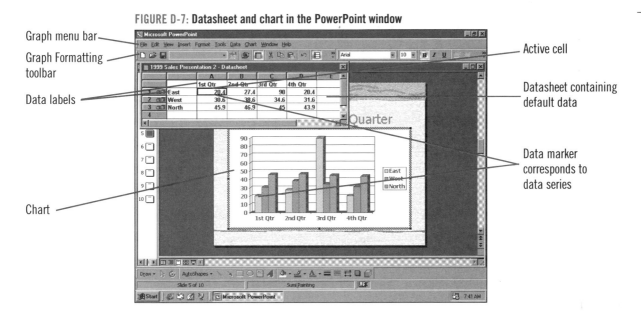

FIGURE D-8: **Chart object on a slide**

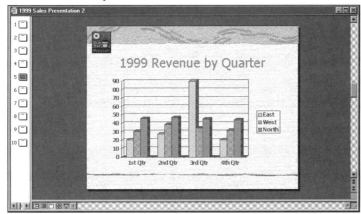

TABLE D-1: **Microsoft Graph chart types**

| chart type | looks like | use to |
|---|---|---|
| Column | | Track values over time or across categories |
| Bar | | Compare values in categories or over time |
| Line | | Track values over time |
| Pie | | Compare individual values to the whole |
| XY (Scatter) | | Compare pairs of values |
| Area | | Show contribution of each data series to the total over time |
| Doughnut | | Compare individual values to the whole with multiple series |
| Radar | | Show changes in values in relation to a center point |
| Surface | | Show value trends across two dimensions |
| Bubble | | Indicate relative size of data points |
| Stock | | Show stock market information or scientific data |
| Cylinder, cone, pyramid | | Track values over time or across categories |

# Entering and Editing Data in the Datasheet

After you embed the default datasheet and chart into your presentation, you need to change the data label and cell information in the sample datasheet to create the chart you need. Although you can import information from a spreadsheet, it is often easier to use Graph and type in the information. As you enter data or make changes to the datasheet, the chart automatically changes to reflect your alterations. ▰▰▰ Maria enters the 1999 quarterly sales figures by division that she wants to show to the employees. She first changes the data labels and then the series information in the cells.

## Steps 1 2 3 4

**1.** Double-click the **chart** on slide 5

The graph is selected and the datasheet appears. The labels representing the quarters across the top are correct, but the row labels need adjusting, and the data needs to be replaced with MediaLoft's quarterly sales figures for each division.

**2.** Click the **East row label**, type **MediaLoft East**, then press **[Enter]**

After you press [Enter], the first data label changes from East to MediaLoft East (although you cannot see all of it right now), and the data label in row 2, the cell directly below the active cell, becomes selected. Don't worry that the column is not wide enough to accommodate the label; you'll fix that after you enter all the labels.

**3.** Type **MediaLoft West**, press **[Tab]**, then press **[↑]**

Pressing [Tab] moves the active cell one column to the right and pressing [↑] moves it up one row—cell A1 is the active cell. Notice that in the chart itself, below the datasheet, the data labels you typed are now in the legend to the right of the chart.

**4.** Position the pointer on top of the column divider to the left of the letter A so that ⊹ changes to ✛ and double-click

The data label column automatically widens to accommodate all the column label text.

**5.** With cell A1 selected, type **600,000**, press **[Enter]**, type **300,000**, press **[Tab]**, then press **[↑]** to move to cell B1, to the top of the second data series column

Notice that the heights of the columns in the chart change to reflect the numbers you typed.

**6.** Enter the rest of the numbers shown in Figure D-9 to complete the datasheet

### Trouble?

The datasheet window can be manipulated in the same ways other windows are. If you can't see a column or a row, use the scroll bars to move another part of the datasheet into view, or resize the datasheet window so you can see all the data.

**7.** Click the **row 3 row number**, then press **[Delete]**

The chart columns adjust to reflect the new information, and the default information in row no longer appears. The chart currently shows the columns grouped by quarter (the legend represents the rows in the datasheet). It would be more effective if the columns were grouped division (with the legend representing the columns in the datasheet).

**8.** Click **Data** on the menu bar, then click **Series in Columns**

The division labels are now on the horizontal axis, and the quarters are listed in the legend. The groups of data markers (the columns) now represent the sales for each division by quarter. Notice that the small column chart graphics that used to be in the row labels have now moved to the column labels, indicating that the series are now in columns.

**9.** Click in the Presentation window outside the chart area, compare your chart to Figure D-10, then save the presentation

The datasheet closes, allowing you to see your entire chart. This chart layout clearly shows MediaLoft East's sales have exceeded MediaLoft West's, but that MediaLoft West's sales increasing steadily.

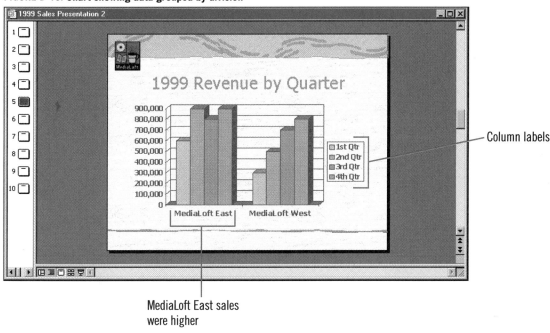

hic shows
series are
ntly in

7

Bars automatically show
the new values

FIGURE D-10: **Chart showing data grouped by division**

Column labels

MediaLoft East sales
were higher

## Series in Rows vs. Series in Columns

you have difficulty visualizing the difference
tween the Series in Rows and the Series in Columns
mmands on the Data menu, think about the legend.
**eries in rows** means that the information in the
ws will become the legend in the chart (and the col-
mn labels will be on the horizontal axis). **Series in**

**Columns** means that the information in the columns
will become the legend in the chart (and the row
labels will be on the horizontal axis). Microsoft Graph
places a small graphic representing the chart type on
the axis items that are currently represented by the
chart series items (bars, etc.).

# Formatting a Chart

Graph lets you change the appearance of the chart to emphasize certain aspects of the information you are presenting. You can change the chart type, create titles, format the chart labels, move the legend, or add arrows. ◄━━ Maria wants to improve the appearance of her chart by formatting the vertical and horizontal axes and by inserting a title.

## Steps 1234

1. **Double-click the chart to reopen Microsoft Graph, then click the Close button in the Datasheet window to close the datasheet**
   The Microsoft Graph menu and toolbar remain at the top of the window.

▶ **Trouble?**

Click the More Buttons button to locate buttons that are not visible on your toolbar.

2. **Click the sales numbers on the vertical axis to select the axis, then click the Currency Style button ⑤ on the Chart Formatting toolbar**
   The numbers on the vertical axis appear with dollar signs and two decimal places. You don't need to show the two decimal places, because all the values are whole numbers.

▶ **Trouble?**

If the Office Assistant appears with a tip in the balloon-shaped dialog box, drag it out of the way or click OK in the Office Assistant dialog balloon.

3. **Click the Decrease Decimal button 🔢 on the Chart Formatting toolbar twice**
   The numbers on the vertical axis now have dollar signs and show only whole numbers. The division names on the horizontal axis would be easier to see if they were larger.

4. **Click either of the division names on the horizontal axis, click the Font Size list arrow on the Chart Formatting toolbar, then click 20**
   The font size changes from 18 points to 20 points for both labels on the horizontal axis. Viewers would understand the chart more readily if it had a title and axis labels.

5. **Click Chart on the menu bar, click Chart Options, then click the Titles tab**
   The Chart Options dialog box opens, in which you can change the chart title, axes, grid lines, legend, data labels, and the table.

6. **Click in the Chart title text box, then type MediaLoft 1999 Sales by Division**
   The preview box changes to show you the chart with the title.

7. **Press [Tab] twice to move the cursor to the Value (Z) axis text box, then type Sales**
   In a 3-D chart, the vertical axis is called the Z-axis, and the depth axis, which you don't usually work with, is the Y-axis. See Figure D-11 for the completed Titles tab.

8. **Click the Legend tab, click the Bottom option button, then click OK**

9. **Double-click the border of the "Sales" label on the vertical axis, click the Alignment tab, drag the red diamond in the Orientation section up to a vertical position so the spin box reads 90 degrees, click OK, then click a blank area of the Presentation window**
   Graph closes and the PowerPoint toolbars and menu bar appear. See Figure D-12.

### CLUES TO USE

### Customizing Charts

You can easily customize the look of any chart in Microsoft Graph. Click the chart to select it, then double-click any data series element (a column, for example) to open the Format Data Series dialog box. Use the tabs to change the element's fill color, border, shape, or data label. You can even use the same fill effects you apply to a presentation background. In 3-D charts, you can change the chart depth as well as the distances between series.

FIGURE D-11: Titles tab in the Chart Options dialog box

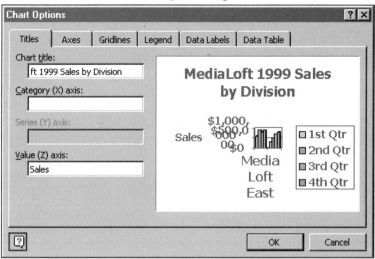

FIGURE D-12: Slide showing formatted chart

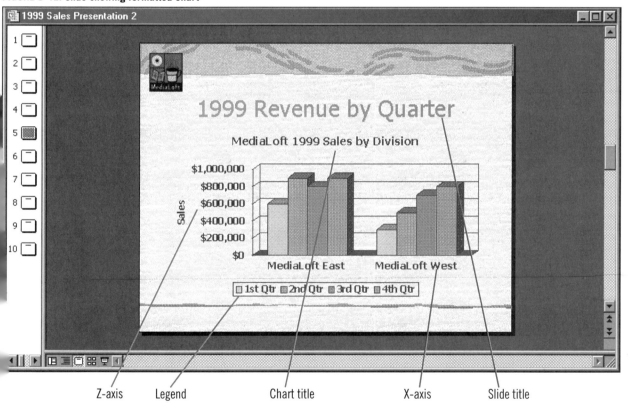

Z-axis          Legend          Chart title          X-axis          Slide title

# Using Slide Show Commands

With PowerPoint, you can show a presentation on any compatible computer using Slide Show view. As you've seen, Slide Show view fills your computer screen with the slides of your presentation, showing them one at a time—similar to how a slide projector shows slides. Once your presentation is in Slide Show view, you can use a number of slide show options to tailor the show. For example, you can draw on, or **annotate**, slides or jump to a specific slide. Maria runs a slide show of her presentation and practices using some of the custom slide show options to make her presentation more effective.

## Steps

1. Go to **slide 1**, then click the **Slide Show button** 🖳
   The first slide of the presentation fills the screen.

2. Press **[Spacebar]**
   Slide 2 appears on the screen. Pressing [Spacebar] or clicking the left mouse button is the easiest way to move through a slide show. You can also use the keys listed in Table D-2. You can also use the Slide Show pop-up menu for on-screen navigation during a slide show.

> **QuickTip**
> You can also access the Slide Show menu by moving the mouse pointer, then clicking the Slide Show menu icon that appears in the lower-left corner of the screen.

3. Right-click anywhere on the screen, point to **Go** on the pop-up menu, then click **Slide Navigator**
   The Slide Navigator dialog box opens and displays a list of the presentation slides.

4. Click **6. Reasons for Our Growth** in the Slide titles list box, then click **Go To**
   The slide show jumps to slide 6. You can emphasize major points in your presentation by annotating the slide during a slide show using the Pen.

5. Right-click the slide, point to **Pointer Options** on the pop-up menu, then click **Pen**
   The pointer changes to ✎.

6. Press and hold **[Shift]** and drag ✎ to draw a line under each of the bulleted points on the slide
   Holding down [Shift] constrains the Pen tool to straight horizontal or vertical lines. Compare your screen to Figure D-13. While the annotation pen is visible, mouse clicks do not advance the slide show. However, you can still move to the next slide by pressing [Spacebar] or [Enter].

7. Right-click to view the Slide Show pop-up menu, point to **Screen**, click **Erase Pen**, then press **[Ctrl][A]**
   The annotations on slide 6 are erased and the pointer returns to ▷.

> **QuickTip**
> If you know the slide number of the slide you want to jump to, type the number, then press [Enter].

8. Right-click anywhere on the screen to view the Slide Show pop-up menu, point to **Go**, point to **By Title**, then click **4 1999 Sales by Division** on the pop-up menu
   Slide 4 appears.

9. Press **[Home]**, then click the mouse, press **[Spacebar]**, or press **[Enter]** to advance through the slide show
   After the black slide that indicates the end of the slide show appears, the next click ends slide show and returns you to Slide view.

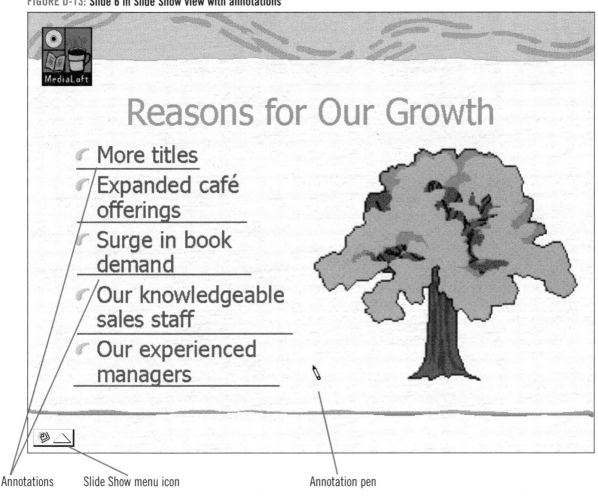

Annotations    Slide Show menu icon                    Annotation pen

TABLE D-2: Slide show keyboard controls

| control | description |
| --- | --- |
| [ ] | Erases the annotation drawing |
| [Enter], [Spacebar], [PgDn], [N], [↓] or [→] | Advances to the next slide |
| [ ] | Displays a hidden slide |
| [ ] or [PgUp] | Returns to the previous slide |
| [ ] | Changes the screen to white; press again to return |
| [ ] | Pauses the slide show; press again to continue |
| [ ] | Changes the screen to black; press again to return |
| [ ][P] | Changes pointer to ✎ |
| [CTRL][A] | Changes pointer to ☖ |
| [ ] | Stops the slide show |

# Creating Tables in PowerPoint

As you create your PowerPoint presentations, you may need to insert information in a row and column format. A table you create in PowerPoint is ideal for this type of information layout. There are two ways to create a table in PowerPoint: the Table command on the Insert menu and the Table slide layout. Once you have created a table, you can use the buttons on the Tables and Borders toolbar to format it, as well as the buttons on the Formatting toolbar. Maria uses the Table command on the Insert menu to create a table describing MediaLoft's competition.

## Steps 1 2 3 4

**1.** Go to **slide 7**, click **Insert** on the menu bar, then click **Table**

The Insert Table dialog box opens, allowing you to specify the number of columns and rows you want in your table. The default of 2 columns is correct but you want 4 rows.

### Trouble?

If the Tables and Borders toolbar does not open, click View on the menu bar, click Toolbars, then click Tables and Borders. If the toolbar obscures part of the table, drag it out of the way.

**2.** Press **[Tab]**, type **4**, then click **OK**

A table with 2 columns and 4 rows appears on the slide, and the Tables and Borders toolbar opens. See Table D-3 to learn about the buttons on this toolbar.

**3.** Type **Seller**, press **[Tab]**, type **# of Titles**, then press **[Tab]**

**4.** Enter the rest of the table information shown in Figure D-14, pressing **[Tab]** after each entry except the last one

**5.** Drag the table by its border down below the slide title

See Figure D-14. The table would look better if it were formatted.

**6.** Drag to select the column headings in the top row of the table

The column headings row becomes highlighted.

### QuickTip

You can change the height or width of any table cell by dragging its top or side borders.

**7.** Click the **Center Vertically button** 🔲 on the Tables and Borders toolbar, click the **Fill Color list arrow** 🎨▾ on the Tables and Borders toolbar, then click the light purple color in the second row

**8.** With the column headings still selected, click the **Center button** 🔲 on the Formatting toolbar, then click in a blank area of the presentation window

The column headings are centered horizontally and vertically and the row is filled with purple.

**9.** Vertically center the text in the other three rows, then fill these three rows with the **light orange color** in the second row

The table would look better if the last three rows were a little farther away from the cell edges.

### QuickTip

You can use the Format Table dialog box to apply a diagonal line through any table cell. Click the Borders tab, then click the diagonal line button.

**10.** With the bottom three rows still selected, click **Format** on the menu bar, click **Table**, click the **Text Box tab**, click the **Left up scroll arrow** twice so it reads .2, click **OK**, click outside the table, then save the presentation

The Tables and Borders toolbar closes and the table is no longer selected. Compare your screen with Figure D-15.

FIGURE D-14: **The new table before formatting**

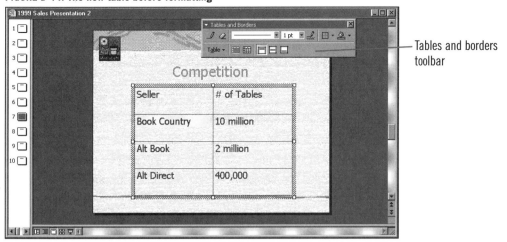

Tables and borders toolbar

FIGURE D-15: **The formatted table**

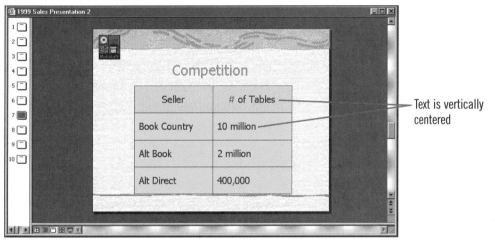

Text is vertically centered

BLE D-3: **The buttons on the Tables and Borders toolbar**

| utton | name | What it does |
|---|---|---|
| | **Draw Table** | Changes the pointer to ✏, which lets you drag to create a table or draw lines in an existing table |
| | **Eraser** | Changes the pointer to ✎, which lets you click any line in a drawn table to erase the line |
| | **Border Style** | Lets you change the border style of the next line you draw with the Pencil pointer |
| pt | **Border Width** | Lets you change the width of the next line you draw with the Pencil pointer |
| | **Border Color** | Changes the color of any table border |
| | **Outside Border** | Lets you choose a border, horizontal, or vertical line for any selected table cell(s) |
| | **Fill Color** | Lets you change the fill color of any selected table cell(s) |
| ble | **Table Menu** | Lets you insert a table, insert or delete rows or columns, merge or split cells, select parts of a table, or modify borders and fills |
| | **Merge Cells** | Lets you merge two selected table cells into one |
| | **Split Cells** | Lets you split a selected table cell into two cells |
| , □, □ | **Align top, center vertically, align bottom** | Let you change the vertical alignment of selected cell text |

# Setting Slide Show Timings and Transitions

In a slide show, you can preset when and how each slide appears on the screen. You can set the **timing**, which is the amount of time a slide is visible on the screen. Each slide can have the or different timing. Setting the right slide timing is important because it determines the am of time you have to discuss the material on each slide. You can also set slide transitions, the sp visual and audio effects you apply to a slide that determine how it moves in and out of view ing the slide show. Maria decides to set her slide timings for 10 seconds per slide a set the transitions for all slides but the last one to fade to black before the next slide appears.

## Steps 1 2 3 4

1. Click the **Slide Sorter View button**
   Slide Sorter view shows a miniature image of the slides in your presentation. The num of slides you see on your screen depends on the current zoom setting. Notice that the Sorter toolbar appears below the Standard and Formatting toolbars.

**QuickTip**

You also can click Slide Show on the menu bar, then click Slide Transition.

2. Right-click one of the slides, then click **Slide Transition** on the pop-up menu
   The Slide Transition dialog box, shown in Figure D-16, opens.

3. In the Advance section, make sure the **On mouse click check box** is selected, the **Automatically after check box** to select it, type **10** in the Automatically text box, then click **Apply to All**
   The timing between slides is 10 seconds, which appears under each slide. When you ru slide show, each slide will remain on the screen for 10 seconds. If you finish talking ir time and want to advance more quickly, press [Spacebar] or click the mouse button.

4. Right-click one of the slides, click **Slide Transition** on the pop-up menu, then the **Effect list arrow** in the top section
   A drop-down menu appears, showing all the transition effects.

**QuickTip**

You also can click Edit on the menu bar, click Select All, then click the Transition list arrow on the Slide Sorter toolbar to apply a transition effect to all the slides.

5. Scroll down the list, click **Fade Through Black**, note that the Preview picture ir Effect section demonstrates the selected effect, click **Apply to All**, then click blank area of the Presentation window to deselect the slide
   As shown in Figure D-17, each slide in Slide Sorter view now has a small transition under it, indicating there is a transition effect set for the slides.

6. Click the **transition icon** under any slide
   The previous slide appears briefly, then the transition effect appears; in this case the ir fades then the current slide appears.

7. Scroll down the Presentation window, right-click the **last slide**, click **Slide Transi** on the pop-up menu, click the **Effect list arrow**, then click **Split Vertical Out**
   As the preview shows, the last slide will now appear with a split from the center of the sc

8. Click the **Sound list arrow**, scroll down the list, click **Drum Roll** or choose anc sound effect, then click **Apply**
   Make sure you did not click Apply to All this time. The last slide now has a different v effect and a drum roll transition applied to it.

9. Press **[Home]**, click the **Slide Show button** and watch the slide show advanc
   To move more quickly, press [Spacebar] or [Enter].

10. When you see the black slide at the end of the slide show, press **[Enter]**
    The slide show ends.

FIGURE D-16: Slide Transition dialog box

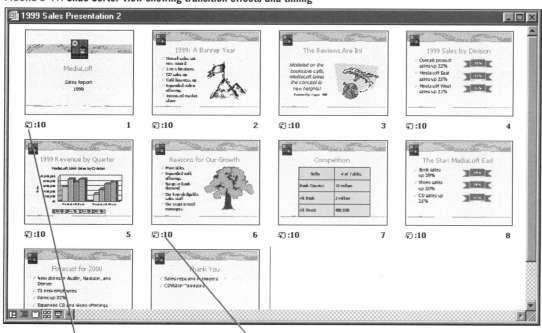

Click to apply to all slides in the presentation

Click to apply only to selected slide

Click to set transition effect

Set timing characteristics here

FIGURE D-17: Slide Sorter view showing transition effects and timing

Indicates a slide show transition is set for this slide

Indicates slide will remain on screen for 10 seconds

## Rehearsing slide show timing

You can set different slide timings for each slide. For example, you can have the title slide appear for 20 seconds, the second slide for 3 minutes, and so on. You also can set timings by clicking the Rehearse Timings button on the Slide Sorter toolbar or by choosing the Rehearse Timings command on the Slide Show menu. The Rehearsal dialog box shown in Figure D-18 opens. It contains buttons to pause between slides and to advance to the next slide. After opening the Rehearsal dialog box, practice giving your presentation. PowerPoint keeps track of how long each slide appears and sets the timing accordingly. You can view your

rehearsed timings in Slide Sorter view. The next time you run the slide show, you can use the timings you rehearsed.

FIGURE D-18: Rehearsal dialog box

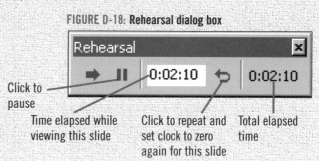

Click to pause

Time elapsed while viewing this slide

Click to repeat and set clock to zero again for this slide

Total elapsed time

**ENHANCING A PRESENTATION** POWERPOINT D-17 ◀

PowerPoint 2000

# Setting Slide Animation Effects

Animation effects let you control how the graphics and main points in your presentation appear on the screen during a slide show. You can animate text, images, or even individual chart elements, or you can add sound effects. Keep in mind that the animation effects you choose give a certain "flavor" to your presentation. They can be serious and businesslike or humorous. Choose appropriate effects for your presentation content and audience. Maria wants to animate the text and graphics of several slides in her presentation.

## Steps 1234

1. **Click slide 2, press and hold down [Ctrl], then click slides 4, 6, 8, 9, and 10**
   The selected slides have bullets on them. The bullets can be animated to appear on the slide individually when you click the mouse during the slide show.

> **QuickTip**
>
> Use the ScreenTips to see the names of the Slide Sorter toolbar buttons.

2. **On the Slide Sorter toolbar, click the Preset Animation list arrow, then click Fly From Left**
   Slide 10 previews the bullets flying in from the left side of the slide, and because this slide has a custom animation applied to it, you also hear the drum roll. When you run the slide show, instead of appearing all at once, the bullets of the selected slides will appear one at time, "flying" in from the left each time you click the mouse button.

> **QuickTip**
>
> If you want a grouped object, like the ribbons on slides 4 and 8, to fly in individually, then you must ungroup them first.

3. **Click slide 1, then run the slide show**
   The bullets fly in from the left. (Some of the graphics on these slides may also fly in from the left.) To set custom animation effects, the target slide must be in Slide view.

4. **Double-click slide 6 to view it in the previous view, which in this case is Slide view, click Slide Show on the menu bar, then click Custom Animation**
   The Custom Animation dialog box opens. Objects that are already animated appear in the Animation Order section in the order in which they will be animated.

5. **In the Check to animate slide objects list box, click Object 3**
   Make sure you do not click the Object 3 check box and remove its checkmark. Object 3 represents the tree, which becomes highlighted in the preview. See Figure D-19.

> **QuickTip**
>
> To preview animation in Normal view, Slide Sorter view, or Slide view, click Slide Show on the menu bar, then click Animation Preview.

6. **Click the Effects tab, click the top left list arrow in the Entry animation and sound section, click Dissolve, click Preview in the upper-right corner of the dialog box, see the new animation effect, then click OK**

7. **Change the animation effect to Dissolve for the mountain graphic on slide 2 and the airplane graphic on slide 3**

8. **Run the Slide Show again from slide 1, then return to Slide Sorter view**
   The special effects make the presentation easier to understand and more interesting.

9. **Click the Zoom text box on the Standard toolbar, type 50, press [Enter], click Window on the menu bar, then click Fit to Page**
   Figure D-20 shows the completed presentation in Slide Sorter view at 50% zoom.

10. **Click View on the menu bar, click Header and Footer, click the Notes and Handouts tab, type your name in the Footer text box, click Apply to All, save your presentation, print it as handouts, six slides per page, then exit PowerPoint**

FIGURE D-19: Custom Animation dialog box

Slide objects
listed here with
a check mark
are added to
Animation order
list below

Click here to
change animation
effects

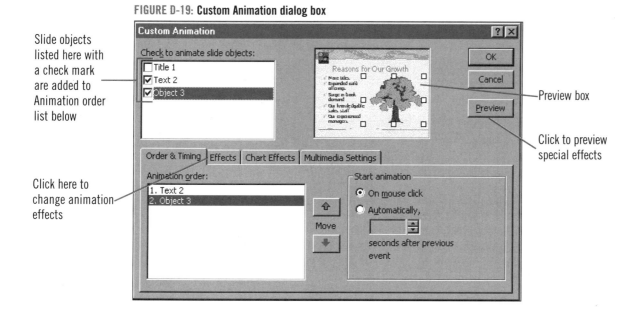

Preview box

Click to preview
special effects

FIGURE D-20: Completed presentation in Slide Sorter view

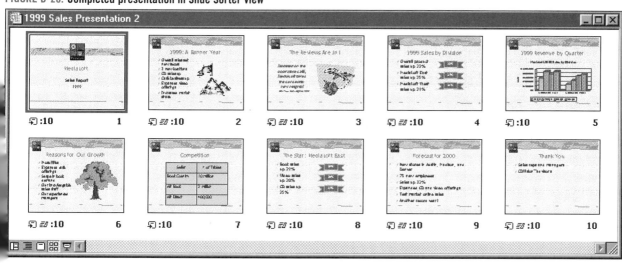

## Presentation Checklist

You should always rehearse your slide show. If possible, rehearse your presentation in the room and with the computer that you will use. Use the following checklist to prepare for the slide show.

Is **PowerPoint** or **PowerPoint Viewer** installed on the computer?

Is your **presentation file** on the hard drive of the computer you will be using? Try putting a shortcut for the file on the desktop. Do you have a backup copy of your presentation file on a floppy disk?

Is the **projection device** working correctly? Can the slides be seen from the back of the room?

✓Do you know how to control **room lighting** so that the audience can both see your slides and their handouts and notes? You may want to designate someone to control the lights if the controls are not close to you.

✓Will the **computer** be situated so you can advance and annotate the slides yourself? If not, designate someone to advance them for you.

✓Do you have enough copies of your **handouts**? Bring extras. Decide when to hand them out, or whether you prefer to have them waiting at the audience members' places when they enter.

PowerPoint 2000

**ENHANCING A PRESENTATION** POWERPOINT D-19 ◄

# Practice

## ► Concepts Review

Label each element of the PowerPoint window shown in Figure D-21.

FIGURE D-21

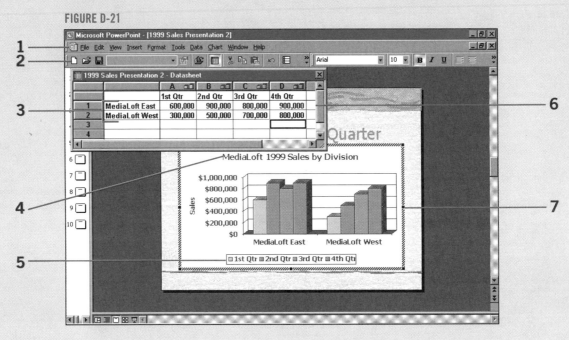

Match each term with the statement that describes it.

8. Chapt

9. Embedded object

10. Animation effect

11. Data series markers

12. Clip Gallery

13. Scaling

a. Resizing an object by a specific percentage

b. A graphic representation of a datasheet

c. Graphic representations of data series

d. The way bulleted items and images appear on a slide

e. A copy of an object from which you can access another program's tools

f. A file index system that organizes images

Select the best answer from the list of choices.

14. PowerPoint animation effects let you control

  a. The order in which text and objects are animated.

  b. The direction from which animated objects appear.

  c. Which text and images are animated.

  d. All of the above.

15. Which of the following is *not* true of a Microsoft Graph chart?

  a. A graph is made up of a datasheet and chart.

  b. You can double-click a chart to view its corresponding datasheet.

  c. An active cell has a black selection rectangle around it.

  d. You cannot import data from other programs into a datasheet.

# ► Skills Review

**1. Insert clip art.**

   **a.** Open the presentation PPT D-3 on your Project Disk, save it as "CD Product Report" to your Project Disk.

   **b.** Go to slide 2 and insert the musical notes graphic from the Music category in the Clip Gallery.

   **c.** On the Size tab of the Format Picture dialog box, deselect Relative to original picture size, scale the graphic to 125% of its current size, and center it in the blank space.

   **d.** Align the top of the main text placeholder with the top of the graphic, and adjust their position as necessary.

**2. Insert, crop, and scale a picture.**

   **a.** Change the layout of slide 6 to the Text & Object layout, and insert PPT D-4 into the object placeholder.

   **b.** Crop about ¾" off the left side of the picture.

   **c.** Align the tops of the text box and the graphic.

   **d.** Scale the graphic to an appropriate percentage of its original size so it is approximately the same size as the main text box.

   **e.** Reposition the graphic, then make the background of the graphic transparent.

**3. Embed a chart.**

   **a.** Go to slide 3, "1999 CD Sales by Quarter," and apply the Chart AutoLayout.

   **b.** Start Microsoft Graph.

   **c.** Move the mouse pointer around on the datasheet and note the different pointer shapes.

   **d.** Deselect the chart object.

**4. Enter and edit data in the datasheet.**

   **a.** Open Graph again, and for the row 1 datasheet label, enter "MediaLoft East."

   **b.** Enter the information shown in Table D-4 into the datasheet and widen the column to fit all the data.

   **c.** Delete any unused rows of default data.

   **d.** Place the Data Series in Columns.

TABLE D-4

|                | 1st Qtr | 2nd Qtr | 3rd Qtr | 4th Qtr |
| -------------- | ------- | ------- | ------- | ------- |
| MediaLoft East | 36      | 40      | 45      | 43      |
| MediaLoft West | 44      | 50      | 52      | 53      |

**5. Format a chart.**

   **a.** Close the datasheet but leave Graph running.

   **b.** Change the region names on the X-axis to 20 points.

   **c.** Apply the Currency Style with no decimals to the values on the vertical axis.

   **d.** Insert the chart title "1999 CD Sales."

   **e.** Add the text "Sales in 000s" to the Z-axis, then change the orientation of the Z-axis to vertical.

   **f.** Place the legend below the graphic.

   **g.** Exit Graph.

**6. Use slide show commands.**

   **a.** Begin the slide show at slide 1, then proceed through the slide show to slide 3.

   **b.** On slide 3, use the Pen to draw straight-line annotations under the labels on the horizontal axis.

   **c.** Erase the pen annotations, then change the pointer back to an arrow.

   **d.** Go to slide 2 using the Go command on the slide show pop-up menu.

   **e.** Use [End] to move to the last slide.

   **f.** Return to Slide view.

**7. Create a table.**

   **a.** Add a slide using the title only format after slide 2.

   **b.** Add the slide title "CD Sales by Type."

   **c.** Insert a PowerPoint table with 2 columns and 5 rows.

   **d.** For the header row, enter Type and Sales.

   **e.** In the left column, add the following types: Rock, Folk, Classical, and Jazz/Blues.

   **f.** In the right column, add realistic sales figures for each CD type.

   **g.** Reposition the table so it doesn't obscure the slide title.

   **h.** Format the table using fills, horizontal and vertical alignment, or any other features.

**8. Set slide show timings and transitions.**

   **a.** Switch to Slide Sorter view.

   **b.** Open the Slide Transition dialog box using the pop-up menu.

   **c.** Specify that all slides should advance after 15 seconds, unless the mouse is clicked first.

   **d.** Apply the Box Out transition effect to all slides.

   **e.** In Slide Sorter view, preview the transition effect on two slides.

   **f.** Apply the Cover Down transition effect to the last slide in the presentation.

   **g.** View the slide show to verify the transitions are correct.

**9. Set slide animation effects.**

   **a.** In Slide Sorter view, apply the Peek from Right animation effect to the bulleted list on slide 5.

   **b.** Go to slide 2 in Slide or Normal view, and using the Custom Animation dialog box, apply the Dissolve effect to the Music graphic and preview the effect in the dialog box.

   **c.** Specify that the bulleted list text object should spiral in after the musical notes graphic appears, and preview the effect. (*Hint:* Check the Order & Timing tab to make sure the musical notes graphic is first in the list.)

   **d.** Run the slide show from the beginning to check the animation effects.

   **e.** Save the presentation.

   **f.** Add your name as a footer to the notes and handouts, then print the presentation as handouts, six slides per page

   **g.** Close the presentation and exit PowerPoint.

# ▶ Independent Challenges

**1.** You are a financial management consultant for Pacific Coast Investments, located in San José, California. One
your primary responsibilities is to give financial seminars on different financial investments and how to determi
which funds to invest in. In this challenge, you enhance the look of the slides by adding and formatting objects a
adding animation effects and transitions.

  To complete this independent challenge:

   **a.** Open the file PPT D-5 on your Project Disk, and save it as "Fund Seminar" to your Project Disk.

   **b.** Add your name as the footer on all slides and handouts.

   **c.** Apply the Chart layout to slide 6, and enter the data in Table D-5 into the datasheet.

   **d.** Format the chart. Add titles as necessary.

   **e.** Add an appropriate clip art item to slide 2.

   **f.** On slide 4, use the Align, Group, and Order commands to organize the shapes.

   **g.** Spell check the presentation, then save it.

   **h.** View the slide show, evaluate your presentation and add a template of your choice. Make changes if necessary.

TABLE D-5

| | 1 year | 3 year | 5 year | 10 year |
|---|---|---|---|---|
| Bonds | 4.2% | 5.2% | 7.9% | 9.4% |
| Stocks | 7.5% | 8.3% | 10.8% | 12.6% |
| Mutual Funds | 6.1% | 6.3% | 6.4% | 6.1% |

   **i.** Set animation effects, slide transitions, and slide tim-
ings, keeping in mind that your audience includes potential investors who need the information you are pres
ing to make decisions about where to put their hard-earned money. View the slide show again.

   **j.** Print the slides of the presentation as handouts, six slides per page, then close the presentation.

**2.** You are the communications director at Heridia Design, Inc, an international advertising agency. One of your responsibilities is to create an on-screen presentation for a presentation contest at the National Association of Advertising Agencies (NAAA) convention. Create a presentation using any type of company. The presentation can be aimed to either convince or educate your audience.

To complete this independent challenge:

**a.** Plan and create the slide show presentation. Add interesting visuals, and use a color scheme appropriate to the type of business you choose. Use a chart to show how well the company has performed. Add a table to one of the slides.

**b.** Use slide transitions, animation effects, and slide timings. Remember, your audience consists of a group of advertising executives who create eye-catching ads every day. View the slide show to evaluate the effects you added.

**c.** Add your name as a footer to slides and handouts. Spell check and save the presentation as "NAAA Presentation" to your Project Disk. Print it as handouts, six slides per page.

**3.** You are the manager of the Maryland University Student Employment Office. The office is staffed by work-study students; new, untrained students start work every semester. Create a presentation that you can use to make the training easier. You can create your own content, or use the following: the work-study staff needs to learn about the main features of the office, including its employment database, library of company directories, seminars on employment search strategies, interviewing techniques, and resume development, as well as its student consulting and resume bulk-mailing services.

To complete this independent challenge:

**a.** Plan and create the slide presentation. Use Microsoft Clip Gallery to help create visual interest.

**b.** Save the presentation as "Student Employment" to your Project Disk. View the slide show and evaluate the contents of your presentation. Make any necessary adjustments.

**c.** Add transitions, special effects, and timings to the presentation. Remember, your audience is university students who need to assimilate a lot of information in order to perform well in their new jobs. View the slide show again.

**d.** Add your name as a footer to slides and handouts. Spell check, save, and print the presentation.

**4.** MediaLoft gives monthly Brown Bag seminars during lunchtime to interested employees. MediaLoft has asked Asset Advisors, a successful investment service company, to give a Brown Bag presentation on sound investment principles. You work for Asset Advisors, and your manager, Kevin Leong, has asked you to prepare the presentation for the MediaLoft session. He knows that MediaLoft's corporate values include socially responsible investing, so Kevin has asked you to include something in the presentation about this topic.

To complete this independent challenge:

**a.** Open the file PPT D-6 from your Project Disk, and save it as "Investment Presentation" to your Project Disk.

**b.** Look through the presentation and adjust the content as necessary. Add clip art if you like.

**c.** Create a Graph chart and embed it on slide 7. Enter the data in Table D-6 into the datasheet.

**d.** Format the chart, and title the chart "Investment Risk Over Time."

**e.** Format the objects in the presentation. Use the Align and Group commands to organize the shapes.

**f.** Connect to the Internet, go to the MediaLoft intranet site at http://www.course.com/illustrated/MediaLoft and click the Research Center link. From there, click the Socially Responsible Investing link, and examine the sites listed there and some of the sites listed within them. Create two new slides in your presentation, one about organizations that promote socially responsible investing and another about investment funds that invest only in socially responsible organizations.

**.** Fill in the appropriate information on the last two slides in the presentation.

**.** Make changes to the color scheme and add the new color scheme to the color scheme list. Change the slide background to a 2-color background with the gradient of your choice.

Spell check the presentation and evaluate the presentation. Set appropriate animations, slide transitions, and slide timings. View the slide show again.

Add your name as a footer to slides and handouts. Save the presentation and print the slides, six handouts per page. Close the presentation and disconnect from the Internet.

TABLE D-6

|  | 1 year | 3 year | 5 year | 10 year |
|---|---|---|---|---|
| Bonds | 8.2% | 7.5% | 5.6% | 2.9% |
| Stocks | 17.3% | 8.9% | 6.1% | 3.2% |
| Mutual Funds | 15.4% | 6.1% | 5.2% | 4.7% |

## ▶ Visual Workshop

Create a slide that looks like the example in Figure D-22. Add your name as a footer on the slide. Save the presentation as "Costs" to your Project Disk.

FIGURE D-22

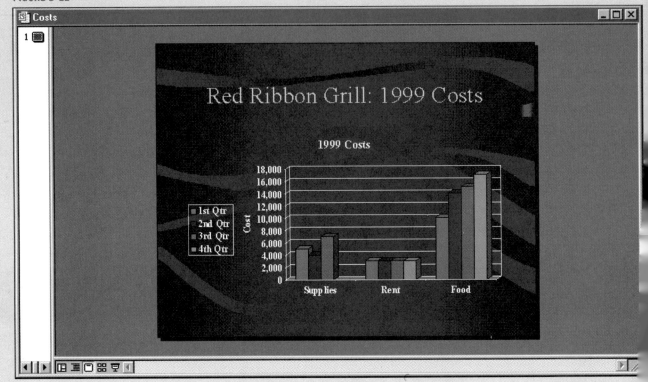

# Integrating
## Word, Excel, Access, and PowerPoint

## Objectives

► **Insert a Word outline into a PowerPoint presentation**
► **Embed a Word table into a PowerPoint slide**
► **Embed an Excel chart into a PowerPoint slide**
► **Link an Excel worksheet to a PowerPoint slide**
► **Update a linked Excel worksheet in PowerPoint**
► **Export a PowerPoint presentation to Word**

PowerPoint, the fourth component of Microsoft Office, can be easily integrated with the other Office programs. For example, to help you develop a PowerPoint presentation, you can insert a document from Word or embed objects like a Word table or an Excel worksheet directly into the slides of your presentation. An embedded object is one that is created in one program, known as a **source program**, and then stored as an independent file in another program, such as your PowerPoint presentation. In this unit, Maria Abbott, MediaLoft's general sales manager, creates a company status presentation that will be used at this year's executive meeting. To complete the presentation, Maria gathers some data herself and collects more from various MediaLoft regions. Because everyone at MediaLoft uses Microsoft Office, Maria knows all the files are compatible.

# Inserting a Word Outline into a PowerPoint Presentation

Although it is very easy to create an outline in PowerPoint, it is unnecessary if the outline already exists in a Word document. You can easily insert a Word document into PowerPoint to create a presentation outline. When you insert the Word outline, the heading styles in the outline are converted to text levels in PowerPoint. For example, every Word paragraph with the style Heading 1 is converted to a new slide, and every Word paragraph with the style Heading 2 is converted to a subpoint under a slide title. If the outline you are inserting has no styles, the text is converted into an outline based on the structure of the document; each hard return indicates a new slide and each hard return followed by a tab indicates a subpoint. ✦ Maria inserts a Word outline created by Alice Wegman, MediaLoft's marketing manager, into her presentation.

**1.** Start PowerPoint

The PowerPoint startup dialog box opens.

**2.** Click the **Open an existing presentation option button**, click **More Files** in the list box, then click **OK**

The Open dialog box opens.

**3.** Open the file **INT C-1** from your Project Disk, then save it as **Company Status** to your Project Disk

**4.** Insert your name as the footer on all handouts

**5.** Click **Window** on the menu bar, then click **Arrange All**

Now your screen matches the figures in this unit. The outline of the presentation appears shown in Figure C-1. The presentation currently contains two slides.

**6.** Click anywhere in the text of slide 2 in the Outline pane

When you insert the Word document, it begins with a new slide after the current slide.

**7.** Click **Insert** on the menu bar, then click **Slides from Outline**

The Insert Outline dialog box opens.

**8.** Select the file **INT C-2** from your Project Disk, click **Insert**, then scroll in the Outli pane to see the new slides

The Word document is inserted as six new slides. See Figure C-2. You can insert a Word document in the Slide or Outline pane in Normal view or in Slide or Outline view. Once an outline is inserted into a presentation, you can edit it as if it had been created in PowerPoint.

**9.** Make sure **slide 3** is selected, click the **Slide View button** 🖳, then click the N Slide button ⬇ below the vertical scroll bar five times to view the new slides

### Trouble?

If you have any other presentations open, close them, then repeat step 5.

### Trouble?

If you see a message saying that PowerPoint needs to install this feature, insert your Office 2000 CD in the appropriate drive and click Yes. See your instructor or technical support person for assistance.

FIGURE C-1: Maria's slide presentation

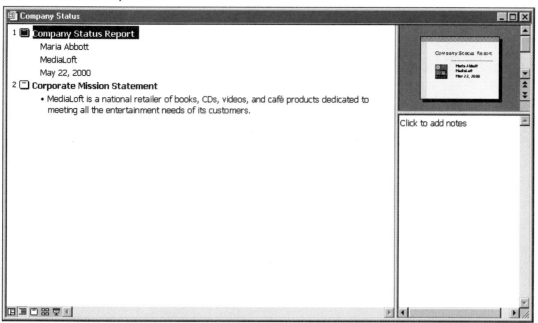

FIGURE C-2: New slides inserted in Outline view

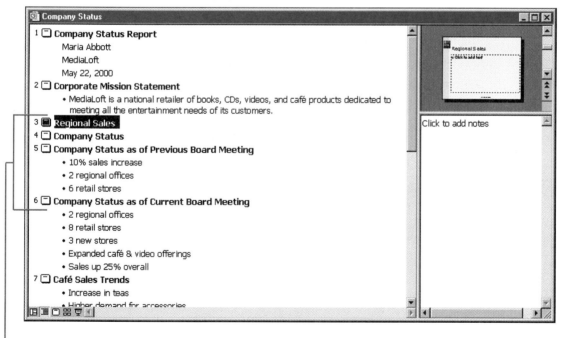

Slides inserted
after slide 2

# Embedding a Word Table into a PowerPoint Slide

You may need to insert a Word table that you can modify using the commands on the Word Table menu, such as AutoFormat or Sort, which are not available on the PowerPoint Table menu. To do this, embed a Word table into a slide. An **embedded** object is a copy of a table, chart, or graphic that you have inserted in a document. You can double-click the embedded object to view the editing tools of the program that created it. However, changes you make to the embedded copy do not affect the original. To embed a Word table into a PowerPoint presentation, you use the Picture command on the Insert menu. Maria wants to create a table and format it using the Word AutoFormat command, so she decides to embed a Word table into a slide illustrating recent MediaLoft growth.

## Steps

1. Click the **slide icon** ☐ for slide 4 in the Outline pane, press and hold **[Shift]** and click the main text placeholder in the Slide pane, then press **[Delete]**

2. Click **Insert** on the menu bar, point to **Picture**, then click **Microsoft Word Table**
   The Insert Table dialog box opens. See Figure C-3.

> **QuickTip**
> You can also embed an existing Word table by copying it from Word and then pasting it into PowerPoint using the Paste Special command.

3. Type **3** in the Number of columns text box, press **[Tab]**, type **4** in the Number of rows text box, then click **OK**
   A Word table opens. The PowerPoint title bar and presentation window remain on the screen, but the PowerPoint menus and toolbars are replaced with Word menus and toolbars, indicating that you are now working on an embedded Word object in PowerPoint.

4. Press **[Tab]**, type **1998**, press **[Tab]**, type **1999**, press **[Tab]**, then enter the rest of the information in Figure C-4 in a similar manner, using **[Tab]** to move from cell to cell

5. Click **Table** on the menu bar, click **Table AutoFormat**, then scroll to and click the **Colorful 3** format

6. Click the **Borders** and **AutoFit check boxes** to deselect them, click **OK**, then click on the slide outside the table
   The PowerPoint menu bar and toolbars return. The table would look better if the numbers were centered and if there were a little more space after each item.

> **Trouble?**
> Click the More Buttons button ⟩⟩ to locate buttons that are not visible on your toolbars.

7. Double-click the table to return to Word, drag to select the two columns containing numbers, then click the **Center button** ▦ on the Formatting toolbar

8. Drag to select the first column, click **Format** on the menu bar, click **Paragraph**, in the Spacing area click the **After up arrow** once so that the text box reads 6 pt, then click **OK**

> **QuickTip**
> The commands on the PowerPoint Tables and Borders toolbar cannot be used on an embedded Word table. You must double-click the table and use Word editing tools.

9. Double-click the **border** between the first and second columns
   The first column widens so that the word "Employees" fits on one line

10. Click on the slide outside the table to return to PowerPoint, drag the table so that is centered in the blank area under the slide title, click on a blank area of the slide to deselect the table, then click the **Save button** ▦ on the Standard toolbar to save the presentation
    The completed table is shown in Figure C-5.

FIGURE C-3: The Insert Table dialog box

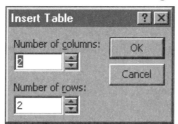

FIGURE C-4: The table in Word

|  | 1998 | 1999 |
|---|---|---|
| Retail stores | 5 | 8 |
| Product lines | 3 | 4 |
| Employees | 122 | 160 |

FIGURE C-5: The completed table

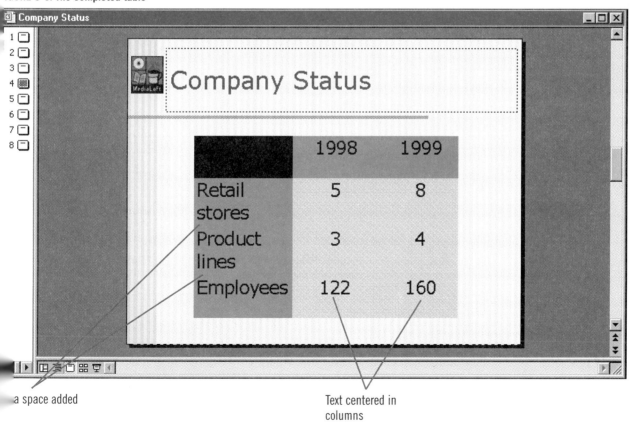

a space added

Text centered in columns

# Embedding an Excel Chart into a PowerPoint Slide

You can easily embed an Excel chart into a PowerPoint presentation. Because it is embedded, you can double-click a chart to edit it using Excel tools. The original Excel chart object remains unchanged. ◀▬▬ Maria includes in her presentation an Excel chart that she received from the Accounting department. Maria wants to format the chart after she adds it to her presentation, so she decides to embed it.

## Steps

1. Click the **slide icon** □ for slide 3 in the Outline pane, click the **Common Tasks menu button** on the Formatting toolbar, click **Slide Layout**, click the **Object layout** (fourth row, fourth column), then click **Apply**

2. Double-click the **object placeholder**
   The Insert Object dialog box opens.

3. Click the **Create from file option button**, click **Browse**, click the **Look in list arrow**, click the **drive** containing your Project Disk, click **INT C-3**, click **OK**, then click **OK** in the Insert Object dialog box
   The Excel chart appears on the slide.

4. Position and resize the **chart object**, as shown in Figure C-6

5. Click the **Fill Color list arrow** on the Drawing toolbar, then click the **light gray square**, third from the right
   The chart text would be more readable if it were larger.

6. Double-click the **chart object**
   The PowerPoint menu bar and toolbars are replaced with the Excel menu bar and toolbars and the Excel Chart toolbar appears.

7. Click the **Chart Objects list arrow** on the Chart toolbar, click **Chart title**, click the **Format Chart Title button** 🖼 on the Chart toolbar, click the **Font tab**, click **36** in the Size list, then click **OK**
   The change in the Excel chart is reflected in the embedded object in PowerPoint. Because this is an embedded object, editing the object does not alter the original Excel file.

8. Double-click the **vertical axis** to open the Format Axis dialog box, click the **Font tab**, click **16** in the size list, click **OK**, then repeat for the **horizontal axis**

9. Repeat step 8 to make the **legend** larger, then resize the legend to display all the text (if necessary)

10. Click in the Presentation window outside the chart to exit Excel, click the **chart object** once to select it, drag the **sizing handles** to resize the chart to be as large as possible, center it, then click in the presentation window outside the chart object to deselect it
    Compare your slide to Figure C-7.

### Trouble?
If the Excel chart toolbar appears, click in the Presentation window outside the chart, click it once to select it, then try step 4 again.

### Trouble?
If the Chart toolbar does not appear, click View on the menu bar, point to Toolbars, then click Chart.

**FIGURE C-6: Resizing the chart object**

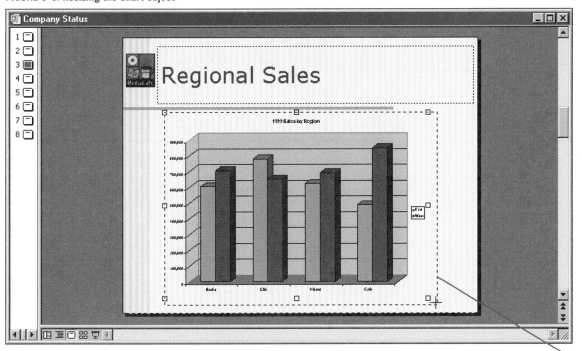

Border of sizing box

**FIGURE C-7: Excel object embedded in a slide**

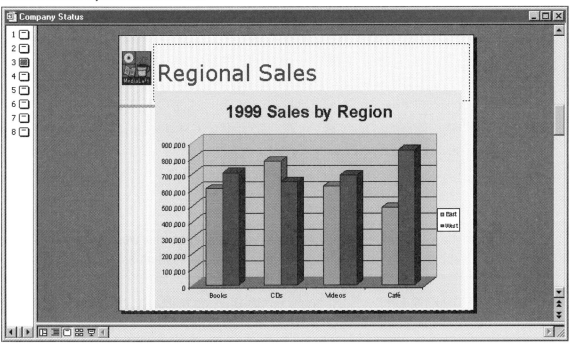

### Embedding objects using Paste Special

You can also embed an object or selected information from another Microsoft Office program into PowerPoint by copying and pasting the information. For example, assume you want to embed a worksheet from a Microsoft Excel file. Open the Microsoft Excel file that contains the worksheet, select the worksheet, and copy it to the Clipboard. Open your PowerPoint presentation, click Edit on the menu bar, click Paste Special, then click OK in the Paste Special dialog box.

# Linking an Excel Worksheet to a PowerPoint Slide

You can connect objects to your presentation by establishing a link between the file that cr the object and the PowerPoint presentation that contains the object. Unlike an embedded ob which is stored directly in a slide, a linked object is stored in its original file (called the source f When you **link** an object to a PowerPoint slide, a representation, or picture, of the object ap on the slide instead of the actual object, and this representation of the object is connecte linked, to the original file. Changes made to a linked object's source file are reflected in the li object. Some of the objects that you can link to PowerPoint include movies, PowerPoint s from other presentations, and Microsoft Excel worksheets. Table C-1 provides information to you decide whether to link or embed an object. ◆━━━ Maria needs to insert an Excel works from Jeff Shimada, the director of café operations, into her presentation. Jeff saved the works to MediaLoft's company network of computers. Maria decides to link the worksheet because knows Jeff will have to update the worksheet before the presentation.

## Steps

QuickTip

If you plan to do the steps in this unit again, be sure to make and use copy of the Excel file Cafe Profit.

1. Click the **slide icon** ▭ for slide 7 in the Outline pane, click the **Common Ta menu button** on the Formatting toolbar, click **Slide Layout**, click the **Text over Ob layout** (fifth row, fourth column), then click **Apply**

2. Double-click the **object placeholder**
   The Insert Object dialog box opens. You want to create a linked object from an existing

3. Click the **Create from file option button**, click **Browse**, click the **Look in list arr** click the **drive** containing your Project Disk, click **Cafe Profit**, then click **OK**

4. Click the **Link check box** in the Insert Object dialog box to select it
   Compare your screen to Figure C-8.

5. Click **OK**
   The Excel worksheet is linked to the PowerPoint slide. The worksheet would be easie read if it were larger.

QuickTip

If Excel opens while you are trying to resize or move the worksheet, click the Close button in the Excel program window.

6. Drag the corner sizing handles and reposition the worksheet object until i approximately the same size and in the same position as in Figure C-9
   The chart text is difficult to read against the background.

7. Click the **Fill Color list arrow** on the Drawing toolbar, click **Automatic**, then clic a blank area of the Presentation window to deselect the object
   Compare your screen to Figure C-9.

8. Save your work

FIGURE C-8: Insert Object dialog box

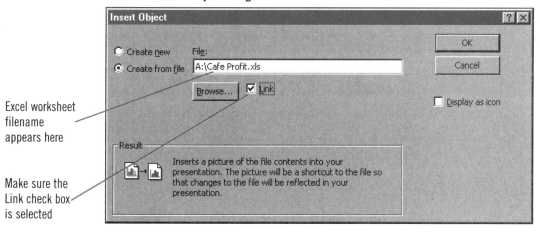

Excel worksheet
filename
appears here

Make sure the
Link check box
is selected

FIGURE C-9: Linked Excel worksheet on slide

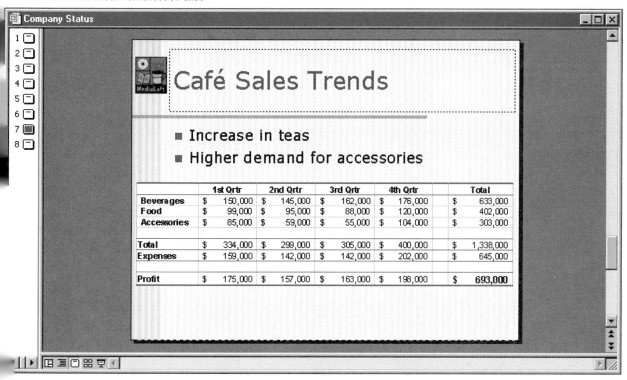

LE C-1: Embedding vs. Linking

| tion | situation |
|---|---|
| bed | You are the only user of an object and you want the object to be a part of your presentation |
| bed | You want to access the object in its source application, even if the original file is not available |
| bed | You want to update the object manually while working in PowerPoint |
| k | You always want the latest information in your object |
| k | The object's source file is shared on a network or where other users have access to the file and can change it |
| k | You want to keep your presentation file size small |

Integration 2000

# Updating a Linked Excel Worksheet in PowerPoint

To edit or change the information in a linked object, you must open the object's source file. You can open the object's source file and the program it was created in by double-clicking the linked object. When you modify a linked object's source file, PowerPoint asks you if you want to automatically update the file in the linked presentation when you open the PowerPoint file. Maria needs to update the linked worksheet because the wrong number was reported for accessory sales for the third quarter.

## Steps

**QuickTip**

To edit or open a linked object in your presentation, the object's source program and source file must be available on your computer or network.

1. Double-click the **worksheet object** on slide 7
   Microsoft Excel opens in a small window, showing the linked worksheet, and the Excel icon appears on the taskbar.

2. Click the **Maximize button** in the Excel program window if necessary

3. Double-click cell **D4**, edit the entry to **60,000**, then press **[Enter]**

4. Click the **Close button** in the Excel program window, then click **Yes** to save the changes
   Microsoft Excel closes and the linked Excel worksheet shows the change you made in Excel. Compare your screen to Figure C-10.

**Trouble?**

If you don't see 📋 on the Standard toolbar, click the More Buttons button ⏩

5. Click the **Spelling button** 📋 on the Standard toolbar and correct any spelling errors in the presentation

6. Click the **Save button** 💾 on the Standard toolbar to save the changes you made

7. Click the **Slide Sorter View button** 🈸 to the left of the horizontal scroll bar
   Compare your screen to Figure C-11.

8. Click **Slide 1**, then click the **Slide Show button** 🖵 and view the final presentation

9. Click **File** on the menu bar, click **Print**, click the **Pure black and white check box** to select it, select **Handouts** in the Print what list, select **6** Slides per page, then click **O** to print the slides

### Updating links

If the PowerPoint file is closed when you change the source file, the linked object will still reflect the changes you make to the source file. When you open the file containing the linked object, a dialog box opens reminding you that the file contains links and asking if you want to update the links now. Click OK to update the links or Cancel to leave the linked object unchanged. If you choose Cancel, you can still update the link later. Click Edit on the menu bar, then click Links to open the Links dialog box. Click the filename of the link you want to update, then click Update Now.

**FIGURE C-10:** Modifications reflected in linked chart

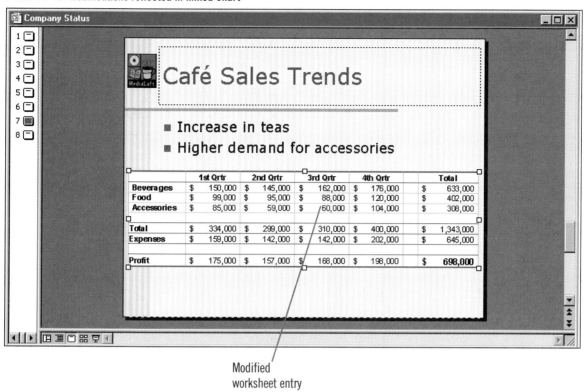

Modified
worksheet entry

**FIGURE C-11:** The final presentation in Slide Sorter view

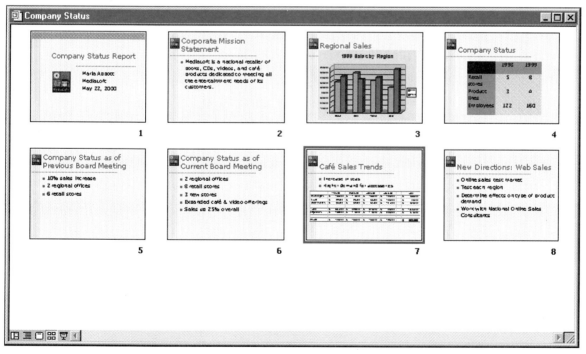

# Exporting a PowerPoint Presentation to Word

You can export a PowerPoint presentation to Word. When you choose the Send To Microsoft Word command on the File menu, Word starts and the outline of the current PowerPoint presentation is exported to Word as a Word document. You can choose one of five layouts for the Word document. Once the PowerPoint outline is in Word, you can save and edit the document. ✐ Maria wants to create handouts with blank lines so the audience can take notes during the presentation.

## Steps 1234

**1.** Click **File** on the menu bar, point to **Send To**, then click **Microsoft Word**
The Write-Up dialog box opens. See Figure C-12.

**2.** Click the **Blank lines next to slides option button**
You want your handouts to automatically reflect any changes you make to the presentation.

**3.** Click the **Paste link option button** at the bottom of the dialog box

**4.** Click **OK**
Microsoft Word opens and the slides appear in a table in a new document. This process may take a little while.

**5.** Click the **Maximize button** on the Word program window if necessary, then scroll up to page 1
See Figure C-13. The slide numbers are in the first column, the slides are in the second column, and blank lines appear next to the slides in the third column. There are three slides per page.

**6.** Select the first column, then click the **Bold button** ⬛ on the Formatting toolbar

**7.** Press **[Ctrl][End]**, then type your name

**8.** Save the Word file as **Handouts for Company Summary** to your Project Disk, then click the **Print button** 🖨 on the Standard toolbar
The handouts print.

**9.** Click the **Close button** on the Word program window, then click the **Close button** the PowerPoint program window without saving any changes
The programs close. Do not save changes when prompted by the alert box.

FIGURE C-12: **Write-Up dialog box**

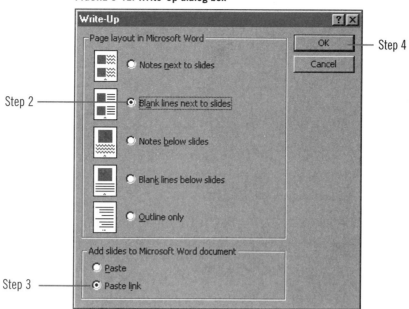

FIGURE C-13: **Exported PowerPoint presentation in Word**

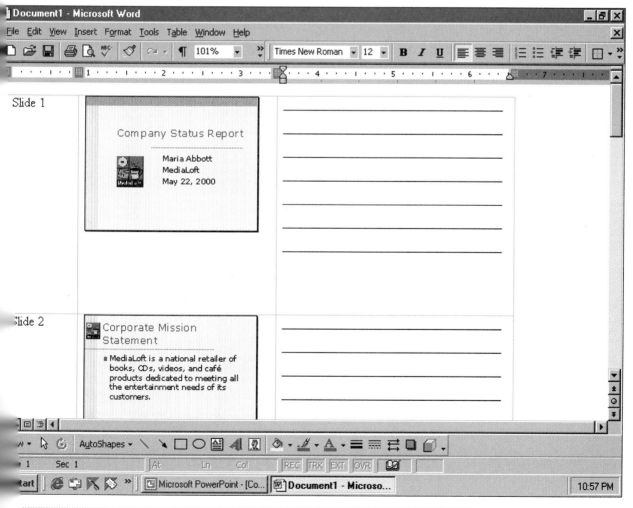

# ▶ Independent Challenges

**1.** You are responsible for recommending which software packages your company should purchase. You have decided to recommend Microsoft Office. Create a PowerPoint presentation illustrating the advantages of each program in the Microsoft Office suite. Your presentation should contain slides that show how first-time computer users feel about computers and why Microsoft Office is a good choice for them. This information is provided in the Word file INT C-4 on your Project Disk. Think about what you want the presentation to say and what graphics you want to use.

To complete this independent challenge:

a. Plan your presentation, determining its purpose and the look that will help communicate your message. Sketch on paper how you want the slides to look.

b. Start PowerPoint, create a presentation, save it as "Office Review" to your Project Disk, and then insert your name as the footer on all slides and handouts.

c. Insert the Word document INT C-4 from your Project Disk into your presentation outline. This file contains information about how first-time computer users feel about computers. Use this outline to help you create your presentation. Your presentation should contain at least 10 slides.

d. Create the title slide for your presentation, then save your work.

e. Add appropriate formatting, a design, graphics, and slide show special effects into the presentation.

f. Check the spelling in your presentation.

g. Run the slide show and evaluate your presentation. Is your message clear? Are the slides visually appealing? Make any changes necessary and save the presentation.

h. Print the slides and outline of your presentation, then close all open applications.


**2.** To augment the Census Bureau's data on marriage and birthrate statistics, you have been asked to prepare PowerPoint presentation that will run continuously in the lobby at the local census office. Charts on the data need be linked to PowerPoint slides because data is occasionally updated. Use the data found in the two worksheets in the Excel file INT C-5 on your Project Disk. Create a presentation that explains this data.

To complete this independent challenge:

a. Start Excel, open the file INT C-5 from your Project Disk, then save it as "Statistics" to your Project Disk.

b. Create at least four charts using the data in the Marriages worksheet, and create one chart using the data in the Birthrates worksheet.

c. Create a new Word document containing an outline for your presentation, type your name at the top, then sav it as "Stat Outline" to your Project Disk. Print this outline.

d. Open a new PowerPoint presentation. Apply a template of your choice. Insert your name as a footer on all slid and handouts. Save it as "Bureau" to your Project Disk.

e. Create a title slide for the presentation, then insert the Word outline into the presentation.

f. Add slide show special effects, such as transitions and animation effects, to the slides.

g. Link the four charts in the Marriages worksheet to slides in the presentation. Update one of the numbers in t worksheet from within PowerPoint and verify that the number in the presentation is also updated.

h. Embed the chart in the Birthrates worksheet in a slide in the presentation.

i. Create handouts in Word so the audience can take notes. Link the presentation in case you make changes. T your name as the last line in the file. Save this file as "Bureau Handouts" to your Project Disk.

j. Check the spelling in your presentation, then run the final slide show and evaluate your presentation.

k. Save and print the slides of your presentation.

l. After you have saved the final presentation, go back to Bureau Handouts in Word, update the link, then sav and print the document. (*Hint*: To update the link, use the Links command on the Edit menu.)

m. Close all open applications.

**3.** You have been hired as an associate in the Marketing department at Nomad Ltd., an outdoor sporting gear and adventure travel company. Nomad recently completed a big marketing campaign promoting its bicycle tours, but the company neglected its nonbicycle tours. Sales of the bungee jumping tours especially have fallen off. It is your job to develop a marketing strategy to restore the sales levels of nonbicycle tours. Concerned about the falling sales, the Nomad board of directors has suggested adding rock climbing and jeep tours to the Nomad tour line to broaden Nomad's customer base.

You decide to send a questionnaire to customers who have taken the bungee jumping tour to ask how this tour can be improved. You also decide to create a PowerPoint presentation that suggests advertising strategies for promoting the new tours. You need several charts to show the current nonbicycle tour trends and the potential sales for the new tours.

To complete this independent challenge:

**a.** Start Word and open the file INT C-6 from your Project Disk. Save it as "Cover Letter" to your Project Disk. Add your name to the bottom of the letter. This is the cover letter to the questionnaire.

**b.** Use the Insert Picture command to add the Nomad logo to the top of the letter. The logo is in the file Nomad on your Project Disk. Save and close the file.

**c.** Start Access and open the file Customer Data from your Project Disk. Create a query that lists all of the information about customers who have taken the bungee tour. Save the query as "Bungee Customers."

**d.** Use Mail Merge to merge the cover letter and the Access query you have created. Print the current page.

**e.** Start Excel and open the file INT C-7 from your Project Disk. Save it as "Tour Type" to your Project Disk. This worksheet contains data for road bike, mountain bike, and bungee tour sales. Create two charts on this worksheet: one that compares the sales numbers of the tours and the other that shows the tours as a percentage of all tours. Use drawing tools and color, if appropriate, to point out weak sales. Name this worksheet "Current."

**f.** Copy the data from the Current worksheet to a new worksheet. In the new worksheet, add a formula that calculates an increase in the bungee tour sales numbers by 20%, then show this increase in your charts. Use drawing tools and color, if appropriate, to indicate which figures are speculative. Name this worksheet "Bungee Increase."

**g.** Copy the increased bungee tour sales data to another new worksheet, then add two more rows for the rock climbing and jeep tours. Assume their sales equal the sales of the increased bungee tour sales. Create two more charts to show the new tours. Use drawing tools and color, if appropriate, to indicate which figures are speculative and to point out the new tours. Name this worksheet, "New Tours."

**h.** Add titles to all three charts to identify them. Use drop shadows and other formatting effects to make them more attractive.

**i.** Start PowerPoint and create a new presentation titled "Tour Evaluation" and save it to your Project Disk. This presentation illustrates your marketing ideas to increase sales.

**j.** Create a title slide, then insert the Word outline INT C-8 from your Project Disk after the title slide. Add to the outline your own ideas on how to strengthen bungee tours sales and generate new sales for the new tours. You can suggest additional tours, too.

**k.** Include all of the Excel charts on your slides by using the method you feel is best: pasting, linking, or embedding, or a combination of the three.
Use templates, clip art, animation effects, and any other PowerPoint features you want to create an effective and professional-looking presentation.

**l.** Insert your name as a footer on all sides and handouts, print the presentation as handouts (6 slides per page), then close all open applications.

**Practice**

**4.** Karen Rosen, MediaLoft's human resources director, has asked you to create a PowerPoint presentation profiling MediaLoft employees. She wants to use this presentation at the next manager's meeting to show general information about employees, the average amount of revenue generated per employee, as well as a separate slide for the two most recent employees-of-the-month.

She knows you won't have time to input all the MediaLoft employees but wants you to base the presentation on information for six employees as a sample. Once the presentation looks right, she'll have someone else enter the rest of the employee information.

To complete this independent challenge:

a. Connect to the Internet, go to the MediaLoft intranet site at http://www.course.com/illustrated/MediaLoft, and click the Human Resources link. Use the Personnel Database table there to create a database in Access. Adapt the fields in the database so the table contains fields representing the columns in the employee table. Save the database as "Employee Data" to your Project Disk and name the table "Employee Data." Enter the data for the first six employees.

b. Create a Word outline that contains the text of your presentation, with information that will create at least eight slides. You could create information about employee experience required or why MediaLoft is an attractive place to work. Skim the rest of this independent challenge to get ideas for slides you will need. Save it as "Employee Profile Outline."

c. Insert the outline into a new PowerPoint presentation and save it as "MediaLoft Employees."

d. Export the Employee Data table in Access to Excel to create an Excel worksheet that lists the name, store location, and year-to-date sales of MediaLoft salespeople. Calculate the average year-to-date sales of the employees. Save your changes to the worksheet. Embed the worksheet in the MediaLoft Employees presentation on an appropriate slide. Format the embedded worksheet using Excel formatting tools.

e. In the presentation, create two slides, each one featuring an employee-of-the-month. On the MediaLoft intranet site, there are pictures of the two most recent employees-of-month. Include these pictures in your presentation. To find the photographs, go to the MediaLoft intranet site at http://www.course.com/illustrated/MediaLoft and click the MediaLoft Fun link. Right-click each image, then click Save Image As to save the photos to your disk. Then embed the photos on the appropriate slides. Create a few bullets next to each photo.

f. Insert a table in a presentation slide that shows what percentage of a typical store's employees work in each of the four departments. Use these percentages: Books – 30%, Videos – 25%, CDs – 27%, and Café – 18%. Format the table.

g. Use templates, clip art, transitions, and any other PowerPoint features you want to create an effective and professional-looking presentation.

h. Insert your name as a footer on all slides and handouts, then save and print the presentation as handouts, two per page.

# Creating
## a Web Publication

▶ **Plan Web publication content**
▶ **Create a Web page document**
▶ **Format a Web page**
▶ **Create a Web page from a Word document**
▶ **Create a Web page from an Access table**
▶ **Create a Web page from an Excel workbook**
▶ **Create Web pages from a PowerPoint presentation**
▶ **Add hyperlinks**

Microsoft Office 2000 offers features that help you create your own Web pages from scratch or convert existing Office documents to **Hypertext Markup Language** (**HTML**). HTML is the language used to describe the content and format of Web pages. ✐━━ Karen Rosen is the director of human resources at MediaLoft. Karen wants to create a set of Web pages that she will eventually place, or **publish**, on the MediaLoft intranet to help new MediaLoft employees learn more about employee benefits and programs. Karen will use Office 2000 to create the new Web pages.

**Internet**

# Planning Web Publication Content

It is important to plan your Web pages carefully before creating them. Planning is especially crucial when you are creating a **Web publication**, or a group of associated Web pages focusing on a particular theme or topic. Following a step-by-step process can help you organize tasks logically and also help to ensure that you identify and complete the necessary steps involved. Before she actually begins creating any Web pages, Karen plans their content and organization as well as the tasks involved in preparing them.

In planning her Web pages Karen is careful to:

### Sketch outlines of the pages

Draw a sketch of how you want each page to look, including the links between pages. Karen identifies the documents she wants to include on the intranet, sketches the layout, and adds notes, as shown in Figure B-1.

### For each page, perform the following tasks:

- **Create a new document and enter the page's text, or use the Office 2000 programs to create a Web page from an existing file.**
  You can use a Web page template as a guide to create your Web page. If you want to create a Web page from an existing file, you can use the features in each Office 2000 program to convert the file to HTML for use on the Web. Karen will create a new Web page in Word and then convert several existing Office documents to HTML files.

- **Format page appearance**
  You can use Word to edit any Web page document—even those not created with Word—to apply visual themes and backgrounds and to add images. Karen will use Word's tools to enhance each page's appearance. She also will apply a common visual theme to her pages and insert the MediaLoft company logo at the top of the first page of her Web publication.

- **View pages using a Web browser**
  Confirm that your completed Web page appears as desired by viewing it in your Web browser window. If necessary, you can use Word to make corrections. Karen will view her pages in Internet Explorer to confirm their appearance.

### Format hyperlinks

After finalizing the text and graphics of your Web pages, you can add hyperlinks to connect them. Karen's sketch indicates that she will eventually create links to the MediaLoft home page and the MediaLoft Human Resources page after publishing her pages on the MediaLoft intranet.

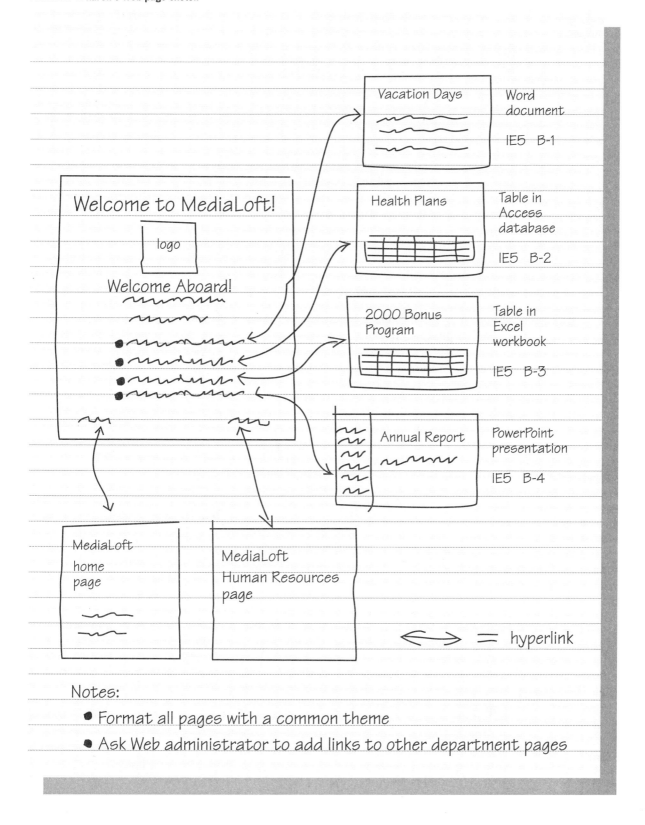

# Unit B
## Internet

# Creating a Web Page Document

To create a Web page, you must prepare a document that uses HTML formatting. HTML places codes, called **tags**, around all the elements in your document that describe how they should appear when viewed using a Web browser. The Microsoft Office Web tools simplify this process by inserting codes for you. Additionally, the Web Pages tab, shown in Figure B-2, in Word includes templates that you can use to create your Web pages, such as a table of contents or a right-aligned column. Karen uses a Web page template in Word to create the basic structure of the MediaLoft Welcome page. When completed, the Welcome page will include links to a description of vacation days, a comparison of health plans, and other links of interest to new MediaLoft employees.

## Steps

**1. Start Word, then make sure the Standard and Formatting toolbars are visible and the Office Assistant is hidden**
You use the Web Pages tab to select a Web page template.

**Trouble?**

If you see a message saying you need to install the feature, insert your Office 2000 CD in the appropriate drive and click OK. See your instructor or technical support person for assistance.

**2. Click File on the menu bar, click New, click the Web Pages tab, then double-click the Simple Layout icon**
A new Web page document based on the Simple Layout template opens in your document window. Note the appearance of placeholder text, which you will delete when you add your own information.

**3. Click Format on the menu bar, then click Theme**
The Theme dialog box opens and displays a list of themes that you can apply to your Web page. When you click a theme in the Choose a Theme list box, its preview appears in the dialog box.

**Trouble?**

If you do not have the Blends theme, or if this theme is not installed, select any other available theme and then continue with Step 5.

**4. In the Choose a Theme list box, click Blends, then click OK**
The Blends theme is applied to your Web page.

**5. Click the Save button 🖫 on the Standard toolbar, in the Save As dialog box click Change Title, in the Set Page Title dialog box type Welcome to MediaLoft!, click OK type Welcome in the File name text box, make sure the location of your Project Disk is displayed in the Save in list box, then click Save**
The file is saved in HTML format with the HTML tags inserted. The Welcome page redisplay

**6. Select the heading Main Heading Goes Here, type Welcome to MediaLoft!, replac the heading Section 1 Heading Goes Here with Welcome Aboard!, then replace t next paragraph with the paragraph shown in Figure B-3**

**Trouble?**

Click the More Buttons button 🔅 to locate buttons that are not visible on your screen.

**7. Press [Enter] twice, click the Bullets button 🗎 on the Formatting toolbar, ty Number of employee vacation days, press [Enter], then repeat this procedure enter the text for the remaining bullets shown in Figure B-3**
To add a bullet, press [Enter] when the insertion point appears at the end of a bulleted li You will add the appropriate text for links to the other MediaLoft pages here; however, y will create the actual links later.

**8. Press [Enter] twice, type MediaLoft home page, press [Enter], then type MediaL Human Resources page**
You have entered all the text for the Welcome page.

**9. Use the mouse pointer to select the next line of text to the end of the page, pr [Delete], then save and close your document**

FIGURE B-2: **Web Pages tab in New dialog box**

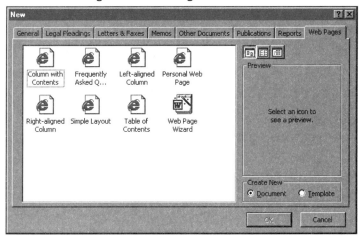

FIGURE B-3: **Text entered for the Welcome page**

Page's filename

Your toolbars may differ

Headings inserted

Text to replace existing paragraph

More Buttons button on Formatting toolbar

More Buttons button on Standard toolbar

Bulleted list

## Choosing Web page content and style

Before finalizing the appearance of your Web publication, analyze other types of Web pages. Their style, layout, and content can suggest new ideas about how to present your information. By viewing a wide variety of pages, you also might learn about Web page formatting features that have only recently become available. Remember, however, that a Web publication expresses your company's or your own identity; include personal touches rather than simply copying other pages.

# Formatting a Web Page

In addition to working with Web pages in Word, you can also create and edit Web documents in **FrontPage Express**, a program specifically designed for Web page production that is included as part of the Internet Explorer 5 suite. Like Word, FrontPage Express includes many tools and templates for creating and editing Web pages. Table B-1 lists some HTML-specific buttons available on the FrontPage Express toolbars. ◄━━━ Although Karen likes the template and visual style she selected for her Web page, she wants to change some of its formatting and add a graphic. She uses FrontPage Express to make these changes.

## Steps

**Trouble?**

If you cannot locate FrontPage Express, ask your instructor or technical support person for assistance.

1. Click the **Start button**, point to **Programs**, point to **Internet Explorer**, then click **FrontPage Express**
   FrontPage Express opens and a blank page appears in the document window.

2. If necessary, maximize the FrontPage Express window

3. Click the **Open button** 📂 on the Standard toolbar, in the Open File dialog box click **Browse**, make sure the location of your Project Disk is displayed in the Look in list box, then double-click **Welcome** in the file list
   The heading should be centered on the page.

4. At the top of the page, click anywhere in the heading **Welcome to MediaLoft!**, then click the **Center button** ▤ on the Formatting toolbar

**QuickTip**

The Change Style list only contains styles compatible with HTML.

5. Click anywhere in the heading **Welcome Aboard!**, click the **Change Style list arrow** on the Formatting toolbar, then click **Heading 2**
   The current heading now reflects the Heading 2 style, as shown in Figure B-4. Next you will insert the logo.

6. Click at the end of the **Welcome to MediaLoft!** line, then press **[Enter]**
   This new centered line will be the location for the MediaLoft logo.

7. Click the **Insert Image button** 🖼 on the Standard toolbar, click **Browse**, make sure the location of your Project Disk is displayed in the Look in list box, click **MLoft** in the file list, then click **Open**
   The MediaLoft logo appears in the blank paragraph, as shown in Figure B-5. Usually, the final step in creating a Web page is to confirm its appearance using your Web browser. However, because your page contains only simple formatting and no advanced elements such as tables, FrontPage Express displays the page exactly as it would appear in your browser window. Therefore, you do not need to open the page in Internet Explorer.

8. Save and close the file, then close FrontPage Express

FIGURE B-4: Headings and list formatted

Insert Image button

Formatted headings

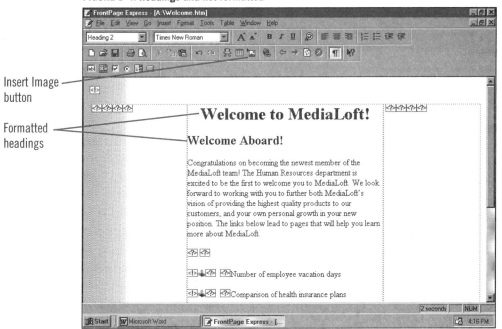

FIGURE B-5: Completed Welcome page

Graphic inserted

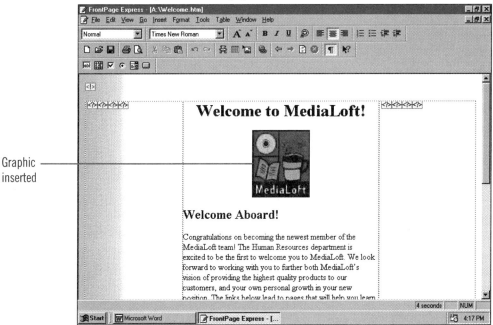

TABLE B-1: FrontPage Express formatting buttons

| button | function |
| --- | --- |
| A˄ | Increases the font size of selected text to the next highest HTML-standard size |
| A˅ | Decreases the font size of selected text to the next lowest HTML-standard size |
| | Displays available text colors and lets you create custom colors |
| | Inserts an automated Web page component, such as a Java script, to perform a task automatically |
| | Refreshes the current page's appearance |
| | Inserts an existing graphic in the active document at the location of the insertion point |

# Creating a Web Page from a Word Document

In addition to offering tools that help you create new Web pages, Office 2000 makes creating Web pages from existing files easy. You can use the Web features in Office to convert files from their Office formats to HTML, which is necessary to make them available on the Web. As noted in her original sketch, Karen wants to create Web pages using several of her existing Office documents. She starts by creating a Web page from a description of company vacation days stored in a Word file.

## Steps

**Trouble?**

If the file IE5 B-1 does not appear in the list of files on your Project Disk in the Open dialog box, change the Files of type list box to display "All Files" or "All Word Documents."

**1.** In Word, open the file **IE5 B-1** from your Project Disk

The file contains a description of the number of vacation days for MediaLoft employees.

**2.** Click **File** on the menu bar, then click **Save as Web Page**

The Save As dialog box opens. In order to save a Web page, you need to specify its filename and page title.

**3.** Click **Change Title**, in the Set Page Title dialog box type **Vacation Days**, click **OK**, in the File name text box type **Vacation**, make sure the location of your Project Disk is displayed in the Save in list box, then click **Save**

Word saves a copy of the document in HTML format and switches to Web Layout view. Now you can change some of the page's formatting.

**Trouble?**

If the Style list arrow or the Center button do not appear on your Formatting toolbar, click the More Buttons button to display additional toolbar buttons.

**4.** Select the heading **Vacation Days**, click the **Style list arrow** on the Formatting toolbar, click **Heading 1**, click the **Center button** on the Formatting toolbar, press **[Ctrl][End]** to move the insertion point to the end of the document, press **[Enter]** then type **Return to Welcome page**

Your Vacation Days Web page should match Figure B-6. "Vacation" appears in the title bar because Word automatically uses the filename as the Web page title instead of the page title that you entered in Step 3. In Internet Explorer, the page's title will appear in the title bar. Next you decide to add a theme to the new page that matches the Welcome page; you will format the "Return to Welcome page" text as a hyperlink later in this unit.

**5.** Click **Format** on the menu bar, click **Theme**, in the Choose a Theme list box click **Blends** (or the style that you selected in the previous lesson), then click **OK**

The Blends theme is applied to the Web page, as shown in Figure B-7. Your complete Vacation Days Web page now matches the appearance of the Welcome page you created.

**6.** Save the Vacation Days Web page, then close it

### Web browsers and Web page appearance

When you use a browser other than Internet Explorer 5, such as Netscape Navigator or Lynx (a text-only browser), remember that the appearance of your Web pages might differ. Depending on your browser's options, you can change settings, such as always using a certain font or selecting a certain window size, that affect the appearance of Web pages. Using common fonts and simple backgrounds is one way to ensure that the appearance of your Web pages is consistent between browsers.

**FIGURE B-6: Vacation Days Web page**

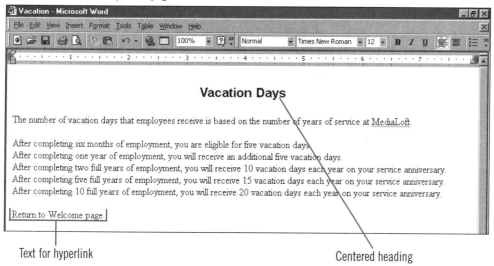

Text for hyperlink                                                    Centered heading

**FIGURE B-7: Completed Vacation Days Web page**

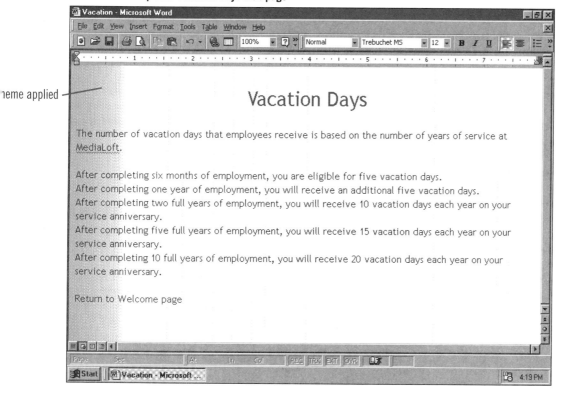

ıeme applied

# Creating a Web Page from an Access Table

Like Word, Access offers a tool for converting existing files to Web pages. You can save each element of a database that you select as a separate HTML file. Then you can use Word to format the HTML file. ✏️ Karen wants to create a Web page that contains a table comparing various health insurance plans available to MediaLoft employees. This information is currently stored in an Access database table.

## Steps

**Trouble?**

If the Office Assistant appears, hide it.

1. **Start Access, open the file IE5 B-2 from your Project Disk, then click Tables on the Objects bar in the IE5 B-2 Database window**
   The Health Plans table is selected automatically. You will export the table to HTML and then edit it using Word.

2. **Click File on the menu bar, then click Export**
   The Export Table 'Health Plans' To dialog box opens, as shown in Figure B-8. You have the option of exporting only the data, in which case you just click Save, or you can export the data and the table format.

3. **Click the Save as type list arrow, click HTML Documents, click the Save formatted check box, then click Save**
   The HTML Output Options dialog box opens. Access needs an existing HTML document on which to base the exported table. You will use the Template file on your Project Disk as an output sample.

4. **Press [Delete] to delete the current text, click Browse, click the file Template on your Project Disk, click OK, then click OK**
   After a few moments, the table is exported.

**Trouble?**

If a dialog box asking if you want to make Word your default Web page editor opens, click No.

5. **Close Access, open the file Health Plans in Word, click Format on the menu bar, click Theme, in the Choose a Theme list box click Blends, then click OK**
   The theme is applied as shown in Figure B-9.

6. **Press [Ctrl][End] to scroll to the bottom of the table, press [Enter], then type Return Welcome page**
   Notice that the fonts used on the page are different. You can select all text and then apply the theme's Normal style to it to make the fonts consistent.

7. **Press [Ctrl][A] to select the entire page, click the Style list arrow on the Formatting toolbar, click Normal, then click anywhere outside the table to deselect it**
   The page appears as shown in Figure B-10; the same font style is applied to all text. Later in this unit you will format the hyperlink text to link to the Welcome page.

8. **Save your changes, then close the file in Word**

### Static and dynamic pages

You can use Access to create static and dynamic Web pages. A **static** HTML page only contains the current information in the table that you are converting. A **dynamic** HTML page, on the other hand, links your Web page to the original database file that you used to create it. When you change the original object in the database, the content of a dynamic page changes to reflect your updates, while the contents of a static page will remain unchanged. Use a dynamic Web page if you expect to change your original Access object often. However, to use this feature, you must locate the database file containing the object on the same file server that contains the dynamic Web page.

FIGURE B-8: Export Table 'Health Plans' To dialog box

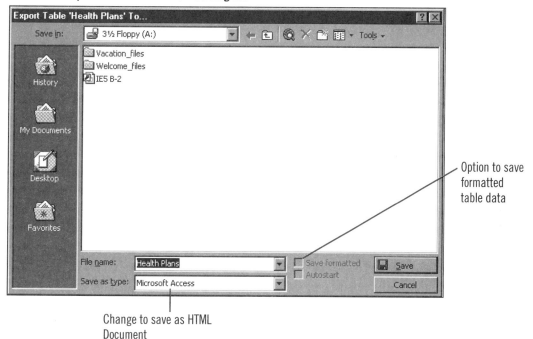

Option to save formatted table data

Change to save as HTML Document

FIGURE B-9: Health Plans Web page in Word

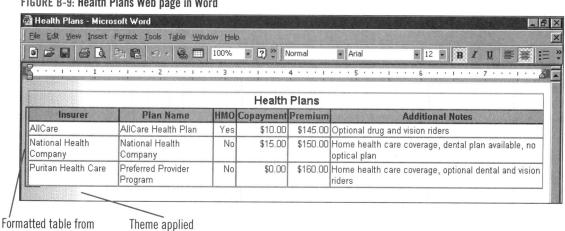

Formatted table from Access database

Theme applied

FIGURE B-10: Completed Health Plans Web page

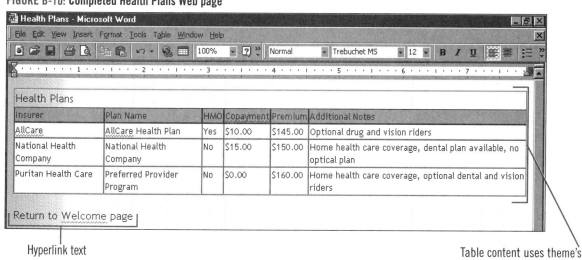

Hyperlink text

Table content uses theme's Normal style

Internet

# Creating a Web Page from an Excel Workbook

Like Word and Access, you can create Web pages using existing Excel files. However, Excel lets you select specific worksheet ranges to use as sources for Web pages, instead of having to include all of the worksheets or cells in an entire workbook. Karen wants to add another Web page to the Welcome publication. Titled 2000 Bonus Program, this page will highlight MediaLoft's bonus program estimates for the year. Karen creates this page from an Excel workbook to show the estimated bonus percentages for employees by quarter and department.

**Trouble?**
If the Office Assistant appears, hide it.

**1.** Start Excel, open the file **IE5 B-3** from your Project Disk, click and drag to select the range **A1:G7**, click **File** on the menu bar, then click **Save as Web Page**
The Save As dialog box opens. As with Access, you use this dialog box in Excel to specify the Web page's filename and title.

**2.** Click the **Selection: $A$1:$G$7 option button** in the Save As dialog box, click **Change Title**, in the Set Title dialog box type **2000 Bonus Program**, click **OK**, in the File name text box type **Bonus**, click **Save**, then close Excel without saving changes to the file IE5 B-3
Now view and edit your new HTML file in Word.

**Trouble?**
If you do not see the Bonus file, click the Files of type list arrow, then click All Files. If the file opens in Excel, close Excel, then repeat Step 3. Make sure you click the Open in Microsoft Word option to open the file correctly.

**3.** In Word, click the **Open button** 📂 on the Standard toolbar, click the **Bonus** file, click the **Open button list arrow** in the Open dialog box, then click **Open in Microsoft Word**
The 2000 Bonus Program Web page opens in Word, as shown in Figure B-11. You will add the theme and then delete the first row of the table because it repeats the page's title. You also will add text at the bottom of the page to use as a hyperlink, and then change the columns so their widths are equal.

**4.** Click **Format** on the menu bar, click **Theme**, in the Choose a Theme list box click **Blends**, then click **OK**

**Trouble?**
If you see Delete Cells on the pop-up menu instead of Delete Rows, click Delete Cells, click the Delete entire row option button, then click OK.

**5.** Select the first row of the table (which contains the repeated heading), right-click the selected row, on the pop-up menu click **Delete Rows**, press **[Ctrl][End]**, press **[Enter]**, then type **Return to Welcome page**

**6.** Select the table, click **Table** on the menu bar, point to **AutoFit**, then click **Distribute Columns Evenly**

**7.** With the table still selected, click the **Style list arrow** on the Formatting toolbar, click **Normal**, then click anywhere outside the table to deselect it
Now the table and the Web page have the same theme and font style as the other pages the Web, as shown in Figure B-12.

**8.** Save your changes, click **Yes** to overwrite the file, then close the file

**9.** Click 📂 in Word, click **Bonus** in the file list, click the **Open button list arrow**, click **Open in Browser**, then view your completed 2000 Bonus Program Web page
The page opens in Internet Explorer, as shown in Figure B-13.

FIGURE B-11: 2000 Bonus Program Web page in Word

File opened in Word

Repeated headings

Table from Excel workbook

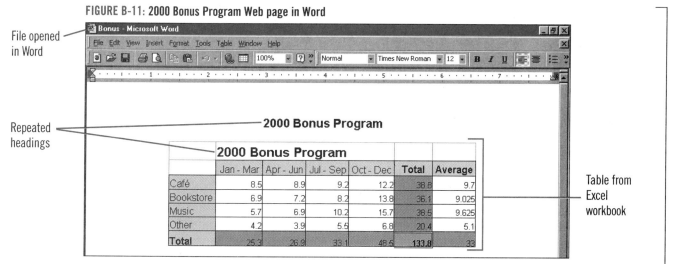

FIGURE B-12: Completed 2000 Bonus Program Web page

Theme applied

One heading

t for erlink

Table after distributing columns evenly and applying Normal style

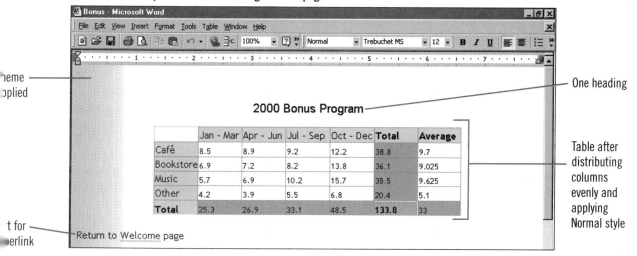

FIGURE B-13: Web page in Internet Explorer

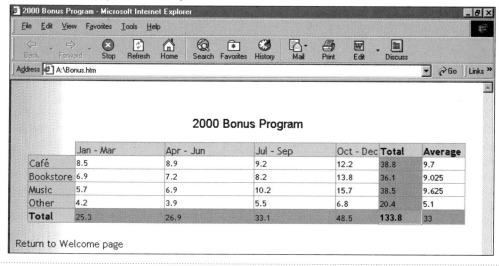

# Creating Web Pages from a PowerPoint Presentation

Unlike other Office files, PowerPoint presentations contain multiple screens of information, called slides. When you convert a PowerPoint presentation to HTML format, PowerPoint creates a separate page for each slide and groups the pages in a folder. When viewing your presentation on the Web, your audience can then navigate through it much like they would in PowerPoint. Karen wants to convert a PowerPoint presentation containing six slides from the company's annual report to HTML format. The presentation outlines the company's recent accomplishments and immediate goals.

**Trouble?**
If the Office Assistant appears, hide it.

**1.** Start PowerPoint, open the file **IE5 B-4** from your Project Disk, then use the slide navigation buttons to view the presentation
The presentation's six slides outline the company's accomplishments and goals.

**Trouble?**
It might take several minutes to save the file.

**2.** Click **File** on the menu bar, click **Save as Web Page**, click **Change Title**, in the Set Page Title dialog box type **Annual Report**, click **OK**, in the File name text box type **Annual**, then click **Save**
Because PowerPoint creates a group of Web pages, you could consider the Web pages based on this presentation as a publication within your publication. PowerPoint exports the current presentation to HTML format. Preview the PowerPoint presentation in your Web browser.

**3.** Click **File** on the menu bar, then click **Web Page Preview**
The presentation opens in Internet Explorer, as shown in Figure B-14. You can click a page title in the left frame to open that page, or click the arrows that appear to the right and left of the "Slide 1 of 6" text at the bottom of the window to view the slides.

**Trouble?**
Click the More Buttons buttons on the Standard and Formatting toolbars to locate buttons that are not visible on your toolbars.

**4.** Click the **PowerPoint program button**, click I at the end of the **1999** line on the title slide, press **[Enter]** twice, click the **Decrease Font Size button** A on the Formatting toolbar three times, then type **Return to Welcome page**
The title page now contains a link back to the Welcome page. Because your PowerPoint Web publication is a group of pages instead of a single page, you must use PowerPoint to create the actual link, whereas in the other Office files you can create all of your links in Word.

**5.** Select the text **Return to Welcome page**, click the **Insert Hyperlink button** on the Standard toolbar, in the Browse for section click **File**, then double-click the **Welcome** file on your Project Disk

**6.** Click **OK** in the Insert Hyperlink dialog box, then save your changes
The hyperlink is now created; you will test the link in the next lesson.

**7.** Click **File** on the menu bar, then click **Web Page Preview** and view your presentation
Internet Explorer displays the first slide from the presentation, as well as navigation tools for the remaining slides in frames, as shown in Figure B-15.

**8.** Close Internet Explorer and PowerPoint

FIGURE B-14: PowerPoint presentation in Internet Explorer

Highlight indicates current slide in main frame

Each presentation slide's title appears in this frame; clicking a slide's title displays the slide in the main frame

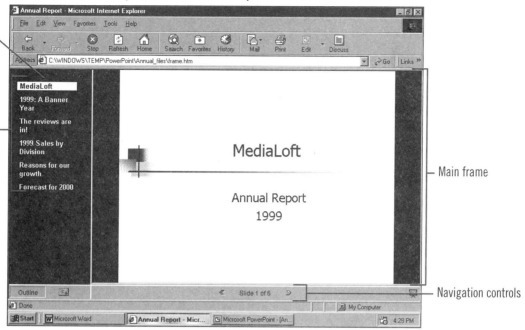

Main frame

Navigation controls

FIGURE B-15: Presentation title slide with hyperlink added

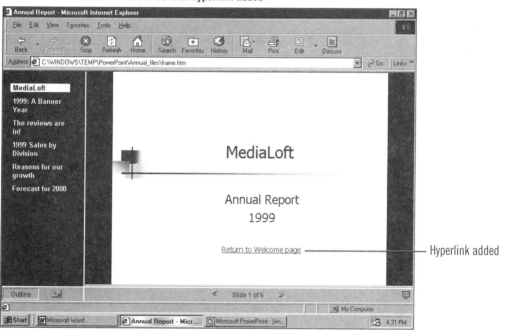

Hyperlink added

## Using frames

rames help you to navigate a group of associated
eb pages. Frame formatting is most useful when
u want to use common navigation elements for all
ges. Although frames are convenient, remember
t not all Web browsers support them. A popular
y to address this problem is to create two versions
a publication—one with frames and one without—
d to offer a choice between the two on the publica-
n's home page. If time or resources limit you to

one version, then base your decision on your audience's capabilities. For example, if you create a page
for a company intranet and know that every computer
has the latest version of a browser installed, adding
frames to your publication makes sense. However, if
you create a page for a Web publication and want the
largest possible audience, choosing frames excludes
some users from viewing your document.

Internet

# Adding Hyperlinks

After you create your page, you need to add hyperlinks both between publication pages and to other Web pages to make it easy for your audience to navigate your pages. You can use hyperlinks to navigate between unpublished documents or published Web pages. ◄─── Karen's sketch shows links from her Welcome page to each associated page as well as a link back to the Welcome page from each associated page. Eventually, she will add the links on the Welcome page to take users to other MediaLoft pages of interest. She starts by adding the links to her Welcome page.

## Steps 1234

**1.** Open the **Welcome** file from your Project Disk in Word, then if necessary, scroll down until you see all of the bulleted items in the document window
Next you create the links to the associated pages using **relative links**, or links that give another page's address in relation to the current page. Once you complete the links, you can publish the pages to the Web in their current directory structure, and the links will remain accurate.

**2.** Select the text to the right of the first bullet, but not the bullet itself, then click the **Insert Hyperlink button** 🔳 on the Standard toolbar
The Insert Hyperlink dialog box opens, as shown in Figure B-16.

**3.** In the Browse for section click **File**, double-click the **Vacation** file on your Project Disk, then click **OK** in the Insert Hyperlink dialog box to close it
The text beside the first bullet changes to underlined text, indicating it is now a hyperlink

**4.** Move the mouse pointer over the hyperlink next to the first bullet
As shown in Figure B-17, the mouse pointer changes to 🖑, indicating that this text is hyperlink. The linked page's path and filename appears above the link. Now you can use th Welcome page to finish the remaining pages.

**5.** Repeat Steps 2 through 3 to create relative links for the remaining lines of bullete text—link the second bullet to the Health Plans file, link the third bullet to the Bonu file, link the fourth bullet to the Annual file, then save the Welcome file
Your final tasks are to add a link to the Welcome page at the bottom of each associated pa and to check all the links you have inserted.

**6.** Click the first bullet character in the list to select it, press **[Delete]** twice, repeat th for each bullet, click **Format** on the menu bar, click **Theme**, in the Choose a Ther list box click **Blends**, click **OK**, then click the **Save button** 🔳 on the Standard toolb Now the bullets and the theme will be displayed correctly in the browser.

**7.** Click the link **Number of employee vacation days**, click the **Edit button** 🔳 in Inter Explorer, select the text **Return to Welcome page** in the Word document that opens, c 🔳, click **File**, double-click **Welcome**, click **OK**, then save and close your document
Now the Vacation Days Web page contains a hyperlink to return to the Welcome page.

**8.** Save your changes, close **Word**, click the **Back button** ⇐ on the Internet Explo toolbar, then repeat Step 7 to add the hyperlink back to the Welcome page on the of your Web pages

**9.** Save the **Welcome** file in Word, use the hyperlinks in your Web site in Inte Explorer to view the pages, then close Internet Explorer and Word
You have successfully created and tested the links between the files in your Web publica

FIGURE B-16: Insert Hyperlink dialog box

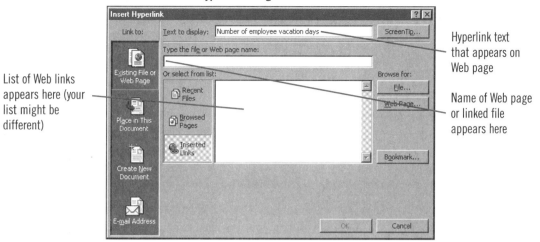

List of Web links appears here (your list might be different)

Hyperlink text that appears on Web page

Name of Web page or linked file appears here

FIGURE B-17: Welcome page with hyperlink added

Mouse pointer over hyperlink

## Publishing your Web pages

Your Web publication is not available to anyone outside your local computer network or workgroup until you publish it, either by placing a copy on the Web or on an intranet server. Remember that links that you create on your home page are one-way: they help users viewing your page to find other interesting pages but do not help locate your page in the first place. Try the following to advertise your Web publication: ask friends and colleagues to create links to your home page on their pages; ask the administrator of your server to add your home page to the index of the site's Web pages; or e-mail information about your publication to groups, organizations, or people with Web sites. To publish effectively on an intranet, send a memo to employees who you think might be interested in your page or ask the network administrator and the owners of other relevant pages to add links to your publication on their pages.

# Practice

## ► Concepts Review

**Label each element of the FrontPage Express window shown in Figure B-18.**

FIGURE B-18

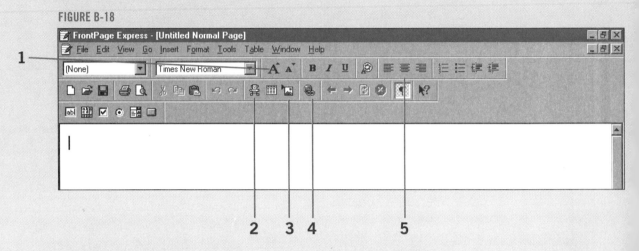

**Match each term with the statement that describes it.**

6. Frames     **a.** Language for describing Web page contents and formats

7. HTML     **b.** Page linked to original database file

8. Home page     **c.** Web page editing tool

9. Dynamic page     **d.** A format that creates borders between screen elements

10. FrontPage Express     **e.** First page of a Web publication

## Select the best answer from the list of choices.

**11. Frames are most useful for**
 **a.** Navigating a group of associated Web pages.
 **b.** Creating hyperlinks.
 **c.** Formatting headings.
 **d.** Creating a home page.

**12. Once you've created Web pages, they become available to users outside your local network only**
 **a.** If you save them on your hard drive.
 **b.** After you format them.
 **c.** If you publish the pages on a Web or intranet server.
 **d.** If you use frames.

**13. The final step in creating a Web publication is**
 **a.** Viewing each page and making final corrections.
 **b.** Formatting hyperlinks.
 **c.** Creating Web pages based on existing files.
 **d.** Creating a home page.

**4. To add a theme to a Web page in Word, you**
 **a.** Click , select the theme, then click OK.
 **b.** Click , select the theme, then click Apply.
 **c.** Click Format on the menu bar, click Theme, select the theme, then click OK.
 **d.** Cannot add a theme to a Web page in Word.

## ▶ Skills Review

**1. Plan Web publication content.**

    **a.** Sketch an outline of a Web publication for the MediaLoft sales department, including a home page, a recent letter sent to past customers, a table of contact information for past customers, a table of the most recent sales figures, and a presentation on MediaLoft's cafe.

    **b.** Draw arrows on your sketch indicating hyperlinks between the pages in your publication.

**2. Create a Web page document.**

    **a.** Start Word.

    **b.** Create a new document using the Table of Contents Web page template. (*Hint*: You may need to install the feature.)

    **c.** Add the Blends theme, then save the document on your Project Disk using the filename "TOC" and the Web page title "MediaLoft Sales Department." (If you don't have this theme, select one that you do have.)

    **d.** Change the main heading to "Sales Information," then change the first section heading to "Company Vision."

    **e.** Replace the paragraph beneath the first section heading with the following text: To provide the highest quality publications possible for our customers.

    **f.** Change the second section heading to: Use these links to access the latest information about MediaLoft.

    **g.** Replace the text under the second section heading with a bulleted list containing the following items: Letter accompanying survey sent to past customers, Customer list, Most recent sales figures, and Café division overview presentation.

    **h.** Change the third section heading to "Research."

    **i.** Add the following bullets under the Research heading: MediaLoft home page and MediaLoft New Employee Orientation.

    **j.** Delete the rest of the text on the page. Save your changes, then close the file.

**3. Format a Web page.**

    **a.** Start FrontPage Express, then open the TOC file from your Project Disk.

    **b.** Apply the Heading 3 style to the "Company Vision" heading, apply the Heading 2 style to the company vision statement, click to the left of the "C" in the line "Company Vision," then press [Enter].

    **c.** Insert the MediaLoft graphic (MLoft.jpg) from your Project Disk on the blank line you created.

    **d.** Save your changes, then close the file and FrontPage Express.

    **e.** Open Internet Explorer, click File on the menu bar, click Open, click Browse, click the TOC file on your Project Disk, click Open, then click OK. Review the appearance of your Web page in the browser window.

**4. Create a Web page from a Word document.**

    **a.** Open the file IE5 B-5 from your Project Disk in Word.

    **b.** Save the file as a Web page with the page title "Customer Survey Letter" and the filename "Survey."

    **c.** Add the Blends theme to the page.

    **d.** Delete the three lines for customer address information and the blank paragraph that follows it, and then delete the text block beginning with "Very truly yours," to the end of the document.

    **e.** Type "Return to MediaLoft home page" at the end of the document.

    **f.** Apply the Heading 2 style to the first line of the document, then center it.

    **g.** Save your changes to the Customer Survey Letter page, then close it.

**5. Create a Web page from an Access table.**

   **a.** Start Access and then open the file IE5 B-6 from your Project Disk.

   **b.** Export the Customers table as a formatted HTML document. Use the filename "Customers", and the Template file as an HTML document output sample.

   **c.** Apply the Blends theme to the page.

   **d.** Scroll to the bottom of the table, then type "Return to MediaLoft home page." Change the text on the page to use the theme's Normal style.

   **e.** Save your changes, close the file, then close Access.

**6. Create a Web page from an Excel workbook.**

   **a.** Start Excel, and then open the file IE5 B-7 from your Project Disk.

   **b.** Click and drag to select the range A1 to H6, then save the selected range as a Web page with the filename "Regions" and the page title "MediaLoft Regions Monthly Sales."

   **c.** Close Excel without saving changes, then open the Regions file in Word. Delete the table's heading (the one without the colored background).

   **d.** Apply the Blends theme to the page.

   **e.** At the end of the document, type "Return to MediaLoft home page."

   **f.** Save your changes, click Yes to overwrite the file, then close the file.

**7. Create Web pages from a PowerPoint presentation.**

   **a.** Start PowerPoint, open the file IE5 B-8 from your Project Disk, then use the slide navigation buttons to page through the presentation quickly.

   **b.** Create a hyperlink to return to the MediaLoft home page on the title slide. The Web address is http://www.course.com/Illustrated/MediaLoft.

   **c.** Save the presentation as a Web page with the title "Eastern Division Report" and the filename "Eastern" on your Project Disk.

   **d.** Preview the presentation in your browser window.

   **e.** Navigate the slides in Internet Explorer, then close the file and PowerPoint.

**8. Add hyperlinks.**

   **a.** In Word, open the file TOC.htm from your Project Disk, then scroll down if necessary so you can see the bulleted lists in the document window.

   **b.** Create hyperlinks for each of the bulleted items in the second section heading to the appropriate Web pages that you created in the previous steps.

   **c.** Create hyperlinks in the documents that you created so the "Return to MediaLoft home page" link opens the Web page with the address http://www.course.com/Illustrated/MediaLoft when clicked. Return to the TOC file, then create a hyperlink using the "MediaLoft New Employee Orientation" link that opens the Employee.htm page on your Project Disk. (*Hint:* If you make a mistake and link the wrong file to a hyperlink, right-click the hyperlink, point to Edit Hyperlink, click Remove Hyperlink, then create the hyperlink again.)

   **d.** Use the procedure you learned in the "Adding Hyperlinks" lesson to reapply the bullets and theme, then save the TOC file.

   **e.** Print the first page of each of your Web pages using the Print button in Internet Explorer, then close Word and Internet Explorer.

# ► Independent Challenges

**1.** You are a volunteer at the Safe Haven Emergency Shelter for families in crisis. Knowing that you have experience creating Web publications, staff members mention that they want to put information about their services and resource requests on the Internet and ask you to create pages for them using existing files for their printed materials.

To complete this independent challenge:

**a.** Sketch the Safe Haven Web publication. In addition to a home page, the publication should include a list of items sought for donation, a table detailing the programs the shelter offers, a chart showing last year's income and expenses, and a presentation summarizing the shelter's recent activities and immediate goals. Be sure to include links between the pages.

**b.** Create a home page for Safe Haven using the Simple Layout template and the Passport theme. (If you do not have this theme, select one that you do have.) Use "Safe Haven Emergency Shelter" as the heading, and create a brief mission statement, or summary of the shelter's function (to help families survive homelessness and domestic violence) to replace the sample paragraph. Create a "More About Us" section heading, and then create appropriate text for links to associated pages on the topics Making Donations, Shelter Programs, Financial Report, and Year in Review. Delete other template text as necessary. Create a third section named "Related Pages," and then create a bulleted list of hyperlinks with the names of national or local organizations whose missions are similar to Safe Haven's. (Search the Web to find organization names if necessary.) Save your home page as "Home" on your Project Disk with the page title "Safe Haven Home Page."

**c.** Create a Web page from the Word file IE5 B-9 from your Project Disk. Save your Web page as "Donations" with a page title of "Safe Haven Donations," and then apply the Passport theme. Change the appearance of the Web page as necessary, and be sure to insert text at the bottom of the page for a link back to the home page. Save your changes, then close the file.

**d.** Create a formatted Web page from the Programs table in the Access database IE5 B-10 from your Project Disk using the Template HTML file on your Project Disk. Apply the Passport theme. Distribute the table's columns evenly and then apply the Normal style (from the theme) to the cells. Add a hyperlink to return to the home page. Save your changes, close the file, then close Access.

**e.** Create a Web page from the range A1:F20 in the Excel workbook IE5 B-11 from your Project Disk. Save the range as a Web page named "Report" and titled "Financial Report." Close Excel without saving changes, and then open the Report file in Word. Apply the Passport theme, and then format the page as necessary so the table is easy to read. Make sure the page has only one heading; delete table rows if necessary. Be sure to insert text for a link to the home page. Save your changes and click Yes to overwrite the existing file. Close the file.

**f.** Create a Web page named "Goals" and titled "Annual Report" from the PowerPoint presentation file IE5 B-12 from your Project Disk. Create a hyperlink on the title slide to return to the home page. Save your changes, and then close the file and PowerPoint.

**g.** Add link addresses to the bulleted list of links on your home page, and then test the links while adding the return links from each of the associated pages. Use the procedure you learned in the "Adding Hyperlinks" lesson to reapply the bullets and theme, then save the Home file. Save your changes, then preview your documents in Internet Explorer.

**h.** Print the first page of each of your Web pages using Internet Explorer, then close Internet Explorer and Word.

**2.** You work in the public relations office at Fox Oil Corporation. Recognizing public concern following recent oil spills by other companies, Fox Oil wants to publicize the steps it is taking to guard against oil-tanker spills. Your supervisor asks you to adapt documents created for print and television ad campaigns to create a Web publication for Fox's Internet site.

To complete this independent challenge:

**a.** Files you will adapt include a press release, a table of Fox's oil-spill prevention programs, a table summarizing recent oil spills by company, and a presentation detailing Fox's oil-spill record and the steps it is taking to ensure that no future spills occur. Sketch how this Web publication should look. Be sure to indicate links between the home page and associated documents.

**b.** Create a home page for the oil-spill publication. Use an appropriate template and theme. Enter text for the home page, format it, then save the file as "Fox Home" with the title "Fox Oil Home Page" on your Project Disk. Include text for a link to the Fox Oil corporate home page, and add the Fox company logo located in the file Fox.jpg on your Project Disk. (*Hint:* To insert the logo in Word, place the insertion point in the correct location, click Insert on the menu bar, point to Picture, click From File, and then open your Project Disk and insert the Fox.jpg file. You might need to resize the logo after inserting it to make it fit. Select the image and then use the resize handles to decrease the image's size.) Save and close the file.

**c.** Convert the Word document IE5 B-13 on your Project Disk to HTML using the filename "Press" and the title "Press Release;" add, delete, and format the text as necessary; apply a theme; and make other necessary changes. Create a hyperlink to return to the Fox home page. Save your changes, then close the file.

**d.** Convert the Prevention Programs table in the Access database IE5 B-14 on your Project Disk to a formatted HTML document using the Template HTML file on your Project Disk. Edit the resulting Web page as necessary, apply a theme, and make other appropriate changes. Create a hyperlink to return to the Fox home page. Save your changes, close the file, and then close Access.

**e.** Convert the table in the Excel spreadsheet IE5 B-15 on your Project Disk to HTML using the filename "Spills" and the title "Oil Spills." Edit the resulting Web page as necessary, apply a theme, and make other appropriate changes. Create a hyperlink to return to the Fox home page. Save your changes, click Yes to overwrite the changes, and then close the file. Close Excel without saving changes.

**f.** Convert the PowerPoint presentation IE5 B-16 on your Project Disk to a set of HTML documents with the filename "Prevention" and the title "Prevention Presentation." Create a hyperlink to return to the Fox home page. Save your changes and then close PowerPoint.

**g.** Format and test the hyperlinks between pages in your Web publication, and then test them in Internet Explorer. If necessary, delete and reapply the bullets on the Fox home page and reapply the theme. Then save the Fox Home file.

**h.** Print the first page of each of your Web pages using Internet Explorer, then close Internet Explorer and Word.

Internet

▶ **Visual Workshop**

You are an employee at the Lakeview Café. The manager wants to post information about the restaurant's specials on the restaurant's Web site. Use the Left-aligned Column Web page template in Word to create the café's specials page shown in Figure B-19. Sketch what a publication for this restaurant should look like, and then create an appropriate home page to accompany the specials page with a link to open it. Create at least two other associated Web pages by creating files in Office programs and then converting them to HTML and formatting them. Finally, add links between your pages. Print the first page of each of your Web pages using Internet Explorer. (*Hint:* The graphic is included in the Web page template.)

**FIGURE B-19**

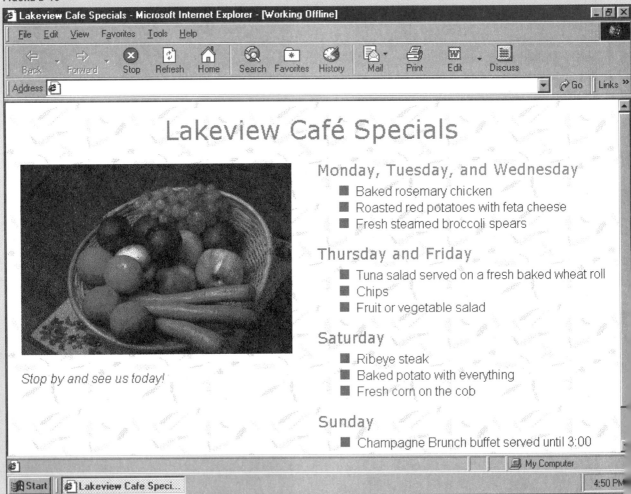

# Getting
## Started with Publisher 2000

### Objectives

► **Define desktop publishing software**
► **Start Publisher and view the Publisher window**
► **Create a publication using a wizard**
► **Replace frame text**
► **Format text**
► **Resize and move frames**
► **Insert a picture**
► **Save, preview, and print a publication**
► **Close a publication and exit Publisher**

Microsoft Publisher 2000 is a desktop publishing program that helps you transform your ideas into visually appealing publications and Web sites. You can use Publisher to create publications and Web sites for your business, organization, or home. In this unit, you will learn how to use a wizard to create a publication that includes text and graphics. Then, you will save and print your publication before closing it and exiting Publisher. ✎ Karen Rosen is the director of human resources at MediaLoft, a nationwide chain of bookstore cafés that sells books, CDs, and videos in eight locations. Karen is planning the MediaLoft company picnic for the San Francisco-based employees. She uses Publisher to create a flyer announcing the event.

**Publisher**

# Defining Desktop Publishing Software

A **desktop publishing program** lets you integrate text, pictures, drawings, tables, and charts in one document using your personal computer. A document created in Publisher is called a **publication**. You can design your publications from scratch, or you can use one of Publisher's wizards to quickly create a publication based on a template. A **template** is a predesigned publication that contains placeholder text and graphics that you can replace with your own text and graphics. **Wizards** walk you through the process of customizing a template by asking you questions about the publication you are creating and replacing the sample text and pictures based on your answers. Figure A-1 shows a publication created with a wizard in Publisher. Table A-1 describes the choices a wizard may ask you to make when creating a new publication. Karen wants her flyer announcing the MediaLoft company picnic to be informative and eye-catching. She knows she wants the flyer to include both text and pictures, so she decides to create it using Publisher.

### Publisher allows you to:

#### Create professionally designed publications
You don't have to be a graphic designer to create powerful and attractive publications quickly and easily with Publisher. Publisher includes more than 1,000 templates for creating newsletters, flyers, calendars, and many other types of publications. Templates include sample text and graphics, a sample layout, and sample color palettes that look great together. You can use a Publisher wizard to walk you through the process of customizing the layout and content of a template.

#### Create a set of publications with a common design
Publisher includes **design sets**, groups of publication templates with the same design theme. For example, you could use a design set to create business cards, letterhead, fax cover sheets, forms, and newsletters for your company.

#### Change your publication's color scheme
Publisher includes more than 50 preset color schemes that you can apply to the publications you create with a wizard. Each color scheme contains five colors that work well together.

#### Insert text and graphics created in other applications and insert clip art
You can insert files created in other programs into your publications. For example, you can insert text from a Word file into a company newsletter. Also you can insert photos, scanned images, or images drawn using Publisher or another drawing program. The Clip Gallery, included with Publisher, contains thousands of pictures, sounds, and motion clips that you can also add to your publications.

#### Arrange text and graphics easily
All elements of a publication are **objects**—text or graphic frames that you can easily move, flip, resize, overlap, or color to control the overall appearance of a publication.

#### Format text
Publisher includes a wide variety of text-formatting options that you can use to enhance the appearance of your publications.

#### Print publications on your own printer or prepare a publication for commercial printing
Publisher's commercial printing technology supports process color, spot color and black and white printing, the four major color models (RGB, HSL, CMYK, and PANTONE), automatic and manual color trapping, and the ability to link graphics to your publication.

#### Publish to the Web
You can create professional-looking Web sites using Publisher's Web Site Wizard. Publisher includes more than 200 Web page backgrounds and more than 300 animated GIF files you can use to add eye-catching motion to your Web site.

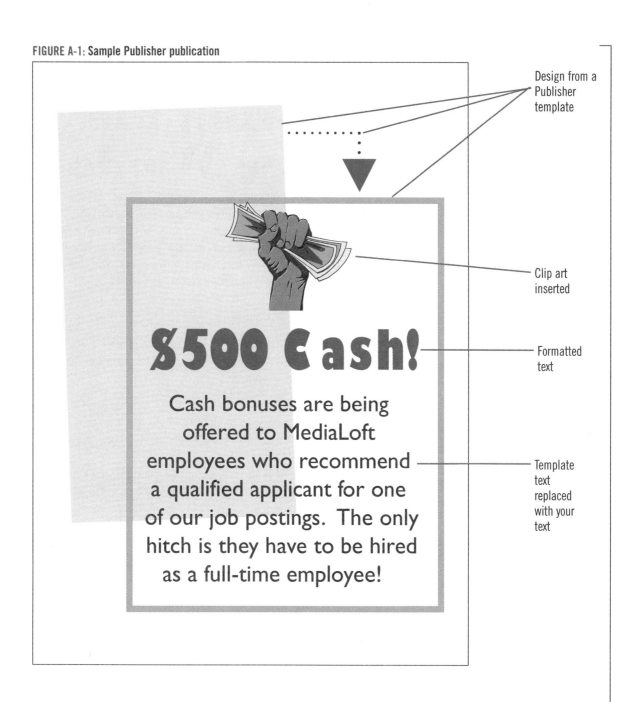

Design from a Publisher template

Clip art inserted

Formatted text

Template text replaced with your text

TABLE A-1: Elements of a publication created with a wizard

| you can choose | to do this, you |
| --- | --- |
| Type of publication | Select a wizard for the type of publication you want to create, such as a newsletter, business card, or catalog |
| Design Style | Select a template with a layout and design that best matches the look and feel you want for your publication |
| Color Scheme | Select the set of coordinated colors you want to appear in your publication |
| Page Size | Select a page orientation for your publication; "portrait" is vertical, and "landscape" is horizontal |
| Layout | Decide how you want the text and graphics to be organized within your publication |
| Personal Information | Select the information you want Publisher to use to replace the placeholder text in your publication; you can also replace placeholder text yourself |

**Publisher**

# Starting Publisher and Viewing the Publisher Window

You start Publisher just as you would start any other Windows application—by using the Start menu. When you start Publisher, the Microsoft Publisher Catalog dialog box opens. You can use this dialog box to select a wizard to create a publication based on a template, or you can choose from a variety of blank publication layouts. You can also close the Catalog dialog box to view the Publisher window. In this lesson, you will familiarize yourself with the elements of the Publisher window. Karen starts Publisher and prepares to create her flyer.

1. Click the **Start button** on the taskbar

**Trouble?**

If the Microsoft Publisher Catalog dialog box does not open, skip Step 3.

2. Point to **Programs** on the Start menu, then click **Microsoft Publisher**
   Publisher and the Microsoft Publisher Catalog dialog box open. You'll learn to use the Catalog dialog box in the next lesson.

3. Click **Exit Catalog**
   A blank one-page publication appears in the publication window, as shown in Figure A-2. The Publisher window includes the following elements:

 The **title bar** contains the name of your publication and the program name. Until you save a publication and give it a name, the temporary name is Unsaved Publication. The title bar also contains the Minimize, Restore, and Close buttons.

 The **menu bar** lists the names of menus that contain Publisher commands. Clicking a menu name displays a list of commands from which you can choose.

 Three **toolbars** appear by default when you start Publisher—the Standard toolbar, the Formatting toolbar, and the Objects toolbar. The **Standard toolbar** includes buttons for the mostly commonly used commands, such as opening, saving, or printing a publication. The **Formatting toolbar** contains buttons for the most frequently used formatting commands, such as changing the font, font size, and font color, applying bold to text, or aligning text. The **Objects toolbar** includes buttons for selecting and creating text and picture frames, as well as buttons for working with other types of objects.

 The **publication window** includes the **publication page** or pages and a **desktop workspace** for storing text and graphics prior to placing them in your publication.

 The **wizard pane** appears to the left of the publication window. It includes options for changing the layout of a publication created with a wizard. You can hide the wizard pane to enlarge the size of the publication window.

 The **vertical and horizontal rulers** help you to size and align text and graphics precisely in your publications.

 The **vertical and horizontal scroll bars** work like scroll bars in any Windows program—you use them to display different parts of your publication in the publication window.

 The **status bar**, located below the publication window, displays the position and size of the selected object in a publication and shows the current page. You can use the **Page Navigation buttons** to jump to a specific page in your publication. You can use the **Object Position indicator** to precisely position an object containing text or graphics and the **Object Size indicator** to accurately gauge the size of an object.

FIGURE A-2: **Blank one-page publication**

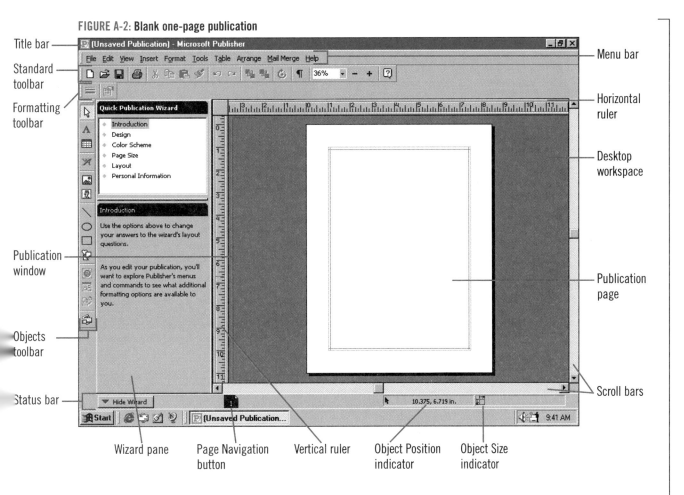

Title bar
Standard toolbar
Formatting toolbar
Publication window
Objects toolbar
Status bar

Menu bar
Horizontal ruler
Desktop workspace
Publication page
Scroll bars

Wizard pane — Page Navigation button — Vertical ruler — Object Position indicator — Object Size indicator

## Getting Help

Publisher includes an extensive Help system that you can use to learn about features and commands. You can get help while working with Publisher by using the Office Assistant, the Help menu, or by logging on to the Microsoft Web site. The Office Assistant, shown in Figure A-3, is an animated character that appears to give tips while you work. To get Help from the Office Assistant, simply click the Office Assistant and then type your question. This unit assumes the Office Assistant is hidden. If the Office Assistant appears on your screen you can hide it by right-clicking the character and then clicking Hide on the pop-up menu. If you've hidden the Office Assistant, press [F1] to ask for help. If you've turned off the Office Assistant, you can access the Help menu by clicking Help on the menu bar and then clicking Microsoft Publisher Help. To access Help online, click Help on the menu bar, then click Microsoft Publisher Web Site. You must be able to connect to the Internet to access the Web site.

FIGURE A-3: **Office Assistant**

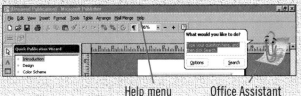

Help menu          Office Assistant

Publisher 2000

**Publisher**

# Creating a Publication Using a Wizard

The easiest way to create a publication that contains text and graphics is to use a wizard to customize a template. A **template** is a model publication designed to be used as the basis of a new publication. Templates contain placeholder text and images that you replace with your own text and images. Publisher's wizards allow you to create professionally designed publications quickly by using templates and asking you questions about the information you want to include in your publication. You enter your answers to the questions in the wizard, and Publisher replaces the text in the template. The wizards are located in the Catalog, which opens when you start Publisher. You can also access the Catalog using the New command on the File menu. ◄▬▬▬ Karen uses a wizard to create her flyer for the company picnic. She picks a template that most closely matches the publication she is planning to create.

## Steps

1. Click **File** on the menu bar, then click **New**

   The Microsoft Publisher Catalog dialog box opens with the Publications by Wizard tab displayed. The left pane of the tab lists the types of publications you can create using the wizard. The right pane shows the templates available for the publication type selected in the left pane.

2. On the Publications by Wizard tab, click **Flyers** in the left pane, then click **Event** in the expanded list of flyer types that appears

3. Scroll down to and click the **Company Picnic Flyer** in the right pane, as shown in Figure A-4, then click **Start Wizard**

   The Company Picnic Flyer template appears in the publication window and an introduction to the Flyer Wizard displays in the wizard pane. You use the Back and Next buttons in the wizard pane to navigate the wizard and begin customizing the design and content of the template.

4. Read the introduction to the Flyer Wizard in the wizard pane, then click **Next** to begin

   The Flyer Wizard Color Scheme list appears in the wizard pane, as shown in Figure A-5. Each color scheme in this list includes five colors that work well together in publications. Click the name of a color scheme in the list to preview the color scheme applied to the current publication. You can change the color scheme of a publication created with a wizard at any time, so feel free to experiment with colors.

5. Click the **Sunrise** color scheme in the wizard pane, then click **Next**

   A question appears in the wizard pane asking you if you'd like to include a placeholder for the customer's address. This publication does not require that information.

6. Click the **No option button** if necessary, then click **Next**

   The wizard asks which personal information set you would like to use for the publication. A **personal information set** includes information about you, your business, or your organization, such as names, addresses, phone numbers, or logos. You enter this information in Publisher. When you create a publication with the wizard, you can choose to automatically replace template text with information stored in a personal information set. You have not created a personal information set for MediaLoft, so you'll skip this question.

7. Click **Finish**

   You have successfully created a publication! The company picnic template appears in the publication window with the options you chose. You can change your answers to any of the wizard's questions at any time by clicking the option you want to change in the top pane of the Flyer Wizard, and then making the correction in the bottom pane of the Flyer Wizard. Your publication will be updated automatically.

8. Click **Hide Wizard** to view more of your workspace

   In the next lesson, you will replace the placeholder text in the flyer with your own text.

**Trouble?**

If a Publisher dialog box opens asking you to enter information about yourself, click OK, then click Cancel in the Personal Information dialog box that appears. See your instructor or technical support person for assistance.

**Trouble?**

If the Next button isn't available, skip to Step 7.

**Trouble?**

If an alert box appears telling you it's time to save, click No. You will learn how to save your publication later in this unit.

**FIGURE A-4:** Microsoft Publisher Catalog dialog box

Publications by Design tab

Left pane lists types of publications

Company Picnic Flyer template

Click to open a saved publication

Blank Publications tab

Right pane displays templates for event flyers

Click to start the wizard

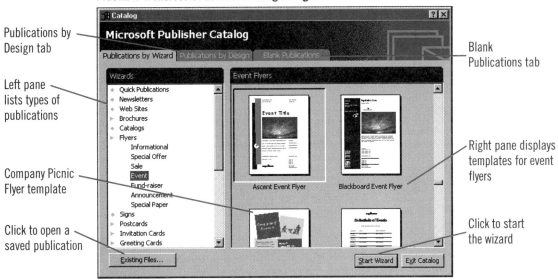

**FIGURE A-5:** Publication Wizard

Flyer Wizard Color Scheme list

unrise color cheme

lick to return the previous uestion

ick to lvance to the xt question

Company picnic flyer template

Click to exit the wizard

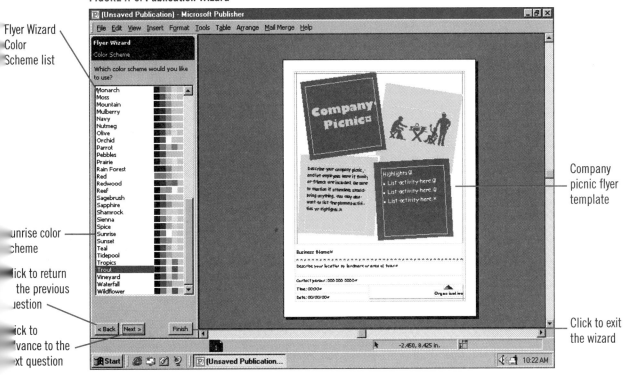

There are three tabs in the Microsoft Publisher Catalog dialog box. The Publications by Wizard tab lists wizards and templates organized by type of publication. You can use this tab to view and select the different templates available for the type of publication you want to create. The Publications by Design tab lists the design sets available in Publisher and includes the templates for each type of publication included in each design set. Use this tab to view and create a set of publications with a common design theme, such as business cards, letterhead, envelopes, business forms, and fax cover sheets. The Blank Publications tab includes different paper sizes and orientations that you can select from to create a publication from scratch. For example, you can select Business Card on the Blank Publications tab to begin a blank publication the size of a standard business card.

**Publisher**

# Replacing Frame Text

Unlike when you use a word processor, you cannot just type text anywhere in a publication. Before you type text, you must create a frame to hold the text. A **frame** is an object that contains text or graphics. Frames can be resized and moved anywhere in your publication. Also, frames can be linked to each other to create an object comprised of several frames. Once you create a frame, you can type text into the frame, or you can insert text from a Word file into a frame. To enter text in a frame or to resize or move it, first you must select the frame. When you click a frame to select it, **handles** (little black squares) appear around the frame to indicate the frame is selected. To select the text in a frame, you must first select the frame. To insert text into a frame, right-click the frame, then choose from the commands on the pop-up menu that appears. Karen is ready to replace the template text with her own text. She types some of the text directly into the frames and inserts text describing the company picnic from a Word file she created last week.

## Steps 1234

**Trouble?**

If an alert box appears telling you it's time to save, click No. You will learn how to save your publication later in this unit.

**1.** Click in the center of the **"Highlights" frame** to select the placeholder text

The bulleted placeholder items are selected and handles appear around the text frame.

**2.** Press **[F9]**

Pressing [F9] zooms in on the selected section of your publication, making it easier to see your work in detail. The [F9] key is a **toggle key**—press it once to zoom in and again to zoom back out. Use the [F9] key as often as necessary in this unit to zoom in and out on your publication.

**3.** Type the following, pressing **[Enter]** after all but the last line:
**Beach Barbecue**
**Volleyball Tournament**
**Swimming**
**Fun in the Sun!**

**QuickTip**

Press [Ctrl][A] to quickly select all the text in a frame.

**4.** Click in the **"Business Name" frame** to select it, select the text **Business Name** then type **MediaLoft Summer 2000 Company Picnic at Stinson Beach!**

**QuickTip**

Type one space between the end of a sentence and the start of a new sentence. Publisher automatically adjusts the space after punctuation.

**5.** Click in the **"Describe your location" frame**, select all the text in the frame if necessary, then type **Directions: Route 101 North to Highway 1. Take Stinson Beach exit—23 miles north of San Francisco.**

**6.** Select **555 555 5555**, then type your name and **x5140**

**7.** Select **00:00**, then type **11 AM to dusk**

**8.** Select **00/00/00**, then type **July 28**

Next, you'll replace the template text with text stored in a Word file.

**9.** Right-click in the yellow **"Describe your company picnic" frame**, point to **Change Text** on the pop-up menu, then click **Text File** on the Change Text menu

The Insert Text dialog box opens. You need to locate and then select the file you plan to insert.

**Trouble?**

If you see a message saying the feature is not installed, insert your Office 2000 Disk 2 CD in the appropriate drive and click Yes. See your instructor or technical support person for assistance.

**10.** In the Insert Text dialog box, locate the files on your Project Disk, click the file **PB A** as shown in Figure A-6, then click **OK**

The placeholder text is replaced with the text from the Word file.

**11.** Press **[F9]** to zoom out, if necessary

Compare your flyer with Figure A-7. In the next lesson, you will format the text you just inserted.

FIGURE A-6: Insert Text dialog box

Location of Project — Disk (yours may differ)

File PB A-1

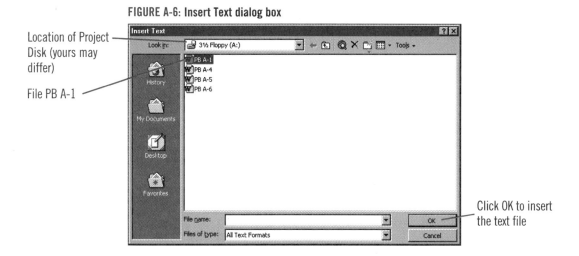

Click OK to insert the text file

FIGURE A-7: Company Picnic flyer with placeholder text replaced

Text inserted from Word

Text you entered

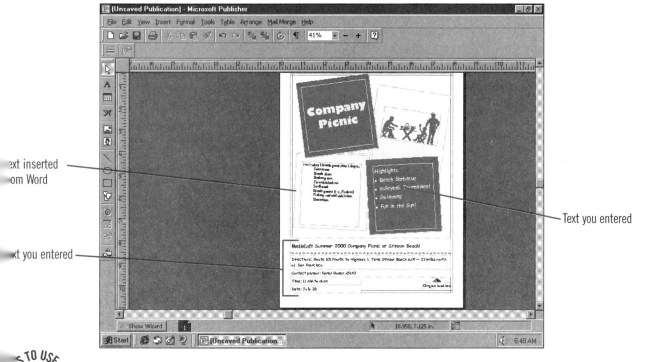

Text you entered

## Creating text frames

f you need additional text frames in your publica-ion, or if you are creating a publication from cratch, you can create a new text frame easily. To reate a text frame, click the Text Frame Tool utton A on the Objects toolbar. The pointer hanges to a crosshair pointer ┼. Position the ointer where you want one corner of the text ame to appear, press and hold the mouse button, en drag diagonally to create a rectangular frame, s shown in Figure A-8. Release the mouse button hen the text frame is the size and shape that you ant. Then you can enter text in the frame by cking in the frame and typing.

FIGURE A-8: Creating a text frame

Text Frame Tool button

Outline of new text frame

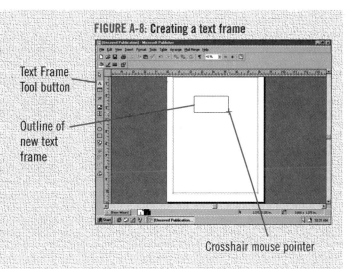

Crosshair mouse pointer

**Publisher**

# Formatting Text

Once you enter text in your publication, you can format it by selecting the text and then apply-ing formatting to enhance its appearance. You can format text using the Formatting toolbar, which includes buttons for changing the **font**, or the design of the set of characters, and the **font size**, or the physical size of the characters measured in points. The Formatting toolbar also includes buttons for boldfacing, italicizing, and underlining text, and for changing text align-ment and text color. Another formatting feature is Autofit. **Autofit** automatically sizes text to fit it in a frame. ✐▬▬ Now that Karen has finished entering text in her flyer, she formats the text to make the flyer more attractive and readable.

## Steps

**Trouble?**

If an alert box appears telling you it's time to save, click No. You will learn how to save your publication later in this unit.

**QuickTip**

It is a good idea to limit the number of fonts you use in a publication to no more than two. Too many fonts can make a publication look cluttered and disjointed.

1. Click in the **"For Friday's beach party" frame** to select it, if necessary
   The font and font size of the text in the selected frame is displayed on the Formatting tool-bar. The font is Times New Roman, and the font size is 12.

2. Press **[Ctrl][A]** to select all the text in the frame, then press **[F9]** to zoom in

3. Click the **Font list arrow** on the Formatting toolbar, scroll down the list of fonts, then click **Comic Sans MS** on the Font drop-down list, as shown in Figure A-9
   The names of the fonts in the Font list are formatted in the font they represent. The font in the selected frame now matches the font in the other text frames.

4. With the text still selected, click the **Increase Font Size button** A on the Formatting toolbar
   Publisher automatically increases the font size of the selected text, but there is now more text than the frame can hold. When there is too much text to fit in a frame, a Text Overflow icon
   A ▪▪▪ appears at the bottom of the text frame. To fix this, you can either reduce the font size of the text, increase the size of the frame, or autofit the text. You decide to experiment with AutoFit.

5. Click **Format** on the menu bar, point to **AutoFit Text**, then click **Best Fit**
   The font size is automatically reduced to 12.5 points and the text now fits in the frame, shown in Figure A-10.

**QuickTip**

Press [Ctrl][B] to quickly bold text after you select it.

6. Scroll down to the bottom of the publication, select **Contact person:**, then click the **Bold button** B on the Formatting toolbar
   The selected text is now boldface, or thicker and darker, and easier to notice.

7. Boldface **Time:** and **Date:** using the instructions in Step 6
   The flyer is looking good. Next, you will learn how to resize and move text frames.

**FIGURE A-9: Choosing a font**

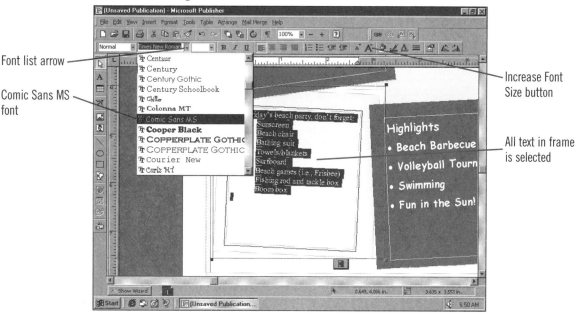

Font list arrow

Comic Sans MS font

Increase Font Size button

All text in frame is selected

**FIGURE A-10: Autofitting text in a frame**

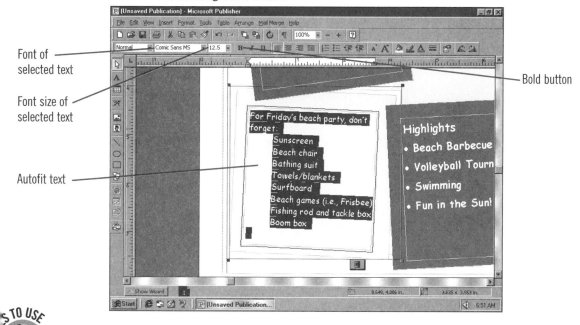

Font of selected text

Font size of selected text

Autofit text

Bold button

## Spell checking your publication

Before you finalize a publication, you should check it for spelling errors. To have Publisher check for spelling errors in your publication, click Tools on the menu bar, point to Spelling, then click Check Spelling. In the Check Spelling dialog box, shown in Figure A-11, you can choose to ignore or change the words Publisher identifies as misspelled. You can also add a word to the dictionary. To check the spelling in every text frame in your publication, make sure the Check all stories check box is selected in the Check Spelling dialog box.

**FIGURE A-11: Check Spelling dialog box**

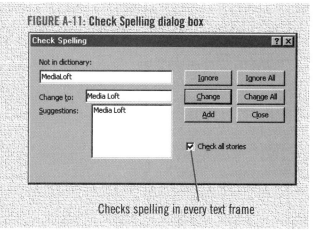

Checks spelling in every text frame

**Publisher**

# Resizing and Moving Frames

In the course of creating a publication, you might find it necessary to resize or move a text frame. For example, you might want to make a frame smaller because there is too much white space, or you might want to move a text frame closer to the graphic it describes. Once you learn how to resize or move a text frame, you can resize and move any Publisher object, such as a picture or a table. To move or resize a frame, you must first select it. To size a frame, you drag a handle. To move a frame, you click anywhere on the frame (except on a handle) and drag the frame to a new location. ◢▬▬ Karen resizes the text frames at the bottom of the flyer to align their right edges. She also decides to move the picture frame up and to the right so that it doesn't overlap the other yellow frame.

## Steps 1234

**Trouble?**

If an alert box appears telling you it's time to save, click No. You will learn how to save your publication later in this unit.

**Trouble?**

If the rulers do not appear, click View on the menu bar, then click Rulers.

**QuickTip**

To change the length and width of a frame at the same time, drag a corner handle. To keep the center of the frame in the same location, press [Ctrl] as you drag.

1. Click the **"Directions" frame** to select it
   Handles appear around the frame.

2. Position the mouse pointer over the middle-right handle
   When you position the mouse pointer over a handle, a Resize pointer ⊕ appears. See Table A-2 for a list of common pointer shapes.

3. Drag the **middle-right handle** to the 5" mark on the horizontal ruler, as shown in Figure A-12
   The text automatically wraps to fill the new frame area.

4. Select the **"Contact person" frame**, then drag the **middle-right handle** to the 5" mark on the horizontal ruler

5. Resize the **"Time"** and **"Date" frames** to align their right edge with the 5" mark on the horizontal ruler

6. Scroll to the top of the flyer and position the mouse pointer over the **picnic graphic** in the yellow frame
   The pointer changes to the Move pointer 🚚. You use this pointer to move any Publisher object. You want to move the frame so that it does not overlap the other yellow frame.

7. Click and drag the **picnic graphic frame** up and to the right slightly until it doesn't touch the other yellow frame, as shown in Figure A-13, then release the mouse button
   Be careful not to drag the frame off the page. If you make a mistake, click the Undo button 🔙 on the Standard toolbar, then try to move the frame again.

8. Press **[F9]** to zoom out and see the entire publication
   In the next lesson, you will replace the placeholder graphics with your own images.

**TABLE A-2: Common Pointer Shapes**

| pointer shape | use to | pointer shape | use to |
|---|---|---|---|
| 🔲 🔲 🔲 ⊕ RESIZE RESIZE RESIZE RESIZE | Resize an object | ✛ | Draw a frame |
| 🚚 MOVE | Move an object to a new location | ✛ CROP | Crop an object |
| ⬁ DRAG | Drag selected text to a new location | 📥 | Insert overflow text |

FIGURE A-12: Resizing a frame

Directions frame

Contact person frame

Time frame

Date frame

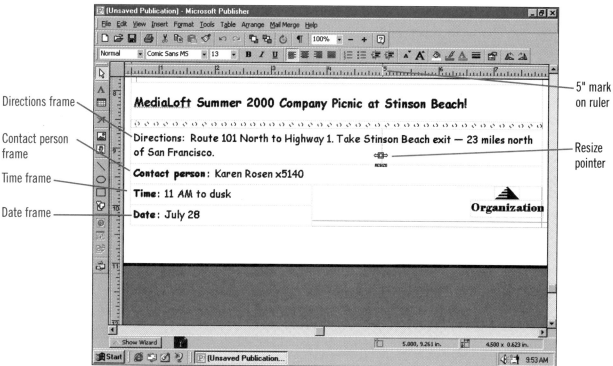

5" mark on ruler

Resize pointer

FIGURE A-13: Moving a frame

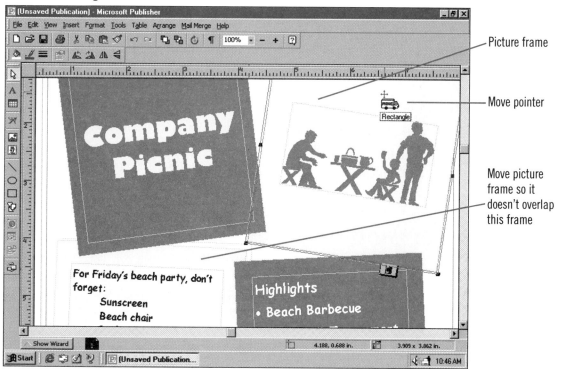

Picture frame

Move pointer

Move picture frame so it doesn't overlap this frame

**Publisher**

# Inserting a Picture

Publications usually include both text and graphics. With Publisher, you can insert many types of graphic images into your publications, including clip art, images created in other applications, such as a logo or a chart, scanned images, or photographs taken with a digital camera. The Microsoft **Clip Gallery** is a library of art, pictures, sounds, video clips, and animations that all Office applications share. You can easily preview and insert images from the Clip Gallery in your publications. Also, you can insert other images that are stored on a disk directly into your publication. See Table A-3 for a list of the picture file formats that Publisher supports.　　　Karen replaces the temporary clip art in her flyer with a photograph from last year's company outing. She also replaces the placeholder logo with the MediaLoft logo.

## Steps

**Trouble?**

If an alert box appears telling you it's time to save, click No. You will learn how to save your publication later in this unit.

1. Right-click the **picnic graphic frame**, point to **Change Picture**, point to **Picture**, then click **From File**

   The Insert Picture dialog box opens. The left pane of the Insert Picture dialog box lists the picture files stored on the current drive or in the current folder. The right pane shows a preview of the selected picture file.

2. Use the **Look in list arrow** to locate the files stored on your Project Disk, click the file **PB A-2**, wait for the preview of the picture to appear in the dialog box, then click **Insert**, as shown in Figure A-14

   A status box telling you that the file is being inserted appears briefly. Then the photo you inserted appears, replacing the temporary graphic image. You can also use a wizard to replace a placeholder picture with your own image.

3. Scroll to the bottom of the flyer, click the **logo placeholder** in the lower-right corner of the flyer, then click the **Wizard button** that appears beneath the logo placeholder when you select it

   The Logo Creation Wizard dialog box opens. You can use the wizard to create a new logo or to modify an existing logo. You'll use the wizard to insert the MediaLoft logo.

4. Click the **Picture file that I already have option button**, then click **Insert Picture**

5. Click the file **PB A-3** in the Insert Picture dialog box, wait for the preview of the image to appear, then click **Insert**

   The MediaLoft logo replaces the placeholder in the flyer.

6. Click the **Close button** in the Logo Creation Wizard dialog box

7. Press **[F9]** to zoom in on the logo if necessary, drag the **upper-left handle** of the logo until it reaches 5" on the horizontal ruler and 8¾" on the vertical ruler, as shown Figure A-15, then release the mouse button

   Congratulations, you have successfully completed the flyer! In the next lesson, you will save and print your publication.

**CLUES TO USE**

### Inserting clip art in a publication

To replace a clip art placeholder in your publication, double-click the placeholder image to open the Clip Gallery. In the Insert ClipArt dialog box, first select the tab for the type of clip art you want—Pictures, Sounds, or Motion Clips. Then, scroll through the images to find the picture you want to include in your publication. Click the picture you want to insert, and then click the Insert Clip button on the Clip Art shortcut toolbar. Click the Close button in the Insert Clip Art dialog box to close it.

**FIGURE A-14: Importing a picture**

Location of Project Disk (yours may differ)

File PB A-2

File name text box

Look in list arrow

Preview of picture

Inserts picture

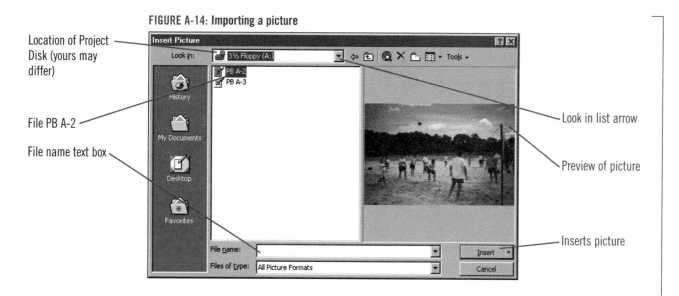

**FIGURE A-15: Resizing MediaLoft's logo**

Logo sized to 8¾" mark on vertical ruler

Resize pointer

Logo sized to 5" mark on horizontal ruler

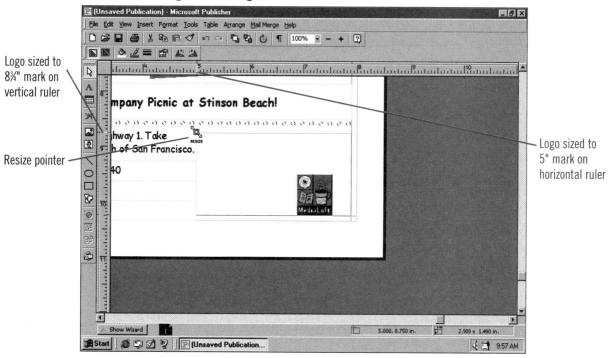

**LE A-3: Image file formats supported by Publisher**

| age file format | extension | image file format | extension |
|---|---|---|---|
| dows Bitmap | .bmp | Kodak Photo CD and Pro Photo CD | .pcd |
| elDraw! | .cdr | PC Paintbrush | .pcx |
| Graphics | .cgm | Macintosh Picture | .pict |
| dows Enhanced Metafile | .emf | Portable Network Graphics | .png |
| psulated PostScript | .eps | Tagged Image File | .tif |
| hics Interchange Format | .gif | Windows Metafile | .wmf |
| Photographics Expert Group | .jpeg or .jpg | WordPerfect Graphics | .wpg |

**Publisher**

# Saving, Previewing, and Printing a Publication

You need to save your work in order to store it permanently on a disk. You should save your work every 10 to 15 minutes and before you print your publication. By default, Publisher automatically reminds you to save your work every 10 minutes. To save a file for the first time, you can use the Save or Save As commands, or the Save button. After you've named the file, you can use the Save command or the Save button to save any new changes to the publication. Once you have saved a publication, you can print it using the Print command. It's a good idea to proof your publications before you print so that you can catch and fix any mistakes. You can proof your publication by changing the zoom level. Karen saves the flyer, checks it for mistakes, and then prints it so she can copy it to distribute to the MediaLoft employees.

**Steps**

**QuickTip**

After you've saved your publication for the first time, click the Save button on the Standard toolbar to quickly save changes to your publication.

1. Click **File** on the menu bar, then click **Save**

   The Save As dialog box opens. You must give the publication its own unique name before you save it to your Project Disk. You'll name the file Picnic.

2. Click the **Save in list arrow**, click the location of your Project Disk, type **Picnic** in the File name text box, compare your dialog box with Figure A-16, then click **Save**

3. Click **No** in the alert box that appears asking if you want to add the MediaLoft logo to your personal information set

4. Click **View** on the menu bar, point to **Zoom**, and then click **Whole Page**

   The zoom level adjusts so that the whole page fits in the publication window. When you change the zoom level, you can select a specific zoom percentage, or a specific view. You can also click the Zoom list arrow on the Standard toolbar to change the zoom level of your publication. After you proof your publication for mistakes, you are ready to print it.

**QuickTip**

Press [Ctrl][P] to quickly access the Print dialog box. Click the Print button on the Standard toolbar to print the publication with the current settings.

5. Click **File** on the menu bar, then click **Print**

   The Print dialog box opens, as shown in Figure A-17. You can use this dialog box to select print options.

6. Make sure the number of copies is **1**, then click **OK**

   Your publication prints in color if you have a color printer, or in black and white if you don't have a color printer. Figure A-18 shows a copy of the completed flyer.

### Using the Pack and Go Wizard

When you want to take your publication to another computer or to a commercial printing service, you can use the **Pack and Go Wizard** to assemble and compress all the files necessary for viewing and printing your publication in a different location. Packing your publication (that is, including the fonts and graphics that you used in your publication) ensures that it will look the same on another computer as it does on yours. If you're packing your publication to disks, Publisher automatically compresses and splits the files so they fit on multiple disks and includes a program to unpack the files on other computers. To use the Pack and Go Wizard, click File on the menu bar, point to Pack and Go, and then click Take to Another Computer or Take to a Commercial Printing Service. Read the Wizard screens and make your selections, clicking Next after each choice. Click Finish when you have answered all of the Wizard questions.

FIGURE A-16: **Save As dialog box**

Location of
Project Disk
(yours may differ)

File name text box

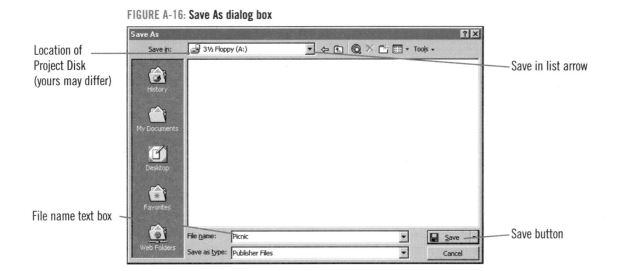

Save in list arrow

Save button

FIGURE A-17: **Print dialog box**

Click to select
how many pages
of the publication
to print

Click to select
additional print
settings

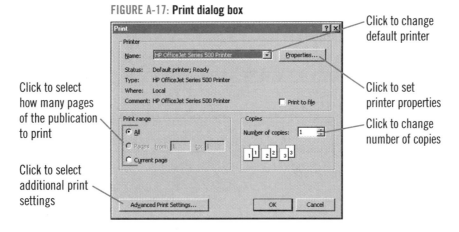

Click to change
default printer

Click to set
printer properties

Click to change
number of copies

FIGURE A-18: **Completed publication**

**Publisher**

# Closing a Publication and Exiting Publisher

When you are finished working on a publication or when you want to create or open another publication, you must close the current publication. In Publisher, you cannot have two publications open at the same time. You close a publication using the Close command on the File menu. When you are finished working with Publisher, you can exit the program using the Exit command on the File menu. ✎ Karen closes the flyer and exits Publisher.

## Steps

1. Click **File** on the menu bar, then click **Close**, as shown in Figure A-19

2. If an alert box appears asking if you want to save changes before closing, click **Yes** to save changes

   The flyer closes and a new, blank publication appears in the workspace along with the Quick Publication Wizard. You can create or open a publication, or you can close the program. You are finished working with Publisher, so you'll exit the program.

**QuickTip**

Click the Close button on the title bar to close the publication and exit Publisher at the same time.

3. Click **File** on the menu bar, then click **Exit**, as shown in Figure A-20

FIGURE A-19: **Closing a publication**

File menu ⎯

Click to close a publication ⎯

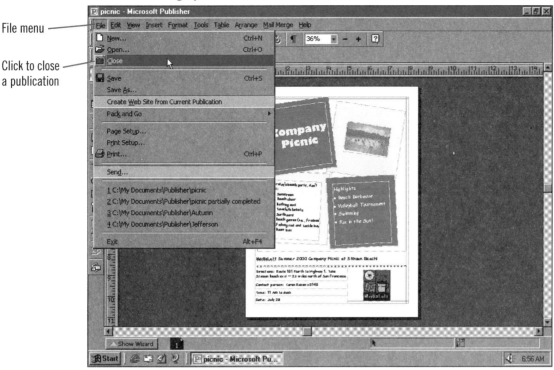

FIGURE A-20: **Exiting Publisher**

Click to close a publication and exit Publisher at the same time

ck to exit
lisher ⎯

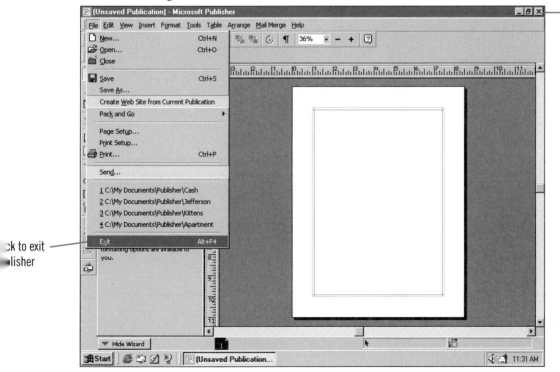

# Practice

## ► Concepts Review

Label each element of the publication window shown in Figure A-21.

FIGURE A-21

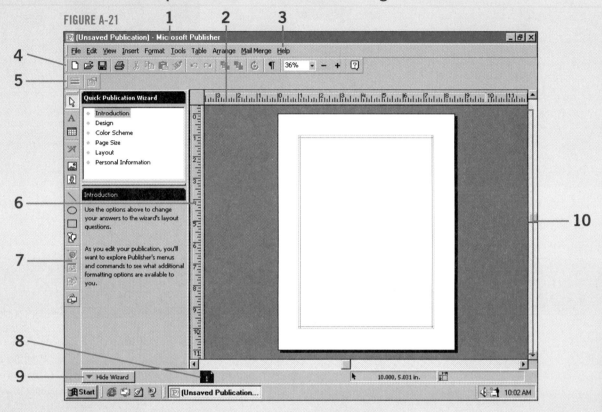

Match each term with the statement that describes it.

11. **Publication**     a. Object that may contain text or graphics and can be moved or resized
12. **Template**        b. Library of art, pictures, sounds, video, and animations that all Office programs shar
13. **Frame**           c. Publication that includes sample text and graphics in an attractive layout
14. **Handles**         d. Document created in Microsoft Publisher
15. **Clip Gallery**    e. Black squares that appear around a frame to indicate it is selected

16. **Which mouse pointer shape would you use to change the size of a frame?**
    a. ⊞
    b. 🖑
    c. ⬉ DRAG
    d. ⬍ RESIZE

17. **Which part of the Microsoft Publisher Catalog dialog box would you use to create a variety of publication all based on a single design set?**
    a. Publications by Wizard tab
    b. Publications by Design tab
    c. Blank Publications tab
    d. Existing Files button

## Skills Review

1. **Start Publisher and view the Publisher window.**
   a. Start Publisher and exit the Catalog.
   b. Identify as many parts of the publication window as you can without referring to the unit material.
2. **Create a publication using the Publication Wizard.**
   a. Open the Microsoft Publisher Catalog.
   b. Select the Apartment for Rent Flyer in the Sale Flyers category.
   c. Start the Wizard, then click Next to begin.
   d. Change the color scheme to a palette of your choice, then click Next.
   e. Click No for the Customer Address, then click Finish.
3. **Replace frame text.**
   a. Type "9/1/00" for the Available date.
   b. Select the "Amount of rent" text frame, press [F9], and then type the following information, pressing [Enter] after each bullet except the last:
   $800/month
   6- or 12-month lease
   $1,600 deposit required at lease signing
   5 rooms (2 bedrooms)
   2 bathrooms
   Great deck overlooks bike path!
   No pets allowed
   Nonsmokers only
   5-minute walk to public transportation and shopping
   c. Select the "Describe your location" text frame, and insert the text file PB A-4 from your Project Disk into the frame.
   d. Select the "Contact person" frame, and replace the frame text with "Call [insert your name] for more information: (781) 555-1000."
   e. Select one of the tear-off "Name" frames at the bottom of the flyer and type your name and the phone number "(781) 555-1000." (*Hint:* Click a frame to select it, then start typing.)
   f. Click another tear-off "Name" frame to automatically update all the identical frames with your new text.
4. **Format text.**
   a. Select the first tear-off "Your Name" frame at the bottom of the flyer, and then press [Ctrl][A] to select all of the text in the frame.
   b. Bold the text in that frame, and then click another "Your Name" frame to automatically format all the identical frames.
   c. Italicize the text in the "Available" frame. (*Hint:* Scroll if necessary to locate the frame.)
   d. Increase the font size of the text in the "$800/month" frame to 20 points.
   e. Change the text color of the "Call Your Name frame" to red. (*Hint:* Use the Font Color button on the Formatting toolbar to choose another color in the scheme.)
   f. Select the "Located in" frame, press [Ctrl][A], and then format the text to autofit, best fit.
**Resize and move frames.**
   a. Select the "Located in" frame if necessary, then drag the right-middle resizing handle to the 4¼" mark on the horizontal ruler.
   b. Select the "Call Your Name" frame, drag the middle-left resizing handle to the 4¼" mark on the horizontal ruler.
   c. Drag the "Call Your Name" frame up to the 7" mark on the vertical ruler to position it next to the "Located in" frame.

**Publisher 2000**

   **d.** Select the "Located in" frame and drag the lower-middle resizing handle down to the 8" mark on the vertical ruler. Notice that the text automatically resizes. Delete the extra line at the end of the paragraph to resize the text again to 11.3 points.

   **e.** Press [F9] to zoom back out and see more of your publication.

**6. Insert a picture.**

   **a.** Double-click the house picture frame at the top of the flyer to open the Insert Clip Art dialog box.

   **b.** Select the last clip in the list and then click the Insert Clip button on the ClipArt shortcut bar. (*Hint:* The ClipArt shortcut bar appears when you select an image. The Insert Clip button is the first button on the shortcut bar.)

   **c.** Close the Insert Clip Art dialog box, then resize the image if necessary.

**7. Save, proof, and print a publication.**

   **a.** Save the publication as "Apartment" to your Project Disk.

   **b.** Switch to Whole Page view to proof your publication and make any last-minute changes.

   **c.** Save your changes, then print your publication.

**8. Close a publication and exit Publisher.**

   **a.** Close the publication.

   **b.** Exit Publisher.

# ▶ Independent Challenges

**1.** Your dog just had puppies and you would like to place them in good homes. You decide to use a Publisher template to create a flyer to post at the local veterinary clinic.

   To complete this independent challenge:

   **a.** Start Publisher, select the Pets Available Flyer template in the Catalog, and respond to the wizard questions.

   **b.** Using Figure A-22 as a guide, replace the placeholder text and format that text.

   **c.** Replace the "Describe" text frame with the text file PB A-5 located on your Project Disk.

**FIGURE A-22**

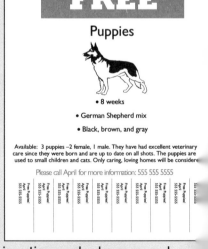

   **d.** Replace the placeholder dog graphic with the German Shepherd dog located in the third row of the ClipArt gallery, and size the picture frame appropriately. Choose a different image if necessary.

   **e.** Replace the name April with your name in the "Please call" text frame and in the tear off "Free Puppies" frames.

   **f.** Save the publication as "Puppies" to your Project Disk.

   **g.** Proof the flyer for mistakes, then print a copy and close the publication.

**2.** You've volunteered to create a home page for your son's elementary school's Web site. After researching other school Web sites for inspiration, you create a home page using a Publisher template.

   To complete this independent challenge:

   **a.** Start Publisher, select the School Web Site template in the Catalog, and then start the wizard.

   **b.** Respond to the wizard questions by accepting Reef as the color scheme, inserting a calendar page, and accepting the defaults for the remaining options.

   **c.** On page 1 of the Web site, replace the text with the text in Table A-4.

   **d.** Resize the "Vision" frame to the 8½" mark on the vertical ruler.

   **e.** Increase the font size for "Vision" and "Mission", apply bold, and change the text color to Teal. (*Hint:* Use the Font Color button.)

**f.** Click the logo placeholder, and use the Logo Creation Wizard to design a Publisher created logo with the open oval design, without a placeholder graphic, and with three lines of text. (*Hint:* Click each option in the top pane of the wizard and select from the choices in the bottom pane.)

TABLE A-4

| Placeholder text frame | Replace with |
| --- | --- |
| Home Page Title | Jefferson Elementary School |
| Business Name | Established in 1969 |
| Your home page…. | Text File PB A-6. (Click No to have Publisher fit the text.) |
| Your business tag line here | Making Education Count! |
| Primary Business Address | Your Name |
| | Jefferson Elementary School |
| | 23 School Street |
| | Waverly, WA 12345 |

**g.** Close the Logo Creation Wizard, and replace "Organization Name Placeholder" with "Jefferson Elementary School." (*Hint:* Increase the zoom level to enlarge the logo.)

**h.** Save the publication as "Jefferson" to your Project Disk. Click No if asked to save the logo to the Primary Business personal information set.

**i.** Proof your publication, and then print and close the publication.

**3.** Create a calendar for next month using a Publisher template.
To complete this independent challenge:

**a.** Start Publisher, select a full-page calendar template from the Catalog, and start the wizard.

**b.** Respond to the wizard questions, being sure to create a monthly calendar and to change the start date to next month. Do not include a schedule of events.

**c.** Replace the placeholder text with text of your own, making sure to include your name in the publication, and then format the text appropriately.

**d.** Customize the logo if a logo placeholder is part of the template. Replace the clip art if a clip art placeholder is part of the template.

**e.** Save the publication as "Calendar" to your Project Disk. Click No if asked to save the logo to the Primary Business personal information set.

**f.** Proof your publication, and then print and close the publication.

**4.** You have just been hired as a designer for MediaLoft in Kansas City. You decide to use a Publisher template to create a business card for your new job. To gather the information you need, you connect to the MediaLoft intranet site. An intranet is a group of connected networks that uses Internet software to handle data communications, such as e-mail and Web pages, within an organization. These pages often provide company-wide information.
To complete this independent challenge:

**a.** Connect to the Internet, go to the MediaLoft intranet site at http://www.course.com/illustrated/MediaLoft, and then click the link for the About page. Write down the address and phone number for MediaLoft Kansas City, then disconnect from the Internet.

**.** Start Publisher, select any business card template in the Catalog, and then accept all the default wizard settings.

**.** Replace the address and phone number placeholder text with the information from the intranet site, and change the fax and e-mail address.

**.** Replace the placeholder text with your name, your title "Designer," and the organization name "MediaLoft."

**.** Replace the placeholder logo with the logo file PB A-3 on your Project Disk.

Use the top and bottom panes of the Business Card Wizard to select a different design and color scheme for your business card. (*Hint:* Click Show Wizard if necessary.)

Save the publication as "Business Card" to your Project Disk, and then print the publication and close it.

# ▶ Visual Workshop

Create a calendar for the month of September 2000 using a Publisher Wizard template. Use Figure A-23 as a guide in creating your calendar. (*Hints*: Start with the Art Left Calendar template. Select and delete the gray shadow frame. Also, type "autumn" in the Search for clips text box to find the appropriate image in the Clip Gallery.) Save the publication as "Autumn" to your Project Disk.

**FIGURE A-23**

## September 2000

| Sun | Mon | Tue | Wed | Thu | Fri | Sat |
|-----|-----|-----|-----|-----|-----|-----|
|     |     |     |     |     | 1   | 2   |
| 3   | 4   | 5   | 6   | 7   | 8   | 9   |
| 10  | 11  | 12  | 13  | 14  | 15  | 16  |
| 17  | 18  | 19  | 20  | 21  | 22  | 23  |
| 24  | 25  | 26  | 27  | 28  | 29  | 30  |

# Getting
## Started with Outlook 2000

### Objectives

► **Understand electronic mail**
► **Start Learning Outlook 2000 E-mail**
► **View the Learning Outlook 2000 E-mail window**
► **Reading and replying to messages**
► **Create and send new messages**
► **Forward messages**
► **Manage your Inbox**
► **Create a Personal Distribution List**
► **Send a message to a Personal Distribution List**

Microsoft Outlook 2000 is an integrated desktop information management program that lets you manage your personal and business information and communicate with others. Using Outlook, you can manage information such as your electronic messages, appointments, contacts, tasks, and files. In this unit, you will focus on the electronic mail features of Outlook. You will work with a program called "Learning Outlook 2000 E-mail," a simulation program specifically designed for use with this book that looks and feels like Outlook. You will be able to use the skills learned in this unit to work with the actual Outlook program. ◢▬▬ Alice Wegman is the marketing manager at MediaLoft, a chain of eight bookstore cafés. MediaLoft sells books, CDs, and videos. Alice will use Learning Outlook 2000 E-mail to communicate with other MediaLoft employees.

# Understanding Electronic Mail

Electronic mail software, popularly known as **e-mail**, is software that lets you send and receive electronic messages over a network. A **network** is a group of computers connected to each other with cables and software. Figure A-1 illustrates how e-mail messages can travel over a network. MediaLoft employees use e-mail because of its speed and ease of use. E-mail is often an effective way to communicate with co-workers or colleagues.

Following are some of the benefits of using e-mail:

### Provides a convenient and efficient way to communicate

You can send messages whenever you wish; the recipients do not have to be at their computers to receive your message. Other users can also send you electronic messages, even if you are not currently running your e-mail program. Any new messages sent to you will be waiting when you start your e-mail program.

### Allows you to send large amounts of information

Your messages can be as long as you wish, so you are not limited to the short time typically allowed on some voice mail systems. You can also attach a file (such as a spreadsheet or word processing document) to a message.

### Lets you communicate with several people at once

You can create your own electronic address book containing the names of the people with whom you frequently communicate. You can then send a message to multiple individuals at one time (without going to the copy machine first).

### Ensures delivery of information

With Outlook, you have the option of receiving a notification message when a recipient receives and reads your e-mail. To receive a notification message, the sender must be on your network and using Outlook.

### Lets you communicate from a remote place

If you have a modem and communications software, you can connect your computer at home to the computers at your office over the phone lines. This gives you the flexibility to send and receive messages when you are not at the office. You can also join a commercial online service and send e-mail to people on the **Internet**, which is a network that connects millions of computer users around the world.

### Provides a record of communications

You can organize your sent and received messages in a way that best suits your work style. Organizing your saved messages lets you keep a record of communications, which can be very valuable in managing a project or business.

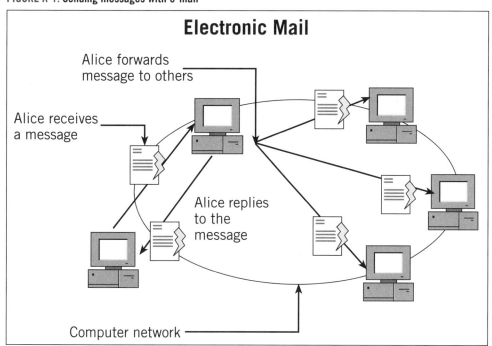

## Electronic mail etiquette

When you compose a message, take extra care in what you say and how you say it. The recipient of your message doesn't have the benefit of seeing your body language or hearing the tone of your voice to interpret what you are saying. For example, using all capital letters in the text of a message is the e-mail equivalent of screaming and is not appropriate. Carefully consider the content of your messages before you send them, and don't send confidential or sensitive material. Remember, once you send a message, you may not be able to prevent it from being delivered. If your e-mail account is a company account, it's a good idea to learn whether your company permits sending personal messages. All messages you send have been legally interpreted as property of the company for which you work, so don't assume that your messages are private.

Outlook 2000

# Starting Learning Outlook 2000 E-mail

Before you can read or send messages, you must start Outlook and enter a secret password. In this lesson and throughout this unit, you will work with the Learning Outlook 2000 E-mail program, which is installed in the Course Programs program group on the Start menu. (If you were using Microsoft Outlook, it would be installed in a different program group.) *You need to complete this unit in one sitting; do not exit Learning Outlook 2000 E-mail until instructed.* Alice needs to start Learning Outlook 2000 E-mail and sign into her mail account using a password.

## Steps

1. **Click the Start button on the taskbar, point to Programs, then point to Course Programs**
See Figure A-2. Note that the actual Microsoft Outlook program would be stored in a different program group on your computer.

2. **Click Learning Outlook 2000 E-mail**
You see a message box describing the Learning Outlook 2000 E-mail simulation program.

> **QuickTip**
>
> Depending on how your e-mail system is set up, you may be required to follow different steps to log into your electronic mailbox.

3. **Click Continue**
The message box describing the Learning Outlook 2000 E-mail simulation program closes and the Learning Outlook 2000 E-mail program starts. The Enter Password dialog box appears as shown in Figure A-3. Alice Wegman is already entered as the user name. The domain name is MEDIALOFT. A **domain** is a collection of computers that the network manager groups together because the computers are used for the same task. The domain name MEDIALOFT is a fictional domain name. If this were your mail account, you would enter mailbox name and domain name provided by your system administrator. On many networks before you can use Outlook, you must enter a secret password identifying yourself.

4. **Click in the Password text box**
Passwords are case sensitive; that is, *PASSWORD* is different from *password*.

> **QuickTip**
>
> To keep your password secret, do not write it down in a visible place, share it with others, or use a familiar or common name. Such passwords are easy for others to guess.

5. **In the Password text box, type any password you wish, using up to 19 characters, then press [Enter]**
Four messages show up at first. After a minute, a total of nine messages appear.

### CLUES TO USE

#### Keeping your password secure

In Learning Outlook 2000 E-mail, you can enter any password you wish using up to 19 characters. If you are on a network using Outlook, however, your system administrator will probably provide you with your own unique and secret password. After you have been assigned a password, you can then change it to one of your own choosing. It is a good idea to change your password every two months to keep it secure. Make sure you choose a password that is easy for you to remember, but difficult for others to guess. As a security benefit, your password does not appear in the Sign In dialog box as you type it. Instead, you see "*" as you type each letter.

**FIGURE A-2: Course Programs program group**

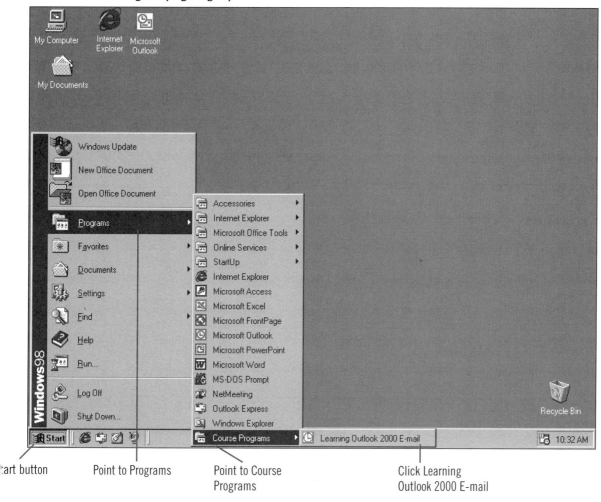

Start button    Point to Programs    Point to Course Programs    Click Learning Outlook 2000 E-mail

**FIGURE A-3: Enter Password dialog box**

Enter your password here which will appear as a series of asterisks

# Viewing the Learning Outlook 2000 E-mail Window

Before you can use Outlook, you need to understand the parts of the Outlook window. Use the list below and Figure A-4 to learn about each part of the window.

## Details

 In the center of Learning Outlook 2000 E-mail window is Alice's **Inbox**, which shows a list of message headers for the e-mail she has received. Each **message header** identifies the sender of the message, the subject, and the date and time the message was received. Message headers of unread messages appear in boldface. By default, Outlook displays the Inbox with a **preview pane**, the lower pane of the Inbox. You use the preview pane to read and scroll through messages without opening them.

 **Message header icons** to the left of the sender's name identify the attributes of the message. For example, an icon that looks like a closed envelope indicates that the message has not been read. See Table A-1 for a description of the icons that appear in the Inbox.

 **Column headings**, above the message headers, identify the sections of the message header.

 On the left side of the Learning Outlook 2000 E-mail window is the **Outlook Bar**. The Outlook Bar contains shortcuts to frequently used folders. The Inbox folder is currently open. To open a different folder, you simply click the folder icon. The Inbox folder contains all the messages other users have sent you. Other folders include the Sent Items, Outbox, and Deleted Items folders. The Sent Items folder contains messages you have sent. The Outbox folder contains messages you have sent, but which Outlook has not yet delivered. The Deleted Items folder contains messages you have deleted.

 At the top of the window, the **title bar** displays the name of the program, Learning Outlook 2000 E-mail. When you are reading messages, the subject of the message appears in the title bar.

 The **menu bar** (as in all Windows programs) contains the names of the menu items. Clicking a menu item on the menu bar displays a list of related commands. For example, you use the commands on the Edit menu to edit the text of your message.

 Under the menu bar, the **toolbar** contains buttons that give you quick access to the most frequently used commands.

 Just below the toolbar, the **folder banner** displays the name of the open folder to the left and the icon of the open folder to the right.

 The **status bar** at the bottom of the window indicates the total number of messages that the open folder contains, as well as the number of those messages that have not been read.

Title bar

Menu bar

Toolbar

Folder banner

Message header

Inbox

Message header icon

Outlook Bar

Preview pane

Status bar

Column heading

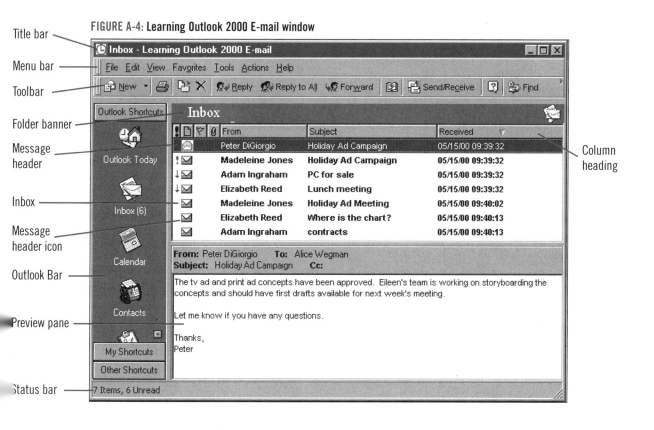

Outlook 2000

TABLE A-1: Message header icons

| on | description |
| --- | --- |
| | High importance message |
| | Low importance message |
| | Unread message |
| | Read message |
| | Forwarded message |
| | Replied to message |
| | Notification of a delivered message |
| | Notification of a read message |
| | Message has an attachment |
| | Message has been flagged for follow up |

# Reading and Replying to Messages

To read a message in your Inbox, you can select it and then preview it in the preview pane, or you can double-click anywhere in the message header to open it in its own window. After reading a message, you can delete it, file it in another folder, or keep it in your Inbox. You can also send a response back to the sender of the message using the Reply button on the toolbar. The Reply command automatically addresses your comments to the original sender and includes the text of the original sender's message. Alice reads a few messages and sends a reply.

## Steps

1. **Click the message containing Lunch meeting in the Subject column to select it, then read the message in the preview pane**
   The message appears in the lower pane of the Inbox, as shown in Figure A-5. Now you can read another message in the Inbox.

2. **Double-click the message from Madeleine Jones containing Holiday Ad Campaign in the Subject column**
   The message appears in the message window. For longer messages, it is sometimes easier to open the message in its own window. You might need to scroll to see the entire message. The yellow **InfoBar** below the message toolbar provides information about the message.

3. **Click the Reply button** 📨 Reply **on the message toolbar**
   A new message window appears in front of the original message window, as shown in Figure A-6, with the blinking insertion point in the message area above a copy of the original message text. The Subject text box contains the same subject as the original message.

4. **Type I prefer the Friday 4:00 time. I am working on an outline of my presentation right now and I'll send a draft to you soon. Because I will be relying on my assistant for a good part of this project, I think he should be at the meeting as well. What do you think?**

5. **Click the Send button** 📧 Send **on the message toolbar**
   The reply message window closes, and the reply is sent to the original sender. The InfoBar in the original message to which you replied now displays text recording the date and time that you replied to this message. See Figure A-7. In addition, Outlook stores a copy of the reply in your Sent Items folder. Messages stay in this folder until you delete them. Next, you will reply to a message that has already been read, which is indicated with an icon that looks like an opened envelope.

6. **Click the Close button** ❎ **in the Holiday Ad Campaign message window**
   The message window closes. In the Inbox, the icon for this message changes from the Unread message icon ✉️ to the Replied to message icon 📬.

7. **Select the Holiday Ad Campaign message from Peter DiGiorgio, then click** 📨 Reply
   You do not need to open a message to reply to it. The message window appears.

8. **Type I am pleased that you are on the Holiday Ad Campaign team. I will let you know if I have any questions.**
   Your reply is entered into the message area.

9. **Click** 📧 Send
   Outlook sends the reply back to the original sender, Peter DiGiorgio, the reply message window closes, and the icon for the original message changes to 📬.

FIGURE A-5: Reading a message in the preview page

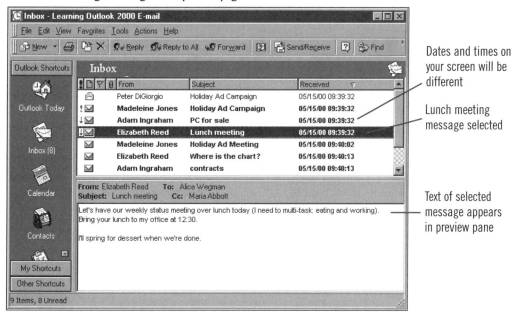

Dates and times on your screen will be different

Lunch meeting message selected

Text of selected message appears in preview pane

FIGURE A-6: Message window for replying to messages

RE: indicates message reply

Enter text of reply here

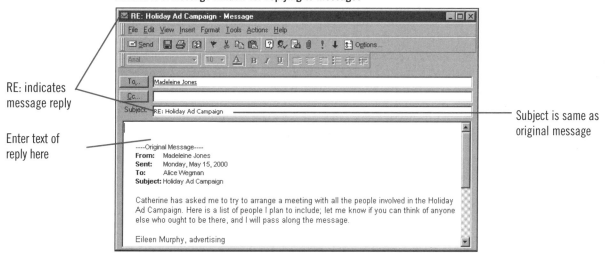

Subject is same as original message

FIGURE A-7: Record of reply in replied to message

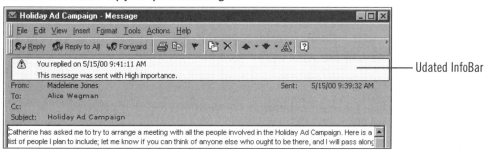

Udated InfoBar

## Emoticons

If you see something like this :-) in an e-mail message, you are looking at an emoticon. **Emoticons** are faces created by simple keyboard characters — in this example the colon, dash, and end parenthesis — to express an emotion or mood. (Turn the page sideways to see the face.) The possibilities are endless and they are a fun way to get your point across.

# Creating and Sending New Messages

A critical facet of using e-mail is being able to create new messages and send them to other users on your network. When you create a message, you must indicate for whom the message is intended and specify any other recipients who should receive a copy. You also need to enter a meaningful subject for the message. Then you write the text of your message and send it. Alice wants to know if her assistant, Peter DiGiorgio, might be able to complete his assignment for the Holiday Ad Campaign earlier than originally planned, so she sends him a message. She decides to send Catherine Favreau, the Director of Advertising, a copy of this message.

1. **Click the New Mail Message button** 🗐 **New on the toolbar**
   The new mail message window appears, as shown in Figure A-8. In this window, you enter address information and compose your message. Although you could type the information directly in the To box, to ensure that you address the message properly, you use the Address Book feature to look up the correct information.

> **QuickTip**
> In the new message window, you can also click the To button or the Cc button to open the Select Names dialog box.

2. **Click the Address Book button** 📖 **on the new message window toolbar**
   The Select Names dialog box opens, as shown in Figure A-9. In this dialog box, you can view the user names of all the users connected to the mail system. These names belong to an **address book** (which is simply a collection of names and e-mail addresses) called the Global Address List. If you are not on a network, the names in this list are from your Contacts list in Outlook.

> **QuickTip**
> In the Select Names dialog box, double-clicking a name is a fast way to enter a name in the To box.

3. **Scroll down and click the name Peter DiGiorgio to select it, then click the To button**
   The name "Peter DiGiorgio" appears in the To box in the Select Names dialog box.

4. **Scroll up and click the name Catherine Favreau, then click the Cc button**
   The name "Catherine Favreau" appears in the Cc box (for courtesy copy).

> **QuickTip**
> To change the way the names in the Address Book in Outlook are sorted, click the Address Book button in the Inbox window, then in the Address Book window, click View on the menu bar, point to Sort By, then click Last Name.

5. **Click OK**
   The Select Names dialog box closes and the new message window appears again.

6. **Click in the Subject text box, then type New deadline**
   The text you type in the Subject box appears in the recipient's Inbox, so that the reader can quickly get an idea of the contents of the message.

7. **Press [Tab], then type There is an important Holiday Ad Campaign meeting Friday and I would like to show our ideas at that time. Let me know what I can do facilitate your work.**
   Pressing [Tab] moves the insertion point from the Subject text box to the message box.

8. **Click the Send button** 📧 Send
   Outlook sends the message.

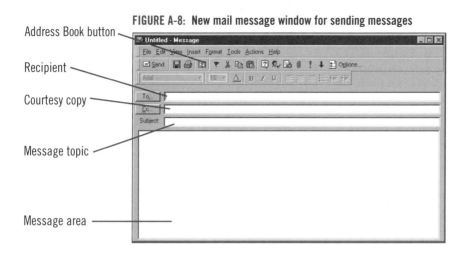

FIGURE A-8: New mail message window for sending messages

Address Book button

Recipient

Courtesy copy

Message topic

Message area

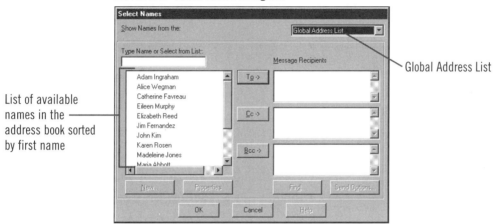

FIGURE A-9: Select Names dialog box

Global Address List

List of available names in the address book sorted by first name

## RULES TO USE

## Options when sending messages

In Outlook, there are several options that affect how messages are delivered. To change these options, click the Options button [Options...] on the message toolbar to display the Message Options dialog box shown in Figure A-10. You can, for example, assign a level of importance and a level of sensitivity so that the reader can prioritize messages. You can also encrypt the message for privacy. When you want to know when a message has been received or read, you can enable the Request a delivery receipt for this message or the Request a read receipt for this message check boxes. Messages you send are automatically saved in the Sent Items folder. To have Outlook delete the messages, disable the Save sent message to check box. Examine the Message options dialog box to familiarize yourself with the other options.

FIGURE A-10: Message Options dialog box

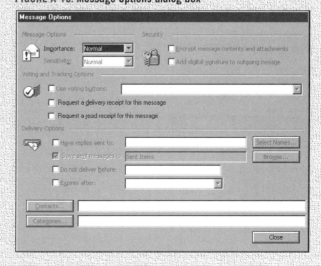

# Forwarding Messages

Messages you receive from others might contain information that would be useful to someone else. With Outlook, you can forward a message to another user. The recipient of the forwarded message can then read and respond to it. Alice has received an agenda for the Holiday Ad Campaign meeting. She would like her assistant, Peter, to attend the meeting and review the agenda before the meeting, so she forwards the message to him.

## Steps 1 2 3 4

1. **In the Inbox window, scroll down and click the message with Agenda in the Subject heading, then click the Forward button** ⬛Forward **on the toolbar**
   The Forward message window appears, as shown in Figure A-11. The subject text box already contains the subject from the original message.

2. **Click the Address Book button** 📖, **then scroll down and double-click the name Peter DiGiorgio**
   The name "Peter DiGiorgio" appears in the To box in the Select Names dialog box.

3. **Click OK**
   You return to the message window. Because the subject is already completed, you continue by composing a brief introduction to the message you are forwarding.

4. **Click in the message area, then type Glad to hear you are making progress. In fact, I think you should attend Friday's meeting. Here is the agenda from Madeleine.**
   If you want to be notified when the recipient has read your message, you need to change this option before you send the message.

5. **Click the Options button** ⬛Options... **on the message toolbar, then click the Request read receipt for this message check box**
   The Tracking option is enabled, as shown in Figure A-12.

6. **Click Close in the Message Options dialog box, then click the Send button** ⬛Send **on the message toolbar**
   The message is forwarded to Peter DiGiorgio. After a few moments you receive a notification that the forwarded message was read. This notification message is called a **read report**.

7. **If necessary scroll down the list of messages in the Inbox window, then double-click the message from Peter DiGiorgio with the subject Read: FW: Agenda**
   The Read message opens, as shown in Figure A-13. The Read message displays the details of the message and when it was read.

8. **Click the Close button** ❎ **on the message window**
   The message window closes.

### Trouble?

If your Inbox window is not maximized you will know that you have received the notification message because the screen will flicker briefly. In Outlook, the default is for new messages to appear at the top of the message list, but in this simulation, they appear at the bottom.

FIGURE A-11: Forward message window

FW indicates the message has been forwarded

Default subject for message

Enter new text here

Text of original message

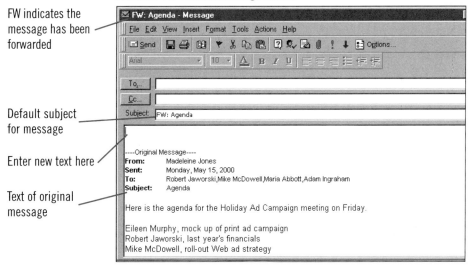

FIGURE A-12: Message Options dialog box

Request a delivery receipt for this message check box

Request a read receipt for this message check box

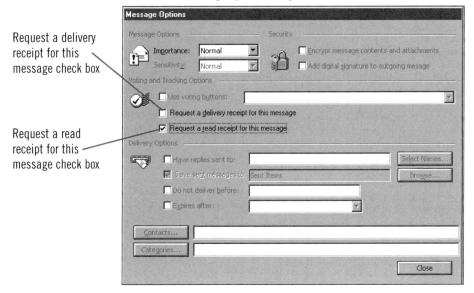

FIGURE A-13: Read Report message

Indicates Read notification message

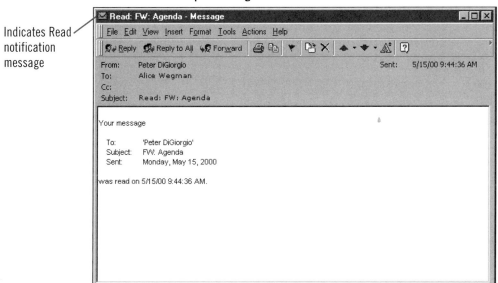

Outlook 2000

# Managing Your Inbox

As you work with Outlook, the messages you receive and read accumulate in your Inbox. To keep track of important messages and prevent the Inbox from becoming too big and inefficient, Outlook offers several options. For example, you can sort messages to quickly identify the messages you need, you can print messages that you need to keep on paper, and you can delete messages you have read and no longer need. Outlook also lets you store messages in other folders, that you create. Currently the messages in the Inbox are sorted by date with the oldest message appearing at the top of the Inbox.  Alice decides to clean up her Inbox by sorting the messages and deleting the messages she no longer needs. She also decides to print a message containing directions to the Holiday Ad campaign meeting.

## Steps

1. Click **View** on the menu bar, point to **Current View**, click **Customize Current View**, then click **Sort**
   The Sort dialog box opens, as shown in Figure A-14.

   > **QuickTip**
   > Clicking a column heading is a fast way to sort messages by a particular heading in the Inbox. Each time you click the column heading, the messages are sorted by that heading in either ascending or descending order.

2. Click the **Sort Items by list arrow**, then scroll up and select **From** in the list of available fields

3. Click **OK**, then click **OK** again
   The messages in the Inbox are sorted alphabetically by the sender's first name

4. Scroll up and click the message that contains **Lunch meeting** in the Subject column, then click the **Delete button** ☒ on the toolbar
   The message is removed from the Inbox and is now stored in the Deleted Items folder. If you accidentally delete a message you intended to retain, you can open the Deleted Items folder and retrieve the message.

5. Click **View** on the menu bar, point to **Current View**, click **Customize Current View**, click **Sort**, select **Received** in the Sort Items by list box, click the **Descending option button**, click **OK** twice, then scroll to the top of the Inbox if necessary
   The newest messages appear at the top of the Inbox and the oldest messages appear at the bottom of the Inbox, as shown in Figure A-15.

6. Scroll down and click the message from Peter DiGiorgio with Holiday Ad campaign in the Subject column, then click ☒
   It is a good idea to permanently delete all unwanted messages from the Deleted Items folder since they take up disk space.

7. Click **Tools** on the menu bar, then click **Empty "Deleted Items" Folder**
   An alert box appears, asking you to confirm that you wish to permanently delete all the items and subfolders in the Deleted Items folder.

8. Click **Yes**
   All the messages in the Deleted Items folder are permanently deleted.

   > **QuickTip**
   > To print with the default settings, click the print button 🖨 on the toolbar.

9. Scroll to the top of the message list, select the **directions to meeting message** the Inbox, click **File**, then click **Print**
   The Print dialog box opens, as shown in Figure A-16. In the actual Microsoft Outlook program, you can specify the number of copies to print and other printing options.

10. Click **OK**
    After you click OK, the dialog box closes and you return to the Inbox. Outlook prints message on your printer.

**FIGURE A-14: Sort dialog box**

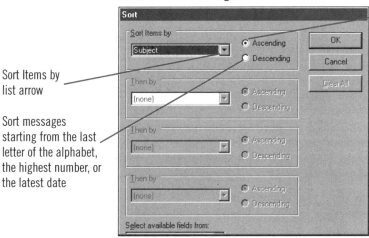

Sort Items by list arrow

Sort messages starting from the last letter of the alphabet, the highest number, or the latest date

Sort messages starting from the first letter of the alphabet, the lowest number, or the earliest date

**FIGURE A-15: Messages sorted by date received**

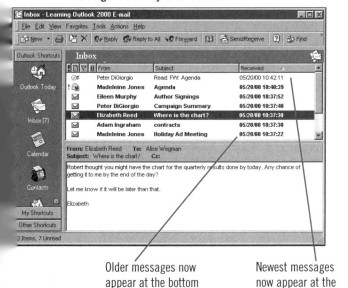

Older messages now appear at the bottom of the list

Newest messages now appear at the top of the list

**FIGURE A-16: Print dialog box**

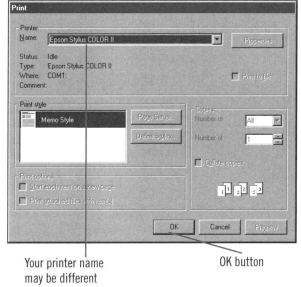

Your printer name may be different

OK button

## Using folders to manage your Inbox

In the actual Outlook program you can use folders to organize your messages. On the File menu, point to New, then click Folder to create a folder to help you organize your messages. The new folder is automatically added to the folder list. To see a list of all available folders, click the folder name in the Folder banner. For example, for easy reference you might want to create a folder called "Technical" to store messages related to system procedures or using your PC. In addition, you can create folders within folders, allowing you to create a hierarchical structure for your Inbox. For instance, the "Technical" folder could contain the additional folders "Network" and "PC" so that you can further categorize your messages, as shown in Figure A-17. After creating a folder, you simply drag (or use the Cut, Copy, and Paste commands) to place messages in the desired folder.

Note that the ability to create folders is not available in the Learning Outlook 2000 E-mail program.

**FIGURE A-17: Folders in Microsoft Outlook**

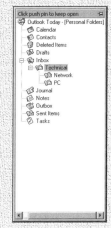

# Creating a Personal Distribution List

When you address a message, you may choose a name from a global distribution list or from the **Contacts folder** in the Outlook Address Book. The contacts folder is your e-mail address book and information storage for the people and businesses you communicate with. If there are many names in the Contacts folder, it can be time consuming to scroll through all the names to select the ones you want. Fortunately, Outlook provides an easy way to manage the user names you use most often. You can create a **Personal Distribution List**, which is a collection of contacts to whom you regularly send the same messages. For example, if you send messages reminding your staff of a weekly meeting, you can create a Personal Distribution List called "Team" that contains the names of your staff. When you want to send a message to everyone on the team, you simply select "Team" from the Select Names dialog box, instead of selecting each user name. Personal Distribution Lists are automatically added to the Contacts folder. ◄▬▬ Alice finds that she regularly sends messages to members of her Holiday Ad Campaign team. She creates a Personal Distribution List containing these names.

1. Click the **Address Book button** 📖 on the toolbar
   The Address Book window opens.

2. Click the **New Entry button** 🖳 on the Address book toolbar
   The New Entry dialog box opens, as shown in Figure A-18. In this dialog box you can select the type of entry you want to make and in which address book the new entry will reside. Currently, there are no Personal Distribution Lists, so you need to create one.

3. Click **New Distribution List** in the Select the entry type box, then click **OK**
   The Untitled Distribution List dialog box opens, as shown in Figure A-19.

4. In the Name text box, type **Holiday Ad**, then click **Select Members**
   Outlook displays the list of names stored in the Global Address list. From this list, you select the names to include in the Holiday Ad distribution list.

5. Click the name **Catherine Favreau**, then press and hold [**Ctrl**] as you click each of the following names: **Eileen Murphy**, **Madeleine Jones** and **Peter DiGiorgio**
   With these names selected, you add them to the list.

### Trouble?
If you accidentally click the wrong name, press and hold [Ctrl], then click the name again to deselect it.

6. Click the **Members button**
   Verify that all four names appear in the Personal Distribution List area of the dialog box, shown in Figure A-20.

7. Click **OK**
   The Holiday Ad dialog box displays the new Holiday Ad distribution list and its members.

8. Click the **Save and Close button** in the Holiday Ad Distribution List window
   Outlook adds the Holiday Ad distribution list to the Personal Address Book in the Contacts folder.

9. Click the **Close button** ☒ in the Address Book window, then click **Contacts** in the Outlook Bar
   The contacts folder is displayed. Notice the name "Holiday Ad" in the left column.

10. Click **Inbox** in the Outlook Bar, then click **OK** in the alert box
    The Inbox folder appears again.

FIGURE A-18: New Entry dialog box

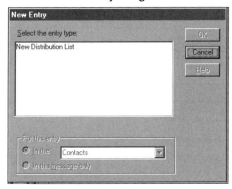

FIGURE A-19: Untitled Distribution List dialog box

Enter a name for
your distribution
list here

Click to add names
to the list

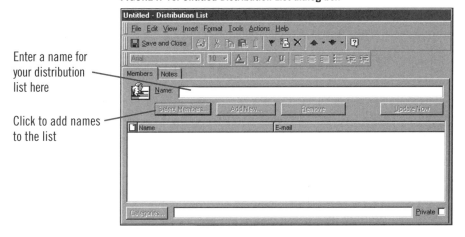

FIGURE A-20: Edit members of Holiday Ad dialog box

All four names
added to
distribution list

OK button

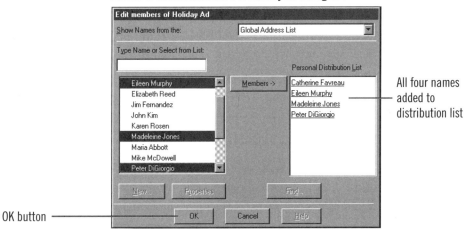

## Adding names to the Contacts folder

In Microsoft Outlook, the names of the people in your Personal Distribution Lists are automatically added to your Contacts folder, so that you can send messages to individual members without necessarily sending them to all the members of the distribution list. You can also add individual names to your Contacts folder without adding them to a distribution list. In the Address Book dialog box, click the New Entry button on the toolbar, and then double-click New Contact and enter the information for that contact. To see the contents of the Contacts folder, select Contacts in the Show names from the list box.

# Sending a Message to a Personal Distribution List

In the same way you can send a message to an individual user, you can send a message to several users at once using a Personal Distribution List. ✒ Now that Alice has created a distribution list consisting of her team members, she can send a single message to all of her team using one easy-to-remember distribution list name.

## Steps

1. Click the **New Mail Message button** 🖅 New on the toolbar
   You want to send a message to all the people on the team.

2. In the new mail message window, click the **Address Book button** 📖 on the message toolbar
   Because you need to send this message to members of a Personal Distribution List, make sure you are in the Contacts folder.

3. Click the **Show Names from the list arrow**, then select **Contacts**
   The Contacts folder is displayed in the Select Names dialog box, as shown in Figure A-21. Outlook displays distribution list names in boldface, with the icon 📇 to the left of the name. If you had any other contacts listed, the names woud not be in boldface.

4. Double-click **Holiday Ad** in the list

5. Click **OK** to return to the new mail message window
   The To box in the new mail message window contains the Holiday Ad distribution list. Now you enter the subject of the message.

6. Click in the **Subject text box**, then type **No team meeting this week**
   After typing the subject of the message, you enter the text.

7. Press [Tab], then type **Because we will all be attending the Holiday Ad Campaign meeting Friday afternoon, we will not have our usual staff meeting at that time. Instead, let's get together to review the project status at 3:00 PM Thursday. Let me know if anyone has a problem with that.**

8. Click the **Send button** 📧 Send on the message toolbar
   Clicking this button sends the message to all the people in the Holiday Ad distribution list.
   *Do not exit Learning Outlook 2000 E-mail, if you plan to complete the Skills Review.*

9. Click **File** on the menu bar, then click **Exit** to exit Learning Outlook 2000 E-mail

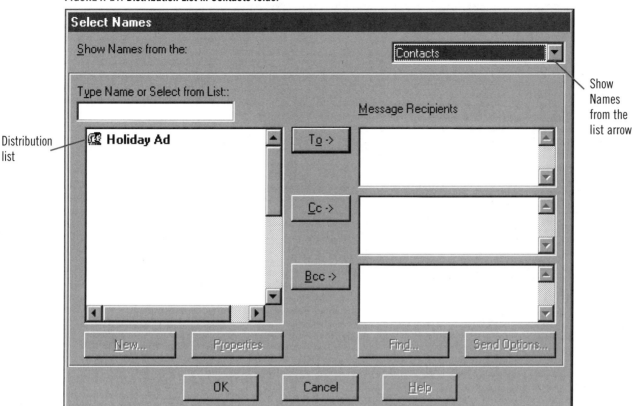

Distribution list

Show Names from the list arrow

Outlook 2000

## What is Microsoft Outlook Express?

Microsoft Outlook Express is a program that you can use to exchange e-mail and join newsgroups. It comes with Windows 98. Because it focuses primarily on e-mail, it is not as robust as Outlook. Outlook comes with Microsoft Office 2000 Professional and Premium Editions. Remember that Outlook is an integrated desktop information manager that combines the Inbox function with a Calendar, Contacts database, Tasks database, and Notes database. (See the Appendix for more information on the additional features of Outlook.) However, once you learn how to use the e-mail capabilities of Outlook, you will be able to apply those skills to Outlook Express. They share many of the same menus and toolbars. For that matter, you can apply the skills you learned in this unit to any other e-mail program.

# Practice

## ▶ Concepts Review

Label the elements of the Learning Outlook 2000 E-mail window shown in Figure A-22.

FIGURE A-22

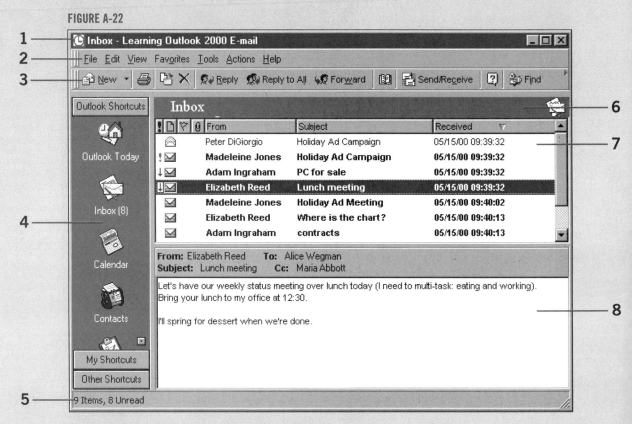

## Match each term with the statement that best describes it.

9. Electronic mail

10. Personal Distribution List

11. Contacts folder

12. Read report

13. Inbox

14. Message Header

a. Stores all of the user names to whom you can send messages

b. A list of users to which you have assigned a name

c. Message you receive when someone reads the message you sent

d. Information sent and received over a computer network

e. Contains all the messages you have received

f. Identifies the sender, subject, and date of the message

Select the best answer from the list of choices.

**15. A group of computers connected to each other with cables and software is called**
   **a.** the Internet.
   **b.** a network.
   **c.** a modem.
   **d.** electronic mail.

**16. Which of the following is the popular abbreviated name for "electronic mail"?**
   **a.** Mail-net
   **b.** Electro-mail
   **c.** Learning Mail
   **d.** E-mail

**17. After signing into Outlook, you see your messages in the**
   **a.** Inbox.
   **b.** Message window.
   **c.** Mail window.
   **d.** Display window.

**18. To read a message, you**
   **a.** Click View, then click Read.
   **b.** Double-click a message.
   **c.** Click the Read button on the toolbar.
   **d.** Click the Inbox folder.

**9. After reading and closing a message**
   **a.** The next message opens so you can read it.
   **b.** You can click the Read button to open the next message.
   **c.** An icon in the message header indicates you have read the message.
   **d.** The message is automatically deleted from the Inbox.

**0. To forward a selected message to another user, you**
   **a.** Click File, then click Forward.
   **b.** Click the Forward button.
   **c.** Click the Send button.
   **d.** Click Tools, then click Forward.

**. To create a new message, you**
   **a.** Click the New Mail Message button.
   **b.** Click the Create button.
   **c.** Click the Mail button.
   **d.** Click the Send button.

**To send the same message to multiple recipients, which of the following is *not* an option?**
   **a.** Drag the message to each of the recipient names
   **b.** In the Select Names dialog box, you can select multiple names from the Contacts folder
   **c.** You can enter multiple names in the To box
   **d.** Create a Personal Distribution List containing the names of the users

## ▶ Skills Review

If you exited from the Learning Outlook 2000 E-mail program before continuing on to this Skills Review, you will need to practice sending and deleting a few messages before you continue. You do not need to perform these steps if you did not exit Learning Outlook 2000 E-mail at the end of the unit.

1. Start Learning Outlook 2000 E-mail.
2. Send three different messages to any three different users.
3. Delete any two messages from any two users.
4. Send one more message to any user.

After a minute or so, the messages described in the Skills Review exercises will begin to appear, so you can continue.

1. **Read and reply to messages.**
   a. Double-click the message containing "contracts" in the Subject column.
   b. Click the Close button in the message window.
   c. Double-click the message containing "Author Signings" in the Subject column.
   d. Click the Reply button on the message toolbar.
   e. Type "Stephen King lives on the East Coast and might be interested. Can't hurt to start big! Let me know how it goes."
   f. Click the Send button on the Reply message toolbar.
   g. Click the Close button in the message window.

2. **Create and send new messages.**
   a. Click the New Mail Message button on the toolbar.
   b. Click the Address Book button on the message toolbar.
   c. Click the name "Peter DiGiorgio" to select it, then click the To button.
   d. Click the name "Elizabeth Reed," then click the Cc button.
   e. Click OK.
   f. Type "New chart" in the Subject text box.
   g. Press [Tab] and type "I think the Results chart for Elizabeth should include a pie chart as well as a bar graph.'
   h. Click the Send button in the message toolbar.

3. **Forward a message.**
   a. In the Inbox window, double-click the message with "Where is the chart?" in the Subject heading, then clic
      the Forward button on the toolbar.
   b. Click the Address Book button, then double-click the name "Peter DiGiorgio."
   c. Click OK.
   d. Click the insertion point in the message area and type "Glad to hear you are making progress on the charts
      am passing along a message from Elizabeth. You can respond directly to her."
   e. Click the Options button, click the Request a read receipt for this message check box, then click close.
   f. Click the Send button in the Forward message toolbar.
   g. Click the Close button in the message window.
   h. Double-click the message from Peter DiGiorgio with the subject "Read: FW: Where is the chart?"
   i. Click the Close button in the message window.

**4. Manage your Inbox.**
- **a.** Click View on the menu bar, point to Current View, click Customize Current View, then click Sort.
- **b.** Click the Sort Items by list arrow, click From, click the Descending option button, then click OK twice.
- **c.** Click the message that contains "Holiday Ad Meeting" in the Subject column and click the Delete button on the toolbar.
- **d.** Click View on the menu bar, point to Current View, click Customize Current View, then click Sort.
- **e.** Click the Sort Items by list arrow, select Importance, click the Descending option button, then click OK twice.
- **f.** Click the message that contains "Agenda" in the Subject column, click File on the menu bar, then click Print.
- **g.** Click OK.

**5. Create a Personal Distribution List.**
- **a.** Click the Address Book button.
- **b.** Click the New Entry button on the Address Book toolbar.
- **c.** Click New Distribution List in the Select the entry type box, then click OK.
- **d.** In the Name box, type Systems Committee, then click Select Members.
- **e.** Click Robert Jaworski, then choose the following names by pressing [Ctrl] as you click each name: Madeleine Jones, Adam Ingraham.
- **f.** Click the Members button.
- **g.** Click OK.
- **h.** Click the Save and Close button on the message toolbar.
- **i.** Click the Close button in the Address Book window.

**6. Send a message to a Personal Distribution List.**
- **a.** Click the New Mail Message button.
- **b.** In the new mail message window, click the Address Book button.
- **c.** Click the Show Names from the list arrow, then click contacts.
- **d.** Double-click "Systems Committee" from the list.
- **e.** Click OK.
- **f.** In the Subject text box, type "Next systems meeting."
- **g.** In the message area, type "At next Thursday's meeting, we will review the proposals from the training companies. Please come prepared to defend your preferences."
- **h.** Click Send.

f you have been assigned Independent Challenge 1, do not exit the Learning Outlook 2000 E-mail program before ontinuing.

# ▶ Independent Challenges

In Order to complete Independent Challenge 1, you must have completed the Skills Review.

**1.** To help you become more comfortable using the Outlook program, you can start the part of the Learning Outlook 2000 E-mail program that is designed to give you the freedom to experiment with Outlook features and procedures. After you complete the Skills Review, you will receive a number of messages at random in your Inbox.
   To complete this independent challenge:

   **a.** Reply to, forward, delete, sort, and print these new messages.
   **b.** Create and send new messages of your own.
   **c.** Explore using the different send options described in this unit.
   **d.** Click File, then click Exit to exit Learning Outlook 2000 E-mail.

**2.** If you have access to Microsoft Outlook 2000 or any other e-mail program, you can apply the skills you've learned in this unit (working with the simulation) to the actual program.
   To complete this independent challenge:

   **a.** Send a message (composed of any text) with a high priority to any user in your Contacts folder.
   **b.** Reply to a message that was sent to you.
   **c.** Forward a message to another user.
   **d.** Delete a message you don't need anymore.
   **e.** Create a Personal Distribution List called "Jokes" that you will use to forward jokes that you receive.
   **f.** Print the high priority message that you sent in Step A. This should now reside in your Sent Items folder.

# Appendix

## Beyond E-mail: Understanding Additional Outlook Features

### Objectives

► **Manage your appointments and tasks**
► **Manage your contacts**
► **Preview your day**

To effectively use Microsoft Outlook 2000 in managing your business and personal information, it is important to know not only how to use the Inbox to send and receive electronic messages, but also how to use the additional components in Outlook. Outlook integrates several tools, including Inbox, Calendar, Contacts, Tasks, Notes, and Outlook Today to provide you with a uniquely comprehensive information manager.

Now that you know how to manage your electronic messages with Inbox, you will learn how Outlook combines e-mail with its other components to create a new class of program: an integrated desktop information manager.

# Managing Your Appointments and Tasks

The Calendar and Tasks tools in Microsoft Outlook provide convenient, effective means to manage your appointments and tasks. **Calendar** is the electronic equivalent of your desk calendar, while **Tasks** is an electronic to-do list. Calendar defines an **appointment** as an activity that does not involve inviting other people or scheduling resources; a **meeting** as an activity you invite people to or reserve resources for; and an **event** as an activity that lasts 24 hours or longer. You can specify the subject and location of the activity, and its start and end times. You can also ensure that you do not forget the activity by having Outlook sound a reminder prior to the start of the activity. Outlook will notify you if the activity conflicts with, or is adjacent to, another scheduled activity. You can view any period of time that you desire in Calendar. For example, you can look at and plan activities for next month or even next year.

## Details

### Review the following features of Calendar and Tasks:

 To schedule your appointments, meetings, and events, open the **Outlook Shortcuts** on the Outlook Bar, click the **Calendar folder**, and then click the **New Appointment button** or the toolbar. See Figure AP-1. To make your screen match the figure, click View on the menu bar, point to CurrentView, click Day/Week/Month, then click the Day button on the toolbar.

 To facilitate planning and scheduling your activities, you can choose to view Calendar by day, week, or month, and you can use the **Date Navigator** to quickly select even nonadjacent days. Dates displayed in boldface on the Date Navigator indicate days on which you have scheduled appointments.

 Use Calendar to schedule a meeting by having Outlook check the availability of all the invitee internally as well as over the Internet. Once you have selected a meeting time and location, you can send invitations in meeting requests. If the invitee accepts the invitation, Outlook will po the meeting automatically to the invitee's calendar.

 Save Calendar as an HTML file to publish it over the Web. It can then be shared over a corpora **intranet** (an internal internet) or over the Internet to aid others in working with your schedul

 To manage your business and personal to-do list, open the **Tasks folder** on the Outlook ba See Figure AP-2.

 Click the **New Task button** to create new tasks. Once you create a task, you can work wi that task in several ways. Click the **Organize button** to organize your tasks by groupi them in **categories** such as ideas or competition. View your tasks in several different wa including by subject, by status, and by due date. You can mark your progress on tasks by p centage complete, and you can have Outlook create status summary reports in e-mail messa and then send the update to anyone on the update list.

 Use the **New Task Request** command on the Actions menu to assign tasks to a co-worker assistant and have Outlook automatically update you on the status of the task completion. help you coordinate your tasks and your appointments, the task list from Tasks is automatic displayed in the **TaskPad** in Calendar. To schedule time to complete a task, simply drag a t from the TaskPad to a time block in the Calendar. Any changes you make to a task are reflec in both the TaskPad in Calendar and the task list in Tasks.

 If you want to quickly write down an idea or a note concerning an appointment or a task, sin open the **Notes folder** on the Outlook bar and click the **New Note button** on the toolbar. Figure AP-3. **Notes** is the electronic version of the popular colored paper sticky notes.

**FIGURE AP-1:** Appointments, meetings, and events displayed in the Calendar window

New Appointment button

Outlook Bar

Calendar folder

Date Navigator

TaskPad

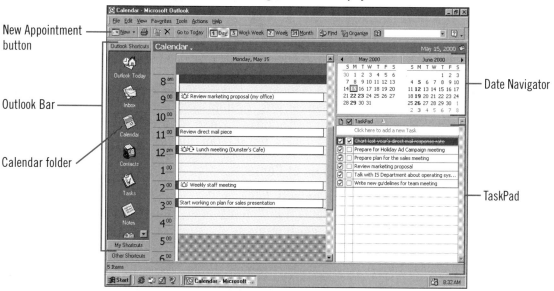

**FIGURE AP-2:** Tasks list displayed in the Tasks window

New Task button

Organize button

Tasks organized by category

Tasks folder

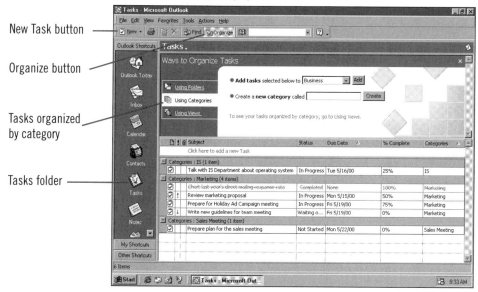

**FIGURE AP-3:** Notes displayed in the Notes window

New Note button

Notes folder

Outlook 2000

# Managing Your Contacts

The **Contacts** tool in Microsoft Outlook enables you to manage all your business and personal contact information. With Contacts, you can store each contact's general information such as full name, company, job title, as well as up to three street addresses, three e-mail addresses, and more than a dozen telephone numbers. You also can store each contact's Web page address.

### Review the following features of Contacts:

 To open Contacts, click the **Contacts folder** in the Outlook group on the Outlook Bar. See Figure AP-4. Click the **New Contact button** 📧 on the toolbar to enter new contact information and to begin using the Contacts features.

 Click the **Full Name button** to enter the full name for the contact, including title, first name, middle name, last name, and suffix if appropriate. See Figure AP-5. You can easily sort and group your contacts by any part of their names.

 Click the **Address button** to enter an address for a contact. The address can include the street, city, state/province, postal code, and country/region. Click the **Details tab** to store each contact's detailed information, including the department or office in which he or she works, the assistant's or manager's name, the contact's birthday, anniversary, or even the contact's nickname. In addition to facilitate finding a contact quickly, Outlook allows you to file each contact under any name that you choose, including under a first name, a last name, a company name, or any word such as "architect" or "caterer." Outlook will automatically present you with several naming options under which to file each contact, but you are free to choose any word you like. Once you have entered your contacts' information, you can view your contacts in a variety of ways, including as detailed address cards, as a phone list, or by company, category, or location.

 If you have a modem, use automatic dialing to quickly dial a contact telephone number. Click the **Dial button** 📞 on the Contacts toolbar, select a contact, click **Start Call**, click **Dialing Options**, click **Line Properties**, then select the modem and connections options you want on the General, Connections and Options tabs. After Outlook has dialed the phone number, pick up the phone handset and click **Talk.**

 Keep track of all e-mail, tasks, appointments, and documents relating to a specific contact by linking any item or document to a contact. For example, when you create a new Microsoft Outlook item, such as a task, you can link it to the contact to which it relates. You can also link any items that already exist in folders to a contact. And, you can link documents to a contact. For more information on these features, refer to Microsoft Outlook Help and enter the phrase **linking an item to a contact.**

 Send contact information over the Internet by using Internet **vCards**, the Internet standard for creating and sharing virtual business cards. You can save a contact as a save vCards sent in mail messages. To send a vCard to someone in e-mail, click **Contacts**, click the contact you want to send as a vCard, click **Actions**, and then click **Forward as vCard.**

 If you want to create a mailing list that's a subset of your Contacts folder, you can filter the Contacts list and then use the filtered list to begin a mail merge from Outlook. When you filter a list, you search for only specific information—for example, only those contacts that live in Kansas. You can create a variety of merged documents in Microsoft Word, and you can begin your mail merge from Outlook. You can create form letters, print mailing labels, or print addresses on envelopes. You can also send bulk e-mail messages or faxes to your contacts. To start a mail merge to a filtered set of your contacts, click the **View menu** in Contacts, point to **Current View**, and then click **Customize Current View**. Click **Filter** and then select the options you want. Once you have the view created, start the mail merge by clicking **Mail Merge** on the Tools menu.

FIGURE AP-4: Contacts displayed in the Contacts window

New Contact button

Dial button

Contacts folder

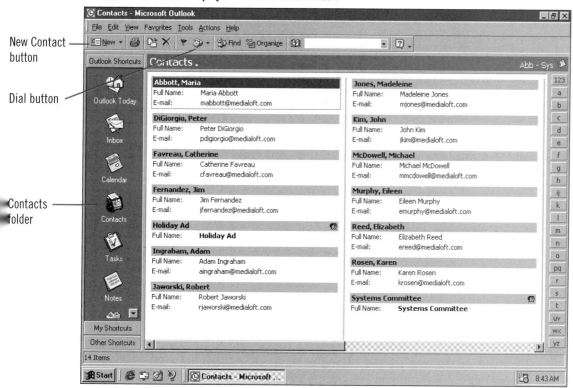

FIGURE AP-5: Individual contact in the Contact dialog box

Details tab

Full Name button

Address button

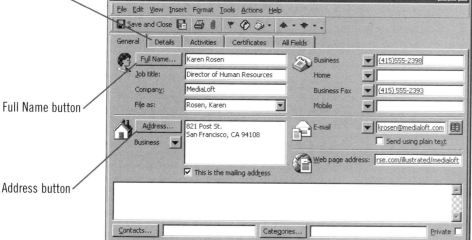

# Previewing Your Day

The **Outlook Today page** provides a preview of your day at a glance. It is the electronic version of your day planner book and provides a snapshot view of the activities, tasks, contacts, and notes that you've entered into various Outlook tools. Just as with a paper-based daily planner, you can customize how you view Outlook Today to fit your personal style and work habits. See Figure AP-6.

## Details

### Review the following features of Outlook Today:

 View how many messages are in your Inbox, Outbox, and Drafts folders. The right pane of Outlook Today displays your message information. You can customize Outlook Today to show any of your Personal Folders in the Messages pane.

 Outlook allows you to view your appointments over the next few days. These appear in the Calendar section of Outlook Today, which is located in the left pane. You can choose to show anywhere from 1–7 days of appointments and tasks in your Calendar.

 Tasks appear in the center pane of Outlook Today, allowing you to list all of your tasks in one convenient place. You can customize Outlook Today to show all your tasks or just today's tasks. You can also sort your tasks by Importance, Due Date, Creation Time, or Start Date, and in ascending or descending order. In addition, you can keep track of tasks by checking off task items that you've accomplished. You can click the checkbox to the left of the task to indicate you've completed it. The task list will be updated automatically in the Tasks folder.

 For detailed information on a Calendar item, you can double-click the appointment or meeting. Clicking the appointment or meeting opens the Appointment or Meeting dialog box. You can see more details at a glance and then close the dialog box to view Outlook Today again.

 Customize the page for the way you work by clicking the **Customize Outlook Today button** in the Outlook Today window. You can change the tasks that appear on the Outlook Today page, change how many appointments appear on the Outlook Today page, determine from where mail messages are sent and received, and change the style of Outlook Today (how it looks). You can also make the Outlook Today page your default page when you start Outlook.

**FIGURE AP-6: Outlook Today page**

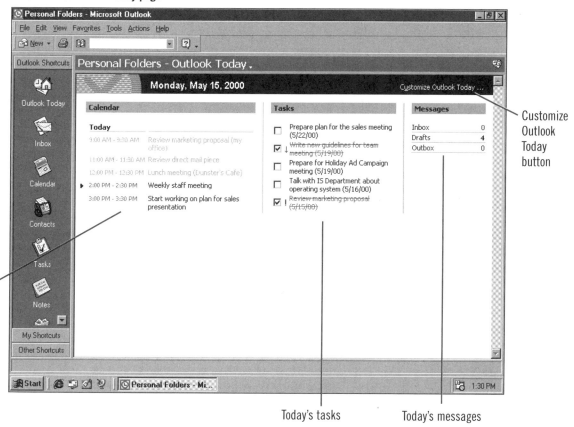

Customize Outlook Today button

Today's Calendar

Today's tasks

Today's messages

# Practice

## ► Concepts Review

Label the elements of the calendar window shown in Figure AP-7.

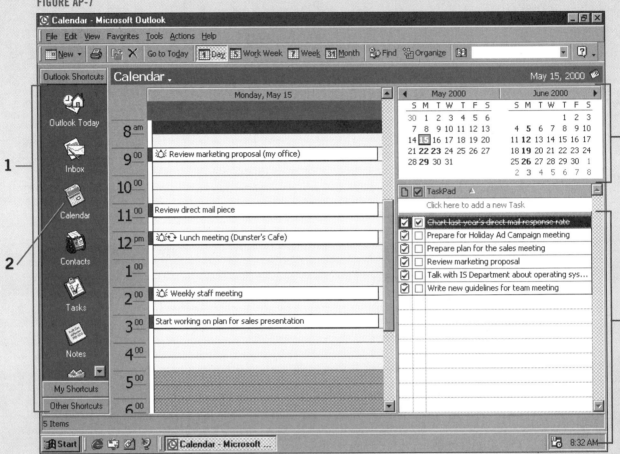

Select the best answer from the list of choices.

**5. Which of the following is *not* one of the Outlook tools:**
   **a.** Inbox      **b.** Meeting Planner      **c.** Calendar      **d.** Notes

**6. Use the _____ feature to schedule your appointments, meetings, and events.**
   **a.** Calendar      **b.** Tasks      **c.** Notes      **d.** Contacts

**7. Use the _____ feature to manage your business and personal to-do list.**
   **a.** Calendar      **b.** Tasks      **c.** Notes      **d.** Contacts

**8. Use the _____ feature to supplement the information stored in Calendar and Tasks.**
   **a.** Calendar      **b.** Tasks      **c.** Notes      **d.** Contacts

Unit A

# Bonus Exercises
## for Office 2000

### Including

- ► **Word**
- ► **Excel**
- ► **Access**
- ► **PowerPoint**
- ► **Integration**
- ► **Internet Explorer**
- ► **Publisher**

This unit contains bonus exercises for Word, Excel, Access, PowerPoint, Integration, Internet Explorer, and Publisher. These exercises were created to enhance the Office 2000 skills you learned in earlier units and to offer further practice.

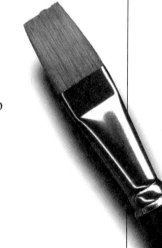

# ► Skills Review Word Unit A

**1. Start Word 2000.**
    **a.** Click the Start button on the taskbar, point to Programs, then start Microsoft Word.
    **b.** Click the Normal view button if necessary. Hide the Office Assistant if it appears.
    **c.** Reset your usage data to return your toolbars and menus to the default settings.

**2. View the Word program window.**
    **a.** Identify the title bar, the menu bar, the status bar, and the Standard and Formatting toolbars.
    **b.** Click the More Buttons button on each toolbar to view your other toolbar buttons.
    **c.** Identify as many other elements in the Word program window as you can.

**3. Create a document.**
    **a.** A local TV show called "Our Town Today" is looking for interns, and you decide to write to request an interview. Begin a letter by typing today's date.
    **b.** For the inside address, type "Mr. John Campbell, Executive Producer, Our Town Today, Central Studios". Then type a street address, town, state, and zip code of your choosing.
    **c.** For the greeting, type "Dear Mr. Campbell:". (If the Office Assistant appears, click Cancel.)
    **d.** In the body of the letter, explain that you are interested in pursuing a broadcasting career and that you would like to interview for an intern position. Provide two reasons why you are qualified for the job, and include a phone number where you can be reached.
    **e.** For a closing, type "Sincerely,", press [Enter] four times, then type your name.
    **f.** Correct any grammatical or spelling errors you made as you typed the letter.
    **g.** Using the [Backspace] key, change the closing to "Very truly yours,".
    **h.** Using the [Delete] key, change the name of the studio to "General Studios".

**4. Save a document.**
    **a.** Save the document on your Project Disk with the filename "Intern Letter".
    **b.** Change Mr. John Campbell's title to "Senior Executive Producer".
    **c.** Save the changes to the letter.

**5. Preview and print a document.**
    **a.** Click the Print Preview button, click the document to zoom in, then proofread the letter.
    **b.** Zoom out on the document, then close Print Preview.
    **c.** Save the document, then print a copy of the letter, using the default print settings.

**6. Get Help.**
    **a.** Use the Office Assistant to search for help on saving a document.
    **b.** Read about the different ways to save documents in Word, scrolling to the bottom of the Help window.
    **c.** Click the Show button on the Help window toolbar, then type "How do I prevent loss of work in the event of power outage?" on the Answer Wizard tab.
    **d.** Click the topic About preventing loss of work, read about using AutoRecover, then close the Help window and hide the Office Assistant.

**7. Close a document and exit Word.**
    **a.** Close the Intern Letter document, saving your changes if necessary.
    **b.** Exit Word.

# Visual Workshop Word Unit A



Create the document shown in Figure A-1. Save it on your Project Disk with the filename "Vertigo Follow-up Letter", then print the document.

**FIGURE A-1**

April 15, 2001

Ms. Barbara Jacobson
Human Resources Director
Vertigo Publishing
105 Elm Street
Chestnut Hill, MA  02167

Dear Ms. Jacobson:

Thank you for taking the time to meet with me to discuss the marketing assistant position at Vertigo Publishing. After much consideration, I have decided to accept another position at an Internet start-up company that markets specialty food items over the Web. I am looking forward to putting my excellent Microsoft Office skills to work there.

Thank you again for your time and consideration, and best of luck filling the marketing assistant position.

Sincerely,

Your Name

1. **Open and save a new document.**
   a. Start Word.
   b. Open the file BWD-1 from your Project Disk and save it as "Harmony Cruises".

2. **Select and replace text.**
   a. Select "Mr. Robert Bailey" on the first line of the inside address and replace it with "Ms. Paula Jeffries".
   b. Select "Vice President, Sales and Marketing" on the second line of the inside address and replace it with "National Sales Manager".
   c. Select "Mr. Bailey" on the salutation line and replace it with "Ms. Jeffries".
   d. Delete the last sentence of the first paragraph that begins "This letter summarizes ... ".
   e. Undo the deletion, then replace "this morning" in that sentence with "yesterday".
   f. Select "Spirit" in the first line of the second paragraph and replace it with "Destiny". In the same paragraph, replace the other two instances of "Spirit" with "Destiny" using the Repeat Typing command.
   g. Select "Joanne Smithers" in the closing and replace it with your name.

3. **Move text.**
   a. Display the Clipboard toolbar.
   b. Using the cut-and-paste method, move the first sentence of the fourth paragraph ("To reserve this cruise ship ... ") to the end of the second paragraph.
   c. Using the drag-and-drop method, reverse the order of the second and third paragraphs. If necessary, add line spaces between the paragraphs after you complete the move.

4. **Copy text.**
   a. Copy "BroadNet" from the inside address and paste it immediately after the word "annual" in the first paragraph.
   b. Copy "Harmony Cruises" from the first paragraph and paste it underneath Corporate Account Executive in the closing.
   c. Paste "BroadNet" from the Clipboard toolbar just before the word "employees" at the end of the second paragraph.
   d. Close the Clipboard toolbar.

5. **Check spelling and grammar.**
   a. Press [Ctrl][Home], then use the Spelling and Grammar command to review and correct errors.
   b. Use the Thesaurus to find alternate words for "venue" and "suitable" in the third paragraph. If the Thesaurus is not installed on your computer, think of different words on your own.

6. **Create and use AutoCorrect entries.**
   a. Create an AutoCorrect entry for "BroadNet Systems", using the abbreviation "bn".
   b. In the first line of the second paragraph, place the insertion point before "employees," then type "bn" followed by [Spacebar].

7. **Find and replace text.**
   a. Press [Ctrl][Home], then use the Replace command to replace all instances of "cabins" with "rooms".
   b. Save your changes, print the document, close the document, then exit Word.

Create the letter shown in Figure A-2 using the Professional Letter template. Save it as "Executive Retreat Letter" on your Project Disk, then print a copy of the letter.

**FIGURE A-2**

**Candlesticks, Inc.**    1400 Water View Drive
Portland, OR 97201

September 20, 2001

Mr. Bill Stone
14 Fiske Street
Pacific Palisades, CA 90272

Dear Mr. Stone:

I am delighted that you have agreed to perform your comedy act at our upcoming Senior Management Retreat scheduled for October 12-15 in Palm Springs, California. The primary goal of this three-day summit is to focus our executive team on core strategies for the coming year. An important secondary goal is to have fun and enjoy wholesome entertainment together. Our president, Kathryn Stephens, saw your show in Portland last summer and is especially pleased that you will be performing for us.

Your performance is scheduled for dinner on the third night, when the team will be ready to unwind and have some fun. It would be great if you could incorporate some humor about our products into your show. I have enclosed a catalog to give you some ideas.

I have reserved a room for you at the Palmetto Inn on October 15. Once we have arranged your flight details, I will reserve a limo to meet you at the airport.

If there is anything I can do to assist you in your trip, please don t hesitate to call.

Sincerely,

Your Name
Vice President, Human Resources

1. **Change fonts and font sizes.**
   a. Start Word, open the file BWD-2 from your Project Disk, and save it as "Welcome Kit".
   b. Format the top two lines of the document in 24-point Tahoma.
   c. Midway down the document, format the heading "Facilities" in 18-point Tahoma, then format the headings "Tennis Center", "Aquatics Center", and Fitness Center" in 14-point Tahoma.
   d. At the bottom of the document, format the heading "Other Services" in 18-point Tahoma.

2. **Apply font effects.**
   a. In the list following the first body paragraph, apply superscript formatting to the TM after the word "PermaShine."
   b. Format "Facilities" in bold, then use the format painter to apply the same formatting to "Other Services".
   c. Under Other Services, format "Restaurants" and "Babysitting" in bold italic.

3. **Change paragraph alignment.**
   a. Center the top two lines of the document.
   b. Type your name at the bottom of the document, change the font size to 10 points, then right-align the text.

4. **Indent paragraphs.**
   a. Indent the three-line list following the first body paragraph 1 inch.
   b. Select the quote under the Fitness Center heading, drag the Left Indent marker to the 1 inch mark on the horizontal ruler, then drag the Right Indent marker to the 5 inch mark on the horizontal ruler.

5. **Change line spacing.**
   a. Change the line spacing of the list following the first body paragraph to 1.5 lines.

6. **Change paragraph spacing.**
   a. Change the paragraph spacing after "New Member Welcome Kit", "Facilities", and "Other Services" to 6 points.

7. **Align text with tabs.**
   a. In the Tennis Center section, insert a blank line after "times shown below:".
   b. Set tab stops at 1.5" and at 3".
   c. Press [Tab], type "Clinic Level", press [Tab], type "Clinic Time", then press [Enter].
   d. Press [Tab], type "Beginner", press [Tab], type "Mondays, 9-11", then press [Enter].
   e. Press [Tab], type "Intermediate", press [Tab], type "Tuesdays, 9-11", then press [Enter].
   f. Press [Tab], type "Advanced", press [Tab], type "Wednesdays, 9-11" then press [Enter].
   g. Underline "Clinic Level" and "Clinic Time", select the next three lines, then format the 3 inch tab stop with dotted leader.

8. **Create bulleted and numbered lists.**
   a. Apply square bullets to the three-line list following the first body paragraph.
   b. Apply numbered list formatting to the Restaurants and Babysitting paragraphs under Other Services.

9. **Apply borders and shading.**
   a. Apply a single-line border above and below "Emerson Fitness Center New Member Welcome Kit", then appl[y] 12.5% gray shading to the paragraphs.
   b. Apply a single-line border under the headings "Facilities" and "Other Services".
   c. Apply 10% gray shading to the member quote, save your changes, then print the document.

# ► Visual Workshop Word Unit C

Create the contest announcement shown in Figure A-3 and save it as "Contest Flyer" on your Project Disk. Use 26-point Arial Black for the title, 15-point Arial Black for the headings, and 15-point Times New Roman for the body text. Use 12.5% shading. Add your name to the box at the bottom of the flyer, then print a copy of the completed flyer.

**FIGURE A-3**

## Refer-a-Friend Contest

At WEBVISION, INC., we know the most valuable asset we have is our people. And good people like you know other good people who would be valuable to our organization. Realizing this, we are pleased to announce a contest to reward employees who refer new employees to WEBVISION, INC.

### How does the contest work?

Submit resumes of qualified people to the Human Resources department. For every referral we hire, we will pay you a bonus.

### How much will I be paid if my referral gets hired?

It depends on what position your referral accepts. Below is a sampling of current open positions and the associated bonus amount:

| Position | Bonus Amount |
|---|---|
| Chief Technology Officer | $5,000 |
| Corporate Sales Director | $3,000 |
| Web Designer | $1,000 |

### Is money the only reward?

No! You will also enjoy the following benefits:

- ✓ the joy of working with people you refer
- ✓ the satisfaction of helping the company stay on the cutting edge
- ✓ the chance to win a week's vacation to Maui (awarded to the person who recruits the most employees)

*If you know of strong candidates for the above positions, contact* **Your Name** *in Human Resources today.*

**1. Create a table.**

   **a.** Start Word, type your name at the top of the document, press [Enter] twice, then type "Deer Falls Community Arts Schedule".

   **b.** Press [Enter] twice, create a table that contains three columns and four rows, then enter the following text in the table:

| | | |
|---|---|---|
| March | Oklahoma! | Deer Falls High School Auditorium |
| June | Barbershop Quartet Festival | Deer Falls Park |
| October | Witness for the Prosecution | Elementary School Gym |
| November | Deer Falls Ballet Performance | Hanes Community Center |

   **c.** Add a row at the top and enter the headings "Month", "Event", and "Location".

   **d.** Save the document as "Arts Schedule" to your Project Disk.

**2. Adjust table rows and columns.**

   **a.** Select the entire table, then distribute the rows evenly.

   **b.** Drag the right border of the last column to the 5" mark on the horizontal ruler.

   **c.** Distribute the columns evenly, center the table on the page, then save your changes.

**3. Add and delete rows and columns.**

   **a.** Add a new row to the bottom of the table, then type "December", "Chorale Concert", and "Unitarian Church" in the new cells.

   **b.** Delete the March row, move the October row up to the second row, then change "October" to "March".

   **c.** Add a new column to the right of Location, type "Director" as the heading, then enter four names in the column.

   **d.** Save your changes to the table.

**4. Format a table.**

   **a.** AutoFormat the table in the Professional preset format.

   **b.** Apply 12.5% shading to the bottom four rows of the table.

   **c.** Center the text in the top row of the table.

   **d.** Apply a 1.5-point border around the outer edge of the table. (*Hint*: Use the Line Weight and Outside Border list arrows on the Tables and Borders toolbar.)

   **e.** Save, print, and close the document.

**5. Calculate data in a table.**

   **a.** Open the file BWD-3 from your Project Disk and save it as "Tour Sales".

   **b.** Type your name at the top of the document, then press [Enter] twice.

   **c.** In each appropriate cell in the Total column, enter a formula that calculates the sum of the values of the cells to the left.

   **d.** In each cell in the Total row, enter a formula that calculates the sum of the values of the cells above.

   **e.** Save your changes.

**6. Sort a table.**

   **a.** Sort rows 2 through 5 in descending order by the values in the Total column.

   **b.** Sort the table alphabetically by the Destination column, making sure to sort only rows 2 through 5.

   **c.** Save, print, and close the document.

# ▶ Visual Workshop Word Unit D

Create the document shown in Figure A-4 and save it as "Order Confirmation" on your Project Disk. Be sure to align the text in the cells as shown in the figure. (*Hint*: Use the Table Properties dialog box to align text vertically.)

**FIGURE A-4**

## ORDER CONFIRMATION

The Casual Connection
*"Comfortable Clothes for Everyday Living"*
555 Timberwood Industrial Park
Madison, WI 53703

Your Name
17 Ridgeway Drive
Manchester, NH 03102

Thank you for your online order! Below is summary of the items you ordered. Your order will arrive in 3 to 5 business days.

| Item Number | Description | Item size | Color | Monogramming Initials | | | Qty. | Price |
|---|---|---|---|---|---|---|---|---|
| 778-532 | Suede boots | 10 | Brown | | | | 1 | $129.95 |
| 445-009 | Canvas bag | Large | Navy | C | J | H | 1 | $29.95 |
| 223-859 | Wool socks | Large | Gray | | | | 1 | $9.95 |
| | | | | | | | | |
| | | | | | | | | |
| | | | | | | | | |
| *Thank you for shopping with The Casual Connection!* | | | | Total price of items | | | | $169.85 |
| | | | | Monogramming | | | | $15.00 |
| | | | | Shipping charges | | | | $9.95 |
| | | | | **Total charges** | | | | **$194.80** |

# ► Skills Review Excel Unit A

## 1. Start Excel 2000.
**a.** Point to Programs on the Start menu.
**b.** Click the Microsoft Excel program icon.

## 2. View the Excel window.
**a.** Identify the title bar, the menu bar, and the Standard and Formatting toolbars.
**b.** Click the More Buttons button on each toolbar to view your other toolbar buttons.
**c.** Identify the name box and the active cell.

## 3. Open and Save a workbook.
**a.** Open the workbook BEX-1 from your Project Disk by clicking the Open button.
**b.** Save the workbook as "Delectable Pastries" by clicking File on the menu bar, then clicking Save As.

## 4. Enter labels and values.
**a.** Enter the labels shown in Figure A-5, the Delectable Pastries worksheet.
**b.** Enter the values shown in Figure A-5.
**c.** Change cell C3 to "Price" instead of "Sale Price".
**d.** Type your name in cell A14.
**e.** Save the workbook by clicking the Save button.

**FIGURE A-5**

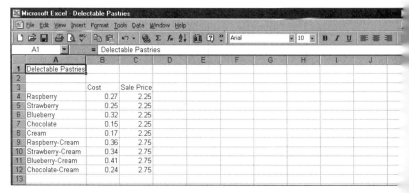

## 5. Preview and print a worksheet.
**a.** Click the Print Preview button.
**b.** Use the Zoom button to see more of your worksheet.
**c.** Print one copy of the worksheet.

## 6. Get Help.
**a.** Click the Office Assistant button if the Assistant is not displayed.
**b.** Ask the Office Assistant for information about previewing a worksheet before you print it.
**c.** Print information offered by the Office Assistant using the Print button on the Help window toolbar.
**d.** Close the Help window.

## 7. Close a workbook and exit Excel.
**a.** Click the Close Window button on the menu bar.
**b.** If asked if you want to save the worksheet, click No.
**c.** If necessary, close any other worksheets you might have opened.
**d.** Click the Close button on the title bar.

# ▶ Visual Workshop Excel Unit A

Create a worksheet similar to Figure A-6 using the skills you learned in this unit. Save the workbook as "Princeton Health and Fitness" on your Project Disk. Type your name in cell A13, then preview and print the worksheet.

FIGURE A-6

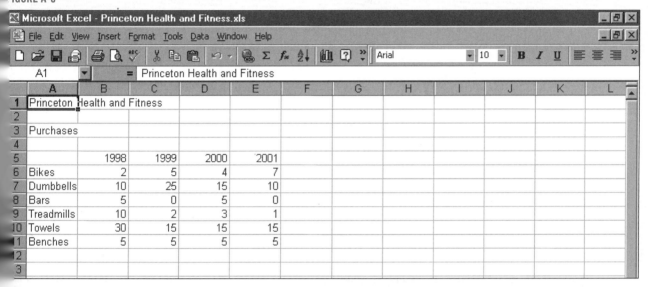

# ▶ Skills Review Excel Unit B

1. **Edit cell entries and work with ranges.**
   a. Start Excel, open the workbook BEX-2 from your Project Disk, and save it as "Summer Maintenance Expenses".
   b. Change the Paint expense for June to 1400, change the Tools expense for August to 58, and change the label "Sponges" to "Mops".
   c. Type your name in cell A25, then save your work.

2. **Enter formulas.**
   a. Type the label "Total" in cell A11.
   b. Click cell B11, then enter the formula B4+B5+B6+B7+B8+B9.
   c. Save your work, then preview the data in the Summer Maintenance Expenses worksheet.

3. **Introduce Excel functions.**
   a. Click cell C11, then enter the function SUM(C4:C9).
   b. Type the label "Average" in cell A12.
   c. Create a formula in cell B12 that determines the average expense amount for June, then save your work.

4. **Copy and move cell entries.**
   a. Select the range A4:A9, then copy the range to cell A18.
   b. Use the drag-and-drop method to copy the title in cell B1 to cell B15, then save your work.

5. **Copy formulas with relative cell references.**
   a. Click cell E4, then create a formula that sums B4:D4.
   b. Use the Office Clipboard to copy the formula in E4 into cells E5:E9.
   c. Use the Office Clipboard to copy the formula in E4 into cells E18:E23.
   d. Copy the formula in cell C11 into cells D11 and E11.
   e. Copy the formula in B12 into cells C12, D12, and E12. Show only one decimal place. (*Hint*: Click the Decrease Decimal button on the Formatting toolbar until only one decimal place displays.)
   f. Save and preview the worksheet.

6. **Copy formulas with absolute cell references.**
   a. Click cell H1 and type the value 15,000.
   b. Click cell F4, then create a formula that divides E4 by H1, with H1 being an absolute reference. Show two decimal places.
   c. Copy the formula in F4 into cells F5:F9 and into cell F11.
   d. Copy the formula in F4 into cells F18:F23.
   e. Change the amount in cell H1 to 10,000.
   f. Save the worksheet.

7. **Name and move a sheet.**
   a. Name the Sheet1 tab "Expenses", then move the Expenses sheet so it comes after Sheet3.
   b. Name the Sheet2 tab "Workers", then move the Workers sheet after the Expenses sheet.
   c. Delete Sheet3.
   d. Save, preview, print, and close the workbook, then exit Excel.

# ► Visual Workshop Excel Unit B

Create a worksheet similar to Figure A-7 using the skills you learned in this unit. Save the workbook as "Highway Traffic" on your Project Disk. Type your name in cell A19, then preview and print the worksheet.

**FIGURE A-7**

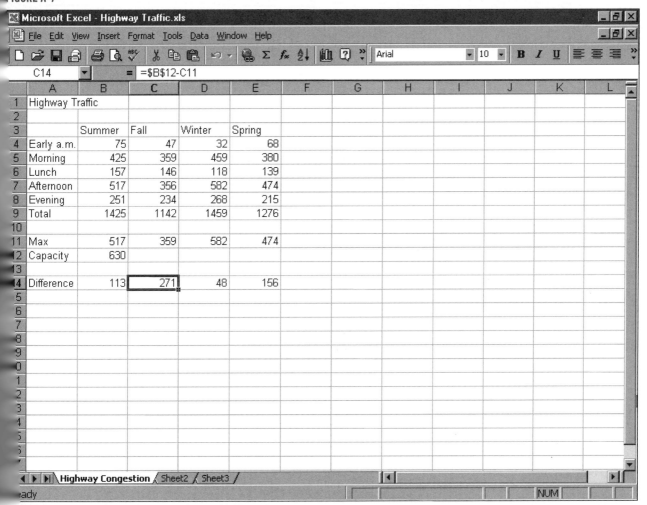

## 1. Format values.

**a.** Start Excel, open a new workbook, then save it as "Slippery Slide".

**b.** Type "Slippery Slide Inc." in cell A1, then type "Park Revenue" in cell A2.

**c.** Enter the information from Table A-1 into your worksheet. Begin in cell A3, and do not leave any blank rows or columns.

**d.** Apply bold and italics to the Area, Price, Tickets Sold, and Revenue column headings.

**e.** Apply the Comma format to the Tickets Sold data, but do not show any decimal places. (*Hint*: Use the Decrease Decimal button.)

**f.** Insert formulas in the Revenue column (multiply the Price by the Tickets Sold), then apply bold and italics to the Revenue data.

**g.** Apply the Currency format to the Price and Revenue data, but do not show any decimal places. Save your changes.

## 2. Use fonts and font sizes.

**a.** Change the font of the worksheet title, "Slippery Slide Inc.", and subtitle, "Park Revenue", to Times New Roman. Increase the font size to 18 and 14 points, respectively.

**b.** Change the font of cells A3:D7 to Comic Sans MS, then apply bold to the labels in the Area column.

**c.** Change the font size of the column headings to 14 points, resize the columns as necessary, then save your changes.

**TABLE A-1**

| Area | Price | Tickets Sold | Revenue |
|------|-------|--------------|---------|
| Mini-golf | 8 | 156 | |
| Bumper boats | 5 | 245 | |
| Go-carts | 5 | 678 | |
| Water Park | 23 | 2540 | |

## 3. Change attributes and alignment of labels.

**a.** Apply boldface and underlining to the worksheet title.

**b.** Use the Merge and Center button to center the title and the subtitle over columns A through D.

**c.** Center the Price, Tickets Sold, and Revenue headings, then save your changes.

## 4. Adjust column widths.

**a.** Use the Format menu to resize the Area column to 14 and the Tickets Sold column to 17.

**b.** Use the AutoFit feature to resize the Price and Revenue columns, then save your changes.

## 5. Insert and delete rows and columns.

**a.** Insert a new row between rows 6 and 7, then type "Parking" in cell A7.

**b.** Enter "5" for the parking price and "3215" for the tickets sold.

**c.** Use the fill handle to copy the formula from cell D6 to D7, then save your changes.

## 6. Apply colors, patterns, and borders.

**a.** Add a single-line border around cells A1:D8.

**b.** Apply a turquoise background to the title and a light turquoise background to the subtitle.

**c.** Change the font color of the Water Park row to blue.

**d.** Apply a pattern fill to the heading and labels in the Area column.

## 7. Use conditional formatting.

**a.** Create conditional formatting that changes the Mini-golf revenue value to red if it is less than 2000.

**b.** Use the Format Painter to format the Bumper boats, Go-carts, and Parking revenue values in the same way.

**c.** Save your changes.

## 8. Check spelling.

**a.** Use the spell checker to check the spelling in the worksheet and then correct any errors.

**b.** Type your name in cell A10, save your changes, then preview and print the workbook.

# ► Visual Workshop Excel Unit C

Create the worksheet shown in Figure A-8, using skills you learned in this unit. Open the file BEX-3 on your Project Disk and save it as "Employee Expenditures for March". Create a conditional format in the Total Expenditures column so that entries greater than $1000 are displayed in red and boldface. (*Hint*: The only additional font used in this exercise is Times New Roman. It is 18 points in row 1 and 14 points in row 2.) Type your name in cell A14, save, then print the worksheet.

**FIGURE A-8**

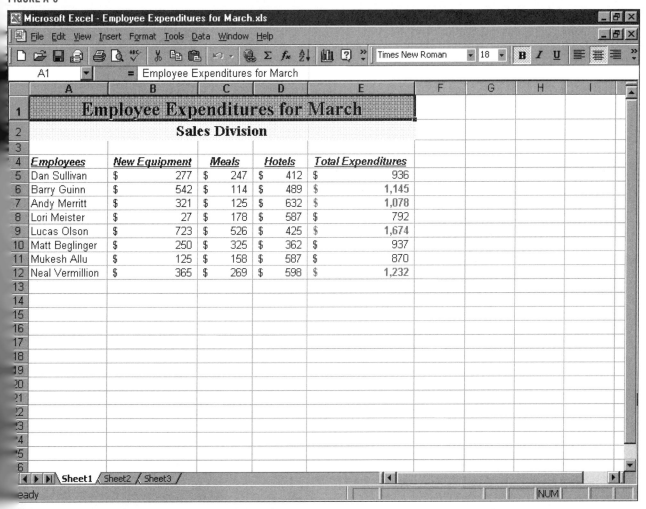

# ► Skills Review Excel Unit D

## 1. Create a chart.
**a.** Start Excel, open the workbook BEX-4 from your Project Disk, then save it as "Vending Machine Products".
**b.** Select the range A1:E7, then click the Chart Wizard button.
**c.** Complete the Chart Wizard dialog boxes. Build a line chart, title it "Products Sold by Location", and locate it on the same sheet as the data.
**d.** Save your work.

## 2. Move and resize a chart.
**a.** Make sure the chart is still selected, then move it beneath the data.
**b.** Drag the chart's selection handles so it is as wide as the screen.
**c.** Move the legend to align with the top of the plot area, then save your work.

## 3. Edit a chart.
**a.** Change cell A2 to "Beverages". Change cell D6 to "700". Notice the changes in the chart.
**b.** Select the chart, then click the Chart Type list arrow on the Chart toolbar.
**c.** Click the 3-D line chart button, then rotate the chart to move the data.
**d.** Change the chart back to a line chart, then save your work.

## 4. Format a chart.
**a.** Make sure the chart is still selected.
**b.** Use the Chart Options dialog box to turn off the displayed gridlines.
**c.** Change the Hospital, School, Apartment, and Telephone Co. lines to a heavier line weight with no markers. (*Hint:* Double-click each line.)
**d.** Turn the major Y-axis gridlines back on, then save your work.

## 5. Enhance a chart.
**a.** Open the Chart Options dialog box, then click the Titles tab.
**b.** Type "Product" in the Category (X) axis text box, type "Number Sold" in the Value (Y) axis text box, then click OK.
**c.** Change the chart title font to 14-point Times New Roman, change the font color to blue, and add a drop shadow to the title.
**d.** Save your work.

## 6. Annotate and draw on a chart.
**a.** Select the chart, then create the text annotation "Discontinue pretzels at school".
**b.** Change the font size of the annotation to 10 points, if necessary, then drag it under the legend.
**c.** Draw an arrow that points from the text annotation to the School Pretzels data point, then save your work.

## 7. Preview and print a chart.
**a.** Select the chart, then preview it to see how it will look when printed.
**b.** Change the paper orientation to landscape, then make any necessary adjustments.
**c.** Add a footer to the page that includes your name. (*Hint:* Click the Header/Footer tab in the Page Setup dialog box, click Custom Footer, then type your name in the Left Section text box.)
**d.** Click Print in the Print Preview window, then save your work.

# ► Visual Workshop Excel Unit D

Create the chart shown in Figure A-9 using the skills you learned in this unit. Open the file BEX-5 from your Project Disk, and save it as "Richmond Rain Levels". Create the chart, then preview the worksheet and make any necessary adjustments. Type your name in cell A20, save, then print your results.

**FIGURE A-9**

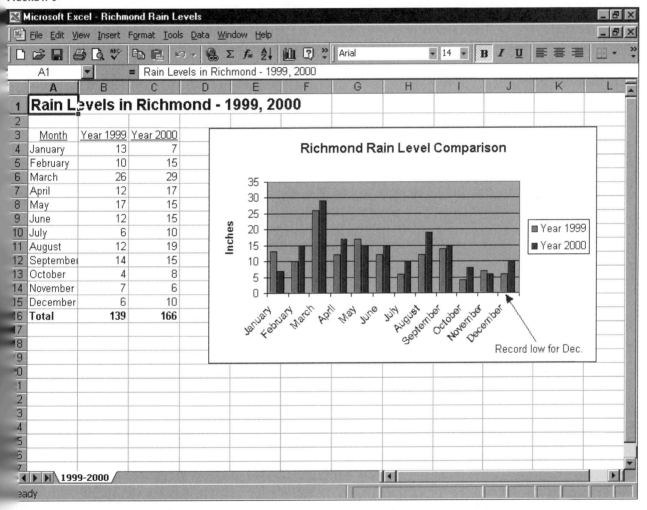

**Skills Review Access Unit A**

### 1. Define database software and learn database terminology.
- **a.** Write two brief paragraphs that describe how a business can use database software.
- **b.** List and define four key database terms.
- **c.** List the seven Access objects, and identify the object that stores the data in a database.

### 2. Start Access and open a database.
- **a.** Start Access.
- **b.** Using the Open dialog box, open the EasternUniversity-A database file from your Project Disk.

### 3. View the database window.
- **a.** Maximize both the Access window and the EasternUniversity-A: Database window.
- **b.** Click each of the objects on the Objects bar, and view the list of objects and object shortcuts for each object type. Notice how the toolbars change slightly for each type of object.
- **c.** Click Tables on the Objects bar, then open the Students table.

### 4. Navigate records.
- **a.** Move through the fields of the first record, then move to the last field of the last record.
- **b.** Press [Ctrl][Up Arrow] to move to the last field of the first record.
- **c.** Press [Ctrl][Home] to move to the first field of the first record.
- **d.** Press [Tab] three times to move to the Address field for Kelsey (the first record).
- **e.** Use the Next Record navigation button to scroll to the 8888 Godiva Hill record.
- **f.** Click the Last Record navigation button to quickly move to the Ford Street record.

### 5. Enter records.
- **a.** Click the New Record button and add yourself to the table as the last record (record 12). You are an IT major, your Social Security number is 111-11-1111, you are a full-time student, and your balance is $1,000.00.
- **b.** Move the Gender field so that it follows the LastName field in the datasheet; it will be the fourth column.

### 6. Edit records.
- **a.** Change the FirstName field in record 7 from Susan to Suzanne.
- **b.** Change the Major field in all appropriate records from MIS to IT.

### 7. Preview and print a datasheet.
- **a.** Preview the Students table datasheet.
- **b.** Use the Page Setup option on the File menu to change the page orientation from portrait to landscape.
- **c.** Preview using the Multiple Pages button, then print both pages.

### 8. Get Help and exit Access.
- **a.** Close the Students table object, saving your changes.
- **b.** Use the Office Assistant to learn more about printing.
- **c.** Close the database, then exit Access.

# ► Visual Workshop Access Unit A

Open the BrunildasBakedGoods-A database on your Project Disk. Modify the existing Products table so that it includes the fields shown in the datasheet in Figure A-10, enter the records shown in the figure, and then print the datasheet. If you need your name on the printed solution, enter your name in the Category field for the last record.

**FIGURE A-10**

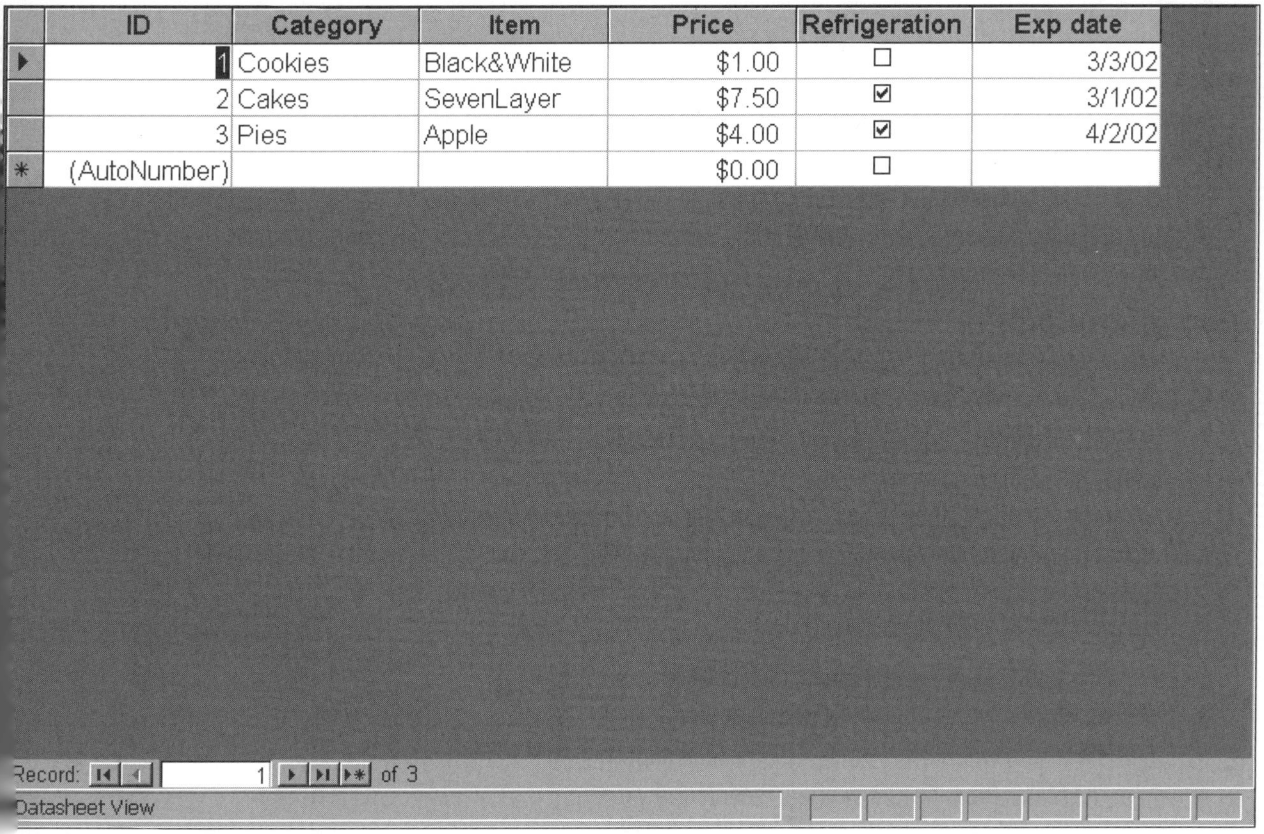

| | ID | Category | Item | Price | Refrigeration | Exp date |
|---|---|---|---|---|---|---|
| ► | 1 | Cookies | Black&White | $1.00 | ☐ | 3/3/02 |
| | 2 | Cakes | SevenLayer | $7.50 | ☑ | 3/1/02 |
| | 3 | Pies | Apple | $4.00 | ☑ | 4/2/02 |
| * | (AutoNumber) | | | $0.00 | ☐ | |

Record: ◄◄ ◄ 1 ► ►► ►* of 3

Datasheet View

# ► Skills Review Access Unit B

## 1. Create a table.
a. Start Access, then create a blank database called "Photograph-B" on your Project Disk.
b. Use the Table Wizard to create a new table based on the Photographs sample table in the Personal category.
c. Choose the following fields: PhotographID, DateTaken, TimeTaken, PlaceTaken, Flash, PrintSize, and Notes.
d. Rename the PhotographID field as PhotoID, then move to the next dialog box.
e. Name the table "Photographs", allow Access to set the primary key, then click Finish.

## 2. Use Table Design View.
a. In the first blank row, add a new field called "PrintForSale" with a Yes/No data type. Enter the description "Will print copies to sell at show".
b. Insert a field named "Subject" with a text data type between the Flash and PlaceTaken fields. Change the Field size property to "25".
c. Change the Required field property for the PlaceTaken field to "Yes".
d. Save and view the datasheet, then add one record that includes your name in the subject field.
e. Close the Photographs database but don't exit Access.

## 3. Format a datasheet.
a. Open the EasternUniversity-B database from your Project Disk, then open the Students datasheet.
b. Enter your name as the last record. You live in NJ and have a balance of $1500.00.
c. Change the font to 11-point Comic Sans MS.
d. Change the gridline color to red and the background color to aqua.
e. Remove the horizontal gridline so that it appears as a transparent border.
f. Change the page orientation to landscape, change the right and left margins to 0.25", then view the datasheet.
g. Hide the SSN field, resize the columns so the datasheet fits on one page, then print the datasheet.

## 4. Sort records and find data.
a. Sort the records in ascending order by last name, then sort in descending order by account balance.
b. Find the records where the Phone number field contains 201 in any part of the field, then find the records where the Major field is IT. How many records did you find?

## 5. Filter records.
a. Filter the records by form for all students with an account balance greater than $4500.
b. Filter by Selection for all students from NY with an account balance greater than $4500.
c. Print the datasheet, then remove the filter.

## 6. Create a query.
a. Create a new query based on the Students table using Last Name, City, State, Major, AccountBalance, and FullTime.
b. Name the query "StudentsFromNJ", then view the datasheet.
c. In Query Design View, add the criteria NJ to the state field, then view the datasheet.

## 7. Use Query Design View.
a. Modify the StudentsFromNJ query to include only those whose account balance is less than $9000.00.
b. Save the query with the name "StudentsFromNJLessThan9000", then print the query results.
c. Modify the query so that the records are sorted in ascending order by Account Balance. Also add "PhoneNumber as the second field in the datasheet".
d. Save the sorted query's datasheet as "StudentsFromNJ Sorted-LessThan9000".
e. Print the query results, close the datasheet, close the database, then exit Access.

# ► Visual Workshop Access Unit B

Open the BrunildasBakedGoods-B database and create the query shown in Figure A-11. The query is based on the Products table. Notice the order of the fields, that only products that require refrigeration are displayed, and that the records are sorted in descending order on the Price field. If you need your name on the printed solution, enter your name as a record in the Products table, making sure to check the refrigeration field. Save the query as "Products Query" and print the datasheet.

FIGURE A-11

**Products Query : Select Query**

| Category | Price | Refrigeration | Item | Exp date |
|----------|-------|---------------|------|----------|
| Cakes | $7.50 | ☑ | SevenLayer | 3/1/02 |
| Pies | $5.43 | ☑ | Strawberry | 4/3/02 |
| Cakes | $4.50 | ☑ | Chocolate | 5/1/02 |
| Pies | $4.00 | ☑ | Apple | 4/2/02 |
| * | $0.00 | ☐ | | |

Record: I◄ ◄ 1 ► ►I ►* of 4

**Skills Review Access Unit C**

### 1. Create a form.
**a.** Start Access and open the EasternUniversity-C database from your Project Disk.
**b.** Use the Form Wizard to create a form based on the Students Query. Select all the available fields.
**c.** Use a Columnar layout and a Rice Paper style, then title the form Student Data Entry Form.
**d.** Display the form in Form view.

### 2. Move and resize controls.
**a.** Open and maximize the Design View window for the form.
**b.** Widen the form so that the right edge is at the 6¼" mark on the horizontal ruler.
**c.** Move and resize the controls so that the form is logical, has a two-column design, and is attractive. For example, move the LastName controls to the right of the FirstName controls. Delete any unnecessary labels.

### 3. Modify labels.
**a.** Right-align all of the labels. Use the Format menu to bottom-align the controls that are next to each other so they appear to be on one line.
**b.** Change the label "Gender" to "M or F".

### 4. Modify text boxes.
**a.** Add a new text box to the right of or below the AccountBalance controls.
**b.** Type the following expression in the new unbound text box: "=[AccountBalance]*0.06". (*Hint*: You must use the exact field names in a calculated expression.)
**c.** Change the calculated text box label to "LATEFEE", then right-align the label.
**d.** In the property sheet for the new calculated control, change the Format property to "Currency".
**e.** Move, resize, and align the controls so that the form looks good and is easy to use.

### 5. Modify tab order.
**a.** Change the Tab order so that pressing [Tab] moves you through the text boxes in a logical order.

### 6. Enter and edit records.
**a.** Use the form to enter yourself and a friend as new records, then print your own record.
**b.** Find the record for Maria Lee, change her balance to "$700", notice the change in the late fee, then print that record.
**c.** Filter for all records with a City entry of New York. How many records did you find?
**d.** Sort the filtered New York records in ascending order by Last Name, print the first one, then remove the filter

### 7. Add an image.
**a.** Expand the Form Header section to the 1½" mark on the vertical ruler.
**b.** Add a label with your name to the Form Header. Format it in a 14-point font of your choice, with blue text and a green fill.
**c.** Use the Image control to insert the Diploma.wmf file found on your Project Disk in the Form Header. Before resizing the image, open the Property Sheet and change the Size Mode to Zoom.
**d.** Resize the image so it is about 1" wide and 1½" tall, then move it next to the label with your name.
**e.** Adjust the size of the Form Header section if necessary, then view the form in Form view.
**f.** Print the final form with your record, close the form, close the database, then exit Access.

# ▶ Visual Workshop Access Unit C

Using the BrunildasBakedGoods-C database, create the entry form shown in Figure A-12. The database and the graphic file BBGLogo are found on your Project Disk. The form is based on the Inventory Query and uses the Expedition style. Name the form Baked Goods Entry Form. The font in the form header is Haettenschweiler (choose a different font if this is not available to you). Notice the formatting of the labels and the alignment and placement of the fields. After rearranging the fields, use AutoOrder to set the tab order. If you need your name on the printed solution, enter your name as a label in the form's header section. Print the form for one record.

**FIGURE A-12**

# ▶ Skills Review Access Unit D

## 1. Create a report.
a. Start Access and open the EasternUniversity-D database on your Project Disk.
b. Enter your name and address in record 16 in the Students table.
c. Use the Report Wizard to create a report based on the Students Query.
d. Include all the fields in the report except FullTime, Student ID, and Gender.
e. Do not add any grouping. Sort in ascending order by LastName, use the Tabular layout and Landscape orientation, use the Soft Gray style, then name the report "Students Report – Your Name".
f. Preview the new one-page report.

## 2. Group records.
a. In Report Design view, delete the City, State, Postal Code, and Major labels from the Page Header.
b. Open the Sorting and Grouping dialog box. Click the second Field/Expression list arrow, click the Major field, sorting in ascending order, then open the Group Header and Group Footer sections for the Major field.
c. Click the Major field selector, then drag the Major field so that it is the first field in the Sorting and Grouping dialog box.
d. Move the Major unbound text box from the Detail section to the left side of the Major Header.
e. Preview the first page of the new report.

## 3. Change the sort order.
a. In Report Design view, open the Sorting and Grouping dialog box, then add "AccountBalance" as a sort field in descending order immediately below the Major field.
b. Close the dialog box, then preview the first page of the report.

## 4. Modify an expression.
a. In Report Design View, add a text box control in the Major Footer section directly below the Account Balance text box in the Detail section. Change the label to "Outstanding Balance" for each major, adjusting the size of the label.
b. Modify the unbound text box to subtotal the Account Balance field. *Hint*: =Sum([AccountBalance]).

## 5. Align controls.
a. In Report Design view, right-align the new calculated control in the Footer section, then align it with the AccountBalance field in the Detail section and the AccountBalance label in the header.
b. Preview the report, then return to Report Design view to resize and arrange the labels and fields so that all text is visible in the report. Make sure the labels in the header are aligned with the fields they represent.

## 6. Format controls.
a. Select the calculated control, click the Properties button, change the Format property on the Format tab to "Currency", then close the property sheet.
b. Select the Major field in the Header section, change the font to 12-point Arial, apply bold and italic, then change the background color to bright yellow.
c. Preview, save, print, then close the report.

## 7. Create labels.
a. Use the Label Wizard and the Students table to create mailing labels using Avery 5160 labels.
b. Sort the labels by the State field, then name the report "Mailing Labels – Your Name".
c. Print the labels, save, close the report, then exit Access.

# Visual Workshop Access Unit D

Use the BrunildasBakedGoods-D database on your Project Disk to create the printed report shown in Figure A-13. The report is based on the Products Query table and was created using the Report Wizard and the Casual style with a stepped layout. Note that the records are grouped by the Baker field and sorted by price. Name the report "YourNameBakingReport". Make sure to adjust the labels in the Page header and format the controls as shown. A calculated control that counts the number of records is displayed in the group footer, which you have to create.

**FIGURE A-13**

## YourNameBakingReport

| Baker | Price | ID | | Item | Refrigeration needed | Exp date |
|---|---|---|---|---|---|---|
| Jan | | | | | | |
| | $0.75 | 7 | Cookies | Oreo | ☐ | 3/9/03 |
| | $1.00 | 1 | Cookies | Black&White | ☐ | 3/3/02 |
| | $1.25 | 10 | Cookies | Mint | ☐ | 5/9/03 |
| | $3.75 | 9 | Pies | Chocolate | ☑ | 5/7/02 |
| | $4.50 | 5 | Cakes | Chocolate | ☑ | 5/1/02 |
| | | | **Total Items:** | | 5 | |
| Maureen | | | | | | |
| | $4.00 | 3 | Pies | Apple | ☑ | 4/2/02 |
| | $5.00 | 8 | Cakes | Angel Food | ☑ | 4/7/02 |
| | $5.43 | 4 | Pies | Strawberry | ☑ | 4/3/02 |
| | | | **Total Items:** | | 3 | |
| Ruth | | | | | | |
| | $1.50 | 6 | Cookies | Chocolate Chip | ☐ | 12/2/02 |
| | $7.50 | 2 | Cakes | SevenLayer | ☑ | 3/1/02 |
| | | | **Total Items:** | | 2 | |

Monday, November 20, 2000 Page 1 of 1

# ► Skills Review PowerPoint Unit A

## 1. Start PowerPoint and use the AutoContent Wizard.
a. Start PowerPoint.
b. Create a new presentation using the AutoContent Wizard.
c. In the AutoContent Wizard, select Company Meeting as the presentation type and on-screen presentation as the output type. (*Hint*: You may need to install the feature.)
d. Type "Sun Visions Quarterly Report" as the presentation title, enter your name in the footer, and finish the wizard to show the first slide of the presentation.

## 2. View the PowerPoint window.
a. Identify the Standard, Formatting, and Drawing toolbars.
b. Click the More Buttons button on the Standard and Formatting toolbars to view your other toolbar buttons.
c. Display the Common Tasks drop-down menu.
d. Identify as many other elements of the PowerPoint window as you can without referring to the unit material.

## 3. View a presentation.
a. View all the slides in your presentation in Slide Show view.
b. Switch to Outline view and review the presentation contents.
c. Switch to Notes page view and scroll through the presentation to see if any of the slides contain notes.
d. Switch to Slide view and view each slide.
e. View all of the slides in the presentation in Slide Sorter view.

## 4. Save a presentation.
a. Open the Save As dialog box.
b. Save your presentation as "Qtr 4 Report" to your Project Disk, making sure to embed the fonts in your presentation.
c. Return to Normal view, then save your changes.

## 5. Get Help.
a. If the Office Assistant is open, click it. If not, open the Office Assistant.
b. Search for information on printing a presentation.
c. Select About printing and then read the information in the Help window, exploring any additional topics that interest you.
d. Click the Show button to expand the Help window.
e. On the Contents tab, double-click the Designing Slide Shows book icon, and then read the Help topic The 4Ps of presenting.
f. On the Index tab, search for information on a topic that interests you.
g. Close the Help window and hide the Office Assistant.

## 6. Print and close the file, and exit PowerPoint.
a. Save your presentation.
b. Open the Print dialog box and explore the different print options.
c. Print slides 3 and 5 as handouts in grayscale.
d. Print all of the slides in Outline view, in pure black and white.
e. Close your presentation and exit PowerPoint.

# ▶ Visual Workshop PowerPoint Unit A

Create the presentation shown in Figure A-14 using the Project Post-Mortem AutoContent Wizard in the Projects category. Save the presentation as "UniGraphix" to your Project Disk. Print slides 1 and 3 as handouts, two slides per page, in black and white, framed.

FIGURE A-14

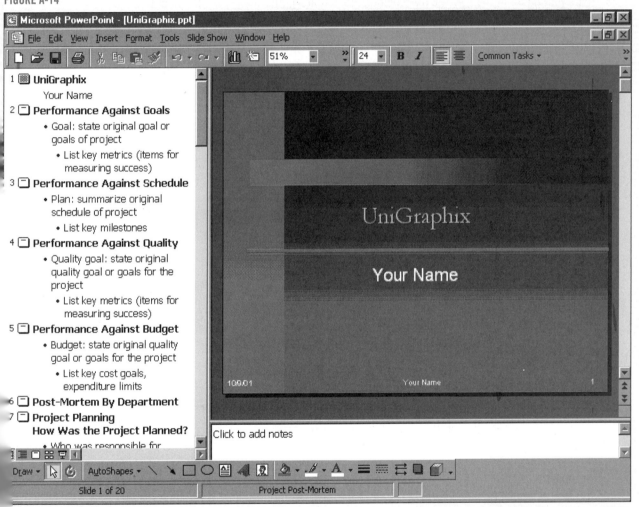

**1. Choose a look for a presentation.**
   **a.** Start PowerPoint and open a new presentation by clicking the Design Template option button or by clicking New on the File menu.
   **b.** Display the Design Templates tab, then open a presentation using the Factory template.
   **c.** In the New Slide dialog box, select Title Slide as the first slide.
   **d.** Save the presentation as "2001 Goals" to your Project Disk.

**2. Enter slide text.**
   **a.** Type "Year 2001 Goals" in the title placeholder.
   **b.** Type your name in the subtitle placeholder, press [Enter], and then type today's date.
   **c.** Deselect the text object, and then save your changes to the presentation.

**3. Create new slides.**
   **a.** Add a new slide to the presentation. Select the Bulleted List AutoLayout for slide 2.
   **b.** Type "What's New" as the title of slide 2.
   **c.** Type the following items in the main text object as a bulleted list: "New locations", "Executive positions", "Warehouse positions", "Advertising campaigns".

**4. Work in Outline view.**
   **a.** Switch to Outline view, then create a new bulleted list slide as slide 3.
   **b.** In the Outline pane, type "What's Revised" as the title for slide 3.
   **c.** Type the following items as a bulleted list on slide 3: "Chain of command", "Shipping/receiving procedures", "Work shifts", "Office upgrade".
   **d.** Create a new bulleted list slide as slide 4. Type "New Changes" as the title and add the following as a bulleted list: "Work shifts added", "Equipment upgrade", "Position advancement".
   **e.** Create a new bulleted list slide as slide 5. Type "Employee Benefits" as the title and add the following as a bulleted list: "Profit share percent up", "In-house promotions", "Year-end bonuses".
   **f.** On slide 2, move the first bulleted item, "New locations", to the third bullet position.
   **g.** On slide 3, move "Shipping/receiving procedures" to the fourth bullet position and "Office upgrade" to the second bullet position.

**5. Enter notes.**
   **a.** Go to slide 2, switch to Notes Page view, and adjust the zoom level to 100%.
   **b.** Click the notes placeholder, then type "We will hire within the company to fill new positions before advertising in the paper".
   **c.** Switch to Normal view, go to slide 3, then place the insertion point in the Notes pane.
   **d.** Type "A memo outlining the new chain of command for each location will be sent next week."

**6. Check spelling in the presentation.**
   **a.** Spell check the presentation. Correct any misspelled words and ignore any words that are spelled correctly.
   **b.** Add your name as a footer and "Employee Meeting 2001 Goals" as a header to all notes and handouts.

**7. Evaluate your presentation.**
   **a.** View the presentation in Slide Show view and evaluate it using the points described in the lesson.
   **b.** Switch to Slide Sorter view, move slide 2 to the slide 3 position, move slide 5 to the slide 4 position, then delete the last slide.
   **c.** Change the design template to Blueprint for all slides in the presentation.
   **d.** Switch to Normal view, save your changes, then print the Notes pages in grayscale with a frame around the pa

# ► Visual Workshop PowerPoint Unit B

reate the presentation shown in Figures A-15 and A-16. Save the presentation as "Grand Opening" to your Project
isk. Review your slides in Slide Show view, add your name as a footer to all notes and handouts, then print the notes
age for slide 2 and print the outline.

GURE A-15

URE A-16

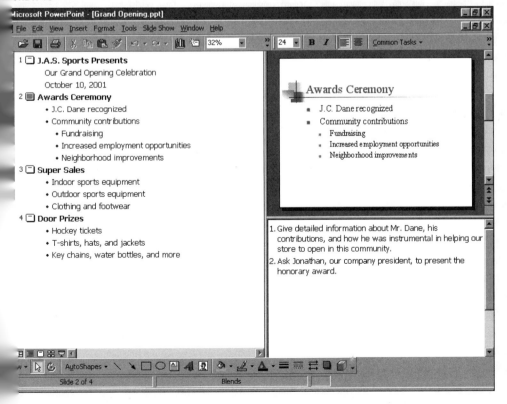

### 1. Open an existing presentation.
  **a.** Open the file BPPT-1 from your Project Disk and save it as "Company Picnic".

### 2. Draw and modify an object.
  **a.** Make sure the horizontal and vertical rulers are displayed. (*Hint*: Click Ruler on the View menu.)
  **b.** On slide 4, add the AutoShape Right Arrow from the Block Arrows category on the AutoShapes menu. Using the rulers as guides, draw the arrow 4" long and 1" deep.
  **c.** Change the fill color to turquoise, change the line color to no line, and apply 3-D Style 7 to the arrow.

### 3. Edit drawing objects.
  **a.** Move the arrow to the left side of the slide, just under the title.
  **b.** Make a copy of the arrow and place the copy in the lower-right corner of the slide. Make two more copies and arrange them between the first two arrows in stair-step fashion.
  **c.** Insert the text "Top sales award" on the first arrow, "Employee of the month" on the second arrow, "Raffle drawing" on the third arrow, and "First place winners" on the fourth arrow.

### 4. Align and group objects.
  **a.** Select all four arrows, then distribute them horizontally and vertically. (*Hint*: Use the Align or Distribute command on the Draw button menu.)
  **b.** Group the arrows.
  **c.** Change the arrow text font to Arial, then change the text color to black.
  **d.** Copy the group of arrows and paste them on slide 2. Change the text on the arrows to the following: "Family guests", "Side dish or dessert", "Beach toys", "Lawn chairs".

### 5. Add and arrange text.
  **a.** Go to slide 3 and display the guides.
  **b.** Move the vertical guide left to about 1.33 and move the horizontal guide up to about 1.58.
  **c.** Starting at the intersection of the guides, create a word-processing box about 5" wide.
  **d.** Type the following as a list in the text object: "Chicken and beef BBQ", "Soft drinks, juice, and coffee", "Games and races for all ages", "Location maps or 10 am carpool".
  **e.** Turn off the guides in the presentation.

### 6. Format text.
  **a.** Select the entire text object, increase the font size to 28 points, change the font to Arial, then apply bold and italic.
  **b.** On slide 1, select the subtitle text object, then change the font size to 28 points and apply bold and italic.

### 7. Customize the color scheme and background.
  **a.** Open the Color Scheme dialog box, then apply the upper-middle color scheme to all slides.
  **b.** Open the Background dialog box, click the Background fill list arrow, and then open the Fill Effects dialog box
  **c.** On the Gradient tab, select a two-color gradient. For color one, select the light yellow Follow Accent Scheme Color; for color two, select the gold Follow Accent and Followed Hyperlink Scheme Color. Apply this background to all slides.

### 8. Correct text automatically.
  **a.** On slide 5, type the title "Saturday Raffle Prizes".
  **b.** Type the following items as a bulleted list: "Sony DiscMan(tm)", "Disney Video Collection(c)", Tropical Vacation(r) for two".
  **c.** Add your name to the footer of all notes and handouts.
  **d.** Save your changes, and then print the slides as handouts, six slides per page.

reate a one-slide presentation that looks like the one shown in Figure A-17. Add your name as a footer on the slide.
ve the presentation as "Beach Activities" to your Project Disk, then print the slide in Slide View.

**URE A-17**

# ► Skills Review PowerPoint Unit D

## 1. Insert clip art.
a. Open the presentation BPPT-2 from your Project Disk and save it as "Employee Meeting".
b. Go to slide 2, then apply the Text & ClipArt AutoLayout to the slide.
c. Insert an appropriate graphic from the Business category of the Clip Gallery.

## 2. Insert, crop, and scale a picture.
a. Change slide 5 to the Text & Object layout, then insert the file Celebrate.bmp from your Project Disk into the object placeholder.
b. Crop the graphic to eliminate the man on the left, then make the background transparent.
c. Scale the graphic so its height and width is 120% of the original, move it to the left about 1", then align the top of the graphic with the top of the text object.

## 3. Embed a chart and enter and edit data in a datasheet.
a. Go to slide 6 and apply the Chart AutoLayout.
b. Start Microsoft Graph, and then enter the information shown in Table A-2 into the datasheet.
c. Delete column D, then close the datasheet but leave Graph running.

## 4. Format a chart.
a. Apply currency style with no decimals to the values on the vertical axis.
b. Insert the chart title "Amberlings Sales Report", then format it in 18-point Arial.
c. Place the Legend at the bottom of the chart, then exit Graph.

TABLE A-2

|          | 1998 | 1999 | 2000 |
|----------|------|------|------|
| Jonathan | 4508 | 5236 | 5579 |
| Jessica  | 4365 | 4778 | 6847 |
| Maric    | 3845 | 5482 | 5744 |

## 5. Use slide show commands.
a. Begin the slide show at slide 1, then use the Go command to advance to slide 4.
b. Use a magenta pen to circle "Warehouse positions", then erase the pen annotations and change the pointer back to an arrow.
c. Press [End] to move to the last slide, then return to Normal view.

## 6. Create a table.
a. On slide 7, apply the Table AutoLayout. Add a table with three columns and six rows.
b. Type "What", "When", and "Where" in the header row.
c. In the first column, add the names of meetings or events, in the second column add the names of months, and in the third column add locations for the events.
d. Adjust the columns to fit the text and center the table on the slide.
e. Center the column headings vertically and horizontally, apply bold, and then increase the font size to 32 point
f. Apply a fill color to the header row background and a different fill color to the background of the remaining row

## 7. Setting slide show timings and transitions.
a. Switch to Slide Sorter View. Open the Slide Transition dialog box and set the slides to automatically advanc after 4 seconds.
b. Apply the Split Horizontal In slide transition to slides 1, 3, 5, and 7. Apply the Split Vertical In slide transiti to slides 2, 4, 6, and 8.
c. View the slide show to verify the transitions are correct.

## 8. Set slide animation effects.
a. Apply the Flying preset animation effect to slides 1, 3, 4, 5, and 7. Apply the Animate Chart preset animati effect to slide 6.
b. Apply the Dissolve animation effect to the graphic on slide 2, then view the slide show to check the animation eff
c. Add your name as a footer to notes and handouts, save your changes, then print the presentation as hand outs, six slides per page.

Bonus Exercises

eate the Table slide shown in Figure A-18. Save the presentation as "Banquet Schedule" to your Project Disk. Add ur name to the slide footer and print the slide in pure black and white, framed. (*Hint*: Use the Format Table dialog x to add a diagonal line to a cell.)

URE A-18

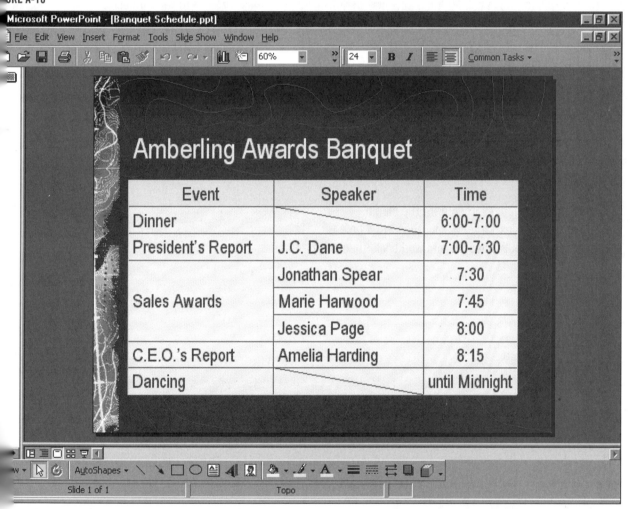

# ▶ Skills Review Integration

## 1. Open multiple programs.
   **a.** Start Word, then minimize the program window.
   **b.** Start Excel, then minimize the program window.
   **c.** Tile the windows vertically so that both program windows are in view on your screen.

## 2. Copy Word data into Excel.
   **a.** In Word, open the file BINT-1 from your Project Disk and save it as "Sales Target Memo".
   **b.** Replace Martin Flanders' name with your name.
   **c.** Select the table in the Word document, press [Ctrl], then drag the table to the Excel worksheet and paste it that the outline of the table is positioned in the range A1:D7.
   **d.** Resize the column widths for columns A, C, and D so that the ScreenTip indicates 12 pixels.
   **e.** Type your name in cell A9, then save the workbook as "Q1 Sales Targets" to your Project Disk.
   **f.** Print the Q1 Sales Targets workbook, then close it. Do not exit Excel.

## 3. Create a dynamic link between Excel and Word.
   **a.** In the Excel program window, open the file BINT-2 and save it as "2002 Sales Targets" to your Project Disk.
   **b.** Select the chart in the Excel workbook, copy it, then use the Paste Special command to paste link it in the Word document below the sentence "The chart below shows our sales targets for the rest of 2002:".
   **c.** Position the chart so its left edge is aligned with the left edge of the paragraph above it. (*Hint*: Select the chart, then drag it to the right.)
   **d.** In the Excel worksheet, change the price of Lavender Shower Gel to $20.00. Notice the change in the chart the memo.
   **e.** Save your changes, then print the memo.
   **f.** Close the Sales Target Memo, then exit Word.
   **g.** Close the 2002 Sales Targets workbook, then exit Excel.

# ► Visual Workshop Integration

sing Word, Excel, and Access, create the form letter shown in Figure A-19. Merge the names and addresses contained the Sales Rep Table in the Access database Aunt Martha Cookies, found on your Project Disk, with a document you eate in Word. Use the Paste Special command to copy the chart from the Excel worksheet BINT-3 on your Project isk into the letter. (*Hints*: For the letter, use 14-point Times New Roman. Add the chart to the letter before you per- rm the merge.) Save the merge document as "Sales Letters" to your Project Disk. Your completed file should contain ven letters. Print the first letter.

URE A-19

January 15, 2002

John Brown
44 Sand Hill Lane
Atlanta, GA  30339

Dear John:

Congratulations on another great sales year! As the chart below illustrates, you and your sales colleagues succeeded in increasing sales of Aunt Martha's Cookies by 40% in 2001.

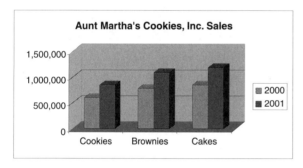

To acknowledge your efforts, I'm pleased to enclose a box of Aunt Martha's chocolate chip cookies, along with a gold watch embossed with the Aunt Martha's Cookies, Inc. logo. Great job!

Sincerely,

Your Name
Vice President, Sales
Aunt Martha's Cookies, Inc.

**1. Create a Web page document.**
   **a.** Start Word and create a new document using the Personal Web Page template.
   **b.** Apply the Bold Stripes theme, then save the document on your Project Disk using the filename "Personal Web Page" and the Web page title "My Web Page".
   **c.** Change the main heading to your name.
   **d.** Delete the Work Information and Current Projects hyperlinks and bullets under the Contents heading, then delete the Work Information and Current Projects sections and their subheadings (including the Back to top hyperlink) from the rest of the document.
   **e.** Under the heading Contact Information, delete the Office phone heading and the corresponding paragraph.
   **f.** In the Contact section, replace the text under the E-mail address heading with your e-mail address, then replace the text under the Web address heading with "mywebpage.com".
   **g.** Replace the text under the Biographical Information heading with appropriate information about you.
   **h.** Replace the text under the Personal Interests heading with a bulleted list containing the following three items: "Books", "Music", and "Hiking".
   **i.** Save your changes and close the file.

**2. Format a Web page.**
   **a.** Start FrontPage Express, then open the Personal Web Page file from your Project Disk.
   **b.** Right-align the page title, which should be your name, and then insert the My Graphic.gif file from your Project Disk to the left of your name. Add a space between the graphic and your name.
   **c.** Save your changes, then close the file and Front Page Express.
   **d.** Start Internet Explorer, then open the Personal Web Page file to review its appearance in the browser window. When you are finished, exit Internet Explorer.

**3. Create a Web page from an Excel workbook.**
   **a.** Start Excel, and then open the file BIE5-1 from your Project Disk.
   **b.** Click and drag to select the range A1:D13, then save the selected range as a Web page with the filename "Books.htm" and the page title "Favorite Books".
   **c.** Exit Excel without saving changes, then open the Books.htm file in Word.
   **d.** Apply the Bold Stripes theme to the page, and make any necessary adjustments to the format of the table.
   **e.** Delete the extra rows at the bottom of the table if necessary, save your changes, click Yes to overwrite the f then close the file.

**4. Add hyperlinks.**
   **a.** In Word, open the Personal Web Page.htm file from your Project Disk. Under the Favorite Links heading, replace the text next to the first bullet with a hyperlink named "Amazon.com" that opens the Web page wit the address http://www.amazon.com.
   **b.** Replace the text next to the second and third bullets with hyperlinks to "Barnes and Noble" (http://www.bn.com) and "Billboard.com" (http://www.billboard.com).
   **c.** Under the Personal Interest heading, create a hyperlink for the first bullet that links to the Books Web pag you created in Step 3.
   **d.** Use the procedure you learned in the "Adding Hyperlinks" lesson to reapply the bullets and the Bold Stripe theme, then save and close the Personal Web Page file.
   **e.** View and print the first page of each of your Web pages in Internet Explorer, then exit Word and Internet Explorer.

# ► Visual Workshop Internet Explorer

ou are a science teacher at West High School. You will be starting a new unit on the NASA Space Program and will
quire your students to complete a related project. You want to post information about the project on the school's
eb site. Use the Right-aligned Column Web page template in Word to create the NASA Space Program Project page
own in Figure A-20. Sketch and create a Web page for the science curriculum at West High School, with a link to the
ASA Space Program Project page. Create at least two other associated Web pages by creating files in Office programs
d then converting them to HTML and formatting them. Finally, add links between your pages. Print the first page of
ch of your Web pages using Internet Explorer. (*Hint*: The graphic is included in the Web page template.)

URE A-20

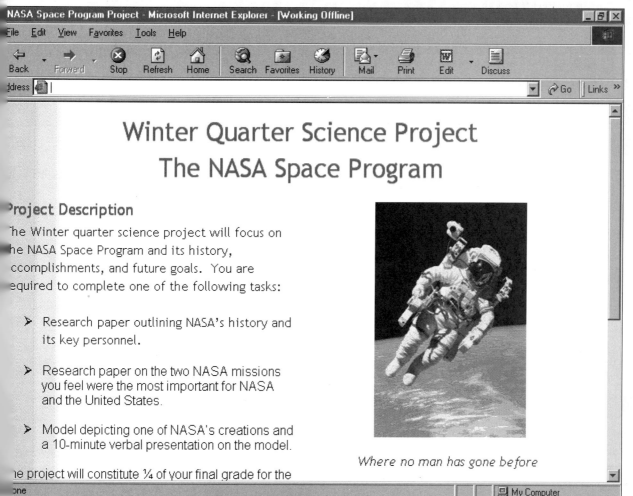

## ► Skills Review Publisher Unit A

1. **Start Publisher and view the Publisher window.**
   a. Start Publisher and exit the Catalog.
   b. Press [F1] to open the Office Assistant, search Help for information on toolbars, then close the Help window and hide the Office Assistant.

2. **Create a Publication using the Publication Wizard.**
   a. Open the Microsoft Publisher Catalog.
   b. Select the Play Announcement Flyer in the Announcement Flyers category, then start the Wizard.
   c. Choose the Lagoon color scheme, choose No for the customer address, click Finish, then hide the Wizard.

3. **Replace frame text.**
   a. Type "The Seagull" for the Play Title, then type "Anton Chekhov" for the Author name.
   b. In the text frame above the "Presents" text frame, type "Jasper Actors Guild".
   c. Type "7/5/02" for the date and "8:00" for the time.
   d. In the Describe your location text frame, insert the text file BPB-1 from your Project Disk.
   e. Delete the phone number, type your name as the contact person, then type "$8.00" for the Ticket Price.
   f. At the bottom, delete the middle and right logo placeholders and the three Organization Name text frames.
   g. Type "Tasty Donuts" as the organization in the remaining logo placeholder.

4. **Format text.**
   a. Change the font color of the text "Jasper Actors Guild" to green.
   b. Change the text "Hunter Pavilion, at Elm Tree Park" to 14-point Gil Sans MT. (*Hint*: If the font size does not change to 14 points, point to AutoFit Text on the Format menu, click None, then try again.)
   c. Change the font of the text in the Contact text box to Gil Sans MT, then format the text to autofit, best fit.

5. **Resize and move frames.**
   a. Resize the graphic frame by dragging the lower-right sizing handle to the 5½" mark on the horizontal ruler the 8½" mark on the vertical ruler.
   b. Move the "Sponsored by" and "Tasty Donuts" text frames so their left edges align at the 1½" mark on the horizontal ruler.

6. **Insert a picture.**
   a. Double-click the city graphic frame to open the Insert Clip Art dialog box.
   b. Type "seagull" in the Search for clips text box, then press [Enter].
   c. Insert one of the images using the Insert clip button, then close the dialog box. If the seagull images are r available to you, insert a different clip from the Clip Gallery.
   d. Click Tasty Donuts, click the Wizard button, then create a logo that has the Open Oval design, no placeholde graphic, and one line of text.

7. **Save, proof, print, and close a publication.**
   a. Save the publication as "Seagull" to your Project Disk.
   b. View your publication in Whole Page view, then make any necessary changes.
   c. Save your changes, print the publication, close the publication, then exit Publisher.

~reate the postcard shown in Figure A-21 using the Art Exhibit Announcement Wizard template in the Postcard category.
~e the Trout color scheme and include promotional text on the Address Side. To create the logo, use the Logo Creation
~izard and choose the Crossed Corner design. (*Hint*: To add the crayon graphic to the logo, double-click the graphic
~ceholder to open the Clip Gallery, then type "crayons" in the Search for clips text box. Insert another appropriate clip if
~e crayons clip is not available to you.) Save the publication as "Art Exhibit" to your Project Disk, then print a copy.

**~URE A-21**

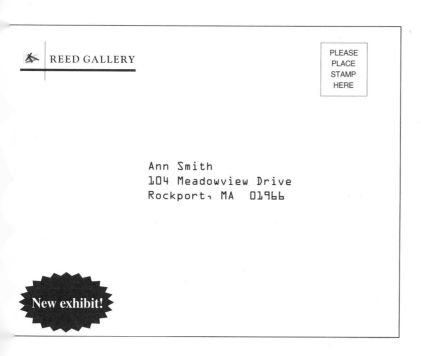

# Formatting
## a Disk

A **disk** is a device on which you can store electronic data. Disks come in a variety of sizes and have varying storage capacities. Your computer's **hard disk**, one of its internal devices, can store large amounts of data. **Floppy disks**, on the other hand, are smaller, inexpensive, and portable. Most floppy disks that you buy today are 3½" (the diameter of the inside, circular part of the disk). Disks are sometimes called **drives**, but this term really refers to the name by which the operating system recognizes the disk (or a portion of the disk). The operating system typically assigns a drive letter to a drive (which you can reassign if you want). For example, on most computers the hard disk is identified by the drive letter "C" and the floppy drive by the drive letter "A." The amount of information a disk can hold is called its **capacity**, usually measured in megabytes (Mb). The most common floppy disk capacity is 1.44 Mb. Newer computers come with other disk drives, such as a **Zip drive**, a kind of disk drive made to handle **Zip disks**. These disks are portable like floppy disks, but they can contain 100 Mb, far more than regular floppy disks.  In this appendix, you will prepare a floppy disk for use.

**Windows 2000**

# Formatting a Disk

In order for an operating system to be able to store data on a disk, the disk must be form **Formatting** prepares a disk so it can store information. Usually, floppy disks are form when you buy them, but if not, you can perform this function yourself using Windows To complete the following steps, you need a blank floppy disk or a disk containing you no longer need. Do not use your Project Disk for this lesson, as all information on the will be erased.

**Trouble?**

This unit assumes that the drive that will contain your floppy disks is drive A. If not, substitute the correct drive any time you are instructed to use the 3½ Floppy (A:) drive.

**1.** Start Windows if necessary, then place a 3½" floppy disk in drive A

**2.** Double-click the **My Computer icon** on the desktop
My Computer opens, as shown in Figure AP-1. This window lists all the drives and pr that you can use on your computer. Because computers have different drives, printers grams, and other devices installed, your window will probably look different.

**3.** Right-click the **3½ Floppy (A:) icon**
When you click with the right mouse button, a pop-up menu of commands that ap the item you right-clicked appears. Because you right-clicked a drive, the Format mand is available.

**Trouble?**

Windows cannot format a disk if it is write-protected; therefore, you may need to slide the write-protect tab over until it clicks to continue. See Figure AP-3 to locate the write-protect tab on your disk.

**4.** Click **Format** on the pop-up menu
The Format dialog box opens, as shown in Figure AP-2. In this dialog box, you s the capacity of the disk you are formatting, the File system, the Allocation unit size, the of formatting you want to do, and if you want, a volume label. You are doing a standar mat so you will accept the default settings.

**5.** Click **Start**, then, when you are warned that formatting will erase all data on the click **OK** to continue
Windows formats your disk. After the formatting is complete, you will probably see a mary about the size of the disk; it's okay if you don't.

**6.** Click **OK** when the message telling you that the format is complete appears, click **Close** in the Format dialog box

**QuickTip**

Once a disk is formatted, you do not need to format it again. However, some people use the Quick Format option to erase the contents of a disk quickly, rather than having to select the files and then delete them.

**7.** Click the **Close button** in the My Computer window
My Computer closes and you return to the desktop.

**FIGURE AP-1: My Computer window**

ve con-
ning
r disk

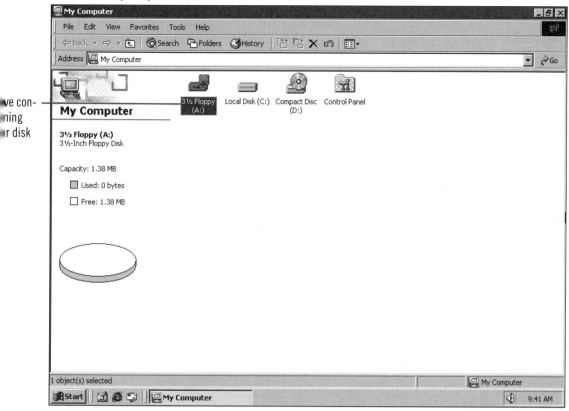

**FIGURE AP-2: Format dialog box**

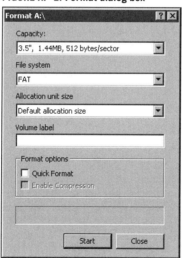

**FIGURE AP-3: Write-protect tab**

Move write-protect tab
down to protect disk, or up
to remove protection

3.5" disk

# Appendix A:
## Formatting a Disk

A **disk** is a device on which you can store electronic data. Disks come in a variety of sizes and have varying storage capacities. Your computer's **hard disk**, one of its internal devices, can store large amounts of data. **Floppy disks**, on the other hand, are smaller, inexpensive, and portable. Most floppy disks that you buy today are 3½" (the diameter of the inside, circular part of the disk). Disks are sometimes called **drives**, but this term really refers to the name by which the operating system recognizes the disk (or a portion of the disk). The operating system typically assigns a drive letter to a drive (which you can reassign if you want). For example, on most computers the hard disk is identified by the drive letter "C" and the floppy drive by the drive letter "A." The amount of information a disk can hold is called its **capacity**, usually measured in megabytes (Mb). The most common floppy disk capacity is 1.44 Mb. Newer computers come with devices, such as a **Zip drive**, a new kind of disk drive made to handle **Zip disks**. These disks are portable like floppy disks, but they can contain 100 Mb, far more than regular floppy disks. In this appendix, you will prepare a floppy disk for use.

# Formatting a Disk

For an operating system to be able to store data on a disk, the disk must be formatte **Formatting** prepares a disk so it can store information. Usually disks are formatted when y buy them, but if not, you can perform this function yourself using Windows 98. complete the following steps, you need a blank disk or a disk containing data you no lon need. Do not use your Project Disk for this lesson, as all information will be erased.

## Steps 1234

**Trouble?**

This unit assumes that the drive that will contain your floppy disks is drive A. If not, substitute the correct drive any time you are instructed to use the 3½ Floppy (A:) drive.

**1.** Start Windows if necessary, then place a 3½" floppy disk in drive A

**2.** Double-click the **My Computer icon** on the desktop

My Computer opens, as shown in Figure AP-1. This window lists all the drives and print that you can use on your computer. Because computers have different drives, printers, p grams, and so forth installed, your window will probably look different.

**3.** Right-click the 3½ **Floppy (A:) icon**

When you click with the right mouse button, a pop-up menu of commands that apply to item you right-clicked appears. You right-clicked a drive so the Format command is availa

**Trouble?**

Windows cannot format a disk if it is write-protected; therefore, you need to move the write-protect tab to continue. See Figure AP-3 to locate the write-protect tab on your disk.

**4.** Click **Format** on the pop-up menu

The Format dialog box opens, as shown in Figure AP-2. In this dialog box, you spe the capacity of the disk you are formatting and the kind of formatting you want to do. Table AP-1 for a description of formatting options.

**5.** Click the **Full option button**, then click **Start**

Windows formats your disk. By selecting the Full option, you ensure that your computer read the disk. After the formatting is complete, you will probably see a summary about size of the disk; it's okay if you don't.

**6.** Click **Close** in the Format Results dialog box, then click **Close** in the Format dialog

**QuickTip**

Once a disk is formatted, you do not need to format it again. However, some people use the Quick (erase) option to quickly erase the contents of a disk rather than having to select the files and then delete them.

**7.** Click the **Close button** in the My Computer window

My Computer closes and you return to the desktop.

**TABLE AP-1: Options in the Format dialog box**

| option | description |
|---|---|
| Capacity | Use to specify the amount of information your disk is made to hold |
| Quick (erase) | Use for an already-formatted disk that contains files you want to erase; it takes less time than the Full option |
| Full | Use for a new, unformatted disk; this option initializes the disk, preparing it to receive data and requiring more ti to complete than the Quick option |
| Copy system files only | Use to make an already-formatted disk bootable, meaning you will be able to start your computer with it |
| Label | Use to give your disk a name to make it easier to identify later |
| Display summary when finished | Use to see information about the disk after formatting is finished, such as how much space is available on the di |
| Copy system files | Use to format the disk and then make it bootable after formatting is complete by copying system files to it |

FIGURE AP-1: **My Computer window**

e containing
disk

icons may
different

FIGURE AP-2: **Format dialog box**

to format a new,
matted disk

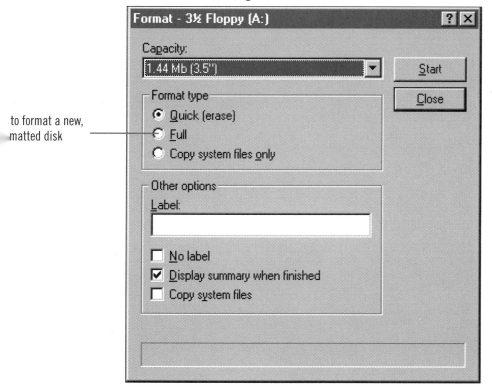

FIGURE AP-3: **Write-protect tab**

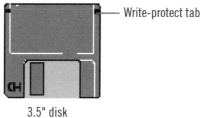

Write-protect tab

3.5" disk

# Word 2000 MOUS Certification Objectives

...low is a list of the Microsoft Office User Specialist program objectives for Core Word 2000 skills showing where each ...OUS objective is covered in the Lessons and the Practice. This table lists the Core MOUS certification skills covered ... the units in this book (Units A–D). The core skills without page references are covered in *Microsoft Office 2000— ...strated Second Course* (Units E–H). For more information on which Illustrated titles meet MOUS certification, ...ase see the inside cover of this book.

| ...OUS ...andardized ...ding number | Activity | Lesson page where skill is covered | Location in lesson where skill is covered | Practice |
|---|---|---|---|---|
| ...000.1 | **Working with text** | | | |
| ...000.1.1 | Use the Undo, Redo, and Repeat command | WORD B-6 | Clues to Use | Skills Review |
| ...000.1.2 | Apply font formats (Bold, Italic and Underline) | WORD C-4 | Steps 2–8 | Skills Review, Independent Challenges 1–4 |
| ...000.1.3 | Use the SPELLING feature | WORD B-14 | Steps 3–7 | Skills Review, Independent Challenges 1, 2, 4 |
| ...000.1.4 | Use the THESAURUS feature | WORD B-15 | Clues to Use | Skills Review, Independent Challenge 2 |
| ...000.1.5 | Use the GRAMMAR feature | WORD B-14 | Steps 3–7 | Skills Review, Independent Challenges 1, 2, 4 |
| ...00.1.6 | Insert page breaks | | | |
| ...00.1.7 | Highlight text in document | WORD C-4 | Clues to Use | Independent Challenge 2 |
| ...00.1.8 | Insert and move text | WORD B-10 | Steps 1–9 | Skills Review, Independent Challenges 1–4 |
| ...00.1.9 | Cut, Copy, Paste, and Paste Special using the Office Clipboard | WORD B-8 WORD B-10 WORD B-12 | Details Steps 1–6 Steps 1–6 | Skills Review, Independent Challenges 1–4 |
| ...00.1.10 | Copy formats using the Format Painter | WORD C-6 | Clues to Use | Skills Review |
| ...00.1.11 | Select and change font and font size | WORD C-2 | Steps 3–8 | Skills Review, Independent Challenges 1–4, Visual Workshop |
| ...00.1.12 | Find and replace text | WORD B-18 | Steps 1–6 | Skills Review, Independent Challenges 1, 4 |
| ...00.1.13 | Apply character effects (superscript, subscript, strikethrough, small caps and outline) | WORD C-4 | Steps 4–8 | Skills Review, Independent Challenges 1, 4 |
| ...0.1.14 | Insert date and time | | | |
| ...0.1.15 | Insert symbols | | | |
| ...0.1.16 | Create and apply frequently used text with AutoCorrect | WORD B-16 | Steps 1–5 | Skills Review, Independent Challenge 3 |
| ...0.2 | **Working with paragraphs** | | | |
| ...0.2.1 | Align text in paragraphs (Center, Left, Right and Justified) | WORD C-6 | Steps 1–4 | Skills Review, Independent Challenges 1–4, Visual Workshop |

| MOUS standardized coding number | Activity | Lesson page where skill is covered | Location in lesson where skill is covered | Practice |
|---|---|---|---|---|
| W2000.2.2 | Add bullets and numbering | WORD C-16 | Steps 1–7 | Skills Review, Independent Challenges 1, 2, Visual Workshop |
| W2000.2.3 | Set character, line, and paragraph spacing options | WORD C-4 WORD C-10 WORD C-12 | QuickTip Steps 1–5 Steps 1–7 | Skills Review, Independent Challenges 3, 4, Visual Workshop |
| W2000.2.4 | Apply borders and shading to paragraphs | WORD C-18 | Steps 1–7 Clues to Use | Skills Review, Independent Challenges 2, 3, 4, Visual Workshop |
| W2000.2.5 | Use indentation options (Left, Right, First Line and Hanging Indent) | WORD C-8 | Steps 1–6 Clues to Use | Skills Review, Independent Challenges 1, 2, 3 |
| W2000.2.6 | Use TABS command (Center, Decimal, Left and Right) | WORD C-14 | Steps 1–7 | Skills Review, Independent Challenges 2, 3 |
| W2000.2.7 | Create an outline style numbered list | WORD C-17 | Clues to Use | |
| W2000.2.8 | Set tabs with leaders | WORD C-14 | Steps 3–7 | Skills Review |
| **W2000.3** | **Working with documents** | | | |
| W2000.3.1 | Print a document | WORD A-12 | Steps 5–6 | Skills Review, Independent Challenges 1–4, Visual Workshop |
| W2000.3.2 | Use print preview | WORD A-12 | Steps 1–4 | Skills Review, Independent Challenges 1–4 |
| W2000.3.3 | Use Web Page Preview | | | |
| W2000.3.4 | Navigate through a document | | | |
| W2000.3.5 | Insert page numbers | | | |
| W2000.3.6 | Set page orientation | | | |
| W2000.3.7 | Set margins | | | |
| W2000.3.8 | Use GoTo to locate specific elements in a document | | | |
| W2000.3.9 | Create and modify page numbers | | | |
| W2000.3.10 | Create and modify headers and footers | | | |
| W2000.3.11 | Align text vertically | | | |
| W2000.3.12 | Create and use newspaper columns | | | |
| W2000.3.13 | Revise column structure | | | |
| W2000.3.14 | Prepare and print envelopes and labels | | | |
| W2000.3.15 | Apply styles | | | |
| W2000.3.16 | Create sections with formatting that differs from other sections | | | |
| W2000.3.17 | Use click & type | | | |

| MOUS Standardized Coding number | Activity | Lesson page where skill is covered | Location in lesson where skill is covered | Practice |
|---|---|---|---|---|
| 2000.4 | **Managing files** | | | |
| 2000.4.1 | Use Save | WORD A-10 | Steps 1–4 | Skills Review, Independent Challenges 1–4, Visual Workshop |
| 2000.4.2 | Locate and open an existing document | WORD B-4 | Steps 2–5 | Skills Review, Independent Challenges 1, 2 |
| 2000.4.3 | Use Save As (different name, location or format) | WORD B-4 | Steps 6–7 | Skills Review, Independent Challenges 1, 2 |
| 2000.4.4 | Create a folder | WORD B-4 | QuickTip | |
| 2000.4.5 | Create a new document using a Wizard | WORD B-3 | Clues to Use | Independent Challenge 4 |
| 2000.4.6 | Save as Web Page | | | |
| 2000.4.7 | Use templates to create a new document | WORD B-3 | Clues to Use | Visual Workshop |
| 2000.4.8 | Create hyperlinks | | | |
| 2000.4.9 | Use the Office Assistant | WORD A-14 | Steps 1–8 | Skills Review, Independent Challenges 1, 3 |
| 2000.4.10 | Send a WORD document via e-mail | | | |
| 2000.5 | **Using tables** | | | |
| 2000.5.1 | Create and format tables | WORD D-2 | Steps 4–10 | Skills Review, Independent Challenges 1–3, Visual Workshop |
| 2000.5.2 | Add borders and shading to tables | WORD D-8 | Steps 1–5 Clues to Use | Skills Review, Independent Challenges 1–4, Visual Workshop |
| 2000.5.3 | Revise tables (insert & delete rows and columns, change cell formats) | WORD D-6 | Steps 1–5 | Skills Review, Independent Challenges 1–4 |
| 2000.5.4 | Modify table structure (merge cells, change height and width) | WORD D-4 WORD D-16 | Steps 1–4 Steps 1–5 | Skills Review, Independent Challenges 1–4, Visual Workshop |
| 2000.5.5 | Rotate text in a table | WORD D-14 | Clues to Use | Skills Review, Independent Challenge 2 |
| 2000.6 | **Working with pictures and charts** | | | |
| 2000.6.1 | Use the drawing toolbar | | | |
| 2000.6.2 | Insert graphics into a document (WORDArt, ClipArt, images) | | | |

# Excel 2000 MOUS Certification Objectives

elow is a list of the Microsoft™ Office User Specialist program objectives for Core Excel 2000 skills showing where ch MOUS objective is covered in the Lessons and Practice. This table lists the Core MOUS certification skills covered in the units in this book (Units A-D). The core skills without page references are covered in *Microsoft Office 2000-ustrated Second Course* (Units E-H). For more information on which Illustrated titles meet MOUS certification, ease see the inside cover of this book.

| OUS andardized oding number | Activity | Lesson page where skill is covered | Location in lesson where skill is covered | Practice |
|---|---|---|---|---|
| **2000.1** | **Working with cells** | | | |
| 2000.1.1 | Use Undo and Redo | Excel B-4 | Steps 7-8, QuickTip | Skills Review |
| 2000.1.2 | Clear cell content | Excel A-10 | Trouble, Step 2 | Skills Review |
| 2000.1.3 | Enter text, dates, and numbers | Excel A-10 | Steps 2-7 | Skills Review, Independent Challenges 2-4 |
| 2000.1.4 | Edit cell content | Excel B-4 | Steps 3-10 | Skills Review, Independent Challenges 2-3 |
| 2000.1.5 | Go to a specific cell | | | |
| 2000.1.6 | Insert and delete selected cells | | | |
| 2000.1.7 | Cut, copy, paste, paste special and move selected cells, use the Office Clipboard, Paste Special | Excel B-10 Excel B-11 Excel B-14 | Steps 2-4, QuickTips Step 2 QuickTip | Skills Review, Independent Challenges 1-4 |
| 2000.1.8 | Use Find and Replace | | | |
| 2000.1.9 | Clear cell formats | Excel C-6 | QuickTip | Skills Review |
| 2000.1.10 | Work with series (AutoFill) | Excel B-14 Excel B-15 | Step 3 Clues to Use | Skills Review |
| 2000.1.11 | Create hyperlinks | | | |
| **2000.2** | **Working with files** | | | |
| 2000.2.1 | Use Save | Excel A-10 | Step 8 | |
| 2000.2.2 | Use Save As (different name, location, format) | Excel A-8 | Steps 5-6 | Skills Review |
| 2000.2.3 | Locate and open an existing workbook | Excel A-8 | Steps 1-4 | Skills Review, Independent Challenges 2-4, Visual Workshop |
| 2000.2.4 | Create a folder | | | |
| 2000.2.5 | Use templates to create a new workbook | | | |
| 2000.2.6 | Save a worksheet/workbook as a Web Page | | | |
| 2000.2.7 | Send a workbook via email | | | |
| 2000.2.8 | Use the Office Assistant | Excel A-14 | Steps 1-6 Clues to Use | Independent Challenge 1 |
| **2000.3** | **Formatting worksheets** | | | |
| 2000.3.1 | Apply font styles (typeface, size, color and styles) | Excel C-4 Excel C-6 | Steps 2-5, Clues to Use Steps 2-7 | Skills Review, Independent Challenges 1-4, Visual Workshop |

| MOUS standardized coding number | Activity | Lesson page where skill is covered | Location in lesson where skill is covered | Practice |
|---|---|---|---|---|
| XL2000.3.2 | Apply number formats (currency, percent, dates, comma) | Excel C-2 | Steps 3-5 | Skills Review, Independent Challenges 1-4, Visual Workshop |
| XL2000.3.3 | Modify size of rows and columns | Excel C-8 Excel C-9 | Steps 1-7 Clues to Use | Skills Review, Independent Challenges 1-4 |
| XL2000.3.4 | Modify alignment of cell content | Excel C-6 | Step 7 | Skills Review, Independent Challenges 1-4 |
| XL2000.3.5 | Adjust the decimal place | | | |
| XL2000.3.6 | Use the Format Painter | Excel C-3 Excel C-14 | Clues to Use Step 6 | Skills Review, Independent Challenges 1-4 |
| XL2000.3.7 | Apply autoformat | Excel C-7 | Clues to Use | |
| XL2000.3.8 | Apply cell borders and shading | Excel C-12 | Steps 2-8 | Skills Review, Independent Challenges 1-4 |
| XL2000.3.9 | Merging cells | Excel C-6 | Step 6 | Skills Review, Independent Challenge 2 |
| XL2000.3.10 | Rotate text and change indents | | | |
| XL2000.3.11 | Define, apply, and remove a style | | | |
| **XL2000.4** | **Page setup and printing** | | | |
| XL2000.4.1 | Preview and print worksheets & workbooks | Excel A-12 | Steps 1-5 | Skills Review, Independent Challenges 2-4, Visual Workshop |
| XL2000.4.2 | Use Web Page Preview | | | |
| XL2000.4.3 | Print a selection | | | |
| XL2000.4.4 | Change page orientation and scaling | | | |
| XL2000.4.5 | Set page margins and centering | | | |
| XL2000.4.6 | Insert and remove a page break | | | |
| XL2000.4.7 | Set print, and clear a print area | | | |
| XL2000.4.8 | Set up headers and footers | | | |
| XL2000.4.9 | Set print titles and options (gridlines, print quality, row & column headings) | | | |
| **XL2000.5** | **Working with worksheets & workbooks** | | | |
| XL2000.5.1 | Insert and delete rows and columns | Excel C-10 | Steps 1-6 | Skills Review |
| XL2000.5.2 | Hide and unhide rows and columns | | | |
| XL2000.5.3 | Freeze and unfreeze rows and columns | | | |
| XL2000.5.4 | Change the zoom setting | | | |
| XL2000.5.5 | Move between worksheets in a workbook | Excel B-18 | Steps 1-2 | Skills Review, Independent Challenges 1-4, |
| XL2000.5.6 | Check spelling | Excel C-16 | Steps 1-5 | Skills Review |
| XL2000.5.7 | Rename a worksheet | Excel B-18 | Steps 3-4 | Skills Review, Independent Challenges 1-4 |
| XL2000.5.8 | Insert and Delete worksheets | Excel B-18 | QuickTip | Skills Review |

| MOUS Standardized Coding number | Activity | Lesson page where skill is covered | Location in lesson where skill is covered | Practice |
|---|---|---|---|---|
| 2000.5.9 | Move and copy worksheets | Excel B-18<br>Excel B-19 | Step 6<br>Clues to Use | Skills Review,<br>Independent Challenge 1 |
| 2000.5.10 | Link worksheets & consolidate data using 3D References | | | |
| **2000.6** | **Working with formulas & functions** | | | |
| 2000.6.1 | Enter a range within a formula by dragging | Excel B-8 | Steps 4-6 | Skills Review,<br>Independent Challenges 1-4 |
| 2000.6.2 | Enter formulas in a cell and using the formula bar | Excel B-6 | Steps 1-4 | Skills Review,<br>Independent Challenges 1-4 |
| 2000.6.3 | Revise formulas | Excel B-16 | Steps 6-7 | Skills Review,<br>Independent Challenges 1-4 |
| 2000.6.4 | Use references (absolute and relative) | Excel B-12<br>Excel B-14<br>Excel B-16 | Details<br>Steps 1-8<br>Steps 1-8 | Skills Review,<br>Independent Challenges 1, 4 |
| 2000.6.5 | Use AutoSum | Excel B-8 | Steps 2-4 | Skills Review |
| 2000.6.6 | Use Paste Function to insert a function | Excel B-8 | Steps 7-9 | Skills Review |
| 2000.6.7 | Use basic functions (AVERAGE, SUM, COUNT, MIN, MAX) | Excel B-8<br>Excel B-9 | Steps 8-9<br>Clues to Use | Skills Review |
| 2000.6.8 | Enter functions using the formula palette | | | |
| 2000.6.9 | Use date functions (NOW and DATE) | | | |
| 2000.6.10 | Use financial functions (FV and PMT) | | | |
| 2000.6.11 | Use logical functions (IF) | | | |
| **2000.7** | **Using charts and objects** | | | |
| 2000.7.1 | Preview and print charts | Excel D-16 | Steps 2-8 | Skills Review,<br>Independent Challenges 1-4,<br>Visual Workshop |
| 2000.7.2 | Use chart wizard to create a chart | Excel D-4 | Steps 2-7 | Skills Review,<br>Independent Challenges 1-4,<br>Visual Workshop |
| 2000.7.3 | Modify charts | Excel D-6<br>Excel D-8<br>Excel D-10 | Steps 2-8<br>Steps 2-6<br>Steps 2-6 | Skills Review,<br>Independent Challenges 1-4,<br>Visual Workshop |
| 2000.7.4 | Insert, move, and delete an object (picture) | | | |
| 2000.7.5 | Create and modify lines and objects | Excel D-12<br>Excel D-14 | Steps 4-8<br>Steps 2-8 | Skills Review,<br>Independent Challenges 1-4,<br>Visual Workshop |

# Access 2000 MOUS Certification Objectives

Below is a list of the Microsoft™ Office User Specialist program objectives for Core Access 2000 skills showing where each MOUS objective is covered in the Lessons and Practice. This table lists the Core MOUS certification skills covered in the units in this book (Units A-D). The core skills without page references are covered in *Microsoft Office 2000—Illustrated Second Course* (Units E-H). For more information on which Illustrated titles meet MOUS certification, please see the inside cover of this book.

| MOUS Standardized Coding number | Activity | Lesson page where skill is covered | Location in lesson where skill is covered | Practice |
|---|---|---|---|---|
| 2000.1 | **Planning and designing databases** | | | |
| 2000.1.1 | Determine appropriate data inputs for your database | Access B-2 | Details Table B-1 | Skills Review, Independent Challenges 1-4, Visual Workshop |
| 2000.1.2 | Determine appropriate data outputs for your database | Access A-4 | Table A-2 | Skills Review, Independent Challenges 1-4 |
| 2000.1.3 | Create table structure | Access B-4 | Steps 2-7 | Skills Review, Independent Challenges 1-4 |
| 2000.1.4 | Establish table relationships | | | |
| 2000.2 | **Working with Access** | | | |
| 2000.2.1 | Use the Office Assistant | Access A-18 | Steps 3-6 | Skills Review |
| 2000.2.2 | Select an object using the Objects Bar | Access B-8 | Steps 1-2 | Skills Review, Independent Challenges 1-4 |
| 2000.2.3 | Print database objects (tables, forms, reports, queries) | Access A-16 | Steps 1-7 | Skills Review, Independent Challenges 1-4 |
| 2000.2.4 | Navigate through records in a table, query, or form | Access A-10 | Steps 2-6 | Skills Review, Independent Challenges 1-4 |
| 2000.2.5 | Create a database (using a Wizard or in Design View) | | | |
| 2000.3 | **Building and modifying tables** | | | |
| 2000.3.1 | Create tables by using the Table Wizard | Access B-4 | Step 1 | Skills Review, Independent Challenges 1-2 |
| 2000.3.2 | Set primary keys | Access B-4 | Steps 6-7 | Skills Review, Independent Challenges 1-4 |
| 2000.3.3 | Modify field properties | Access B-6 | Steps 5-6 | Skills Review, Independent Challenges 1-4 |
| 2000.3.4 | Use multiple data types | Access B-6 | Step 2 | Skills Review, Independent Challenges 1-4 |
| 2000.3.5 | Modify tables using Design View | Access B-6 | Steps 1-8 | Skills Review, Independent Challenges 1-4 |
| 2000.3.6 | Use the Lookup Wizard | | | |
| 2000.3.7 | Use the input mask wizard | | | |
| 2000.4 | **Building and modifying forms** | | | |
| 2000.4.1 | Create a form with the Form Wizard | Access C-4 | Steps 1-3 | Skills Review, Independent Challenges 1-3 |

| MOUS standardized coding number | Activity | Lesson page where skill is covered | Location in lesson where skill is covered | Practice |
|---|---|---|---|---|
| AC2000.4.2 | Use the Control Toolbox to add controls | Access C-10<br>Access C-16 | Steps 1-7<br>Steps 2-5 | Skills Review,<br>Independent Challenges 2-3 |
| AC2000.4.3 | Modify Format Properties (font, style, font size, color, caption, etc.) of controls | Access C-8<br>Access C-10 | Steps 2-5<br>Steps 5-6 | Skills Review,<br>Independent Challenges 2-3 |
| AC2000.4.4 | Use form sections (headers, footers, detail) | Access C-6<br>Access C-12<br>Access C-16 | Steps 1-6<br>Steps 2-5<br>Steps 2-5 | Skills Review,<br>Independent Challenges 2-3 |
| AC2000.4.5 | Use a Calculated Control on a form | Access C-10 | Steps 2-7 | Skills Review,<br>Independent Challenges 2 |
| **AC2000.5** | **Viewing and organizing information** | | | |
| AC2000.5.1 | Use the Office Clipboard | Access D-10 | Clues to Use | Skills Review,<br>Independent Challenges 2-3 |
| AC2000.5.2 | Switch between object Views | Access B-6<br>Access B-18 | Step 7<br>Step 6 | Skills Review,<br>Independent Challenges 1-4<br>Visual Workshop |
| AC2000.5.3 | Enter records using a datasheet | Access A-12 | Steps 2-4 | Skills Review,<br>Independent Challenges 3-4<br>Visual Workshop |
| AC2000.5.4 | Enter records using a form | Access C-14 | Step 2 | Skills Review,<br>Independent Challenge 1,<br>Visual Workshop |
| AC2000.5.5 | Delete records from a table | Access A-14 | Step 9 | Skills Review |
| AC2000.5.6 | Find a record | Access B-10<br>Access B-12<br>Access B-14 | Details<br>Steps 4-7<br>Steps 4-8 | Skills Review,<br>Independent Challenge 1,<br>Visual Workshop |
| AC2000.5.7 | Sort records | Access B-10<br>Access B-12 | Details<br>Steps 1-3 | Skills Review,<br>Independent Challenges 1-4 |
| AC2000.5.8 | Apply and remove filters (filter by form and filter by selection) | Access B-10<br>Access B-14 | Details<br>Steps 1-6 | Skills Review |
| AC2000.5.9 | Specify criteria in a query | Access B-16<br>Access B-18 | Step 6<br>Step 4 | Skills Review,<br>Independent Challenges 1-4<br>Visual Workshop |
| AC2000.5.10 | Display related records in a subdatasheet | | | |
| AC2000.5.11 | Create a calculated field | Access C-10 | Steps 1-6 | Skills Review,<br>Independent Challenge 3 |
| AC2000.5.12 | Create and modify a multi-table select query | | | |
| **AC2000.6** | **Defining relationships** | | | |
| AC2000.6.1 | Establish relationships | | | |
| AC2000.6.2 | Enforce referential integrity | | | |
| **AC2000.7** | **Producing reports** | | | |
| AC2000.7.1 | Create a report with the Report Wizard | Access D-4 | Steps 2-5 | Skills Review,<br>Independent Challenges 1-<br>Visual Workshop |

| MOUS Standardized coding number | Activity | Lesson page where skill is covered | Location in lesson where skill is covered | Practice |
|---|---|---|---|---|
| 2000.7.2 | Preview and print a report | Access D-6 | Step 7 | Skills Review, Independent Challenges 1-4, Visual Workshop |
| 2000.7.3 | Move and resize a control | Access D-12 | Steps 2-5 | Skills Review, Independent Challenges 1-4, Visual Workshop |
| 2000.7.4 | Modify format properties (font, style, font size, color, caption, etc.) | Access D-14 | Steps 2-7 | Skills Review, Independent Challenges 1-4, Visual Workshop |
| 2000.7.5 | Use the Control Toolbox to add controls | Access D-6 | Steps 3-6 | Skills Review, Independent Challenges 1-4, Visual Workshop |
| 2000.7.6 | Use report sections (headers, footers, detail) | Access D-3 Access D-6 | Table D-1, Figure D-5 Steps 1-7 | Skills Review, Independent Challenges 1-4, Visual Workshop |
| 2000.7.7 | Use a Calculated Control in a report | Access D-12 | Step 4 | Skills Review, Independent Challenge 1 |
| **2000.8** | **Integrating with other applications** | | | |
| 2000.8.1 | Import data to a new table | | | |
| 2000.8.2 | Save a table, query, form as a Web page | | | |
| 2000.8.3 | Add Hyperlinks | | | |
| **2000.9** | **Using Access Tools** | | | |
| 2000.9.1 | Print Database Relationships | | | |
| 2000.9.2 | Backup and Restore a database | | | |
| 2000.9.3 | Compact and Repair a database | | | |

# PowerPoint 2000 MOUS Certification Objectives

...low is a list of the Microsoft™ Office User Specialist program objectives for Core PowerPoint 2000 skills showing where ...h MOUS objective is covered in the Lessons and Practice. This table lists the Core MOUS certification skills covered ...the units in this book (Units A-D). The core skills without page references are covered in *Microsoft Office 2000— ...ustrated Second Course* (Units E-H). For more information on which Illustrated titles meet MOUS certification, please ...the inside cover of this book.

| OUS andardized ding number | Activity | Lesson page where skill is covered | Location in lesson where skill is covered | Practice |
|---|---|---|---|---|
| 2000.1 | **Creating a presentation** | | | |
| 2000.1.1 | Delete slides | PowerPoint B-8 | QuickTip | Skills Review, Independent Challenges 1, 2, 4 |
| 2000.1.2 | Create a specified type of slide | PowerPoint B-4 PowerPoint B-8 PowerPoint B-9 | Steps 4-5 Steps 1-2 Table B-3 | Skills Review, Independent Challenges 1-4, Visual Workshop |
| 2000.1.3 | Create a presentation from a template and/or a Wizard | PowerPoint B-4 | Steps 1-5 | Skills Review, Independent Challenges 1-4, Visual Workshop |
| 000.1.4 | Navigate among different views (slide, outline, sorter, tri-pane) | PowerPoint A-10 | Steps 1-8 | Skills Review |
| 000.1.5 | Create a new presentation from existing slides | PowerPoint C-2 PowerPoint C-12 | Steps 1-9 Clues to Use | Skills Review, Independent Challenge 2 |
| 000.1.6 | Copy a slide from one presentation into another | PowerPoint C-12 | Clues to Use | Skills Review |
| 000.1.7 | Insert headers and footers | PowerPoint B-13 PowerPoint B-14 | Clues to Use Steps 5-7 | Skills Review, Independent Challenges 1-4 |
| 000.1.8 | Create a blank presentation | PowerPoint A-7 PowerPoint B-4 | Table A-2 Table B-1 | |
| 000.1.9 | Create a presentation using the AutoContent Wizard | PowerPoint A-6 | Steps 1-8 | Skills Review, Independent Challenges 2, 3, Visual Workshop |
| 000.1.10 | Send a presentation via e-mail | | | |
| 000.2 | **Modifying a presentation** | | | |
| 00.2.1 | Change the order of slides using Slide Sorter view | PowerPoint B-16 | Step 3 | Skills Review, Independent Challenges 1-2, 4 |
| 00.2.2 | Find and replace text | PowerPoint C-15 | Clues to Use | Skills Review |
| 00.2.3 | Change the layout for one or more slides | PowerPoint D-2 | Steps 3-4 | Skills Review, Independent Challenge 1 |
| 00.2.4 | Change slide layout (Modify the Slide Master) | | | |

| MOUS standardized coding number | Activity | Lesson page where skill is covered | Location in lesson where skill is covered | Practice |
|---|---|---|---|---|
| PP2000.2.5 | Modify slide sequence in the outline pane | PowerPoint B-10<br>PowerPoint B-11 | QuickTip<br>Table B-4 | |
| PP2000.2.6 | Apply a design template | PowerPoint B-4<br>PowerPoint B-5<br>PowerPoint B-17 | Steps 1-4<br>Clues to Use<br>Clues to Use | Skills Review |
| **PP2000.3** | **Working with text** | | | |
| PP2000.3.1 | Check spelling | PowerPoint B-14 | Steps 1-4 | Skills Review,<br>Independent Challenges 1-4 |
| PP2000.3.2 | Change and replace text fonts (individual slide and entire presentation) | PowerPoint C-14<br>PowerPoint C-15 | Steps 7-8<br>Clues to Use | Skills Review,<br>Visual Workshop |
| PP2000.3.3 | Enter text in tri-pane view | PowerPoint B-6<br>PowerPoint B-8 | Steps 3-9<br>Steps 1-8 | Skills Review,<br>Independent Challenges 1—4 |
| PP2000.3.4 | Import text from Word | PowerPoint C-13 | Clues to Use | Skills Review |
| PP2000.3.5 | Change the text alignment | PowerPoint C-14 | Step 9 | Skills Review |
| PP2000.3.6 | Create a text box for entering text | PowerPoint C-12 | Steps 2-4, QuickTip | Skills Review,<br>Independent Challenge 3,<br>Visual Workshop |
| PP2000.3.7 | Use the Wrap text in TextBox Autoshape feature | PowerPoint C-12<br>PowerPoint C-14 | Steps 2-4<br>QuickTip | Skills Review |
| PP2000.3.8 | Use the Office Clipboard | PowerPoint C-7 | Clues to Use | |
| PP2000.3.9 | Use the Format Painter | | | |
| PP2000.3.10 | Promote and Demote text in slide & outline panes | PowerPoint B-8<br>PowerPoint B-10<br>PowerPoint B-11 | Steps 6-9<br>Steps 4-9<br>Table B-4 | |
| **PP2000.4** | **Working with visual elements** | | | |
| PP2000.4.1 | Add a picture from the Clip Art Gallery | PowerPoint D-2 | Steps 4-7 | Skills Review,<br>Independent Challenges 1, |
| PP2000.4.2 | Add and group shapes using WordArt or the Drawing Toolbar | PowerPoint C-4<br>PowerPoint C-10 | Steps 5-6<br>Steps 1, 4 | Skills Review |
| PP2000.4.3 | Apply formatting | PowerPoint C-4<br>PowerPoint C-14 | Steps 8-9<br>Steps 1-9 | Skills Review |
| PP2000.4.4 | Place text inside a shape using a text box | PowerPoint C-6 | Steps 7-8 | Skills Review |
| PP2000.4.5 | Scale and size an object including Clip Art | PowerPoint D-2<br>PowerPoint D-4 | Step 8<br>Step 8 | Skills Review,<br>Independent Challenges 3<br>Visual Workshop |

| MOUS Standardized Coding number | Activity | Lesson page where skill is covered | Location in lesson where skill is covered | Practice |
|---|---|---|---|---|
| 2000.4.6 | Create tables within PowerPoint | PowerPoint D-14 | Steps 1-2 | Skills Review, Independent Challenge 2 |
| 2000.4.7 | Rotate and fill an object | PowerPoint C-11 PowerPoint C-4 | Clues to Use Step 9 | Skills Review, Independent Challenges 2-4 |
| **2000.5** | **Customizing a presentation** | | | |
| 2000.5.1 | Add AutoNumber bullets | | | |
| 2000.5.2 | Add speaker notes | PowerPoint B-12 | Steps 1-7 | Skills Review, Independent Challenges 1-4 |
| 2000.5.3 | Add Graphical bullets | | | |
| 2000.5.4 | Add slide transitions | PowerPoint D-16 | Steps 1-8 | Skills Review, Independent Challenges 1-4 |
| 2000.5.5 | Animate text and objects | PowerPoint D-18 | Steps 1-7 | Skills Review, Independent Challenges 1-4 |
| **2000.6** | **Creating output** | | | |
| 2000.6.1 | Preview presentation in black and white | PowerPoint A-17 | Clues to Use | |
| 2000.6.2 | Print slides in a variety of formats | PowerPoint A-16 | Steps 1-7, QuickTips | Skills Review, Independent Challenges 2, 3, Visual Workshop |
| 2000.6.3 | Print audience handouts | PowerPoint A-16 | Steps 3-6 | Skills Review, Independent Challenge 2, Visual Workshop |
| 2000.6.4 | Print speaker notes in a specified format | PowerPoint B-14 | Step 9 | Skills Review |
| **2000.7** | **Delivering a presentation** | | | |
| 2000.7.1 | Start a slide show on any slide | | | |
| 2000.7.2 | Use on-screen navigation tools | PowerPoint D-12 | Steps 2-4, Steps 8-9 | Skills Review |
| 2000.7.3 | Print a slide as an overhead transparency | PowerPoint A-16 | QuickTip | Skills Review |
| 2000.7.4 | Use the pen during a presentation | PowerPoint D-12 | Steps 5-7 | Skills Review |
| **2000.8** | **Managing files** | | | |
| 2000.8.1 | Save changes to a presentation | PowerPoint A-12 | Step 5 | Skills Review |

| MOUS standardized coding number | Activity | Lesson page where skill is covered | Location in lesson where skill is covered | Practice |
|---|---|---|---|---|
| PP2000.8.2 | Save as a new presentation | PowerPoint A-12 | Steps 1-3 | Skills Review, Independent Challenges 2, 3, Visual Workshop |
| PP2000.8.3 | Publish a presentation to the Web | | | |
| PP2000.8.4 | Use Office Assistant | PowerPoint A-14 | Steps 1-9, Trouble? QuickTips | Skills Review, Independent Challenges 1, 4 |
| PP2000.8.5 | Insert hyperlink | | | |

# Project Files List

complete many of the lessons and practice exercises in this book, students need to use a
ject File that is supplied by Course Technology and stored on a Project Disk. Below is a list
the files that are supplied, and the unit or practice exercise to which the files correspond. For
ormation on how to obtain Project Files, please see the inside cover of this book. The follow-
list only includes Project Files that are supplied; it does not include the files students create
m scratch or the files students create by revising the supplied files.

| it | File supplied on Project Disk | Location file is used in unit |
|---|---|---|
| dows 98 Unit A | No files supplied | |
| dows 98 Unit B | WIN B-1.bmp | Lessons |
| | WIN B-2.bmp | Skills Review |
| ce 2000 Introduction | No files supplied | |
| ernet Explorer 5 Unit A | No files supplied | |
| d Unit A | No files supplied | |
| d Unit B | WD B-1.doc | Lessons |
| | WD B-2.doc | Skills Review |
| | WD B-3.doc | Independent Challenge 1 |
| | WD B-4.doc | Independent Challenge 2 |
| d Unit C | WD C-1.doc | Lessons |
| | WD C-2.doc | Skills Review |
| | WD C-3.doc | Independent Challenge 1 |
| | WD C-4.doc | Independent Challenge 2 |
| d Unit D | WD D-1.doc | Lessons |
| | WD D-2.doc | Skills Review |
| | WD D-3.doc | Independent Challenge 3 |
| l Unit A | EX A-1.xls | Lessons |
| | EX A-2.xls | Skills Review |
| l Unit B | EX B-1.xls | Lessons |
| | EX B-2.xls | Skills Review |
| | EX B-3.xls | Independent Challenge 3 |
| l Unit C | EX C-1.xls | Lessons |
| | EX C-2.xls | Skills Review |
| | EX C-3.xls | Independent Challenge 1 |
| | EX C-4.xls | Independent Challenge 2 |
| | EX C-5.xls | Visual Workshop |
| Unit D | EX D-1.xls | Lessons |
| | EX D-2.xls | Independent Challenge 1 |
| | EX D-3.xls | Independent Challenge 2 |
| | EX D-4.xls | Independent Challenge 3 |
| | EX D-5.xls | Visual Workshop |
| ration Unit A | INT A-1.doc | Lessons |
| | INT A-2.xls | |
| | INT A-3.xls | Independent Challenge 1 |
| | INT A-4.doc | |

| Unit | File supplied on Project Disk | Location file is used in unit |
|---|---|---|
| **Access Unit A** | MediaLoft-A.mdb | Lessons |
| | Recycle-A.mdb | Skills Review |
| | Recycle-A.mdb | Independent Challenge 2 |
| | Recycle-A.mdb | Independent Challenge 3 |
| | MediaLoft-A.mdb | Independent Challenge 4 |
| | Recycle-A.mdb | Visual Workshop |
| **Access Unit B** | MediaLoft-B.mdb | Lessons |
| | Doctors-B.mdb | Skills Review |
| | Doctors-B.mdb | Independent Challenge 2 |
| | MediaLoft-B.mdb | Independent Challenge 4 |
| | MediaLoft-B.mdb | Visual Workshop |
| **Access Unit C** | MediaLoft-C.mdb | Lessons |
| | Smallmedia.bmp | |
| | Membership-C.mdb | Skills Review |
| | Handin1.bmp | |
| | Clinic-C.mdb | Independent Challenge 1 |
| | Clinic-C.mdb | Independent Challenge 2 |
| | Clinic-C.mdb | Independent Challenge 3 |
| | Medical.bmp | |
| | Clinic-C.mdb | Visual Workshop |
| | Medstaff.bmp | |
| **Access Unit D** | MediaLoft-D.mdb | Lessons |
| | Club-D.mdb | Skills Review |
| | Therapy-D.mdb | Independent Challenge 1 |
| | Therapy-D.mdb | Independent Challenge 2 |
| | Club-D.mdb | Visual Workshop |
| **Integration Unit B** | MediaLoft-IB.mdb | Lessons |
| | INT B-1.doc | |
| | MediaLoft-IB.mdb | Independent Challenge 2 |
| **PowerPoint Unit A** | No files supplied | |
| **PowerPoint Unit B** | No files supplied | |
| **PowerPoint Unit C** | PPT C-1.ppt | Lessons |
| | PPT C-2.ppt | Skills Review |
| | PPT C-3.ppt | |
| | PPT C-4.doc | |
| | PPT C-5.ppt | Independent Challenge 2 |
| | PPT C-6.doc | |
| **PowerPoint Unit D** | PPT D-1.ppt | Lessons |
| | PPT D-2.bmp | |
| | PPT D-3.ppt | Skills Review |
| | PPT D-4.bmp | |
| | PPT D-5.ppt | Independent Challenge 1 |
| | PPT D-6.ppt | Independent Challenge 4 |

| Unit | File supplied on Project Disk | Location file is used in unit |
| --- | --- | --- |
| Integration Unit C | INT C-1.ppt | Lessons |
| | INT C-2.doc | |
| | INT C-3.xls | |
| | Cafe Profit.xls | |
| | INT C-4.doc | Independent Challenge 1 |
| | INT C-5.xls | Independent Challenge 2 |
| | INT C-6.doc | Independent Challenge 3 |
| | Nomad.bmp | |
| | Customer Data.mdb | |
| | INT C-7.xls | |
| | INT C-8.doc | |
| Internet Explorer Unit B | MLoft.jpg | Lessons |
| | IE5 B-1.doc | |
| | IE5 B-2.mdb | |
| | IE5 B-3.xls | |
| | IE5 B-4.ppt | |
| | Template.htm | |
| | MLoft.jpg | Skills Review |
| | IE5 B-5.doc | |
| | IE5 B-6.mdb | |
| | IE5 B-7.xls | |
| | IE5 B-8.ppt | |
| | Template.htm | |
| | Employee.htm and | |
| | Employee_files folder and | |
| | associated files | |
| | (filelist.xml; image001.gif; | |
| | image002.gif) | |
| | IE5 B-9.doc | Independent Challenge 1 |
| | IE5 B-10.mdb | |
| | IE5 B-11.xls | |
| | IE5 B-12.ppt | |
| | Template.htm | |
| | Fox.jpg | Independent Challenge 2 |
| | IE5 B-13.doc | |
| | IE5 B-14.mdb | |
| | IE5 B-15.xls | |
| | IE5 B-16.ppt | |
| | Template.htm | |
| Publisher Unit A | PB A-1.doc | Lessons |
| | PB A-2.jpg | |
| | PB A-3.jpg | |
| | PB A-4.doc | Skills Review |
| | PB A-5.doc | Independent Challenge 1 |
| | PB A-3.jpg | Independent Challenge 4 |
| Outlook Unit A | No files supplied | |
| Outlook Appendix | No files supplied | |

| Unit | File supplied on Project Disk | Location file is used in unit |
|---|---|---|
| **Bonus Exercises** | BWD-1.doc | Skills Review Word Unit B |
| | BWD-2.doc | Skills Review Word Unit C |
| | BWD-3.doc | Skills Review Word Unit D |
| | BEX-1.xls | Skills Review Excel Unit A |
| | BEX-2.xls | Skills Review Excel Unit B |
| | BEX-3.xls | Skills Review Excel Unit C |
| | BEX-4.xls | Skills Review Excel Unit D |
| | BEX-5.xls | Visual Workshop Excel Unit B |
| | EasternUniversity-A.mdb | Skills Review Access Unit A |
| | BrunildasBakedGoods-A.mdb | Visual Workshop Access Unit A |
| | EasternUniversity-B.mdb | Skills Review Access Unit B |
| | BrunildasBakedGoods-B.mdb | Visual Workshop Access Unit B |
| | EasternUniversity-C.mdb Diploma.wmf | Skills Review Access Unit C |
| | BrunildasBakedGoods-C.mdb BBGLogo.wmf | Visual Workshop Access Unit C |
| | EasternUniversity-D.mdb | Skills Review Access Unit D |
| | BrunildasBakedGoods-D.mdb | Visual Workshop Access Unit D |
| | BPPT-1.ppt | Skills Review PowerPoint Unit C |
| | BPPT-2.ppt Celebrate.bmp | Skills Review PowerPoint Unit D |
| | BINT-1.doc BINT-2.xls | Skills Review Integration |
| | BINT-3.xls Aunt Martha Cookies.mdb | Visual Workshop Integration |
| | BIE5-1.xls My Graphic.gif | Skills Review Internet Explorer |
| | BPB-1.doc | Skills Review Publisher Unit A |

# Glossary

**essories** Built-in programs that come with Windows 98.

**ve Desktop** The screen that appears when you first Windows 98, providing access to your computer's grams and files and to the Internet. *See also* Desktop.

**ve program** The program that you are using, differen- d from other open programs by a highlighted program on on the taskbar and a differently colored title bar.

**ve window** The window that you are currently g, differentiated from other open windows by a dif- itly colored title bar.

**ess Bar** The area below the toolbar in My puter and Windows Explorer that you use to open display a drive, folder, or Web page.

**up** To save files to another location in case you computer trouble and lose files.

**vser** A program, such as Microsoft Internet rer, designed to access the Internet.

**t mark** A solid circle that indicates that an option bled.

**city** The amount of information a disk can hold, ly measured in megabytes (Mb).

**ading menu** A list of commands from a menu with an arrow next to it; pointing at the arrow dis- a submenu from which you can choose additional nands.

**nel Bar** The bar on the right side of the Active op that shows buttons to access the Internet and Web pages known as active channels (like those on sion).

**box** A square box in a dialog box that you click n an option on or off.

**mark** A mark that indicates that a feature is d.

**ic style** A Windows 98 setting in which you single- o select items and double-click to open them.

To press and release the left mouse button once.

**ard** Temporary storage space on your computer's lisk containing information that has been cut or .

**Close** To quit a program or remove a window from the desktop. The Close button is usually located in the upper- right corner of a window.

**Command** A directive that provides access to a pro- gram's features.

**Command button** In a dialog box, a button that carries out an action. A command button usually has a label that describes its action, such as Cancel or Help. If the label is followed by an ellipses (…), clicking the button displays another dialog box.

**Context-sensitive help** Help that is specifically related to what you are doing.

**Control Panel** Used to change computer settings such as desktop colors or mouse settings.

**Copy** To place information onto the Clipboard in order to paste it in another location, but also leaving it in the original location.

**Cut** To remove information from a file and place it on the Clipboard, usually to be pasted into another location.

**Default** Settings preset by the operating system or program.

**Delete** To place a file or folder in the Recycle Bin, where you can either remove it from the disk permanently or restore it to its original location.

**Desktop** The screen that appears when you first start Windows 98, providing access to your computer's pro- grams and files and to the Internet. *See also* Active Desktop.

**Dialog box** A window that opens when more informa- tion is needed to carry out a command.

**Document** A file that you create using a program such as WordPad.

**Double-click** To press and release the left mouse button twice quickly.

**Drag** To move an item to a new location using the mouse.

**Drive** A device that reads and saves files on a disk and is also used to store files; floppy drives read and save files on floppy disks, whereas hard drives read and save files on your computer's built-in hard disk.

**Edit** To change the content or format of an existing file.

**Explorer Bar** The pane on the left side of the screen in Windows Explorer that lists all drives and folders on the computer.

**File** An electronic collection of information that has a unique name, distinguishing it from other files.

**File hierarchy** A logical structure for folders and files that mimics how you would organize files and folders in a filing cabinet.

**File management** The process of organizing and keeping track of files and folders.

**Floppy disk** A disk that you insert into a disk drive of your computer (usually drive A or B) to store files.

**Folder** A collection of files and/or other folders that helps you organize your disks.

**Font** The design of a set of characters (for example, Times New Roman).

**Format** To enhance the appearance of a document by, for example, changing the font or font size, adding borders and shading to a document.

**Graphical user interface (GUI)** An environment made up of meaningful symbols, words, and windows in which you can control the basic operation of a computer and the programs that run on it.

**Hard disk** A disk that is built into the computer (usually drive C) on which you store files and programs.

**Highlighting** When an icon is shaded differently indicating it is selected. *See also* Select.

**Icon** Graphical representation of computer elements such as files and programs.

**Inactive** Refers to a window or program that is open but not currently in use.

**Input device** An item, such as a mouse or keyboard, that you use to interact with your computer.

**Insertion point** A blinking vertical line that indicates where text will appear when you type.

**Internet** A worldwide collection of over 40 million computers linked together to share information.

**Internet style** A Windows 98 setting in which you point to select items and single-click to open them. *See also* Web style.

**Keyboard shortcut** A keyboard alternative for exec ing a menu command (for example, [Ctrl][X] for Cu

**List box** A box in a dialog box containing a list of ite to choose an item, click the list arrow, then click desired item.

**Maximize** To enlarge a window so it fills the er screen. The Maximize button is usually located in upper-right corner of a window.

**Menu** A list of related commands in a program example, the File menu).

**Menu bar** A bar near the top of the program win that provides access to most of a program's fea through categories of related commands.

**Minimize** To reduce the size of a window. The Mini button is usually located in the upper-right corner window.

**Mouse** A hand-held input device that you roll on desk to position the mouse pointer on the Windows top. *See also* Mouse pointer.

**Mouse buttons** The two buttons on the mouse (righ left) that you use to make selections and issue comma

**Mouse pointer** The arrow-shaped cursor on the s that follows the movement of the mouse. The shape mouse pointer changes depending on the program the task being executed. *See also* Mouse.

**Multi-tasking** Working with more than one windc program at a time.

**My Computer** A program that you use to manag drives, folders, and files on your computer.

**Open** To start a program or open a window; also u describe a program that is running but not active.

**Operating system** A computer program that co the basic operation of your computer and the pro; you run on it. Windows 98 is an example of an ope system.

**Option button** A small circle in a dialog box th; click to select an option.

**Paint** A drawing program that comes with Windc

**Pane** A section of a divided window.

**Point** To position the mouse pointer over an it your computer screen; also a unit of measur (1/72nd inch) used to specify the size of text.

**nter trail** A shadow of the mouse pointer that ears when you move the mouse; helps you locate the nter on your screen.

**-up menu** A menu that appears when you right- k an item on the desktop.

**gram** Task-oriented software that you use for a par- lar kind of work, such as word processing or database agement. Microsoft Access, Microsoft Excel, and rosoft Word are all programs.

**gram button** A button on the taskbar that represents pen program or window.

**perties** Characteristics of a specific computer ele- t (such as the mouse, keyboard, or desktop display) you can customize.

**ck Launch toolbar** A toolbar located next to the t button on the taskbar that contains buttons to start rnet-related programs and show the desktop.

**dom access memory (RAM)** The memory that rams use to perform necessary tasks while the com- r is on. When you turn the computer off, all infor- on in RAM is lost.

**ycle Bin** An icon that appears on the desktop that esents a temporary storage area on your computer's disk for deleted files, which remain in the Recycle ntil you empty it.

**ore** To reduce the window to its previous size e it was maximized. The Restore button is usually ed in the upper-right corner of a window.

**t-click** To press and release the right mouse button

**enTip** A description of a toolbar button that rs when you position the mouse pointer over the n.

**l bar** A bar that appears at the bottom and/or right of a window whose contents are not entirely visible; lick the arrows or drag the box in the direction you to move. *See also* Scroll box.

**box** A rectangle located in the vertical and hori- scroll bars that indicates your relative position in a w. *See also* Scroll bar.

**t** To click and highlight an item in order to per- some action on it. *See also* Highlighting.

**cut** A link that you can place in any location that ou instant access to a particular file, folder, or pro- on your hard disk or on a network.

**Shut down** The action you perform when you have fin- ished working with Windows 98; after you shut down it is safe to turn off your computer.

**Slider** An item in a dialog box that you drag to set the degree to which an option is in effect.

**Spin box** A box with two arrows and a text box; allows you to scroll in numerical increments or type a number.

**Start button** A button on the taskbar that you use to start programs, find and open files, access Windows Help and more.

**Tab** A place in a dialog box where related commands and options are organized.

**Taskbar** A strip at the bottom of the screen that con- tains the Start button, Quick Launch toolbar, and shows which programs are running.

**Text box** A rectangle in a dialog box in which you type text.

**Title bar** The area along the top of the window that indicates the filename and program used to create it.

**Toolbar** A strip with buttons that allow you to activate a command quickly.

**Web page** A document that contains highlighted words, phrases, and graphics that link to other documents on the Internet.

**Web site** A computer on the Internet that contains Web pages.

**Web style** A Windows 98 setting in which you point to select items and single-click to open them. *See also* Internet style.

**Window** A rectangular frame on a screen that can con- tain icons, the contents of a file, or other usable data.

**Windows Explorer** A program that you use to manage files, folders, and shortcuts; allows you to work with more than one computer, folder, or file at once.

**Windows Help** A "book" stored on your computer, com- plete with an index and a table of contents, that contains information about Windows 98.

**WordPad** A word processing program that comes with Windows 98.

**World Wide Web** Part of the Internet that consists of Web sites located on different computers around the world.

**Zip disk** A portable disk that can contain 100 Mb, far more than a regular floppy disk.

**Zip drive** A drive that can handle Zip disks.

# Glossary

**Word 2000**

**Alignment** The horizontal position of text relative to page margins or tab stops; for example, left, center, or right.

**Application** See *Program.*

**Ascending order** The sequence in which items are sorted from smallest to largest, or from A to Z.

**AutoCorrect** A feature that automatically corrects misspelled words and grammatical errors as you type. Word provides many entries for common mistakes, but you can also add your own.

**AutoFit** A table formatting feature that automatically adjusts the width of a table to fit to the document margins.

**AutoRecover** A feature that automatically saves document changes in a temporary file at specified intervals, so that you can recover some of your changes if power to your computer is interrupted.

**Bold** Formatting in which text appears thicker and darker.

**Border** A vertical or horizontal line that you can add to the top, bottom or sides of paragraphs; also the line that divides cells in a table. You can format borders with different line styles and colors.

**Bullet** A small graphic symbol, usually a round or square dot, often used to identify items in a list.

**Cell** The intersection of a row and a column in a table.

**Cell reference** An address or name that identifies a cell's position in a table; it consists of a letter that identifies the cell's column and a number that identifies its row; for example, cell B3.

**Center** A form of paragraph alignment in which the lines of text are centered between the left and right margins.

**Character spacing** A form of character formatting that allows you to expand or condense the amount of space between characters, adjust the width (or scale) of characters, raise or lower characters, and adjust kerning.

**Click** To press and release a mouse button in one motion.

**Clipboard** A temporary storage area for cut or copied items that are available for pasting. See *office clipboard.*

**Clipboard toolbar** A toolbar that shows the contents of the Office Clipboard; contains buttons for copying and pasting items to and from the Office Clipboard.

**Column** A vertical arrangement of cells in a table.

**Copy** A command that copies a selected part of a document and places it on the Clipboard.

**Cut** A command that removes a selected part of a document and places it on the Clipboard.

**Default** The original setting, such as page margins or tab spacing, set by the program.

**Delete** To remove selected text or a graphic from a docum

**Descending order** The sequence in which rows are so from Z to A or from largest to smallest.

**Dialog box** A window that opens when more informatio needed to carry out a command.

**Document window** The rectangular area of the Word gram window where you view and work on a document.

**Drag** To hold down the mouse button while moving mouse.

**Edit** To add, delete, or change text and graphics.

**File** An electronic collection of information that has a un name, distinguishing it from other files. In Word, all docum are stored as files.

**Filename** The name assigned to a file; the name you assig a document when you save it to a disk.

**Folders** Subdivisions of a disk that work like a filing syste help you organize files.

**Font** The typeface or design of a set of characters (le numerals, symbols, and punctuation marks).

**Font effects** Enhanced formatting you can apply to text, as bold, italics, shadows, or all caps.

**Font size** The size of text, measured in points (pts). The er the number of points, the bigger the font size.

**Format** The appearance of a document, including color, attributes, borders, and shading.

**Format Painter** A feature used to copy the formatting ap to one set of text to another.

**Formatting toolbar** A toolbar that contains buttons fo most frequently used formatting commands.

**Formula** A set of instructions used to perform numeric lations (adding, multiplying, averaging, etc.).

**Global replace** Replacing all occurrences of specific te document without having to review and change each o rence individually.

**Graphics** A picture, chart, or drawing in a document.

**Hanging indent** A paragraph format in which the first a paragraph starts farther to the left than the subsequent

**Horizontal ruler** A graphical bar across the top of the ment window that you can use to place and align text.

**ent**  The distance between the beginning or end of a line of and the page margins. A paragraph can have left, right, -line, and hanging indents.

**ent markers**  Movable buttons on the horizontal ruler that rmine the indent settings for the selected paragraph.

**ertion point**  A blinking vertical line in the document win- that indicates where text will appear when you type.

**cs**  Formatting in which the text appears slanted.

**ify**  A form of paragraph alignment in which both the left right edges of a paragraph are flush with the margins.

**ing**  A form of character formatting that allows you to st the space between standard combinations of characters, as "W" followed by "a".

**oard shortcut**  A combination of keys or function keys an press to perform an operation in Word. Using keyboard cuts is often faster than using the menus and commands.

**align**  A form of paragraph alignment in which the left of a paragraph is even, usually flush with the left margin.

**spacing**  The amount of space between lines of text, mea- in lines or points.

**rcase**  The small letters of a character set (a, b, c, d…).

**in**  The empty space between the edge of the text, or the d area, and the edge of the page. A document's margins sible in Print Preview or Print Layout view.

**bar**  A bar beneath the title bar that contains menus that e program's commands.

**e**  Combing two or more cells in a table to form a sin- l.

**Buttons button**  The button you click to display toolbar as that are not currently visible.

**rinting characters**  Marks displayed on the screen to te characters that do not print, such as tab characters or aph marks. You can control the display of special charac- th the Show/Hide ¶ button on the Standard toolbar.

**l view**  The document view in which you do not see the f the page; useful for most editing and formatting tasks.

**Assistant**  An animated character that appears to offer swer questions, and provide access to the program's Help

**Clipboard**  A temporary storage area shared by all programs that can be used to cut, copy and paste multi- ns within and between Office programs. The Office rd can hold up to 12 items collected from any Office n. See also *Clipboard toolbar*.

**Open**  The operation of retrieving and displaying a document in the document window.

**Overtype mode**  A feature that lets you replace, or overwrite, existing text as you type.

**Paragraph spacing**  The amount of space between para- graphs, measured in points.

**Paste**  A command that inserts cut or copied items into a doc- ument from the Clipboard.

**Point**  The unit of measurement for fonts and space between paragraphs and text characters. There are 72 points per inch.

**Print Layout view**  A view that mimics the look of a printed page; especially useful for viewing margins, alignment, and text flow.

**Print Preview**  A command you can use to display the docu- ment as it will look when printed.

**Program**  Task-oriented software (such as Excel or Word) that enables you to perform a certain type of task such as data cal- culation or word processing.

**Redo**  A command that repeats a reversed edit or formatting change; only reversed changes can be repeated with the Redo command.

**Replace**  The command you use to locate and change a specific occurrence of text. Also, refers to the operation of selecting and typing over existing text to replace it.

**Reset usage data**  An option that allows adapted toolbars and menus to be returned to their default settings.

**Right-align**  A form of paragraph alignment in which only the right edge of a paragraph is even, usually flush with the right margin.

**Row**  A horizontal arrangement of cells in a table.

**Sans serif font**  A font whose characters do not include serifs, the small strokes at the ends of the characters. Arial is a sans serif font.

**Save**  The command used to permanently store your docu- ment and any changes you make to a file on a disk. See also *Filename*.

**ScreenTip**  A pop-up label that appears when you point to a button. It provides descriptive information about the button.

**Scroll**  To move within a window to display parts of a docu- ment that are not currently visible.

**Scroll bars**  Bars at the right and bottom edges of the docu- ment window used to view different parts of a document not currently visible in the document window.

**Scroll box**  The movable box in the scroll bars that you drag to move around in a document.

**Search**  To use the Find command to locate specific text in a document.

**Select** To highlight text with the mouse. Most formatting and editing commands in Word require that you select the text that you want to format or edit.

**Selection bar** An unmarked column at the left edge of a document window that can be used to select text. In a table, each cell, row, and column also has its own selection bar.

**Serif font** A font that has small strokes (called serifs) at the ends of the characters. Times New Roman and Palatino are serif fonts.

**Shading** A background color or pattern you can apply to text, tables, or graphics.

**Sort** An operation that arranges rows in a table (or paragraphs of text) in a sequence, such as chronological, alphabetical, or numerical order.

**Sort criterion** The detail of a table or list by which rows or paragraphs are sorted, for example, last name.

**Split cells** A command used to divide a cell in a table into two or more cells.

**Standard toolbar** The toolbar containing buttons that perform some of the most frequently used commands.

**Status bar** A bar at the bottom of the Word window that indicates the current page number and section number, the total number of pages in the document, and the vertical position (in inches) of the insertion point.

**Superscript** Formatting in which the text is raised above and is several points smaller than adjacent text. Copyright and trademark symbols, as well as certain notations in equations, are often superscripted.

**Tab** A key you press to position text so that it is located at a specific horizontal position in a document.

**Table** A grid of rows and columns divided by borders; commonly used to display text, numbers, or other items for quick reference and analysis.

**Tab leaders** A solid or dotted line that appears in front of tabbed text.

**Table AutoFormat** A feature that includes preset formats that can be applied to format a table with shading, fonts, and borders.

**Tab stop** A measured position used for placing and aligning text horizontally at a specific location in a document. Word has five kinds of tab stops, left-aligned (the default), centered, right-aligned, decimal, and bar.

**Template** A formatted document that contains place ho text you can replace with your own text. Word includes t plates for creating memos, letters, faxes, and other kind commonly used documents.

**Title bar** The bar at the top of a window that displays the gram name and the filename of the current document.

**Tone** The feeling of a document, affected by its content visual appearance.

**Toolbar** A bar that contains buttons that give you quick ac to the most frequently used commands. Word includes n different toolbars related to specific tasks. For example, Tables and Borders toolbar contains buttons that are u when you create tables.

**Undo** A command that reverses previous edits or forma changes you made to a document; you can undo up to 100 vious actions.

**Uppercase** The capital letters of a character set (A, B, C, I

**Vertical alignment** The placement of text on a page or cell in relation to the top, bottom, or center of the page or

**Vertical ruler** A graphical bar at the left edge of the docu window in Print Layout view.

**View** A format for displaying a document in the docu window that offers features useful for working on dif types of documents. Word includes four views: No Outline, Print Layout, and Web Layout.

**View buttons** Buttons on the horizontal scroll bar that you to switch between views.

**Wizard** An interactive set of dialog boxes that guide through the process of creating a document; it asks you tions about document preferences and creates the doc according to your specifications.

**Word processing program** A software application u create documents efficiently.

**Wordwrap** A feature that automatically moves the ins point to the next line of a paragraph as you type.

# Glossary

**Excel 2000**

**…olute reference** A cell reference that contains a dollar sign …ore the column letter and/or row number to indicate the …olute, or fixed, contents of specific cells. For example, the …nula $A$1+$B$1 calculates only the sum of these specific … no matter where the formula is copied in the workbook.

**…ive cell** The current location of the cell pointer.

**…ress** The location of a specific cell or range expressed by …coordinates of column and row; for example, A1.

**…nment** The horizontal placement of cell contents; for …nple, left, center, or right.

**…hors** Cells listed in a range address. For example, in the …nula =SUM(A1:A15), A1 and A15 are anchors.

**… chart** A line chart in which each area is given a solid …r or pattern to emphasize the relationship between the …es of charted information.

**…uments** Information a function needs to create the …wer. In an expression, multiple arguments are separated by …mas. All of the arguments are enclosed in parentheses; for …nple, =SUM(A1:B1).

**…metic operator** A symbol used in a formula, such as + or -, …, to perform mathematical operations.

**…bute** The styling features such as bold, italics, and under-…g that can be applied to cell contents.

**…Complete** A feature that automatically completes labels …ed in adjoining cells in a column.

**…Fill** A feature that creates a series of text or numbers …a range is selected using the fill handle.

**…Fit** A feature that automatically adjusts the width of a col-…to accommodate its widest entry when the boundary to the …of the column selector is double-clicked.

**…ormat** Preset schemes that can be applied to format a range …tly. Excel comes with 16 AutoFormats that include colors, …and numeric formatting.

**…Sum** A feature that automatically creates totals using the …um button.

**…round color** The color applied to the background of

**…hart** A chart that shows information as a series of (hori-…) bars.

**…r** The edge of a selected area of a worksheet. Lines and …an be applied to borders.

**…l button** The X in the formula bar; it removes informa-…om the formula bar and restores the previous cell entry.

**…he** intersection of a column and row in a worksheet.

**…ddress** The unique location identified by intersecting …n and row coordinates.

**Cell pointer** A highlighted rectangle around a cell that indicates the active cell.

**Cell reference** The address or name that identifies a cell's position in a worksheet; it consists of a letter that identifies the cell's column and a number that identifies its row; for example, cell B3. Cell references in worksheets can be used in formulas and are relative or absolute.

**Chart** A graphic representation of information from a worksheet. Types include 2-D and 3-D column, bar, pie, area, and line charts.

**Chart sheet** A separate sheet that only contains a chart linked to worksheet data.

**Chart title** The name assigned to a chart.

**Chart Wizard** A series of dialog boxes that helps create or modify a chart.

**Check box** A square box in a dialog box that can be clicked to turn an option on or off.

**Clear** A command on the Edit menu used to erase a cell's contents, formatting, or both.

**Clipboard** A temporary storage area for cut or copied items that are available for pasting. See *office clipboard*.

**Clipboard toolbar** A toolbar that shows the contents of the Office Clipboard; contains buttons for copying and pasting items to and from the Office Clipboard.

**Close** A command that closes the file so you can no longer work with it, but keeps Excel open so that you can continue to work on other workbooks.

**Column chart** The default chart type in Excel that displays information as a series of (vertical) columns.

**Column selector button** The gray box containing the letter above the column.

**Conditional format** The format of a cell based on its value or outcome of a formula.

**Control menu box** A box in the upper-left corner of a window used to resize or close a window.

**Copy** A command that copies the selected cells contents and places it on the Clipboard.

**Cut** A command that removes the cell contents from the selected area of a worksheet and places them on the Clipboard.

**Data marker** A graphical representation of a data point, such as a bar or column.

**Data point** Individual piece of data plotted in a chart.

**Data series** The selected range in a worksheet that Excel converts into a graphic and displays as a chart.

**Delete** A command that removes cell contents from a worksheet.

**Dialog box** A window that opens when more information is needed to carry out a command.

**Dummy column/row** Blank column or row included at the end of a range that enables a formula to adjust when columns or rows are added or deleted.

**Edit** A change made to the contents of a cell or worksheet.

**Electronic spreadsheet** A computer program that performs calculations on data and organizes information into worksheets. A worksheet is divided into columns and rows, which form individual cells.

**Enter button** The check mark in the formula bar used to confirm an entry.

**Exploding pie slice** A slice of a pie chart that has been pulled away from the whole pie to add emphasis.

**Fill color** Cell background color.

**Fill Down** A command that duplicates the contents of the selected cells in the range selected below the cell pointer.

**Fill handle** A small square in the lower-right corner of the active cell used to copy cell contents.

**Fill Right** A command that duplicates the contents of the selected cells in the range selected to the right of the cell pointer.

**Find** A command used to locate information the user specifies.

**Find & Replace** A command used to find one set of criteria and replace it with new information.

**Floating toolbar** A toolbar within its own window; not anchored along an edge of the worksheet.

**Font** The typeface or design of a set of characters (letters, numbers, symbols, and punctuation marks).

**Format** The appearance of text and numbers, including color, font, attributes, borders, and shading. See also *Number format*.

**Format Painter** A feature used to copy the formatting applied to one set of text or in one cell to another.

**Formula** A set of instructions used to perform numeric calculations (adding, multiplying, averaging, etc.).

**Formula bar** The area below the menu bar and above the Excel workspace where you enter and edit data in a worksheet cell. The formula bar becomes active when you start typing or editing cell data. It includes the Enter button and the Cancel button.

**Function** A special, predefined formula that provides a shortcut for a commonly used calculation; for example, AVERAGE.

**Gridlines** Horizontal and/or vertical lines within a chart that make the chart easier to read.

**Input** Information that produces desired results in a worksheet.

**Insertion point** Blinking I-beam that appears in the formula bar during entry and editing.

**Label** Descriptive text or other information that identifies rows and columns of a worksheet. Labels are not included calculations.

**Label prefix** A character that identifies an entry as a label controls the way it appears in the cell.

**Landscape orientation** A print setting which positions worksheet on the page so the page is wider than it is tall.

**Legend** A key explaining how information is represented colors or patterns in a chart.

**Line chart** A graph of data that is mapped by a series of li Line charts show changes in data or categories of data over t and can be used to document trends.

**Mixed reference** Formula containing both a relative absolute reference.

**Mode indicator** A box located at the lower-left corner of status bar that informs you of the program's status. For ex ple, when Excel is performing a task, the word "Wait" appe

**More Buttons button** A button you click on the toolba view toolbar buttons that are not currently visible.

**Mouse pointer** A symbol that indicates the current locatic the mouse on the desktop. The mouse pointer changes its s at times; for example, when you insert data, select a range, tion a chart, change the size of a window, or select a topic in I

**Moving border** The dashed line that appears around a c range that is copied to the Clipboard.

**Name box** The left-most area in the formula bar that s the cell reference or name of the active cell. For exampl refers to cell A1 of the active worksheet. You can also get a names in a workbook using the Name list arrow.

**Named range** A range of cells given a meaningful na retains its name when moved and can be referenced in a for

**Number format** A format applied to values to express nu concepts, such as currency, date, and percentage.

**Object** A chart or graphic image that can be moved resized and contains handles when selected.

**Office Assistant** An animated character that appears to tips, answer questions, and provide access to the program' system.

**Office Clipboard** A temporary storage area shared Office programs that can be used to cut, copy and paste ple items within and between Office programs. The Clipboard can hold up to 12 items collected from any program. See also *Clipboard toolbar*.

**Open** A command that retrieves a workbook from a di displays it on the screen.

**Order of precedence** The order in which Excel cal parts of a formula: (1) exponents, (2) multiplication an sion, and (3) addition and subtraction.

**Output** The end result of a worksheet.

**...ste** A command that moves information on the Clipboard ...a new location. Excel pastes the formula, rather than the ...lt, unless the Paste Special command is used.

**...te Function** A series of dialog boxes that lists and ...cribes all Excel functions and assists the user in function ...tion.

**...chart** A circular chart that represents data as slices of pie. ...ie chart is useful for showing the relationship of parts to a ...le; pie slices can be extracted for emphasis. See also ...loding pie slice.

**...t** A unit of measure used for fonts and row height. One ...equals 72 points.

**...ting method** Specifying formula cell references by select-...the desired cell with your mouse instead of typing its cell ...ence; it eliminates typing errors.

**...rait orientation** A print setting which positions the work-...t on the page so the page is taller than it is wide.

**...t Preview** A command you can use to view the worksheet ...will look when printed.

**...ram** Task-oriented software (such as Excel or Word) that ...les you to perform a certain type of task, such as data cal-...ion or word processing.

**...rams menu** The Windows 95/98 Start menu that lists all ...able programs on your computer.

**...ge** A selected group of adjacent cells.

**...ge format** A format applied to a selected range in a ...sheet.

**...tive cell reference** A type of cell reference used to indi-...relative position in the worksheet. It allows you to copy ...nove formulas from one area to another of the same ...nsions. Excel automatically changes the column and row ...ers to reflect the new position.

**...t usage data** An option that allows adapted toolbars and ...s to be returned to their default settings.

**...height** The vertical dimension of a cell.

**...selector button** The gray box containing the number to ...t of the row.

**...** A command used to permanently store your workbook ...ny changes you make to a file on a disk. The first time you ...workbook you must give it a filename.

**...As** A command used to create a duplicate of the current ...ook with a new filename. Used the first time you save a ...ook.

**...tion handles** Small boxes appearing along the corners ...des of charts and graphic images that are used for moving ...sizing.

**... of labels** Pre-programmed series, such as days of the ...and months of the year. They are formed by typing ...t word of the series, then dragging the fill handle to the ...cell.

**Sheet** A term used for a worksheet.

**Sheet tab** A description at the bottom of each worksheet that identifies it in a workbook. In an open workbook, move to a worksheet by clicking its sheet tab. Also known as *Worksheet tab*.

**Sheet tab scrolling buttons** Buttons that enable you to move among sheets within a workbook.

**Spell check** A command that attempts to match all text in a worksheet with the words in the dictionary.

**Start** To open a software program so you can use it.

**Status bar** The bar at the bottom of the Excel window, that provides information about various keys, commands, and processes.

**Text annotations** Labels added to a chart to draw attention to a particular area.

**Text color** The color applied to the text within a cell.

**Tick marks** Notations of a scale of measure on a chart axis.

**Title bar** The bar at the top of the window that indicates the program name and the name of the current worksheet.

**Toggle button** A button that turns a feature on and off.

**Toolbar** A bar that contains buttons that give you quick access to the most frequently used commands.

**Truncate** To shorten the display of a cell based on the width of a cell.

**Values** Numbers, formulas, or functions used in calculations.

**What-if analysis** A decision-making feature in which data is changed and automatically recalculated.

**Window** A rectangular area of a screen where you view and work on a worksheet.

**Workbook** A collection of related worksheets contained within a single file.

**Worksheet** An electronic spreadsheet containing 256 columns by 65,536 rows.

**Worksheet tab** See *Sheet tab*.

**Worksheet window** The worksheet area in which data is entered.

**X-axis** The horizontal line in a chart.

**X-axis label** A label describing the x-axis of a chart.

**Y-axis** The vertical line in a chart.

**Y-axis label** A label describing the y-axis of a chart.

**Zoom** A feature that enables you to focus on a larger or smaller part of the worksheet in Print Preview.

Excel 2000

# Glossary

**And criteria** Criteria placed in the same row of the query design grid. All criteria on the same row must be true in order for a record to appear on the resulting datasheet.

**Arguments** The pieces of information a function needs to create the final answer. In an expression, multiple arguments are separated by commas. All of the arguments are surrounded by a single set of parentheses.

**Ascending order** A sequence in which information is placed in alphabetical order or from smallest to largest. For a text field, numbers sort first, then letters.
Text ascending order: 123, 3H, 455, 98, 98B, animal, Iowa, New Jersey
Date ascending order: 1/1/57, 1/1/61, 12/25/61, 5/5/98, 8/20/98, 8/20/99
Number ascending order: 1, 10, 15, 120, 140, 500, 1200, 1500

**AutoNumber** A data type in which Access enters a sequential integer for each record added into the datasheet. Numbers cannot be reused even if the record is deleted.

**Bound control** A control used in either a form or report display data from the underlying record source; also used to edit and enter new data in a form.

**Bound image control** A bound control used to show OLE data such as a picture on a form or report.

**Calculated control** A control that uses information from existing controls to calculate new data such as subtotals, dates, or page numbers; used in either a form or report.

**Caption property** A field property used to override the technical field name with an easy-to-read caption entry when the field name appears on datasheets, forms, and reports.

**Check box** Bound control used to display "yes" or "no" answers for a field. If the box is "checked" it indicates "yes" information in a form or report.

**Clipboard toolbar** A toolbar that shows the contents of the Office Clipboard; contains buttons for copying and pasting items to and from the Office Clipboard.

**Combo box** A bound control used to display a list of possible entries for a field in which you can also type an entry from the keyboard. It is a "combination" of the list box and text box controls.

**Command button** An unbound control used to provide an easy way to initiate an action or run a macro.

**Control** Any element on a form or report such as a label, text box, line, or combo box. Controls can be bound, unbound, or calculated.

**Criteria** The entry that determines which records are displayed when finding or filtering records in a datasheet or form, or when building a query.

**Currency** A data type used for monetary values.

**Current record symbol** A black triangle symbol that app in the record select box to the left of the record that has focus in either a datasheet or a form.

**Data** The unique entries of information that you enter the fields of the records.

**Data access page** See "Page".

**Database** A collection of data associated with a topic example, sales of products to customers).

**Database software** Software used to manage data that ca organized into lists of things such as customers, products, dors, employees, projects, or sales.

**Database window** The window that includes common ments such as the Access title bar, menu bar, and toolbar. It contains an Objects bar to quickly work with the seven di ent types of objects within the database by clicking the ap priate object button.

**Datasheet** A spreadsheet-like grid that shows field columns and records as rows.

**Datasheet view** A view that lists the records of the obje a datasheet. Table, query, and most form objects ha Datasheet view.

**Data type** A required property for each field that define type of data that can be entered in each field. Valid data include AutoNumber, Text, Number, Currency, Date/ OLE Object, Memo, Yes/No, and Hyperlink.

**Date/Time** A data type used for date and time fields.

**Descending order** A sequence in which information is in reverse alphabetical order or from largest to smallest. text field, letters sort first, then numbers.
Text descending order: Zebra, Victory, Langguth, Bunin 9854, 77, 740, 29, 270, 23500, 1
Date descending order: 1/1/99, 1/1/98, 12/25/97, 5 8/20/61, 8/20/57
Number descending order: 1500, 1400, 1200, 140, 120, 15

**Design view** A view in which the structure of the object manipulated. Every Access object has a Design view.

**Detail section** The section of the form or report that co the controls that are printed for each record in the unde query or table.

**Edit mode** The mode in which Access assumes you are to edit that particular field, so keystrokes such as [Ctrl] [Ctrl][Home], [←], and [→] move the insertion point the field.

**t record symbol** A pencil-like symbol that appears in the ord selector box to the left of the record that is currently ng edited in either a datasheet or a form.

**ression** A combination of values, functions, and operators calculates to a single value. Access expressions start with an al sign and are placed in a text box in either Form or Report ign view.

**d** The smallest piece or category of information in a data- such as the customer's name, city, state, or phone number.

**d list** A list of the available fields in the table or query that oresents.

**d names** The names given each field in Table Design or e Datasheet view. Field names can be up to 64 charac- long.

**d Property** See *Properties*.

**r** A temporary view of a subset of records. A filter can be I as a query object if you wish to apply the same filter later out recreating it.

**r window** A window that appears when you click the r by Form button when viewing data in a datasheet or in a window. The Filter window allows you to define the filter ·ia.

**s** The property that refers to which field would be edited started typing.

**·r** Information that prints at the bottom of every printed (or section when using forms and reports).

 An Access object that provides an easy-to-use data entry n that generally shows only one record at a time.

**atting** Enhancing the appearance of the information in a report or datasheet.

 **Design toolbar** The toolbar that appears when working rm Design View with buttons that help you modify a s controls.

 **View toolbar** The toolbar that appears when working in View with buttons that help you print, edit, find, filter, lit records.

**ion** A special, predefined formula that provides a short- r a commonly used calculation, for example, AVERAGE.

**ic** See *Image*.

 **Footer section** The section of the report that contains ·ls that print once at the end of each group of records.

 **Header section** The section of the report that contains ls that print once at the beginning of each group of s.

**es** See *Sizing handles*.

**·r** Information that prints at the top of every printed or section when using forms and reports).

**Help system** Pages of documentation and examples that are available through the Help menu option, the Microsoft Access Help button on the Database toolbar, or the Office Assistant.

**Hyperlink** A data type that stores World Wide Web addresses.

**Image** A nontextual piece of information such as a picture, piece of clip art, drawn object, or graph. Because images are graphical (not numbers or letters), they are sometimes referred to as *graphical images*.

**Key field** A field that contains unique information for each record. Also known as *Primary key field*. A key field cannot con- tain a null entry.

**Key field symbol** In a table's Design view, the symbol that appears as a miniature key in the field indicator box to the left of the field name. It identifies the field that contains unique information for each record.

**Label** An unbound control that displays static text on forms and reports.

**Line control** An unbound control used to draw lines on a form or report that divide it into logical groupings.

**List box** A bound control that displays a list of possible choices from which the user can choose. Used mainly on forms.

**Lookup wizard** Specifying a lookup data type for a field invokes a wizard that helps link the current table to another table. The final data type of the field is determined by choices made in the wizard. A field created with the lookup data type will consist of data from another table or list.

**Macro** An Access object that stores a collection of keystrokes or commands such as printing several reports in a row or pro- viding a toolbar when a form opens.

**Memo** A data type used for lengthy text such as comments or notes. It can hold up to 64,000 characters of information.

**Module** An Access object that stores Visual Basic program- ming code that extends the functions and automated processes of Access.

**Navigation buttons** Buttons in the lower-left corner of a datasheet or form that allow you to quickly navigate between the records in the underlying object as well as add a new record.

**Navigation mode** A mode in which Access assumes that you are trying to move between the fields and records of the datasheet (rather than edit a specific field's contents), so keystrokes such as [Ctrl][Home] and [Ctrl][End] move you to the first and last field of the datasheet, respectively.

**New Record button** A button that, when clicked, presents a new record for data entry. It is found on both the Form View and Datasheet toolbars as well as part of the Navigation buttons.

**Null** The term that refers to a state of "nothingness" in a field. Any entry such as 0 in a numeric field or an invisible space in a text field is *not* null. It is common to search for empty fields by using the criteria "Is Null" in a filter or query. "Is Not Null" criteria finds all records where there is an entry of any kind.

**Number** A data type used for numeric information used in calculations, such as quantities.

**Object** A table, query, form, report, page, macro, or module.

**Objects bar** In the opening database window, the toolbar that presents the seven Access objects. When you click an object button on the Objects bar, options and wizards to create an object of that type as well as existing objects of that type appear in the main portion of the database window.

**Office Assistant** An animated character that appears to offer tips, answer questions, and provide access to the program's Help system.

**Office Clipboard** A temporary storage area shared by all Office programs that can be used to cut, copy and paste multiple items within and between Office programs. The Office Clipboard can hold up to 12 items collected from any Office program. See also *Clipboard toolbar*.

**OLE Object** A data type that stores pointers that tie files created in other programs to a record such as pictures, sound clips, word-processing documents, or spreadsheets.

**Option button** A bound control used to display a limited list of possible choices for field such as "female" or "male" for a gender field in a form or report.

**Or criteria** Criteria placed on different rows of the query design grid. A record will appear in the resulting datasheet if it is true for any single row.

**Page** An Access object that creates Web pages from Access objects as well as provides Web page connectivity features to an Access database. Also called Data Access page.

**Page Footer section** The section of the form or report that contains controls that print once at the bottom of each page.

**Page Header section** The section of the form or report that contains controls that print once at the top of each page. On the first page of the report, the Page Header section prints below the Report Header section.

**Primary key field** See *Key field*.

**Primary sort field** In a query grid, the left-most field that includes sort criteria. It determines the order in which the records will appear and can be specified "ascending" or "descending."

**Print Preview** A window that displays how the physical printout will appear if the current object is printed.

**Properties** Characteristics that further define the field (if field properties), control (if control properties), section (if section properties), or object (if object properties).

**Property sheet** A window that displays an exhaustive lis properties for the chosen control, section, or object within form or report Design view.

**Query** An Access object which provides a spreadsheet-like of the data similar to tables. It may provide the user with a su of fields and/or records from one or more tables. Queries are ated when a user has a "question" about the data in the datab

**Raw data** The individual pieces of information stored in database in individual fields.

**Record** A group of related fields, such as all demogra information for one customer.

**Record selector box** The small square to left of a record datasheet that marks the current record or edit record sy when the record has focus or is being edited. Clicking the re selector box selects the entire record. In Form view, the re selector box expands to the entire height of the form bec only one record is viewed at a time.

**Record source** In a form or report, either a table or query c that contains the fields and records that the form will display the most important property of the form or report object. A b control on a form or report also has a record source proper this case, the record source property identifies the field to whic control is bound.

**Rectangle control** An unbound control used to draw re gles on the form that divide the other form controls into l groupings.

**Relational database** A database in which more than table, such as the customer, sales, and inventory tables, can information. The term "relational database" comes from fact that the tables are linked or "related" with a commor of information. An Access database is relational.

**Report** An Access object which creates a professional pri of data that may contain such enhancements as headers, ers, and calculations on groups of records.

**Report Footer section** On a report, a section that co controls that print once at the end of the last page of the r

**Report Header section** On a report, a section that co controls that print once at the top of the first page of the

**Row selector** The small square to the left of a field in Design view.

**ScreenTip** A pop-up label that appears when you poi button. It provides descriptive information about the bu

**Secondary sort field** In a query grid, the second field the left that includes sort criteria. It determines the or which the records will appear if there is a "tie" on the p sort field. (For example, the primary sort field might State field. If two records both contained the data "IA" field, the secondary sort field, which might be the Cit would determine the order of the IA records in the re datasheet.)

**...tion** A location of a form or report that contains controls. ... section in which a control is placed determines where and ... often the control prints.

**...ng handles** Small squares at each corner of a selected ...trol. Dragging a handle resizes the control. Also known as ...dles.

**...:** To place records in an order (ascending or descending) ...d on the values of a particular field.

**...rce document** The original paper document that ...rds raw data such as an employment application. In some ...bases, there is no source document because raw data is ...red directly into the computer.

**...cific record box** Part of the Navigation buttons that indi- ... the current record number. You can also click in the spe- ...record box and type a record number to quickly move to ...record.

**...us bar** The bar at the bottom of the Access window that ...ides informational messages and other status information ...a as whether the Num Lock is active or not).

**...control** An unbound control used to create a three- ...nsional aspect to a form so that other controls can be orga- ...l and shown in Form view by clicking the "tabs."

**...order** The sequence in which the controls on the form ...e the focus when pressing [Tab] or [Enter] in Form view.

**...:** An Access object which is a collection of records for a ... subject, such as all of the customer records. Tables can be ...l with a common field to share information and therefore ...nize data redundancy.

**...Datasheet toolbar** The toolbar that appears when you ...ewing a table's datasheet.

**...** A data type that allows text information or combinations ...t and numbers such as a street address. By default, it is ...aracters but can be changed to 50 characters. The maxi- ...length of a text field is 255 characters.

**Text box** A common control used on forms and reports to display data bound to an underlying field. A text box can also show calculated controls such as subtotals and dates.

**Toggle button** A bound control used to indicate "yes" or "no" answers for a field. If the button is "pressed" it displays "yes" information.

**Toolbox toolbar** The toolbar that has common controls that you can add to a report or form when working in the report or form's Design view.

**Unbound controls** Controls that do not change from record to record and exist only to clarify or enhance the appearance of the form, such as labels, lines, and clip art.

**Unbound image control** An unbound control used to display clip art that doesn't change as you navigate from record to record on a form or report.

**Wildcard characters** Special characters used in criteria to find, filter, and query data. The asterisk (*) stands for any group of characters. For example, the criteria I* in a State field criteria cell would find all records where the state entry was IA, ID, IL, IN, or Iowa. The question mark (?) wildcard stands for only one character. The pound sign (#) can only be used as a wildcard in a numeric field and stands for a single number.

**Wizard** An interactive set of dialog boxes that guides you through an Access process such as creating a query, form, or report.

**Yes/No** A data type that stores only one of two values (Yes/No, On/Off, True/False).

**Access 2000**

# Glossary

**PowerPoint 2000**

**Active cell** A selected cell in a Graph datasheet or an Excel worksheet.

**Adjustment handle** A small diamond positioned next to a sizing handle that changes the dimensions of an object.

**Align** To place objects' edges or centers on the same plane.

**Annotation** A freehand drawing on the screen made by using the Annotation tool. You can annotate only in Slide Show view.

**AutoContent Wizard** A wizard that helps you get your presentation started by supplying a sample outline and a design template.

**AutoLayout** A predesigned slide layout that contains placeholders for titles, main text, clip art, graphs, and charts.

**Background** The area behind the text and graphics on a slide.

**.bmp** The abbreviation for the bitmap graphics file format.

**Bullet** A small graphic symbol, usually a round or square dot, often used to identify items in a list.

**Cell** The intersection of a column and row in a worksheet, datasheet, or table.

**Chart** A graphical representation of information from a datasheet or worksheet. Types include 2-D and 3-D column, bar, pie, area, and line charts.

**Clip art** Professionally designed pictures that come with PowerPoint.

**Clipboard toolbar** A toolbar that shows the contents of the Office Clipboard; contains buttons for copying and pasting items to and from the Office Clipboard.

**Clip Gallery** A library of art, pictures, sounds, video clips, and animations that all Office applications share.

**Color scheme** The basic eight colors that make up a PowerPoint presentation; a color scheme assigns colors for text, lines, objects, and background color. You can change the color scheme on any presentation at any time.

**Common Tasks menu** A menu located on the Formatting toolbar that contains commands for common tasks performed in PowerPoint.

**Control boxes** The gray boxes along the left and top of a Graph datasheet that contain the row and column identifiers.

**Crop** To hide part of a picture or object using the Cropping tool.

**Data label** Information that identifies the data in a column or row in a datasheet.

**Data series** A column or row in a datasheet.

**Data series marker** A graphical representation of a data series, such as a bar or column.

**Datasheet** The component of a graph that contains the information you want to depict on your Graph chart.

**Design templates** Prepared slide designs with formatting color schemes that you can apply to an open presentation.

**Dialog box** A window that opens when more informatic needed to carry out a command.

**Drawing toolbar** A toolbar that contains buttons that let create lines and shapes.

**Embedded object** An object that is created in another a cation and is copied to a PowerPoint presentation. Embe objects maintain their identity as files in their original app tion for easy editing.

**File format** A file type, such as .wmf or .gif.

**Folder** A subdivision of a disk that works like a filing sy to help you organize files.

**Formatting toolbar** The toolbar that contains buttons fo most frequently used formatting commands, such as font and size.

**.gif** The abbreviation for the graphics interchange format

**Graph** The program that creates a datasheet and cha graphically depict information.

**Grid** Evenly spaced horizontal and vertical lines that d appear on the slide.

**Group** To combine multiple objects into one object.

**Keyword** A word you use to quickly find an object.

**Main text** Sub-points or bullet points on a slide und slide title.

**Main text placeholder** A reserved box on a slide for the text points.

**Master text placeholder** The placeholder on the Master that controls the formatting and placement Main text placeholder on each slide. If you modify the M text placeholder, each Main text placeholder is affected entire presentation.

**Master title placeholder** The placeholder on the Slide that controls the formatting and placement of the Title holder on each slide. If you modify the Master title place each Title placeholder is affected in the entire presentati

**Menu bar** The bar beneath the title bar that contains that list the program's commands.

**More Buttons button** A button you click to view toolb tons that are not currently visible.

**Normal view** A presentation view that divides the pr tion window into Outline, Slide, and Notes panes.

**tes pane** In Normal view, the pane that shows speaker ⌐es for the current slide; also in Notes Page view, the area ⌐w the slide image that contains speaker notes.

**⌐ect** The component you place or draw on a slide. Objects ⌐drawn lines and shapes, text, clip art, imported pictures, and ⌐edded objects.

**⌐ce Assistant** An animated character that appears to offer ⌐, answer questions, and provide access to the program's Help ⌐em.

**⌐ce Clipboard** A temporary storage area shared by all ⌐ce programs that can be used to cut, copy and paste multi-⌐ items within and between Office programs. The Office ⌐board can hold up to 12 items collected from any Office ⌐ram. See also *Clipboard toolbar*.

**⌐nization chart** A diagram of connected boxes that shows ⌐rting structure in a company or organization.

**⌐ine pane** The presentation window section that shows ⌐entation text in the form of an outline with a small slide ⌐ representing each slide.

**⌐ine view** A presentation view that lists the titles and main ⌐of all the slides in your presentation. Also shows a small ver-⌐of the current slide.

**⌐ining toolbar** The toolbar that contains buttons for the ⌐-used outlining commands, such as moving and indenting ⌐ines.

**⌐e** A section of the presentation window, such as the ⌐ine or Slide pane.

**⌐eholder** A dashed line box where you place text or objects.

**⌐rPoint Viewer** A special application designed to run a ⌐rPoint slide show on any compatible computer that does ⌐ave PowerPoint installed.

**⌐rPoint window** A window that contains the running ⌐rPoint application. The PowerPoint window includes the ⌐rPoint menus, toolbars, and Presentation window.

**⌐entation software** A software program used to organize ⌐resent information.

**⌐entation window** The area or "canvas" where you work ⌐iew your presentation. You type text and work with objects ⌐ Presentation window.

**⌐e** To change the size of a graphic a specific percentage of ⌐ginal size.

**⌐l** To move within a window to see parts of a document ⌐re not currently visible.

**⌐tion box** A slanted line border that appears around a ⌐oject or placeholder indicating it is ready to accept text.

**⌐ handles** The small squares at each corner of a selected ⌐. Dragging a handle resizes the object.

**⌐ icon** A symbol that appears next to a slide in ⌐e view.

**⌐ indicator box** A small box that appears when you drag ⌐rtical scroll box in Slide and Notes Page view identifying ⌐ slide you are on.

**Slide miniature** A reduced version of the current slide that appears in a small window.

**Slide pane** The presentation window section that contains a single slide, including text and graphics.

**Slide Show view** A view that shows a presentation as an electronic slide show.

**Slide Sorter view** A presentation view that provides a miniature picture of all slides in the order in which they appear in your presentation; used to rearrange slides and add special effects.

**Slide view** A presentation view with a large Slide pane and a reduced Outline pane.

**Stacking order** The order in which objects are placed on the slide. The first object placed on the slide is on the bottom, the last object placed on the slide is on the top.

**Standard toolbar** The toolbar containing the buttons that perform some of the most frequently used commands.

**Status bar** The bar at the bottom of the PowerPoint window that contains messages about what you are doing and seeing in PowerPoint, such as the current slide number or a description of a command or button.

**Text label** A text object you create using the Text Box button.

**Text object** Any text you create using the Text Box button or enter into a placeholder. Once you enter text into a placeholder, the placeholder becomes a text object.

**Text placeholder** A box with a dashed border and text that you replace with your own text.

**Timing** The time a slide stays on the screen during a slide show.

**Title** The first line or heading on a slide.

**Title placeholder** A box on a slide reserved for the title of a presentation or slide.

**Title slide** The first slide in your presentation.

**Toggle button** A button that turns a feature on and off.

**Transition** The effect that moves one slide off the screen and the next slide on the screen during a slide show. Each slide can have its own transition effect.

**View** A way of looking at your presentation, such as Slide view, Normal view, Notes Page view, Slide Sorter view, and Slide Show view.

**View buttons** The buttons next to the horizontal scroll bar that you click to switch among views.

**Window** A rectangular area of the screen where you view and work on presentations.

**Wizard** An interactive set of dialog boxes that guides you through the process of creating a presentation; it asks you questions about presentation preferences and creates the presentation according to your specifications.

**.wmf** The abbreviation for the Windows metafile file format, which is the format of much clip art.

**Word-processing box** A text object you draw using the Text Box button that automatically wraps text inside a box.

# Glossary

**Internet**

**Absolute link** A link that contains a fixed address; used when you don't want the link's address to change.

**Address bar** The bar that indicates the address of the Web page currently opened in the Web browser window.

**Computer network** Two or more connected computers that can share information and resources.

**Crawl** The process by which a Web search engine methodically catalogs the entire Internet to create huge databases with links to Web pages and their URLs.

**Document window** See *Web page area*.

**Dynamic HTML page** A method of linking a Web page to the original database file that was used to create it.

**Explorer Search bar** The frame that opens in the left pane and contains the Search Assistant when you use Internet Explorer's search feature.

**Favorites list** A list of frequently visited Web pages that you can open by clicking a link in the list.

**FrontPage Express (FrontPage)** A program that is included as part of the Internet Explorer 5 suite specifically designed for Web page production. It provides tools for creating new Web pages and editing existing ones.

**Hits** The result of an Internet search that, when clicked, opens a Web page or category.

**Home page** The first page that opens every time you start Internet Explorer.

**Hyperlinks** Web pages that contain highlighted words, phrases, or graphics that open other Web pages when clicked. Also known as *Links*.

**Hypertext Markup Language (HTML)** The language used to describe the content and format of Web pages.

**Internet** A communications system that connects computers and computer networks located around the world using telephone lines, cables, satellites, and other telecommunications media.

**Internet Explorer 5** A popular browser from Microsoft that comes with Microsoft Office 2000.

**Intranet** A computer network that connects computers in a local area only, such as computers in a company's office.

**Links** See *Hyperlinks*.

**Menu bar** The bar beneath the title bar that lists the me that contain the program's commands.

**Mosaic** The first graphical Web browser.

**NetMeeting** An Internet Explorer suite component enables you to set up audio and video links to people at di ent locations for a live discussion.

**Outlook Express** An Internet Explorer suite component allows you to read and send e-mail messages as well as read post messages in newsgroups (discussions organized arc specific topics).

**Personal Web Server** An Internet Explorer suite compo that lets you use your personal computer to host a Web sit

**Publish** The process of placing Web pages on an intran the Web so people can access them using a Web browser.

**Relative link** A link that gives another page's address in tion to the current page.

**Scroll box** A movable box in the scroll bar that you dr move around in a Web page.

**Search Assistant** A search feature that lists search op for finding Web pages, people, businesses, previous sea or maps.

**Search engine** An Internet site that lets you enter a key or phrase describing the information you want to find and provides you with a list of related Web sites.

**Static HTML page** A Web page that contains the cu information in an Access database table that you are conv to a Web page.

**Status bar** A bar located at the bottom of the Web br window that displays information about your conn progress whenever you open a new Web page, notifies you you connect to another Web site, and identifies the percen information transferred from the Web server to your brov also displays the Web addresses of any links on the Wel when you move your mouse pointer over them.

**Status indicator** The Internet Explorer logo on the t that animates while a new Web page loads.

**Surfing** The process of using the Web and navigating Web pages and sites.

**‹s** The codes that HTML places around all the elements in ·/eb document that describe how they should appear when wed using a Web browser.

**e bar** The bar at the top of the window that indicates the ne of the program and the name of the Web page currently ɔlayed in the Web browser window.

**lbar** A bar that contains buttons that give you quick access he most frequently used commands, such as moving from ~ Web page to another, printing Web pages, and searching for ·rmation on the Internet.

**‹form Resource Locator (URL)** A Web page's address.

**·ical scroll bar** A scroll bar that allows you to move the ·ent Web page up or down in the Web browser window.

**Web browsers** Software programs used to access and open Web pages.

**Web page area** The specific area where the current Web page appears.

**Web publication** A group of associated Web pages focusing on a particular theme or topic.

**Windows Media Player** An Internet Explorer suite component that lets you listen to and/or view live and prerecorded sounds, images, and videos.

**World Wide Web (Web or WWW)** A part of the Internet containing Web pages that are linked together.

**Publisher 2000**

# Glossary

**AutoFit**  A formatting feature that automatically sizes text to fit in a frame.

**Clip Gallery**  A library of art, pictures, sounds, video clips, and animations that all Office applications share.

**Desktop publishing program**  A program that lets you easily integrate text, pictures, drawings, tables, and charts in one document using your personal computer.

**Desktop workspace**  The area around the publication page you can use to store text and graphics prior to placing them in a publication.

**Font**  The typeface or design of a set of characters (letters, numbers, symbols, and punctuation marks).

**Font size**  The physical size of characters measured in points.

**Frame**  An object that contains text or graphics.

**Handles**  Little black squares that appear around a frame to indicate the frame is selected.

**Menu bar**  A bar beneath the title bar that lists the menus that contain the program's commands.

**Object Position indicator**  A part of the status bar used to precisely position an object containing text or graphics.

**Object Size indicator**  A part of the status bar used to accurately gauge the size of an object.

**Office Assistant**  An animated character that appears to offer tips, answer questions, and provide access to the program's Help system.

**Pack and Go Wizard**  A wizard that allows you to package your presentation to take to another computer or to a commercial printing service.

**Page Navigation buttons**  A button used to jump to a specific page in your publication.

**Publication**  A document created in Publisher.

**Publication page**  A visual representation of your publicat...

**Publication window**  The area that includes the publica... page or pages and a desktop workspace for storing text graphics prior to placing them in your publication.

**Rulers**  Vertical and horizontal bars (or rulers) that help position text and graphics in your publications.

**Scroll bars**  Bars at the right bottom edges of the docur... window used to view different parts of your document not rently visible in the window.

**Status bar**  The bar at the bottom of the Publication win... that indicates the position and size of the selected object publication and shows the current page.

**Templates**  Preset publications that include sample text graphics, a sample layout, and sample color palettes that all great together.  Used as a basis for a new publication.

**Title bar**  The bar at the top of the window that indicate... name of the program and the name of the current docum...

**Toggle key**  A key that toggles between two options – ... once to turn the option on, press again to turn it off.

**Toolbar**  A bar that contains buttons that give you quick a... to the most frequently used commands.  Publisher's d... toolbars are the Standard toolbar, the Formatting toolbar the Objects toolbar.

**Wizard**  An interactive series of dialog boxes that guide... through the process of creating a publication, asks you ... tions about publication preferences and creates the public according to your specifications.

**Wizard pane**  A part of the screen that appears to the left ... publication window and includes the various wizard o... in the top pane and details about those options in the ... tom pane.

# Glossary

**ress book**  A collection of user names.

**ointment**  An activity that does not involve inviting other
le or scheduling resources.

**ndar**  A tool within Outlook that is the electronic equiva-
of your daily desk calendar.

**gories**  A method for organizing your tasks.

**puter network**  Two or more connected computers that
hare information and resources.

**tacts**  A tool in Outlook that enables you to manage all
business and personal contact information.

**acts folder**  A feature of Contacts that allows you to view,
and create contacts.

**Navigator**  A feature in Calendar that allows you to
ly select even, nonadjacent days.

**ted Items folder**  A folder in the Inbox folder that con-
messages you have deleted.

**ils tab**  A tab in the Contact dialog box used to store each
ct's detailed information.

**il**  Electronic mail software that lets you send and receive
onic messages over a network.

**ticons**  Faces created by simple keyboard characters to
ss an emotion or mood.

**t**  An activity that lasts 24 hours or longer.

To search for specific information.

**r banner**  The horizontal bar that indicates the name of
en folder to the left and the icon of the open folder to
ht.

**l Address List**  An address book that contains all the
ames of the people connected to the mail system.

Part of the e-mail window that contains the e-mail you
eceived.

**et**  A communication system that connects comput-
d computer networks located around the world using
one lines, cables, satellites, and other telecommuni-
s media.

**ng Outlook 2000 E-mail**  Software that simulates the
d functionality of Microsoft Outlook 2000.

**ng**  An activity you invite people to or reserve
ces for.

**Message header**  The area at the top of a message that identifies the sender of the message, the subject, and the date and
time the message was received.

**Network**  A group of computers connected to each other
with cables and software to allow users to share applications,
disk storage, printers, and send and receive electronic messages from one another.

**Notes**  A tool in Outlook that is an electronic version of the
popular colored paper sticky notes.

**Notes folder**  A feature in Notes that allows you to quickly
write down an idea or a note concerning an appointment
or task.

**Outbox folder**  A folder in the Inbox folder that contains messages you have sent, but which Outlook has not yet delivered.

**Outlook bar**  The bar located on the left side of the e-mail window that contains shortcuts to frequently used folders.

**Outlook Express**  An Internet Explorer suite component that
allows you to exchange e-mail and join newsgroups.

**Outlook Today page**  A tool within Outlook that provides a
preview of your day at a glance.

**Personal Distribution List**  A collection of contacts to whom
you regularly send the same messages.

**Preview pane**  The lower pane of the Inbox that allows you to
read and scroll through your messages without opening them.

**Report message**  A message you receive when the e-mail
recipient either receives or opens a message you sent.

**Sent Items folder**  A folder in the Inbox folder that contains
messages you have sent.

**Status bar**  The bar at the bottom of the Outlook window that
indicates the total number of messages that the open folder
contains, as well as the number of those messages that have not
been read.

**TaskPad**  An area in Calendar that displays your task list.

**Task requests**  A feature in Tasks that allows you to assign tasks
to co-workers or assistants and have Outlook automatically
update you on the status of task completion.

**Tasks**  A tool within Outlook that is an electronic to-do list.

**Tasks folder**  A feature in Tasks that allows you to manage
your business and personal to-do list.

**Vcards**  The Internet standard for creating and sharing virtual
business cards.

# Index

# Index

# Index

# Index

# Index

# Index

# Index

# Index